Education at a Glance

OECD INDICATORS 2002

OECD

ORGANISATION FOR ECONOMIC CO-OPERATION AND DEVELOPMENT

ORGANISATION FOR ECONOMIC CO-OPERATION AND DEVELOPMENT

Pursuant to Article 1 of the Convention signed in Paris on 14th December 1960, and which came into force on 30th September 1961, the Organisation for Economic Co-operation and Development (OECD) shall promote policies designed:

- to achieve the highest sustainable economic growth and employment and a rising standard of living in Member countries, while maintaining financial stability, and thus to contribute to the development of the world economy;

- to contribute to sound economic expansion in Member as well as non-member countries in the process of economic development; and

- to contribute to the expansion of world trade on a multilateral, non-discriminatory basis in accordance with international obligations.

The original Member countries of the OECD are Austria, Belgium, Canada, Denmark, France, Germany, Greece, Iceland, Ireland, Italy, Luxembourg, the Netherlands, Norway, Portugal, Spain, Sweden, Switzerland, Turkey, the United Kingdom and the United States. The following countries became Members subsequently through accession at the dates indicated hereafter: Japan (28th April 1964), Finland (28th January 1969), Australia (7th June 1971), New Zealand (29th May 1973), Mexico (18th May 1994), the Czech Republic (21st December 1995), Hungary (7th May 1996), Poland (22nd November 1996), Korea (12th December 1996) and Slovak Republic (14th December 2000). The Commission of the European Communities takes part in the work of the OECD (Article 13 of the OECD Convention).

The Centre for Educational Research and Innovation was created in June 1968 by the Council of the Organisation for Economic Co-operation and Development and all Member countries of the OECD are participants.

The main objectives of the Centre are as follows:

- *analyse and develop research, innovation and key indicators in current and emerging education and learning issues, and their links to other sectors of policy;*

- *explore forward-looking coherent approaches to education and learning in the context of national and international cultural, social and economic change; and*

- *facilitate practical co-operation among Member countries and, where relevant, with non-member countries, in order to seek solutions and exchange views of educational problems of common interest.*

The Centre functions within the Organisation for Economic Co-operation and Development in accordance with the decisions of the Council of the Organisation, under the authority of the Secretary-General. It is supervised by a Governing Board composed of one national expert in its field of competence from each of the countries participating in its programme of work.

Publié en français sous le titre :

Regards sur l'éducation
Les indicateurs de l'OCDE 2002

FOREWORD

Compelling incentives for individuals, economies and societies to raise levels of education have been the driving force behind increased participation in a widening range of learning activities – by people of all ages, from earliest childhood to advanced adulthood. As the demand for learning spreads and becomes more diverse, the challenge for governments is to ensure that the nature and types of learning opportunities respond in a cost-effective manner to real, dynamic needs.

In searching for effective education policies that enhance individuals' social and economic prospects, provide incentives for greater efficiency in schooling and help to mobilise resources in order to meet rising demands for education, governments are paying increasing attention to international comparisons. Through co-operation within the OECD framework, countries are seeking to learn from each other about how to overcome barriers to investment in education and to secure the benefits of education for all, how to foster competencies for the knowledge society, and how to manage teaching and learning in order to promote learning throughout life.

As part of the drive to enhance the OECD's work in this area and to better respond to the needs of citizens and governments, the OECD has elevated the education group in its Secretariat to the level of an independent Directorate. A central part of the Directorate for Education's strategy is the development and analysis of quantitative indicators that provide an opportunity for governments to see their education system in the light of other countries' performances. Together with OECD's country policy reviews, the indicators are designed to support and review efforts which governments are making towards policy reform.

The publication *Education at a Glance – OECD Indicators 2002* is a key instrument for disseminating the indicators to a range of users, from governments seeking to learn policy lessons, academics requiring data for further analysis, to the general public wanting to monitor how its nation's schools are progressing in producing world-class students. It does so by providing a rich, comparable and up-to-date array of indicators that reflect a consensus among professionals on how to measure the current state of education internationally.

The 2002 edition of *Education at a Glance* adds three important improvements to its predecessors: First, OECD's Programme for International Student Assessment (PISA), which governments launched to monitor student performance regularly within an internationally agreed framework, provides now comparable information on the outcomes of education and learning as well as on key factors shaping these outcomes. Such information has long been a critical gap in the indicator set. Second, a growing proportion of the indicators now looks beyond aggregate country performance and incorporates variations within countries that allow an examination of issues of equity in the provision and outcomes of education, on dimensions such as gender, age, socio-economic background, type of institution, or field of education. Third, the work is now being organised within a new framework that groups the indicators according to whether they speak to educational outcomes for individuals and countries, the policy levers or circumstances that shape these outcomes, or to antecedents or constraints that set the context for policy choices.

The publication is the product of a longstanding, collaborative effort between OECD governments, the experts and institutions working within the framework of OECD's education indicators programme (INES), and the OECD Secretariat. The publication was drafted by the Division for Education Indicators and Analysis, under the responsibility of Andreas Schleicher, in co-operation with Eric Charbonnier, Hannah Cocks, Jean-Luc Heller, Judit Kadar-Fülop, Karine Tremblay and Claire Shewbridge. The development of the publication was steered by INES National Co-ordinators in Member countries and facilitated by the financial and material support of the three countries responsible for co-ordinating the INES Networks - the Netherlands, Sweden and the United States. In addition, work on the publication has been aided by a grant from the National Center for Education Statistics (NCES) in the United States. The Annex lists the members of the various bodies as well as the individual experts who have contributed to this publication and the OECD education indicators more generally.

While much progress has been accomplished in recent years, significant further work is needed to link better a broad range of policy needs with the best available data. Future work will need to continue to address various challenges and tradeoffs: First, the indicators need to respond to educational issues that are high on national policy agendas, and where the international comparative perspective can offer important added value to what can be accomplished through national analysis and evaluation. Second, while the indicators need to be as comparable as possible, they also need to be as country-specific as is necessary to allow for historical, systemic and cultural differences between countries. Third, the indicators need to be presented in as straightforward a manner as possible, but remain sufficiently complex to reflect multifaceted educational realities. Fourth, there is a general desire to keep the indicator set as small as possible, but it needs to be large enough to be useful to policy-makers in countries that face different educational challenges.

The new organisational structure at the OECD provides the framework to address these challenges more vigorously and to pursue not just the development of indicators in areas where it is feasible and promising to develop data, but also to advance in areas where a considerable investment still needs to be made in conceptual work.

The report is published on the responsibility of the Secretary-General of the OECD.

Barry McGaw
Director for Education
OECD

TABLE OF CONTENTS

INTRODUCTION

THE 2002 EDITION OF EDUCATION AT A GLANCE

The OECD indicators represent the consensus of professional thinking on how to measure the current state of education internationally.

Education at a Glance – OECD Indicators 2002 provides a rich, comparable and up-to-date array of indicators that reflect a consensus among professionals on how to measure the current state of education internationally. They provide information on the human and financial resources invested in education, on how education and learning systems operate and evolve, and on the returns to educational investments. The indicators are organised thematically, and each is accompanied by background information. The 2002 edition of *Education at a Glance* adds three important improvements to its predecessors:

Comparable information on learning outcomes adds a new dimension to the OECD indicators,…

OECD's Programme for International Student Assessment (PISA), which governments launched to monitor student performance regularly within an internationally agreed framework, provides now comparable information on the outcomes of education and learning as well as on key factors shaping these outcomes. Such information has long been a critical gap in the indicator set. PISA aims to provide a new basis for policy dialogue such that countries can work together to define educational goals that are both innovative and realistic, and that reflect judgements concerning the skills that are relevant to adult life. PISA is part of a shift in focus from education inputs and institutions to outcomes. The shift is designed to support policy-makers as they attempt to improve schooling that prepares young people for adult life during an era of rapid change and increasing global interdependence.

…better information on disparities in individual and institutional performance improves the examination of equity issues in the provision and outcomes of education,…

A growing proportion of the indicators now looks beyond aggregate country performance and incorporates variations within countries that allow an examination of issues of equity in the provision and outcomes of education on dimensions such as gender, age, socio-economic background, type of institution, or field of education.

…and a new organising framework for the indicators makes them easier to use .

The OECD education indicators are being progressively integrated into a new framework. This framework:

- distinguishes between the actors in education systems: individual learners, instructional settings and learning environments, educational service providers, and the education system as a whole;

- groups the indicators according to whether they speak to learning outcomes for individuals and countries, policy levers or circumstances that shape these outcomes, or to antecedents or constraints that set policy choices into context; and

- identifies the policy issues to which the indicators relate, with three major categories distinguishing between the quality of educational outcomes and educational provision, issues of equity in educational outcomes and educational opportunities, and the adequacy and effectiveness of resource management.

The following matrix describes the first two dimensions:

	Education and learning outputs and outcomes	Policy levers and contexts shaping educational outcomes	Antecedents or constraints that contextualise policy
Individual partici-pants in education and learning	1. The quality and distribution of individual educational outcomes	5. Individual attitudes, engagement, and behaviour	9. Background characteristics of the individual learners
Instructional settings	2. The quality of instructional delivery	6. Pedagogy and learning practices and classroom climate	10. Student learning conditions and teacher working conditions
Education providers	3. The output of educational institutions and institutional performance	7. School environment and organisation	11. Characteristics of the service providers and their communities
Education system as a whole	4. The overall performance of the education system	8. System-wide institutional settings, resource allocations, and policies	12. The national educational, social, economic, and demographic context

CONTENTS AND HIGHLIGHTS

The 2002 edition of *Education at a Glance* is divided into four chapters.

Chapter A examines the outcomes of education and learning, in terms of...
...current output of educational institutions and educational attainment of the adult population,...

Chapter A begins by examining graduation rates in upper secondary and tertiary levels of education (**Indicators A1** and **A2**). These indicators speak both to the institutional and the system-level output of education systems. To gauge progress in educational output, current graduation rates are compared to the educational attainment of older persons who left the education system at different points in time.

Countries' progress is also reviewed in closing the gender gap in educational attainment and graduation rates, both overall and across different fields of education (**Indicators A1, A2** and **A4**).

Dropout and survival rates (**Indicator A2**) provide some indication of the internal efficiency of education systems. Students leave educational programmes before their completion for many reasons - they realise that they have chosen the wrong subject or educational programme, they fail to meet the standards set by their educational institution, or they may want to work before completing their programme. Nevertheless, high dropout rates indicate that the education system is not meeting the needs of its clients. Students may find that the educational programmes do not meet their expectations or their needs in order to enter the labour market, or that the programmes require more time outside the labour market than they can justify.

- The proportion of individuals in the population who have not completed upper secondary education has been falling in almost all OECD countries, and rapidly in some. In all but five OECD countries, the ratio of upper secondary graduates to the population at the typical age of graduation now exceeds 70 per cent, and in many countries, it exceeds 90 per cent (p. 32).

- An average of 26 per cent of persons at the typical age of graduation complete the tertiary-type A level of education. This figure ranges from about one-third or more in Australia, Finland, Iceland, Poland, the United Kingdom and the United States, to less than 20 per cent in Austria, the Czech Republic, Denmark, Germany, Italy and Switzerland (p. 42).

- Among older age groups, women have attained lower levels of upper secondary education than men, but for younger people, this pattern is now reversing. Today, graduation rates for women exceed those for men in most countries (p. 34).

- In the humanities, arts, education, health and welfare, more than two-thirds of the tertiary-type A graduates are women, on average in OECD countries, whereas it is less than one-third in mathematics and science and less than one-quarter in engineering, manufacturing and construction (p. 58).

- The adult population now possesses a greater stock of university-level skills, but most of this increase is due to significant increases in tertiary graduation rates in a comparatively small number of countries (p. 43).

- On average, one-third of OECD students drop out before they complete their first tertiary-level degree (p. 44).

Counting the numbers of graduates alone does not inform us about the quality of learning outcomes. To address this, **Indicators A5** and **A6** reflect the reading, mathematical and scientific literacy of 15-year-old students both with regard to the relative performance of countries and to the equality of learning outcomes within each country. Reading, mathematics and science are viewed as important basic skills in all OECD countries and student assessments in these areas therefore provide essential indicators for gauging the quality of educational performance. Nevertheless, there is a growing acknowledgement that there are a much wider range of competencies that are important for the success of individuals and societies. **Indicator A8** begins to address this with a comparative review of civic knowledge and attitudes of 14-year-olds.

- On average across OECD countries, 10 per cent of 15-year-olds have acquired Level 5 literacy skills, which involve evaluating information and building hypotheses, drawing on specialised knowledge, and accommodating concepts contrary to expectations. The percentage varies from 19 per cent in Finland and New Zealand to below 1 per cent in Mexico. An average of 12 per cent of 15-year-olds have only acquired the most basic literacy skills at Level 1, and 6 per cent fall even below that (p. 65).

- 15-year-olds in Japan have the highest mean scores in mathematical literacy. Their scores cannot be distinguished statistically, however, from those of students in Korea and New Zealand, two other top-performing countries. In scientific literacy, students in Korea and Japan demonstrate the highest average performance (p. 76).

- The difference in mean performance between countries is large, but the variation in the performance of 15-year-olds within each country is many times larger. Wide disparities in performance are not a necessary condition for a country to attain a high level of overall performance, however. Five of the countries with the smallest variation in mathematical literacy – Canada, Finland, Iceland, Japan and Korea – all perform well overall (p. 78).

- Generally, 14-year-olds consider that obeying the law and voting are very important adult responsibilities. They also value activities that promote human rights, protect the environment, and benefit the community. They give less value to engaging in political discussions or joining a political party (p. 92).

...and how this varies between schools and students...

Indicators A5 and **A6** show that, in most countries, there are considerable differences in performance within each education system. This variation may reflect differences in school and student backgrounds, the human and financial resources available to schools, curricular differences, selection policies and practices, or the way that teaching is organised and delivered.

Some countries have non-selective school systems that seek to provide all students with the same opportunities for learning, and allow each school to cater to all levels of student performance. Other countries respond to diversity explicitly by forming groups of students of similar performance levels through selection either within or between schools, with the aim of serving students according to their specific needs. Other countries combine the two approaches. Even in comprehensive school systems, schools may vary significantly in response to the socio-economic and cultural characteristics of the communities that they serve or their geography. **Indicator A7** sheds light on such performance differences between schools and the factors to which these relate.

- On average, differences in the performance of 15-year-olds between schools account for 36 per cent of the OECD average variation in student performance, but this proportion varies from 10 per cent in Finland and Sweden to more than 50 per cent in Austria, Belgium, the Czech Republic, Germany, Greece, Hungary, Italy and Poland (p. 85).

- Some variation between schools can be attributed to geography, institutional factors, or the selection of students by ability. Differences are often compounded by family background, particularly in countries with differentiated school systems, since results are associated not only with individual students' backgrounds but, to a greater extent, with the backgrounds of other students (p. 87).

...equity in educational opportunities and outcomes...

Students come from a variety of socio-economic and cultural backgrounds. Schools must therefore provide appropriate and equitable opportunities for a diverse student body. Diverse backgrounds and interests can enhance a learning environment but heterogeneous levels of ability and differences in school preparedness increase the challenges of meeting the needs of students from very different socio-economic backgrounds.

To pursue this policy issue, **Indicators A9** and **A10** examine the relationship between student performance in reading literacy and their parents' occupational status, place of birth, and the language spoken at home. Although these characteristics do not lend themselves directly to educational policy, identifying the characteristics of the students most likely to perform poorly can help educators and policy-makers locate areas for policy intervention. If it can be shown that some countries find it easier than others to accommodate different background factors, important policy insights can be generated and used in other countries.

- 15-year-olds whose parents have higher-status jobs show higher literacy performance on average but the advantage is much greater in some countries than in others, particularly in Belgium, Germany, Luxembourg and Switzerland (p. 99).

- Socio-economic background remains one of the most powerful factors influencing performance. Some countries, however, most notably Canada, Finland, Iceland, Ireland, Japan and Korea, demonstrate that high average quality and social equity in educational outcomes can go together (p. 99).

- In most countries with significant immigrant populations, first-generation 15-year-olds read well below the level of native students even if they were themselves born in the country, but the disadvantage varies widely across countries (p. 105).

- Not surprisingly, students who do not speak the majority language at home perform much less well than students who do. In all countries, these students are much more likely to score among the lowest quarter of students, but again, the disadvantage varies widely across countries (p. 106).

...and the returns to education for individuals and society.

As levels of skill tend to rise with educational attainment, the social costs incurred when those with higher levels of education do not work also rise; and as populations in OECD countries age, higher and longer participation in the labour force can lower dependency ratios and help to alleviate the burden of financing public pensions. **Indicators A11** and **A12** examine the relationship between educational attainment and labour force activity, comparing rates of participation in the labour force first, and then rates of unemployment.

Markets also provide incentives to individuals to develop and maintain appropriate levels of skills through wage differentials, especially through higher earnings for persons completing additional education. Acquiring higher levels of education can also be viewed as an investment in human capital, which includes the stock of skills that individuals maintain or develop, through education or training, and then offer, in return for earnings, on the labour market. The higher the earnings from increased human capital, the higher the returns on the investment and the premium paid for enhanced skills and/or higher productivity. Indicators **A13** and **A14** seek to measure the returns to education for individuals, in terms of higher earnings; for taxpayers, in terms of higher fiscal income from better educated individuals; and for economies more generally, in terms of the relationship between education and economic growth. Together, these indicators shed light on the longer-term impact of education for individuals and societies.

- Labour force participation rates rise with educational attainment in most OECD countries. With very few exceptions, graduates of tertiary education have markedly higher participation rates than upper secondary graduates. The gap in male participation rates is particularly wide between upper secondary graduates and those with no upper secondary qualification (p. 112).

- Although there is a gender gap in labour force participation for those with tertiary educational attainment, the gap is much narrower than for those with lower qualifications (p. 113).

- A 15-year-old can expect to hold a job for 6.5 of the 15 years to come, to be unemployed for a total of 0.8 years, and to be out of the labour market for 1.4 years. Countries vary most in terms of the average length of periods of unemployment, which primarily reflects differences in youth employment rates (p. 120).

- Education and earnings are positively linked, and this link is particularly pertinent in upper secondary education, which constitutes a watershed in many countries. Education beyond upper secondary brings a particularly high premium and, while women still earn less than men with similar levels of educational attainment, the differences are smaller at higher levels (p. 124).

- In all countries, the private rate of return to investment in education is higher than real interest rates, and often significantly so. Social returns are still well above risk-free real interest rates, but tend to be lower than private returns, due to the significant social costs of education (p. 127).

- Earnings differentials and the length of education tend to be the prime determinants of the returns, but there are other factors, including taxes which reduce the returns, lower risks of unemployment which increase the returns, tuition fees which reduce the returns, and public grant or loan arrangements which boost returns (p. 128).

- The improvement in human capital has been a strong and common factor behind economic growth in recent decades, and in some countries accounted for more than half a percentage point of growth in the 1990s (p. 136).

Chapter B considers the financial and human resources invested in education, in terms of...

Financial resources are a central policy lever for improving educational outcomes. As an investment in human skills, education can help to foster economic growth and enhance productivity, contribute to personal and social development, and reduce social inequality. But like any investment, education has returns and costs. After Chapter A examined the returns to education, Chapter B provides a comparative examination of spending patterns in OECD countries. By giving more emphasis to trends in spending patterns, *Education at a Glance 2002* analyses how different demand and supply factors interact and how spending on education, compared to spending on other social priorities, has changed.

...the resources that each country invests in education relative to its number of students enrolled...

Effective schools require the right combination of trained and talented personnel, adequate facilities, state-of-the-art equipment, and motivated students ready to learn. The demand for high-quality education, however, can translate into higher costs per student, and must therefore be weighed against undue burdens for taxpayers. No absolute standards exist for measuring the per student resources needed to ensure optimal returns for individual students or society as a whole. Nonetheless, international comparisons can provide a starting point for discussion by evaluating the variation that exists between OECD countries in educational investment. **Indicator B1** examines direct public and private expenditure on educational institutions in relation to the number of their full-time equivalent (FTE) students. It also reviews how OECD countries apportion per capita education expenditure between different levels of education.

- As a whole, OECD countries spend US$ 4 229 per primary student, US$ 5 174 per secondary student, and US$ 11 422 per tertiary student. These averages mask a broad range of expenditure across countries, however (p. 148).

- On average, OECD countries spend 2.3 times as much per student at the tertiary level as at the primary level (p. 154).

- In some OECD countries, low annual expenditure per tertiary-level student still translates into high overall costs of tertiary education, because of the length of studies (p. 154).

- At the tertiary level, education spending has not always kept pace with rapidly expanding enrolments.

- Lower unit expenditure cannot automatically be equated with poorer quality educational services. Australia, Finland, Korea and the United Kingdom, for example, which have moderate per student education expenditure at primary and lower secondary levels, are among the OECD countries with 15-year-old students performing best in mathematics (p. 150).

...and relative to national income and the size of public budgets,...

Indicator B2 examines the proportion of national resources that goes to educational institutions and the levels of education to which they go. The proportion of national financial resources allocated to education is one of the key choices made by each OECD country; it is an aggregate choice made by governments, enterprises, and individual students and their families. **Indicator B2** also shows how the amount of educational spending relative to the size of national wealth and in absolute terms has evolved over time in OECD countries.

Indicator B3 completes the picture of the resources invested in education by examining changes in public spending on education in absolute terms and relative to changes in overall public spending. All governments are involved in education, funding or directing the provision of services. Since markets offer no guarantee of equal access to educational opportunities, governments fund educational services to ensure that they are within the reach of their populations. Public expenditure on education as a percentage of total public expenditure indicates the value of education relative to the value of other public investments such as health care, social security, defence and security.

- OECD countries spend 5.8 per cent of their collective GDP on their educational institutions (p. 162).

- In 14 of 18 OECD countries, public and private investment in education increased by more than 5 per cent between 1995 and 1999 (p. 163).

- On average, OECD countries devote 12.7 per cent of total public expenditure to educational institutions (p. 175).

- In real terms, public expenditure on education increased by more than 5 per cent in four out of five OECD countries between 1995 and 1999 (p. 177).

- Public expenditure on education tended to grow faster than total government spending, but not as fast as GDP. In Italy, the Netherlands, Sweden and the United Kingdom, public expenditure on education increased between 1995 and 1999, despite falling public budgets in real terms (p. 177).

...the ways in which education systems are financed, and the sources of the funds,...

Cost-sharing between the participants in education and society as a whole is an issue that is under discussion in many OECD countries. This is a particularly relevant question at the early and late stages of education – pre-primary and tertiary – where full or nearly full public funding is less common. As new client groups participate in education, the range of educational opportunities, programmes and providers is growing, and governments are forging new partnerships to mobilise the necessary resources. Public funding is now being looked upon increasingly as providing only a part, albeit a very substantial part, of the investment in education. Private funding is playing an increasingly important role. To shed light on these issues, **Indicator B4** examines the relative proportions of funds for educational institutions from public and private sources, and how these figures have evolved since 1995.

New funding strategies aim not only at mobilising the required resources from a wider range of public and private sources, but also at providing a broader range of learning opportunities and improving the efficiency of schooling. In the majority of OECD countries, publicly funded primary and secondary education is also organised and delivered by public institutions. However, in a fair number of OECD countries the public funds are then transferred to private institutions or given directly to households to spend in the institution of their choice. In the former case, the final spending and delivery of education can be regarded as subcontracted by governments to non-governmental institutions, whereas in the latter instance, students and their families are left to decide which type of institution best meets their requirements. Also the allocation of funds between public and private sources is examined in **Indicator B4**.

- The private share of total payments to educational institutions ranges from about 3 per cent or less in Finland, Norway, Portugal, the Slovak Republic, Sweden and Turkey to as much as 40 per cent in Korea (p. 182).

- In some OECD countries, governments pay most primary and secondary education costs, but leave the management of educational institutions to the private sector to broaden the range of learning opportunities without limiting the participation of students from low-income families. In Belgium and the Netherlands, the majority of primary and secondary students are enrolled in such government-dependent private institutions. In Australia, France, Korea, Spain and the United Kingdom, the proportion is still more than 20 per cent (p. 182).

- Very few primary and secondary educational institutions are financed predominantly by households as compared to governments (p. 183).

- Tertiary institutions tend to mobilise a far higher proportion of their funds from private sources than do primary, secondary and post-secondary non-tertiary institutions. The share ranges from 3 per cent or less in Austria, the Flemish Community of Belgium, Denmark, Finland, Greece and Switzerland, to 78 per cent in Korea (p. 185).

- In ten out of 19 OECD countries, private expenditure on tertiary education grew by more than 30 per cent between 1995 and 1999. In most countries, however, this growth in private spending was not associated with a decrease in public-sector spending on tertiary education (p. 185).

...different financing instruments...

The primary financing mechanism of education in most OECD countries remains direct spending on educational institutions. However, governments are looking increasingly towards greater diversity in financing instruments. Comparing these instruments helps to identify policy alternatives. Subsidies to students and their families, the subject of **Indicator B5,** constitute one such alternative to direct spending on institutions. Governments subsidise the costs of education and related expenditure in order to increase access to education and reduce social inequalities. Furthermore, public subsidies play an important role in indirectly funding educational institutions. Channelling institutional funding through students may heighten institutional competition and therefore the efficiency of education funding. Since aid for student living costs can also serve as a substitute for work as a financial resource, public subsidies may enhance educational attainment by enabling students to study full-time and to work fewer hours or not at all.

Public subsidies come in many forms: means-based subsidies, family allowances for all students, tax allowances for students or parents, or other household transfers. Should household subsidies take the form of grants or loans? Do loans effectively help increase the efficiency of financial resources invested in education and shift some of the costs to the beneficiaries? Or are student loans less appropriate than grants for encouraging low-income students to pursue their education? **Indicator B5** cannot answer these questions, but it does provide a useful overview of the subsidy policies being pursued in different OECD countries.

- An average of 16 per cent of public spending on tertiary education goes, in the form of subsidies, to supporting students, households and other private entities. In Australia, Denmark and the United Kingdom, public subsidies account for one-third or more of public tertiary education budgets (p. 194).

- Subsidies are particularly important in systems where students are expected to pay at least part of their education costs (p. 196).

- In most OECD countries, the beneficiaries of public subsidies enjoy considerable discretion in spending them. In all reporting OECD countries, subsidies are spent mainly outside educational institutions, and in one out of three countries, they are spent exclusively outside (p. 196).

...and how the money is invested and apportioned among different resource categories.

Chapter B concludes with an examination of how financial resources are invested and apportioned among resource categories (**Indicator B6**). The allocation of resources can influence the quality of instruction (through the relative expenditure on teachers' salaries, for example), the condition of educational facilities (through expenditure on school maintenance), and the ability of the education system to adjust to changing demographic and enrolment trends. A comparison of how OECD countries apportion their educational expenditure among resource categories can provide some insight into the differences in organisational structure and operation of educational institutions. Systemic budgetary and structural decisions on allocating resources eventually make themselves felt in the classroom; they affect teaching and the conditions under which teaching takes place.

- On average, one-quarter of the expenditure on tertiary education is earmarked for R&D at tertiary educational institutions. OECD countries differ significantly in how they emphasise R&D in tertiary institutions, which explains part of the wide differences in expenditure per tertiary student (p. 202).

- Expenditure on ancillary services at primary, secondary and post-secondary non-tertiary levels represent, on average, 5 per cent of total spending on educational institutions. This is usually more than what OECD countries spend on household subsidies (p. 202).

- In primary, secondary and post-secondary non-tertiary education combined, current expenditure accounts for 92 per cent of total spending on average across all OECD countries. In all but four OECD countries, 70 per cent or more of current expenditure goes to staff salaries (p. 203).

- At the tertiary level, OECD countries tend to devote a higher proportion of current expenditure to services that are sub-contracted or bought in (p. 205).

Chapter C looks at access to education, participation and progression, in terms of...

A well-educated population has become a defining feature of a modern society. Education is seen as a mechanism for instilling civic values, and as a means for developing individuals' productive and social capacity. Early childhood programmes prepare young children socially and academically for primary education. Primary and secondary education provides basic skills that serve as a foundation for young people to become productive members of society. Tertiary education provides opportunities for acquiring advanced knowledge and skills, either immediately after initial schooling or later. Many employers encourage ongoing training, and assist workers in upgrading or re-orienting their skills to meet the demands of changing technologies. Chapter C sketches a comparative picture of access, participation and progression in education across OECD countries.

...the expected duration of schooling, overall and at the different levels of education,...

Indicators on the expected duration of schooling, and on enrolment rates at different educational levels (**Indicator C1**) can help to elucidate the structure of education systems and access to educational opportunities in them. Enrolment trends at the different education levels and types of institutions show how education supply and demand are balanced in different countries.

- In 25 of 27 OECD countries, individuals participate in formal education for between 15 and 20 years, on average. Most of the variation comes from differences in upper secondary enrolments (p. 215).

- School expectancy increased between 1995 and 2000 in 18 out of 20 OECD countries. In Australia, the Czech Republic, Finland, Greece, Hungary, Korea, Poland and the United Kingdom, the increase exceeded one year over this relatively short period (p.216).

- In two-fifths of OECD countries, more than 70 per cent of three to four-year-olds are enrolled in either pre-primary or primary programmes. At the other end of the spectrum, a 17-year-old can expect to spend an average of 2.5 years in tertiary education (p. 216).

- In the majority of OECD countries, women can expect to receive more years of education than men – an additional 0.5 years, on average. However, in Korea, Switzerland and Turkey, men can expect to have between 0.7 to 2.8 more years of education (p. 216).

...entry to and participation in different types of educational programmes and institutions,...

Virtually all young people in OECD countries can expect to go to school for 11 years. However, participation patterns and progression through education vary widely. Both the timing and participation rate in pre-school and after the end of compulsory education differ considerably between countries. Some countries have extended participation in education, for example, by making pre-school education almost universal by the age of three, by retaining the majority of young people in education until the end of their teens, or by maintaining 10 to 20 per cent participation among up to the late 20s. High tertiary entry and participation rates help to ensure the development and maintenance of a highly educated population and labour force. Rates of entry to both types of tertiary education (**Indicator C2**) are an indication, in part, of the degree to which the population is acquiring high-level skills and knowledge valued by the labour market in knowledge societies.

While the successful graduation from upper secondary education is becoming the norm in most OECD countries, routes to it are becoming increasingly varied. Upper secondary programmes can differ in their curricular content, often depending on the type of further education or occupation for which the programmes are intended to prepare students. Most upper secondary programmes in OECD countries are primarily designed to prepare students for further studies at the tertiary level. The orientation of these programmes can be general, pre-vocational or vocational. Besides the programmes primarily preparing students for further education, in most OECD countries there are also upper secondary programmes designed to prepare students for direct entry to the labour market. Enrolment in these different types of educational programmes is also examined in **Indicator C2**.

- Today, four out of ten school leavers are likely to attend tertiary programmes leading to the equivalent of a bachelors' or higher tertiary-type A degree. In some OECD countries, the figure can be as high as one of every two school leavers (p. 223).

- With the exception of France, Germany and Turkey, participation in tertiary education grew in all OECD countries between 1995 and 2000; in the majority of OECD countries by more than 15 per cent, and in the Czech Republic, Hungary, Korea and Poland by more than 50 per cent (p. 225).

- The majority of students in primary and secondary education are enrolled in public institutions. However, 11 per cent of primary level students, 14 per cent of lower secondary level students, and 19 per cent of upper secondary level students, on average, are enrolled in privately managed schools. At all levels, the majority of students in Belgium and in the Netherlands are enrolled in privately managed schools, and in Korea and the United Kingdom, the majority of students in upper secondary education are enrolled in privately managed schools (p. 229).

- In most OECD countries, the majority of tertiary students are enrolled in public institutions. However, in Belgium, Japan, Korea, the Netherlands and the United Kingdom, privately managed institutions enrol the majority of students (p. 229).

...learning beyond initial education...

There is ample evidence that more secondary and tertiary education for young people improves their individual economic and social prospects. There is also growing, albeit less direct evidence, of a pay-off for societies at large from having a more highly educated population (**Indicators A13** and **A14**). But as rapidly changing technology and globalisation transform the pattern of demand for skilled labour world-wide, increasing the proportion of young people who participate in upper secondary or higher education can only be one part of the solution, for several reasons. First, an inflow of better-educated young people can only gradually change the overall educational level of the existing workforce. Second, educational attainment is only one component of human capital accumulation since knowledge and skills continue to be acquired lifelong, not only in education settings but also through family life, from experience with communities and in business. Strategies for developing lifelong learning opportunities must therefore look beyond mainstream educational programmes and qualifications if they are to ensure optimal investment in human capital. **Indicator C4** brings together evidence from the International Adult Literacy Survey (1994-1998) and national household surveys on adult education and training, which both provide some understanding of participation in job-related education and training of the employed.

- For half of the reporting OECD countries, more than 40 per cent of the adult population participated in some form of continuing education and training within a 12-month period (p. 248).

- The incidence and intensity of continuing education and training varies greatly between OECD countries. Participation rates range from 18 per cent or lower in Hungary, Poland and Portugal, to more than 50 per cent in Denmark, Finland, Sweden and the United States (p. 248).

- In 11 out of the 19 OECD countries, adults with tertiary qualifications are between two and three times more likely to participate in job-related training than adults who have not completed upper secondary education; thus education combines with other influences to make adult training least common among those who need it most (p. 248).

- Women with lower levels of educational attainment tend to receive less job-related continuing education and training but the pattern becomes less pronounced for women with upper secondary and tertiary qualifications (p. 248).

...and cross-border movements of students.

The international dimension of higher education is receiving more and more attention. The general trend towards freely circulating capital, goods and people, coupled with changes in the openness of labour markets, have increased the demand for new kinds of skills and knowledge in OECD countries. Governments are looking increasingly to higher education to play a role in broadening the horizons of students and allowing them to develop a deeper understanding of the multiplicity of languages, cultures and business methods in the world.

One way for students to expand their knowledge is to attend higher educational institutions in countries other than their own. International student mobility involves costs and benefits to students and institutions in sending and host countries alike. While the direct short-term monetary costs and benefits of this mobility are relatively easy to measure, the long-term social and economic benefits to students, institutions and countries are more difficult to quantify. The number of students studying in other countries (**Indicator C3**), however, provides some idea of the extent of student mobility.

- Five countries (Australia, France, Germany, the United Kingdom and the United States) attract seven out of ten foreign students studying in the OECD area (p. 237).

- In absolute numbers, Greek, Japanese and Korean students represent the largest sources of foreign students from OECD countries, while students from China and Southeast Asia make up the largest numbers of foreign students from non-OECD countries (p. 239).

- In relative terms, foreign students in OECD countries constitute from below 1 per cent to almost 17 per cent of tertiary enrolments. Proportional to their size, Australia, Austria, Belgium, Switzerland and the United Kingdom show the largest proportions of foreign students, measured as a percentage of their tertiary enrolments (p. 240).

Chapter D examines the learning environment and organisation of schools, in terms of...

Chapters A, B and C examined financial resources invested in education, patterns of participation, and the results of education in terms of student achievement and the labour market outcomes of education. Chapter D now looks at teaching and learning conditions in education systems. Learning in schools is mostly organised in classroom settings where teachers are the primary agents for planning, pacing and monitoring learning. In the first five indicators, school conditions are analysed from the learners' point of view, while the last two indicators present system-level information on the working conditions of the teaching force.

...student learning conditions,...

How effectively learning time is used depends on how appropriate study programmes are, and on how much instruction time a student receives. **Indicator D1** examines instruction time available for various study areas for students between 9 and 14 years of age. The size of the learning group that shares teacher time is another variable for measuring the use of classroom learning time. **Indicator D2** looks at the variation in average class size, and the ratio of students to teaching staff across OECD countries to estimate the human resources available for individual students.

- Students between the ages of 9 and 11 spend an average of 841 hours per year in the classroom. Students between the ages of 12 and 14 spend nearly 100 hours more, although the figures vary significantly across countries (p. 279).

- On average across countries, reading and writing in the language of instruction, mathematics, and science, comprise about half the compulsory curriculum for 9 to 11 year-olds, and 40 per cent for 12 to 14-year-olds (p. 279).

- 15-year-old students spend an average of 4.6 hours per week on homework and learning in the language of instruction, mathematics and science in addition to instruction time spent in the classroom (p. 280).

- On average, one in three 15-year-olds receive, at least occasionally, private tutoring or private instruction (p. 281).

- The average class size in primary education is 22 students, but the figure varies from 36 students in Korea to fewer than half that number in Greece, Iceland and Luxembourg (p. 288).

...the availability and use of information technology at school and at home...

In addition to classroom time and human resources, new technologies assume an increasingly important role in education. They not only equip students with important skills to participate effectively in the modern world, but also foster the development of self-regulated learning strategies and skills, as part of an essential foundation for lifelong learning. The mere presence of modern information and communication technology (ICT) in schools does not guarantee its effective use, but its availability is critical for improving teaching and learning conditions in schools and for providing equitable education for all. **Indicator D3** looks at the availability of ICT in students' homes and schools, and the use of technology in teaching and learning. **Indicator D4** goes further by analysing the attitudes and experiences of young males and females in using information technology.

- On average across countries, the typical 15-year-old attends a school with 13 students for one computer but this varies widely across countries and, in some countries, between regions and schools (p. 296).

- On average across countries, about one-third of 15-year-old students reported using a computer at school daily or at least a few times per week but the frequency of using a computer at home is almost double this. However, the percentage of 15-year-olds who say that they never have a computer available to them is 10 percentage points higher for the home than for school, which suggests that schools may play an important role in bridging the educational gap between the "information have and have-nots" (p. 297).

- On average in OECD countries, 15-year-old males are significantly more confident in their perceived ability to use computers than females. Gender differences are greatest in Denmark, Finland and Sweden, and smallest in Australia, New Zealand, Scotland and the United States (p. 309).

- With the exception of Ireland, Mexico and the United States, 15-year-old males report significantly higher levels of interest in computers than females (p. 309).

...classroom and school climate ...

Teachers act as professionals with a relatively high degree of freedom to organise students' learning activities and to evaluate their progress. Their subject knowledge, pedagogical skills, discipline, enthusiasm and commitment are important for determining the learning climate of the classroom and, more generally, the school. Other factors such as student discipline, the availability of educational resources, and school autonomy also influence the working climate of the school which, in turn, significantly affects education outcomes. **Indicator D5** first examines those aspects of classroom climate that appear to favour learning of 15-year-olds, and the differences between countries with respect to these. Next, the indicator presents indices on the working climate of schools showing patterns of differences between countries with respect to relevant school climate factors.

- Compared to the OECD mean, 15-year-olds in Australia, Canada, New Zealand, Portugal, Sweden, the United Kingdom and the United States reported receiving more support from their teachers than those in Austria, Belgium, the Czech Republic, Germany, Italy, Korea, Luxembourg and Poland (p. 318).

- On average across countries, one 15-year-old in three reported that more than five minutes are spent at the start of the class doing nothing; more than one in four complained about noise and disorder (p. 318).

- More than half the 15-year-olds in Australia, Denmark, Ireland, New Zealand, Norway, Sweden and the United Kingdom reported that they regularly use the science laboratory compared to less than 10 per cent in Finland and Hungary (p. 320).

- School resources tend to be used more frequently, schools tend to have a higher level of autonomy, teachers' morale and commitment tend to be higher, and teacher-student relations tend to be relatively better in high performing countries, whereas in countries with relatively low performance, negative school climate indices tend to cluster, and the indices on the use of school resources, teachers' morale and commitment, school autonomy and teacher-student relations tend to fall below the OECD average (p. 322).

...and teachers' working conditions.

Chapter D concludes with a comparative review of teachers' working conditions. Education systems employ a large number of professionals in increasingly competitive market conditions. Ensuring a sufficient number of skilled teachers is a key concern in all OECD countries. Key determinants of the supply of qualified teachers are the salaries and working conditions of teachers, including starting salaries and pay scales, and the costs incurred by individuals to become teachers, compared with salaries and costs in other occupations. Both affect the career decisions of potential teachers and the types of people attracted to the teaching profession. At the same time, teachers' salaries are the largest single factor in the cost of providing education. Teacher compensation is thus a critical consideration for policy-makers seeking to maintain the quality of teaching and a balanced education budget. The size of education budgets naturally reflects trade-offs between a number of interrelated factors, including teachers' salaries, the ratio of students to teaching staff, the quantity of instruction time planned for students, and the designated number of teaching hours. To shed light on these issues, **Indicator D6** shows the starting, mid-career and maximum statutory salaries of teachers in public primary and secondary education, and incentive schemes and bonuses used in teacher rewards systems.

Together with class size and the ratio of students to teaching staff (**Indicator D2**), hours of instruction for students (**Indicator D1**) and teachers' salaries (**Indicator D6**), the amount of time that teachers spend in the classroom teaching influences the financial resources which countries need to invest in education. While the number of teaching hours and the extent of non-teaching responsibilities are important parts of a teacher's working conditions, they also affect the attractiveness of the profession itself. **Indicator D7** examines the statutory working time of teachers at different levels of education, as well as the statutory teaching time, *i.e.*, the time that full-time teachers are expected to spend teaching students. Although working time and teaching time only partly determine the actual workload of teachers, they do give some insight into differences between countries in what is demanded of teachers.

- The mid-career salaries of lower secondary teachers range from less than US $ 10 000 in the Czech Republic and Hungary to US $ 40 000 and more in Germany, Japan, Korea, Switzerland and the United States. Some countries make a major investment in human resources despite lower levels of national income (p. 332).

- An upper secondary teacher's salary per contact hour is, on average, 42 per cent higher than that of a primary teacher. This difference in compensation per teaching hour between these two levels is 10 per cent or less in Australia, New Zealand, Scotland and the United States, and more than 80 per cent in Spain and Switzerland (p. 334).

- Teachers in Australia, Denmark, England, New Zealand and Scotland reach the highest step on the salary scale in 11 years or less. More than 30 years of service are required for a teacher to reach the maximum salary level in Austria, the Czech Republic, France, Greece, Hungary, Italy, Japan, Korea and Spain (p. 334).

- Schools have at least some responsibility in deciding the levels and extent of compensation for additional responsibilities and overtime in about half of OECD countries (p. 335).

- Public primary school teachers teach an average of 792 hours per year; the figure ranges from 583 hours to 1 139 hours (p. 343).

- At the lower secondary level, teachers teach an average of 720 hours, but the figure ranges from 555 hours to 1 182 hours. Regulations of teachers' working time vary. In most countries, teachers are formally required to work a specific number of hours. Some countries specify teaching time in lessons per week, in others, time is set aside for non-teaching school activities, and in some countries, the hours when teachers are required to be at school are specified (p. 343).

FURTHER RESOURCES

The web site *www.oecd.org/els/education/eag2002* provides a rich source of information on the methods employed for the calculation of the indicators, the interpretation of the indicators in the respective national contexts and the data sources involved. The web site also provides access to the data underlying the indicators.

The web site *www.pisa.oecd.org* provides information on the OECD Programme for International Student Assessment (PISA), on which many of the indicators in this publication draw.

Education Policy Analysis is a companion volume to *Education at a Glance*, which takes up selected themes of key importance for governments. The five chapters in this year's edition of *Education Policy Analysis* reviews five themes: Eight key strategies for improving access to quality early childhood education and care are identified; the characteristics of countries that achieve high quality reading skills of 15-year-olds from all social backgrounds are analysed; policies that countries can use to attract, develop and retain effective teachers are explored; and the growth of education across national borders is documented, and its challenges for national policy making discussed. In addition, a broader concept of "human capital" is developed that helps bridge the gap between education's economic mission, and its wider social and personal benefits.

READER'S GUIDE

Coverage of the statistics

Although a lack of data still limits the scope of the indicators in many countries, the coverage extends, in principle, to the entire national education system regardless of the ownership or sponsorship of the institutions concerned and regardless of education delivery mechanisms. With one exception described below, all types of students and all age groups are meant to be included: children (including students with special needs), adults, nationals, foreigners, as well as students in open distance learning, in special education programmes or in educational programmes organised by ministries other than the Ministry of Education, provided the main aim of the programme is the educational development of the individual. However, vocational and technical training in the workplace, with the exception of combined school and work-based programmes that are explicitly deemed to be parts of the education system, is not included in the basic education expenditure and enrolment data.

Educational activities classified as "adult" or "non-regular" are covered, provided that the activities involve studies or have a subject-matter content similar to "regular" education studies or that the underlying programmes lead to potential qualifications similar to corresponding regular educational programmes. Courses for adults that are primarily for general interest, personal enrichment, leisure or recreation are excluded.

Calculation of international means

For many indicators a country mean is presented and for some an OECD total.

The *country mean* is calculated as the unweighted mean of the data values of all countries for which data are available or can be estimated. The country mean therefore refers to an average of data values at the level of the national systems and can be used to answer the question of how an indicator value for a given country compares with the value for a typical or average country. It does not take into account the absolute size of the education system in each country.

The *OECD total* is calculated as a weighted mean of the data values of all countries for which data are available or can be estimated. It reflects the value for a given indicator when the OECD area is considered as a whole. This approach is taken for the purpose of comparing, for example, expenditure charts for individual countries with those of the entire OECD area for which valid data are available, with this area considered as a single entity.

Note that both the country mean and the OECD total can be significantly affected by missing data. Given the relatively small number of countries, no statistical methods are used to compensate for this. In cases where a category is not applicable (code "a") in a country or where the data value is negligible (code "n") for the corresponding calculation, the value zero is imputed for the purpose of calculating country means. In cases where both the numerator and the denominator of a ratio are not applicable (code "a") for a certain country, this country is not included in the country mean.

For financial tables using 1995 data, both the country mean and OECD total are calculated for countries providing both 1995 and 1999 data. This allows comparison of the country mean and OECD total over time with no distortion due to the exclusion of certain countries in the different years.

Classification of levels of education

The classification of the levels of education is based on the revised International Standard Classification of Education (ISCED-97). The biggest change between the revised ISCED and the former ISCED (ISCED-76) is the introduction of a multi-dimensional classification framework, allowing for the alignment of the educational content of programmes using multiple classification criteria. ISCED is an instrument for compiling statistics on education internationally and distinguishes among six levels of education. The *Glossary and the notes in Annex 3 (Indicator A2)* describe in detail the ISCED levels of education, and Annex 1 shows corresponding theoretical graduation ages of the main educational programmes by ISCED level.

Symbols for missing data

Four symbols are employed in the tables and graphs to denote missing data:

a   Data not applicable because the category does not apply.

c   There are too few observations to provide reliable estimates *(i.e.,* there are fewer than five schools or fewer than 30 students with valid data for this cell).

m   Data not available.

n   Magnitude is either negligible or zero.

x   Data included in another category or column of the table *(e.g., x(2)* means that data included in column 2 of the table).

Country codes

OECD Member countries

Australia	AUS	Korea	KOR
Austria	AUT	Luxembourg	LUX
Belgium	BEL	Mexico	MEX
Belgium (Flemish Community)	BFL	Netherlands	NLD
Canada	CAN	New Zealand	NZL
Czech Republic	CZE	Norway	NOR
Denmark	DNK	Poland	POL
Finland	FIN	Portugal	PRT
France	FRA	Slovak Republic	SVK
Germany	DEU	Spain	ESP
Greece	GRC	Sweden	SWE
Hungary	HUN	Switzerland	CHE
Iceland	ISL	Turkey	TUR
Ireland	IRL	United Kingdom	UKM
Italy	ITA	United States	USA
Japan	JPN		

Countries participating in the OECD/UNESCO World Education Indicators programme

Argentina, Brazil, Chile, China, Egypt, India, Indonesia, Jamaica, Jordan, Malaysia, Paraguay, Peru, Philippines, Russian Federation, Thailand, Tunisia, Uruguay and Zimbabwe participate in the OECD/UNESCO World Education Indicators (WEI) programme. Data for these countries are collected using the same standards and methods that are applied for OECD countries and therefore included in this publication. Israel has observer status in OECD's activities on education and has contributed to the OECD indicators on educational finance.

Chapter

THE OUTPUT OF
EDUCATIONAL INSTITUTIONS
AND THE IMPACT OF LEARNING

OVERVIEW

Indicator A1: Current upper secondary graduation rates and attainment of the adult population

Table A1.1. Upper secondary graduation rates (2000)
Table A1.2. Population that has attained at least upper secondary education (2001)
Table A1.3. Post-secondary non-tertiary graduation rates (2000)

Chapter A examines the outcomes of education and learning, in terms of…

Indicator A2: Current tertiary graduation and survival rates and attainment of the adult population

Table A2.1. Tertiary graduation rates (2000)
Table A2.2. Survival rates in tertiary education (2000)
Table A2.3. Population that has attained tertiary education (2001)

…the current output of educational institutions and educational attainment of the adult population,…

Indicator A3: Educational attainment of the labour force and adult population

Table A3.1a. Educational attainment of the population (2001)
Table A3.1b. Educational attainment of the labour force (2001)
Table A3.1c. Educational attainment of the population, by gender (2001)

Indicator A4: Graduates by field of study

Table A4.1. Tertiary graduates, by field of study and level of education (2000)
Table A4.2. Percentage of tertiary qualifications awarded to women, by type of tertiary education and by subject category (2000)

Indicator A5: Reading literacy of 15-year-olds

Table A5.1. Reading proficiency of 15-year-olds (2000)
Table A5.2. Variation in performance in reading literacy of 15-year-olds (2000)

…the quality of learning outcomes and how this varies among schools and students,…

Indicator A6: Mathematical and scientific literacy of 15-year-olds

Table A6.1. Variation in performance in mathematical literacy of 15-year-olds (2000)
Table A6.2. Variation in performance in scientific literacy of 15-year-olds (2000)

Indicator A7: How student performance varies between schools

Table A7.1. Sources of variation in performance in reading literacy of 15-year-old students (2000)

Indicator A8: Civic knowledge and engagement

Table A8.1. Civic attitudes and civic engagement of 14-year-olds (1999)

Indicator A9: Occupational status of parents and student performance

Table A9.1. Student performance and socio-economic status (2000)

…equity in educational opportunities and outcomes…

A

...and the returns to education for individuals and society.

Indicator A10: Place of birth, language spoken at home, and reading literacy of 15-year-olds

Table A10.1. Performance in reading literacy and country of birth of 15-year-olds and their parents (2000)

Table A10.2. Performance in reading literacy and language spoken at home of 15-year-olds (2000)

Indicator A11: Labour force participation by level of educational attainment

Table A11.1. Labour force participation rates, by level of educational attainment (2001)

Table A11.2. Unemployment rates, by level of educational attainment (2001)

Indicator A12: Expected years in education, employment and non-employment between the ages of 15 and 29

Table A12.1. Expected years in education and not in education for 15 to 29-year-olds, by gender and work status (2001)

Indicator A13: The returns to education: Private and social rates of return to education and their determinants

Table A13.1. Relative earnings of the population with income from employment

Table A13.2. Differences in earnings between women and men

Table A13.3. Private internal rates of return to education (1999-2000)

Table A13.4. Social rates of return to education (1999-2000)

Indicator A14: The returns to education: Links between human capital and economic growth

Table A14.1. Decomposition of changes in annual average growth rates of GDP per capita (1980-1997)

Indicators A5, A6, A7, A9 and A10 draw on data from the Programme of International Student Assessment (PISA). Detailed information on this programme is available on the web site *www.pisa.oecd.org.*

CURRENT UPPER SECONDARY GRADUATION RATES AND ATTAINMENT OF THE ADULT POPULATION

A1

- In the majority of OECD countries for which comparable data are available, the ratio of upper secondary graduates to the population at the typical age of graduation exceeds 70 per cent. In Germany, Hungary, Japan, Poland and the Slovak Republic, graduation rates are 90 per cent or above. The challenge now is to ensure that the remaining fraction is not left behind, with the risk of social exclusion that this may entail.

- Comparing the attainment of the population aged 25 to 34 years with that of the population aged 45 to 54 shows that the proportion of individuals who have not completed upper secondary education has been shrinking in almost all OECD countries, and in some rapidly.

- Among older age groups, women have attained lower levels of upper secondary education than men, but for younger people the pattern is now reversing. Today, graduation rates of women exceed those of men in most countries.

Chart A1.1.

Upper secondary graduation rates (2000)

Ratio of unduplicated count of all upper secondary graduates to population at typical age of graduation

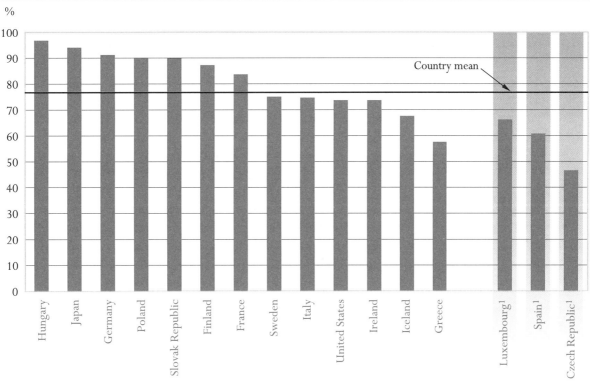

1. A significant proportion of the youth cohort is not covered by this indicator.
Countries are ranked in descending order of total upper secondary graduation rates.
Source: OECD. Table A1.1. See Annex 3 for notes *(www.oecd.org / els / education / eag2002).*

A1

To gauge the share of the population that has obtained the minimum credentials for successfully entering the labour market ...

...this indicator shows the current upper secondary graduate output of educational institutions...

...as well as historical patterns of upper secondary completion.

In 11 out of 13 OECD countries with comparable data, upper secondary graduation rates exceed 70 per cent...

...and in Germany, Hungary, Japan, Poland and the Slovak Republic they are 90 per cent or above.

Policy context

Rising skill demands in OECD countries have made qualifications at the upper secondary level of education the minimum credential for successful labour market entry. Upper secondary education serves as the foundation for advanced learning and training opportunities, as well as preparation for direct entry into the labour market. Although many countries do allow students to leave the education system at the end of the lower secondary level, young people in OECD countries who leave without an upper secondary qualification tend to face severe difficulties in entering the labour market (see Indicators A11 to A14).

The upper secondary graduation rate reflects the current output of education systems, *i.e.*, the percentage of the typical upper secondary school age population that follow and successfully complete upper secondary programmes. Although high upper secondary graduation rates do not guarantee that an education system has adequately equipped its graduates with the basic skills and knowledge necessary to enter the labour market – this indicator does not capture the quality of educational outcomes – it is one indication of the extent to which education systems succeed in meeting the minimum requirements of the labour market.

By comparing educational attainment levels between different generations one can identify the evolution of education levels within the population, reflecting both changing demands of the labour market and changing educational policies.

Evidence and explanations

Upper secondary graduation rates are estimated as the number of persons, regardless of their age, who graduate for the first time from upper secondary programmes per 100 people at the age at which students typically graduate from upper secondary education (see Annex 1). The graduation rates take into account students graduating from upper secondary education at the modal or typical graduation ages, and older students (*e.g.*, those in "second chance" programmes). In 11 out of 13 of the OECD countries with comparable data, upper secondary graduation rates exceed 70 per cent (Chart A1.1).

In five of the 13 countries for which comparable numbers of graduates are available, graduation rates are 90 per cent or above (Germany, Hungary, Japan, Poland and the Slovak Republic). Caution should be used in interpreting the graduation rates displayed in Chart A1.1 for the following countries: In the Czech Republic and Spain, the length of secondary programmes was recently extended, which leads to an underestimation of graduation rates, and many Luxembourg nationals study in neighbouring countries.

Some countries provide "second chance" opportunities for obtaining upper secondary credentials by offering examinations rather than providing upper secondary programmes for adults. In the United States, students who do not successfully complete the last year of upper secondary education – a relatively large proportion – often take and pass a test of General Educational Development (GED) at a later point in time. This qualification is formally regarded as the equivalent of an upper secondary qualification.

A comparison of the levels of educational attainment between older and younger age groups indicates marked progress with regard to the percentage of the population graduating from upper secondary education (Chart A1.2). On average, only 60 per cent of 45 to 54 year-olds have attained an upper secondary level of education, compared to 74 per cent of 25 to 34-year-olds.

Upper secondary attainment levels have increased in almost all countries…

This is especially striking in countries whose adult population generally has a lower attainment level. In younger age groups, differences between countries in the level of educational attainment are less pronounced. As a result, many countries currently showing low attainment in the adult population are expected to move closer to those with higher attainment levels. In Korea, Portugal and Spain, the proportion of individuals aged 25 to 34 with at least upper secondary attainment is around twice as high as that in the age group 45 to 54.

…and many countries with traditionally low levels of education are catching up.

Chart A1.2.

Percentage of the population that has attained at least upper secondary education[1], by age group (2001)

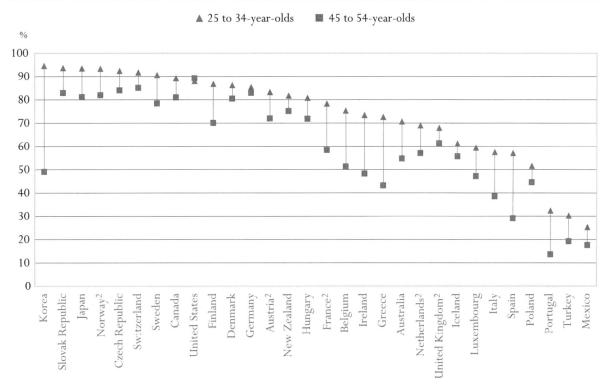

▲ 25 to 34-year-olds   ■ 45 to 54-year-olds

Note: Not all ISCED 3 programmes meet minimum requirements for ISCED 3C long programmes. See Annex 3 for notes.
1. Excluding ISCED 3C short programmes.
2. Year of reference 2000.
Countries are ranked in descending order of the percentage of 25 to 34-year-olds who have attained at least upper secondary education.
Source: OECD. Table A1.2. See Annex 3 for a description of ISCED-97 levels, ISCED-97 country mappings and national data sources *(www.oecd.org/els/education/eag2002).*

A1

Gender differences in graduation rates

Among older age groups, women have lower levels of education than men...

The balance of educational attainment among men and women in the adult population is unequal in most OECD countries: historically women did not have sufficient opportunities and/or incentives to reach the same level of education as men. Women are generally over-represented among those who did not proceed to upper secondary education and under-represented at the higher levels of education (see also Indicator A3).

...but for younger people the pattern is now reversing.

However, these differences are mostly attributable to the large gender differences in the attainment of older age groups and have been significantly reduced or reversed among younger age groups.

Today, graduation rates for women exceed those for men in most countries.

Today, graduation rates no longer show significant differences between men and women in half of the countries with available data (Table A1.1). Further, in 14 out of 16 OECD countries for which upper secondary graduation rates can be compared between the genders, graduation rates for women exceed those for men in Finland, Greece, Iceland, Ireland, Italy and Spain by 10 percentage points or more. In the majority of OECD countries, the gender ratio for upper secondary programmes designed to lead to further tertiary-type A education (ISCED 3A) strongly favours women, only in Korea and Turkey do more men graduate than women.

Graduation from post-secondary non-tertiary programmes

In some countries, a significant proportion of students broaden their knowledge at the upper secondary level after completing a first upper secondary programme.

Post-secondary non-tertiary programmes straddle the boundary between upper secondary and post-secondary education from a comparative point of view, even though they might clearly be considered upper secondary or post-secondary programmes in a national context. Although their content may not be significantly more advanced than upper secondary programmes, they serve to broaden the knowledge of participants who have already gained an upper secondary qualification. The students tend to be older than those enrolled at the upper secondary level.

In Canada, Hungary and Ireland 28 per cent or more of a typical age cohort complete a post-secondary non-tertiary programme.

Typical examples of such programmes would be trade and vocational certificates in Canada and the United States, nursery teacher training in Austria and Switzerland or vocational training in the dual system for holders of general upper secondary qualifications in Germany. In most countries, post-secondary non-tertiary programmes are vocationally oriented.

In half of OECD countries where post-secondary non-tertiary programmes are offered, a significant proportion of upper secondary graduates also graduate from a post-secondary non-tertiary programme, either instead of or in addition to tertiary education (OECD average 9 per cent). In Canada, Hungary and Ireland, 28 per cent or more of a typical age cohort complete a post-secondary non-tertiary programme (Table A1.3).

In almost two-thirds of OECD countries with available data, the majority of post-secondary non-tertiary students graduate from ISCED 4C programmes, which are designed primarily to prepare graduates for direct entry into the labour market. Apprenticeships that are designed for students who have already graduated from an upper secondary programme are also included in this category. However, in Belgium, the Czech Republic, Germany, the Slovak Republic and Spain, the majority of post-secondary non-tertiary graduates are from ISCED 4A programmes, most of which are designed to provide direct access to tertiary-type A education.

Definitions and methodologies

Upper secondary graduates are those who successfully complete the final year of upper secondary education, regardless of their age. In some countries, successful completion requires a final examination; in others it does not.

Graduate data refer to the school year 1999–2000 and are based on the UOE data collection on education statistics that is administered annually by the OECD.

Gross graduation rates for ISCED 3A, 3B and 3C programmes cannot be added, as some individuals graduate from more than one upper secondary programme and would thus be counted twice. The same applies for graduation rates by programme orientation, *i.e.*, general or vocational. The unduplicated total count of graduates is calculated by netting out those students who graduated from another upper secondary programme in a previous year.

For some countries, an unduplicated count of post-secondary non-tertiary graduates is unavailable and graduation rates may be overestimated because graduates complete multiple programmes at the same level. These countries are marked with a footnote in Table A1.3.

Pre-vocational and vocational programmes include both school-based programmes and combined school and work-based programmes that are recognised as part of the education system. Entirely work-based education and training that is not overseen by a formal education authority is not taken into account.

Data on population and educational attainment are taken from OECD and EUROSTAT databases, which are compiled from National Labour Force Surveys. See Annex 3 at *www.oecd.org/els/education/eag2002* for national sources.

Educational attainment data derive from National Labour Force Surveys and use the International Standard Classification of Education (ISCED-97).

The attainment profiles are based on the percentage of the population aged 25 to 64 years that has completed a specified level of education. The International Standard Classification of Education (ISCED-97) is used to define the levels of education. See Annex 3 at *www.oecd.org/els/education/eag2002* for a description of ISCED-97 education levels and mappings for each country.

Table A1.1.
Upper secondary graduation rates (2000)
Ratio of upper secondary graduates to total population at typical age of graduation (multiplied by 100) in public and private institutions, by programme destination, programme orientation and gender

	Total (unduplicated)			ISCED 3A (designed to prepare for direct entry to tertiary-type A education)		ISCED 3B (designed to prepare for direct entry to tertiary-type B education)		ISCED 3C (long) similar to duration of typical 3A or 3B programmes		ISCED 3C (short) shorter than duration of typical 3A or 3B programmes		General programmes		Pre-vocational/Vocational programmes	
	M + F	Males	Females	M + F	Females	M + F	Females	M + F	Females	M + F	Females	M + F	Females	M + F	Females
	(1)	(2)	(3)	(4)	(5)	(6)	(7)	(8)	(9)	(10)	(11)	(12)	(13)	(14)	(15)
Australia	m	m	m	67	73	m	m	m	m	m	m	m	m	m	m
Austria	m	m	m	m	m	m	m	m	m	m	m	m	m	m	m
Belgium	m	m	m	60	64	a	a	19	19	11	15	36	40	54	57
Canada	m	m	m	m	m	m	m	m	m	m	m	m	m	m	m
Czech Republic[1]*	47	50	42	18	21	n	n	a	a	31	23	8	10	41	35
Denmark	m	m	m	52	64	a	a	54	64	a	a	52	64	54	64
Finland	87	81	94	87	94	a	a	a	a	a	a	53	64	72	77
France	84	81	86	49	57	10	8	2	2	37	32	31	37	67	62
Germany	91	89	94	33	36	58	57	a	a	a	a	33	36	58	57
Greece	58	50	66	56	64	m	m	26	22	m	m	56	64	26	22
Hungary	97	98	95	58	65	1	2	x(10)	x(11)	37	28	26	32	70	62
Iceland	67	60	76	47	58	n	n	22	14	14	16	47	58	36	30
Ireland	74	67	80	74	80	a	a	5	5	a	a	59	63	20	23
Italy	75	68	81	74	80	1	1	a	a	19	18	29	39	64	60
Japan	94	92	96	69	73	1	n	24	23	x(8)	x(9)	69	73	26	24
Korea	m	m	m	60	58	a	a	37	38	a	a	60	58	37	38
Luxembourg[1]*	66	63	69	39	47	6	5	20	17	a	a	26	29	40	40
Mexico	m	m	m	28	30	a	a	4	5	x(8)	x(9)	28	30	4	5
Netherlands	m	m	m	63	68	a	a	32	29	x(8)	x(9)	37	41	57	56
New Zealand	m	m	m	65	70	45	52	12	14	x(8)	x(9)	m	m	m	m
Norway	m	m	m	64	79	a	a	52	44	m	m	64	79	52	44
Poland	90	87	94	70	78	a	a	a	a	29	21	32	41	67	58
Portugal	m	m	m	m	m	m	m	m	m	m	m	m	m	m	m
Slovak Republic	90	90	90	72	80	n	n	1	1	24	17	18	21	79	77
Spain[1]*	61	54	67	46	53	n	n	9	9	13	15	46	53	22	24
Sweden	75	72	78	74	77	a	a	1	n	a	a	42	46	32	31
Switzerland	m	m	m	19	22	50	42	13	19	n	n	m	m	m	m
Turkey*	m	m	m	37	31	a	a	m	m	a	a	20	19	16	13
United Kingdom	m	m	m	m	m	m	m	m	m	m	m	m	m	m	m
United States	74	73	74	m	m	m	m	m	m	m	m	m	m	m	m
Country mean	77	74	80	55	61	8	7	15	15	12	10	40	45	45	44
Argentina[2]	48	40	55	48	55	a	a	a	a	a	a	26	34	21	21
Brazil[2]	a	a	a	62	70	m	m	a	a	a	a	m	m	m	m
Chile[2]	a	a	a	34	39	28	28	a	a	a	a	34	39	28	28
China[2]	a	a	a	17	15	a	a	20	21	4	m	m	m	m	m
India	34	40	28	34	28	a	a	m	m	m	m	m	m	m	m
Indonesia[3]	a	a	a	19	20	13	11	a	a	a	a	19	20	13	11
Israel	m	m	m	59	67	26	23	3	1	a	a	59	67	26	23
Jamaica	a	a	a	65	67	n	n	a	a	a	a	65	67	n	n
Jordan	a	a	a	68	75	a	a	3	n	a	a	55	63	13	13
Malaysia[2]	m	m	m	14	19	a	a	53	63	a	a	65	81	2	1
Paraguay[2]	a	a	a	35	38	a	a	m	m	a	a	28	31	8	8
Peru[2]	a	a	a	50	50	x(4)	x(5)	a	a	a	a	41	42	9	8
Philippines[2]	a	a	a	66	72	a	a	a	a	a	a	66	72	a	a
Russian Federation[3]	a	a	a	53	m	a	a	m	m	m	m	m	m	m	m
Thailand	a	a	a	27	30	18	18	a	a	a	a	27	30	18	18
Tunisia	a	a	a	26	29	2	1	2	1	a	a	26	29	4	2
Zimbabwe[3]	a	a	a	3	3	1	1	m	m	m	m	m	m	m	m

Note: x indicates that data are included in another column. The column reference is shown in brackets after "x". *e.g.,* x(2) means that data are included in column 2.
1. Significant proportion of the youth cohort is missing.
2. Year of reference 1999.
3. Year of reference 2001.
*See Annex 3 for notes (*www.oecd.org/els/education/eag2002*).
Source: OECD.

A1

Table A1.2.
Population that has attained at least upper secondary education (2001)
Percentage of the population that has attained at least upper secondary education[1], by age group

	Age group				
	25-64	25-34	35-44	45-54	55-64
Australia	59	71	60	55	44
Austria[2]	76	83	80	72	63
Belgium[2]	59	75	63	51	38
Canada	82	89	85	81	67
Czech Republic	86	92	90	84	76
Denmark	80	86	80	80	72
Finland	74	87	84	70	51
France[1]	64	78	67	58	46
Germany	83	85	86	83	76
Greece	51	73	60	43	28
Hungary	70	81	79	72	44
Iceland	57	61	60	56	46
Ireland	58	73	62	48	35
Italy	43	57	49	39	22
Japan	83	94	94	81	63
Korea	68	95	77	49	30
Luxembourg	53	59	57	47	42
Mexico	22	25	25	17	11
Netherlands[2, 3]	65	74	69	60	51
New Zealand	76	82	80	75	60
Norway[2]	85	93	90	82	70
Poland	46	52	48	44	36
Portugal	20	32	20	14	9
Slovak Republic	85	94	90	83	66
Spain	40	57	45	29	17
Sweden	81	91	86	78	65
Switzerland	87	92	90	85	81
Turkey	24	30	24	19	13
United Kingdom[3]	63	68	65	61	55
United States	88	88	89	89	83
Country mean	*64*	*74*	*68*	*60*	*49*

OECD COUNTRIES

1. Excluding ISCED 3C short programmes.
2. Year of reference 2000.
3. Not all ISCED 3 programmes meet minimum requirements for ISCED 3C long programmes. See Annex 3 for notes (*www.oecd.org/els/education/eag2002*)
Source: OECD. See Annex 3 for a description of ISCED-97 levels, ISCED-97 country mappings and national data sources (*www.oecd.org/els/education/eag2002*).

Table A1.3.
Post-secondary non-tertiary graduation rates (2000)
Ratio of post-secondary non-tertiary graduates to total population at typical age of graduation (multiplied by 100) in public and private institutions,
by programme destination and gender

	Total (unduplicated)			ISCED 4A (designed to prepare for direct entry to tertiary-type A education)		ISCED 4B (designed to prepare for direct entry to tertiary-type B education)		ISCED 4C	
	M + F	Males	Females	M + F	Females	M + F	Females	M + F	Females
	(1)	(2)	(3)	(4)	(5)	(6)	(7)	(8)	(9)
Australia	m	m	m	m	m	m	m	m	m
Austria	m	m	m	m	m	m	m	m	m
Belgium[1]	17.8	16.1	19.6	10.2	10.3	a	a	7.6	9.2
Canada[1]	28.1	31.5	24.7	n	n	n	n	28.1	24.7
Czech Republic[1]	9.0	9.7	8.2	9.0	8.2	a	a	n	n
Denmark[1]	1.7	2.9	0.4	0.1	n	a	a	1.6	0.4
Finland	1.5	1.6	1.4	a	a	a	a	1.9	1.9
France[1]	1.2	0.8	1.7	0.7	0.8	a	a	0.6	0.9
Germany	14.8	16.0	13.5	9.3	8.7	5.5	4.8	a	a
Greece[1]	15.3	11.6	19.2	a	a	a	a	15.3	19.2
Hungary[1]	31.2	29.1	33.5	5.8	6.1	a	a	25.3	27.2
Iceland	6.1	8.3	3.9	a	a	a	a	6.2	4.0
Ireland	28.9	15.1	43.4	a	a	a	a	28.9	43.4
Italy	3.1	2.3	4.0	a	a	a	a	3.1	4.0
Japan	m	m	m	m	m	m	m	m	m
Korea	a	a	a	a	a	a	a	a	a
Luxembourg[1]	3.1	4.5	1.8	a	a	a	a	3.1	1.6
Mexico	a	a	a	a	a	a	a	a	a
Netherlands[1]	1.0	1.5	0.4	a	a	a	a	1.0	0.4
New Zealand[1]	2.6	1.7	3.6	n	0.1	0.2	0.2	2.3	3.3
Norway[1]	11.4	16.4	6.2	4.8	3.2	a	a	6.6	3.0
Poland[1]	12.6	8.4	16.9	a	a	12.6	16.9	a	a
Portugal	m	m	m	m	m	m	m	m	m
Slovak Republic[1]	2.2	1.3	3.1	2.2	3.1	a	a	a	a
Spain	9.8	9.2	10.5	9.5	10.1	0.3	0.4	n	n
Sweden	m	m	m	m	m	m	m	0.5	0.3
Switzerland[1]	17.6	16.1	19.1	3.0	2.0	14.6	17.2	n	n
Turkey	a	a	a	a	a	a	a	a	a
United Kingdom	m	m	m	m	m	m	m	m	m
United States	6.6	5.8	7.3	a	a	a	a	6.6	7.3
Country mean	*9.4*	*8.7*	*10.1*	*2.3*	*2.2*	*1.4*	*1.7*	*5.5*	*6.0*
Argentina [2]	a	a	a	a	a	a	a	a	a
Brazil[2]	a	a	a	a	a	m	m	a	a
China[2]	a	a	a	a	a	a	a	2.0	2.0
Indonesia[3]	a	a	a	a	a	a	a	a	a
Jordan	a	a	a	a	a	a	a	a	a
Malaysia[2]	m	m	m	0.6	0.6	0.7	0.2	0.3	0.3
Paraguay[2]	a	a	a	a	a	a	a	a	a
Peru[2]	a	a	a	a	a	a	a	m	m
Philippines[2]	a	a	a	6.0	m	x(4)	m	x(4)	m
Russian Federation[3]	a	a	a	a	a	a	a	32.5	22.7
Thailand	a	a	a	a	a	a	a	m	m
Tunisia	a	a	a	a	a	n	n	a	a

Note: x indicates that data are included in another column. The column reference is shown in brackets after "x". *e.g.*, x(2) means that data are included in column 2.
1. Gross graduation rate may include some double counting.
2. Year of reference 1999.
3. Year of reference 2001.
Source: OECD.

CURRENT TERTIARY GRADUATION AND SURVIVAL RATES AND ATTAINMENT OF THE ADULT POPULATION

A2

• On average across OECD countries, 26 per cent of persons at the typical age of graduation currently complete the tertiary-type A level of education - a figure which ranges from about a third or more in Australia, Finland, Iceland, Poland, the United Kingdom and the United States to below 20 per cent in Austria, the Czech Republic, Denmark, Germany, Italy and Switzerland.

• On average, one-third of OECD students "drop out" before they complete their first degree, regardless of whether they are following tertiary-type A or tertiary-type B programmes.

• As measured by educational attainment, there has been an increase in the stock of university-level skills in the adult population. But most of that increase is due to significant increases in tertiary graduation rates in a comparatively small number of countries.

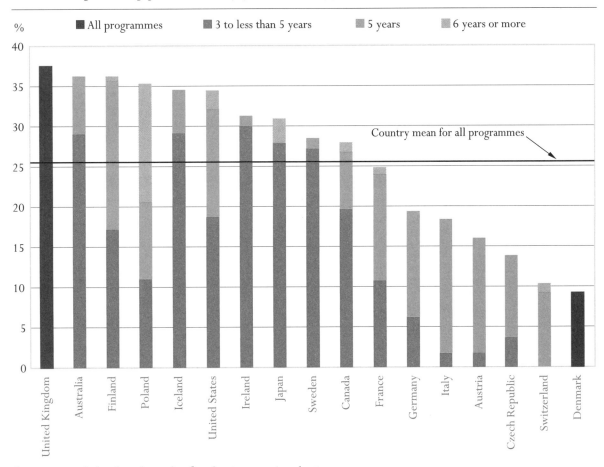

Chart A2.1.

Graduation rates in tertiary-type A education, by duration of programme (2000)

Ratio of number of graduates to the population at the typical age of graduation (multiplied by 100)

Countries are ranked in descending order of total tertiary-type A graduation rates.
Source: OECD. Table A2.1. See Annex 3 for notes *(www.oecd.org / els / education / eag2002).*

A₂

This indicator shows tertiary graduation rates as well as historical patterns of tertiary educational attainment...

...and sheds light on the internal efficiency of tertiary education systems.

Policy context

Tertiary graduation rates are an indicator of the current production rate of advanced knowledge by each country's education system. Countries with high graduation rates at the tertiary level are the most likely to be developing or maintaining a highly skilled labour force. Measures of educational attainment show the evolution of advanced knowledge in the population.

Tertiary level dropout and survival rates can be useful indicators of the internal efficiency of tertiary education systems but the specific reasons for leaving a tertiary programme are varied: students may realise that they have chosen the wrong subject or educational programme; they may fail to meet the standards set by their educational institution, particularly in tertiary systems that provide broader access; or they may find attractive employment before completing their programme. "Dropping out" is not necessarily an indication of failure by individual students, but high dropout rates may well indicate that the education system is not meeting the needs of its clients. Students may not find that the educational programmes offered meet their expectations or their labour market needs. It may also be that students find that programmes take longer than the number of years which they can justify being outside the labour market.

Evidence and explanations

Graduation rates at the tertiary level

Tertiary programmes vary widely in structure and scope between countries.

Tertiary graduation rates are influenced both by the degree of access to tertiary programmes, as well as by the demand for higher skills in the labour market. They are also affected by the way in which the degree and qualification structures are organised within countries.

This indicator distinguishes between different categories of tertiary qualifications: *i)* degrees at tertiary-type B level (ISCED 5B); *ii)* degrees at tertiary-type A level (ISCED 5A); and *iii)* advanced research qualifications at the doctorate level (ISCED 6).

Tertiary-type A programmes are subdivided in accordance with the theoretical duration of studies to allow for comparisons that are independent of differences in national degree structures.

Tertiary-type A programmes are largely theoretically-based and designed to provide sufficient qualifications for entry to advanced research programmes and professions with high skill requirements. Countries differ in the way in which tertiary-type A studies are organised, both in universities and in other institutions. The duration of programmes leading to a first type-A qualification ranges from three years (*e.g.*, the Bachelor's degree in most colleges in Ireland and the United Kingdom in most fields of study and the *Licence* in France) to five years or more (*e.g.*, the *Diplom* in Germany and the *Laurea* in Italy).

Whereas, in many countries, there is a clear distinction between first and second university degrees, *i.e.,* undergraduate and graduate programmes, this distinction is not made in other countries where degrees that are comparable internationally at the "Master's level" are obtained through a single programme of long duration. To ensure international comparability, it is therefore necessary to compare degree programmes of similar cumulative duration, as well as completion rates for first-degree programmes.

To allow for comparisons that are independent of differences in national degree structures, tertiary-type A degrees are subdivided in accordance with the total theoretical duration of studies at the tertiary level. For the purpose of this indicator, degrees are divided into those of medium (three to less than five years), long (five to less than six years) and very long (more than six years) duration. Degrees obtained from short programmes of less than three years' duration are not considered equivalent to the completion of the tertiary-type A level of education and are therefore not included in this indicator. Second-degree programmes are classified according to the cumulative duration of the first and second-degree programme and individuals who already hold a first degree are netted out of these.

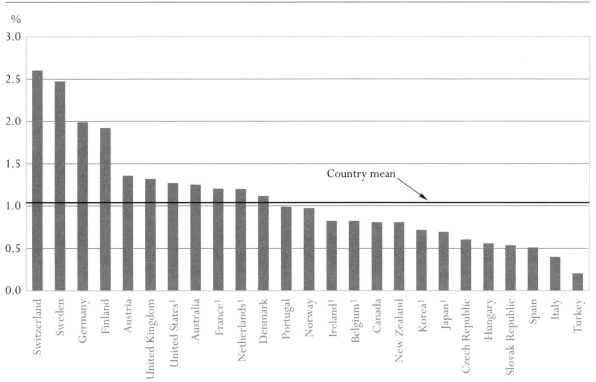

Chart A2.2.

Graduation rates for advanced research programmes (2000)

Sum of graduation rates over single years of age (multiplied by 100)

1. Gross graduation rates were used for these countries, which were calculated as the ratio of the number of graduates to the population at the typical age of graduation, multiplied by 100.
Countries are ranked in descending order of graduation rates for advanced research programmes.
Source: OECD. Table A2.1. See Annex 3 for notes. *(www.oecd.org/els/education/eag2002).*

A2

On average in OECD countries, 26 per cent of persons at the typical age of graduation complete tertiary-type A education...

On average in OECD countries, about 26 per cent of persons at the typical age of graduation complete tertiary-type A education. This figure ranges from over a third in Australia, Finland, Iceland, Poland, the United Kingdom and the United States to below 15 per cent in the Czech Republic, Denmark and Switzerland (Chart A2.1). In general, in countries with higher graduation rates the majority of students complete medium length programmes (3 to less than 5 years). Notable exceptions to this rule are Finland and Poland where the majority of students complete longer programmes. The pattern for countries with lower tertiary-type A graduation rates is more obvious. In Austria, the Czech Republic, Germany, Italy and Switzerland, the majority of students complete longer programmes (of at least 5 years duration) and graduation rates are below 20 per cent.

...while the graduation rate at the tertiary-type B level is 11 per cent...

Tertiary-type B programmes are more occupationally-oriented and lead to direct labour market access. The programmes are typically of shorter duration than type A programmes (typically two to three years). Generally they are not deemed to lead to university-level degrees. Graduation rates for tertiary-type B programmes account, on average in OECD countries, for around 11 per cent of an age cohort (Table A2.1). In Denmark and Japan, around 25 per cent of the population at the typical age of graduation complete the tertiary-type B level of education, and this figure is between 11 and 15 per cent in Finland, Germany and Ireland.

Chart A2.3.

Percentage of the population that has attained at least tertiary education, by age group (2001)

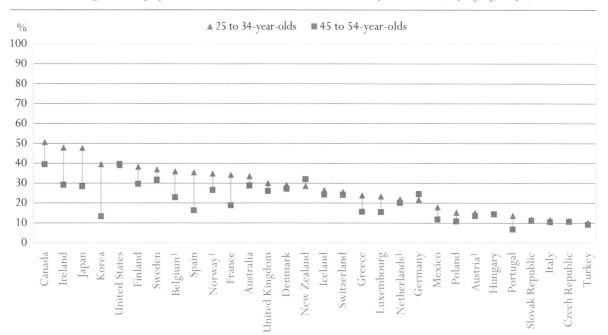

1. Year of reference 2000.
Countries are ranked in descending order of the percentage of 25 to 34-year-olds who have attained at least tertiary education.
Source: OECD. Table A2.3. See Annex 3 for a description of ISCED-97 levels, ISCED-97 country mappings and national data sources *(www.oecd.org/els/education/eag2002).*

On average across OECD countries, 1 per cent of the population obtain an advanced research qualification, such as a Ph.D. In Sweden and Switzerland this is around 2.5 per cent and in Finland and Germany almost 2 per cent (Chart A2.2).

The rising skill requirements of labour markets, an increase in unemployment during recent years and higher expectations by individuals and society have influenced the proportion of young people who obtain at least a tertiary qualification. As measured by tertiary qualifications, there has been a general increase in the stock of higher-level skills in the adult population. Across OECD countries, only 14 per cent of 45 to 54 year-olds hold tertiary-type A and advanced research qualifications, whereas 18 per cent of 25 to 34 year-olds do so (Chart A2.3). In some countries this increase has been marked. In Korea and Spain, for example, only 16 and 13 per cent of 45 to 54-year-olds, respectively, have obtained a tertiary qualification compared to 40 and 36 per cent among 25 to 34-year-olds.

... and 1 per cent obtain an advanced research qualification.

There has been an increase in the proportion of young people who have attained a qualification equivalent to tertiary-type A and advanced research programmes.

A₂

Chart A2.4.

Survival rates in tertiary-type A education, by duration of programme (2000)

Number of graduates divided by the number of new entrants in the typical year of entrance to the specified programme

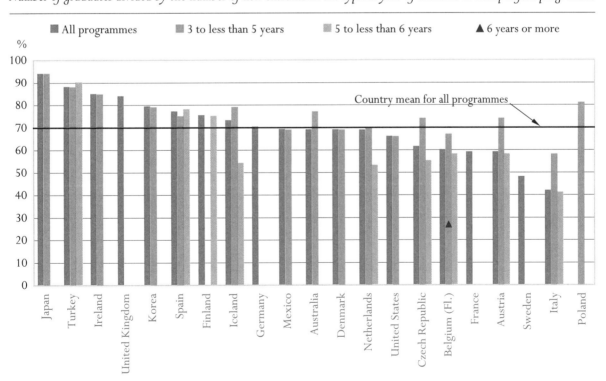

Countries are ranked in descending order of tertiary-type A survival rate for all programmes.
Source: OECD. Table A2.2. See Annex 3 for notes *(www.oecd.org/els/education/eag2002).*

Survival rates at the tertiary level

Tertiary-type A survival rates are generally higher in countries with more flexible qualification structures…

Tertiary-type A survival rates differ widely between OECD countries, ranging from above 80 per cent in Ireland, Japan, Turkey and the United Kingdom to below 60 per cent in Austria, France, Italy and Sweden (Chart A2.2). In both Austria and Italy the majority of students who do successfully complete a first tertiary-type A programme have followed longer programmes lasting 5 to 6 years. In contrast, the majority of students in Ireland, Japan, Korea, Turkey and the United Kingdom, where survival rates are around 80 per cent or above, have completed a medium first tertiary-type A programme (3 to 5 years long) (see Table A2.2).

…a pattern that is not as clearly visible at the tertiary-type B level.

Tertiary-type B survival rates range from above 80 per cent in Denmark, the Flemish Community of Belgium, Japan, Mexico, Poland and Sweden, to around 50 per cent in Ireland and Italy. In general, tertiary-type B programmes are of a shorter duration than tertiary-type A programmes. In the majority of countries with available data, most, if not all, students successfully complete short programmes (2 to 3 years). It is however interesting to note that both Denmark and the Flemish Community of Belgium have the majority of students graduating from medium length type B programmes (in the Flemish Community the only tertiary-type B programme option) and the highest survival rates at the tertiary-type B level (see Table A2.2).

For advanced research programmes, survival rates are high in Italy, Japan and Korea.

In Italy, Japan and Korea, survival rates for students following advanced research programmes are 85 per cent or higher. Conversely, students are far likelier to drop out of such programmes in France and Iceland (36 and 50 per cent survival rate respectively).

Definitions and methodologies

Data on graduates refer to the academic year 1999-2000 and are based on the UOE data collection on education statistics that is administered annually by the OECD.

Tertiary graduates are those who obtain a tertiary-type A or tertiary-type B qualification in the specified reference year. This indicator distinguishes between different categories of tertiary qualifications: *i)* qualifications at the tertiary-type B level (ISCED 5B); *ii)* tertiary-type A qualifications (ISCED 5A); and *iii)* advanced research degrees of doctorate standard (ISCED 6). For some countries, data are not available for the categories requested. In such cases, the OECD has assigned graduates to the most appropriate category. Tertiary-type A degrees are also subdivided in accordance with the total theoretical duration of studies at the level of ISCED 5A, to allow for comparisons that are independent of differences in national degree structures.

Graduation rates for first tertiary programmes (tertiary-type A and type B) are calculated as gross graduation rates. In order to calculate gross graduation rates, countries identify the age at which graduation typically occurs (see Annex 1). The graduates themselves, however, may be of any age. The number of graduates is then divided by the population at the typical graduation age. In many countries, defining a typical age of graduation is difficult, however, because graduates are dispersed over a wide range of ages.

A2

A net graduation rate is calculated for second and advanced tertiary programmes (where duplication of certificates awarded does not pose a problem) as the sum of age-specific graduation rates. The net graduation rate can be interpreted as the percentage of persons within a virtual age cohort who obtain a tertiary qualification, and are thus unaffected by changes in population size or typical graduation age. Gross graduation rates are presented for those countries that cannot provide such detailed data.

Survival rate at the tertiary level is defined as the proportion of new entrants to the specified level of education who successfully complete a first qualification. Dropouts are defined as those students who leave the specified level in the educational system without obtaining a first qualification. The first qualification refers to any degree, regardless of the duration of study, obtained at the end of a programme which does not have as a prerequisite a previous degree at the same level. The survival rate is calculated as the ratio of the number of students who are awarded an initial degree to the number of new entrants to the level n years before, n being the number of years of full-time study required to complete the degree.

Data on population and education attainment are taken from OECD and EUROSTAT databases, which are compiled from National Labour Force Surveys. See Annex 3 at *www.oecd.org/els/education/eag2002* for national sources.

The attainment profiles are based on the percentage of the population aged 25 to 64 years that has completed a specified level of education. The International Standard Classification of Education (ISCED-97) is used to define the levels of education. See Annex 3 at *www.oecd.org/els/education/eag2002* for a description of ISCED-97 education levels and mappings for each country.

Educational attainment data are derived from National Labour Force Surveys and use the International Standard Classification of Education (ISCED-97).

Table A2.1.
Tertiary graduation rates (2000)
Ratio of tertiary graduates to the population at the typical age of graduation, multiplied by 100, by programme destination and duration of programme

| | Tertiary-type B programmes (first programmes) | Tertiary-type A programmes (first programmes) | | | | Advanced research programmes[1] |
		All programmes	3 to less than 5 years (excluding students who subsequently completed a longer programme)	5 years	6 years or more	
	(1)	(2)	(3)	(4)	(5)	(6)
Australia	m	36.3	29.1	7.1	n	1.3
Austria	m	16.0	1.8	14.2	n	1.4
Belgium	m	m	m	m	m	0.8
Canada	m	27.9	19.7	7.1	1.2	0.8
Czech Republic*	4.8	13.6	3.7	10.1	a	0.6
Denmark	24.5	9.2	m	m	m	1.1
Finland*	14.3	36.3	17.2	18.4	0.6	1.9
France	18.3	24.6	10.8	13.2	0.9	1.2
Germany	10.7	19.3	6.2	13.1	a	2.0
Greece	m	m	m	m	m	m
Hungary	m	m	m	m	m	0.6
Iceland*	5.5	33.2	29.2	5.4	n	n
Ireland	15.2	31.2	30.0	1.2	x(4)	0.8
Italy	0.6	18.1	1.8	16.6	n	0.4
Japan	28.8	30.9	27.2	x(3)	3.3	0.7
Korea	m	m	m	m	m	0.7
Luxembourg	m	m	m	m	m	m
Mexico	m	m	m	m	m	m
Netherlands	m	m	m	m	m	1.2
New Zealand	m	m	m	m	m	0.8
Norway	m	m	m	m	m	1.0
Poland	m	34.4	11.0	9.6	14.7	m
Portugal	m	m	m	m	m	1.0
Slovak Republic	2.2	m	m	m	m	0.5
Spain	7.8	m	m	m	m	0.5
Sweden	4.2	28.1	27.2	1.2	a	2.5
Switzerland	m	10.4	n	9.3	1.1	2.6
Turkey	m	m	m	m	m	0.2
United Kingdom	m	37.5	m	m	m	1.3
United States	8.3	33.2	18.8	13.3	2.3	1.3
Country mean	*11.2*	*25.9*	*15.6*	*10.0*	*1.7*	*1.0*

Note: x indicates that data are included in another column. The column reference is shown in brackets after "x". *e.g.*, x(2) means that data are included in column 2.
1. Net graduation rate is calculated by summing the graduation rates by single year of age, except for Belgium, France, Ireland, Japan, Korea, the Netherlands and the United States.
*See Annex 3 for notes (*www.oecd.org/els/education/eag2002*).
Source: OECD.

Table A2.2.
Survival rates in tertiary education (2000)
*Number of graduates divided by the number of new entrants in the typical year of entrance, by programme destination,
and distribution of graduates by duration of programme*

		Tertiary-type A education			Tertiary-type B education				Advanced research programmes
	Survival rate for all tertiary-type A programmes	Survival rate for programmes of duration:			Survival rate for all tertiary-type B programmes	Survival rate for programmes of duration:			
		3 to less than 5 years	5 to less than 6 years	6 years or more		2 to less than 3 years	3 to less than 5 years	5 years or more	
	(1)	(2)	(3)	(4)	(5)	(6)	(7)	(8)	(9)
Australia*	69	77	m	n	m	m	a	a	m
Austria	59	74	58	n	m	m	m	m	m
Belgium (Fl.)*	60	67	58	27	88	a	88	a	m
Czech Republic	61	74	55	a	77	75	78	a	m
Denmark	69	69	a	a	84	65	90	a	m
Finland	75	m	75	a	m	m	m	m	m
France*	59	m	m	m	72	72	n	a	36
Germany	70	a	a	a	75	a	a	a	m
Iceland	73	79	54	n	55	73	31	n	50
Ireland	85	85	x(2)	x(2)	50	50	x(6)	a	m
Italy	42	58	41	a	51	a	51	a	89
Japan	94	94	x(2)	x(2)	86	86	x(6)	x(6)	85
Korea	79	79	x(2)	a	74	73	78	a	95
Mexico	69	69	x(2)	a	81	81	x(6)	a	54
Netherlands	69	70	53	a	58	59	50	a	m
Poland	m	81	m	a	84	84	a	a	m
Spain	77	75	78	n	74	74	n	n	m
Sweden	48	m	m	a	85	m	m	a	m
Turkey	88	88	90	a	77	77	a	a	a
United Kingdom*	83	m	m	m	m	m	m	m	m
United States*	66	66	a	a	62	62	x(6)	x(6)	m
Country mean	*70*	*76*	*62*	*2*	*73*	*72*	*67*	*n*	*58*
Israel	70	m	m	m	91	m	m	m	m

Note: x indicates that data are included in another column. The column reference is shown in brackets after "x". *e.g.*, x(2) means that data are included in column 2.
*See Annex 3 for notes (*www.oecd.org/els/education/eag2002*).
Source: OECD.

Table A2.3.
Population that has attained tertiary education (2001)
Percentage of the population that has attained tertiary-type B education and tertiary-type A or advanced research programmes, by age group

	Tertiary-type B education					Tertiary-type A and advanced research programmes				
	25-64	25-34	35-44	45-54	55-64	25-64	25-34	35-44	45-54	55-64
	(1)	(2)	(3)	(4)	(5)	(6)	(7)	(8)	(9)	(10)
Australia	10	10	10	10	9	19	24	19	19	12
Austria[1]	7	8	8	7	5	7	7	8	6	4
Belgium[1]	15	19	16	13	9	12	17	13	10	8
Canada	21	25	23	20	15	20	25	20	20	15
Czech Republic	x(6)	x(7)	x(8)	x(9)	x(10)	11	11	13	11	9
Denmark	19	18	20	21	16	8	11	8	6	4
Finland	17	20	21	16	12	15	18	16	13	11
France	11	17	12	9	6	12	18	11	10	8
Germany	10	8	11	10	10	13	14	15	15	10
Greece	5	7	7	4	3	12	17	14	12	6
Hungary	x(6)	x(7)	x(8)	x(9)	x(10)	14	15	15	14	12
Iceland	6	6	8	6	4	19	21	21	19	11
Ireland	22	28	23	18	13	14	20	14	11	8
Italy	x(6)	x(7)	x(8)	x(9)	x(10)	10	12	11	10	6
Japan	15	23	19	11	5	19	24	25	17	10
Korea	7	15	6	2	1	17	25	20	11	8
Luxembourg	7	8	6	6	5	11	15	11	10	8
Mexico	2	3	2	1	0	13	15	15	11	7
Netherlands[1]	3	2	3	3	2	21	24	22	20	15
New Zealand	15	12	16	18	17	14	17	15	14	7
Norway[1]	3	3	3	3	2	26	32	26	23	19
Poland	x(6)	x(7)	x(8)	x(9)	x(10)	12	15	11	11	10
Portugal	2	3	3	2	2	7	11	7	5	3
Slovak Republic	1	1	1	1	0	10	11	11	10	8
Spain	7	12	7	3	2	17	24	18	13	8
Sweden	15	17	17	14	10	17	20	16	17	15
Switzerland	10	10	11	9	8	16	16	18	15	13
Turkey	x(6)	x(7)	x(8)	x(9)	x(10)	9	10	8	9	6
United Kingdom	8	9	9	8	7	18	21	18	18	12
United States	9	9	10	10	7	28	30	28	30	24
Country mean	*8*	*10*	*9*	*7*	*6*	*15*	*18*	*16*	*14*	*10*

Note: x indicates that data are included in another column. The column reference is shown in brackets after "x". *e.g.*, x(2) means that data are included in column 2.
1. Year of reference 2000.
Source: OECD. See Annex 3 for a description of ISCED-97 levels, ISCED-97 country mappings and national data sources (*www.oecd.org/els/education/eag2002*).

EDUCATIONAL ATTAINMENT OF THE LABOUR FORCE AND ADULT POPULATION

A3

- Educational attainment is generally higher among people in the labour force than among adults of working age outside it.

- In Mexico, Portugal and Turkey more than two-thirds of the labour force aged 25 to 64 have not completed the upper secondary level of education and around half in Italy and Spain. The proportion of the labour force aged 25 to 64 who have completed upper secondary education is at least 85 per cent in Canada, the Czech Republic, Germany, Japan, Norway, Poland, the Slovak Republic, Switzerland, the United Kingdom and the United States.

Chart A3.1.

Educational attainment of the adult population (2001)

Distribution of 25 to 64-year-olds, by level of educational attainment

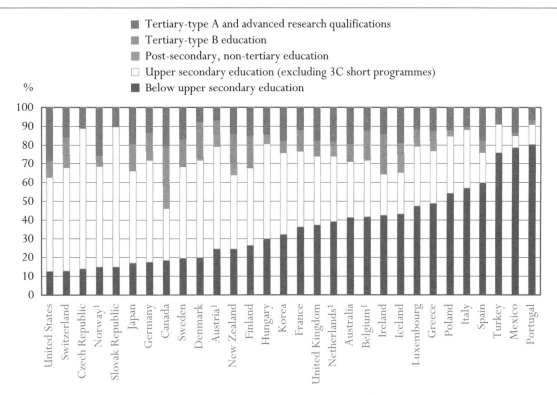

Note: Not all ISCED 3 programmes meet minimum requirements for ISCED 3C long programmes. See Annex 3 for notes *(www.oecd.org/els/education/eag2002)*.
1. Year of reference 2000.
Countries are ranked in ascending order of the percentage of 25 to 64-year-olds who have completed below upper secondary education.
Source: OECD. Table A3.1a. See Annex 3 for a description of ISCED-97 levels, ISCED-97 country mappings and national data sources *(www.oecd.org/els/education/eag2002)*.

A₃

This indicator shows a profile of the educational attainment of the labour force and the adult population as a proxy for the knowledge and skills available to economies and societies.

Countries differ widely in the distribution of educational attainment in their labour force.

Educational attainment is generally higher among people in the labour force than among working age adults outside it.

Policy context

A well-educated and well-trained labour force is important for the social and economic well-being of countries and individuals. Education plays a key role in providing individuals with the knowledge, skills and competencies to participate effectively in society and the economy. Education also contributes to an expansion of scientific and cultural knowledge. This indicator shows the distribution of levels of educational attainment in the labour force and adult population.

Evidence and explanations

In 20 out of the 30 OECD countries, 60 per cent or more of the labour force aged 25 to 64 has completed at least the upper secondary level of education (Table A3.1b). This refers to those who have completed educational programmes at ISCED-97 levels 3A or 3B, or long programmes at ISCED-97 level 3C. The proportion is equal to or exceeds 80 per cent in 13 OECD countries: Austria, Canada, the Czech Republic, Denmark, Germany, Japan, Hungary, New Zealand, Norway, the Slovak Republic, Switzerland, Sweden and the United States. In other countries, especially but not only in southern Europe, the educational structure of the adult population shows a different profile: in Italy, Mexico, Portugal, Spain and Turkey, more than half of the labour force aged 25 to 64 years have not completed upper secondary education.

A comparison between the distribution of educational attainment in the labour force aged 25 to 64, and the distribution of educational attainment in the total population in the same age range shows a higher percentage of people in the labour force with upper secondary and tertiary qualifications (see Table A3.1b). Across OECD countries, an average of 66 per cent of the adult population have completed at least upper secondary education, but in the adult labour force this figure is 71 per cent. In Belgium, Hungary and Italy, upper secondary and tertiary attainment in the adult population and in the labour force differ by 9 percentage points or more whereas the difference is less than 2 percentage points in Iceland, Japan, Korea and Switzerland.

Chart A3.2.

Gender differences in educational attainment, by age group (2001)

Difference between female and male 25 to 34 and 45 to 54-year-olds in the percentage of the population that has attained at least upper secondary or at least tertiary education

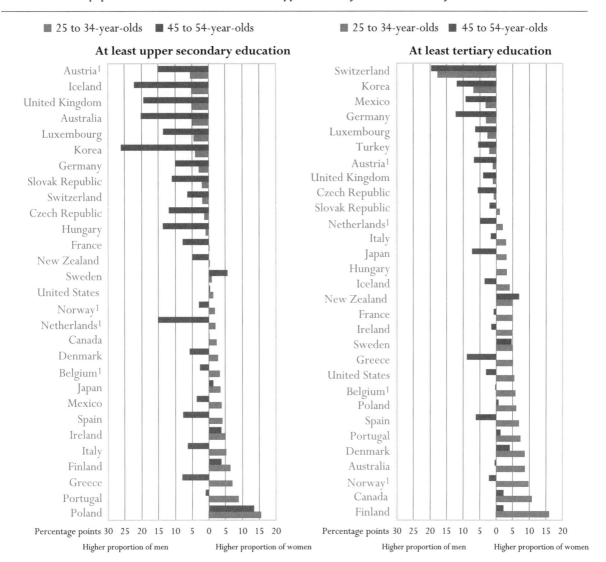

Note: Not all ISCED 3 programmes meet minimum requirements for ISCED 3C long programmes. See Annex 3 for notes *(www.oecd.org/els/education/eag2002)*.

1. Year of reference 2000.

Countries are ranked in ascending order of the difference between women and men as a percentage of 25 to 34-year-olds who have attained at least upper secondary or tertiary education.

Source: OECD. Table A3.1c. See Annex 3 for a description of ISCED-97 levels, ISCED-97 country mappings and national data sources *(www.oecd.org/els/education/eag2002)*.

A₃

Definitions and methodologies

The attainment profiles shown here are based on the percentage of the population or of the labour force aged 25 to 64 years that has completed a specified level of education. The International Standard Classification of Education (ISCED-97) is used to define the levels of education. The post-secondary non-tertiary level (ISCED 4) covers programmes that straddle the boundary between upper secondary and tertiary education.

Tertiary education comprises two levels (ISCED 5 and ISCED 6). ISCED 5 consists of programmes that do not lead directly to an advanced research qualification, while ISCED 6 is reserved for programmes leading to advanced research qualifications, such as a Ph.D. Tertiary education (ISCED 5) is further sub-divided into two categories, ISCED 5A and 5B. ISCED 5A, tertiary-type A education, covers more theoretical programmes that give access to advanced research programmes and to professions with high general skills requirements, while ISCED 5B, tertiary-type B education, covers more practical or occupationally specific programmes that provide participants with a qualification of immediate relevance to the labour market.

Data on population and educational attainment are taken from OECD and EUROSTAT databases, which are compiled from National Labour Force Surveys. See Annex 3 at *www.oecd.org/els/education/eag2002* for national sources.

Table A3.1a.
Educational attainment of the population (2001)
*Distribution of the **population** of 25 to 64-year-olds, by highest level of education attained*

| | Pre-primary and primary education | Lower secondary education | Upper secondary education | | | Post-secondary non-tertiary education | Tertiary-type B education | Tertiary-type A and advanced research programmes | All levels of education |
			ISCED 3C Short	ISCED 3C Long / 3B	ISCED 3A				
	(1)	(2)	(3)	(4)	(5)	(6)	(7)	(8)	(9)
Australia	x(2)	41	a	11	19	x(5)	10	19	100
Austria[1]	x(2)	24	a	48	7	7	7	7	100
Belgium[1]	20	22	a	7	23	1	15	12	100
Canada	6	12	a	x(5)	28	12	21	20	100
Czech Republic	x(2)	14	x(4)	42	33	x(5)	x(8)	11	100
Denmark	n	20	x(2)	46	6	2	19	8	100
Finland	x(2)	26	a	a	42	x(5)	17	15	100
France	18	18	28	3	10	n	11	12	100
Germany	2	16	a	52	3	5	10	13	100
Greece	39	10	a	4	24	5	5	12	100
Hungary	3	27	a	28	23	5	n	14	100
Iceland	2	34	7	a	22	10	6	19	100
Ireland	25	18	a	a	22	x(5,7)	22	14	100
Italy	22	33	2	6	25	2	x(8)	10	100
Japan	x(2)	17	a	x(5)	49	x(9)	15	19	100
Korea	17	15	a	x(5)	44	a	7	17	100
Luxembourg	28	20	x(2)	18	14	3	7	11	100
Mexico	55	23	a	7	a	a	2	13	100
Netherlands[1]	13	22	x(4)	24	13	4	3	21	100
New Zealand	x(2)	24	a	21	19	7	15	14	100
Norway[1]	1	14	a	42	12	3	3	26	100
Poland	x(2)	19	35	a	31	3	x(8)	12	100
Portugal	68	12	x(5)	x(5)	11	x(5)	2	7	100
Slovak Republic	1	14	a	39	35	a	1	10	100
Spain	35	25	x(5)	6	11	x(7)	7	17	100
Sweden	9	10	a	x(5)	49	x(7)	15	17	100
Switzerland	3	9	a	49	6	7	10	16	100
Turkey	66	9	a	6	10	a	x(8)	9	100
United Kingdom	x(2)	17	27	15	15	x(9)	8	18	100
United States	5	8	x(5)	x(5)	50	x(5)	9	28	100
Country mean	*15*	*19*	*3*	*16*	*22*	*3*	*8*	*15*	*100*

OECD COUNTRIES

Note: x indicates that data are included in another column. The column reference is shown in brackets after "x". *e.g.,* x(2) means that data are included in column 2.
1. Year of reference 2000.
Source: OECD. See Annex 3 for a description of ISCED-97 levels, ISCED-97 country mappings and national data sources (*www.oecd.org/els/education/eag2002*).

Table A3.1b.
Educational attainment of the labour force (2001)
*Distribution of the **labour force** for 25 to 64-year-olds, by highest level of education attained*

	Pre-primary and primary education	Lower secondary education	Upper secondary education			Post-secondary non-tertiary education	Tertiary-type B education	Tertiary-type A and advanced research programmes	All levels of education
			ISCED 3C Short	ISCED 3C Long/3B	ISCED 3A				
	(1)	(2)	(3)	(4)	(5)	(6)	(7)	(8)	(9)
Australia	x(2)	35	a	12	20	x(5)	11	22	100
Austria[1]	x(2)	19	a	50	6	8	8	8	100
Belgium[1]	12	21	a	8	26	1	18	15	100
Canada	4	10	a	x(5)	28	13	23	22	100
Czech Republic	x(2)	10	x(4)	43	35	x(5)	x(8)	13	100
Denmark	n	16	x(2)	48	5	2	21	9	100
Finland	x(2)	21	a	a	43	x(5)	19	17	100
France	13	18	29	3	11	n	13	13	100
Germany	1	12	a	52	2	5	11	16	100
Greece	32	10	a	5	24	7	6	16	100
Hungary	1	18	a	32	25	6	n	18	100
Iceland	2	33	7	a	22	10	6	20	100
Ireland	18	17	a	a	23	x(5,7)	25	17	100
Italy	12	33	2	7	30	2	x(8)	13	100
Japan	x(2)	15	a	x(5)	49	x(9)	14	22	100
Korea	15	15	a	x(5)	43	a	7	19	100
Luxembourg	23	18	x(2)	19	15	3	8	14	100
Mexico	50	25	a	6	n	a	2	17	100
Netherlands[1]	8	20	x(4)	25	15	5	3	24	100
New Zealand	x(2)	20	a	22	19	7	16	15	100
Norway[1]	n	12	n	42	12	3	3	28	100
Poland	x(2)	14	36	a	32	4	x(8)	14	100
Portugal	64	13	x(5)	x(5)	12	x(5)	3	8	100
Slovak Republic	n	9	a	41	37	a	1	12	100
Spain	26	26	x(5)	7	11	x(7)	8	21	100
Sweden	7	10	a	x(5)	50	x(7)	15	18	100
Switzerland	3	8	a	48	6	7	11	17	100
Turkey	59	10	a	7	11	a	x(8)	12	100
United Kingdom	x(2)	12	27	16	16	x(9)	9	20	100
United States	3	6	x(5)	x(5)	50	x(5)	10	31	100
Country mean	*12*	*17*	*3*	*16*	*23*	*3*	*9*	*17*	*100*

OECD COUNTRIES

Note: x indicates that data are included in another column. The column reference is shown in brackets after "x". *e.g.,* x(2) means that data are included in column 2.
1. Year of reference 2000.
Source: OECD. See Annex 3 for a description of ISCED-97 levels, ISCED-97 country mappings and national data sources (*www.oecd.org/els/education/eag2002*).

Table A3.1c.
Educational attainment of the population, by gender (2001)
Percentage of the population that has attained at least upper secondary education or at least tertiary education, by age group and gender

A_3

		At least upper secondary education[1]					At least tertiary education (tertiary-type A education, tertiary-type B education and advanced research programmes)				
		25-64	25-34	35-44	45-54	55-64	25-64	25-34	35-44	45-54	55-64
Australia	Males	66	73	67	65	54	27	29	27	29	22
	Females	52	68	54	45	34	31	38	32	29	21
Austria[2]	Males	82	86	85	79	73	17	16	19	17	15
	Females	69	81	75	64	52	11	14	14	10	5
Belgium[2]	Males	59	74	61	53	42	27	33	28	23	20
	Females	58	77	65	50	35	28	39	31	23	14
Canada	Males	81	88	83	81	68	39	45	39	38	30
	Females	82	91	86	81	65	44	56	46	40	30
Czech Republic	Males	91	93	93	90	86	13	12	14	14	12
	Females	82	92	87	78	68	9	11	12	8	7
Denmark	Males	82	85	82	83	75	24	25	24	25	21
	Females	79	88	79	78	69	29	34	32	29	19
Finland	Males	72	84	81	68	51	29	30	32	28	25
	Females	76	90	87	72	51	36	46	42	31	22
France[3]	Males	67	78	69	62	52	22	32	21	19	16
	Females	61	78	66	55	40	24	37	24	18	13
Germany	Males	87	87	88	88	85	28	23	30	31	28
	Females	78	84	83	78	67	18	20	21	18	12
Greece	Males	54	69	62	47	33	20	21	24	20	13
	Females	49	76	58	40	23	16	27	19	11	6
Hungary	Males	75	81	82	79	49	14	13	13	14	14
	Females	66	80	75	65	40	15	16	18	14	10
Iceland	Males	64	64	67	66	58	24	25	27	26	16
	Females	49	59	54	44	33	25	29	31	22	15
Ireland	Males	55	71	59	46	35	35	45	37	30	22
	Females	60	76	66	50	36	36	50	36	28	20
Italy	Males	44	55	48	42	26	10	10	11	11	8
	Females	43	60	51	35	18	10	13	11	10	5
Japan	Males	83	92	93	80	65	36	46	46	32	20
	Females	83	95	95	82	61	32	49	41	25	11
Korea	Males	76	95	84	61	45	30	42	34	19	15
	Females	59	91	68	35	16	18	35	17	7	3
Luxembourg	Males	58	62	61	54	53	21	25	20	19	20
	Females	47	57	53	40	31	15	22	15	12	8
Mexico	Males	22	23	25	19	12	18	20	22	17	10
	Females	22	27	24	16	10	12	16	13	7	4
Netherlands[2,3]	Males	63	73	71	67	62	26	27	27	27	22
	Females	61	75	67	53	41	21	26	22	18	13
New Zealand	Males	77	82	80	78	65	26	26	27	29	23
	Females	74	82	79	73	55	32	31	34	35	26
Norway[2]	Males	86	93	90	83	73	28	30	28	28	23
	Females	84	94	91	80	66	29	40	30	25	18
Poland	Males	39	44	39	38	34	11	12	9	10	11
	Females	52	60	56	51	38	13	18	13	11	10
Portugal	Males	19	28	19	14	10	7	10	7	6	5
	Females	21	37	21	13	7	11	17	11	7	4
Slovak Republic	Males	90	95	92	89	79	11	11	11	12	10
	Females	81	93	88	78	56	11	12	12	10	7
Spain	Males	42	55	46	34	22	24	32	25	19	14
	Females	40	59	46	26	14	23	39	25	13	7
Sweden	Males	79	90	84	76	63	30	34	31	29	24
	Females	82	91	88	81	67	34	39	35	34	25
Switzerland	Males	90	93	92	88	87	35	35	37	34	33
	Females	85	91	88	82	75	16	17	21	15	8
Turkey	Males	28	35	28	23	15	10	11	9	11	8
	Females	19	25	18	13	10	7	9	7	6	4
United Kingdom[3]	Males	69	70	70	71	63	27	30	28	28	20
	Females	57	65	59	52	42	25	29	26	24	17
United States	Males	87	87	88	89	83	37	36	37	41	35
	Females	88	89	89	89	82	37	42	38	38	27
Country mean	*Males*	*66*	*73*	*70*	*64*	*54*	*24*	*26*	*25*	*23*	*18*
	Females	*62*	*74*	*67*	*57*	*43*	*22*	*29*	*24*	*19*	*13*

1. Excluding ISCED 3C short programmes.
2. Year of reference 2000.
3. Not all ISCED 3 programmes meet minimum requirements for ISCED 3C long programmes. See Annex 3 for notes (*www.oecd.org/els/education/eag2002*).
Source: OECD. See Annex 3 for a description of ISCED-97 levels, ISCED-97 country mappings and national data sources (*www.oecd.org/els/education/eag2002*).

OECD COUNTRIES

GRADUATES BY FIELD OF STUDY

- On average across OECD countries, every third tertiary-type A graduate obtains a degree in the social sciences, business or law. The second most popular fields are the humanities, arts and education.

- In the humanities, arts, education, health and welfare, on average in OECD countries, more than two-thirds of the tertiary-type A graduates are women, whereas there are less than one-third in mathematics and computer science and less than one-quarter in engineering, manufacturing and construction.

- In OECD countries, men are still more likely than women to earn advanced research qualifications, such as doctorates.

- Social sciences, business and law, and education are also popular at the tertiary-type B level.

A4

Chart A4.1.
Tertiary graduates by field of study (2000)
Graduates with tertiary-type A and advanced research qualifications, by field of study

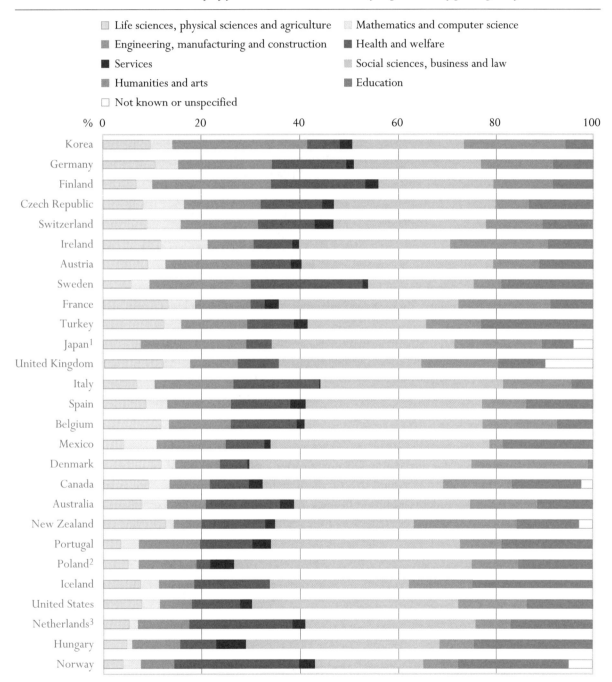

- ☐ Life sciences, physical sciences and agriculture
- ☐ Mathematics and computer science
- ☐ Engineering, manufacturing and construction
- ■ Health and welfare
- ■ Services
- ☐ Social sciences, business and law
- ☐ Humanities and arts
- ☐ Education
- ☐ Not known or unspecified

Korea
Germany
Finland
Czech Republic
Switzerland
Ireland
Austria
Sweden
France
Turkey
Japan[1]
United Kingdom
Italy
Spain
Belgium
Mexico
Denmark
Canada
Australia
New Zealand
Portugal
Poland[2]
Iceland
United States
Netherlands[3]
Hungary
Norway

Countries are ranked in descending order of the proportion of qualifications in life sciences, physical sciences and agriculture, mathematics and computer science, and engineering, manufacturing and construction.
1. Mathematics and computer science are included in the category "life sciences, physical sciences and agriculture".
2. Excludes tertiary-type A second degree programmes and advanced research programmes.
3. Excludes advanced research programmes.
Source: OECD. Table A4.1. See Annex 3 for notes *(www.oecd.org / els / education / eag2002)*.

A4

This indicator shows the distribution of tertiary graduates across fields of study.

Policy context

Changing opportunities in the job market, relative earnings in different occupations and sectors, and admission policies and practices among tertiary education institutions may affect the fields which students choose to study. In turn, the relative popularity of the various fields of study affects the demand for courses and teaching staff, as well as the supply of new graduates. This indicator sheds light on the distribution of tertiary graduates across fields of study as well as the relative share of women among graduates in the different fields of study.

Evidence and explanations

Graduates by field of study

On average in OECD countries, every third tertiary-type A graduate obtains a degree in the social sciences, law or business.

In 24 of the 28 countries providing data, the largest concentration of tertiary-type A and advanced research qualifications awarded is in the combined fields of social sciences, business and law (Table A4.1). On average in OECD countries, every third tertiary-type A graduate obtains a degree in the social sciences, business or law. The percentage of tertiary-type A qualifications awarded in the social sciences, business and law ranges from under 25 per cent in Finland, Korea, Norway, Sweden and Turkey, to over 40 per cent in Denmark, Mexico, Poland and the United States. In Finland and Korea the largest concentration of tertiary-type A and advanced research qualifications awarded is in the fields of engineering, manufacturing and construction, and in Norway and Sweden in the fields of health and welfare.

The second most popular fields are humanities, arts and education.

Typically, one out of every three or four students graduates from the fields of humanities, arts or education. The percentage of students in science-related fields (engineering, manufacturing and construction, life sciences, physical sciences and agriculture, mathematics and computing, but not including health and welfare) ranges from less than 19 per cent in Hungary, Iceland, the Netherlands, Norway and the United States, to 34 per cent in Finland and Germany, and 42 per cent in Korea.

Individual preferences, admission policies and degree structures influence the prevalence of the different fields of study.

The distribution of qualifications awarded by field of study is driven by the relative popularity of these fields among students, the relative number of students admitted to these fields in universities and equivalent institutions, and the degree structure of the various disciplines in a particular country.

Part of the variation in graduation rates between countries (Table A2.1) can also be accounted for by differences in the number of tertiary-type A degrees earned in the fields of education and the humanities. Countries with high graduation rates, on average, have a higher proportion of graduates in education and humanities and a lower proportion of graduates in science-related fields. In other words, there is less variation in graduation rates in science-related fields between countries than in overall graduation rates.

Social sciences, business and law, and education are also popular at the tertiary-type B level.

The picture is much the same for tertiary-type B education, where programmes are more occupationally oriented: the combined field of the social sciences, business and law has the largest concentration of graduates (26 per cent), followed by the combined field of the humanities, arts and education (21 per cent).

A4

However, health and welfare graduates are more common at this level than engineering, manufacturing and construction graduates (19 and 15 per cent respectively) (see Table A4.1).

The selection of a field of study at this level is heavily dependent on opportunities to study similar subject matter, or to prepare for similar occupations at the post-secondary non-tertiary or tertiary-type A level. For example, if nurses in a particular country were trained primarily in tertiary-type B programmes, the proportion of students graduating with qualifications in medical sciences from that level would be higher than if nurses were primarily trained in upper secondary or tertiary-type A programmes.

Gender differences in tertiary graduation

First tertiary-type A graduation rates for women equal or exceed those for men in 21 out of 27 OECD countries. On average in OECD countries, 54 per cent of all first tertiary-type A graduates are women. However, major differences remain between fields of study. In the humanities, arts, education, health and welfare, more than two thirds of the tertiary-type A graduates are women, on average in OECD countries, whereas less than one third of mathematics and computer science graduates and less than a fifth of engineering, manufacturing and construction graduates are women.

Tertiary-type A graduation rates for women equal or exceed those for men in most countries...

Chart A4.2.

Proportion of tertiary qualifications awarded to women (2000)

For all fields of study for women with tertiary-type A and advanced research qualifications

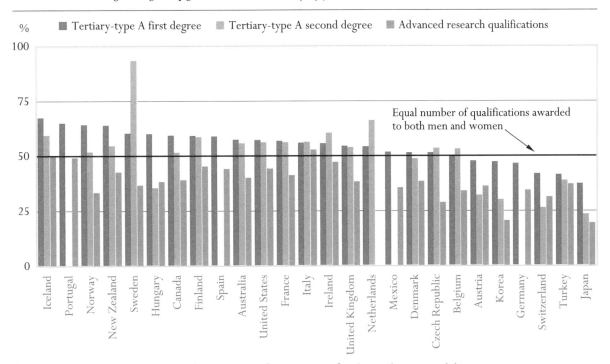

Countries are ranked in descending order of the percentage of tertiary-type A first degrees that are awarded to women.
Source: OECD. Table A4.2. See Annex 3 for notes *(www.oecd.org/els/education/eag2002)*.

A4

…except in Austria, Germany, Japan, Korea, Switzerland and Turkey.

In Iceland, New Zealand, Norway and Portugal, the proportion of women obtaining a first tertiary-type A qualification exceeds 60 per cent but it is 48 per cent or below in Austria, Germany, Japan, Korea, Switzerland and Turkey (Tables A4.2 and A3.1c).

In OECD countries, men are still more likely than women to earn advanced research qualifications, such as doctorates.

Men remain more likely than women to obtain advanced research qualifications in OECD countries (Table A4.2). Graduation rates from advanced research, *e.g.,* Ph.D. programmes, are lower for women than for men in all countries, except Italy. On average in OECD countries, nearly two-thirds of all graduates at this level are men. In Japan and Korea, around 80 per cent of advanced research qualifications are awarded to men.

Definitions and methodologies

Data on graduates refer to the academic year 1999–2000 and are based on the UOE data collection on education statistics that is annually administered by the OECD.

Tertiary graduates are those who obtain a tertiary-type A or tertiary-type B qualification or equivalent in the specified reference year. This indicator distinguishes between different categories of tertiary qualifications: *i)* qualifications at the tertiary-type B level (ISCED 5B); and *ii)* qualifications at the tertiary-type A (ISCED 5A) and *iii)* advanced research qualifications (ISCED 6). For some countries, data are not available for the categories requested. In such cases, the country has assigned graduates to the most appropriate category.

Table A4.2 shows the percentage distribution of qualifications among women by subject category. Tertiary graduates who receive their qualification in the reference year are divided into categories based on their subject of specialisation. These figures cover graduates from all tertiary degrees reported in Table A2.1.

A4

Table A4.1.

Tertiary graduates, by field of study and level of education (2000)

			Education	Humanities and arts	Social sciences, business and law	Services	Engineering, manufacturing and construction	Agriculture	Health and welfare	Life sciences	Physical sciences	Mathematics and statistics	Computing	Not known or unspecified
		(1)	(2)	(3)	(4)	(5)	(6)	(7)	(8)	(9)	(10)	(11)	(12)	(13)
OECD COUNTRIES	Australia	A	11.3	13.9	36.0	2.8	7.9	1.2	15.0	5.6	1.1	0.5	4.6	a
		B	m	m	m	m	m	m	m	m	m	m	m	m
	Austria	A	10.7	9.6	39.1	2.2	17.3	2.9	8.1	3.2	3.1	0.8	2.8	0.2
		B	32.8	1.8	2.9	7.9	33.9	5.6	12.9	n	1.4	0.3	0.6	a
	Belgium[1]	A	7.3	15.5	36.3	1.6	12.5	3.5	13.3	6.3	2.0	0.6	1.0	n
		B	22.6	6.9	25.2	2.3	10.8	0.5	26.6	0.5	0.3	n	4.2	a
	Canada	A	14.2	14.2	36.8	2.8	8.2	1.3	7.9	5.9	2.1	1.4	2.8	2.4
		B	4.5	7.8	29.0	12.8	16.9	3.3	18.6	0.1	0.1	n	6.0	0.8
	Czech Republic	A	13.1	7.1	32.9	2.3	15.5	3.8	12.5	2.2	2.2	1.0	7.3	a
		B	a	8.1	35.4	8.0	6.1	2.6	35.1	a	a	a	4.7	a
	Denmark	A	1.0	23.6	44.7	0.3	8.9	3.2	5.5	4.2	4.3	1.0	1.8	n
		B	19.2	2.2	7.9	5.4	12.4	1.1	49.2	n	n	n	2.7	0.1
	Finland*	A	8.2	12.4	23.5	2.6	24.0	2.3	19.3	1.9	2.7	1.0	2.2	n
		B	0.3	4.2	22.1	16.9	19.5	1.5	31.5	a	a	a	4.0	a
	France	A	8.3	19.0	36.6	2.8	11.2	0.8	2.9	6.7	5.8	2.8	2.7	0.3
		B	a	1.5	39.5	5.6	25.2	n	20.2	1.8	2.4	0.4	3.3	a
	Germany	A	8.1	15.0	25.9	1.6	19.0	1.9	15.0	3.0	5.8	1.9	2.8	n
		B	10.9	1.2	9.6	9.6	13.7	3.4	50.3	a	n	a	0.3	1.0
	Greece	A	m	m	m	m	m	m	m	m	m	m	m	m
		B	m	m	m	m	m	m	m	m	m	m	m	m
	Hungary[1]	A	24.4	7.1	39.5	6.0	9.8	3.6	7.3	0.5	0.7	0.1	1.0	a
		B	n	n	38.9	53.5	4.2	n	n	n	n	3.4	n	a
	Iceland	A	24.8	13.0	28.4	n	7.1	0.7	15.3	4.9	2.1	0.5	3.3	a
		B	6.4	14.0	47.5	n	n	n	n	n	n	n	32.2	a
	Ireland	A	9.0	20.2	30.8	1.4	9.3	1.7	7.8	6.9	3.3	1.1	8.4	0.2
		B	0.9	6.9	31.5	6.0	19.6	0.7	8.9	2.7	4.5	n	17.8	0.5
	Italy	A	4.3	14.2	37.3	0.3	16.0	2.1	17.3	3.0	1.8	2.8	0.9	n
		B	38.7	61.3	a	a	a	a	a	a	a	a	a	a
	Japan	A	6.3	18.1	37.2	x(13)	21.3	3.4	5.2	4.4	x(9)	x(9)	x(9)	4.0
		B	8.1	17.9	9.6	22.7	16.9	0.7	18.1	n	x(9)	x(9)	x(9)	6.0
	Korea	A	5.6	20.9	22.8	2.5	27.4	3.2	6.6	2.1	4.4	2.1	2.4	a
		B	8.6	14.8	19.7	5.0	38.0	1.3	8.9	n	0.1	n	3.4	a
	Luxembourg	A	m	m	m	m	m	m	m	m	m	m	m	m
		B	25.2	a	59.4	a	5.8	a	9.6	a	a	a	a	a
	Mexico	A	18.6	2.8	44.6	1.3	14.0	2.0	7.8	0.8	1.5	0.4	6.3	a
		B	n	0.7	34.4	3.8	37.7	1.8	7.2	0.6	a	0.1	13.7	a
	Netherlands[2]	A	16.8	7.3	34.8	2.6	10.4	2.3	20.9	1.1	1.9	0.3	1.5	n
		B	a	a	39.7	11.1	2.3	a	37.7	a	a	a	9.2	a
	New Zealand	A	12.6	21.3	28.3	2.0	5.6	1.4	12.9	n	11.3	0.1	1.6	2.8
		B	27.8	13.2	22.4	18.1	3.4	2.4	7.7	n	0.3	n	3.2	1.5
	Norway	A	22.7	7.2	22.1	3.3	6.8	1.4	25.3	1.2	1.4	0.3	3.3	4.9
		B	a	5.5	51.0	5.2	14.9	0.1	1.0	n	a	a	21.6	0.7
	Poland[3]	A	15.1	9.7	48.5	4.8	12.0	2.4	2.8	1.6	1.1	1.0	0.9	a
		B	100.0	a	a	a	a	a	a	a	a	a	a	a
	Portugal[1]	A	18.7	8.5	38.6	3.7	12.4	1.7	10.6	0.9	1.0	0.7	3.0	a
		B	18.7	8.5	38.6	3.7	12.4	1.7	10.6	0.9	1.0	0.7	3.0	a
	Slovak Republic	A	21.0	5.5	30.1	8.3	15.4	4.4	8.5	1.0	1.2	0.6	4.1	a
		B	3.2	12.5	5.0	7.1	6.9	1.5	63.7	n	n	n	n	a
	Spain	A	13.6	9.3	36.0	3.2	12.9	3.0	11.9	2.5	3.3	1.4	2.9	n
		B	4.4	6.7	30.9	12.8	23.6	0.5	10.6	n	n	n	10.3	0.1
	Sweden	A	18.8	5.7	21.6	1.0	20.5	1.0	22.8	2.3	2.4	0.6	3.1	n
		B	4.9	6.3	14.6	14.3	23.3	7.1	8.9	0.1	0.1	0.2	20.5	a
	Switzerland	A	9.9	11.8	31.1	3.8	15.7	1.4	11.4	3.3	4.3	1.1	5.8	0.4
		B	14.4	2.7	39.3	10.5	12.6	1.4	12.3	n	n	n	6.8	n
	Turkey	A	23.0	11.2	24.2	2.8	13.3	5.1	9.5	2.1	5.3	2.8	0.7	a
		B	a	3.7	34.8	6.8	37.6	6.3	5.4	a	n	a	5.4	a
	United Kingdom	A	10.0	15.7	28.8	n	9.9	1.1	8.3	6.0	5.0	1.3	4.2	9.8
		B	6.1	7.6	22.6	n	9.2	1.6	28.4	1.6	1.5	0.3	7.1	13.9
	United States	A	13.1	14.2	42.2	2.4	6.5	2.3	9.8	4.1	1.5	0.9	2.8	0.3
		B	2.5	0.2	33.4	8.6	18.6	1.9	27.9	a	a	a	6.2	0.8
	Country mean	*A*	*13.2*	*12.6*	*33.5*	*2.5*	*13.2*	*2.3*	*11.5*	*3.1*	*3.0*	*1.1*	*3.1*	*0.9*
		B	*13.0*	*7.6*	*25.8*	*9.0*	*14.7*	*2.4*	*18.8*	*n*	*n*	*n*	*6.8*	*0.9*
NON-OECD COUNTRY	**Israel**	A	18.2	13.6	43.1	m	8.5	0.7	5.7	2.7	1.7	5.9	x(11)	a
		B	17.7	7.5	18.2	a	47.6	a	3.5	a	a	n	x(11)	5.4

Note: Column 1 specifies the level of education, where A equals tertiary-type A and advanced research programmes, and B equals tertiary-type B programmes.
Note: x indicates that data are included in another column. The column reference is shown in brackets after "x". *e.g.*, x(2) means that data are included in column 2.
1. Excludes tertiary-type B second degree programmes.
2. Excludes advanced research programmes.
3. Excludes tertiary-type A second degree programmes and advanced research programmes.
* See Annex 3 for notes (*www.oecd.org/els/education/eag2002*).
Source: OECD.

Table A4.2.
Percentage of tertiary qualifications awarded to women, by type of tertiary education and by subject category (2000)

	All fields of study					Health and welfare		Life sciences, physical sciences and agriculture		Mathematics and computer science		Humanities, arts and education		Social sciences, business, law and services		Engineering, manufacturing and construction	
	Tertiary-type B (First degree)	Tertiary-type B (Second degree)	Tertiary-type A (First degree)	Tertiary-type A (Second degree)	Advanced research degrees	Tertiary-type B education	Tertiary-type A and advanced research programmes	Tertiary-type B education	Tertiary-type A and advanced research programmes	Tertiary-type B education	Tertiary-type A and advanced research programmes	Tertiary-type B education	Tertiary-type A and advanced research programmes	Tertiary-type B education	Tertiary-type A and advanced research programmes	Tertiary-type B education	Tertiary-type A and advanced research programmes
	(1)	(2)	(3)	(4)	(5)	(6)	(7)	(8)	(9)	(10)	(11)	(12)	(13)	(14)	(15)	(16)	(17)
OECD COUNTRIES																	
Australia	m	m	57	56	40	m	76	m	50	m	27	m	70	m	52	m	21
Austria	48	79	48	32	36	78	59	24	46	39	15	76	66	72	49	11	18
Belgium	61	m	50	53	34	79	59	33	40	12	25	70	65	58	52	22	21
Canada	57	n	59	52	39	84	74	50	53	29	28	70	68	62	58	17	23
Czech Republic	72	a	51	53	29	91	70	52	45	39	12	58	71	70	54	29	27
Denmark	66	75	51	49	38	85	59	27	48	10	28	69	69	39	44	32	26
Finland	65	a	59	59	45	89	84	47	51	42	35	71	77	70	65	21	19
France	54	a	57	56	41	81	60	47	49	19	31	57	73	68	59	13	24
Germany	62	a	46	a	34	79	56	13	38	14	23	87	69	50	43	7	20
Greece	m	m	m	m	m	m	m	m	m	m	m	m	m	m	m	m	m
Hungary	69	m	60	35	38	a	70	a	42	48	17	a	71	73	51	14	21
Iceland	48	a	67	59	50	a	82	a	57	34	22	65	83	51	57	a	25
Ireland	52	52	55	60	47	93	75	60	53	50	41	61	69	61	57	11	24
Italy	64	a	56	56	53	a	58	a	51	a	54	64	82	a	55	a	28
Japan	68	a	37	23	19	81	50	49	38	x(8)	x(9)	87	67	75	26	16	9
Korea	54	34	47	30	20	82	50	37	42	51	49	71	70	57	40	32	23
Luxembourg	m	m	m	m	m	m	m	m	m	m	m	m	m	m	m	m	m
Mexico	40	m	52	m	36	69	61	41	41	49	43	79	65	48	55	23	22
Netherlands	56	a	54	66	m	79	76	a	37	12	16	a	71	48	49	8	13
New Zealand	65	66	64	54	43	83	79	35	46	26	34	70	73	65	53	31	33
Norway	47	a	64	52	33	92	82	m	46	36	15	70	75	57	48	10	27
Poland	83	a	m	68	m	a	68	a	64	a	58	83	78	a	64	a	24
Portugal	70	m	65	x(3)	49	80	77	59	61	34	37	88	78	67	64	36	35
Slovak Republic	81	a	52	a	38	94	69	71	41	n	17	67	71	65	50	33	30
Spain	52	a	59	m	44	80	76	25	52	25	34	68	72	68	60	16	27
Sweden	53	a	60	93	37	95	79	59	53	50	39	54	75	63	57	25	25
Switzerland	44	42	42	26	31	81	54	11	33	18	16	75	62	38	35	5	11
Turkey	43	a	41	39	37	57	53	48	44	30	42	66	45	56	39	26	24
United Kingdom	59	x(1)	54	54	38	88	71	41	52	26	27	59	67	57	55	12	20
United States	60	a	57	56	44	87	75	38	51	43	33	77	68	64	53	14	21
Country mean	*59*	*44*	*54*	*51*	*38*	*83*	*68*	*41*	*47*	*31*	*30*	*70*	*70*	*60*	*52*	*19*	*23*
Argentina[1]	70	77	m	m	m	m	m	m	m	m	m	m	m	m	m	m	m
Brazil[1]	m	m	61	m	54	m	m	m	m	m	m	m	m	m	m	m	m
Chile[1]	48	a	51	51	29	m	m	m	m	m	m	m	m	m	m	m	m
China[1]	m	a	m	34	20	m	m	m	m	m	m	m	m	m	m	m	m
India[1]	25	a	40	40	m	m	m	m	m	m	m	m	m	m	m	m	m
Indonesia[2]	28	m	42	m	38	m	m	m	m	m	m	m	m	m	m	m	m
Israel	53	a	62	55	44	m	m	m	m	m	m	m	m	m	m	m	m
Jamaica[3]	68	m	74	66	x(4)	m	m	m	m	m	m	m	m	m	m	m	m
Jordan	72	a	47	36	17	m	m	m	m	m	m	m	m	m	m	m	m
Malaysia[1]	49	66	57	38	30	m	m	m	m	m	m	m	m	m	m	m	m
Paraguay[1]	76	85	63	68	m	m	m	m	m	m	m	m	m	m	m	m	m
Russian Federation[2]	m	a	m	a	40	m	m	m	m	m	m	m	m	m	m	m	m
Thailand	53	n	57	n	49	m	m	m	m	m	m	m	m	m	m	m	m
Tunisia	46	a	49	37	m	m	m	m	m	m	m	m	m	m	m	m	m
Uruguay[1]	77	83	56	83	55	m	m	m	m	m	m	m	m	m	m	m	m
Zimbabwe[2]	51	a	m	m	m	m	m	m	m	m	m	m	m	m	m	m	m

(Left margin: OECD COUNTRIES / NON-OECD COUNTRIES)

Note: x indicates that data are included in another column. The column reference is shown in brackets after "x". *e.g.*, x(2) means that data are included in column 2.
1. Year of reference 1999.
2. Year of reference 2001.
3. Public institutions only.
Source: OECD.

READING LITERACY OF 15-YEAR-OLDS

A5

- On average across OECD countries, 10 per cent of 15-year-olds have acquired Level 5 literacy skills, which involve evaluation of information and building of hypotheses, drawing on specialised knowledge, and accommodating concepts contrary to expectations. However, this percentage varies from 19 per cent in Finland and New Zealand to below 1 per cent in Mexico.

- An average of 12 per cent of 15-year-olds have only acquired the most basic literacy skills at Level 1 and a further 6 per cent fall even below that.

- Some countries, most notably Finland, Japan and Korea, achieve both a high level of average performance and a narrow range of disparities of student performance.

Chart A5.1.

Reading proficiency of 15-year-olds (2000)

Percentage of 15-year-olds at each level of proficiency on the PISA reading literacy scale

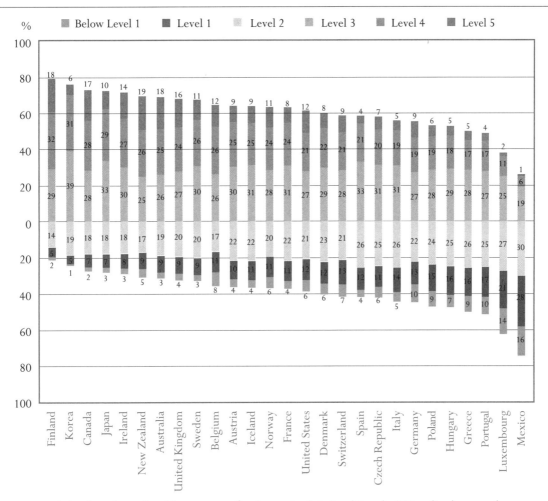

Countries are ranked in descending order of the percentage of students at Levels 3, 4 and 5 on the PISA reading literacy scale.
Source: OECD PISA database, 2001. Table A5.1. See Annex 3 for notes on methodology *(www.oecd.org/els/education/eag2002)* and *www.pisa.oecd.org.*

A5

This indicator shows the performance of 15-year-olds in reading literacy.

Policy context

The ability to read, understand, and use information is at the heart of learning both in school and throughout life. This indicator shows the performance of 15-year-olds on tasks based on a concept of reading literacy that goes beyond the notion of decoding written material and literal comprehension. Reading in PISA incorporates understanding and reflecting on texts. Literacy involves the ability to use written information to fulfil goals, and the consequent ability of complex modern societies to use written information effectively.

Evidence and explanations

Percentage of 15-year-olds proficient at each level of reading literacy

PISA provides an interpretative framework for performance levels in reading literacy.

This indicator examines reading literacy in several ways (see Box A5.1 for an explanation of reading literacy in PISA). First, it describes proficiency in terms of the range of scores that 15-year-olds achieve in each country. Proficiency in reading is examined at five levels, each representing tasks of increasing complexity, with Level 5 being the highest. Second, this indicator describes performance in terms of the mean scores achieved by 15-year-olds and the distribution of scores across student populations.

Box A5.1. What is reading literacy in PISA?

Reading Literacy is the ability to understand, use and reflect on written texts in order to achieve one's goals, to develop one's own knowledge and potential, and to participate effectively in society. This definition goes beyond the notion that reading means decoding written material and literal comprehension. Rather, reading also incorporates understanding and reflecting on texts, for a variety of reasons and in a variety of contexts. PISA's assessment of reading literacy reflects three dimensions: aspect of reading task; form of reading material; and the use for which the text is constructed.

What scales are reported? PISA's assessment of reading literacy is reported on three scales. A "retrieving information" scale is based on students' ability to locate information in a text. An "interpreting" scale is based on the ability to construct meaning and draw inferences from written information. A "reflection and evaluation" scale is based on students' ability to relate a text to their knowledge, ideas and experiences. In addition, a combined reading literacy scale summarises the results from the three reading scales. Indicator A5 focuses on the combined scale only which is referred to as the "reading literacy scale".

What do the scale scores mean? The scores on each scale represent degrees of proficiency in each dimension or aspect of reading literacy (here, the combined scale). For example, a low score on a scale indicates that a student has limited skills, whereas a high score indicates that a student has advanced skills in this area.

What are proficiency levels? In an attempt to capture this progression of difficulty, each of the reading literacy scales is divided into five levels based on the type of knowledge and skills students need to demonstrate at a particular level. Students at a particular level not only demonstrate the knowledge and skills associated with that level but also the proficiencies defined by lower levels. For instance, all students proficient at Level 3 are also proficient at Levels 1 and 2.

Chart A5.1 presents an overall profile of proficiency on the reading literacy scale with the length of the coloured components of the bars showing the percentage of 15-year-olds proficient at each level (see Box A5.2). As can be seen from the chart, the percentage of students reaching each level of literacy and the patterns of distribution across the levels varies from country to country. Across countries, on average, 10 per cent of students reach proficiency Level 5, 32 per cent reach Level at least 4 (*i.e.*, Levels 4 and 5), 61 per cent reach at least Level 3, 82 per cent reach at least Level 2, and 94 per cent reach at least Level 1.

Examining individual countries' performance level by level shows that, in five countries (Australia, Canada, Finland, New Zealand and the United Kingdom), 15 per cent or more of students reach the highest level of proficiency in reading literacy. In an additional three countries (Belgium, Ireland and the United States), between 12 and 15 per cent of students reach this level. Only five per cent or less of the students in Brazil, Greece, Latvia, Luxembourg, Mexico, Portugal, Spain and the Russian Federation reach the highest level of proficiency.

10 per cent of 15-year-olds in OECD countries have acquired Level 5 literacy skills, which involve to evaluate information and build hypotheses, draw on specialised knowledge, and to accommodate concepts contrary to expectations but this proportion ranges across countries from 19 to less than 1 per cent.

**Box A5.2. What can students at each
proficiency level do and what scores are associated with the levels?**

Students proficient at **Level 5 (over 625 points)** are capable of completing sophisticated reading tasks, such as managing information that is difficult to find in unfamiliar texts; showing detailed understanding of such texts and inferring which information in the text is relevant to the task; and being able to evaluate critically and build hypotheses, draw on specialised knowledge, and accommodate concepts that may be contrary to expectations.

Students proficient at **Level 4 (553 to 625 points)** are capable of difficult reading tasks, such as locating embedded information, construing meaning from nuances of language and critically evaluating a text.

Students proficient at **Level 3 (481 to 552 points)** are capable of reading tasks of moderate complexity, such as locating multiple pieces of information, drawing links between different parts of the text, and relating it to familiar everyday knowledge.

Students proficient at **Level 2 (408 to 480 points)** are capable of basic reading tasks, such as locating straightforward information, making low-level inferences of various types, deciding what a well-defined part of the text means, and using some outside knowledge to understand it.

Students proficient at **Level 1 (335 to 407 points)** are capable of completing only the least complex reading tasks developed for PISA, such as locating a single piece of information, identifying the main theme of a text or making a simple connection with everyday knowledge.

Students performing below **Level 1 (below 335 points)** are not able to show routinely the most basic type of knowledge and skills that PISA seeks to measure. These students may have serious difficulties in using reading literacy as an effective tool to advance and extend their knowledge and skills in other areas.

A large proportion of high performers typically means fewer low performers, but in some countries, there are large disparities.

Although there is a general tendency among countries with a high proportion of 15-year-olds scoring at Level 5 to have fewer students below the lowest level of proficiency (see Finland, for example), this is not always the case. Belgium and the United States, for example, stand out in showing an above-average share of performers at the highest proficiency level while, at the same time, showing an above-average proportion of students scoring below Level 1.

Half of all 15-year-olds in Finland and at least 40 per cent of students in five other countries reach at least Level 4 on the reading literacy scale. With the exception of Luxembourg and Mexico, at least one in five students in each OECD country reaches at least Level 4. In Brazil, the country with the lowest overall performance in reading literacy, only about 4 per cent of students score at Level 4 or above.

In one-third of OECD countries, more than two-thirds of 15-year-olds are proficient at least at Level 3.

In one-third of OECD countries, between 67 and 80 per cent of 15-year-old students are proficient at least at Level 3 on the reading literacy scale: Australia, Canada, Finland, Ireland, Japan, Korea, New Zealand, Sweden and the United Kingdom. Using these nine countries to explore the question "is the pattern of proficiency similar across countries?" several patterns emerge. In Canada and Finland, for instance, relatively large proportions of students reach Level 5 and at least 90 per cent of students in each country reach at least Level 2 — these countries show strong results across the reading literacy scale. In Australia, Ireland, New Zealand and the United Kingdom, there are large numbers of students at the highest level, but over 10 per cent of students perform at or below Level 1. These countries perform well in getting students to higher levels of proficiency but succeed less well than Canada or Finland in reducing the proportion with low skills. The opposite is true in Korea, where less than 6 per cent of students are at Level 1 or below, but where a below-average proportion (6 per cent) reach the highest level of proficiency.

In every OECD country, at least half of all students are at Level 2 or higher. Interestingly, in Spain, where only 4 per cent of students reach Level 5, an above-average 84 per cent reach at least Level 2. However, over 40 per cent of students in Spain have Level 2 as their highest proficiency level.

The simplest tasks in PISA require students to do more than just read words fluently…

Reading literacy, as defined in PISA, focuses on the knowledge and skills required to apply "reading to learn" rather than on the technical skills acquired in "learning to read". Since comparatively few young adults in OECD countries have not acquired technical reading skills, PISA does not therefore seek to measure such things as the extent to which 15-year-old students are fluent readers or how well they spell or recognise words. In line with most contemporary views about reading literacy, PISA focuses on measuring the extent to which individuals are able to construct, expand and reflect on the meaning of what they have read in a wide range of texts common both within and beyond school. The simplest reading tasks that can still be associated with this notion of reading literacy are those at Level 1. Students proficient at this level are capable of completing only the least complex reading tasks developed for

A5

PISA, such as locating a single piece of information, identifying the main theme of a text or making a simple connection with everyday knowledge.

Students performing below 335 points, *i.e.,* below Level 1, are not capable of the most basic type of reading that PISA seeks to measure. This does not mean that they have no literacy skills. In fact, most of these students can probably read in a technical sense, and the majority of them (54 per cent on average across OECD countries) are able to solve successfully at least 10 per cent of the non-multiple choice reading tasks in PISA 2000 (and 6 per cent correctly solve one-quarter of them). Nonetheless, their pattern of answers in the assessment is such that they would be expected to solve fewer than half of the tasks in a test made up of items drawn solely from Level 1, and therefore perform below Level 1. Such students show serious difficulties in using reading literacy as an effective tool to advance and extend their knowledge and skills in other areas. Students with literacy skills below Level 1 may, therefore, be at risk not only of difficulties in their initial transition from education to work but also of failure to benefit from further education and learning opportunities throughout life.

...and while students below Level 1 may have the technical capacity to read, they may face serious difficulties in future life...

Education systems with large proportions of students performing below, or even at, Level 1 should be concerned that significant numbers of their students may not be acquiring the necessary literacy knowledge and skills to benefit sufficiently from their educational opportunities. This situation is even more troublesome in light of the extensive evidence suggesting that it is difficult in later life to compensate for learning gaps in initial education. Adult literacy skills and participation in continuing education and training are strongly related, even after controlling for other characteristics affecting participation in training.

...and, along with those at Level 1, may not acquire the necessary literacy skills to sufficiently benefit from educational opportunities.

In the combined OECD area, 12 per cent of students perform at Level 1, and 6 per cent below Level 1, but there are wide differences between countries. In Finland and Korea, only around 5 per cent of students perform at Level 1, and less than 2 per cent below it, but these countries are exceptions. In all other OECD countries, between 9 and 44 per cent of students perform at or below Level 1. Over 2 per cent and, in half of the OECD countries over 5 per cent, perform below Level 1.

The percentage of students at or below Level 1 varies widely, from a few per cent to nearly half...

The countries with 20 per cent or more of students at Level 1 or below are, in order, Brazil, Mexico, Luxembourg, Latvia, the Russian Federation, Portugal, Greece, Poland, Hungary, Germany, Liechtenstein and Switzerland. In Brazil, Mexico, Luxembourg, Latvia, Portugal and Germany, between close to 10 and 23 per cent of students do not reach Level 1, *i.e.,* are unable routinely to show the most basic skills that PISA seeks to measure. This is most remarkable in the case of Germany, which has the relatively high figure of 9 per cent of its students performing at Level 5.

...and, in some countries, a considerable minority do not reach Level 1.

National means and distribution of performance in reading literacy

Another way to summarise student performance and to compare the relative standing of countries in terms of student performance in PISA 2000 is to display the mean scores for students in each country. To the extent that high average performance at age 15 can be considered predictive of a highly skilled future

Average scores can usefully summarise country performances...

A5

workforce, countries with high average performance will have an important economic and social advantage. It should be noted, however, that average performance charts often mask significant variation in performance within countries, reflecting different performance among many different groups of students.

…but mask wide differences in student performance within countries.

As in previous international studies of student performance, such as the Third International Mathematics and Science Study (TIMSS), only around one-tenth of PISA's total variation in student performance lies between countries and can, therefore, be captured through a comparison of country averages. The remaining variation of student performance occurs within countries, that is between educational programmes, between schools, and between students within schools. Thus, this indicator also presents information on the distribution of reading literacy scores, examining the range of performance between the top and bottom quarter of students in each country.

Finland shows unparalleled overall performance, almost two-thirds of a proficiency level ahead of the OECD average.

On the reading literacy scale, students from Finland perform on average higher than students from any other country participating in the study (see Chart A5.2). Their mean score, 546 points, is almost two-thirds of a proficiency level above the OECD average of 500 points (or in statistical terms, almost half the international standard deviation above the mean). Twelve other countries, Australia, Austria, Belgium, Canada, Iceland, Ireland, Japan, Korea, the Netherlands, New Zealand, Sweden and the United Kingdom, score above the OECD mean. Five countries perform at or about the OECD mean, and 14 countries, including the four non-OECD countries, perform significantly below the OECD mean.

High average scores are not enough: countries also look to raise the level of achievement of poor performers.

Looking at the distribution in student performance (Table A5.2) shows that the variation in student performance on the reading literacy scale within countries is large. The variation within every country far exceeds the range of country mean scores. The difference between the 75th and 25th percentiles, which covers the middle half of the national performance distribution, exceeds the magnitude of one proficiency level (72 score points) in all countries, and about two times the magnitude of one proficiency level in Australia, Belgium, Germany and New Zealand. (The OECD average on this measure is 1.8 times the magnitude of one proficiency level.)

Are these observed disparities inevitable? That is hard to say…

Together, these findings suggest that educational systems in many countries face significant challenges in addressing the needs of all students, including those most in need as well as those performing exceptionally well.

…but some countries contain them within a far narrower range than others…

One can also observe that countries with similar levels of average performance show considerable variation in disparities of student achievement. For example, Korea and the United Kingdom both show above-average mean performance on the reading literacy scale at around 525 score points. The difference between the 75th and 25th percentile in Korea is 92 points, significantly below the OECD average, but in the United Kingdom it is 137 score points, similar to the OECD average. A similar result can be observed for countries scoring below average. Italy and Germany each perform at around 485 score points,

A5

Chart A5.2
Multiple comparisons of mean performance on the PISA reading literacy scale (2000)

	Mean	S.E.	Finland	Canada	New Zealand	Australia	Ireland	Korea	United Kingdom	Japan	Sweden	Austria	Belgium	Iceland	Norway	France	United States	Denmark	Switzerland	Spain	Czech Republic	Italy	Germany	Liechtenstein	Hungary	Poland	Greece	Portugal	Russian Fed.	Latvia	Luxembourg	Mexico	Brazil
		Mean	546	534	529	528	527	525	523	522	516	507	507	507	505	505	504	497	494	493	492	487	484	483	480	479	474	470	462	458	441	422	396
		S.E.	(2.6)	(1.6)	(2.8)	(3.5)	(3.2)	(2.4)	(2.6)	(5.2)	(2.2)	(2.4)	(3.6)	(1.5)	(2.8)	(2.7)	(7.0)	(2.4)	(4.2)	(2.7)	(2.4)	(2.9)	(2.5)	(4.1)	(4.0)	(4.5)	(5.0)	(4.5)	(4.2)	(5.3)	(1.6)	(3.3)	(3.1)
Finland	546	(2.6)	□	▲	▲	▲	▲	▲	▲	▲	▲	▲	▲	▲	▲	▲	▲	▲	▲	▲	▲	▲	▲	▲	▲	▲	▲	▲	▲	▲	▲	▲	▲
Canada	534	(1.6)	▽	□	○	○	○	▲	▲	○	▲	▲	▲	▲	▲	▲	▲	▲	▲	▲	▲	▲	▲	▲	▲	▲	▲	▲	▲	▲	▲	▲	▲
New Zealand	529	(2.8)	▽	○	□	○	○	○	○	○	▲	▲	▲	▲	▲	▲	○	▲	▲	▲	▲	▲	▲	▲	▲	▲	▲	▲	▲	▲	▲	▲	▲
Australia	528	(3.5)	▽	○	○	□	○	○	○	○	▲	▲	▲	▲	▲	▲	○	▲	▲	▲	▲	▲	▲	▲	▲	▲	▲	▲	▲	▲	▲	▲	▲
Ireland	527	(3.2)	▽	○	○	○	□	○	○	○	○	▲	▲	▲	▲	▲	○	▲	▲	▲	▲	▲	▲	▲	▲	▲	▲	▲	▲	▲	▲	▲	▲
Korea	525	(2.4)	▽	○	○	○	○	□	○	○	○	▲	▲	▲	▲	▲	○	▲	▲	▲	▲	▲	▲	▲	▲	▲	▲	▲	▲	▲	▲	▲	▲
United Kingdom	523	(2.6)	▽	▽	○	○	○	○	□	○	○	▲	▲	▲	▲	▲	○	▲	▲	▲	▲	▲	▲	▲	▲	▲	▲	▲	▲	▲	▲	▲	▲
Japan	522	(5.2)	▽	○	○	○	○	○	○	□	○	○	○	○	○	○	○	▲	▲	▲	▲	▲	▲	▲	▲	▲	▲	▲	▲	▲	▲	▲	▲
Sweden	516	(2.2)	▽	▽	▽	○	○	○	○	○	□	○	○	▲	○	▲	○	▲	▲	▲	▲	▲	▲	▲	▲	▲	▲	▲	▲	▲	▲	▲	▲
Austria	507	(2.4)	▽	▽	▽	▽	▽	▽	▽	○	○	□	○	○	○	○	○	○	▲	▲	▲	▲	▲	▲	▲	▲	▲	▲	▲	▲	▲	▲	▲
Belgium	507	(3.6)	▽	▽	▽	▽	▽	▽	▽	○	○	○	□	○	○	○	○	○	▲	▲	▲	▲	▲	▲	▲	▲	▲	▲	▲	▲	▲	▲	▲
Iceland	507	(1.5)	▽	▽	▽	▽	▽	▽	▽	○	▽	○	○	□	○	○	▲	▲	▲	▲	▲	▲	▲	▲	▲	▲	▲	▲	▲	▲	▲	▲	▲
Norway	505	(2.8)	▽	▽	▽	▽	▽	▽	▽	○	○	○	○	○	□	○	○	○	○	▲	▲	▲	▲	▲	▲	▲	▲	▲	▲	▲	▲	▲	▲
France	505	(2.7)	▽	▽	▽	▽	▽	▽	▽	○	▽	○	○	○	○	□	○	○	○	▲	▲	▲	▲	▲	▲	▲	▲	▲	▲	▲	▲	▲	▲
United States	504	(7.0)	▽	▽	○	○	○	○	○	○	○	○	○	▽	○	○	□	○	○	○	○	○	○	○	○	▲	▲	▲	▲	▲	▲	▲	▲
Denmark	497	(2.4)	▽	▽	▽	▽	▽	▽	▽	▽	▽	○	○	▽	○	○	○	□	○	○	▲	▲	▲	▲	▲	▲	▲	▲	▲	▲	▲	▲	▲
Switzerland	494	(4.2)	▽	▽	▽	▽	▽	▽	▽	▽	▽	○	○	▽	○	○	○	○	□	○	○	▲	▲	▲	▲	▲	▲	▲	▲	▲	▲	▲	▲
Spain	493	(2.7)	▽	▽	▽	▽	▽	▽	▽	▽	▽	▽	▽	▽	▽	▽	○	○	○	□	○	○	○	○	▲	▲	▲	▲	▲	▲	▲	▲	▲
Czech Republic	492	(2.4)	▽	▽	▽	▽	▽	▽	▽	▽	▽	▽	▽	▽	▽	▽	○	▽	○	○	□	○	○	○	○	▲	▲	▲	▲	▲	▲	▲	▲
Italy	487	(2.9)	▽	▽	▽	▽	▽	▽	▽	▽	▽	▽	▽	▽	▽	▽	○	▽	▽	○	○	□	○	○	○	○	▲	▲	▲	▲	▲	▲	▲
Germany	484	(2.5)	▽	▽	▽	▽	▽	▽	▽	▽	▽	▽	▽	▽	▽	▽	○	▽	▽	○	○	○	□	○	○	○	○	▲	▲	▲	▲	▲	▲
Liechtenstein	483	(4.1)	▽	▽	▽	▽	▽	▽	▽	▽	▽	▽	▽	▽	▽	▽	○	▽	○	○	○	○	○	□	○	○	○	○	▲	▲	▲	▲	▲
Hungary	480	(4.0)	▽	▽	▽	▽	▽	▽	▽	▽	▽	▽	▽	▽	▽	▽	○	▽	○	○	○	○	○	○	□	○	○	○	▲	▲	▲	▲	▲
Poland	479	(4.5)	▽	▽	▽	▽	▽	▽	▽	▽	▽	▽	▽	▽	▽	▽	▽	▽	○	○	○	○	○	○	○	□	○	○	▲	▲	▲	▲	▲
Greece	474	(5.0)	▽	▽	▽	▽	▽	▽	▽	▽	▽	▽	▽	▽	▽	▽	▽	▽	▽	▽	▽	○	○	○	○	○	□	○	○	○	▲	▲	▲
Portugal	470	(4.5)	▽	▽	▽	▽	▽	▽	▽	▽	▽	▽	▽	▽	▽	▽	▽	▽	▽	▽	▽	○	○	○	○	○	○	□	○	○	▲	▲	▲
Russian Fed.	462	(4.2)	▽	▽	▽	▽	▽	▽	▽	▽	▽	▽	▽	▽	▽	▽	▽	▽	▽	▽	▽	▽	▽	▽	▽	▽	○	○	□	○	▲	▲	▲
Latvia	458	(5.3)	▽	▽	▽	▽	▽	▽	▽	▽	▽	▽	▽	▽	▽	▽	▽	▽	▽	▽	▽	▽	▽	▽	▽	▽	○	○	○	□	▲	▲	▲
Luxembourg	441	(1.6)	▽	▽	▽	▽	▽	▽	▽	▽	▽	▽	▽	▽	▽	▽	▽	▽	▽	▽	▽	▽	▽	▽	▽	▽	▽	▽	▽	▽	□	▲	▲
Mexico	422	(3.3)	▽	▽	▽	▽	▽	▽	▽	▽	▽	▽	▽	▽	▽	▽	▽	▽	▽	▽	▽	▽	▽	▽	▽	▽	▽	▽	▽	▽	▽	□	▲
Brazil	396	(3.1)	▽	▽	▽	▽	▽	▽	▽	▽	▽	▽	▽	▽	▽	▽	▽	▽	▽	▽	▽	▽	▽	▽	▽	▽	▽	▽	▽	▽	▽	▽	□
Upper rank*			1	2	2	2	3	4	5	3	9	11	11	11	11	11	10	16	16	17	17	19	21	20	21	21	23	24	27	27	30	31	32
Lower rank*			1	4	8	9	9	9	9	10	11	16	16	15	16	16	20	19	21	21	21	24	25	26	26	27	28	28	29	29	30	31	32

*Note: Because data are based on samples, it is not possible to report exact rank order positions for countries. However, it is possible to report the range of rank order positions within which the country mean lies with 95 per cent likelihood.

Instructions

Read across the row for a country to compare performance with the countries listed along the top of the chart. The symbols indicate whether the mean performance of the country in the row is significantly lower than that of the comparison country, significantly higher than that of the comparison country, or if there is no statistically significant difference between the mean performance of the two countries.

Note: Countries are presented in descending order of mean performance on the PISA reading literacy scale. Due to low response rates, the Netherlands is excluded from the figure. Assuming negligible to moderate levels of bias due to non-response, the position of the Netherlands may be expected, with 95 per cent confidence, to lie between 2nd and 14th place among countries.

▲ Mean performance statistically significantly higher than in comparison country.
○ No statistically significant difference from comparison country.
▽ Mean performance statistically significantly lower than in comparison country.

Statistically significantly above the OECD average
Not statistically significantly different from the OECD average
Statistically significantly below the OECD average

Source: OECD PISA database, 2001. *See Annex 3* for notes on methodology *(www.oecd.org/els/education/eag2002)* and *www.pisa.oecd.org.*

A5

...and some countries succeed in combining high average performance with low disparities.

significantly below the OECD average. In Italy the difference between the 75th and 25th percentile is 124 points, but in Germany, it is 146 points. Bringing the bottom quarter of students closer to the mean is one way for countries with wide internal disparities to raise overall performance.

Finally, comparing the range of achievement within a country with its average performance shows that some countries attain both relatively low differences between top and bottom-performing students and relatively high levels of overall performance. There is a tendency for high performing countries to show relatively small disparities. For example, the three countries with the smallest differences between the 75th and 25th percentiles, Finland, Japan and Korea are also among the best performing countries in reading literacy. By contrast, one of the three countries with the highest achievement differences, Germany, scores significantly below the OECD average.

Definitions and methodologies

The achievement scores are based on assessments administered as part of the Programme for International Student Assessment (PISA) undertaken by the OECD during 2000.

The target population studied for this indicator was 15-year-old students. Operationally, this refers to students aged between 15 years and 3 (completed) months and 16 years and 2 (completed) months at the beginning of the testing period and enrolled in an educational institution, regardless of the grade level or type of institutions in which they were enrolled and of whether they participated in school full-time or part-time.

To facilitate the interpretation of the scores assigned to students in PISA, the mean score for reading literacy performance across OECD countries was set at 500 and the standard deviation at 100, with the data weighted so that each OECD country contributed equally. These reference points anchor PISA's measurement of student proficiency.

For notes on standard errors, significance tests, and multiple comparisons see Annex 3 at *www.oecd.org/els/education/eag2002*.

Table A5.1.
Reading proficiency of 15-year-olds (2000)
Percentage of 15-year-olds at each level of proficiency on the PISA reading literacy scale

A5

	Proficiency levels											
	Below Level 1 (less than 335 score points)		Level 1 (from 335 to 407 score points)		Level 2 (from 408 to 480 score points)		Level 3 (from 481 to 552 score points)		Level 4 (from 553 to 625 score points)		Level 5 (above 625 score points)	
	%	S.E.	%	S.E.	%	S.E.	%	S.E.	%	S.E.	%	S.E.
Australia	3.3	(0.5)	9.1	(0.8)	19.0	(1.1)	25.7	(1.1)	25.3	(0.9)	17.6	(1.2)
Austria	4.4	(0.4)	10.2	(0.6)	21.7	(0.9)	29.9	(1.2)	24.9	(1.0)	8.8	(0.8)
Belgium	7.7	(1.0)	11.3	(0.7)	16.8	(0.7)	25.8	(0.9)	26.3	(0.9)	12.0	(0.7)
Canada	2.4	(0.3)	7.2	(0.3)	18.0	(0.4)	28.0	(0.5)	27.7	(0.6)	16.8	(0.5)
Czech Republic	6.1	(0.6)	11.4	(0.7)	24.8	(1.2)	30.9	(1.1)	19.8	(0.8)	7.0	(0.6)
Denmark	5.9	(0.6)	12.0	(0.7)	22.5	(0.9)	29.5	(1.0)	22.0	(0.9)	8.1	(0.5)
Finland	1.7	(0.5)	5.2	(0.4)	14.3	(0.7)	28.7	(0.8)	31.6	(0.9)	18.5	(0.9)
France	4.2	(0.6)	11.0	(0.8)	22.0	(0.8)	30.6	(1.0)	23.7	(0.9)	8.5	(0.6)
Germany	9.9	(0.7)	12.7	(0.6)	22.3	(0.8)	26.8	(1.0)	19.4	(1.0)	8.8	(0.5)
Greece	8.7	(1.2)	15.7	(1.4)	25.9	(1.4)	28.1	(1.7)	16.7	(1.4)	5.0	(0.7)
Hungary	6.9	(0.7)	15.8	(1.2)	25.0	(1.1)	28.8	(1.3)	18.5	(1.1)	5.1	(0.8)
Iceland	4.0	(0.3)	10.5	(0.6)	22.0	(0.8)	30.8	(0.9)	23.6	(1.1)	9.1	(0.7)
Ireland	3.1	(0.5)	7.9	(0.8)	17.9	(0.9)	29.7	(1.1)	27.1	(1.1)	14.2	(0.8)
Italy	5.4	(0.9)	13.5	(0.9)	25.6	(1.0)	30.6	(1.0)	19.5	(1.1)	5.3	(0.5)
Japan	2.7	(0.6)	7.3	(1.1)	18.0	(1.3)	33.3	(1.3)	28.8	(1.7)	9.9	(1.1)
Korea	0.9	(0.2)	4.8	(0.6)	18.6	(0.9)	38.8	(1.1)	31.1	(1.2)	5.7	(0.6)
Luxembourg	14.2	(0.7)	20.9	(0.8)	27.5	(1.3)	24.6	(1.1)	11.2	(0.5)	1.7	(0.3)
Mexico	16.1	(1.2)	28.1	(1.4)	30.3	(1.1)	18.8	(1.2)	6.0	(0.7)	0.9	(0.2)
New Zealand	4.8	(0.5)	8.9	(0.5)	17.2	(0.9)	24.6	(1.1)	25.8	(1.1)	18.7	(1.0)
Norway	6.3	(0.6)	11.2	(0.8)	19.5	(0.8)	28.1	(0.8)	23.7	(0.9)	11.2	(0.7)
Poland	8.7	(1.0)	14.6	(1.0)	24.1	(1.4)	28.2	(1.3)	18.6	(1.3)	5.9	(1.0)
Portugal	9.6	(1.0)	16.7	(1.2)	25.3	(1.0)	27.5	(1.2)	16.8	(1.1)	4.2	(0.5)
Spain	4.1	(0.5)	12.2	(0.9)	25.7	(0.7)	32.8	(1.0)	21.1	(0.9)	4.2	(0.5)
Sweden	3.3	(0.4)	9.3	(0.6)	20.3	(0.7)	30.4	(1.0)	25.6	(1.0)	11.2	(0.7)
Switzerland	7.0	(0.7)	13.3	(0.9)	21.4	(1.0)	28.0	(1.0)	21.0	(1.0)	9.2	(1.0)
United Kingdom	3.6	(0.4)	9.2	(0.5)	19.6	(0.7)	27.5	(0.9)	24.4	(0.9)	15.6	(1.0)
United States	6.4	(1.2)	11.5	(1.2)	21.0	(1.2)	27.4	(1.3)	21.5	(1.4)	12.2	(1.4)
OECD total	*6.2*	*(0.4)*	*12.1*	*(0.4)*	*21.8*	*(0.4)*	*28.6*	*(0.4)*	*21.8*	*(0.4)*	*9.4*	*(0.4)*
Country mean	*6.0*	*(0.1)*	*11.9*	*(0.2)*	*21.7*	*(0.2)*	*28.7*	*(0.2)*	*22.3*	*(0.2)*	*9.5*	*(0.1)*
Brazil	23.3	(1.4)	32.5	(1.2)	27.7	(1.3)	12.9	(1.1)	3.1	(0.5)	0.6	(0.2)
Latvia	12.7	(1.3)	17.9	(1.3)	26.3	(1.1)	25.2	(1.3)	13.8	(1.1)	4.1	(0.6)
Liechtenstein	7.6	(1.5)	14.5	(2.1)	23.2	(2.9)	30.1	(3.4)	19.5	(2.2)	5.1	(1.6)
Russian Federation	9.0	(1.0)	18.5	(1.1)	29.2	(0.8)	26.9	(1.1)	13.3	(1.0)	3.2	(0.5)

OECD COUNTRIES / NON-OECD COUNTRIES

Source: OECD PISA database, 2001. See Annex 3 for notes on methodology (*www.oecd.org/els/education/eag2002*) and *www.pisa.oecd.org*.

Table A5.2.
Variation in performance in reading literacy of 15-year-olds (2000)
Performance of 15-year-olds on the PISA reading literacy scale, by percentile

| | Mean | | Standard deviation | | Percentiles | | | | | | | | | | | | |
| | | | | | 5th | | 10th | | 25th | | 75th | | 90th | | 95th | |
	Mean score	S.E.	S.D.	S.E.	Score	S.E.	Score	S.E.	Score	S.E.	Score	S.E.	Score	S.E.	Score	S.E.
Australia	528	(3.5)	102	(1.6)	354	(4.8)	394	(4.4)	458	(4.4)	602	(4.6)	656	(4.2)	685	(4.5)
Austria	507	(2.4)	93	(1.6)	341	(5.4)	383	(4.2)	447	(2.8)	573	(3.0)	621	(3.2)	648	(3.7)
Belgium	507	(3.6)	107	(2.4)	308	(10.3)	354	(8.9)	437	(6.6)	587	(2.3)	634	(2.5)	659	(2.4)
Canada	534	(1.6)	95	(1.1)	371	(3.8)	410	(2.4)	472	(2.0)	600	(1.5)	652	(1.9)	681	(2.7)
Czech Republic	492	(2.4)	96	(1.9)	320	(7.9)	368	(4.9)	433	(2.8)	557	(2.9)	610	(3.2)	638	(3.6)
Denmark	497	(2.4)	98	(1.8)	326	(6.2)	367	(5.0)	434	(3.3)	566	(2.7)	617	(2.9)	645	(3.6)
Finland	546	(2.6)	89	(2.6)	390	(5.8)	429	(5.1)	492	(2.9)	608	(2.6)	654	(2.8)	681	(3.4)
France	505	(2.7)	92	(1.7)	344	(6.2)	381	(5.2)	444	(4.5)	570	(2.4)	619	(2.9)	645	(3.7)
Germany	484	(2.5)	111	(1.9)	284	(9.4)	335	(6.3)	417	(4.6)	563	(3.1)	619	(2.8)	650	(3.2)
Greece	474	(5.0)	97	(2.7)	305	(8.2)	342	(8.4)	409	(7.4)	543	(4.5)	595	(5.1)	625	(6.0)
Hungary	480	(4.0)	94	(2.1)	320	(5.6)	354	(5.5)	414	(5.3)	549	(4.5)	598	(4.4)	626	(5.5)
Iceland	507	(1.5)	92	(1.4)	345	(5.0)	383	(3.6)	447	(3.1)	573	(2.2)	621	(3.5)	647	(3.7)
Ireland	527	(3.2)	94	(1.7)	360	(6.3)	401	(6.4)	468	(4.3)	593	(3.6)	641	(4.0)	669	(3.4)
Italy	487	(2.9)	91	(2.7)	331	(8.5)	368	(5.8)	429	(4.1)	552	(3.2)	601	(2.7)	627	(3.1)
Japan	522	(5.2)	86	(3.0)	366	(11.4)	407	(9.8)	471	(7.0)	582	(4.4)	625	(4.6)	650	(4.3)
Korea	525	(2.4)	70	(1.6)	402	(5.2)	433	(4.4)	481	(2.9)	574	(2.6)	608	(2.9)	629	(3.2)
Luxembourg	441	(1.6)	100	(1.5)	267	(5.1)	311	(4.4)	378	(2.8)	513	(2.0)	564	(2.8)	592	(3.5)
Mexico	422	(3.3)	86	(2.1)	284	(4.4)	311	(3.4)	360	(3.6)	482	(4.8)	535	(5.5)	565	(6.3)
New Zealand	529	(2.8)	108	(2.0)	337	(7.4)	382	(5.2)	459	(4.1)	606	(3.0)	661	(4.4)	693	(6.1)
Norway	505	(2.8)	104	(1.7)	320	(5.9)	364	(5.5)	440	(4.5)	579	(2.7)	631	(3.1)	660	(4.6)
Poland	479	(4.5)	100	(3.1)	304	(8.7)	343	(6.8)	414	(5.8)	551	(6.0)	603	(6.6)	631	(6.0)
Portugal	470	(4.5)	97	(1.8)	300	(6.2)	337	(6.2)	403	(6.4)	541	(4.5)	592	(4.2)	620	(3.9)
Spain	493	(2.7)	85	(1.2)	344	(5.8)	379	(5.0)	436	(4.6)	553	(2.6)	597	(2.6)	620	(2.9)
Sweden	516	(2.2)	92	(1.2)	354	(4.5)	392	(4.0)	456	(3.1)	581	(3.1)	630	(2.9)	658	(3.1)
Switzerland	494	(4.2)	102	(2.0)	316	(5.5)	355	(5.8)	426	(5.5)	567	(4.7)	621	(5.5)	651	(5.3)
United Kingdom	523	(2.6)	100	(1.5)	352	(4.9)	391	(4.1)	458	(2.8)	595	(3.5)	651	(4.3)	682	(4.9)
United States	504	(7.1)	105	(2.7)	320	(11.7)	363	(11.4)	436	(8.8)	577	(6.8)	636	(6.5)	669	(6.8)
OECD total	*499*	*(2.0)*	*100*	*(0.8)*	*322*	*(3.4)*	*363*	*(3.3)*	*433*	*(2.5)*	*569*	*(1.6)*	*622*	*(2.0)*	*653*	*(2.1)*
Country mean	*500*	*(0.6)*	*100*	*(0.4)*	*324*	*(1.3)*	*366*	*(1.1)*	*435*	*(1.0)*	*571*	*(0.7)*	*623*	*(0.8)*	*652*	*(0.8)*
Brazil	396	(3.1)	86	(1.9)	255	(5.0)	288	(4.5)	339	(3.4)	452	(3.4)	507	(4.2)	539	(5.5)
Latvia	458	(5.3)	102	(2.3)	283	(9.7)	322	(8.2)	390	(6.9)	530	(5.3)	586	(5.8)	617	(6.6)
Liechtenstein	483	(4.1)	96	(3.9)	310	(15.9)	350	(11.8)	419	(9.4)	551	(5.8)	601	(7.1)	626	(8.2)
Russian Federation	462	(4.2)	92	(1.8)	306	(6.9)	340	(5.4)	400	(5.1)	526	(4.5)	579	(4.4)	608	(5.3)

Source: OECD PISA database, 2001. See Annex 3 for notes on methodology (*www.oecd.org/els/education/eag2002*) and *www.pisa.oecd.org*.

OECD COUNTRIES

NON-OECD COUNTRIES

MATHEMATICAL AND SCIENTIFIC LITERACY OF 15-YEAR-OLDS

A6

• 15-year-olds in Japan display the highest mean scores in mathematical literacy, although their scores cannot be distinguished statistically from students in two other top-performing countries, Korea and New Zealand. On the scientific literacy scale, students in Korea and Japan demonstrate the highest average performance.

• While there are large differences in mean performance among countries, the variation of performance among 15-year-olds within each country is many times larger. However, wide disparities in performance are not a necessary condition for a country to attain a high level of overall performance. On the contrary, five of the countries with the smallest variation in performance on the mathematical literacy scale, namely Canada, Finland, Iceland, Japan and Korea, all perform significantly above the OECD average, and four of them – Canada, Finland, Japan and Korea – are among the six best-performing countries in mathematical literacy.

Chart A6.1
Multiple comparisons of mean performance on the PISA mathematical literacy scale (2000)

A6

Instructions: Read across the row for a country to compare performance with the countries listed along the top of the chart.

Legend:
- ▲ Mean performance statistically significantly higher than in comparison country.
- ○ No statistically significant difference from comparison country.
- ▽ Mean performance statistically significantly lower than in comparison country.

Comparison country codes (with Mean and S.E.): JP = Japan 557 (5.5); KR = Korea 547 (2.8); NZ = New Zealand 537 (3.1); FI = Finland 536 (2.1); AU = Australia 533 (3.5); CA = Canada 533 (1.4); CH = Switzerland 529 (4.4); UK = United Kingdom 529 (2.5); BE = Belgium 520 (3.9); FR = France 517 (2.7); AT = Austria 515 (2.5); DK = Denmark 514 (2.4); IS = Iceland 514 (2.3); LI = Liechtenstein 514 (7.0); SE = Sweden 510 (2.5); IE = Ireland 503 (2.7); NO = Norway 499 (2.8); CZ = Czech Republic 498 (2.8); US = United States 493 (7.6); DE = Germany 490 (2.5); HU = Hungary 488 (4.0); RU = Russian Fed. 478 (5.5); ES = Spain 476 (3.1); PL = Poland 470 (5.5); LV = Latvia 463 (4.5); IT = Italy 457 (2.9); PT = Portugal 454 (4.1); GR = Greece 447 (5.6); LU = Luxembourg 446 (2.0); MX = Mexico 387 (3.4); BR = Brazil 334 (3.7).

Country	Mean	S.E.	JP	KR	NZ	FI	AU	CA	CH	UK	BE	FR	AT	DK	IS	LI	SE	IE	NO	CZ	US	DE	HU	RU	ES	PL	LV	IT	PT	GR	LU	MX	BR
Japan	557	(5.5)	□	○	○	▲	▲	▲	▲	▲	▲	▲	▲	▲	▲	▲	▲	▲	▲	▲	▲	▲	▲	▲	▲	▲	▲	▲	▲	▲	▲	▲	▲
Korea	547	(2.8)	○	□	○	○	○	▲	▲	▲	▲	▲	▲	▲	▲	▲	▲	▲	▲	▲	▲	▲	▲	▲	▲	▲	▲	▲	▲	▲	▲	▲	▲
New Zealand	537	(3.1)	▽	○	□	○	○	○	○	○	▲	▲	▲	▲	▲	▲	▲	▲	▲	▲	▲	▲	▲	▲	▲	▲	▲	▲	▲	▲	▲	▲	▲
Finland	536	(2.1)	▽	○	○	□	○	○	○	○	▲	▲	▲	▲	▲	▲	▲	▲	▲	▲	▲	▲	▲	▲	▲	▲	▲	▲	▲	▲	▲	▲	▲
Australia	533	(3.5)	▽	○	○	○	□	○	○	○	▲	▲	▲	▲	▲	▲	▲	▲	▲	▲	▲	▲	▲	▲	▲	▲	▲	▲	▲	▲	▲	▲	▲
Canada	533	(1.4)	▽	▽	○	○	○	□	○	○	▲	▲	▲	▲	▲	▲	▲	▲	▲	▲	▲	▲	▲	▲	▲	▲	▲	▲	▲	▲	▲	▲	▲
Switzerland	529	(4.4)	▽	▽	○	○	○	○	□	○	○	○	▲	▲	▲	▲	▲	▲	▲	▲	▲	▲	▲	▲	▲	▲	▲	▲	▲	▲	▲	▲	▲
United Kingdom	529	(2.5)	▽	▽	○	○	○	○	○	□	○	○	▲	▲	▲	▲	▲	▲	▲	▲	▲	▲	▲	▲	▲	▲	▲	▲	▲	▲	▲	▲	▲
Belgium	520	(3.9)	▽	▽	▽	▽	▽	▽	○	○	□	○	○	○	○	○	○	▲	▲	▲	▲	▲	▲	▲	▲	▲	▲	▲	▲	▲	▲	▲	▲
France	517	(2.7)	▽	▽	▽	▽	▽	▽	○	○	○	□	○	○	○	○	○	○	▲	▲	○	▲	▲	▲	▲	▲	▲	▲	▲	▲	▲	▲	▲
Austria	515	(2.5)	▽	▽	▽	▽	▽	▽	▽	▽	○	○	□	○	○	○	○	○	▲	▲	○	▲	▲	▲	▲	▲	▲	▲	▲	▲	▲	▲	▲
Denmark	514	(2.4)	▽	▽	▽	▽	▽	▽	▽	▽	○	○	○	□	○	○	○	○	○	○	○	▲	▲	▲	▲	▲	▲	▲	▲	▲	▲	▲	▲
Iceland	514	(2.3)	▽	▽	▽	▽	▽	▽	▽	▽	○	○	○	○	□	○	○	○	○	○	○	▲	▲	▲	▲	▲	▲	▲	▲	▲	▲	▲	▲
Liechtenstein	514	(7.0)	▽	▽	▽	▽	▽	▽	▽	▽	○	○	○	○	○	□	○	○	○	○	○	○	○	▲	▲	▲	▲	▲	▲	▲	▲	▲	▲
Sweden	510	(2.5)	▽	▽	▽	▽	▽	▽	▽	▽	○	○	○	○	○	○	□	○	○	○	○	▲	▲	▲	▲	▲	▲	▲	▲	▲	▲	▲	▲
Ireland	503	(2.7)	▽	▽	▽	▽	▽	▽	▽	▽	▽	○	○	○	○	○	○	□	○	○	○	○	○	▲	▲	▲	▲	▲	▲	▲	▲	▲	▲
Norway	499	(2.8)	▽	▽	▽	▽	▽	▽	▽	▽	▽	▽	▽	○	○	○	○	○	□	○	○	○	○	▲	▲	▲	▲	▲	▲	▲	▲	▲	▲
Czech Republic	498	(2.8)	▽	▽	▽	▽	▽	▽	▽	▽	▽	▽	▽	○	○	○	○	○	○	□	○	○	○	▲	▲	▲	▲	▲	▲	▲	▲	▲	▲
United States	493	(7.6)	▽	▽	▽	▽	▽	▽	▽	▽	▽	○	○	○	○	○	○	○	○	○	□	○	○	○	○	○	▲	▲	▲	▲	▲	▲	▲
Germany	490	(2.5)	▽	▽	▽	▽	▽	▽	▽	▽	▽	▽	▽	▽	▽	○	▽	○	○	○	○	□	○	○	○	○	▲	▲	▲	▲	▲	▲	▲
Hungary	488	(4.0)	▽	▽	▽	▽	▽	▽	▽	▽	▽	▽	▽	▽	▽	○	▽	○	○	○	○	○	□	○	○	○	▲	▲	▲	▲	▲	▲	▲
Russian Fed.	478	(5.5)	▽	▽	▽	▽	▽	▽	▽	▽	▽	▽	▽	▽	▽	▽	▽	▽	▽	▽	○	○	○	□	○	○	○	▲	▲	▲	▲	▲	▲
Spain	476	(3.1)	▽	▽	▽	▽	▽	▽	▽	▽	▽	▽	▽	▽	▽	▽	▽	▽	▽	▽	○	○	○	○	□	○	○	○	▲	▲	▲	▲	▲
Poland	470	(5.5)	▽	▽	▽	▽	▽	▽	▽	▽	▽	▽	▽	▽	▽	▽	▽	▽	▽	▽	○	○	○	○	○	□	○	○	○	○	○	▲	▲
Latvia	463	(4.5)	▽	▽	▽	▽	▽	▽	▽	▽	▽	▽	▽	▽	▽	▽	▽	▽	▽	▽	▽	▽	▽	○	○	○	□	○	○	○	○	▲	▲
Italy	457	(2.9)	▽	▽	▽	▽	▽	▽	▽	▽	▽	▽	▽	▽	▽	▽	▽	▽	▽	▽	▽	▽	▽	▽	○	○	○	□	○	○	○	▲	▲
Portugal	454	(4.1)	▽	▽	▽	▽	▽	▽	▽	▽	▽	▽	▽	▽	▽	▽	▽	▽	▽	▽	▽	▽	▽	▽	▽	○	○	○	□	○	○	▲	▲
Greece	447	(5.6)	▽	▽	▽	▽	▽	▽	▽	▽	▽	▽	▽	▽	▽	▽	▽	▽	▽	▽	▽	▽	▽	▽	▽	○	○	○	○	□	○	▲	▲
Luxembourg	446	(2.0)	▽	▽	▽	▽	▽	▽	▽	▽	▽	▽	▽	▽	▽	▽	▽	▽	▽	▽	▽	▽	▽	▽	▽	○	○	○	○	○	□	▲	▲
Mexico	387	(3.4)	▽	▽	▽	▽	▽	▽	▽	▽	▽	▽	▽	▽	▽	▽	▽	▽	▽	▽	▽	▽	▽	▽	▽	▽	▽	▽	▽	▽	▽	□	▲
Brazil	334	(3.7)	▽	▽	▽	▽	▽	▽	▽	▽	▽	▽	▽	▽	▽	▽	▽	▽	▽	▽	▽	▽	▽	▽	▽	▽	▽	▽	▽	▽	▽	▽	□

	JP	KR	NZ	FI	AU	CA	CH	UK	BE	FR	AT	DK	IS	LI	SE	IE	NO	CZ	US	DE	HU	RU	ES	PL	LV	IT	PT	GR	LU	MX	BR
Upper rank*	1	2	4	4	4	5	4	6	9	10	10	10	11	9	13	16	17	17	16	20	20	21	23	23	25	26	26	27	29	31	32
Lower rank*	3	3	8	7	9	8	10	10	15	15	16	16	16	18	17	19	20	20	23	22	23	25	25	26	28	28	29	30	30	31	32

*Note: Because data are based on samples, it is not possible to report exact rank order positions for countries. However, it is possible to report the range of rank order positions within which the country mean lies with 95 per cent likelihood.

Instructions

Read across the row for a country to compare performance with the countries listed along the top of the chart. The symbols indicate whether the mean performance of the country in the row is significantly lower than that of the comparison country, significantly higher than that of the comparison country, or if there is no statistically significant difference between the mean performance of the two countries.

Note: Countries are presented in descending order of mean performance on the PISA mathematical literacy scale. Due to low response rates, the Netherlands is excluded from the figure. Assuming negligible to moderate levels of bias due to non-response, the position of the Netherlands may be expected, with 95 per cent confidence, to lie between 1st and 4th place among countries.

- ▲ Mean performance statistically significantly higher than in comparison country.
- ○ No statistically significant difference from comparison country.
- ▽ Mean performance statistically significantly lower than in comparison country.

Statistically significantly above the OECD average
Not statistically significantly different from the OECD average
Statistically significantly below the OECD average

Source: OECD PISA database, 2001. See Annex 3 for notes on methodology *(www.oecd.org / els / education / eag2002)* and *www.pisa.oecd.org.*

Policy context

The need to provide the foundations for the professional training of a small number of mathematicians, scientists and engineers dominated the content of school mathematics and science curricula for much of the past century. With the growing role of science, mathematics and technology in modern life, however, the objectives of personal fulfilment, employment, and full participation in society increasingly require all adults to be mathematically, scientifically and technologically literate.

Mathematics and science today need to be used by the many, not just the few...

Deficiencies in mathematical and scientific literacy can have grave consequences not only on the labour market and earnings prospects of individuals but also on the competitiveness of nations. Conversely, the performance of a country's best students in mathematics and science-related subjects can have implications for the part that country will play in tomorrow's advanced technology sector. Aside from workplace requirements, mathematical and scientific literacy also are important for understanding the environmental, medical, economic and other issues that confront modern societies and that rely heavily on technological and scientific advances.

...if people are to understand and participate in the modern world.

Consequently, policy-makers and educators alike attach great importance to mathematics and science education. Addressing the increasing demand for mathematical and scientific skills requires excellence throughout educational systems, and it is important to monitor how well nations provide young adults with fundamental skills in these areas. The Programme for International Student Assessment (PISA) provides information about how well 15-year-olds perform in these areas with a focus on assessing the knowledge and skills that prepare students for life and lifelong learning (Box A6.1).

This indicator shows the performance of 15-year-olds in mathematical and scientific literacy.

Evidence and explanations

Charts A6.1 and A6.2 order countries by the mean performance of their students on the mathematical and scientific literacy scales. The charts also show which countries perform above, below, or about the same as the OECD average and how their students perform in comparison to students in every other country.

Box A6.1. What are mathematical and scientific literacy in PISA?

What is mathematical literacy? Mathematical literacy in PISA concerns students' ability to recognise and interpret mathematical problems encountered in their world, to translate these problems into a mathematical context, to use mathematical knowledge and procedures to solve the problems within their mathematical context, to interpret the results in terms of the original problem, to reflect upon the methods applied, and to formulate and communicate the outcomes.

What do different points along the mathematical literacy scale mean? The scale can be described in terms of the knowledge and skills students need to demonstrate at various points along the mathematical literacy scale.

- Towards the top end of the mathematical literacy scale, around 750 score points, students typically take a creative and active role in their approach to mathematical problems.

- Around 570 score points on the scale, students are typically able to interpret, link and integrate different representations of a problem or different pieces of information; and/or use and manipulate a given model, often involving algebra or other symbolic representations; and/or verify or check given propositions or models.

- At the lower end of the scale, around 380 score points, students are usually able to complete only a single processing step consisting of reproducing basic mathematical facts or processes or applying simple computational skills.

What is scientific literacy? Scientific literacy reflects students' ability to use scientific knowledge, to recognise scientific questions and to identify what is involved in scientific investigations, to relate scientific data to claims and conclusions, and to communicate these aspects of science.

What do different points along the scientific literacy scale mean? The scale can be described in terms of increasingly difficult tasks required for students:

- Towards the top end of the scientific literacy scale, around 690 score points, students generally are able to create or use simple conceptual models to make predictions or give explanations; analyse scientific investigations in relation to, for example, experimental design or the identification of an idea being tested; relate data as evidence to evaluate alternative viewpoints or different perspectives; and communicate scientific arguments and/or descriptions in detail and with precision.

- Around 550 score points, students typically are able to use scientific concepts to make predictions or provide explanations; recognise questions that can be answered by scientific investigation and/ or identify details of what is involved in a scientific investigation; and select relevant information from competing data or chains of reasoning in drawing or evaluating conclusions.

- Towards the lower end of the scale, around 400 score points, reached by at least three-quarters of the students in almost all countries, students are able to recall simple scientific factual knowledge (*e.g.*, names, facts, terminology, simple rules); and use common science knowledge in drawing or evaluating conclusions.

Japan shows the highest mean score in mathematical literacy...

Students in Japan display the highest mean scores in mathematical literacy, although their scores cannot be distinguished statistically from students in three other top-performing countries: Korea, the Netherlands and New Zealand. Other countries that score significantly above the OECD average include Australia, Austria, Belgium, Canada, Denmark, Finland, France, Iceland, Liechtenstein, Sweden, Switzerland and the United Kingdom.

...and Korea in scientific literacy.

On the scientific literacy scale, students in Korea and Japan demonstrate the highest average performance compared to students in other OECD countries. Australia, Austria, Canada, Czech Republic, Finland, Ireland, New Zealand, Sweden and the United Kingdom are among other countries that score significantly above the OECD average.

Chart A6.2

Multiple comparisons of mean performance on the PISA scientific literacy scale (2000)

A6

Columns (across the top), with Mean and S.E.:

Country	Mean	S.E.
Korea	552	(2.7)
Japan	550	(5.5)
Finland	538	(2.5)
United Kingdom	532	(2.7)
Canada	529	(1.6)
New Zealand	528	(2.4)
Australia	528	(3.5)
Austria	519	(2.5)
Ireland	513	(3.2)
Sweden	512	(2.5)
Czech Republic	511	(2.4)
France	500	(3.2)
Norway	500	(2.7)
United States	499	(7.3)
Hungary	496	(4.2)
Iceland	496	(2.2)
Belgium	496	(4.3)
Switzerland	496	(4.4)
Spain	491	(3.0)
Germany	487	(2.4)
Poland	483	(5.1)
Denmark	481	(2.8)
Italy	478	(3.1)
Liechtenstein	476	(7.1)
Greece	461	(4.9)
Russian Fed.	460	(4.7)
Latvia	460	(5.6)
Portugal	459	(4.0)
Luxembourg	443	(2.3)
Mexico	422	(3.2)
Brazil	375	(3.3)

Upper rank* / Lower rank* (by column order: Korea, Japan, Finland, United Kingdom, Canada, New Zealand, Australia, Austria, Ireland, Sweden, Czech Republic, France, Norway, United States, Hungary, Iceland, Belgium, Switzerland, Spain, Germany, Poland, Denmark, Italy, Liechtenstein, Greece, Russian Fed., Latvia, Portugal, Luxembourg, Mexico, Brazil):

	Upper rank*	Lower rank*
Korea	1	2
Japan	1	2
Finland	3	4
United Kingdom	3	7
Canada	4	8
New Zealand	4	8
Australia	4	8
Austria	8	10
Ireland	9	12
Sweden	9	13
Czech Republic	10	13
France	13	18
Norway	13	18
United States	11	20
Hungary	13	21
Iceland	14	21
Belgium	13	20
Switzerland	13	21
Spain	16	22
Germany	19	23
Poland	19	25
Denmark	21	25
Italy	22	25
Liechtenstein	20	26
Greece	25	29
Russian Fed.	26	29
Latvia	25	29
Portugal	26	29
Luxembourg	30	30
Mexico	31	31
Brazil	32	32

Note: Because data are based on samples, it is not possible to report exact rank order positions for countries. However, it is possible to report the range of rank order positions within which the country mean lies with 95 per cent likelihood.

Instructions

Read across the row for a country to compare performance with the countries listed along the top of the chart. The symbols indicate whether the mean performance of the country in the row is significantly lower than that of the comparison country, significantly higher than that of the comparison country, or if there is no statistically significant difference between the mean performance of the two countries.

Note: Countries are presented in descending order of mean performance on the PISA scientific literacy scale. Due to low response rates, the Netherlands is excluded from the figure. Assuming negligible to moderate levels of bias due to non-response, the position of the Netherlands may be expected, with 95 per cent confidence, to lie between 3rd and 14th place among countries.

Source: OECD PISA database, 2001. *See Annex 3* for notes on methodology *(www.oecd.org/els/education/eag2002)* and *www.pisa.oecd.org*.

▲ Mean performance statistically significantly higher than in comparison country.

○ No statistically significant difference from comparison country.

▽ Mean performance statistically significantly lower than in comparison country.

Statistically significantly above the OECD average
Not statistically significantly different from the OECD average
Statistically significantly below the OECD average

As can be inferred by reading the lists of above-average performers in the previous paragraphs, in general, countries that perform well in one subject area also perform well in the other subject area (*i.e.*, mean mathematics and science scores are highly correlated). However, there are some exceptions. For example, the scores for mathematical literacy of the Czech Republic and Ireland are not significantly different from the OECD average, but their students perform significantly above the OECD average on the scientific literacy scale. Conversely, students in Belgium, France, Iceland, and Switzerland perform significantly above the OECD average on the mathematical literacy scale, but their score in scientific literacy is not statistically different than the OECD average. Students in Denmark and Liechtenstein, while above the OECD mean in mathematical literacy, are below the OECD mean in scientific literacy.

While there are large differences in mean performance among countries, the variation of performance among students within each country is many times larger.

While there are large differences in mean performance among countries, the variation of performance among students within each country is many times larger. Tables A6.1 and A6.2 show how students perform at the 5th, 25th, 75th and 95th percentiles in each county. The distributions of student performance on the mathematical literacy scale in Belgium, Germany, Greece, Hungary, New Zealand, Poland, Switzerland and the United States show a relatively large gap between the 75th and 25th percentiles – between 135 and 149 score points. Finland, Iceland, Ireland, Japan and Korea show comparatively smaller disparities, with 113 score points or less separating the 75th and 25th percentiles.

In scientific literacy, Belgium, Denmark, France, Germany, Hungary, New Zealand, Switzerland and the United States exhibit relatively large gaps between students at the 75th and 25th percentiles – between 140 and 154 score points each – while Finland, Japan, Korea, and Mexico exhibit relatively small differences between these groups of students – with less than 118 score point differences.

Disparities in performance are not a necessary condition for a country to attain a high level of overall performance.

It is useful to relate the range of achievement with average performance. This comparison shows that wide disparities in student performance are not a necessary condition for a country to attain a high level of overall performance. On the contrary, it is striking to see that five of the countries with the smallest differences between the 75th and 25th percentiles on the mathematical literacy scale, namely Canada, Finland, Iceland, Japan and Korea, all perform significantly above the OECD average (Table A6.1). Furthermore, four of them, Canada, Finland, Japan and Korea are among the six best-performing countries in mathematical literacy. A similar pattern is observed for scientific literacy. Again, Canada, Finland, Japan and Korea are among the six countries with the smallest differences between 75th and 25th percentiles, as well as among the six best performing countries.

Conversely, the countries with the largest internal disparities tend to perform below the OECD mean. In mathematical literacy, for example, among the six countries (Belgium, Germany, Greece, Hungary, Poland and the United States) with the largest differences between the students at the 75th and 25th percentiles, only two (Belgium and the United States) do not perform significantly below the OECD average.

Definitions and methodologies

The target population studied for this indicator was 15-year-old students. Operationally, this refers to students aged between 15 years and 3 (completed) months and 16 years and 2 (completed) months at the beginning of the testing period and enrolled in an educational institution, irrespective of the grade level or type of institutions in which they were enrolled and of whether they participated in school full-time or part-time.

To facilitate the interpretation of the scores assigned to students in PISA, the mean score for mathematical and scientific literacy performance across OECD countries was set at 500 and the standard deviation at 100, with the data weighted so that each OECD country contributed equally.

For notes on standard errors, significance tests, and multiple comparisons see Annex 3 at *www.oecd.org/els/education/eag2002*.

The achievement scores are based on assessments administered as part of the Programme for International Student Assessment (PISA) undertaken by the OECD during 2000.

A6

Table A6.1.
Variation in performance in mathematical literacy of 15-year-olds (2000)
Performance of 15-year-olds on the PISA mathematical literacy scale, by percentile

| | Mean | | Percentiles | | | | | | | | | | | |
| | | | 5th | | 10th | | 25th | | 75th | | 90th | | 95th | |
	Mean score	S.E.	Score	S.E.	Score	S.E.	Score	S.E.	Score	S.E.	Score	S.E.	Score	S.E.
Australia	533	(3.5)	380	(6.4)	418	(6.4)	474	(4.4)	594	(4.5)	647	(5.7)	679	(5.8)
Austria	515	(2.5)	355	(5.3)	392	(4.6)	455	(3.5)	581	(3.8)	631	(3.6)	661	(5.2)
Belgium	520	(3.9)	322	(11.0)	367	(8.6)	453	(6.5)	597	(3.0)	646	(3.9)	672	(3.5)
Canada	533	(1.4)	390	(3.2)	423	(2.5)	477	(2.0)	592	(1.7)	640	(1.9)	668	(2.6)
Czech Republic	498	(2.8)	335	(5.4)	372	(4.2)	433	(4.1)	564	(3.9)	623	(4.8)	655	(5.6)
Denmark	514	(2.4)	366	(6.1)	401	(5.1)	458	(3.1)	575	(3.1)	621	(3.7)	649	(4.6)
Finland	536	(2.2)	400	(6.5)	433	(3.6)	484	(4.1)	592	(2.5)	637	(3.2)	661	(3.5)
France	517	(2.7)	364	(6.4)	399	(5.4)	457	(4.7)	581	(3.1)	629	(3.2)	656	(4.6)
Germany	490	(2.5)	311	(7.9)	349	(6.9)	423	(3.9)	563	(2.7)	619	(3.6)	649	(3.9)
Greece	447	(5.6)	260	(9.0)	303	(8.1)	375	(8.1)	524	(6.7)	586	(7.8)	617	(8.6)
Hungary	488	(4.0)	327	(7.1)	360	(5.7)	419	(4.8)	558	(5.2)	615	(6.4)	648	(6.9)
Iceland	514	(2.3)	372	(5.7)	407	(4.7)	459	(3.5)	572	(3.0)	622	(3.1)	649	(5.5)
Ireland	503	(2.7)	357	(6.4)	394	(4.7)	449	(4.1)	561	(3.6)	606	(4.3)	630	(5.0)
Italy	457	(2.9)	301	(8.4)	338	(5.5)	398	(3.5)	520	(3.5)	570	(4.4)	600	(6.1)
Japan	557	(5.5)	402	(11.2)	440	(9.1)	504	(7.4)	617	(5.2)	662	(4.9)	688	(6.1)
Korea	547	(2.8)	400	(6.1)	438	(5.0)	493	(4.2)	606	(3.4)	650	(4.3)	676	(5.3)
Luxembourg	446	(2.0)	281	(7.4)	328	(4.2)	390	(3.8)	509	(3.4)	559	(3.2)	588	(3.9)
Mexico	387	(3.4)	254	(5.5)	281	(3.6)	329	(4.1)	445	(5.2)	496	(5.6)	527	(6.6)
New Zealand	537	(3.1)	364	(6.1)	405	(5.4)	472	(3.9)	607	(4.0)	659	(4.2)	689	(5.2)
Norway	499	(2.8)	340	(7.0)	379	(5.2)	439	(4.0)	565	(3.9)	613	(4.5)	643	(4.5)
Poland	470	(5.5)	296	(12.2)	335	(9.2)	402	(7.0)	542	(6.8)	599	(7.7)	632	(8.5)
Portugal	454	(4.1)	297	(7.3)	332	(6.1)	392	(5.7)	520	(4.3)	570	(4.3)	596	(5.0)
Spain	476	(3.1)	323	(5.8)	358	(4.3)	416	(5.3)	540	(4.0)	592	(3.9)	621	(3.1)
Sweden	510	(2.5)	347	(5.8)	386	(4.0)	450	(3.3)	574	(2.6)	626	(3.3)	656	(5.5)
Switzerland	529	(4.4)	353	(9.1)	398	(6.0)	466	(4.8)	601	(5.2)	653	(5.8)	682	(4.8)
United Kingdom	529	(2.5)	374	(5.9)	412	(3.6)	470	(3.2)	592	(3.2)	646	(4.3)	676	(5.9)
United States	493	(7.6)	327	(11.7)	361	(9.6)	427	(9.7)	562	(7.5)	620	(7.7)	652	(7.9)
OECD total	*498*	*(2.1)*	*318*	*(3.1)*	*358*	*(3.4)*	*429*	*(3.0)*	*572*	*(2.1)*	*628*	*(1.9)*	*658*	*(2.1)*
Country mean	*500*	*(0.7)*	*326*	*(1.5)*	*367*	*(1.4)*	*435*	*(1.1)*	*571*	*(0.8)*	*625*	*(0.9)*	*655*	*(1.1)*
Brazil	334	(3.7)	179	(5.5)	212	(5.2)	266	(4.2)	399	(5.5)	464	(7.5)	499	(8.9)
Latvia	463	(4.5)	288	(9.0)	328	(8.9)	393	(5.7)	536	(6.2)	593	(5.6)	625	(6.6)
Liechtenstein	514	(7.0)	343	(19.7)	380	(18.9)	454	(15.5)	579	(7.5)	635	(16.9)	665	(15.0)
Russian Federation	478	(5.5)	305	(9.0)	343	(7.4)	407	(6.6)	552	(6.6)	613	(6.8)	648	(7.8)

OECD COUNTRIES

NON-OECD COUNTRIES

Source: OECD PISA database, 2001. See Annex 3 for notes on methodology (*www.oecd.org/els/education/eag2002*) and *www.pisa.oecd.org*.

Table A6.2.
Variation in performance in scientific literacy of 15-year-olds (2000)
Performance of 15-year-olds on the PISA scientific literacy scale, by percentile

		Mean		Percentiles											
				5th		10th		25th		75th		90th		95th	
		Mean score	S.E.	Score	S.E.	Score	S.E.	Score	S.E.	Score	S.E.	Score	S.E.	Score	S.E.
OECD COUNTRIES	Australia	528	(3.5)	368	(5.1)	402	(4.7)	463	(4.6)	596	(4.8)	646	(5.1)	675	(4.8)
	Austria	519	(2.6)	363	(5.7)	398	(4.0)	456	(3.8)	584	(3.5)	633	(4.1)	659	(4.3)
	Belgium	496	(4.3)	292	(13.5)	346	(10.2)	424	(6.6)	577	(3.5)	630	(2.6)	656	(3.0)
	Canada	529	(1.6)	380	(3.7)	412	(3.4)	469	(2.2)	592	(1.8)	641	(2.2)	670	(3.0)
	Czech Republic	511	(2.4)	355	(5.6)	389	(4.0)	449	(3.6)	577	(3.8)	632	(4.1)	663	(4.9)
	Denmark	481	(2.8)	310	(6.0)	347	(5.3)	410	(4.8)	554	(3.5)	613	(4.4)	645	(4.7)
	Finland	538	(2.5)	391	(5.2)	425	(4.2)	481	(3.5)	598	(3.0)	645	(4.3)	674	(4.3)
	France	500	(3.2)	329	(6.1)	363	(5.4)	429	(5.3)	575	(4.0)	631	(4.2)	663	(4.9)
	Germany	487	(2.4)	314	(9.5)	350	(6.0)	417	(4.9)	560	(3.3)	618	(3.5)	649	(4.7)
	Greece	461	(4.9)	300	(9.3)	334	(8.3)	393	(7.0)	530	(5.3)	585	(5.3)	616	(5.8)
	Hungary	496	(4.2)	328	(7.5)	361	(4.9)	423	(5.5)	570	(4.8)	629	(5.1)	659	(8.5)
	Iceland	496	(2.2)	351	(7.0)	381	(4.3)	436	(3.7)	558	(3.1)	607	(4.1)	635	(4.8)
	Ireland	513	(3.2)	361	(6.5)	394	(5.7)	450	(4.4)	578	(3.4)	630	(4.6)	661	(5.4)
	Italy	478	(3.1)	315	(7.1)	349	(6.2)	411	(4.4)	547	(3.5)	602	(4.0)	633	(4.4)
	Japan	550	(5.5)	391	(11.3)	430	(9.9)	495	(7.2)	612	(5.0)	659	(4.7)	688	(5.7)
	Korea	552	(2.7)	411	(5.3)	442	(5.3)	499	(4.0)	610	(3.4)	652	(3.9)	674	(5.7)
	Luxembourg	443	(2.3)	278	(7.2)	320	(6.8)	382	(3.4)	510	(2.8)	563	(4.4)	593	(4.0)
	Mexico	422	(3.2)	303	(4.8)	325	(4.6)	368	(3.1)	472	(4.7)	525	(5.5)	554	(7.0)
	New Zealand	528	(2.4)	357	(5.6)	392	(5.2)	459	(3.8)	600	(3.4)	653	(5.0)	683	(5.1)
	Norway	500	(2.8)	338	(7.3)	377	(6.6)	437	(4.0)	569	(3.5)	619	(3.9)	649	(6.2)
	Poland	483	(5.1)	326	(9.2)	359	(5.8)	415	(5.5)	553	(7.3)	610	(7.6)	639	(7.5)
	Portugal	459	(4.0)	317	(5.0)	343	(5.1)	397	(5.2)	521	(4.7)	575	(5.0)	604	(5.3)
	Spain	491	(3.0)	333	(5.1)	367	(4.3)	425	(4.4)	558	(3.5)	613	(3.9)	643	(5.5)
	Sweden	512	(2.5)	357	(5.7)	390	(4.6)	446	(4.1)	578	(3.0)	630	(3.4)	660	(4.5)
	Switzerland	496	(4.4)	332	(5.8)	366	(5.4)	427	(5.1)	567	(6.4)	626	(6.4)	656	(9.0)
	United Kingdom	532	(2.7)	366	(6.8)	401	(6.0)	466	(3.8)	602	(3.9)	656	(4.7)	687	(5.0)
	United States	499	(7.3)	330	(11.7)	368	(10.0)	430	(9.6)	571	(8.0)	628	(7.0)	658	(8.4)
	OECD total	*502*	*(2.0)*	*332*	*(3.3)*	*368*	*(3.1)*	*431*	*(2.8)*	*576*	*(2.1)*	*631*	*(1.9)*	*662*	*(2.3)*
	Country mean	*500*	*(0.7)*	*332*	*(1.5)*	*368*	*(1.0)*	*431*	*(1.0)*	*572*	*(0.8)*	*627*	*(0.8)*	*657*	*(1.2)*
NON-OECD COUNTRIES	Brazil	375	(3.3)	230	(5.5)	262	(5.9)	315	(3.7)	432	(4.9)	492	(7.8)	531	(8.2)
	Latvia	460	(5.6)	299	(10.1)	334	(8.8)	393	(7.7)	528	(5.7)	585	(7.2)	620	(8.0)
	Liechtenstein	476	(7.1)	314	(23.5)	357	(20.0)	409	(12.3)	543	(12.7)	595	(12.4)	629	(24.0)
	Russian Federation	460	(4.7)	298	(6.5)	333	(5.4)	392	(6.2)	529	(5.8)	591	(5.9)	625	(5.7)

Source: OECD PISA database, 2001. See Annex 3 for notes on methodology (*www.oecd.org/els/education/eag2002*) and *www.pisa.oecd.org*.

HOW STUDENT PERFORMANCE VARIES BETWEEN SCHOOLS

- On average, differences in the performance of 15-year-olds between schools account for 36 per cent of the OECD average variation in student performance, but this proportion varies from 10 per cent in Finland and Sweden to more than 50 per cent in Austria, Belgium, the Czech Republic, Germany, Greece, Hungary, Italy and Poland.

- Some of the variation between schools is attributable to geography, institutional factors or the selection of students by ability. The differences are often compounded by family background, particularly in countries with differentiated school systems, since students' results are associated not only with their own individual backgrounds but – to a greater extent – with the backgrounds of others at their school.

- High overall variation can result from high within-school differences, high between-school differences or a combination of the two.

- In school systems with differentiated school types, the clustering of students with particular socio-economic characteristics in certain schools is greater than in systems where the curriculum does not vary significantly between schools. In Austria, Belgium, the Czech Republic, Germany, Italy and the Netherlands, for example, the between-school variation associated with the fact that students attend different types of school is considerably compounded by differences in social and family background.

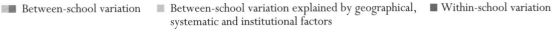

Chart A7.1.

Variation in student performance between schools and within schools
on the PISA reading literacy scale (2000)

Expressed as a percentage of the average variation in student performance in OECD countries

A7

■ Between-school variation   ■ Between-school variation explained by geographical,   ■ Within-school variation
systematic and institutional factors

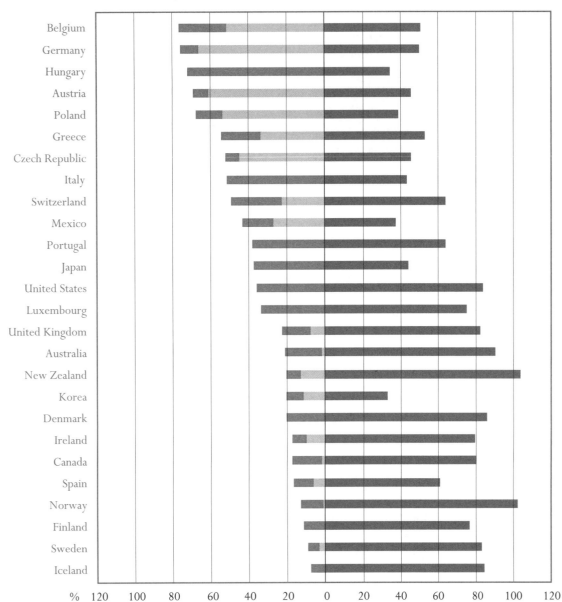

Countries are ranked in descending order of the total between-school variation in student performance on the PISA reading literacy scale.
Source: OECD PISA database, 2001. Table A7.1. See Annex 3 for notes on methodology *(www.oecd.org/els/education/eag2002)* and *www.pisa.oecd.org.*

A7

Many factors account for the performance differences observed by PISA...

Policy context

Indicators A5 and A6 have shown that, in most countries, there are considerable differences in performance within each education system. This variation may result from the background of students and schools, from the human and financial resources available to schools, from curricular differences, from selection policies and practices and from the way in which teaching is organised and delivered.

...and the organisation of the education system can play a significant part in this equation.

Some countries have non-selective school systems that seek to provide all students with the same opportunities for learning and that allow each school to cater to the full range of student performance. Other countries respond to diversity explicitly by forming groups of students of similar performance levels through selection either within or between schools, with the aim of serving students according to their specific needs. And in yet other countries, combinations of the two approaches occur. Even in comprehensive school systems, there may be significant variation between schools due to the socio-economic and cultural characteristics of the communities that the schools serve or due to geographical differences (such as differences between regions, provinces or states in federal systems, or differences between rural and urban areas). Finally, there may be significant variation between individual schools that cannot be easily quantified or otherwise described, part of which could result from differences in the quality or effectiveness of the teaching that those schools provide.

To shed light on this, this indicator examines performance differences between schools.

To examine the impact of such policies and practices, this indicator examines differences between schools in reading literacy performance. The results for mathematical and scientific literacy are broadly similar and therefore not shown in this indicator.

Evidence and explanations

Chart A7.1 compares the extent of variation in student performance within countries...

Chart A7.1 and Table A7.1 show the extent of variation attributable to different factors in each country. The length of the bars indicates the total observed variation in student performance on the reading literacy scale. Note that the values are expressed as percentages of the average variation between OECD countries in student performance on the reading literacy scale. If the sum of the two bars for each country is larger than 100, this indicates that variation in student performance is greater in the corresponding country than in a typical OECD country. Similarly, a combined value smaller than 100 indicates below-average variation in student performance.

...and breaks it down into between-school and within-school differences.

The bar for each country is aligned so that variation between schools is represented by the length to the left of the vertical line down the centre of the chart, and variation within schools is represented by the length to the right of that vertical line. Longer segments to the left of the vertical line indicate greater variation in the mean performance of schools. Longer segments to the right of the vertical line indicate greater variation among students within schools.

As shown in Chart A7.1, in most countries a considerable portion of the variation in student performance lies between schools. On average, across the 26 OECD countries included in this comparison, differences between schools account for 36 per cent of the OECD average between-student variation. In Austria, Belgium, the Czech Republic, Germany, Greece, Hungary, Italy and Poland, more than 50 per cent of the OECD average between-student variation is between schools (see Column 3 in Table A7.1). Where there is substantial variation between schools and less variation between students within schools, students will generally be in schools in which other students perform at levels similar to their own. This selectivity may reflect family choice of school or residential location, or policies on school enrolment, allocation of students or the curriculum.

On average, differences between schools account for 36 per cent of the OECD average between-student variation, but this proportion varies widely across countries

In Korea, overall variation in student performance on the reading literacy scale is about half the OECD average variation, and Korea's variation between schools is only about 20 per cent of the OECD average variation between schools. Korea thus not only achieves high average performance in reading and low overall disparity between students, but does so with relatively little variation in mean performance between schools. Spain also shows low overall variation (around three-quarters of the OECD average) and low between-school variation (16 per cent of the OECD average variation in student performance) but, unlike Korea, has a mean score significantly below the OECD average.

Some countries have low variation between schools and within schools…

The smallest variation in reading performance among schools occurs in Finland, Iceland and Sweden, where the differences account for only between 7 and 11 per cent of the average between-student variation in OECD countries. In these countries performance is largely unrelated to the schools in which students are enrolled. They are thus likely to encounter a similar learning environment in terms of the ability distribution of students. It is noteworthy that overall variation in student performance in these countries is below the OECD average. These education systems succeed both in minimising differences between schools and in containing the overall variation in student performance in reading literacy.

…particularly those with the lowest overall variation.

Australia, New Zealand and Norway (with 112, 126 and 116 per cent of the OECD average between-student variation, respectively) are among the countries with the highest overall variation in reading performance, but only a comparatively small proportion (21, 20 and 13 per cent of the OECD average of student performance) results from differences between schools. In these countries, most variation occurs within schools, suggesting that individual schools need to cater to a more diverse client base.

High overall variation can result from high within-school differences,…

Belgium, Germany and Switzerland (124, 133 and 112 per cent of the average between-student variation in OECD countries) are also countries with comparatively high overall variation in student performance, but a large proportion (76, 75 and 49 per cent of the OECD average variation in student performance) results from differences in performance between schools.

…high between-school differences…

...or a combination of the two.

The United States, another country with comparatively large overall variation in student performance (118 per cent of the average variation between students in OECD countries), is somewhere in the middle, with 35 per cent of the average OECD variation in student performance between schools.

Box A7.1. Factors associated with between-school variation in student performance

Many factors contribute to the variation in average student performance between schools. Some of these are as follows:

- **Sub-national differences:** In several countries school systems operate under sub-national jurisdictions (such as the communities in Belgium, the provinces and territories in Canada, the *Länder* in Germany or the states in Australia and the United States) or vary between a combination of cantons and linguistic communities (as in Switzerland).

- **Rural and urban areas:** Schooling and curricula often differ between urban and rural settings.

- **Publicly and privately managed schools:** In many countries, publicly and privately managed schools compete. In some countries, private schools usually have more selective enrolment policies. In addition, schools that are privately financed may hinder the participation of students from disadvantaged socio-economic backgrounds.

- **Programme type:** Some systems distinguish between types of school, which can differ substantially in the curriculum offered (*e.g.*, preparing students either for university education or for direct entry into the labour market). Even in systems in which differentiation occurs within schools, there may be distinct vocational and general tracks.

- **Level of education:** In a few countries, some 15-years-old students attend upper secondary schools while others attend lower secondary, depending either on their month of birth or on the promotion practices used, or as in the case of Switzerland, because of variation across cantons. In other countries, the same school may host more than one level of education. This means that the variation in student performance attributable to the difference in curriculum between lower and upper secondary education is included in the between-school variation in the former case, and in the within-school between-student variation in the latter.

- **Socio-economic intake:** The socio-economic characteristics of the communities served by schools often vary, although the size of this variation differs greatly between countries. The variation in school intake can affect the performance of the students enrolled.

Some of the variation between schools is attributable to geography, institutional factors or selection of students by ability...

Where does this variation in student performance on the reading literacy scale originate? The answer will vary between countries (see also Box A7.1). Many participating countries provided an indication of those geographical, systemic or institutional aspects of their education systems captured by PISA that they considered most likely to account for differences in performance between schools. The variation in student performance accounted for by these variables is indicated in Chart A7.1 in lighter shading on the left-hand side of the bar.

A7

- In Australia, discounting differences between states and territories reduces the between-school variation in student performance from 21 to 19 per cent of the OECD average between-student variation.

- In Austria, discounting the differences between the various tracks to which students are allocated across six school types reduces the between-school variation from 68 to 8 per cent. In Belgium, discounting differences between the linguistic communities and between school type reduces the between-school variation from 76 to 25 per cent. Discounting differences between school and programme types reduces the between-school variation in Germany from 75 to 10 per cent, in Hungary from 71 to 19, in Poland from 67 to 14 and in Korea from 20 to 9 per cent over the OECD average between-student variation.

- Discounting differences between general and vocational schools, and between upper secondary and lower secondary programmes, reduces the between-school variation from 52 to 7 per cent in the Czech Republic, and in Greece from 54 to 21 per cent.

- In Ireland, discounting differences between school types, between regular schools and schools designated as educationally disadvantaged, and between rural and urban areas, reduces between-school variation from 17 to 7 per cent.

- Discounting level of education and programme type reduces the between-school variation in Italy (*Licei* versus vocational and technical schools) from 51 to 23 per cent, and in Mexico from 43 to 16 per cent.

- In Canada, discounting differences between provinces reduces between-school variation in student performance from 17 to 16 per cent.

- In Iceland, discounting school size and level of urbanisation reduces between-school variation from 7 to 6 per cent.

- In New Zealand, discounting school intake (including average socio-economic status and the proportion of Maori and Pacific students) reduces variation between schools from 20 to 7 per cent.

- Discounting immigrant students reduces variation between schools in Norway from 13 to 12 per cent and in Sweden from 9 to 6 per cent.

- In Spain, discounting differences between publicly and privately managed schools reduces between-school variation from 16 to 10 per cent.

- In Switzerland, discounting differences between programme types and levels of education, and between the linguistic communities in which schools are located, reduces the between-school variation from 49 to 27 per cent.

A7

- In the United Kingdom, discounting differences between schools managed by local authorities versus other bodies such as self-governing trusts and church foundations, between co-educational and single-gender schools, and between regions, reduces the between-school variation from 22 to 15 per cent.

...which can be compounded by the bunching of socially privileged students, particularly in countries with different types of secondary schools...

Broadly, the data also suggest that, in school systems with differentiated school types, the clustering of students with particular socio-economic characteristics in certain schools is greater than in systems where the curriculum does not vary significantly between schools. In Austria, Belgium, the Czech Republic, Germany, Italy and the Netherlands, for example, the between-school variation associated with the fact that students attend different types of school is considerably compounded by differences in social and family background. This may be a consequence of selection or self-selection: when the school market provides some differentiation, students from lower social backgrounds may tend to be directed to, or choose for themselves, less demanding study programmes, or may opt not to participate in the selection procedures of the education system.

...since students' results are associated not only with their own individual backgrounds but – to a greater extent – with the backgrounds of others at their school.

The fuller analysis in the report *Knowledge and Skills for Life* (OECD, 2001) suggests that the overall social background of a school's intake on student performance tends to be greater than the impact of the individual student's social background. Students from a lower socio-economic background attending schools in which the average socio-economic background is high tend to perform much better than when they are enrolled in a school with a below-average socio-economic intake – and the reverse is true for more advantaged students in less advantaged schools. This suggests that institutional differentiation in education systems, often compounded by the social background of a school's intake, self-selection by students and/or their parents as well as judgements on prior achievement, can have a major impact on an individual student's success at school.

Definitions and methodologies

The achievement scores are based on assessments administered as part of the Programme for International Student Assessment (PISA) undertaken by the OECD during 2000.

The target population studied for this indicator was 15-year-old students. Operationally, this refers to students aged between 15 years and 3 (completed) months and 16 years and 2 (completed) months at the beginning of the testing period and enrolled in an educational institution, irrespective of the grade level or type of institutions in which they were enrolled and of whether they participated in school full-time or part-time.

To facilitate the interpretation of the scores assigned to students in PISA, the mean score for reading literacy performance across OECD countries was set at 500 and the standard deviation at 100, with the data weighted so that each OECD country contributed equally. These reference points anchor PISA's measurement of student proficiency.

Variation in Table A7.1 is expressed by statistical variance. This is obtained by squaring the standard deviation referred to earlier in this chapter. The statistical

A7

variance rather than the standard deviation is used for this comparison to allow for the decomposition of the components of variation in student performance. The average is calculated over the OECD countries included in the table. Owing to the sampling methods used in Japan, the between-school variation in Japan includes variation between classes within schools.

For notes on standard errors, significance tests, and multiple comparisons see Annex 3 at *www.oecd.org/els/education/eag2002*.

Table A7.1.
Sources of variation in performance in reading literacy of 15-year-old students (2000)
Between-school and within-school variation in student performance on the PISA reading literacy scale

	Total variation in SP[1]	Total variation in SP expressed as a percentage of the average variation in student performance across OECD countries	Total variation in SP between schools	Total variation in SP within schools	Variation explained by the international socio-economic index of occupational status of students		Variation explained by the international socio-economic index of occupational status of students and schools		Variation explained by geographical/systemic/institutional factors		Variation explained by geographical/systemic/institutional factors and the international socio-economic index of occupational status of students and schools		Total variation between schools expressed as a percentage of the total variation within the country[2]
					Between-school variation explained	Within-school variation explained	Between-school variation explained	Within-school variation explained	Between-school variation explained	Within-school variation explained	Between-school variation explained	Within-school variation explained	
OECD COUNTRIES													
Australia	10 357	111.6	20.9	90.6	8.3	6.7	14.2	6.9	1.8	0.1	15.0	7.0	18.8
Austria	8 649	93.2	68.6	45.7	10.4	0.4	42.6	0.3	60.4	0.0	61.6	0.5	60.0
Belgium	11 455	123.5	76.0	50.9	11.0	1.8	44.2	1.9	50.7	0.0	61.9	1.9	59.9
Canada	8 955	96.5	17.1	80.1	4.6	5.0	7.8	5.1	1.1	0.0	8.4	5.1	17.6
Czech Republic	9 278	100.0	51.9	45.3	8.8	1.8	34.4	1.8	44.5	0.0	46.8	1.8	53.4
Denmark	9 614	103.6	19.6	85.9	10.2	8.0	11.6	8.1	m	m	m	m	18.6
Finland	7 994	86.2	10.7	76.5	1.5	4.6	1.7	4.6	m	m	m	m	12.3
France	m	m	m	m	m	m	m	m	m	m	m	m	m
Germany	12 368	133.3	74.8	50.2	11.7	2.3	51.5	2.3	65.2	0.0	66.9	2.3	59.8
Greece	9 436	101.7	53.8	52.9	7.0	1.1	25.0	1.1	33.3	0.0	40.1	0.4	50.4
Hungary	8 810	95.0	71.2	34.8	8.3	0.3	49.4	0.2	52.5	0.0	58.7	0.1	67.2
Iceland	8 529	91.9	7.0	85.0	1.6	5.0	1.7	5.0	0.9	0.0	2.3	5.0	7.6
Ireland	8 755	94.4	17.1	79.2	5.5	5.7	10.1	5.7	9.7	0.0	12.7	5.5	17.8
Italy	8 356	90.1	50.9	43.4	3.4	0.5	23.8	0.5	27.6	0.0	30.1	0.5	54.0
Japan[3]	7 358	79.3	36.5	43.9	m	m	m	m	m	m	m	m	45.4
Korea	4 833	52.1	19.7	33.0	1.0	0.2	7.1	0.2	10.9	0.0	12.0	0.2	37.4
Luxembourg	10 088	108.7	33.4	74.9	11.1	8.3	26.7	8.2	m	m	m	m	30.8
Mexico	7 370	79.4	42.9	37.4	5.2	0.1	25.7	0.1	26.5	0.0	35.3	0.1	53.4
New Zealand	11 701	126.1	20.1	103.9	7.3	10.9	11.6	11.0	12.9	0.0	14.8	11.0	16.2
Norway	10 743	115.8	12.6	102.4	3.7	8.7	4.9	8.7	0.5	3.8	5.2	10.1	10.9
Poland	9 958	107.3	67.0	38.9	6.3	1.1	42.4	1.1	53.0	0.0	55.9	1.1	63.2
Portugal	9 436	101.7	37.5	64.3	10.6	4.6	23.8	4.6	m	m	m	m	36.8
Spain	7 181	77.4	15.9	60.9	5.4	3.0	9.1	3.1	6.2	0.0	10.9	3.1	20.7
Sweden	8 495	91.6	8.9	83.0	4.5	6.9	5.8	6.9	2.7	2.6	6.9	8.1	9.7
Switzerland	10 408	112.2	48.7	63.7	12.7	4.0	24.3	3.9	22.1	0.0	29.7	4.1	43.4
United Kingdom	10 098	108.9	22.4	82.3	9.6	8.4	16.0	8.7	7.3	0.0	17.1	6.7	21.4
United States	10 979	118.3	35.1	83.6	12.0	5.6	25.5	5.8	m	m	m	m	29.6
NON-OECD COUNTRIES													
Brazil	7 427	80.1	35.8	47.1	6.5	1.9	19.7	2.1	5.3	0.0	21.7	2.1	43.1
Latvia	10 435	112.5	35.1	77.5	4.9	4.4	16.7	4.5	m	m	m	m	31.2
Liechtenstein	m	m	m	m	m	m	m	m	m	m	m	m	43.9
Russian Federation	8 466	91.3	33.6	57.1	4.8	2.4	15.4	2.3	16.6	0.0	21.0	2.3	37.1

1. The total variation in student performance is obtained as the square of the standard deviation shown in Table A5.2. The statistical variance and not the standard deviation is used for this comparison to allow for the decomposition of the components of variation in student performance. For reasons explained in the *PISA 2000 Technical Report*, the sum of the between and within-school variance components may, for some countries, differ slightly from the square of the standard deviation shown in Table A5.2.

2. This index is often referred to as the intra-class correlation (rho).

3. Due to the sampling methods used in Japan, the between-school variance in Japan includes variation between classes within schools.

Source: OECD PISA database, 2001. See Annex 3 for notes on methodology (*www.oecd.org/els/education/eag2002*) and *www.pisa.oecd.org*.

CIVIC KNOWLEDGE AND ENGAGEMENT

A8

- Within the frame of reference of the IEA Civic Education Study, 14-year-olds in most OECD countries typically demonstrate a solid understanding of fundamental democratic values and institutions and skills in interpreting civic-related material such as political cartoons or a mock election leaflet and in distinguishing between statements of opinion and of fact.

- 14-year-olds generally view obeying the law and voting as very important adult responsibilities and also value activities that promote human rights, protect the environment and benefit the community. They value engaging in political discussions or joining a political party less.

Chart A8.1.

Civic knowledge of 14-year-olds (1999)

Mean score and significance of the mean score compared to the international mean on the IEA Civic Education sub-scales of content knowledge and interpretative skills, and the IEA Civic Education total civic score

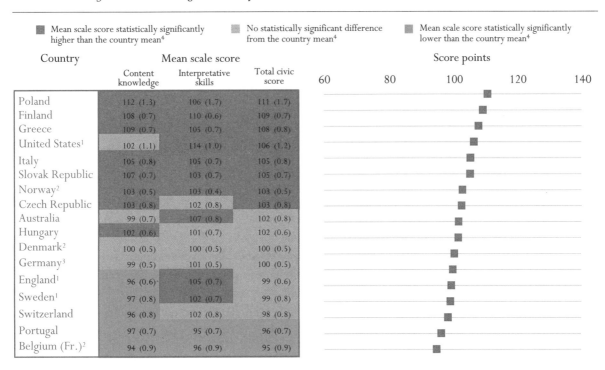

■ Mean scale score statistically significantly higher than the country mean[4]	■ No statistically significant difference from the country mean[4]	■ Mean scale score statistically significantly lower than the country mean[4]					

Country	Content knowledge	Interpretative skills	Total civic score	60	80	100	120	140
Poland	112 (1.3)	106 (1.7)	111 (1.7)					
Finland	108 (0.7)	110 (0.6)	109 (0.7)					
Greece	109 (0.7)	105 (0.7)	108 (0.8)					
United States[1]	102 (1.1)	114 (1.0)	106 (1.2)					
Italy	105 (0.8)	105 (0.7)	105 (0.8)					
Slovak Republic	107 (0.7)	103 (0.7)	105 (0.7)					
Norway[2]	103 (0.5)	103 (0.4)	103 (0.5)					
Czech Republic	103 (0.8)	102 (0.8)	103 (0.8)					
Australia	99 (0.7)	107 (0.8)	102 (0.8)					
Hungary	102 (0.6)	101 (0.7)	102 (0.6)					
Denmark[2]	100 (0.5)	100 (0.5)	100 (0.5)					
Germany[3]	99 (0.5)	101 (0.5)	100 (0.5)					
England[1]	96 (0.6)	105 (0.7)	99 (0.6)					
Sweden[1]	97 (0.8)	102 (0.7)	99 (0.8)					
Switzerland	96 (0.8)	102 (0.8)	98 (0.8)					
Portugal	97 (0.7)	95 (0.7)	96 (0.7)					
Belgium (Fr.)[2]	94 (0.9)	96 (0.9)	95 (0.9)					

1. Date of testing at beginning of school year.
2. Countries' overall participation rate after replacement is less than 85 per cent.
3. Does not cover all of the national population.
4. Country mean includes all countries participating in the IEA Civic Education Study, not just the countries listed in this table.
Countries are ranked in descending order of the mean scale score on the IEA Civic Education total civic knowledge scale.
Source: IEA Civic Education Study (2001).

Policy context

Democratic societies rely not just on a solid foundation of knowledge and skills in subject matter areas such as reading, mathematics and science, but also on the continual preparation of informed citizens who have the knowledge and skills to understand basic forms of political communication. They also rely on individuals who will be engaged in participation as citizens.

This indicator shows 14-year-olds' knowledge of civic-related content, their skills in understanding political communication and their attitudes towards government.

How can schools nurture young people's knowledge of, and engagement in, the civil society and the governmental sphere. To ascertain what students in different countries understand and believe about citizenship, government, and the law, the International Association for the Evaluation of Educational Achievement (IEA) Civic Education Study was designed to identify and examine the ways in which young people are prepared to undertake their role as citizens in democracies, both inside and outside the school. In this study, 14-year-olds in 28 countries, including 17 OECD countries, were tested on their knowledge of civic-related content, their skills in understanding political communication, their concepts and attitudes towards civic issues, and their participation or practice in this area.

Evidence and explanations

Civic knowledge and skills

The IEA Civic Education Study distinguishes between content knowledge and interpretative skills when comparing civic knowledge across countries.

Chart A8.1 shows the mean Civic Knowledge scores of 14-year-olds. The total score is composed of two subscores, entitled "content knowledge" (knowledge of fundamental democratic principles) and "interpretative skills" (skills in interpreting civic-related information, such as political cartoons, election leaflets or newspaper articles). The total scale as well as the two subscales were adjusted to have a mean of 100 and a standard deviation of 20 across all 28 countries participating in the IEA Civic Education study.

The results suggest that the average 14-year-old in most OECD countries has a solid understanding of fundamental democratic values and institutions…

The results suggest that the average student across the participating countries has a solid understanding of fundamental democratic values and institution, within the frame of reference that was established for this by the IEA Civic Education Study. The test results indicate that internationally a majority of students recognise essential functions of laws, private civil society associations and political parties (out of the 38 questions used in the test, 25 were answered correctly by at least 60 per cent of the combined student population across participating countries and 13 questions by more than 70 per cent).

…as well as a substantial level of skills in interpreting civic-related material such as political cartoons or a mock election leaflet and in distinguishing between statements of opinion and of fact.

The average student demonstrated a substantial level of skills in interpreting civic-related material such as political cartoons or a mock election leaflet and in distinguishing between statements of opinion and of fact. Among 14-year-olds, high average skills in interpreting civic and political information are found *primarily* in countries where democracy has been the form of government for more than 40 years. Australia, England, Greece, Finland, Italy, Norway, Poland, the Slovak Republic, Sweden, and the United States all scored above the international mean in the IEA Civic Education Study's sub-scale on Interpretative Skills.

There are no simple explanations for the differences among countries in civic content knowledge and interpretative skills. The high performing countries include not only long standing democracies but also nations that have experienced massive political transitions during the lifetimes of the 14-year-olds that were assessed (*e.g.*, the Czech Republic, Poland and the Slovak Republic). The Czech Republic, Greece, Finland, Hungary, Italy, Norway, Poland and the Slovak Republic all scored above the country mean (which includes all participating countries, not just those that are members of the OECD) in the IEA Civic Education Study's sub-scale on Content Knowledge.

There are wide differences among countries for which there are no simple explanations…

Comparing performance on the two subscales shows some interesting patterns. Students in Australia, England, Sweden, Switzerland and the United States ranked higher in their performance on the items measuring skills in understanding civic-related information than on the items measuring content knowledge of fundamental democratic principles. By contrast, students in the Czech Republic and Hungary ranked higher on the items measuring content knowledge than on the items assessing interpretative skills.

…but some may mirror differences in curricular emphases.

Chart A8.2.

Trust of 14-year-olds in government-related institutions (1999)

Mean score and significance of the mean score compared to the country mean on the IEA Civic Education scale of trust in government-related institutions

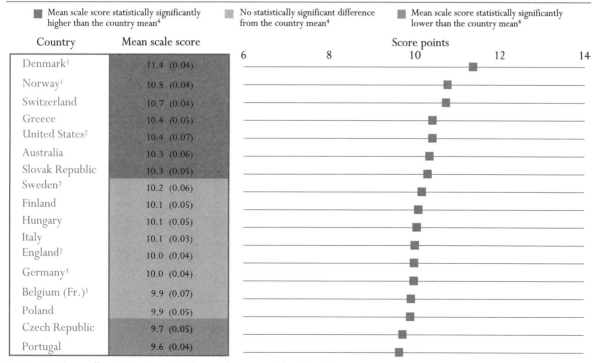

1. Countries' overall participation rate after replacement is less than 85 per cent.
2. Date of testing at beginning of school year.
3. Does not cover all of the national population.
4. Country mean includes all countries participating in the IEA Civic Education Study, not just the countries listed in this table.
Countries are ranked in descending order of the country mean on the IEA Civic Education scale of trust in government-related institutions.
Source: IEA Civic Education Study (2001).

A8

Students were also asked about their trust in government and what they believe is important for adults to be good citizens.

Patterns of trust in government and civic engagement

In the Civic Education Study, students were also asked to what extent certain types of government institutions – national government, local council or government in the town or city in which the student lives, courts, the police, political parties and National Parliament – can be trusted. Chart A8.2 shows the results, with a scale that has a mean of 10 and a standard deviation of 2 across all 28 countries participating in the IEA Civic Education Study. Australia, Denmark, Greece, Norway, the Slovak Republic, Switzerland, and the United States all scored above the international mean, the Czech Republic and Portugal below it. A number of countries with low trust scores were non-OECD countries, which are not included in the chart.

14-year-olds generally view obeying the law and voting as very important adult responsibilities.

Students were also asked questions assessing what they believe is important for adults to do as good citizens. Table A8.1 shows selected responses (for other items see *Citizenship and Education in Twenty-Eight Countries,* IEA 2001). 14-year-olds generally view obeying the law as a very important responsibility of adult citizenship and voting as important.

Chart A8.3.

Likelihood of voting of 14-year-olds (1999)

Percentage of 14-year-olds who say that they are very likely or likely to vote in national elections

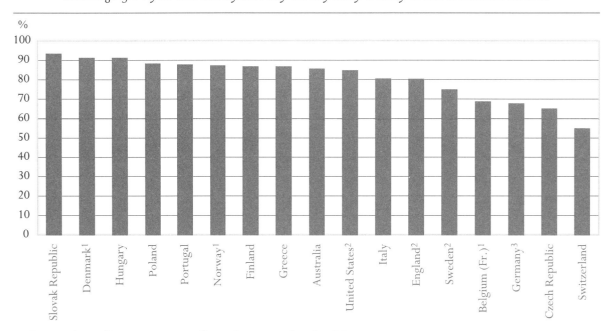

1. Countries' overall participation rate after replacement is less than 85 per cent.
2. Date of testing at beginning of school year.
3. National Desired Population does not cover all International Desired Population.
Countries are ranked in descending order of the percentage of 14-year-old students who say that they are very likely or likely to vote in national elections.
Source: IEA Civic Education Study (2001). Table A8.1.

They also believe that the responsibilities of adult citizens include taking part in activities that promote human rights, protect the environment and benefit the community. In some countries, following political issues in the media is also considered important.

Finally, students were asked to estimate the kinds of political participation they expected to undertake as adults. Only about 20 per cent of the respondents across countries said that they intended to participate in those activities usually associated with conventional adult political involvement, for example joining a political party, writing to newspapers about social and political concerns, or being a candidate for a local or city-wide office. Substantial proportions of 14-year-olds say, however, that they expect that they will vote and think that it is important for adult citizens to vote. In some countries this is considerably higher than the proportion of young adults who actually vote (see Chart A8.3).

They also highly rate activities that promote human rights, protect the environment and benefit the community but far less so engaging in political discussions or joining a political party.

Definitions and methodologies

This indicator was derived from the International Association for the Evaluation of Educational Achievement's (IEA) Civic Education Study, which tested nationally representative samples of 90 000 students from 28 countries in 1999. The target population is defined as the students enrolled in the grade level in which the majority of 14-year-olds are enrolled (8th or 9th grade). In a survey portion of the IEA instrument students were asked to indicate how likely they were to vote and how important they believed it was for good adult citizens to engage in a number of political and civic activities. Those percentages are presented along with standard errors appropriate to the sampling method.

This indicator is based on the IEA Civic Education Study for which data were collected by the IEA in 1999.

For further information see *Citizenship and Education across Countries: Civic Knowledge and Engagement at Age Fourteen* (Torney-Purta, Lehmann, Oswald, and Schulz, published by IEA Amsterdam).

Table A8.1.
Civic attitudes and civic engagement of 14–year–olds (1999)
Percentage of students who say that they are very likely or likely to vote in national elections and percentage of students who believe that it is very important or important that a good citizen participates in selected civic activities

| | Percentage of students who say that they are very likely or likely to vote in national elections | | Percentage of students who believe that it is very important or important that a good citizen … | | | | | | | | | |
| | | | votes in every election | | joins a political party | | engages in political discussions | | participates in activities to benefit people in the community | | takes part in activities to protect the environment | |
	Mean	S.E.	Mean	S.E.	Mean	S.E.	Mean	S.E.	Mean	S.E.	Mean	S.E.
Australia	85	(1.0)	89	(0.8)	17	(1.0)	34	(1.1)	80	(1.0)	74	(1.1)
Belgium (Fr.)[1]	69	(2.0)	82	(1.4)	24	(1.0)	39	(1.4)	54	(2.0)	71	(1.7)
Czech Republic	65	(1.7)	66	(1.1)	18	(1.0)	29	(1.4)	78	(0.9)	84	(1.0)
Denmark[1]	91	(0.7)	60	(1.0)	17	(0.8)	44	(0.9)	86	(0.8)	83	(0.7)
England[3]	80	(1.0)	76	(1.1)	20	(0.9)	42	(1.3)	78	(1.0)	76	(1.1)
Finland	87	(0.7)	59	(1.2)	13	(0.8)	23	(1.1)	60	(1.0)	74	(1.0)
Germany[1]	67	(1.1)	69	(0.9)	18	(0.7)	43	(1.2)	85	(0.9)	72	(1.2)
Greece	86	(0.9)	94	(0.6)	49	(1.0)	59	(1.0)	90	(0.7)	89	(0.7)
Hungary	91	(0.7)	81	(0.9)	29	(0.9)	21	(0.8)	89	(0.6)	77	(1.0)
Italy	80	(1.1)	84	(0.7)	32	(1.0)	49	(1.0)	82	(0.7)	79	(0.8)
Norway[1]	87	(0.7)	71	(0.9)	21	(0.8)	37	(1.0)	83	(0.8)	91	(0.6)
Poland	88	(1.2)	91	(0.8)	35	(1.2)	53	(1.4)	90	(0.8)	77	(0.8)
Portugal	88	(0.8)	71	(0.9)	36	(1.1)	40	(1.0)	94	(0.6)	92	(0.6)
Slovak Republic	93	(0.6)	91	(0.7)	23	(1.3)	51	(1.0)	87	(0.8)	87	(0.8)
Sweden[2]	75	(1.4)	78	(1.0)	21	(0.9)	37	(1.5)	83	(1.2)	81	(1.3)
Switzerland	55	(1.3)	68	(1.2)	23	(1.1)	42	(1.2)	76	(0.9)	70	(1.2)
United States[2]	85	(1.0)	83	(0.9)	48	(1.4)	58	(1.1)	88	(0.8)	83	(0.8)

OECD COUNTRIES

1. Countries' overall participation rate after replacement is less than 85 per cent.
2. National Desired Population does not cover all International Desired Population.
3. Countries with testing date at beginning of school year.
Source: IEA Civic Education Study (2001).

OCCUPATIONAL STATUS OF PARENTS AND STUDENT PERFORMANCE

A9

- 15-year-olds whose parents have higher-status jobs show higher literacy performance on average but the advantage is much greater in some countries than in others, particularly in Belgium, Germany, Luxembourg and Switzerland.

- While socio-economic background remains one of the most powerful factors influencing performance, some countries demonstrate that high average quality and social equity in educational outcomes can go together.

Chart A9.1.

Student performance and equity (2000)

Relationship between average student performance on the PISA reading literacy scale and difference in student performance between the top and bottom quarters of students on the international socio-economic index of occupational status

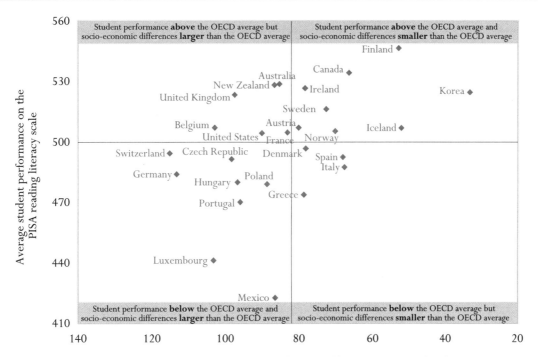

Difference in performance between the top and bottom quarters of students
on the international socio-economic index of occupational status

Source: OECD PISA database, 2001. Table A9.1. See Annex 3 for notes on methodology *(www.oecd.org/els/education/eag2002)* and *www.pisa.oecd.org.*

A9

Policy context

Schools need to cater to children from all backgrounds...

Students come from a variety of family, socio-economic and cultural backgrounds. As a result, schools need to provide appropriate and equitable opportunities for a diverse student body. The learning environment can be enhanced by the variety of students' backgrounds and interests. However, heterogeneous levels of ability and differences in school preparedness increase the challenges that schools face in meeting the needs of students from widely varying socio-economic backgrounds.

...and looking at links between background and performance can help educators to do so more effectively.

Identifying the characteristics of the students most likely to perform poorly can help educators and policy-makers to locate areas for policy intervention. Similarly, identifying the characteristics of students who may flourish academically can assist policy-makers to promote high levels of performance. If it can be shown that some countries find it easier than others to accommodate both groups, this would suggest that it is feasible to foster equity and high performance simultaneously.

To shed light on this, this indicator examines the relationship between 15-year-olds' performance and socio-economic background.

To pursue this question, this indicator examines the relationship between students' performance in reading literacy and one important aspect of their home backgrounds, namely their parents' level of occupational status. The relationship between mathematical and scientific literacy and socio-economic background is similar and therefore not shown in this indicator.

Evidence and explanations

Parental occupation is a measure of socio-economic status and can influence students' aspirations and attitudes.

Higher parental occupational status can influence students' occupational aspirations and expectations and, in turn, their commitment to learning as the means of satisfying those aspirations. High parental occupational status can also increase the range of options of which children are aware. PISA captures this aspect of students' home backgrounds through information on parents' occupations and the activities associated with those occupations in a way that is internationally comparable. The resulting *socio-economic index of occupational status*, which has values ranging from 0 to 90, measures the attributes of occupation that convert a person's education into income. As the required skills increase, so also does the status of the occupation. Therefore, the higher the value on the index, the higher the occupational status of a student's parents. On average across OECD countries, the value of the index is 49 and its standard deviation is 16. Typical occupations among parents of 15-year-olds with between 16 and 35 points on the index include small-scale farming, metalworking, motor mechanics, taxi and lorry-driving, and waiting. Between 35 and 53 index points, the most common occupations are book-keeping, sales, small business management and nursing. Between 54 and 70 index points, typical occupations are marketing management, teaching, civil engineering and accountancy. Finally, between 71 and 90 points, the top international quarter of the index, occupations include medicine, university teaching and law.

As can be seen in Table A9.1, differences in the socio-economic index of occupational status are associated with large differences in reading literacy performance within countries. For those students in the top national quarters of students on the socio-economic index, the mean score of OECD countries on the reading literacy scale is 545 points, or 45 points about the OECD average for all students. By contrast, the average score among the bottom national quarters of students on the socio-economic index is only 463 points. The average gap between the two groups is more than the magnitude of an entire proficiency level in reading.

Students whose parents have higher-status jobs show higher literacy performance on average…

The largest differences, of 100 points or more, are found in Belgium, Germany, Luxembourg and Switzerland. In Germany, the difference is particularly striking. Students whose parents have the highest status jobs (the top quarter on the occupational index) score on average about as well as the average student in Finland, the best-performing country in PISA; those whose parents have the lowest-status jobs score about the same as students in Mexico, the OECD country with the lowest performance.

…but in some countries the advantage is much greater than in others.

The Czech Republic, Hungary, the United Kingdom and the United States also have differences of more than 90 points for students in the top and bottom quarters of the socio-economic index, well above the equivalent of one proficiency level. As in Belgium, Germany and Switzerland, students in these countries who are in the bottom quarter of the occupational index are more than twice as likely as other students also to be among the bottom 25 per cent of their country's performers on the reading literacy scale.

While socio-economic background remains one of the most powerful factors influencing performance…

Although PISA shows that poor performance in school does not automatically follow from a disadvantaged socio-economic background, this still appears to be one of the most powerful factors influencing performance on the PISA reading literacy scale. This represents a significant challenge for public policy, which strives to provide learning opportunities for all students irrespective of their home backgrounds. National research evidence from various countries has generally been discouraging. Schools have appeared to make little difference. Either because privileged families are better able to reinforce and enhance the effect of schools, or because schools are better able to nurture and develop young people from privileged backgrounds, it has often been apparent that schools reproduce existing patterns of privilege rather than delivering equal opportunities in a way that can distribute outcomes more equitably.

The international evidence of PISA is more encouraging. While all countries show a clear positive relationship between home background and educational outcomes, some countries demonstrate that high average quality and equality of educational outcomes can go together. Canada, Finland, Iceland, Korea and Sweden all display above-average levels of student performance on the reading literacy scale and, at the same time, below-average disparities between students from advantaged and disadvantaged socio-economic backgrounds (Chart A9.1).

…some countries demonstrate that high average quality and social equity in educational outcomes can go together.

A9

Conversely, average performance in reading literacy in the Czech Republic, Germany, Hungary, Luxembourg, Poland and Portugal is significantly below the OECD average while, at the same time, there are above-average disparities between students from advantaged and disadvantaged socio-economic backgrounds.

It cannot be assumed, however, that all of these differences are a direct result of the home advantages and higher expectations conferred by parents in higher occupations. Many factors affect students' performance. For example, socio-economic status may be related to where students live and the quality of the schools to which they have access (this would be important in school systems that are dependent on local taxes), to the likelihood that they are enrolled in private schools, to the level of parental support and involvement, etc.

Definitions and methodologies

The achievement scores are based on assessments administered as part of the Programme for International Student Assessment (PISA) undertaken by the OECD during 2000.

The target population studied for this indicator was 15-year-old students. Operationally, this refers to students aged between 15 years and 3 (completed) months and 16 years and 2 (completed) months at the beginning of the testing period and enrolled in an educational institution, regardless of the grade level or type of institutions in which they were enrolled and of whether they participated in school full-time or part-time.

The PISA Socio-Economic Index of Occupational Status was derived from students' responses on parental occupation. The index captures the attributes of occupations that convert parents' education into income. The index was derived by the optimal scaling of occupation groups to maximise the indirect effect of education on income through occupation and to minimise the direct effect of education on income, net of occupation (both effects being net of age). The index is based on either the father's or mother's occupations, whichever is the higher. Values on the index range from 0 to 90; low values represent low socio-economic status and high values represent high socio-economic status. For more information on the methodology, see the *PISA 2000 Technical Report* (OECD, 2002).

For notes on standard errors and significance tests see Annex 3 at *www.oecd.org/els/education/eag2002.*

Table A9.1.
Student performance and socio–economic status (2000)
*International socio-economic index of occupational status (ISEI) and performance on the PISA reading literacy scale,
by national quarters of the index, based on students' self-reports*

A9

| | | International socio-economic index of occupational status | | | | | | | | | | Performance on the PISA reading literacy scale, by national quarters of the international socio-economic index of occupational status[1] | | | | | | | | Change in the PISA reading literacy score per 16.3 units of the international socio-economic index of occupational status[1] | | Increased likelihood of students in the bottom quarter of the ISEI distribution scoring in the bottom quarter of the national reading literacy performance distribution[2] | |
| | | All students | | Bottom quarter | | Second quarter | | Third quarter | | Top quarter | | Bottom quarter | | Second quarter | | Third quarter | | Top quarter | | | | | |
		Mean index	S.E.	Mean index	S.E.	Mean index	S.E.	Mean index	S.E.	Mean index	S.E.	Mean score	S.E.	Mean score	S.E.	Mean score	S.E.	Mean score	S.E.	Change	S.E.	Ratio	S.E.
OECD COUNTRIES	Australia	52.3	(0.5)	31.1	(0.2)	46.3	(0.1)	58.4	(0.2)	73.2	(0.3)	490	(3.8)	523	(4.5)	538	(4.2)	576	(5.4)	31.7	(2.1)	1.9	(0.1)
	Austria	49.7	(0.3)	32.9	(0.2)	44.7	(0.1)	52.2	(0.1)	69.1	(0.3)	467	(3.9)	500	(3.3)	522	(3.4)	547	(3.5)	35.2	(2.1)	2.1	(0.1)
	Belgium	49.0	(0.4)	28.4	(0.1)	42.1	(0.1)	53.5	(0.1)	71.8	(0.2)	457	(6.2)	497	(4.5)	537	(3.2)	560	(3.4)	38.2	(2.2)	2.4	(0.1)
	Canada	52.8	(0.2)	31.3	(0.1)	48.1	(0.1)	58.9	(0.1)	72.9	(0.1)	503	(2.2)	529	(1.9)	545	(1.9)	570	(2.0)	25.7	(1.0)	1.9	(0.1)
	Czech Republic	48.3	(0.3)	31.2	(0.2)	44.4	(0.1)	51.5	(0.0)	66.1	(0.3)	445	(3.1)	487	(2.8)	499	(3.5)	543	(2.9)	43.2	(1.7)	2.3	(0.1)
	Denmark	49.7	(0.4)	29.0	(0.2)	44.0	(0.1)	54.9	(0.2)	71.1	(0.3)	465	(3.3)	490	(3.3)	511	(3.2)	543	(3.6)	29.1	(1.9)	1.8	(0.1)
	Finland	50.0	(0.4)	29.7	(0.2)	43.4	(0.1)	55.1	(0.1)	71.8	(0.2)	524	(4.5)	535	(3.3)	555	(3.1)	576	(3.3)	20.8	(1.8)	1.5	(0.1)
	France	48.3	(0.4)	27.7	(0.2)	41.1	(0.2)	53.1	(0.1)	71.2	(0.2)	469	(4.3)	496	(3.2)	520	(3.1)	552	(3.6)	30.8	(1.9)	2.2	(0.1)
	Germany	48.9	(0.3)	30.0	(0.2)	42.6	(0.1)	52.5	(0.1)	70.2	(0.2)	427	(5.4)	471	(4.0)	513	(3.4)	541	(3.5)	45.3	(2.1)	2.6	(0.2)
	Greece	47.8	(0.6)	25.6	(0.3)	40.2	(0.2)	53.0	(0.1)	72.3	(0.4)	440	(5.6)	460	(7.2)	486	(5.5)	519	(5.5)	28.1	(2.5)	1.8	(0.2)
	Hungary	49.5	(0.5)	30.4	(0.2)	42.6	(0.1)	53.7	(0.1)	71.5	(0.2)	435	(4.9)	461	(4.5)	504	(3.8)	531	(5.9)	39.2	(2.4)	2.2	(0.2)
	Iceland	52.7	(0.3)	31.4	(0.2)	47.3	(0.1)	58.6	(0.2)	73.8	(0.2)	487	(3.1)	496	(3.2)	513	(3.2)	540	(2.5)	19.3	(1.5)	1.5	(0.1)
	Ireland	48.4	(0.5)	28.5	(0.2)	42.7	(0.2)	53.2	(0.1)	69.4	(0.2)	491	(4.3)	520	(4.3)	535	(3.7)	570	(3.7)	30.3	(1.8)	1.9	(0.1)
	Italy	47.1	(0.3)	28.5	(0.1)	40.6	(0.1)	50.3	(0.1)	68.9	(0.4)	457	(4.3)	481	(3.3)	494	(3.6)	525	(3.9)	26.4	(1.8)	1.8	(0.1)
	Japan[1]	m	m	m	m	m	m	m	m	m	m	m	m	m	m	m	m	m	m	m	m	m	m
	Korea	42.8	(0.4)	26.5	(0.1)	35.9	(0.1)	46.0	(0.1)	62.9	(0.5)	509	(4.5)	524	(2.9)	531	(2.8)	542	(3.4)	14.6	(2.1)	1.5	(0.1)
	Luxembourg	44.8	(0.3)	25.1	(0.1)	37.5	(0.1)	50.6	(0.1)	66.1	(0.4)	394	(4.1)	428	(3.4)	473	(3.3)	497	(2.8)	39.2	(2.0)	2.5	(0.1)
	Mexico	42.5	(0.7)	24.4	(0.1)	32.3	(0.1)	46.8	(0.2)	66.5	(0.5)	385	(4.1)	408	(3.7)	435	(4.0)	471	(5.9)	31.8	(2.3)	1.9	(0.2)
	New Zealand	52.2	(0.4)	30.5	(0.3)	47.1	(0.1)	57.7	(0.2)	73.6	(0.2)	489	(4.3)	523	(3.8)	549	(3.4)	574	(4.5)	31.9	(2.1)	2.0	(0.1)
	Norway	53.9	(0.4)	35.6	(0.2)	47.1	(0.1)	59.0	(0.2)	73.9	(0.2)	477	(4.1)	494	(3.8)	514	(3.8)	547	(4.2)	29.7	(2.0)	1.6	(0.1)
	Poland	46.0	(0.5)	27.3	(0.2)	40.0	(0.1)	49.8	(0.1)	67.0	(0.4)	445	(5.6)	472	(4.8)	493	(5.3)	534	(6.4)	35.4	(2.7)	2.0	(0.2)
	Portugal	43.9	(0.6)	26.8	(0.2)	34.5	(0.1)	48.4	(0.1)	65.7	(0.5)	431	(4.9)	452	(4.9)	485	(4.3)	527	(5.0)	38.4	(2.1)	2.0	(0.1)
	Spain	45.0	(0.6)	26.8	(0.1)	36.2	(0.1)	49.6	(0.1)	67.3	(0.5)	461	(3.5)	482	(3.6)	507	(2.7)	529	(3.0)	26.5	(1.6)	1.9	(0.1)
	Sweden	50.6	(0.4)	30.4	(0.2)	44.1	(0.1)	55.7	(0.1)	72.1	(0.2)	485	(2.9)	509	(3.2)	522	(3.1)	558	(3.3)	27.1	(1.5)	1.8	(0.1)
	Switzerland	49.2	(0.5)	29.3	(0.2)	42.5	(0.1)	53.2	(0.1)	71.9	(0.3)	434	(4.3)	492	(4.6)	513	(4.3)	549	(5.3)	40.2	(2.2)	2.7	(0.2)
	United Kingdom	51.3	(0.3)	30.7	(0.2)	45.7	(0.1)	56.9	(0.2)	71.8	(0.2)	481	(3.1)	513	(3.1)	543	(3.5)	579	(3.6)	38.4	(1.6)	2.1	(0.1)
	United States	52.4	(0.8)	30.3	(0.2)	47.4	(0.2)	59.5	(0.2)	72.5	(0.3)	466	(7.5)	507	(5.9)	528	(6.1)	556	(5.9)	33.5	(2.7)	2.1	(0.2)
	OECD total	*49.0*	*(0.2)*	*29.1*	*(0.1)*	*42.5*	*(0.1)*	*54.0*	*(0.1)*	*70.3*	*(0.1)*	*462*	*(2.3)*	*492*	*(1.7)*	*515*	*(1.9)*	*543*	*(2.1)*	*34.0*	*(0.9)*	*2.0*	*(0.1)*
	OECD average	*48.9*	*(0.1)*	*29.3*	*(0.0)*	*42.4*	*(0.0)*	*53.6*	*(0.0)*	*70.2*	*(0.1)*	*463*	*(0.9)*	*491*	*(0.8)*	*515*	*(0.7)*	*545*	*(0.9)*	*33.6*	*(0.4)*	*2.0*	*(0.0)*
NON-OECD COUNTRIES	Brazil	43.9	(0.6)	24.6	(0.2)	34.5	(0.2)	49.6	(0.2)	67.1	(0.4)	368	(3.9)	387	(3.8)	413	(4.0)	435	(4.5)	26.1	(1.9)	1.9	(0.1)
	Latvia	50.2	(0.5)	27.7	(0.1)	40.4	(0.2)	58.5	(0.3)	74.1	(0.3)	428	(6.4)	449	(5.0)	479	(6.7)	492	(6.6)	21.3	(2.2)	1.8	(0.1)
	Liechtenstein	47.5	(0.9)	28.0	(0.6)	41.8	(0.4)	52.1	(0.2)	68.2	(0.9)	437	(11.0)	491	(11.9)	495	(9.1)	523	(9.3)	32.6	(5.2)	2.1	(0.4)
	Russian Federation	49.4	(0.5)	30.0	(0.2)	40.3	(0.1)	53.4	(0.2)	73.9	(0.2)	429	(5.5)	450	(3.8)	472	(4.7)	502	(3.9)	26.5	(1.9)	1.8	(0.1)
	Netherlands[4]	50.9	(0.5)	29.5	(0.2)	45.3	(0.2)	57.3	(0.3)	71.3	(0.2)	495	(5.6)	525	(5.2)	555	(3.6)	566	(4.4)	29.9	(2.4)	2.2	(0.2)

1. Unit changes marked in bold are statistically significant. Where bottom and top quarters are marked in bold this indicates that their difference is statistically significant. 16.3 units on the index corresponds to one international standard deviation.
2. Ratios statistically significantly greater than 1 are marked in bold.
3. Japan was excluded from this comparison because of a high proportion of missing data.
4. Response rate is too low to ensure comparability (see Annex 3 at *www.oecd.org/els/education/eag2002*).
Source: OECD PISA database, 2001. See Annex 3 for notes on methodology (*www.oecd.org/els/education/eag2002*) and *www.pisa.oecd.org*.

PLACE OF BIRTH, LANGUAGE SPOKEN AT HOME, AND READING LITERACY OF 15-YEAR-OLDS

A10

- In most countries with significant immigrant populations, first-generation 15-year-olds read well below the level of native students even if they were themselves born in the country.

- Not surprisingly, students not speaking the majority language at home perform much less well than those who do and are much more likely to score among the lowest quarter of students in each country.

- Students born abroad lag behind even more, although to widely varying degrees in different countries.

- In some countries, students in families that do not speak the test language at home most of the time still do relatively well in reading. For instance, students in Australia and Canada score similarly to the OECD average and similar to the averages in many countries that have few minority-language students.

Chart A10.1.

Place of birth and home language, and student performance on the
PISA reading literacy scale (2000)

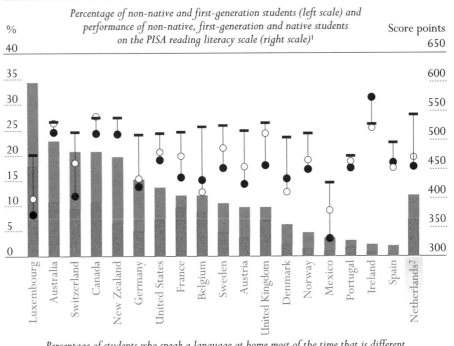

*Percentage of non-native and first-generation students (left scale) and
performance of non-native, first-generation and native students
on the PISA reading literacy scale (right scale)[1]*

Left scale

◼ Percentage of students who were foreign-born and whose parents were also foreign-born ("non-native students")

◼ Percentage of students who were born in the country of assessment but whose parents were foreign-born ("first-generation students")

Right scale

▬ Mean performance on the PISA reading literacy scale of students who were born in the country of assessment with at least one of their parents born in the same country ("native students")

○ Mean performance on the PISA reading literacy scale of students who were born in the country of assessment but whose parents were foreign-born ("first-generation students")

● Mean performance on the PISA reading literacy scale of students who were foreign-born and whose parents were also foreign-born ("non-native students")

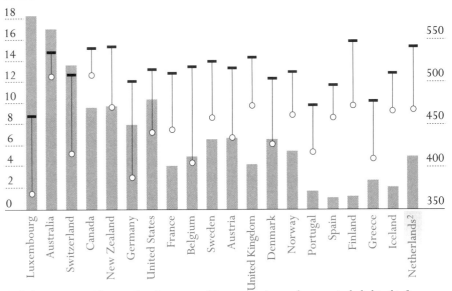

*Percentage of students who speak a language at home most of the time that is different
from the language of assessment, from other official languages or from other
national dialects (left scale) and performance of students on the PISA
reading literacy scale by language group (right scale)[3]*

Left scale

◼ Percentage of students who speak a language at home most of the time that is different from the language of assessment, from other official languages or from other national dialects

Right scale

▬ Mean performance on the PISA reading literacy scale of students who speak a language at home most of the time that is the same as the language of assessment, other official languages or other national dialects

○ Mean performance on the PISA reading literacy scale of students who speak a language at home most of the time that is different from the language of assessment, from other official languages or from other national dialects

1. Only countries with more than 3 per cent of first-generation students are included in this figure.
2. Response rate is too low to ensure comparability (see Annex 3).
3. Only countries with more than 3 per cent of students who speak a language at home most of the
   time that is different from the language of assessment, from other official languages or from other
   national dialects are included in this figure.

Countries are ranked in descending order of the total percentage of non-native and first-generation students.
Source: OECD PISA database, 2001. Tables A10.1 and A10.2. See Annex 3 for notes on methodology
(www.oecd.org/els/education/eag2002) and *www.pisa.oecd.org*.

A10

Increased migration poses challenges for education systems and comparing how successfully countries address these, as done by this Indicator, can provide important policy insights.

Policy context

Migration from one country to another is increasingly common as international trade expands, as employment opportunities attract people to better or different livelihoods, and as nations find themselves providing sanctuary for refugees from political and economic turmoil. For whatever reasons people migrate from one country to another, their school-aged children often find themselves in a new environment in which the language of instruction may be unfamiliar to them. Compelled to learn in a non-native language, and perhaps required to adjust to a new socio-cultural environment, some of these sons and daughters of immigrant parents can be expected to lag academically behind their peers whose first language is also the language of instruction.

Cross-national analysis can provide some insight into the characteristics that help some countries to succeed better than others in accommodating these differences.

Evidence and explanations

PISA allows to relate student performance to their migration status and home language…

To examine the effects of immigrant and language status on proficiency in reading literacy, PISA asked students to indicate whether each of their parents was born in the country in which the students live or in another country, as well as where they themselves were born. In addition, students were asked what language they speak at home most of the time.

…but there are limits to the interpretation of these data.

It is important to recognise the limits of the available data. PISA did not ask students how long they had lived in the country where the assessment took place. Some or even many of the students who were born outside the country may have lived inside the country for most of their lives and be fluent in the language of instruction. Others, by contrast, may be recent arrivals in the midst of their second year of schooling in their "new" country. When interpreting these results, it also needs to be taken into account that students who were unable to read or speak the test language because they had received less than one year of instruction in the language of the assessment were excluded. Likewise, there is no information available about how similar or different a student's first language might be from the language of instruction, which conceivably could have an impact on second language abilities. And finally, the socio-economic composition of the immigrant population may vary across countries.

Place of birth

The analysis compares…

To assess the effect of place of birth on performance, three categories of students are compared:

…"native" students,…

- those students born in the country where the assessment took place and who have at least one parent born in that country (referred to here as "native" students);

A10

- those students born in the country where the assessment took place but both of whose parents were born in another country (referred to here as "first-generation" students); and

…"first-generation" students…

- those students born outside the country where the assessment took place and whose parents were also born in another country (referred to here as "non-native" students).

…and "non-native" students.

For many non-native students, the test language will be a second language (note that the second half of this indicator deals with students' home language), and some will not have many years of experience in the educational system of the country in which they are tested. First-generation students also may be in families in which the first language, or the language spoken at home, is not the language of instruction. Regardless of their place of birth, students in these two categories need to acquire the same knowledge and skills that native-born students are expected to have as they move toward the completion of their formal education.

Language is a key issue for many students born abroad or with immigrant parents.

A comparison of the reading literacy of first-generation students with that of native students in the 14 countries in which first-generation students represent at least 3 per cent of students assessed in PISA 2000, reveals significant differences in favour of native students in ten of the 14 countries (see Chart A10.1). The differences between these students' performance on the reading literacy scale range from 31 to 41 points in France, New Zealand, Sweden and the United States; to about 53 to 62 points in Austria, Liechtenstein and Switzerland in the middle; and to more than 70 points, or nearly a full proficiency level in the Belgium, Germany, Luxembourg and Netherlands, which has the largest difference at 112 points.

In most countries with significant immigrant populations, first-generation students read at levels that are well below the level of native students…

These are troubling differences because both groups of students were born in the country of the test and, presumably, have experienced the same curriculum and benefits that their national education systems offer to all students. Despite the possible similarities in their educational "histories", first-generation students are at a relative disadvantage in these countries in terms of reading literacy. In countries in which first-generation students perform significantly lower than native students and in which there are proportionately large numbers of first-generation students – including Liechtenstein (about 10 per cent), Luxembourg (about 18 per cent) and Switzerland (about 9 per cent) – this may be a particular concern.

…even though they were themselves born in the country – which is disturbing.

A further comparison can be made between non-native and native students. In view of the differences between native and first-generation students in many countries and the differences between first-generation and non-native students in some countries, one would expect the largest overall differences to be between non-native and native students. In 13 of 14 countries, data support this expectation. On average, native students outscore their non-native peers in these 14 countries in reading literacy by 73 points, or by a full proficiency level. The differences range from 103 to 112 points in Liechtenstein, Luxembourg

Students born abroad lag behind even more, although to widely varying degrees in different countries.

and Switzerland and from 72 to 93 points in Austria, Belgium, France, Germany, the Netherlands, Sweden and the United Kingdom. The smallest significant differences are in Canada (27 points), New Zealand (30 points) and the United States (45 points). Australia, with a difference of 19 points, is the only country in which differences between these two groups of students are not significant.

Differences between first-generation and non-native students tend to be smaller.

Comparing first-generation students with non-native students among the same 14 countries reveals no statistically significant differences in reading literacy performance in six of the countries: Australia, Belgium, Germany, the Netherlands, New Zealand and the United States. In other words, in these six countries, PISA does not detect a performance-related disadvantage in reading literacy associated with place of birth (*i.e.*, in or outside the country) among students whose parents were not born in the country. The remaining eight countries in which the differences between first-generation and non-native students *are* statistically significant are Austria, Canada, France, Liechtenstein, Luxembourg, Sweden, Switzerland and the United Kingdom. In these countries, non-native students score from 28 to 58 points lower on the reading literacy scale than do first-generation students, although, in absolute terms, they still score well when compared with non-native students in other countries. Non-native students represent about 2 per cent of students who participated in PISA 2000 in France and the United Kingdom, slightly less than 6 per cent of students in Austria and Sweden, and between 9 and 16 per cent of students in the four other countries in which differences between these groups of students are significant.

Language spoken at home

Not surprisingly, students not speaking the majority language at home perform much less well than those who do...

Another way to examine the immigration issue is to examine what language students speak at home. To assess the effect of language on students' performance in reading literacy, two categories of students are compared.

• those students who speak the language of the test or another national language or dialect most of the time (referred to here as "majority-language students"); and

• those students who routinely converse with their parents and siblings in another language (referred to here as "minority-language" students).

Across the 17 countries in which at least 3 per cent of all students taking the PISA assessments are in the latter group, majority-language students outperform minority-language students (see Chart A10.1). The average difference between the two groups in reading literacy is 66 points. The differences range from about 30 to 34 points in Australia, Canada and the Russian Federation to around 114 points in Belgium and Germany.

One consequence of these differences is that the 15-year-old-students in Belgium, Denmark, Germany, Luxembourg and Switzerland who do not speak the test language at home are at least two and one-half times more likely to be among the lowest 25 per cent of performers in reading literacy as those students who speak the test language most of the time. In Austria, France, Greece, the Netherlands, New Zealand, Sweden and the United States, minority-language students are more than twice as likely as are majority-language students to be in the bottom quarter of performance in reading literacy.

However, in some countries, students in families that do not speak the test language at home most of the time still do relatively well in reading. For instance, students in Australia and Canada score similarly to the OECD average and similar to the averages in many countries that have few minority-language students.

One interesting observation is that minority-language students tend to do relatively well in English-speaking countries. The average difference between minority- and majority-language students in the five predominantly English-speaking countries (Australia, Canada, New Zealand, United Kingdom and the United States) is 54 points in reading literacy. Minority-language students also do reasonably well, with a mean difference of 66 points in reading literacy, in Denmark, the Netherlands, Norway and Sweden, with large proportions of such students. By contrast, minority-language students display the largest deficits, an average of 95 points, in the OECD's German-speaking countries.

Definitions and methodologies

The target population studied for this indicator was 15-year-old students. Operationally, this refers to students aged between 15 years and 3 (completed) months and 16 years and 2 (completed) months at the beginning of the testing period and enrolled in an educational institution, regardless of the grade level or type of institutions in which they were enrolled and of whether they participated in school full-time or part-time.

To address the language issue, PISA's context questionnaire asked students "what language do you speak at home most of the time", to which they could indicate that they speak the language in which the assessment was undertaken, an "other official national language", "other national dialects or languages," or "other languages." The data presented in this indicator compare students in the last group (*i.e.*, "other languages") with students in the first three groups.

In Table A10.2 a measure of the increased likelihood that a student with a particular characteristic will be in the bottom quarter of the distribution on the reading literacy scale is shown. This is a measure of relative probability. For example, the value "2" for the increased likelihood of a student who does not speak the language of assessment at home most of the time to score in the bottom quarter of the achievement distribution says that students from another language background are twice as likely to be among the lowest performers as students who speak the language of the assessment at home most of the time.

For notes on standard errors, significance tests, and multiple comparisons see Annex 3 at *www.oecd.org/els/education/eag2002*.

Table A10.1.
Performance in reading literacy and country of birth of 15-year-olds and their parents (2000)
*Percentage of students and performance on the PISA reading literacy scale, by students' country of birth
and the place of birth of their parents, based on students' self-reports*

| | Native students (students who were born in the country of assessment with at least one of their parents born in the same country) | | | | First-generation students (students who were born in the country of assessment but whose parents were foreign-born) | | | | Non-native students (students who were foreign-born and whose parents were also foreign-born) | | | |
| | | | Performance on the PISA reading literacy scale[2] | | | | Performance on the PISA reading literacy scale[2] | | | | Performance on the PISA reading literacy scale | |
	Percentage of students[1]	S.E.	Mean score	S.E.	Percentage of students[1]	S.E.	Mean score	S.E.	Percentage of students[1]	S.E.	Mean score	S.E.
Australia	77.4	(1.8)	532	(3.6)	10.7	(1.1)	528	(7.1)	11.9	(1.2)	513	(9.3)
Austria	90.4	(0.9)	**515**	(2.4)	3.7	(0.4)	**453**	(9.4)	5.9	(0.6)	422	(8.2)
Belgium	88.0	(1.1)	**522**	(3.8)	8.6	(0.9)	**411**	(8.7)	3.4	(0.4)	431	(9.5)
Canada	79.5	(1.0)	538	(1.5)	10.8	(0.5)	539	(3.1)	9.8	(0.6)	511	(4.9)
Czech Republic	98.9	(0.2)	501	(2.1)	0.6	(0.1)	c	c	0.5	(0.1)	c	c
Denmark	93.8	(0.6)	**504**	(2.2)	2.4	(0.4)	**409**	(13.9)	3.8	(0.4)	433	(7.6)
Finland	98.7	(0.2)	548	(2.6)	0.2	(0.1)	c	c	1.0	(0.2)	468	(12.9)
France	88.0	(0.9)	**512**	(2.8)	9.8	(0.7)	**471**	(6.2)	2.2	(0.3)	434	(11.5)
Germany	84.8	(0.8)	**507**	(2.3)	5.1	(0.5)	**432**	(9.0)	10.1	(0.6)	419	(7.5)
Greece	95.2	(0.9)	478	(4.7)	0.5	(0.1)	c	c	4.3	(0.9)	403	(17.5)
Hungary	98.3	(0.2)	482	(4.0)	0.1	(0.0)	c	c	1.6	(0.2)	486	(11.6)
Iceland	99.2	(0.2)	509	(1.5)	0.2	(0.1)	c	c	0.6	(0.1)	c	c
Ireland	97.7	(0.3)	528	(3.2)	0.9	(0.2)	519	(20.2)	1.4	(0.3)	573	(9.2)
Italy	99.1	(0.2)	489	(2.9)	0.2	(0.1)	c	c	0.8	(0.2)	445	(15.1)
Japan	99.9	(0.1)	525	(5.1)	0.0	(0.0)	c	c	0.1	(0.1)	c	c
Korea[3]	a	a	a	a	a	a	a	a	a	a	a	a
Luxembourg	65.8	(0.7)	**474**	(1.7)	17.8	(0.7)	**399**	(4.6)	16.4	(0.6)	370	(4.7)
Mexico	96.4	(0.4)	**427**	(3.3)	1.1	(0.2)	**378**	(15.3)	2.5	(0.3)	329	(8.2)
New Zealand	80.4	(1.1)	**538**	(2.7)	6.4	(0.5)	**507**	(10.3)	13.2	(0.8)	507	(7.6)
Norway	95.4	(0.4)	**510**	(2.7)	1.5	(0.2)	**464**	(10.6)	3.1	(0.3)	449	(8.5)
Poland	99.7	(0.1)	482	(4.4)	0.0	(0.0)	c	c	0.2	(0.1)	c	c
Portugal	96.9	(0.3)	472	(4.5)	1.8	(0.2)	463	(14.3)	1.4	(0.2)	450	(15.8)
Spain	98.0	(0.4)	**494**	(2.6)	0.6	(0.1)	**450**	(15.9)	1.4	(0.3)	460	(17.8)
Sweden	89.5	(0.9)	**523**	(2.1)	4.7	(0.6)	**485**	(7.3)	5.9	(0.6)	450	(7.2)
Switzerland	79.3	(0.9)	**514**	(4.0)	9.3	(0.6)	**460**	(6.8)	11.4	(0.7)	402	(6.1)
United Kingdom	90.4	(1.2)	528	(2.6)	7.0	(0.9)	510	(9.4)	2.6	(0.4)	456	(15.1)
United States	86.4	(2.1)	511	(6.5)	7.4	(1.4)	478	(19.4)	6.1	(0.9)	466	(10.0)
OECD total	91.3	(0.6)	503	(1.9)	4.6	(0.4)	479	(9.1)	4.1	(0.3)	452	(4.9)
OECD average	91.0	(0.2)	506	(0.6)	4.3	(0.1)	467	(2.8)	4.7	(0.1)	446	(2.5)
Brazil	99.6	(0.1)	398	(3.0)	0.3	(0.1)	c	c	0.1	(0.1)	c	c
Latvia	77.9	(2.4)	**462**	(6.0)	1.5	(0.3)	**423**	(15.1)	20.6	(2.4)	454	(7.3)
Liechtenstein	79.4	(2.1)	**500**	(5.0)	10.2	(1.8)	**446**	(14.8)	10.4	(1.6)	392	(21.4)
Russian Federation	95.4	(0.6)	463	(4.3)	1.8	(0.3)	452	(9.9)	2.8	(0.4)	458	(9.6)
Netherlands[4]	88.1	(1.8)	542	(3.0)	7.4	(1.2)	470	(14.2)	4.5	(0.8)	453	(15.6)

1. Percentage of students participating in the assessment of reading literacy in the respective category.
2. Mean scores marked in bold indicate that the difference in performance between native and first-generation students is statistically significant.
3. This question was not asked in Korea.
4. Response rate is too low to ensure comparability (see Annex 3 at *www.oecd.org/els/education/eag2002*).
Source: OECD PISA database, 2001. See Annex 3 for notes on methodology *(www.oecd.org/els/education/eag2002)* and *www.pisa.oecd.org*.

Table A10.2.

Performance in reading literacy and language spoken at home of 15-year-olds (2000)

Student performance on the PISA reading literacy scale, by language spoken at home, and increased likelihood of students who do not speak the language of assessment at home scoring in the bottom quarter of the national reading literacy performance distribution, based on students' self-reports

		Language spoken at home most of the time IS DIFFERENT from the language of assessment, from other official languages or from other national dialects				Language spoken at home most of the time IS THE SAME as the language of assessment, other official languages or another national dialects				Increased likelihood of students who do not speak the language of assessment at home scoring in the bottom quarter of the national reading literacy performance distribution[3]	
				Performance on the PISA reading literacy scale[2]				Performance on the PISA reading literacy scale[2]			
		Percentage of students[1]	S.E.	Mean score	S.E.	Percentage of students[1]	S.E.	Mean score	S.E.	Ratio	S.E.
OECD COUNTRIES	Australia	17.0	(1.6)	**504**	(7.6)	83.0	(1.6)	**534**	(3.6)	**1.6**	(0.1)
	Austria	6.7	(0.7)	**434**	(7.2)	93.3	(0.7)	**515**	(2.4)	**2.3**	(0.2)
	Belgium	4.9	(0.6)	**403**	(8.6)	95.2	(0.6)	**518**	(3.7)	**2.8**	(0.2)
	Canada	9.4	(0.6)	**506**	(3.8)	90.6	(0.6)	**540**	(1.5)	**1.6**	(0.1)
	Czech Republic	0.8	(0.2)	c	c	99.2	(0.2)	494	(2.2)	c	c
	Denmark	6.7	(0.4)	**425**	(8.1)	93.3	(0.4)	**503**	(2.2)	**2.5**	(0.2)
	Finland	1.3	(0.2)	470	(12.5)	98.7	(0.2)	548	(2.6)	c	c
	France	4.0	(0.5)	**442**	(7.7)	96.0	(0.5)	**510**	(2.6)	**2.3**	(0.2)
	Germany	7.9	(0.8)	**386**	(13.9)	92.1	(0.8)	**500**	(2.9)	**2.9**	(0.3)
	Greece	2.8	(0.6)	**407**	(18.3)	97.2	(0.6)	**477**	(4.8)	**2.3**	(0.4)
	Hungary	m	m	m	m	m	m	m	m	m	m
	Iceland	1.9	(0.3)	**463**	(13.4)	98.1	(0.3)	**509**	(1.5)	c	c
	Ireland	0.9	(0.2)	c	c	99.1	(0.2)	527	(3.2)	c	c
	Italy	0.7	(0.2)	c	c	99.3	(0.2)	491	(3.0)	c	c
	Japan	0.3	(0.1)	c	c	99.7	(0.1)	525	(5.2)	c	c
	Korea[4]	a	a	a	a	a	a	a	a	a	a
	Luxembourg	18.3	(0.7)	**367**	(4.1)	81.7	(0.7)	**460**	(1.6)	**2.8**	(0.1)
	Mexico	0.2	(0.1)	c	c	99.8	(0.1)	422	(3.4)	c	c
	New Zealand	9.6	(0.6)	**469**	(9.6)	90.4	(0.6)	**541**	(2.6)	**2.1**	(0.2)
	Norway	5.3	(0.4)	**459**	(8.4)	94.7	(0.4)	**510**	(2.8)	**1.8**	(0.1)
	Poland	0.5	(0.2)	c	c	99.5	(0.2)	482	(4.4)	c	c
	Portugal	1.5	(0.2)	**416**	(13.8)	98.5	(0.2)	**471**	(4.6)	c	c
	Spain	1.2	(0.2)	**456**	(16.0)	98.8	(0.2)	**495**	(2.6)	c	c
	Sweden	6.7	(0.6)	**456**	(7.1)	93.3	(0.6)	**523**	(2.0)	**2.1**	(0.2)
	Switzerland	13.6	(0.6)	**414**	(6.1)	86.4	(0.6)	**509**	(4.1)	**2.8**	(0.2)
	United Kingdom	4.1	(0.7)	**470**	(12.8)	95.9	(0.7)	**528**	(2.5)	**1.9**	(0.2)
	United States	10.8	(2.4)	**438**	(13.1)	89.2	(2.4)	**514**	(5.8)	**2.1**	(0.2)
	OECD total	5.5	(0.7)	443	(8.2)	94.5	(0.7)	503	(1.8)	2.0	(0.1)
	OECD average	5.5	(0.2)	440	(2.6)	94.5	(0.2)	506	(0.6)	2.1	(0.0)
NON-OECD COUNTRIES	Brazil	0.8	(0.2)	c	c	99.2	(0.2)	397	(3.0)	c	c
	Latvia	0.0	(0.0)	a	a	100.0	(0.0)	460	(5.2)	a	a
	Liechtenstein	20.7	(2.2)	**441**	(14.3)	79.3	(2.2)	**494**	(5.1)	c	c
	Russian Federation	7.3	(2.1)	**432**	(9.3)	92.7	(2.1)	**465**	(4.3)	**1.5**	(0.2)
	Netherlands[5]	6.3	(1.1)	**466**	(13.1)	93.7	(1.1)	**539**	(2.7)	**2.2**	(0.3)

1. Percentage of students participating in the assessment of reading literacy in the respective category.
2. Mean scores marked in bold indicate that the difference in performance between students who do not speak the language of assessment at home and those who do is statistically significant.
3. Ratios statistically significantly greater than 1 are marked in bold.
4. This question was not asked in Korea.
5. Response rate is too low to ensure comparability (see Annex 3 at *www.oecd.org/els/education/eag2002*).
Source: OECD PISA database, 2001. See Annex 3 for notes on methodology (*www.oecd.org/els/education/eag2002*) and *www.pisa.oecd.org*.

LABOUR FORCE PARTICIPATION
BY LEVEL OF EDUCATIONAL ATTAINMENT

A11

- Labour force participation rates rise with educational attainment in most OECD countries. With very few exceptions, the participation rate for graduates of tertiary education is markedly higher than that for upper secondary graduates. The gap in male participation rates is particularly wide between upper secondary graduates and those without an upper secondary qualification.

- The labour force participation rate for women with less than upper secondary attainment is particularly low. Rates for women with tertiary attainment approach or exceed 80 per cent in all but four countries, but remain below those of men in all countries except one.

- The gender gap in labour force participation decreases with increasing educational attainment. Although a gender gap in labour force participation remains among those with the highest educational attainment, it is much narrower than among those with lower qualifications.

A11

Chart A11.1.

Differences between labour force participation rates of males and females, by level of educational attainment for 25 to 64-year-olds (2001)

■ Below upper secondary education
■ Upper secondary and post-secondary non-tertiary education
■ Tertiary-type A and advanced research programmes

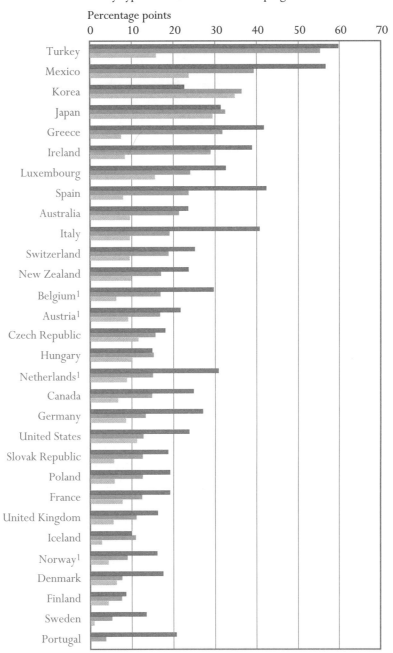

Percentage points

1. Year of reference 2000.
Countries are ranked in descending order of the difference between labour force participation rates of males and females who have upper secondary education and post-secondary non-tertiary education.
Source: OECD. Table 11.1. See Annex 3 for a description of ISCED-97 levels, ISCED-97 country mappings and national data sources *(www.oecd.org/els/education/eag2002).*

A11

This indicator examines the relationship between educational attainment and labour-market status.

Policy context

OECD economies and labour markets are becoming increasingly dependent on a stable supply of well-educated workers to further their economic development and to maintain their competitiveness. As levels of skill tend to rise with educational attainment, the costs incurred when those with higher levels of education do not work also rise; and as populations in OECD countries age, higher and longer participation in the labour force can lower dependency ratios and help to alleviate the burden of financing public pensions.

This indicator examines the relationship between educational attainment and labour force activity, comparing rates of participation in the labour force first, and then rates of unemployment. The adequacy of workers' skills and the capacity of the labour market to supply jobs that match those skills are important issues for policy-makers.

Evidence and explanations

Labour force participation

Labour force participation rates for men vary less between countries than those for women.

Variation between countries in participation by women is a primary factor in the differences in overall participation rates between OECD countries. The overall labour force participation rates for men aged 25 to 64 range from 81 per cent or less in Hungary and Italy to 94 per cent and above in Iceland, Japan, Mexico and Switzerland (Chart A11.1). By contrast, labour force participation among women ranges from 55 per cent or less in Greece, Italy, Mexico, Spain and Turkey, to over 77 per cent in the Nordic countries. Prolonged education and non-employment are two factors which contribute to these disparities, generally increasing the number of people not in the labour force.

Labour force participation rates for men rise with educational attainment in most OECD countries.

Labour force participation rates for men are generally higher among those with higher educational qualifications. With the exception of Mexico, Spain and Turkey, where the trend is less pronounced, the participation rate for graduates of tertiary education is markedly higher than that for upper secondary graduates. The difference ranges from a few percentage points to between 8 and 10 per cent in Austria, Denmark, Germany and Poland. It is very small between the ages of 35 and 44, when most people are in employment, and may stem mainly from the fact that the less skilled leave the labour market earlier. After 55, those with higher educational attainment tend to remain in employment longer than others (Table A11.1).

The gap in male participation rates is particularly wide between those with and those without an upper secondary qualification.

The gap in participation rates of 25 to 64 year-old males is particularly wide between upper secondary graduates and those who have not completed an upper secondary qualification. In 14 out of 29 OECD countries, the difference in the rate of participation between upper secondary graduates and those without such a qualification exceeds ten percentage points. The most extreme case is Hungary, where only half of the male population without upper secondary education, but over 80 per cent with such attainment, participate in the labour force. The gap in participation rates between men with low and men

A11

with high educational attainment is small in Iceland, Korea, Mexico, Portugal, Switzerland and Turkey.

Labour force participation rates for women aged 25 to 64 years show yet more marked differences, not only between those with below upper secondary and those with upper secondary attainment (around 20 percentage points or more in 15 out of the 30 OECD countries) but also between those with upper secondary and those with tertiary attainment (around 10 percentage points or more in 22 countries). Particular exceptions are Japan, Korea and Sweden where participation rates for women with upper secondary qualifications approach those for women with a tertiary qualification (a difference of around 5 to 7 percentage points).

Among women, the difference in labour force participation by level of educational attainment is even wider.

Participation rates for women with less than upper secondary attainment are particularly low, averaging about 50 per cent over all OECD countries and around one-third or below in Hungary, Italy and Turkey. Rates for women with tertiary attainment approach or exceed 80 per cent everywhere except Hungary, Japan, Korea, Luxembourg, Mexico and Turkey, but remain below those of men in all countries (Table A11.1).

Labour force participation among women with qualifications below upper secondary is particularly low...

Although the gender gap in labour force participation remains among those with the highest educational attainment, it is much narrower than among those with lower qualifications. On average across OECD countries, with each additional level attained, the difference between the participation of men and women decreases by 10 percentage points: from not far from 30 percentage points at below upper secondary level, to 20 percentage points at upper secondary and 10 percentage points at tertiary level.

...but the gender gap in labour force participation decreases with increasing educational attainment.

Much of the overall gap between the labour force participation rates of men with differing educational attainment is explained by larger differences in the older populations, particularly among men between the ages of 55 and 64 (Table A11.1). More than 70 per cent of 55 to 64-year-olds with a tertiary-level qualification are active in the labour force in 20 out of 29 countries. Only Greece, Korea, Mexico and Turkey have participation rates as high among those who have not completed upper secondary education. By contrast, the education gap in female labour force participation is relatively wide in all age groups.

The education gap in male participation in the labour force is strongly influenced by differences among the older population.

The patterns observed here reflect a number of underlying causes. Since earnings tend to increase with educational attainment, the monetary incentive to participate is greater for individuals with higher qualifications. In addition, those individuals often work on more interesting and stimulating tasks, and hold functions of higher responsibility, which increase their motivation to remain in the labour force. Conversely, hard physical work, generally associated with rather low levels of education, can lead to a need for early retirement. Moreover, industrial restructuring in many countries has reduced job opportunities for unskilled workers, or for workers with particular skills that have been made obsolete by new technologies. A sizeable number of these people have left the

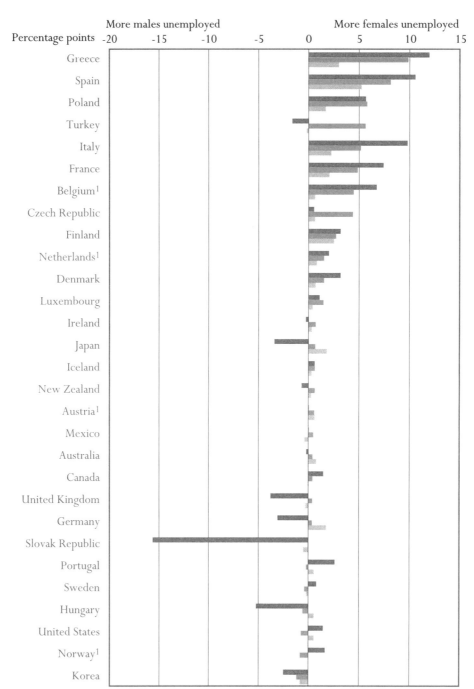

Chart A11.2.

Differences between unemployment rates of females and males,
by level of educational attainment, for 30 to 44-year-olds (2001)

■ Below upper secondary education   ■ Upper secondary and post-secondary non-tertiary education   ■ Tertiary education

1. Year of reference 2000.

Countries are ranked in descending order of the difference between unemployment rates of females and males who have completed upper secondary education or post-secondary non-tertiary education.

Source: OECD. Table A11.2. See Annex 3 for a description of ISCED-97 levels, ISCED-97 country mappings and national data sources (*www.oecd.org/els/education/eag2002*).

labour market either through early retirement schemes or because there are only limited job opportunities. The educational attainment of women and their participation rates in the labour market have been lower historically than those of men, and in spite of considerable advances over the last few decades, current participation rates continue to show the impact of these historical factors.

Unemployment rates by level of educational attainment

The unemployment rate is a measure of a particular economy's ability to supply a job to everyone who wants one. To the extent that educational attainment is assumed to be an indicator of skill, it can signal to employers the potential knowledge, capacities and workplace performance of candidates for employment. The employment prospects of individuals of varying educational attainment will depend both on the requirements of labour markets and on the supply of workers with differing skills. Those with low educational qualifications are at particular risk of economic marginalisation since they are both less likely to be labour force participants and more likely to be without a job if they are actively seeking one.

Those with low educational attainment are both less likely to be labour force participants and more likely to be unemployed.

In 19 out of the 30 OECD countries, male labour force participants aged 25 to 64 with a qualification below upper secondary education are more than 1.5 times as likely to be unemployed as their counterparts who have completed upper secondary education (Chart A11.2). In 17 countries, the unemployment rate for male upper secondary graduates is at least 1.5 times the unemployment rate among tertiary graduates. At the tertiary level, completion of shorter vocationally-oriented programmes (ISCED 5B) is associated with unemployment rates for the adult population which are higher than those for graduates of more theoretical, longer programmes at ISCED level 5A in about half of the countries, but significantly lower in the others (Table A11.2).

Unemployment rates fall with higher educational attainment.

In most countries, the disparities in unemployment rates between levels of educational attainment are particularly strong among men between 30 and 44 years of age. The association between unemployment rates and educational attainment is similar among women, although the gap between upper secondary and tertiary attainment is even wider in many countries. The disadvantage for women is visible for one-third of countries, but the unemployment rates are similar in the others, independently of the levels of attainment. At the tertiary level, the gap is much less obvious, even in the countries where it is a general phenomenon (Chart A11.2).

The wide variation between countries in unemployment rates observed among those with low educational attainment is attributable to a number of factors. In some countries (especially those facing a transition process: the Czech Republic, Hungary, Poland and the Slovak Republic), the high unemployment rates of the poorly educated reflect generally difficult labour market conditions, which affect these individuals in particular. To a lesser extent, this is also the case in Finland, France and Germany. Unemployment rates among those without an

A number of factors contribute to the variation between countries in the association between unemployment rates and educational attainment.

A11

upper secondary qualification are also relatively high in some countries where labour markets are less regulated (Canada, the United Kingdom and the United States). On the other hand, in countries where agriculture is still an important sector of employment (Mexico and Portugal), unemployment rates of persons without upper secondary education tend to be low. Finally, where overall labour market conditions are particularly favourable (Austria, Iceland, Luxembourg, the Netherlands, Norway and Switzerland), jobs appear to be available for workers with low as well as high educational attainment (Table A11.2).

Definitions and methodologies

Data are derived from national labour force surveys.

The labour force participation rate for a particular age group is equal to the percentage of individuals in the population of the same age group who are either employed or unemployed, as defined according to the guidelines of the International Labour Office (ILO).

The unemployed are defined as individuals who are without work, actively seeking employment and currently available to start work. The employed are defined as those who during the survey reference week: *i)* work for pay (employees) or profit (self-employed and unpaid family workers) for at least one hour, or *ii)* have a job but are temporarily not at work (through injury, illness, holiday, strike or lock-out, educational or training leave, maternity or parental leave, etc.) and have a formal attachment to their job.

The unemployment rate is the number of unemployed persons divided by the number of labour force participants (expressed as a percentage). The level of educational attainment is based on the definitions of ISCED-97.

A11

Table A11.1.
Labour force participation rates (2001)
By level of educational attainment and gender for 25 to 64-year-olds and 55 to 64-year-olds

		25 to 64-year-olds					55 to 64-year-olds			
		Below upper secondary education	Upper secondary and post-secondary non-tertiary education	Tertiary-type B education	Tertiary-type A and advanced research programmes	All levels of education	Below upper secondary education	Upper secondary and post-secondary non-tertiary education	Tertiary education	All levels of education
		(1)	(2)	(3)	(4)	(5)	(6)	(7)	(8)	(9)
Australia	Males	79	89	89	92	86	54	67	74	62
	Females	55	68	77	83	66	30	42	61	38
Austria[1]	Males	71	85	87	95	83	32	41	65	42
	Females	49	68	83	86	64	15	18	43	17
Belgium[1]	Males	71	87	92	92	82	29	42	58	38
	Females	41	71	82	86	62	13	22	31	17
Canada	Males	73	88	91	90	86	52	64	66	61
	Females	48	73	81	83	72	28	46	51	41
Czech Republic	Males	70	88	x(4)	94	87	35	55	79	55
	Females	52	73	x(4)	83	70	13	27	61	25
Denmark	Males	75	87	91	96	86	55	65	81	66
	Females	57	79	88	90	77	31	60	67	52
Finland	Males	70	86	90	93	83	43	54	65	51
	Females	61	79	86	88	77	40	53	67	49
France	Males	76	88	92	92	85	36	44	66	44
	Females	57	76	85	84	70	29	36	51	34
Germany	Males	77	84	88	92	84	44	49	67	53
	Females	50	70	81	83	68	26	35	53	34
Greece	Males	82	88	85	90	85	60	48	57	57
	Females	40	57	79	83	52	25	16	30	24
Hungary	Males	50	83	x(4)	89	75	22	46	64	36
	Females	35	67	x(4)	79	58	8	21	43	16
Iceland	Males	95	95	97	98	96	91	92	99	93
	Females	85	84	91	95	87	81	83	82	82
Ireland	Males	79	93	95	94	87	61	72	80	66
	Females	40	64	74	85	60	21	35	50	29
Italy	Males	74	86	x(4)	91	80	36	49	71	41
	Females	34	67	x(4)	81	50	12	29	41	16
Japan	Males	87	95	98	97	95	80	86	86	84
	Females	56	63	66	68	63	48	49	47	49
Korea	Males	84	89	94	91	88	74	67	70	71
	Females	61	53	58	56	57	51	25	42	48
Luxembourg	Males	79	87	92	92	85	22	35	73	36
	Females	46	63	80	77	56	9	20	48	14
Mexico	Males	94	96	97	94	94	81	78	79	80
	Females	37	56	61	70	43	27	37	37	28
Netherlands[1]	Males	77	89	90	92	86	42	53	64	51
	Females	46	73	80	83	64	19	32	45	26
New Zealand	Males	80	91	89	93	89	66	79	80	75
	Females	56	74	77	83	71	41	58	65	52
Norway[1]	Males	75	89	95	94	89	62	75	87	74
	Females	59	80	88	89	80	47	63	86	62
Poland	Males	64	83	x(4)	92	81	35	41	68	41
	Females	45	71	x(4)	86	67	20	24	45	24
Portugal	Males	87	87	94	94	87	63	57	78	64
	Females	66	84	88	95	71	41	32	60	42
Slovak Republic	Males	62	88	89	93	86	25	46	64	43
	Females	43	76	90	88	71	3	12	52	11
Spain	Males	83	90	93	91	86	59	62	73	61
	Females	41	66	77	83	54	20	38	58	24
Sweden	Males	79	88	89	91	87	68	74	82	74
	Females	66	83	86	90	82	56	69	82	68
Switzerland	Males	87	93	96	96	94	78	82	85	83
	Females	62	74	85	86	74	41	58	68	54
Turkey	Males	82	87	x(4)	87	84	52	25	43	49
	Females	22	32	x(4)	71	27	14	5	15	14
United Kingdom	Males	67	88	93	93	86	51	67	73	64
	Females	51	77	85	87	74	44	65	69	58
United States	Males	75	86	90	92	87	55	66	77	68
	Females	52	73	80	81	73	33	54	66	54
Country mean	*Males*	*77*	*88*	*92*	*93*	*86*	*52*	*59*	*72*	*60*
	Females	*50*	*70*	*80*	*83*	*65*	*30*	*39*	*54*	*37*

Note: x indicates that data are included in another column. The column reference is shown in brackets after "x". *e.g.*, x(2) means that data are included in column 2.
1. Year of reference 2000.
Source: OECD. See Annex 3 for a description of ISCED-97 levels, ISCED-97 country mappings and national data sources (*www.oecd.org / els / education / eag2002*).

OECD COUNTRIES

Table A11.2.
Unemployment rates (2001)
By level of educational attainment and gender of 25 to 64-year-olds and 30 to 44-year-olds

		25 to 64-year-olds					30 to 44-year-olds			
		Below upper secondary education	Upper secondary and post-secondary non-tertiary education	Tertiary-type B education	Tertiary-type A and advanced research programmes	All levels of education	Below upper secondary education	Upper secondary and post-secondary non-tertiary education	Tertiary education	All levels of education
		(1)	(2)	(3)	(4)	(5)	(6)	(7)	(8)	(9)
Australia	Males	8.1	4.5	4.5	2.5	5.2	8.6	4.6	2.8	5.3
	Females	7.0	5.2	3.9	2.6	5.1	8.4	5.0	3.5	5.7
Austria[1]	Males	6.9	2.8	1.1	1.8	3.2	6.2	2.3	1.2	2.6
	Females	5.9	3.2	1.3	2.5	3.6	6.2	2.8	1.8	3.3
Belgium[1]	Males	7.7	3.9	2.2	2.4	4.8	8.1	3.2	2.2	4.5
	Females	13.5	7.0	3.0	3.3	7.4	14.8	7.6	2.7	7.6
Canada	Males	10.2	6.2	4.8	4.4	6.2	10.8	6.3	4.8	6.3
	Females	10.2	6.2	4.5	4.4	5.8	12.3	6.7	4.8	6.2
Czech Republic	Males	19.3	4.7	x(4)	1.9	5.4	23.4	4.5	1.8	5.3
	Females	19.1	8.0	x(4)	2.2	8.9	24.0	8.9	2.4	9.7
Denmark	Males	4.0	2.7	3.3	3.5	3.1	4.0	2.3	3.2	2.8
	Females	6.2	4.0	3.1	3.1	4.1	7.2	3.9	3.9	4.3
Finland	Males	10.5	7.9	4.7	3.0	7.2	11.9	7.1	2.8	6.5
	Females	12.7	9.2	5.9	3.6	8.1	15.0	9.8	5.3	8.2
France	Males	9.7	5.1	4.3	4.1	6.2	10.7	4.7	3.5	6.1
	Females	14.4	9.3	5.0	5.6	9.8	18.1	9.5	5.5	10.6
Germany	Males	15.6	8.1	4.4	3.4	7.7	14.2	7.0	2.6	6.5
	Females	11.5	8.4	5.8	4.4	8.1	11.2	7.4	4.4	7.2
Greece	Males	4.9	6.2	4.9	4.5	5.3	4.7	5.1	4.2	4.7
	Females	12.3	15.1	8.3	9.6	12.5	16.7	14.9	7.1	13.2
Hungary	Males	12.5	4.8	x(4)	1.1	5.5	15.1	4.6	0.7	5.6
	Females	7.6	4.2	x(4)	1.3	4.3	9.9	4.1	1.2	4.5
Iceland	Males	2.3	1.2	0.8	1.0	1.5	1.7	1.4	0.6	1.3
	Females	2.4	2.8	2.4	0.2	2.1	2.3	2.0	0.9	1.8
Ireland	Males	5.5	2.3	1.9	1.1	3.3	6.3	2.0	1.6	3.4
	Females	5.1	2.8	2.3	1.0	2.9	6.1	2.7	1.9	3.1
Italy	Males	6.9	4.9	x(4)	3.8	5.8	7.1	3.8	3.9	5.4
	Females	14.0	9.3	x(4)	7.2	10.7	16.8	8.9	6.1	11.1
Japan	Males	6.9	4.8	3.2	2.8	4.4	7.5	3.6	2.0	3.1
	Females	4.3	4.7	3.8	3.1	4.2	4.2	4.2	3.8	4.0
Korea	Males	4.3	3.7	5.0	3.2	3.8	4.9	3.5	2.7	3.4
	Females	1.8	2.7	3.3	2.0	2.3	2.5	2.4	1.9	2.3
Luxembourg	Males	1.5	0.7	0.9	1.1	1.1	1.0	0.6	1.2	0.9
	Females	2.3	1.5	0.4	2.6	1.9	2.1	2.0	1.6	2.0
Mexico	Males	1.4	1.9	2.1	2.2	1.6	1.3	1.2	2.0	1.5
	Females	1.4	1.6	1.8	2.2	1.6	1.3	1.7	1.7	1.5
Netherlands[1]	Males	3.0	1.6	1.5	1.8	2.0	3.0	1.4	1.6	1.9
	Females	5.0	3.1	2.6	2.1	3.4	5.7	3.1	1.7	3.4
New Zealand	Males	7.4	3.0	4.4	2.8	4.0	8.1	3.2	3.4	4.1
	Females	5.9	3.6	2.9	3.2	3.9	7.5	3.8	3.6	4.4
Norway[1]	Males	2.3	3.0	1.9	2.0	2.6	2.3	3.1	1.8	2.7
	Females	2.2	2.2	3.7	1.6	2.0	4.0	2.4	1.8	2.3
Poland	Males	21.7	14.0	x(4)	4.0	13.9	26.3	13.5	1.8	13.7
	Females	23.7	18.3	x(4)	5.9	17.0	31.9	19.3	3.4	18.1
Portugal	Males	2.7	3.1	2.6	2.0	2.7	2.4	3.0	1.4	2.4
	Females	4.6	3.3	2.9	3.3	4.3	5.0	2.8	1.9	4.2
Slovak Republic	Males	44.3	14.8	5.3	4.5	15.7	55.1	14.8	3.9	16.1
	Females	34.6	14.8	11.0	3.4	15.7	39.5	14.8	3.4	15.8
Spain	Males	7.3	5.4	4.1	4.7	6.2	7.6	4.6	3.4	5.8
	Females	16.1	12.8	13.0	8.8	13.3	18.1	12.7	8.6	13.5
Sweden	Males	5.6	5.0	3.4	2.6	4.5	6.3	4.7	2.9	4.3
	Females	6.4	4.2	2.5	2.2	3.8	7.0	4.3	2.7	3.9
Switzerland	Males	m	1.1	m	m	1.1	m	m	m	m
	Females	m	2.9	m	m	3.1	m	3.4	m	3.4
Turkey	Males	9.2	8.0	x(4)	5.6	8.6	9.3	5.5	3.4	7.9
	Females	6.9	13.5	x(4)	6.1	7.7	7.7	11.2	3.2	7.3
United Kingdom	Males	9.4	4.1	2.7	2.0	4.1	11.9	3.9	2.2	4.2
	Females	5.7	3.7	1.7	1.9	3.4	8.2	4.3	2.0	4.0
United States	Males	7.5	4.2	2.5	1.9	3.7	7.4	4.4	1.8	3.7
	Females	8.9	3.4	2.3	2.0	3.3	8.9	3.7	2.3	3.6
Country mean	*Males*	*8.9*	*4.8*	*3.3*	*2.8*	*5.0*	*9.9*	*4.5*	*2.4*	*4.9*
	Females	*9.4*	*6.4*	*4.0*	*3.5*	*6.1*	*11.1*	*6.3*	*3.3*	*6.3*

Note: x indicates that data are included in another column. The column reference is shown in brackets after "x". *e.g.,* x(2) means that data are included in column 2.
1. Year of reference 2000.
Source: OECD. See Annex 3 for a description of ISCED-97 levels, ISCED-97 country mappings and national data sources (*www.oecd.org/els/education/eag2002*).

EXPECTED YEARS IN EDUCATION, EMPLOYMENT AND NON-EMPLOYMENT BETWEEN THE AGES OF 15 AND 29

A12

- On average across countries, a young person aged 15 in 2001 can expect to be in education for a little over six years. In 12 of the 29 countries studied, the figure ranges from six to seven years.

- A young person aged 15 can expect to hold a job for 6.5 of the 15 years to come, to be unemployed for a total of 0.8 years and to be out of the labour market for 1.4 years. It is in the average duration of spells of unemployment that countries vary most, which primarily reflects differences in youth employment rates.

- In absolute terms, young people today can expect to spend less time in unemployment after completing their initial education than they did ten years ago.

Chart A12.1.

Expected years in education and not in education (2001)

By work status for 15 to 29-year-olds

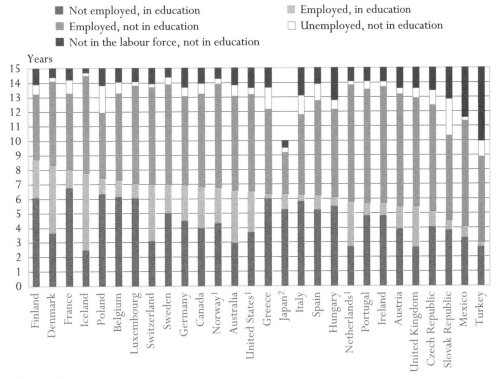

1. Year of reference 2000.
2. Data refer to 15 to 24-year-olds.
Countries are ranked in descending order of the expected years in education of the youth population.
Source: OECD. Table A12.1. See Annex 3 for national data sources *(www.oecd.org/els/education/eag2002).*

A12

This indicator shows the expected years young people spend in education, employment and non-employment.

Policy context

During the past decade, young people have spent longer in initial education, with the result that they delay their entry into the world of work (see the 1998 edition of *Education at a Glance*). Some of this additional time is spent combining work and education, a practice that is widespread in some countries. Once young people have completed their education, access to the labour market is often impeded by spells of unemployment or non-employment, although this situation affects men and women differently. In absolute terms, however, young people today can expect to spend less time in unemployment after completing initial education than they did ten years ago.

Evidence and explanations

On the basis of the current situation of persons between the ages of 15 and 29, this indicator gives a picture of the major trends affecting the transition from school to work.

On average, a 15-year-old can expect to be in the education system for about another six years.

On average, a young person aged 15 in 2001 can expect to be in education for a little over six years (Table A12.1). Between 1985 and 1996, this figure rose by almost 1.5 years. Since 1996, the overall increase has been slower. Countries where young people used to spend relatively little time in education have made up some ground, whereas those in which they stayed in education longest are now recording little increase.

In 12 of the 28 countries studied, a 15-year-old can expect to spend from six to seven years in education. There is, however, a gap of around four years separating the two extreme groups: Denmark, Finland, Iceland and France (eight years on average) on the one hand and Mexico, the Slovak Republic and Turkey (four years on average) on the other.

The average overall figure is marginally higher for women (6.4 compared with 6.2 years). In many countries, the figures are about the same, but Turkey stands out as an exception, with only 2.4 years of expected education for young women aged 15 years. At the other end of the scale, a longer average period of education often goes hand in hand with a relatively higher average for women (Table A12.1).

The figure for expected years of education covers some very different combinations of education and work.

The figure for expected years of education covers some very different combinations of education and work. Employment combined with education includes work-study programmes and part-time jobs. While such combinations are rare in half of the countries studied, in the other half they account for between one and four of the additional six to seven years that young people expect to spend in education.

In addition to the average six years spent in education, a young person aged 15 can expect to hold a job for 6.5 of the 15 years to come, to be unemployed for a total of 0.8 years and to be out of the labour market for 1.4 years, neither in

A12

education nor seeking work. It is worth noting that, in absolute terms, young people can expect to spend less time in unemployment after completion of initial education than they could ten years ago.

It is in the average duration of spells of unemployment that countries vary most, which mainly reflects differences in youth employment rates. The cumulative average duration of unemployment is four months or below in Denmark, Iceland, Luxembourg, Mexico, the Netherlands and Switzerland, but more than 18 months in Greece, Poland, the Slovak Republic and Turkey.

By and large, men and women differ very little in terms of the expected number of years in unemployment. However, while the situation is similar for both genders in many countries, women appear to be at a disadvantage in Greece, Portugal and Spain and at an advantage in Australia, Canada, Germany, Hungary, the Slovak Republic, Turkey and the United Kingdom. In some of the latter countries, however, notably in Australia, the United Kingdom, and in particular Turkey, the lower expectancy for women is largely influenced by the fact that many women leave the labour market, thereby reducing pressure on jobs.

Whereas young men can expect to spend little more than six months neither in education nor in the labour force between the ages of 15 and 29, the average figure for women is near two years. In the Nordic countries (Iceland, Finland and Sweden), young men and young women do not differ in this measure. Conversely, in the Czech Republic, Hungary, Mexico and Turkey there is a much stronger tendency for young women to leave the labour market. In all of the other countries, women between the ages of 15 and 29 spend an average of about one year more than men outside the labour market.

Definitions and methodologies

The statistics presented here are calculated from labour force survey data on age-specific proportions of young people in each of the specified categories. These proportions are then totalled over the 15 to 29 age group to yield the expected number of years spent in various situations. The calculation thus assumes that young persons currently aged 15 years will show the same pattern of education and work between the ages of 15 and 29 as the population between those age limits in the given data year.

Persons in education may include those attending part-time as well as full-time. The definitions of the various labour force statuses are based on the ILO guidelines, except for the category 'youth in education and employed', which includes all work-study programmes whatever their classification according to the ILO guidelines. The data for this indicator were obtained from a special collection with a reference period in the early part of the calendar year, usually the first quarter or the average of the first three months.

Today a 15-year-old can expect to hold a job for 6.5 years, to be unemployed for almost one year and to be out of the labour force for 1.3 years until the age of 29.

Data are derived from national labour force surveys.

Table A12.1.
Expected years in education and not in education for 15 to 29-year-olds, by gender and work status (2001)

		Expected years in education			Expected years not in education			
		Not employed	Employed (including work study programmes)	Sub-total	Employed	Unemployed	Not in the labour force	Sub-total
Australia	Males	3.0	3.6	6.6	6.9	0.9	0.5	8.4
	Females	2.9	3.5	6.4	6.1	0.7	1.8	8.6
	M+F	3.0	3.5	6.5	6.5	0.8	1.2	8.5
Austria	Males	3.6	1.8	5.4	7.9	0.5	1.3	9.6
	Females	4.3	1.1	5.4	7.6	0.4	1.6	9.6
	M+F	3.9	1.5	5.4	7.7	0.4	1.4	9.6
Belgium	Males	5.9	1.3	7.3	6.4	0.8	0.5	7.7
	Females	6.4	0.8	7.2	5.6	0.8	1.4	7.8
	M+F	6.2	1.1	7.2	6.0	0.8	0.9	7.8
Canada	Males	4.0	2.5	6.5	6.8	1.0	0.7	8.5
	Females	4.0	3.0	7.0	6.0	0.5	1.4	8.0
	M+F	4.0	2.8	6.8	6.4	0.8	1.0	8.2
Czech Republic	Males	3.7	1.2	5.0	8.6	1.1	0.3	10.0
	Females	4.4	0.7	5.1	6.0	1.1	2.8	9.9
	M+F	4.1	1.0	5.1	7.3	1.1	1.6	9.9
Denmark	Males	3.4	4.7	8.1	6.2	0.3	0.3	6.9
	Females	4.0	4.5	8.4	5.3	0.3	0.9	6.6
	M+F	3.7	4.6	8.3	5.8	0.3	0.6	6.7
Finland	Males	5.8	2.3	8.1	5.0	0.7	1.1	6.9
	Females	6.3	2.8	9.1	3.9	0.7	1.2	5.9
	M+F	6.1	2.6	8.6	4.5	0.7	1.2	6.4
France	Males	6.6	1.3	7.8	5.9	0.9	0.3	7.2
	Females	7.0	1.2	8.1	4.6	1.0	1.2	6.9
	M+F	6.8	1.2	8.0	5.3	1.0	0.8	7.0
Germany	Males	4.4	2.5	6.9	6.6	0.8	0.8	8.1
	Females	4.6	2.3	6.9	5.7	0.5	1.9	8.1
	M+F	4.5	2.4	6.9	6.1	0.6	1.3	8.1
Greece	Males	6.0	0.3	6.2	6.9	1.3	0.6	8.8
	Females	6.1	0.2	6.3	4.8	1.8	2.1	8.7
	M+F	6.0	0.2	6.3	5.8	1.6	1.3	8.7
Hungary	Males	5.4	0.6	5.9	7.0	0.9	1.2	9.1
	Females	5.6	0.6	6.2	5.1	0.5	3.2	8.8
	M+F	5.5	0.6	6.1	6.0	0.7	2.2	8.9
Iceland	Males	2.6	5.8	8.4	5.8	0.2	0.5	6.6
	Females	2.3	4.7	7.1	7.6	0.3	0.1	7.9
	M+F	2.5	5.2	7.7	6.7	0.3	0.3	7.3
Ireland	Males	4.5	0.7	5.2	8.8	0.5	0.5	9.8
	Females	5.2	0.9	6.0	7.2	0.3	1.4	9.0
	M+F	4.8	0.8	5.6	8.0	0.4	0.9	9.4
Italy	Males	5.6	0.4	6.0	6.4	1.3	1.3	9.0
	Females	6.1	0.4	6.5	4.6	1.4	2.5	8.5
	M+F	5.8	0.4	6.2	5.5	1.4	1.9	8.8
Japan[1]	Males	5.6	1.0	6.6	2.8	0.4	0.3	3.4
	Females	5.0	0.9	5.9	3.0	0.4	0.7	4.1
	M+F	5.3	1.0	6.3	2.9	0.4	0.5	3.7
Luxembourg	Males	6.1	1.1	7.2	7.1	0.4	0.4	7.8
	Females	6.1	0.8	6.8	6.4	0.2	1.5	8.2
	M+F	6.1	0.9	7.0	6.8	0.3	0.9	8.0
Mexico	Males	3.3	0.9	4.2	9.9	0.3	0.6	10.8
	Females	3.3	0.5	3.9	4.9	0.2	6.1	11.1
	M+F	3.3	0.7	4.0	7.3	0.3	3.4	11.0
Netherlands[2]	Males	2.7	3.1	5.8	8.5	0.3	0.5	9.2
	Females	2.7	3.0	5.7	7.6	0.3	1.4	9.3
	M+F	2.7	3.0	5.7	8.0	0.3	0.9	9.3
Norway[2]	Males	4.1	2.0	6.1	7.9	0.5	0.5	8.9
	Females	4.6	2.8	7.3	6.4	0.3	1.0	7.7
	M+F	4.3	2.4	6.7	7.2	0.4	0.7	8.3
Poland	Males	6.2	1.0	7.2	5.2	2.0	0.6	7.8
	Females	6.5	1.0	7.5	3.8	1.9	1.8	7.5
	M+F	6.4	1.0	7.4	4.5	1.9	1.2	7.6
Portugal	Males	4.5	0.8	5.3	8.7	0.4	0.6	9.7
	Females	5.2	0.8	6.0	7.0	0.7	1.3	9.0
	M+F	4.8	0.8	5.6	7.8	0.6	0.9	9.4
Slovak Republic	Males	3.6	0.8	4.3	6.2	3.0	1.5	10.7
	Females	4.1	0.4	4.5	5.5	2.1	2.9	10.5
	M+F	3.8	0.6	4.4	5.9	2.6	2.2	10.6
Spain	Males	4.8	0.9	5.7	7.7	1.0	0.6	9.3
	Females	5.7	1.0	6.7	5.3	1.3	1.6	8.3
	M+F	5.2	0.9	6.2	6.5	1.2	1.1	8.8
Sweden	Males	4.9	1.7	6.6	7.3	0.6	0.5	8.4
	Females	5.2	2.1	7.3	6.5	0.5	0.7	7.7
	M+F	5.0	1.9	6.9	6.9	0.5	0.6	8.1
Switzerland	Males	3.0	4.3	7.3	6.7	0.2	0.8	7.7
	Females	3.2	3.4	6.6	6.7	0.3	1.4	8.4
	M+F	3.1	3.9	7.0	6.7	0.3	1.1	8.0
Turkey	Males	3.1	0.3	3.4	8.2	1.5	1.9	11.6
	Females	2.3	0.2	2.4	3.4	0.6	8.6	12.6
	M+F	2.7	0.2	2.9	5.9	1.1	5.0	12.1
United Kingdom	Males	2.6	2.6	5.2	8.3	0.9	0.7	9.8
	Females	2.7	2.9	5.6	6.7	0.5	2.2	9.4
	M+F	2.7	2.7	5.4	7.5	0.7	1.4	9.6
United States[2]	Males	3.8	2.6	6.4	7.3	0.5	0.8	8.6
	Females	3.7	2.9	6.6	6.1	0.4	1.9	8.4
	M+F	3.7	2.8	6.5	6.7	0.5	1.4	8.5
Country mean	*Males*	*4.3*	*1.9*	*6.2*	*7.2*	*0.8*	*0.7*	*8.8*
	Females	*4.6*	*1.8*	*6.4*	*5.8*	*0.7*	*2.1*	*8.6*
	M+F	*4.5*	*1.8*	*6.3*	*6.5*	*0.8*	*1.4*	*8.7*

1. Data refer to 15 to 24-year-olds.
2. Year of reference 2000.

Source: OECD. See Annex 3 for national data sources (*www.oecd.org/els/education/eag2002*).

OECD COUNTRIES

A12

THE RETURNS TO EDUCATION: PRIVATE AND SOCIAL RATES OF RETURN TO EDUCATION AND THEIR DETERMINANTS

A13

- Education and earnings are positively linked. Upper secondary and post-secondary non-tertiary education form a break point in many countries beyond which additional education attracts a particularly high premium. In all countries, graduates of tertiary-level education earn substantially more than upper secondary and post-secondary non-tertiary graduates. Earnings differentials between tertiary and upper secondary education are generally more pronounced than those between upper secondary and lower secondary or below.

- Earnings of people with below upper secondary education tend to be 60 to 90 per cent of those of upper secondary and post-secondary non-tertiary graduates.

- Women still earn less than men with similar levels of educational attainment.

Chart A13.1.

Relative earnings with income from employment (2001)
*By level of educational attainment and gender for 25 to 64-year-olds
(upper secondary and post-secondary non-tertiary education =100)*

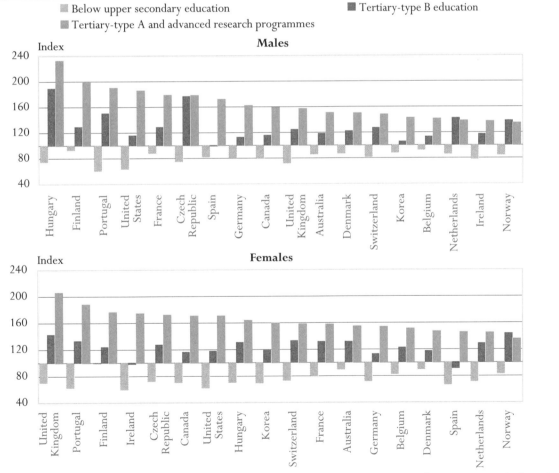

Countries are ranked in descending order of relative earnings for the population having attained the level of tertiary-type A and advanced research programmes.
Source: OECD. Table A13.1. See Annex 3 for national data sources (*www.oecd.org/els/education/eag2002*).

A13

This indicator examines the earnings of workers with differing educational attainment…

…as well as the returns to educational investment and the various costs and benefits influencing them.

Earnings differentials are a measure of the current financial incentives in a particular country for an individual to invest in further education.

Education and earnings are positively linked, whatever the type of socio–economic system or the degree of economic development.

Policy context

One way in which markets provide incentives for individuals to develop and maintain appropriate levels of skills is through wage differentials, in particular through the enhanced earnings accorded to persons completing additional education. The pursuit of higher levels of education can also be viewed as an investment in human capital. Human capital includes the stock of skills that individuals maintain or develop, usually through education or training, and then offer in return for earnings in the labour market. The higher the earnings that result from increases in human capital, the higher the returns on that investment and the premium paid for enhanced skills and/or for higher productivity.

At the same time, education involves costs which need to be considered when examining the returns to investment in education. This indicator examines the returns and the various costs and benefits that influence them.

Evidence and explanations

Education and earnings

Earnings differentials according to educational attainment are a measure of the current financial incentives in a particular country for an individual to invest in further education. Earnings differentials may also reflect differences in the supply of educational programmes at different levels or the barriers in access to those programmes. The earnings benefit of completing tertiary education can be seen by comparing the ratio of the mean annual earnings of those who graduated from tertiary education with the mean annual earnings of upper secondary and post-secondary non-tertiary graduates. The earnings disadvantage from not completing upper secondary or post-secondary non-tertiary education is apparent from a similar comparison. Variations in relative earnings (before taxes) between countries reflect a number of factors, including skill demands in the labour force, minimum wage legislation, the strength of unions, the coverage of collective bargaining agreements, the supply of workers at the various levels of educational attainment, the range of work experience of workers with high and low educational attainment, the distribution of employment between occupations and the relative incidence of part-time and part-year work among workers with varying levels of educational attainment.

Chart A13.1 shows a strong positive relationship between educational attainment and earnings. In all countries, graduates of tertiary-level education earn substantially more than upper secondary and post-secondary non-tertiary graduates. Earnings differentials between tertiary and upper secondary and post-secondary non-tertiary education are generally more pronounced than those between upper secondary and lower secondary or below, suggesting that upper secondary and post-secondary non-tertiary education form a break-point in many countries, beyond which additional education attracts a particularly high premium. Among those countries which report gross earnings, the earnings premium for males aged 25 to 64 years with tertiary-level education ranges from 33 per cent or less in Italy, New Zealand and Norway, to 80 per cent or more in the Czech Republic, Finland, Hungary and Portugal.

The earnings data shown in this indicator differ between countries in a number of ways. Caution should therefore be exercised in interpreting the results. In particular, in countries reporting annual earnings, differences in the incidence of part-year work among individuals with different levels of educational attainment will have an effect on relative earnings that is not reflected in the data for countries reporting weekly or monthly earnings (see definitions below).

Education and gender disparity in earnings

Tertiary education enhances earnings relative to upper secondary and post-secondary non-tertiary education more for females than for males in Australia, Belgium, Canada, Ireland, Korea, the Netherlands, New Zealand, Norway, Switzerland and the United Kingdom, whereas the reverse is true in the remaining countries (Table A13.1).

Although both males and females with upper secondary, post-secondary non-tertiary or tertiary attainment have substantial earnings advantages compared with those of the same gender who do not complete upper secondary education, earnings differentials between males and females with the same educational attainment remain substantial, reinforced by the frequency of part-time work for females.

Earnings differentials between males and females with the same educational attainment remain substantial...

When all levels of education are taken together, the earnings of females between 30 and 44 range from less than 55 per cent of those of males in Switzerland and the United Kingdom to over 75 per cent of those of males in Hungary and Spain (Table A13.2).

Some of the gap in earnings between males and females may be explained by different choices of career and occupation, differences in the amount of time that males and females spend in the labour force, and the relatively high incidence of part-time work among females. Furthermore, earnings data by age suggest that there may be a movement towards more equality of average earnings between males and females across all levels of education, a result which might also be influenced by the increased proportion of females among younger tertiary graduates. In six out of 20 countries, the ratio of female to male earnings at the tertiary-type A and advanced research programmes levels is at least 10 percentage points higher among 30 to 44-year-olds than among 55 to 64-year-olds (Table A13.2).

...with some of the differences explained by career and occupational choices, the amount of time that males and females spend in the labour force, and the relatively high incidence of part-time work among females.

Private internal rates of return to investment in education

The overall incentives to invest in human capital that are embedded in labour market benefits and financing arrangements can be summarised in estimates of the private internal rates of return (Chart A13.2 and Table A13.3). The rate of return represents a measure of the returns obtained, over time, relative to the cost of the initial investment in education. It is expressed as a percentage and is analogous to percentage returns from investing in a savings account (see Annex 3 for an explanation of the methodology at *www.oecd.org/els/education/eag2002*). In its most comprehensive form, the costs equal tuition fees, foregone earnings net of taxes adjusted for the probability of being in employment less the resources made available to students in the form of grants and loans. The benefits are the gains in post-tax earnings adjusted for higher employment probability less the repayment, if any, of public support during the period of study. The calculations assume that the student is full-time in education and has no work activity, hence no earnings while studying. The calculated rates of

Chart A13.2.

Comprehensive private internal rates of return to education (1999-2000)

Impact of length of studies, taxes, unemployment risk, tuition fees and public student support in upper secondary and tertiary education, by gender (in percentage points)

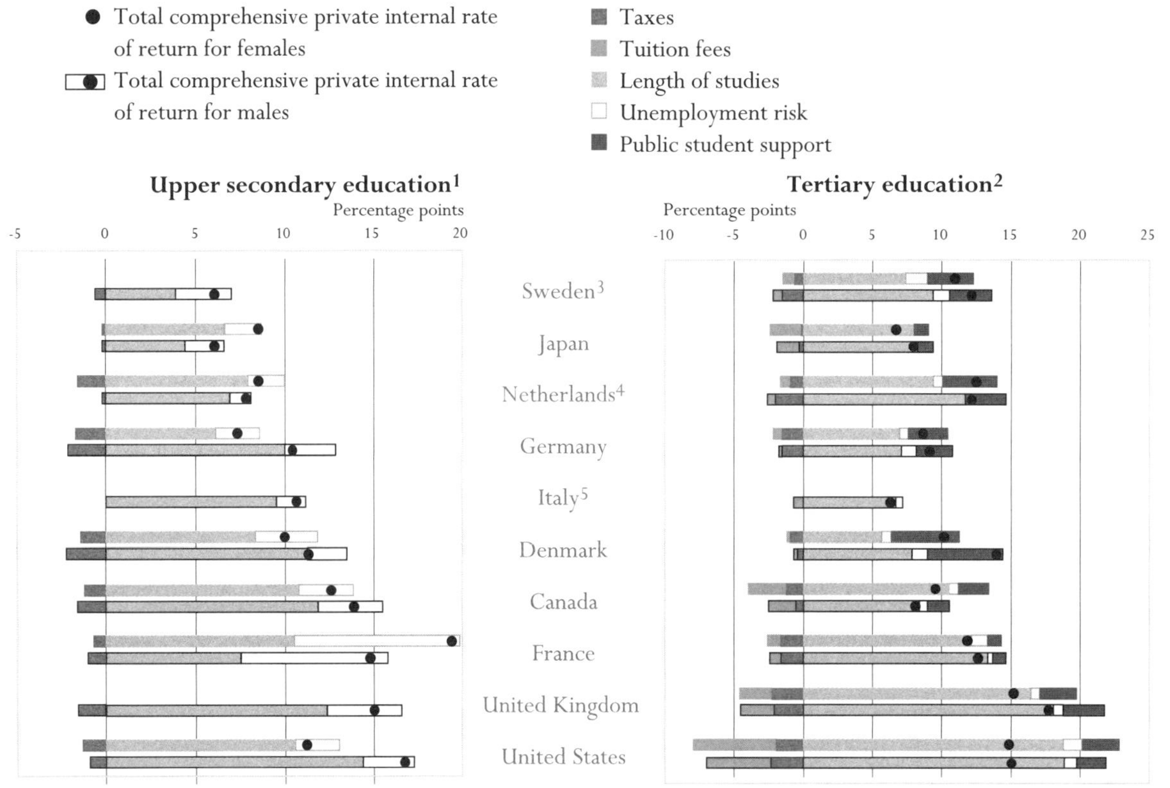

● Total comprehensive private internal rate of return for females

◐ Total comprehensive private internal rate of return for males

■ Taxes
■ Tuition fees
▨ Length of studies
□ Unemployment risk
■ Public student support

Upper secondary education[1]

Tertiary education[2]

Sweden[3]
Japan
Netherlands[4]
Germany
Italy[5]
Denmark
Canada
France
United Kingdom
United States

1. The rate of return to upper secondary education is calculated by comparing the benifits and costs with those of lower secondary education.
2. The rate of return to tertiary education is calculated by comparing the benifits and costs with those of upper secondary education.
3. In tertiary education, the theoretical length of standard tertiary courses is used in the calculations rather than the average theoretical length of different programmes for men and women. For women, earnings differentials between upper and lower secondary levels are not large enough to permit a positive rate of return calculation.
4. Year of reference 1997.
5. Data for males derive from 1998 post-tax earnings data.
Countries are ranked in descending order of the total comprehensive rates of return to education of males in upper secondary education.
Source: OECD. Table A13.3.

The returns to education: Private and social rates of returns to education and their determinants CHAPTER A ■ ·····················

A13

return are, however, likely to be biased upwards as unemployment, retirement and early retirement benefits are not taken into account. The rate-of-return calculations reported in this indicator do not take into account the non-monetary benefits of education.

The estimated private internal rates of return to upper secondary and university education differ significantly across the countries listed in Table A13.3 but are in all cases higher than the real interest rate, and often significantly so, suggesting that human capital investment is an attractive way for the average person to build up wealth. For tertiary studies, three groups of countries can be identified depending on the estimated values of the internal rate of return, which includes the combined effect of earnings, length of studies, taxation, unemployment risk, tuition fees and public student support.

In all countries, the private rate of return is higher than real interest rates, and often significantly so.

- First, with its very high rewards from tertiary education, the United Kingdom is in a group of its own.

- Second, Denmark, France, the Netherlands, Sweden and the United States have relatively high internal rates of return, ranging from 10 to 15 per cent.

- Third, in the remaining countries, rates are below 10 per cent, with the lowest rates recorded for Italy and Japan.

For upper secondary education, the internal rate is calculated to exceed 10 per cent in countries listed in Table A13.3 with the exceptions of Germany (females), Japan, the Netherlands and Sweden.

At the tertiary level, the gender differential in rates of return calculations is limited in most countries. However, at the upper secondary level, gender differences are more marked in Germany and in the United States with returns cut by one-quarter to one-third for females, due to relatively narrow earnings differentials.

As can be seen from Table A13.3, earnings differentials and the length of education are generally the prime determinants of the private internal rates of return. Thus, countries with strong overall incentives to invest in human capital are typically characterised by high education-earnings differentials and/or relatively short education programmes, and *vice versa*. The calculated high rates of return to tertiary education in the United Kingdom, for example, are to an important extent due to relatively short standard university studies, whereas the low rates of return in Germany are strongly influenced by comparatively long study periods. Indeed, if the average length of tertiary studies were shortened by one year without compromising quality, the internal rate of return for males in the countries under review would increase by 1 to 5 percentage points, if all other factors were held constant. To put such a hypothetical shortening of tertiary studies into perspective, it should be noted that to achieve the same

Earnings differentials and the length of education tend to be the prime determinants of the returns…

A13

increase via wider wage differentiation would require an increase in the tertiary wage premium by 5 to 14 percentage points.

There are, however, notable exceptions to this general pattern. Despite narrow wage differentials and long study periods, Denmark and, to a lesser extent, Sweden offer comparatively strong incentives to acquire university education. And France has strong incentives for young people to invest in upper secondary education despite relatively small wage gains compared to the length of such education.

...but there are other factors, including...

The contribution of the various factors to the difference between the narrow internal rate of return, comprising only earnings differentials and the length of education, and the comprehensive rate can be evaluated by adding them successively to the rate-of-return formula:

...taxes, which reduce the returns,...

- *Taxes* reduce the internal rate of return derived from pre-tax earnings and study periods by 1.3 percentage points on average for tertiary education and 1.1 percentage point for upper secondary education in the countries under review. At the tertiary level, the impact of taxes is particularly strong in the United Kingdom and in the United States, mainly reflecting large education-earnings differentials combined with progressive tax systems, but also in the Netherlands and France. At the upper secondary level, the depressing effect of the tax system is most notable in Germany, due to the strong degree of progressivity of the tax system over the relevant earnings range, and in Denmark, while it is the smallest in Japan.

...lower risks of unemployment, which increase the returns,...

- *Unemployment* risk differentials increase the internal rate of return compared with rates based only on pre-tax earnings and the length of study. Reflecting the large differential in unemployment rates between people with lower and upper secondary education, the increase in the internal rate is particularly large for upper secondary education, averaging 3.6 percentage points for males and females for the countries under review. The relatively high unemployment differential in France adds as much as 8.3 to 9.4 percentage points to the internal rate of return. For tertiary education, the differential employment prospects have much less effect on the rates of return, adding on average 0.7 to 0.9 percentage points for males and females, respectively, in the countries included in Table A13.3.

...tuition fees, which reduce the returns...

- *Tuition fees* have a particularly important negative impact on rates of return to tertiary education in the United States, and, to a lesser extent, in Canada and the United Kingdom. In the continental European countries, the impact is significantly smaller due to the much lower level of tuition fees.

...and public grant or loan arrangements, which boost returns.

- *Public student grant and loan arrangements* at the tertiary level give a significant boost to incentives, averaging 2.5 to 3 percentage points in the countries under review, compared with rates of returns excluding such support. The impact is particularly strong in Denmark, the Netherlands and Sweden, while it is weak in France, and absent in Italy.

Social rates of return of investment in education

The benefits to society of additional education can be assessed on the basis of social rates of return. The social internal rate of return needs to reflect the costs and benefits to society of investment in education, which can differ significantly from private costs and benefits. The social cost includes the opportunity cost of having people not participating in the production of output and the full cost of the provision of education rather than only the cost borne by the individual. The social benefit includes the increased productivity associated with the investment in education and a host of possible non-economic benefits, such as lower crime, better health, more social cohesion and more informed and effective citizens. While data on social costs are available for most OECD countries, information about the full range of social benefits is less readily available. To the extent that productivity gains are reflected in labour cost differentials, the latter can be used as a measure of the economic gains for society of education activity. However, the possibility of externalities associated with education suggests that the observed earnings differentials might not fully account for the economy-wide efficiency gains. On the other hand, studies suggest that a (small) part of the wage premia received by better educated individuals is due to educational attainments, signalling inherent abilities to employers rather than productivity differentials due to investment in human capital. And while the non-economic benefits of education are found to be important, it is often difficult to translate them into monetary values for inclusion in rate-of-return calculations.

The benefits to society of additional education can be assessed on the basis of a social rate of return…

In view of the difficulty of constructing comprehensive social rates of return, Table A13.4 presents estimates of a "narrow" definition that abstracts from any externality effects and non-economic benefits. To the extent that there are sizeable positive externalities related to human capital investment by the average student, these estimates will thus be biased downwards.

…which can, however, currently only be estimated in a narrow sense excluding non-economic benefits.

The estimates suggest that the social internal rate of return is particularly high at both the upper secondary and tertiary levels in the United Kingdom and the United States , while it is the lowest in Denmark at both of these education levels. In France, it is moderate for upper secondary education but comparatively high at the tertiary level.

Social returns are still well above risk-free real interest rates, but tend to be lower than private returns, due to the significant social costs of education.

Primarily reflecting that the social cost of education is typically much higher than the private cost, the "narrow" social internal rates of return are significantly lower than the private internal rates of return. At the tertiary level, the differences are particularly large in Denmark and Sweden, with gaps ranging from 4 to almost 7.5 percentage points. At the upper secondary level, differentials between the private and social rates of return are notably wide in France, but comparatively small in Germany and the Netherlands.

A13

The high rates of return can be interpreted as indicating...

The interpretation of the internal rates of return

The private and social internal rates of return reported above are generally well above the risk-free real interest rate. Given that the return on human capital accumulation is subject to considerable uncertainty (as indicated by the wide dispersion of earnings among the better educated), investors are likely to require a compensating risk premium. However, the size of the premium of the internal rates of return over the real interest rate is higher than would seem to be warranted by considerations of risk alone. The high internal rates of return can be interpreted in two different ways.

...a disequilibrium in the market for educated workers, which calls for increasing educational capacity...

One interpretation is that the high rates indicate a serious shortage of better-educated workers driving up their earnings. This might imply a transitory situation, where high returns to education would subsequently generate enough supply response to push the rates into line with returns available on other productive assets. However, the adjustment period could be protracted and the speed of adjustment would depend largely on the capacity of the education system to respond to the derived increase in demand and the capacity of the labour market to absorb the changing relative supplies of labour. The re-balancing mechanism could also be accelerated by better availability of information to students about the returns to different courses of study, thereby helping them to make more informed choices.

...or significantly lower marginal returns than average returns...

Part of the high returns may also be compatible with market equilibrium. This would be the case if the marginal rates are significantly lower than the average rates. The marginal rate would indeed be lower than the average rate if the students at the margin are of lower ability and motivation than the average students, and thus unlikely to be able to command the average wage premium. According to this interpretation, the high internal rates of return would partly reflect economic rents on a scarce resource, namely ability and motivation.

...which would lessen the case for public intervention.

If the returns to education at the margin are lower, the case for public intervention to stimulate human capital accumulation is lessened if the quality of the marginal student cannot be improved. On the other hand, to the extent that the education system can improve cognitive and non-cognitive skills of young people, education policy could make a significant contribution to efficiency and equity in the longer run.

Definitions and methodologies

Data are derived from national labour force surveys and other surveys.

Relative earnings from employment are defined as the mean earnings (income from work before taxes) of persons at a given level of educational attainment divided by the mean earnings of persons with upper secondary education. This ratio is then multiplied by 100. The estimates are restricted to individuals with income from employment during the reference period.

Earnings data in Table A13.1 are annual for most countries but for France, Spain and Switzerland they are monthly. In Belgium and France, data cover the earnings

The returns to education: Private and social rates of returns to education and their determinants **CHAPTER A** ■ ·····················

A13

of employees only. The Spanish data exclude people who work fewer than fifteen hours a week. The observed differences in relative earnings between countries therefore reflect variations not only in wage rates but also in coverage, in the number of weeks worked per year and in hours worked per week. Since lower educational attainment is associated with fewer hours of work (in particular with part-time work) and with less stable employment (more likelihood of temporary employment or more susceptibility to unemployment over the course of a year), the relative earnings charts shown for higher educational attainment in the tables and charts will be greater than what would be evident from an examination of relative rates of pay. The observed differences in relative earnings of males and females within a country can likewise be affected by some of these factors.

For the methods employed for the calculation of the rates of return in Tables A13.3 and A13.4, see Annex 3 at *www.oecd.org/els/education/eag2002*.

Table A13.1.
Relative earnings of the population with income from employment
By level of educational attainment and gender for 25 to 64-year-olds and 30 to 44-year-olds (upper secondary and post-secondary non-tertiary education = 100)

			Below upper secondary education		Tertiary-type B education		Tertiary-type A and advanced research programmes		Tertiary education	
			25-64	30-44	25-64	30-44	25-64	30-44	25-64	30-44
			(1)	(2)	(3)	(4)	(5)	(6)	(7)	(8)
Australia	1999	Males	86	83	118	120	151	149	139	139
		Females	89	88	131	130	155	155	146	146
		M+F	80	78	116	115	144	143	134	133
Belgium	2000	Males	93	x(1)	113	x(3)	141	x(5)	128	x(7)
		Females	82	x(1)	122	x(3)	151	x(5)	132	x(7)
		M+F	92	x(1)	112	x(3)	146	x(5)	128	x(7)
Canada	1999	Males	79	78	116	117	159	159	137	137
		Females	70	69	116	118	171	189	140	148
		M+F	79	79	112	113	162	167	135	138
Czech Republic	1999	Males	75	77	177	182	178	176	178	177
		Females	72	75	127	124	172	176	170	174
		M+F	68	70	151	151	180	182	179	181
Denmark	1999	Males	87	85	122	118	150	145	133	129
		Females	90	90	117	112	147	146	123	120
		M+F	86	85	112	108	151	146	124	120
Finland	1999	Males	93	90	129	125	200	188	167	159
		Females	99	96	124	123	176	172	145	141
		M+F	96	94	120	115	190	179	153	144
France	1999	Males	88	86	128	137	178	181	159	163
		Females	79	81	131	139	158	165	145	152
		M+F	84	84	125	133	169	174	150	155
Germany	2000	Males	80	87	112	110	162	160	141	139
		Females	72	71	113	114	154	153	137	137
		M+F	75	78	115	114	163	160	143	141
Hungary	2001	Males	75	76	189	170	233	237	232	237
		Females	71	74	130	119	164	163	164	162
		M+F	71	73	151	136	194	191	194	190
Ireland	1998	Males	78	84	117	126	137	143	131	136
		Females	59	60	98	83	175	170	145	136
		M+F	79	81	111	117	157	157	142	140
Italy	1998	Males	54	55	x(5)	x(6)	138	142	138	142
		Females	61	56	x(5)	x(6)	115	114	115	114
		M+F	58	57	x(5)	x(6)	127	126	127	126
Korea	1998	Males	88	90	105	109	143	136	132	129
		Females	69	75	118	138	160	181	141	164
		M+F	78	80	106	113	147	142	135	134
Netherlands	1997	Males	86	85	142	128	138	130	139	130
		Females	71	71	128	133	145	150	143	148
		M+F	83	83	136	129	141	136	141	135
New Zealand	2001	Males	76	74	x(7)	x(8)	x(7)	x(8)	130	122
		Females	72	72	x(7)	x(8)	x(7)	x(8)	136	135
		M+F	74	75	x(7)	x(8)	x(7)	x(8)	133	128
Norway	1999	Males	85	88	138	141	134	136	135	137
		Females	83	87	144	150	135	137	135	138
		M+F	84	89	153	153	131	131	133	133
Portugal	1999	Males	60	57	150	155	190	194	180	185
		Females	63	58	133	139	188	206	170	185
		M+F	62	58	141	146	192	202	178	187
Spain	1998	Males	82	76	99	103	172	155	152	138
		Females	66	56	91	89	145	138	137	130
		M+F	80	72	99	101	157	144	144	133
Sweden	1999	Males	87	86	x(7)	x(8)	x(7)	x(8)	138	140
		Females	88	87	x(7)	x(8)	x(7)	x(8)	126	122
		M+F	89	88	x(7)	x(8)	x(7)	x(8)	131	131
Switzerland	2001	Males	81	81	127	128	148	144	139	138
		Females	73	74	133	142	158	167	150	158
		M+F	78	78	144	147	164	162	157	156
United Kingdom	2001	Males	72	67	124	126	157	162	147	151
		Females	70	74	142	133	206	216	183	183
		M+F	67	68	128	124	174	181	159	161
United States	2001	Males	64	63	116	115	186	183	178	175
		Females	62	61	117	119	171	173	164	166
		M+F	65	64	114	113	181	178	172	169

Note: x indicates that data are included in another column. The column reference is shown in brackets after "x". *e.g.*, x(2) means that data are included in column 2.
Source: OECD. See Annex 3 for national data sources (*www.oecd.org/els/education/eag2002*).

OECD COUNTRIES

A13

Table A13.2.
Differences in earnings between women and men
Average annual earnings of women as a percentage of men by level of educational attainment of 30 to 44-year-olds and 55 to 64-year-olds

A13

		Below upper secondary education		Upper secondary and post-secondary non-tertiary education		Tertiary-type B education		Tertiary-type A and advanced research programmes		All levels of education	
		30-44	55-64	30-44	55-64	30-44	55-64	30-44	55-64	30-44	55-64
		(1)	(2)	(3)	(4)	(5)	(6)	(7)	(8)	(9)	(10)
Australia	1999	66	67	63	75	68	66	65	58	65	66
Canada	1999	51	61	58	66	59	57	69	65	63	62
Czech Republic	1999	66	58	67	64	45	62	67	63	63	61
Denmark	1999	76	67	72	67	68	65	72	71	73	65
Finland	1999	74	78	69	77	68	73	63	65	70	70
France	1999	70	62	75	69	76	72	68	64	74	60
Germany	2000	51	49	62	59	64	65	59	62	60	53
Hungary	2001	83	81	84	94	59	48	58	69	77	78
Ireland	1998	50	36	70	55	46	43	83	60	66	43
Italy	1998	71	70	69	43	x(7)	x(8)	56	45	73	57
Korea	1998	57	62	69	70	87	96	92	99	67	50
Netherlands	1997	46	43	55	50	57	39	63	50	55	45
New Zealand	2001	59	57	61	70	x(7)	x(8)	68	54	62	62
Norway	1999	60	61	61	63	64	65	61	61	62	61
Portugal	1999	72	70	70	67	63	57	75	68	73	66
Spain	1998	61	x(1)	81	x(3)	70	x(5)	73	x(7)	79	x(9)
Sweden	1999	74	73	74	69	x(9)	x(10)	x(9)	x(10)	71	70
Switzerland	2001	50	50	55	52	61	42	63	66	54	47
United Kingdom	2001	55	43	50	53	53	81	66	66	54	54
United States	2001	58	65	60	54	62	57	57	50	60	51

Note: x indicates that data are included in another column. The column reference is shown in brackets after "x". *e.g.*, x(2) means that data are included in column 2.
Source: OECD. See Annex 3, Table 6 for national data sources (*www.oecd.org/els/education/eag2002*).

Table A13.3.
Private internal rates of return to education (1999-2000)
The impact of length of studies, taxes, unemployment risk, tuition fees and public student support in upper secondary and tertiary education, by gender (in percentage points)

	Return on upper secondary education (in percentage points)[1]								Return on tertiary education (in percentage points)[2]												
	Comprehensive private internal rate of return		Impact of						Comprehensive private internal rate of return		Impact of										
			Length of studies		Taxes		Unemployment risk				Length of studies		Taxes		Unemployment risk		Tuition fees		Public student support	
	Males	Females	Males	Females	Males	Females	Males	Females	Males	Females	Males	Females	Males	Females	Males	Females	Males	Females	Males	Females
Canada	13.6	12.7	11.9	10.8	-1.6	-1.2	3.6	3.1	8.1	9.4	8.4	10.6	-0.5	-1.3	0.6	0.6	-2.0	-2.7	1.6	2.2
Denmark	11.3	10.5	11.3	8.3	-2.2	-1.4	2.2	3.6	13.9	10.1	7.9	5.7	-0.4	-1.0	1.1	0.7	-0.1	-0.2	5.4	4.9
France	14.8	19.2	7.5	10.5	-1.0	-0.7	8.3	9.4	12.2	11.7	13.3	12.1	-1.6	-1.7	0.4	1.2	-0.8	-0.9	0.9	1.0
Germany	10.8	6.9	10.0	6.1	-2.1	-1.7	2.9	2.5	9.0	8.3	7.1	7.0	-1.5	-1.6	1.1	0.6	-0.3	-0.6	2.6	2.9
Italy[3]	11.2	m	9.5	m	m	m	1.7	m	6.5	m	6.7	m	m	m	0.5	m	-0.7	m	n	m
Japan	6.4	8.5	4.4	6.6	-0.2	-0.2	2.2	2.1	7.5	6.7	8.0	8.0	-0.3	-0.2	0.3	0.0	-1.6	-2.2	1.1	1.1
Netherlands[4]	7.9	8.4	6.9	7.9	-0.2	-1.6	1.2	2.1	12.0	12.3	11.7	9.4	-2.0	-1.0	n	0.7	-0.6	-0.7	2.9	3.9
Sweden[5]	6.4	m	3.9	m	-0.6	m	3.1	m	11.4	10.8	9.4	7.4	-1.5	-0.7	1.2	1.6	-0.7	-0.8	3.0	3.3
United Kingdom	15.1	m	12.4	m	-1.5	m	4.2	m	17.3	15.2	18.1	16.4	-2.1	-2.3	0.7	0.7	-2.4	-2.3	3.0	2.7
United States	16.4	11.8	14.4	10.6	-0.9	-1.3	2.9	2.5	14.9	14.7	18.9	18.8	-2.3	-2.0	0.9	1.4	-4.7	-6.0	2.1	2.7
Country mean[6]	*11.4*	*11.1*	*9.2*	*8.7*	*-1.1*	*-1.1*	*3.6*	*3.6*	*11.8*	*11.3*	*11.4*	*10.6*	*-1.3*	*-1.3*	*0.7*	*0.9*	*-1.5*	*-1.8*	*2.5*	*2.9*

1. The rate of return to upper secondary education is calculated by comparing the benefits and costs with those of lower secondary education.
2. The rate of return to tertiary education is calculated by comparing the benefits and costs with those of upper secondary education.
3. Data for males derive from 1998 post-tax earnings data.
4. Year of reference 1997.
5. In tertiary education, the theoretical length of standard tertiary courses is used in the calculations rather than the average theoretical length of different programmes for men and women. For women, earnings differential between upper and lower secondary levels are not large enough to permit a positive rate of return calculation.
6. Data for men exclude Italy; data for women in upper secondary education exclude Sweden and the United Kingdom.
Source: OECD.

Table A13.4.
Social rates of return to education (1999-2000)
Rates of return to upper secondary and tertiary education, by gender (in percentage points)

| | Social return in upper secondary education[1] | | Social return in tertiary education[2] | |
	Males	Females	Males	Females
Canada[3]	m	m	6.8	7.9
Denmark	9.3	8.7	6.3	4.2
France	9.6	10.6	13.2	13.1
Germany	10.2	6.0	6.5	6.9
Italy[4]	8.4	m	7.0	m
Japan	5.0	6.4	6.7	5.7
Netherlands	6.2	7.8	10.0	6.3
Sweden	5.2	m	7.5	5.7
United Kingdom	12.9	m	15.2	13.6
United States	13.2	9.6	13.7	12.3

1. The rate of return to upper secondary education is calculated by comparing the benefits and costs with those of lower secondary education.
2. The rate of return to tertiary education is calculated by comparing the benefits and costs with those of upper secondary education.
3. In Canada, no data were available on expenditure per student in upper secondary education.
4. In Italy, the sample size of earnings for women was not large enough to allow for the calculation of rates of return.
Source: OECD.

THE RETURNS TO EDUCATION: LINKS BETWEEN HUMAN CAPITAL AND ECONOMIC GROWTH

A14

- The accumulation of physical capital and human capital is important for economic growth, and differences between countries in this respect help significantly to explain the observed differences in growth patterns. In particular, the evidence suggests that investment in education may have beneficial external effects that make social returns to schooling greater than private returns, although improvements to education systems may take time to make significant impacts on average skills in the labour force, especially in ageing populations.

- Public expenditure on health, education and research clearly help to sustain living standards in the long term, and social transfers help to meet social goals, but these must all be financed. The necessary taxation could negatively affect incentives to save and invest.

- Macroeconomic policy geared towards low inflation and stable, sound public finances contributes to growth, for example by encouraging private accumulation of physical capital and a shift in investment towards projects with higher returns.

Chart A14.1.

Decomposition of changes in annual average growth rates of GDP per capita

Estimated effect of changes in explanatory variables to changes in output per capita growth rates over the period 1980s to 1990s

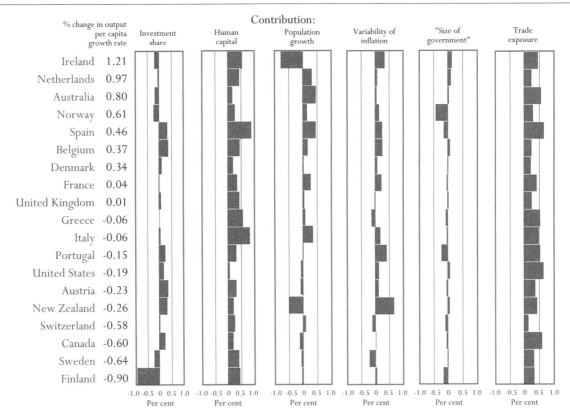

Countries are ranked in descending order of the percentage change in output per capita growth rate.
Source: OECD Economic Outlook, December 2000. Table A14.1.

This indicator estimates the effect of changes in explanatory variables, including human capital, on changes in output per capita growth rates over the period 1980 to 1990.

Policy context

OECD countries have shown wide disparities in growth in recent decades. The 1990s, in particular, saw some relatively affluent countries (notably the United States) pulling further ahead, while growth in many other countries slowed. Persistent differences in the accumulation of different forms of capital (physical, human), market conditions and technological progress – all of which could be influenced by policy and institutions – are potentially important sources of these growth differences between countries. What is the relative importance of education and human capital in this equation? To address this question, this indicator estimates the effect of changes in explanatory variables, including human capital, on changes in output per capita growth rates over the period 1980 to 1990.

Evidence and explanations

Although there is agreement on the importance of policy and institutions for growth, the precise mechanisms linking policy to capital accumulation, economic efficiency, technical progress and, ultimately, output growth are still the subject of intense debate. In particular, policy and institutions may influence private decisions on savings and investment and the formation of human capital. They can also contribute to the overall efficiency with which resources are allocated in the economy over and above their effects on the accumulation of physical and human capital.

The precise mechanisms linking policy to capital accumulation, economic efficiency, technical progress and, ultimately, output growth are still the subject of an intense debate.

Studies on growth typically assume that formal skills and experience embodied in the labour force represent a form of (human) capital. It can be argued, however, that human capital, like physical capital, is subject to some kind of diminishing returns, so that a more highly trained and skilled workforce would enjoy higher levels of income in the long term, but not necessarily permanently higher rates of growth in income. Similarly, investment in human capital (*e.g.*, expenditure on education and training) could have a more permanent impact on growth if high skills and training were to go hand in hand with more intensive research and development and a faster rate of technological progress, or if the existence of a highly skilled labour force were to ease the adoption of new technologies.

The improvement in human capital has been a common factor behind growth in recent decades, and in some countries accounted for more than half a percentage point of growth in the 1990s.

In order to shed light on the impact of policy and institutions on output growth in OECD countries, an empirical analysis based on growth regressions was undertaken (for details see *Economic Outlook,* No. 68). Chart A14.1 shows the estimated effect of changes in explanatory variables on changes in output per capita growth rates from the 1980s to the 1990s.

The improvement in human capital seems to be a common factor behind growth in recent decades in all OECD countries, especially in Greece, Ireland, Italy and Spain, where the increase in human capital accounted for more than half an extra percentage point of growth in the 1990s compared with the previous decade. The impact might be seen to be larger if the measure of human capital used went beyond levels of formal educational attainment. However, although average levels of human capital have typically been rising – and continually feeding through into higher growth – the relatively slow rates of increase (half to one percentage point per decade) need to be borne in mind in evaluating this result.

The magnitude of the impact on growth found in this analysis suggests that the social returns to investment in education may be larger than those experienced by individuals. This possibly reflects spill-over effects, such as links between levels of education and advances in technology, and more effective use of natural and physical resources, and implies that incentives for individuals to engage in education may be usefully enhanced by policy to reap maximum benefits for society as a whole. However, there are some caveats to this interpretation of the results. First, the impacts found in the analysis may be over-estimated because the indicator of human capital may be acting partially as a proxy for other variables, an issue also raised in some microeconomic studies. In addition, the empirical analysis suggests that the impact is determined with some imprecision. In any case, the average level of formal education is bound to react only slowly to changes in education policy, as the latter typically affect only young cohorts entering the labour force. Finally, extending the period of formal education may not be the most efficient way of providing workplace skills, and this aspect of education must also be balanced against other (sometimes competing) goals of education systems. Thus, for those countries at the forefront of educational provision, the growth dividend from further increases in formal education may be less marked than that implied in the empirical analysis.

The magnitude of the impact on growth found in this analysis suggests that the social returns to investment in education may be larger than those experienced by individuals

The contribution stemming from changes in the investment rate is more mixed. Some countries are estimated to have benefited from an increase in the business investment rate in the past decade (*e.g.*, Austria, Belgium, Canada, New Zealand, Portugal and Spain), while others experienced a negative impact from lower investment rates (*e.g.*, Finland, and to a lesser extent Norway and Sweden). There have also been important changes in policy and institutional settings in each country that have contributed to growth, over and above the changes in inputs of physical and human capital. Most countries have benefited, especially in the 1990s, from lower variability in inflation. The most noticeable examples include New Zealand and Portugal, where about half a percentage point of annual output per capita growth is estimated to be due to this factor, other things being equal.

The impact stemming from changes in the investment rate varies.

By contrast, despite greater fiscal discipline, especially in the last decade, the rise in the size of government has contributed to a marginal slowing of growth in many countries. Exceptions include Ireland and the Netherlands, where a reduction in taxes and expenditure as a proportion of GDP marginally boosted output per capita growth in the 1990s.

The size of government has contributed to a marginal slowing of growth in many countries.

Finally, the general process of trade liberalisation in which all OECD countries have been involved is estimated to have increased growth by up to two-thirds

A14

The general process of trade liberalisation is estimated to have increased growth by up to two-thirds of a percentage point annually over the past decade.

of a percentage point annually over the past decade. Despite developments in the 1990s, there remain profound differences in the main determinants of economic growth across the OECD countries.

Definitions and methodologies

Human capital is estimated on the basis of completed levels of education and average years of schooling at each level in the working age population. It should be borne in mind that educational attainment is a crude and somewhat narrow proxy for skills and competencies, taking little account of the quality of formal education or of other important dimensions of human capital. It is derived from OECD data combined with data from de la Fuente and Doménech (2000). For a definition of the other factors (investment share, population growth, variability of inflation, trade exposure and size of government), see *Economic Outlook*, No. 68. Note that government consumption as a percentage of GDP is used as a proxy for the size of government for reasons of data availability. This variable is highly correlated in most countries with tax and non-tax receipts (as a proportion of GDP), although country coverage is more limited.

The calculations are from decompositions of differences in growth rates based on the results of multivariate regressions. Note that the sum of the contributions shown does not correspond to the observed change in output per capita growth rates because the estimated impact of initial levels of GDP per capita and the component unexplained by the regressions are not shown.

Chart A14.1 does not report the estimated effect on growth of different initial conditions (*i.e.*, the convergence process) nor does it show the unexplained country-specific effect. The coefficients used to perform the decomposition are from a growth equation that includes variability in inflation, trade exposure and government consumption (as a proportion of GDP) as a proxy for the potential effect of government "size" on growth.

The changes in growth are based on differences in average growth in GDP per person of working age over each decade. The 1980s cover the period 1981 to 1989; the 1990s cover the period up to 1997.

Table A14.1.
Decomposition of changes in annual average growth rates of GDP per capita (1980-1997)
Estimated effect of changes in explanatory variables to changes in output per capita growth rates over the period 1980s to 1990s[1] (in percentage points)

A14

	% change in output per capita growth rate	Contribution from:					
		Investment share	Human capital	Population growth	Variability of inflation	"Size of government"[2]	Trade exposure
Australia	0.80	-0.16	0.17	0.46	0.05	0.03	0.57
Austria	-0.23	0.37	0.31	-0.07	0.12	-0.02	0.37
Belgium	0.37	0.37	0.45	0.17	0.26	0.06	0.24
Canada	-0.60	0.24	0.19	-0.10	0.01	-0.02	0.60
Denmark	0.34	0.10	0.20	0.03	0.07	0.01	0.22
Finland	-0.90	-0.91	0.44	-0.03	0.05	-0.13	0.33
France	0.04	0.01	0.35	0.27	0.23	-0.02	0.42
Greece	-0.06	n	0.57	0.09	-0.12	-0.05	0.54
Ireland	1.21	-0.17	0.54	-0.75	0.35	0.13	0.46
Italy	-0.06	0.05	0.84	0.36	0.18	-0.01	0.49
Netherlands	0.97	-0.04	0.43	0.32	0.07	0.10	0.25
New Zealand	-0.26	0.33	0.21	-0.47	0.68	0.06	0.44
Norway	0.61	-0.21	0.27	0.15	0.14	-0.41	0.30
Portugal	-0.15	0.25	0.32	0.02	0.42	-0.20	0.53
Spain	0.46	0.33	0.90	0.46	0.25	-0.12	0.67
Sweden	-0.64	-0.19	0.42	-0.05	-0.20	0.02	0.33
Switzerland	-0.58	0.02	0.26	0.09	-0.09	-0.07	0.14
United Kingdom	0.01	0.08	0.44	0.05	n	0.03	0.25
United States	-0.19	0.19	0.07	-0.06	0.13	0.07	0.65

Note: The calculations are from decompositions of differences in growth rates based on the results of multivariate regressions. The sums of the contributions shown do not correspond to the change in output per capita growth rates because the estimated impact of initial levels of GDP per capita and the component unexplained by the regressions are not shown.

1. Changes in growth are based on differences in average growth in GDP per person of working age over each decade. The 1980s include the period 1981 to 1989; the 1990s cover the period up to 1997.

2. Government consumption as a percentage of GDP is used as a proxy for the size of government due to data inavailability. This variable is highly correlated in most countries with tax and non-tax receipts (as a share of GDP) for which, however, country coverage is more limited.

Source: OECD Economic Outlook, December 2000.

FINANCIAL AND HUMAN RESOURCES INVESTED IN EDUCATION

OVERVIEW

Indicator B1: Educational expenditure per student

Table B1.1. Expenditure on educational institutions per student (1999)
Table B1.2. Expenditure on educational institutions per student relative to GDP per capita (1999)
Table B1.3. Cumulative expenditure on educational institutions per student over the average duration of tertiary studies (1999)

Chapter B reviews the financial and human resources invested in education, in terms of...

Indicator B2: Expenditure on educational institutions relative to Gross Domestic Product

Table B2.1a. Expenditure on educational institutions as a percentage of GDP for all levels of education (1995, 1999)
Table B2.1b. Expenditure on educational institutions as a percentage of GDP, by level of education (1995, 1999)
Table B2.1c. Expenditure on educational institutions as a percentage of GDP, by level of education (1999)
Table B2.2. Change of expenditure on educational institutions (1995, 1999)

...the resources that each country invests in education, relative to the number of students enrolled, national income and the size of public budgets,...

Indicator B3: Total public expenditure on education

Table B3.1. Total public expenditure on education (1995, 1999)

Indicator B4: Relative proportions of public and private investment in educational institutions

Table B4.1. Relative proportions of public and private expenditure on educational institutions for all levels of education (1995, 1999)
Table B4.2. Relative proportions of public and private expenditure on educational institutions, by level of education (1995, 1999)
Table B4.3. Distribution of total public expenditure on education (1999)

...the ways in which education systems are financed, and the sources from which the funds originate,...

Indicator B5: Support for students and households through public subsidies

Table B5.1. Public subsides to the private sector as a percentage of total public expenditure on education and GDP for primary, secondary and post-secondary non-tertiary education (1999)
Table B5.2. Public subsides to the private sector as a percentage of total public expenditure on education and GDP for tertiary education (1999)

...different financing instruments,...

Indicator B6: Expenditure on institutions by service category and by resource category

Table B6.1. Expenditure on instruction, research and development (R&D) and ancillary services in educational institutions as a percentage of GDP, and private expenditure on educational goods purchased outside educational institutions as a percentage of GDP (1999)
Table B6.2. Expenditure per student on instruction, ancillary services and research and development (R&D) (1999)
Table B6.3. Expenditure on educational institutions by resource category (1999)

...and how the money is invested and apportioned between different resource categories.

B

Classification of educational expenditure

ducational expenditure in this chapter are classified through three dimensions:

- The first dimension – represented by the horizontal axis in the diagram below – relates to the location where spending occurs. Spending on schools and universities, education ministries and other agencies directly involved in providing and supporting education is one component of this dimension. Spending on education outside these institutions is another.

- The second dimension – represented by the vertical axis in the diagram below – classifies the goods and services that are purchased. Not all expenditure on educational institutions can be classified as direct educational or instructional expenditure. Educational institutions in many OECD countries not only offer teaching services but also various ancillary services to support students and their families, such as meals, transport, housing, etc. In addition, at the tertiary level spending on research and development can be significant. Not all spending on educational goods and services occurs within educational institutions. For example, families may purchase textbooks and materials themselves or seek private tutoring for their children.

- The third dimension – represented by the colours in the diagram below – distinguishes between the sources from which the funds originate. These include the public sector and international agencies (indicated by the light blue colour) and households and other private entities (indicated by the mid-blue colour). Where private expenditure on education is subsidised by public funds, this is indicated by cells in dark blue colour. The diagram is reported at the beginning of each indicator to signal its coverage.

	Spending on educational institutions (e.g., schools, universities, educational administration and student welfare services)	Spending on education outside educational institutions (e.g., private purchases of educational goods and services, including private tutoring)
Spending on educational core services	e.g., public spending on instructional services in educational institutions	e.g., subsidised private spending on books
	e.g., subsidised private spending on instructional services in institutions	e.g., private spending on books and other school materials or private tutoring
	e.g., private spending on tuition fees	
Spending on research and development	e.g., public spending on university research	
	e.g., funds from private industry for research and development in educational institutions	
Spending on educational services other than instruction	e.g., public spending on ancillary services such as meals, transport to schools, or housing on the campus	e.g., subsidised private spending on student living costs or reduced prices for transport
	e.g.., private spending on fees for ancillary services	e.g., private spending on student living costs or transport

  ☐ Public sources of funds   ■ Private sources funds   ■ Private funds publicly subsidised

EDUCATION AT A GLANCE © OECD 2002

EDUCATIONAL EXPENDITURE PER STUDENT

- As a whole, OECD countries spend US$ 4 229 per primary student, US$ 5 174 per secondary student and US$ 11 422 per tertiary student, but these averages mask a broad range of expenditure across countries.

- Lower unit expenditure cannot automatically be equated with a lower quality of educational services. Australia, Finland, Korea and the United Kingdom, for example, which have moderate expenditure on education per student at primary and lower secondary levels, are among the OECD countries with the highest levels of performance by 15-year-olds students in key subject areas.

- On average, OECD countries spend 2.3 times as much per student at the tertiary level than at the primary level.

B1

- In some OECD countries, low annual expenditure per tertiary student still translates into high overall costs of tertiary education because the duration of tertiary studies is long.

- At the tertiary level of education, spending on education has not always kept pace with the rapid expansion of enrolments.

Chart B1.1.

Expenditure on educational institutions per student (1999)

Annual expenditure on educational institutions per student in US dollars converted using PPPs, by level of education, based on full-time equivalents

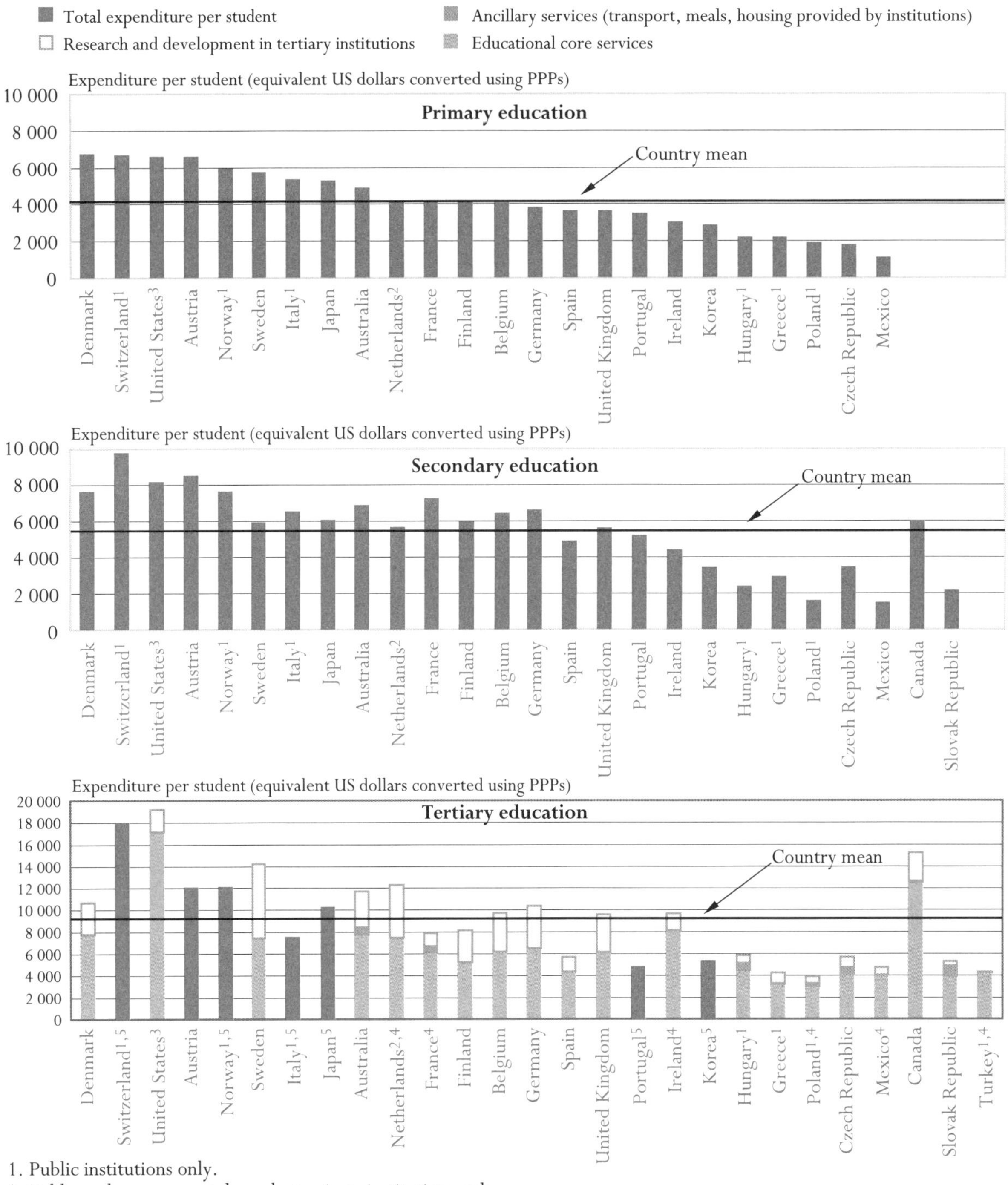

- ■ Total expenditure per student
- □ Research and development in tertiary institutions
- ■ Ancillary services (transport, meals, housing provided by institutions)
- ■ Educational core services

B1

Expenditure per student (equivalent US dollars converted using PPPs)

Primary education

Country mean

Denmark, Switzerland[1], United States[3], Austria, Norway[1], Sweden, Italy[1], Japan, Australia, Netherlands[2], France, Finland, Belgium, Germany, Spain, United Kingdom, Portugal, Ireland, Korea, Hungary[1], Greece[1], Poland[1], Czech Republic, Mexico

Expenditure per student (equivalent US dollars converted using PPPs)

Secondary education

Country mean

Denmark, Switzerland[1], United States[3], Austria, Norway[1], Sweden, Italy[1], Japan, Australia, Netherlands[2], France, Finland, Belgium, Germany, Spain, United Kingdom, Portugal, Ireland, Korea, Hungary[1], Greece[1], Poland[1], Czech Republic, Mexico, Canada, Slovak Republic

Expenditure per student (equivalent US dollars converted using PPPs)

Tertiary education

Country mean

Denmark, Switzerland[1,5], United States[3], Austria, Norway[1,5], Sweden, Italy[1,5], Japan[5], Australia, Netherlands[2,4], France[4], Finland, Belgium, Germany, Spain, United Kingdom, Portugal[5], Ireland[4], Korea[5], Hungary[1], Greece[1], Poland[1,4], Czech Republic, Mexico[4], Canada, Slovak Republic, Turkey[1,4]

1. Public institutions only.
2. Public and government-dependent private institutions only.
3. Public and independent private institutions only.
4. Research and development expenditure at tertiary level and thus total expenditure are underestimated.
5. The bar represents total expenditure at tertiary level and includes research and development expenditure.
Countries are ranked in descending order of expenditure per student in primary education.
Source: OECD. Tables B1.1 and B6.2. See Annex 3 for notes *(www.oecd.org/els/education/eag2002).*

Policy context

Effective schools require the right combination of trained and talented personnel, adequate facilities, state-of-the-art equipment and motivated students ready to learn. The demand for high-quality education, which can translate into higher costs per student, needs to be balanced against placing undue burdens on taxpayers.

This indicator shows annual and cumulative expenditure on education per student in absolute terms…

As a result, the question of whether the resources devoted to education yield adequate returns to the investments made figures prominently in the public debate. Although the optimal volume of resources required to prepare each student for life and work in the modern economy is difficult to assess, international comparisons of spending on education per student can provide a starting point for evaluating the effectiveness of different models of educational provision.

…and relative to GDP per capita.

B1

Policy-makers must also balance the importance of improving the quality of educational services with the desirability of expanding access to educational opportunities, notably at the tertiary level. The comparative review in this indicator of how trends in expenditure on education per student have evolved shows how the expansion of enrolments in many OECD countries, particularly in tertiary education, has not always been paralleled by changes in educational investment.

It also compares trends in the development of expenditure on education per student.

Finally, decisions on the allocation of funds to the various levels of education are also important. For example, some OECD countries emphasise broad access to higher education while others invest in near-universal education for children as young as three or four years of age.

Evidence and explanations

What this indicator covers and what it does not cover

The indicator shows direct public and private expenditure on educational institutions in relation to the number of full-time equivalent students enrolled in these institutions.

Public subsidies for students' living expenses have been excluded to ensure international comparability of the data. Expenditure data for students in private educational institutions are not available for certain OECD countries, and some other countries do not report complete data on independent private institutions. Where this is the case, only the expenditure on public and government-dependent private institutions has been taken into account. Note that variation in expenditure on education per student may reflect not only variation in the material resources provided to students (*e.g.*, variations in the ratio of students to teaching staff) but also variation in relative salary levels.

Coverage diagram (see page 144 for explanations)

While educational expenditure is dominated below the tertiary level by spending on instructional services, at the tertiary level, other services, particularly those related to R&D activities, can account for a significant proportion of educational spending. Indicator B6 provides further information on how spending is distributed by different types of services provided.

Expenditure on education per student in equivalent US dollars

As a whole, OECD countries spend US$ 4 229 per primary student, US$ 5 174 per secondary student and US$ 11 422 per tertiary student...

OECD countries as a whole spend US$ 4 229 per student at the primary level, US$ 5 174 per student at the secondary level and US$ 11 422 per student at the tertiary level. But at the tertiary level, these averages are influenced by high expenditure in a few large OECD countries, most notably the United States. Spending on education per student in the "typical" OECD country, as represented by the simple mean across all OECD countries, amounts to US$ 4 148 at the primary level, US$ 5 465 at the secondary level and US$ 9 210 at the tertiary level of education (Table B1.1).

...but these averages mask a broad range of expenditure across OECD countries.

These averages mask a broad range of expenditure on education per student across OECD countries. At the primary level, expenditure on educational institutions ranges from US$ 1 096 in Mexico to US$ 6 721 in Denmark. Differences between OECD countries are even greater at the secondary level, where spending on education per student varies by a factor of 6.6, from US$ 1 480 in Mexico to US$ 9 756 in Switzerland. Expenditure on education per tertiary student ranges from US$ 3 912 in Poland to US$ 19 220 in the United States (Table B1.1).

These comparisons are based on purchasing power parities, not market exchange rates, and therefore reflect the amount of a national currency that will buy the same basket of goods and services in a given country as that bought by the US dollar in the United States.

R&D expenditure in tertiary institutions amounts to over US$ 3 000 per student in Australia, Belgium, Germany, the Netherlands, Sweden and the United Kingdom.

On average, expenditure on Research and Development at the tertiary level represents one-quarter of all tertiary expenditure. In five out of 20 OECD countries for which tertiary expenditure are separated by type of services, R&D expenditure in tertiary institutions represents more than 35 per cent of tertiary expenditure. On a per student-basis this can translate into significant amounts, as in Australia, Belgium, Germany, the Netherlands, Sweden and the United Kingdom, where expenditure for R&D in tertiary institutions amounts to over US$ 3 000 per student (Chart B1.1 and Table B6.2).

R&D spending in tertiary educational institutions not only depends on total R&D expenditure in a country, but also on the national infrastructure for R&D activities. OECD countries in which most R&D is performed by tertiary educational institutions tend to report higher expenditure per tertiary student than countries in which a large part of R&D is performed in other public institutions or by industry.

The labour intensiveness of education accounts for the predominance of teachers' salaries in overall costs.

The labour intensiveness of the traditional model of classroom education accounts for the predominance of teachers' salaries in overall costs. Differences in the average class size and in the ratio of students to teaching staff (Indicator D2), in staffing patterns, in teachers' salaries (Indicator D6) and in teaching materials

Chart B1.2.

Change in expenditure on educational institutions per student in comparison to underlying factors, by level of education (1995, 1999)

Indices of change in expenditure on educational institutions, enrolment and expenditure per student between 1995 and 1999 (1995=100)

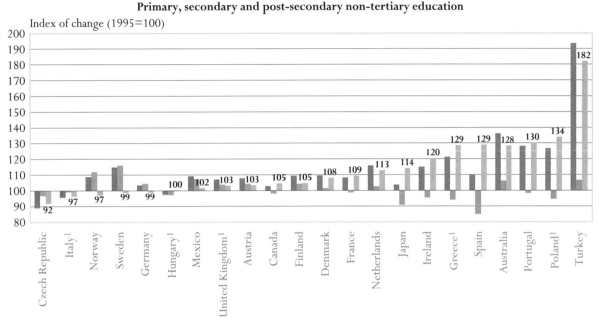

■ Change in expenditure   ■ Change in the number of students   ■ Change in expenditure per student

Primary, secondary and post-secondary non-tertiary education

Index of change (1995=100)

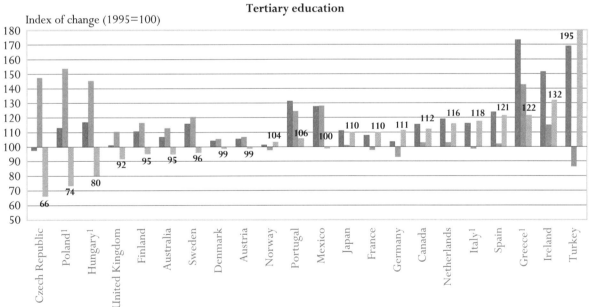

Tertiary education

Index of change (1995=100)

1. Public institutions only.
Countries are ranked in ascending order of change in expenditure per student.
Source: OECD. Table B2.2 and Indicator C1. See Annex 3 for notes *(www.oecd.org/els/education/eag2002).*

B1

and facilities influence the differences in cost between levels of education, types of programme and types of school.

Technology may allow some savings to be made.

Future gains in efficiency may be achieved through the use of new information technologies, both to hold down unit costs and to improve learning outcomes. At the tertiary level, unit cost savings may also be available through the expansion of distance education, whether intensive use is made of technology or not.

B1

Lower unit expenditure cannot simply be equated with lower student performance.

It would be misleading to equate lower unit expenditure generally with lower quality of educational services. Australia, Finland, Korea and the United Kingdom, for example, which have moderate expenditure on education per student at primary and lower secondary levels, are among the OECD countries with the highest levels of performance by 15-year-old students in mathematics (see Indicator A6).

Changes in expenditure on education per student between 1995 and 1999

Expenditure on education per primary, secondary and post-secondary non-tertiary student increased by over 20 per cent in Australia, Greece, Poland, Portugal, Spain and Turkey.

In absolute terms and at 1999 constant prices, expenditure on education per primary, secondary and post-secondary non-tertiary student increased between 1995 and 1999 by over 20 per cent in Australia, Greece, Poland, Portugal, Spain and Turkey. On the other hand, the Czech Republic saw a decline in expenditure on education per primary, secondary and post-secondary non-tertiary student by over 5 per cent. In ten out of the 22 OECD countries, changes remained within plus or minus 5 per cent compared with 1995 (Chart B1.2).

At primary and secondary levels, changes in enrolments were not the main factor driving expenditure...

Although institutional arrangements often adapt to changing demographic conditions only with a considerable time lag, changes in enrolments do not seem to have been the main factor driving changes in expenditure per primary, secondary and post-secondary non-tertiary student. The exceptions to this pattern are Japan and Spain, where a drop of more than 9 per cent in enrolments has led to a significant increase in spending on education per student.

In Norway and Sweden, the two OECD countries with the highest increase in the number of primary, secondary and post-secondary non-tertiary students between 1995 and 1999, increases in expenditure have kept pace with rising enrolments. The parallel increase in both student numbers and expenditure on education in Norway is due to the expansion of primary education from six to seven years, implemented in the school year 1997-1998. In Ireland and Poland, a significant increase in education budgets, coupled with a slight decrease in enrolments, has led to an increase in spending per primary, secondary and post-secondary non-tertiary student of about 20 and 34 per cent, respectively.

...while at the tertiary level, spending on education has not always kept pace with the rapid expansion of enrolments.

The pattern is different at the tertiary level of education. In six out of 22 OECD countries – Australia, the Czech Republic, Finland, Hungary, Poland and the United Kingdom – tertiary expenditure on education per student declined between 1995 and 1999 by 5 per cent or more. In all of these countries, this was mainly the result of the rapid increase in the number of tertiary students

B1

of more than 10 per cent during the same period (Chart B1.2). On the other hand, expenditure per tertiary student rose significantly in Greece and Ireland despite a growth in enrolment of 42 and 15 per cent, respectively. Germany and Turkey were the only OECD countries in which the number of tertiary students actually declined by more than 4 per cent, although in Germany, this decline occurred mainly in the earlier years of this period whereas student numbers have lately begun to increase significantly. All other OECD countries with increases in expenditure per tertiary student of more than 10 per cent saw little or no change in enrolments.

Educational expenditure per student in relation to national GDP

Expenditure on education per student relative to GDP per capita is a spending measure that takes OECD countries' relative wealth into account. Since education is universal at lower levels, spending on education per student relative to GDP per capita at the lower levels of education can be interpreted as the resources spent on young people relative to a country's ability to pay. At higher levels of education, this measure is affected by a combination of national income, spending and enrolment rates.

OECD countries spend an average of 19 per cent of GDP per capita on each primary student, 25 per cent per secondary student and 44 per cent per tertiary student.

At the tertiary level, for example, OECD countries can be relatively high on this measure if a relatively large proportion of their wealth is spent on educating a relatively small number of students. For the OECD as a whole, expenditure on education per student averages 19 per cent of GDP per capita at the primary level, 25 per cent at the secondary level and 44 per cent at the tertiary level (Table B1.2).

As one would expect, there is a clear positive relationship between spending on education per student and GDP per capita (Chart B1.3), showing that poorer OECD countries tend to spend less per student than richer OECD countries. This trend can also be observed when looking at spending as a percentage of GDP per capita (Table B1.2).

Poorer OECD countries tend to spend less per student...

Although the relationship between spending on education per student and GDP per capita is generally positive, there is considerable variation in spending on education per student among both richer and poorer OECD countries. Australia and Austria, for example, are countries with similar levels of GDP per capita which spend very different proportions of their GDP per capita per student. The proportion of national income spent per primary student in Australia, 19 per cent of GDP per capita, is at the level of the OECD average. By contrast, Austria spends 26 per cent of GDP per capita per primary student, which is the highest proportion (Table B1.2).

...but there are many exceptions.

Does growing national income translate into higher spending on education per student? The arrows in Chart B1.4 show, for each OECD country, the changes in expenditure on education per student in relation to the respective changes in GDP per capita in primary, secondary and post-secondary non-tertiary education. The origin of the arrow represents GDP per capita (horizontal axis)

In general, as OECD countries grow richer, expenditure on education per student increases...

Chart B1.3.

Expenditure on educational institutions per student relative to GDP per capita (1999)

*Annual expenditure on educational institutions per student versus GDP per capita
(equivalent US dollars converted using PPPs), by level of education*

B1

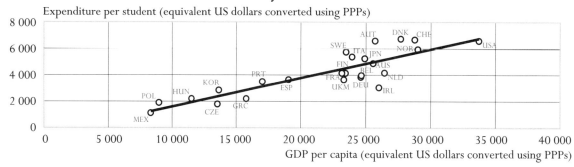

Primary education

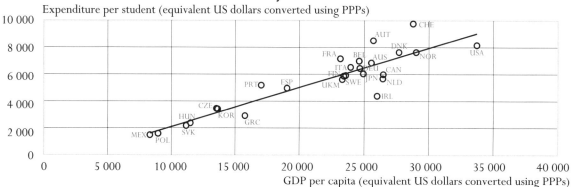

Secondary education

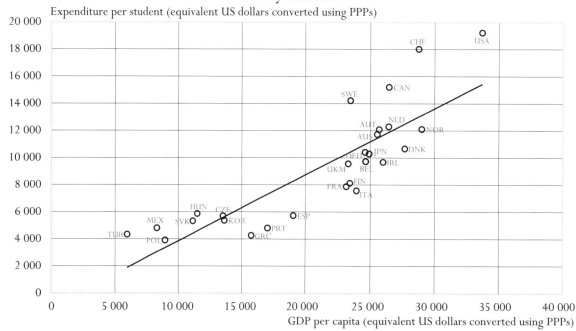

Tertiary education

Note: Please refer to the Reader's Guide for list of country codes and country names used in this chart.
Source: OECD. Tables B1.1 and B1.2 and Annex 2. See Annex 3 for notes *(www.oecd.org/els/education/eag2002).*

and the expenditure on education per student (vertical axis) in 1995 (at 1999 prices and 1999 purchasing power parities), and the end of each arrow shows the corresponding values for 1999.

In general, changes in expenditure on education per student are correlated with changes in GDP per capita. For example, both primary, secondary and post-secondary non-tertiary expenditure on education per student has risen along with GDP per capita in most of the OECD countries.

In six out of 21 OECD countries – Australia, Greece, Japan, Poland, Portugal and Spain – expenditure on education per student has grown faster than GDP per capita between 1995 and 1999. By contrast, primary, secondary and post-secondary non-tertiary expenditure on education per student decreased between 1995 and 1999 in the Czech Republic, Germany, Italy, Norway and Sweden at the same time as GDP per capita increased (Chart B1.4).

...but there are exceptions to this pattern.

B1

Changes in expenditure on educational institutions per student and national income
Change between 1995 and 1999 in expenditure on educational institutions per primary, secondary and post-secondary non-tertiary student compared with GDP per capita
(1999 constant prices and 1999 constant PPPs)

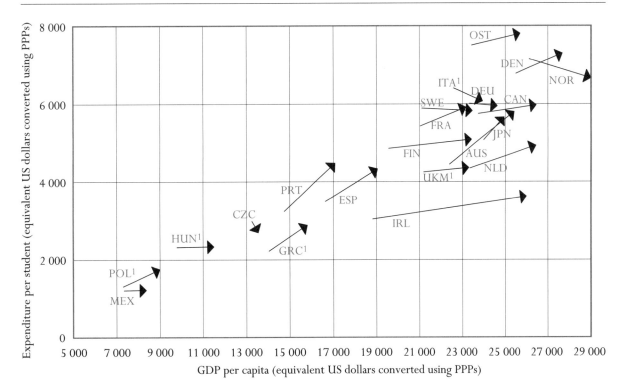

Note: Please refer to the Reader's Guide for list of country codes and country names used in this chart.
The beginning of the arrow indicates spending per student and GDP per capita in 1995.
The end of the arrow indicates the corresponding values for 1999.
1. Public institutions only.
Source: OECD. Table B6.1 and Annex 2. See Annex 3 for notes *(www.oecd.org/els/education/eag2002).*

Differences in educational expenditure per student between levels of education

Expenditure on education per student consistently rises with the level of education.

Expenditure on education per student exhibits a common pattern throughout the OECD: in each OECD country it rises sharply from primary to tertiary education. This pattern can be understood by looking at the main determinants of expenditure, particularly the location and mode of educational provision. The vast majority of education still takes place in traditional school settings with – despite some differences – similar organisation, curriculum, teaching style and management. These shared features are likely to lead to similar patterns of unit expenditure.

B₁

Comparisons of the distribution of expenditure between levels of education are an indication of the relative emphasis placed on education at different levels in various OECD countries, as well as of the relative costs of providing education at those levels. Although expenditure on education per student rises with the level of education in almost all OECD countries, the relative sizes of the differences vary markedly between countries (Chart B1.5). At the secondary level, expenditure on education per student is, on average, 1.3 times that at the primary level, although the difference ranges from 0.8 times the expenditure per primary student in Poland to more than 1.7 times in the Czech Republic, France and Germany.

On average, OECD countries spend 2.3 times as much on education per student at the tertiary level as at the primary level.

Although OECD countries spend, on average, 2.3 times as much on education per student at the tertiary level as at the primary level, spending patterns vary widely between countries. For example, whereas Italy and Portugal only spend 1.4 times as much on a tertiary student as on a primary student, Mexico spends 4.4 times as much (Chart B1.5).

Educational expenditure per student over the average duration of tertiary studies

Annual expenditure on education per student does not always reflect the full cost of tertiary studies.

Since both the typical duration and the intensity of tertiary education vary between OECD countries, the differences between countries in annual expenditure on education per student on educational services as shown in Chart B1.1 do not necessarily reflect the variation in the total cost of educating the typical tertiary student.

Students can choose from a range of institutions and enrolment options.

Today, students can choose from a range of institutions and enrolment options in order to find the best fit between their degree objectives, abilities and personal interests. Many students enrol on a part-time basis while others work while studying, or attend more than one institution before graduating. These varying enrolment patterns can affect the interpretability of expenditure on education per student.

Low annual expenditure may translate into high overall costs of tertiary

In particular, comparatively low annual expenditure on education per student can result in comparatively high overall costs of tertiary education if the typical duration of tertiary studies is long. Chart B1.6 shows the average expenditure that is incurred per student throughout the course of tertiary studies. The figures account for all students for whom expenditure is incurred, including those who do not finish their studies. Although the calculations are based on a number of simplified assumptions and therefore should be treated with some caution (see Annex 3 at *www.oecd.org/els/education/eag2002*), some striking shifts in the rank order of OECD countries between the annual and aggregate expenditure can be noted.

education if the duration of tertiary studies is long.

B1

Chart B1.5.

Differences in expenditure on educational institutions per student relative to primary education (1999)

Ratio of expenditure on educational institutions per student at various levels of education to educational expenditure per student in primary education, multiplied by 100

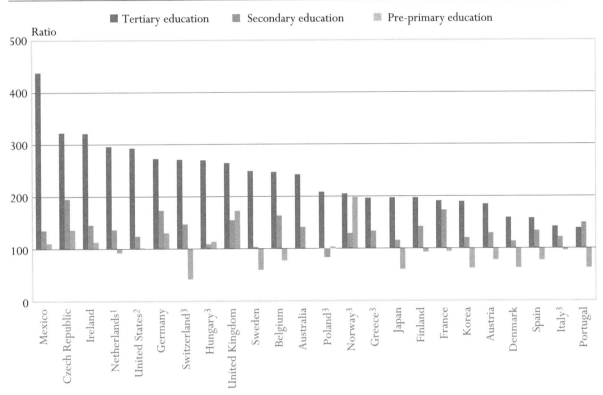

1. Public and government-dependent private institutions only.

2. Public and independent private institutions only.

3. Public institutions only.

A ratio of 500 for tertiary education means that expenditure per tertiary student in a particular country is 5 times the expenditure per primary student.

A ratio of 50 for pre-primary education means that expenditure per pre-primary student in a particular country is half the expenditure per primary student.

Countries are ranked in descending order of expenditure per student in tertiary education relative to educational expenditure per student in primary education.

Source: OECD. Table B1.1. See Annex 3 for notes *(www.oecd.org/els/education/eag2002).*

B1

Chart B1.6.

Cumulative expenditure on educational institutions per student
over the average duration of tertiary studies (1999)

*Annual expenditure on educational institutions per student multiplied by average
duration of studies, in equivalent US dollars converted using PPPs*

Each segment of the bar represents the annual expenditure per student. The number of segments represents the number of years a student remains on average in tertiary education.

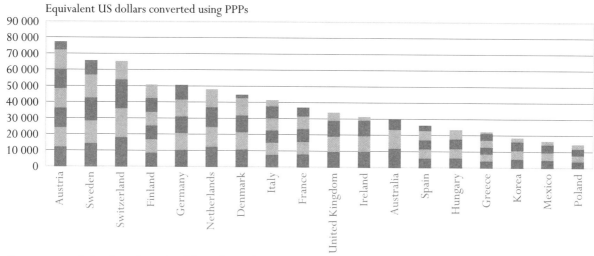

Countries are ranked in descending order of the total expenditure per student over the average duration of tertiary studies.
Source: OECD. Table B1.3. See Annex 3 for notes *(www.oecd.org/els/education/eag2002).*

For example, annual spending per tertiary student in the Netherlands is about the same as in Austria (US$ 12 285 in the Netherlands compared with US$ 12 070 in Austria) (Table B1.1). But because of differences in the tertiary degree structure (Indicator A2), the average duration of tertiary studies is more than one-third longer in Austria than in the Netherlands (6.4 years in Austria, compared with 3.9 years in the Netherlands). As a consequence, the cumulative expenditure for each tertiary student is more than 50 per cent higher in Austria than in the Netherlands (US$ 77 248 compared with US$ 47 911) (Chart B1.6 and Table B1.3).

The total cost of tertiary-type A studies in Switzerland (US$101 334) is more than twice as high as in nine out of ten reporting OECD countries, Germany being the exception (Table B1.3). These differences must, of course, be interpreted in the light of differences in national degree structures as well as possible differences between OECD countries in the academic level of the qualifications of students leaving university. While similar trends are observed in tertiary-type B studies, the total cost of these studies tends to be much lower than those of tertiary type-A programmes, largely because of their shorter duration.

Definitions and methodologies

Data refer to the financial year 1999

Expenditure on education per student on a particular level of education is calculated by dividing the total expenditure on educational institutions at that level by the corresponding full-time equivalent enrolment. Only those educational institutions and programmes are taken into account for which both enrolment and expenditure data are available. Expenditure in national currency is converted into equivalent US dollars by dividing the national currency figure by the purchasing power parity (PPP) index. The PPP exchange rate gives the amount of a national currency that will buy the same basket of goods and services in a given OECD country as that bought by the US dollar in the United States. The PPP exchange rate is used because the market exchange rate is affected by many factors (interest rates, trade policies, expectations of economic growth, etc.) that have little to do with current relative domestic purchasing power in different OECD countries. (Annex 2 gives further details.)

and are based on the UOE data collection on educational statistics administered by the OECD in 2001 (for details see Annex 3).

Charts B1.2 and B1.4 show expenditure on education per student in the financial year 1995. The data on expenditure for 1995 were obtained by a special survey conducted in 2000. OECD countries were asked to collect the 1995 data according to the definitions and the coverage of the UOE 2000 data collection. All expenditure data, as well as the GDP for 1995, are adjusted to 1999 prices using the GDP price deflator.

Data for the financial year 1995 are based on a special survey carried out among OECD countries in 2000.

B1

Expenditure on education per student relative to GDP per capita is calculated by expressing expenditure on education per student in units of national currency as a percentage of GDP per capita, also in national currency. In cases where the educational expenditure data and the GDP data pertain to different reference periods, the expenditure data are adjusted to the same reference period as the GDP data, using inflation rates for the OECD country in question (see Annex 2).

Expected expenditure over the average duration of tertiary studies (Table B1.3) is calculated by multiplying current annual expenditure by the typical duration of tertiary studies. The methodology used for the estimation of the typical duration of tertiary studies is described in Annex 3 at *www.oecd.org/els/ education/eag2002*. For the estimation of the duration of tertiary education, data are based on a special survey carried out in OECD countries in 1997 and 2000.

The ranking of OECD countries by annual expenditure on education per student on educational services is affected by differences in how countries define full-time, part-time and full-time equivalent enrolment. Some OECD countries count every participant at the tertiary level as a full-time student while others determine a student's intensity of participation by the credits which he or she obtains for successful completion of specific course units during a specified reference period. OECD countries that can accurately account for part-time enrolment will have higher expenditure per full-time equivalent student than OECD countries that cannot differentiate between different modes of student attendance.

Note that data appearing in earlier editions of this publication may not always be comparable to data shown in the 2002 edition due to changes in definitions and coverage that were made as a result of the OECD expenditure comparability study (see Annex 3 at *www.oecd.org/els/education/eag2002* for details on changes).

Table B1.1.
Expenditure on educational institutions per student (1999)
Annual expenditure on educational institutions per student in equivalent US dollars converted using PPPs , by level of education, based on full-time equivalents

	Pre-primary education (for children 3 years and older)	Primary education	Lower secondary education	Upper secondary education	All secondary education	Post-secondary non-tertiary education	Tertiary education		
							All tertiary education	Tertiary-type B education	Tertiary-type A and advanced research programmes
	(1)	(2)	(3)	(4)	(5)	(6)	(7)	(8)	(9)
OECD COUNTRIES									
Australia*	m	4 858	6 710	7 066	6 850	7 650	11 725	7 993	12 588
Austria*	5 080	6 568	8 434	8 584	8 504	9 131	12 070	x(7)	x(7)
Belgium*	3 035	3 952	x(5)	x(5)	6 444	x(5)	9 724	x(7)	x(7)
Canada*	4 466	x(5)	x(5)	x(5)	5 981	x(7)	15 211	x(7)	15 470
Czech Republic*	2 404	1 769	2 998	4 043	3 449	832	5 688	1 886	6 679
Denmark*	4 208	6 721	6 904	8 270	7 626	m	10 657	x(7)	x(7)
Finland*	3855	4 138	6 390	5479	5 863	x(5)	8 114	4 500	8 474
France*	3 901	4 139	6 657	7 766	7 152	5 839	7 867	8 458	7 709
Germany *	4937	3 818	4 918	10 107	6 603	11 679	10 393	5 495	11 209
Greece[1]*	x(2)	2 176	x(5)	x(5)	2 904	5 415	4 260	3 439	4 606
Hungary[1]*	2 458	2 179	2 017	2 756	2 368	2 983	5 861	x(7)	x(7)
Iceland	m	m	m	m	m	m	m	m	m
Ireland	3 386	3 018	4 401	4 362	4 383	4 168	9 673	x(7)	x(7)
Italy[1]	5 133	5 354	6 206	6 741	6 518	m	7 552	7 147	7 557
Japan*	3 154	5 240	5612	6 460	6 039	x(4,7)	10 278	7 649	10 749
Korea*	1 752	2 838	3 208	3 597	3 419	a	5 356	3 494	6 612
Luxembourg	m	m	m	m	m	m	m	m	m
Mexico	1 204	1 096	1 129	2 226	1 480	a	4 789	x(7)	x(7)
Netherlands[2]*	3 848	4 162	5 747	5 575	5 670	m	12 285	7 227	12 354
New Zealand	m	m	m	m	m	m	m	m	m
Norway[1]	11 699	5 920	7 387	7819	7 628	x(5)	12 096	x(7)	x(7)
Poland[1]	1 898	1888	x(2)	1 583	1 583	x(4)	3 912	x(7)	3 912
Portugal*	2 165	3 478	4 958	5 422	5 181	a	4 802	x(7)	x(7)
Slovak Republic	1 880	x(3)	1 811	2 637	2 163	x(4)	5 325	x(9)	5 325
Spain	2 789	3 635	x(5)	x(5)	4 864	x(5)	5 707	5 111	5 760
Sweden	3 396	5 736	5 678	6 077	5 911	6 675	14 222	x(7)	x(7)
Switzerland[1, 1]*	2 764	6 663	7 824	11 819	9 756	7 960	17 997	13 421	18 584
Turkey[1]	m	m	m	m	m	m	4 328	x(7)	x(7)
United Kingdom*	6 233	3 627	x(5)	x(5)	5 608	x(5)	9 554	x(7)	x(7)
United States[3]*	6 692	6 582	x(5)	x(5)	8 157	x(7)	19 220	x(7)	x(7)
Country mean	*3 847*	*4 148*	*5 210*	*5 919*	*5 465*	*4 795*	*9 210*	*~*	*~*
OECD total	*3 746*	*4 229*	*~*	*~*	*5 174*	*~*	*11 422*	*~*	*~*
NON-OECD COUNTRIES									
Argentina	1409	1629	2198	2 528	2 327	a	5 606	5 137	6 056
Brazil[1, 5]	1 222	956	1 069	1 172	1 100	m	13 567	m	13 567
Chile	1 431	1 701	1 767	2 041	1 941	a	6 911	3 545	7 652
China	105	372	476	1 768	833	a	5 798	x(7)	x(7)
India[5]	65	303	297	290	295	a	m	m	m
Indonesia[6]	53	81	208	295	242	a	1 047	x(7)	x(7)
Israel	3 415	4 240	x(5)	x(5)	5 164	4 115	11 210	7 965	12 088
Jamaica[1]	386	764	1 065	1 114	1 082	908	6 484	2 650	13 194
Jordan[1]	m	775	782	806	789	a	5 082	x(7)	x(7)
Malaysia[1]	437	1 015	x(5)	x(5)	1 813	8 423	7 924	7 677	7 979
Paraguay	x(2)	877	x(5)	x(5)	1 545	a	5 465	2 796	6 750
Peru	442	483	x(5)	x(5)	579	m	1 414	675	2 057
Philippines[1, 5]	46	474	411	384	406	962	1060	a	1 060
Tunisia[1, 6]	m	988	x(5)	x(5)	1 868	a	5 008	x(7)	x(7)
Uruguay[1]	1 133	1 000	1 114	1 484	1 275	a	2 239	x(7)	x(7)
Zimbabwe[1]	m	537	x(5)	x(5)	813	x(5)	m	m	m

Note: x indicates that data are included in another column. The column reference is shown in brackets after "x". *e.g.*, x(2) means that data are included in column 2.
1. Public institutions only.
2. Public and government-dependent private institutions only.
3. Column 9 refers to tertiary-type A education only.
4. Public and independent private institutions only.
5. Year of reference 1998.
6. Year of reference 2000.
* See Annex 3 for notes (*www.oecd.org/els/education/eag2002*).
Source: OECD.

Table B1.2.
Expenditure on educational institutions per student relative to GDP per capita (1999)
Expenditure on educational institutions per student relative to GDP per capita by level of education, based on full-time equivalents

B1

	Pre-primary education (for children 3 years and older)	Primary education	Lower secondary education	Upper secondary education	All secondary education	Post-secondary non-tertiary education	Tertiary education		
							All tertiary education	Tertiary-type B education	Tertiary-type A and advanced research programmes
	(1)	(2)	(3)	(4)	(5)	(6)	(7)	(8)	(9)
OECD COUNTRIES									
Australia*	m	19	26	28	27	30	46	31	49
Austria*	20	26	33	33	33	36	47	x(7)	x(7)
Belgium*	12	16	x(5)	x(5)	26	x(5)	39	x(7)	x(7)
Canada*	17	x(5)	x(5)	x(5)	23	x(7)	57	x(7)	58
Czech Republic*	18	13	22	30	25	6	42	14	49
Denmark*	15	24	25	30	28	m	39	x(7)	x(7)
Finland*	16	18	27	23	25	x(5)	35	19	36
France*	17	18	29	34	31	25	34	37	33
Germany*	20	16	20	41	27	47	42	22	46
Greece[1]*	x(2)	14	x(5)	x(5)	18	34	27	22	29
Hungary[1]*	21	19	18	24	21	26	51	x(7)	x(7)
Iceland	m	m	m	m	m	m	m	m	m
Ireland	13	12	17	17	17	16	37	x(7)	x(7)
Italy[1]	21	22	26	28	27	m	32	30	32
Japan*	13	21	23	26	24	x(4,7)	41	31	43
Korea*	13	21	24	26	25	a	39	26	48
Luxembourg	m	m	m	m	m	m	m	m	m
Mexico	14	13	14	27	18	a	57	x(7)	x(7)
Netherlands[2]*	15	16	22	21	21	m	46	27	47
New Zealand	m	m	m	m	m	m	m	m	m
Norway[1]	40	20	25	27	26	x(4)	43	x(7)	x(7)
Poland[1]	21	21	x(2)	18	18	x(4)	44	x(7)	44
Portugal*	13	20	29	32	30	a	28	x(7)	x(7)
Slovak Republic	17	x(3)	16	24	19	x(4)	48	x(9)	48
Spain	15	19	x(5)	x(5)	26	x(5)	30	27	30
Sweden	14	24	24	26	25	28	61	x(7)	x(7)
Switzerland[1,4]*	10	23	27	41	34	28	63	47	65
Turkey[1]	m	m	m	m	m	m	73	x(7)	x(7)
United Kingdom*	27	16	x(5)	x(5)	24	x(5)	41	x(7)	x(7)
United States[4]*	20	20	x(5)	x(5)	24	x(7)	57	x(7)	x(7)
Country mean	*18*	*19*	*23*	*28*	*25*	*21*	*44*	*28*	*44*
NON-OECD COUNTRIES									
Argentina	11	13	18	21	19	a	46	42	49
Brazil[1,5]	18	14	15	17	16	m	195	m	195
Chile	17	20	20	24	22	a	80	41	88
China	3	10	13	49	23	a	161	x(7)	x(7)
India[5]	2	12	16	20	17	a	m	m	m
Indonesia[6]	9	3	8	11	9	a	41	x(7)	x(7)
Israel	17	21	x(5)	x(5)	26	21	56	40	61
Jamaica[1]	11	21	30	31	30	25	182	74	371
Jordan[1]	m	20	20	21	20	a	130	x(7)	x(7)
Malaysia[1]	5	12	x(5)	x(5)	22	103	96	93	97
Paraguay	x(2)	20	x(5)	x(5)	35	a	125	64	154
Peru	10	10	x(5)	x(5)	13	m	31	15	45
Philippines[1,5]	2	14	15	15	15	35	42	a	84
Tunisia[1,6]	m	16	x(5)	x(5)	29	a	79	x(7)	x(7)
Uruguay[1]	13	11	13	17	14	a	25	x(7)	x(7)
Zimbabwe[1]	m	19	x(5)	x(5)	28	x(5)	m	m	m

Note: x indicates that data are included in another column. The column reference is shown in brackets after "x". *e.g.,* x(2) means that data are included in column 2.
1. Public institutions only.
2. Public and government-dependent private institutions only.
3. Column 9 refers to tertiary-type A education only.
4. Public and independent private institutions only.
5. Year of reference 1998.
6. Year of reference 2000.
* See Annex 3 for notes (*www.oecd.org/els/education/eag2002*).
Source: OECD.

Table B1.3.
Cumulative expenditure on educational institutions per student over the average duration of tertiary studies (1999)
Average duration of tertiary studies and expenditure on educational institutions over the average duration of studies in equivalent US dollars converted using PPPs, by type of programme

B1

	Method[1]	Average duration of tertiary studies (in years)			Cumulative expenditure per student over the average duration of tertiary studies		
		All tertiary education	Tertiary-type B education	Tertiary-type A and advanced research programmes	All tertiary education	Tertiary-type B education	Tertiary-type A and advanced research programmes
		(1)	(2)	(3)	(4)	(5)	(6)
Australia	CM	2.5	1.6	2.6	29 665	12 548	32 226
Austria[3]	AF	6.4	2.3	7.4	77 248	x(4)	x(4)
Canada[4]	CM	m	m	m	m	m	m
Denmark[3]	AF	4.2	2.1	4.4	44 654	x(4)	x(4)
Finland	CM	6.0	a	6.0	50 760	a	50 760
France[2]	AF	4.7	2.8	5.3	36 832	23 410	40 901
Germany*	CM	4.9	2.4	6.0	50 511	13 408	67 367
Greece[3]	AF	5.2	3.0	7.3	22 197	10 419	33 669
Hungary[3]	CM	4.1	m	4.1	23 735	x(4)	x(4)
Iceland	CM	2.7	2.0	2.8	m	m	m
Ireland*	CM	3.2	2.2	4.0	31 341	x(4)	x(4)
Italy[3]*	CM	5.5	3.3	5.6	41 458	23 371	42 092
Korea[3]*	CM	3.4	2.1	4.2	18 371	7 232	27 904
Mexico[3]	AF	3.4	x(3)	3.4	16 390	x(4)	x(4)
Netherlands[2,4]	CM	3.9	x(1)	x(1)	47 911	x(4)	x(4)
Norway	CM	m	m	m	m	m	m
Poland[3]	CM	3.7	m	3.7	14 395	m	14 395
Spain[3]	AF	4.6	1.5	4.7	25 965	7611	27 113
Sweden	CM	4.6	2.6	4.7	65 529	x(4)	x(4)
Switzerland[3,4]	CM	3.6	2.2	5.5	65 225	29 349	101 334
United Kingdom*	CM	3.5	x(1)	x(1)	33 835	x(4)	x(4)
Country mean		*4.2*	*2.0*	*4.8*	*38 668*	~	~

Note: x indicates that data are included in another column. The column reference is shown in brackets after "x". *e.g.*, x(2) means that data are included in column 2.
1. Either the Chain Method (CM) or an Approximation Formula (AF) was used to estimate the duration of tertiary studies.
2. The duration of tertiary studies is obtained by a special survey conducted in 1997 for the academic year 1995.
3. Public institutions only.
4. Public and government-dependent private institutions only.
* See Annex 3 for notes (*www.oecd.org/els/education/eag2002*).
Source: OECD.

EXPENDITURE ON EDUCATIONAL INSTITUTIONS RELATIVE TO GROSS DOMESTIC PRODUCT

- OECD countries spend 5.8 per cent of their collective GDP on their educational institutions.

- In 14 out of 18 OECD countries, public and private spending on educational institutions increased between 1995 and 1999 by more than 5 per cent but, in contrast to the early 1990s, increases in spending on educational institutions tended to fall behind the growth in national income.

- Two-thirds of expenditure on educational institutions, or 3.7 per cent of combined OECD GDP, is devoted to primary, secondary and post-secondary non-tertiary education, although Canada, Korea and the United States spend more than 2 per cent of their GDP on tertiary education.

B2

Chart B2.1.

Expenditure on educational institutions as a percentage of GDP (1995, 1999)

Direct and indirect expenditure on educational institutions from public and private sources, by level of education, source of fund and year

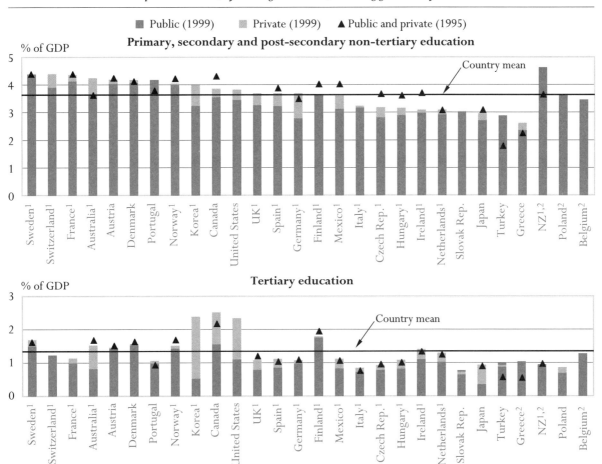

1. Public subsidies included in private funds.
2. Public expenditure only.
Countries are ranked in descending order of total expenditure from both public and private sources on public and private educational institutions in primary, secondary and post-secondary non-tertiary education. Countries presenting public expenditure only are ranked separately.
Source: OECD. Table B2.1b. See Annex 3 for notes *(www.oecd.org/els/education/eag2002).*

B2

Policy context

This indicator provides a measure of the relative proportion of a nation's wealth that is invested in educational institutions.

Expenditure on education is an investment that can help to foster economic growth, enhance productivity, contribute to personal and social development, and reduce social inequality. The proportion of total financial resources devoted to education is one of the key choices made in each OECD country; and is an aggregate choice made by governments, enterprises, and individual students and their families. If the social and private returns on that investment are sufficiently large, there is an incentive for enrolment to expand and total investment to increase.

It also includes a comparative review of changes in educational investment over time.

In appraising how much is spent on education, governments have to assess demands for increased spending in areas such as teachers' salaries and educational facilities. This indicator can provide a point of reference for this as it shows how the volume of educational spending, relative to the size of national wealth and in absolute terms, has evolved over time in various OECD countries.

Evidence and explanations

What this indicator covers and what it does not cover

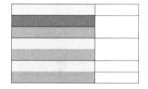

Coverage diagram (see page 144 for explanations)

This indicator covers expenditure on schools, universities and other public and private institutions involved in delivering or supporting educational services. Expenditure on institutions is not limited to expenditure on instructional services but also includes public and private expenditure on ancillary services for students and families, where these services are provided through educational institutions. At the tertiary level, spending on research and development can also be significant and is included in this indicator, to the extent that the research is performed by educational institutions.

Not all spending on educational goods and services occurs within educational institutions. For example, families may purchase textbooks and materials commercially or seek private tutoring for their children outside educational institutions. At the tertiary level, student living costs and forgone earnings can also account for a significant proportion of the costs of education. All such expenditure outside educational institutions is excluded from this indicator, even if it is publicly subsidised. Public subsidies for educational expenditure outside institutions are discussed in Indicators B4 and B5.

Overall investment relative to GDP

As a whole, OECD countries spend 5.8 per cent of their combined GDP on their educational institutions.

All OECD countries invest a substantial proportion of national resources in education. Taking into account both public and private sources of funds, OECD countries as a whole spend 5.8 per cent of their collective GDP on their educational institutions. Under current conditions of tight constraints on public budgets, such a large spending item is subject to close scrutiny by governments looking for ways to reduce or limit the growth of expenditure.

The highest spending on educational institutions can be observed in Korea, with 6.8 per cent of GDP accounted for by public and private spending on educational institutions, followed by Canada, Denmark, Norway and Sweden with more than 6.6 per cent. Eight out of 28 OECD countries, however, spend less than 5 per cent of GDP on educational institutions, and in Greece, the Slovak Republic and Turkey this figure is only between 3.9 and 4.4 per cent (Table B2.1a).

Many factors influence the relative position of OECD countries in this indicator. For example, OECD countries with high spending levels may be enrolling larger numbers of students, while countries with low spending levels may either be limiting access to higher levels of education or delivering educational services in a particularly efficient manner. The distribution of enrolments between sectors and fields of study may also differ, as may the duration of studies and the scale and organisation of related educational research. Finally, large differences in GDP between OECD countries imply that similar percentages of GDP spent on education can translate into very different absolute amounts per student (see Indicator B1).

The national resources devoted to education depend on a number of inter-related factors of supply and demand.

B2

Changes in overall educational spending between 1995 and 1999

In 14 out of the 18 OECD countries for which comparable trend data are available, public and private investment in education increased by over 5 per cent between 1995 and 1999 in real terms. Increases in expenditure on educational institutions amounted to between 20 and 30 per cent in Australia, Ireland and Portugal, and to over 40 per cent in Greece. The trend is similar when public investment is considered separately: direct public expenditure on institutions and public subsidies to households designated for institutions rose by over 5 per cent in 19 out of 23 OECD countries between 1995 and 1999. Greece, New Zealand and Turkey, for which no data on private spending are available, show considerable growth in public spending on educational institutions (Table B2.2).

In 14 out of 18 OECD countries, public and private spending on educational institutions increased between 1995 and 1999 by more than 5 per cent...

In absolute terms, spending on educational institutions increased between 1995 and 1999 but tended to lag behind growth in GDP. Around two-thirds of OECD countries showed a decrease in the proportion of GDP devoted to educational institutions. Most notable are the Czech Republic, Finland, Ireland, Mexico and Norway, where the proportion of GDP spent on education decreased by more than 0.35 percentage points (Table B2.1a).

...but increases in spending on education tended to fall behind the growth in national income.

While the strong growth of GDP in Ireland hides significant increases in spending on educational institutions when spending on education is considered as a proportion of GDP, education in the Czech Republic and Mexico did not benefit significantly from growth in GDP. Both countries were already among the OECD countries spending a lower proportion of GDP on education in 1995 and have now fallen further behind (Table B2.1a).

Expenditure on educational institutions by level of education

Countries differ markedly in their investment in pre-primary educational institutions.

High overall spending on education does not necessarily translate into a high level of spending at all levels of education. Differences in spending on educational institutions are most striking at the pre-primary level of education. Here, spending ranges from less than 0.2 per cent of GDP in Australia, Ireland and Korea to 0.7 per cent or more in Denmark, France, Hungary and Norway (Table B2.1c). Differences at the pre-primary level can be explained mainly by participation rates among younger children (see Indicator C1).

Investing in early childhood education is of key importance in order to build a strong foundation for lifelong learning and to ensure equitable access to learning opportunities later in school. However, high-quality early childhood education and care are not only provided by the educational institutions covered by this indicator. Inferences on access to and quality of early childhood education and care should therefore be made with caution.

Two-thirds of expenditure on educational institutions is devoted to primary, secondary and post-secondary non-tertiary education.

Because of the largely universal enrolment at the primary and lower secondary levels of education in OECD countries, and the high participation rates in upper secondary education (see Indicators C1 and C2), these levels account for the bulk of expenditure on educational institutions, namely 3.7 per cent of the combined OECD GDP (Chart B2.1). At the same time, significantly higher spending on education per student at the upper secondary and tertiary levels of education causes the overall investment in these levels to be higher than enrolment numbers alone would suggest. More than one-quarter of combined OECD expenditure on educational institutions is accounted for by tertiary education.

Canada, Korea and the United States spend more than 2 per cent of their GDP on tertiary education.

Canada, Korea and the United States spend 2.5, 2.4 and 2.3 per cent, respectively, of their GDP on tertiary institutions (Chart B2.1). This accounts for more than one-third of all of their expenditure on educational institutions. Denmark, Finland and Sweden also show high spending levels, with 1.6 per cent or more of GDP devoted to tertiary institutions. On the other hand, France, Portugal and Switzerland spend a below-average proportion of GDP on tertiary institutions but are among the OECD countries with the highest proportion of GDP spent on primary, secondary and post-secondary non-tertiary education. In Switzerland, nevertheless, a low proportion of GDP spent on tertiary institutions translates into one of the highest levels of spending per tertiary student, because of a comparatively low tertiary enrolment rate and a high level of GDP (Tables B2.1b and B1.3).

While some OECD countries have increased spending at all levels of education, others have focused spending increases on specific levels.

Countries vary in the levels of education at which spending has increased. Austria, Finland, France, Germany, the Netherlands, Portugal, Sweden and Turkey, OECD countries with a comparably high increase in absolute spending on educational institutions between 1995 and 1999, invested the additional resources in similar proportions in primary, secondary and post-secondary non-tertiary and tertiary education (Chart B2.2). Australia, Denmark, New

Chart B2.2.

Change in expenditure on educational institutions (1995, 1999)

Index of change between 1995 and 1999 in direct expenditure on educational institutions (1995=100)

■ Change in total direct expenditure on educational institutions   ■ Change in GDP at constant prices

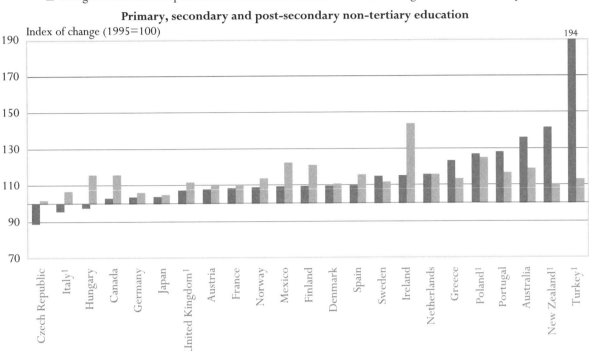

Primary, secondary and post-secondary non-tertiary education

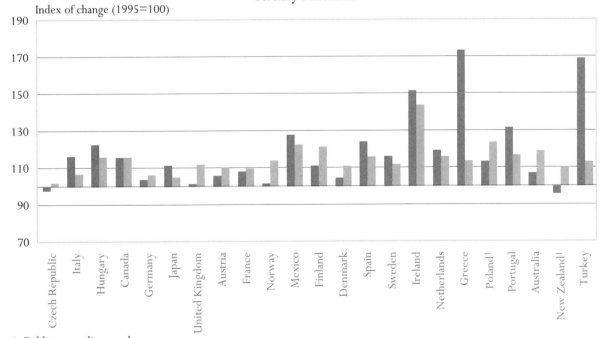

Tertiary education

B₂

1. Public expenditure only.
Countries are ranked in ascending order of change in expenditure on educational institutions at primary, secondary and post-secondary non-tertiary education between 1995 and 1999.
Source: OECD. Table B2.2 and Annex 2. See Annex 3 for notes *(www.oecd.org/els/education/eag2002).*

Zealand, Norway and Poland invested most of the increases made between 1995 and 1999 into primary, secondary and post-secondary non-tertiary education. Conversely, in Canada, Greece, Hungary, Ireland, Italy, Japan, Mexico and Spain, spending on tertiary education increased by more than 10 per cent between 1995 and 1999 while spending on lower levels increased much more slowly. In Hungary and Italy, a significant increase in spending on tertiary institutions was matched by a decrease in spending at the primary, secondary and post-secondary non-tertiary level (Chart B2.2).

Important factors influencing national expenditure on education

The national resources devoted to education depend on a number of inter-related factors of supply and demand, such as the demographic structure of the population, enrolment rates, income per capita, national levels of teachers' salaries and the organisation and delivery of instruction.

The larger the number of young people, the greater the potential demand for educational services.

The size of the school-age population in a particular country (see Indicator A1 in the 2001 edition of *Education at a Glance*) shapes the potential demand for initial education and training. The larger the number of young people, the greater the potential demand for educational services. Among OECD countries of comparable national income, a country with a relatively large youth population will have to spend a higher percentage of its GDP on education so that each young person in that country has the opportunity to receive the same quantity of education as young people in other OECD countries. Conversely, if the youth population is relatively small, the same country will be required to spend less of its wealth on education in order to achieve similar results.

The higher the enrolment rate, the more financial resources will be required.

Although OECD countries generally have little control over the size of their youth populations, the proportion of students participating at various levels of education is indeed a central policy issue. Variations in enrolment rates between OECD countries reflect differences in the demand for education, from pre-primary to tertiary education, as well as the supply of programmes at all levels. Indicator C1 shows that the number of years that a five-year-old child can expect to spend in education ranges among OECD countries from ten to 21. The variation in expected years in tertiary education is even wider, from one year in Mexico to over four years in Finland.

Differences in the length of schooling also influence educational spending.

Differences in the length of schooling are reflected in differences in enrolment rates which, in turn, influence educational expenditure. Chart B2.3 shows the change in expenditure on educational institutions as a percentage of GDP that would be expected if enrolment profiles were equal in all OECD countries and other factors remained the same. Generally, OECD countries that have higher than average enrolment rates, such as Australia, Finland, Norway and Sweden, also spend more of their GDP on education, whereas low expenditure in countries such as the Czech Republic, Hungary, Mexico and Turkey can be partially explained by below-average enrolment rates.

Chart B2.3.

Impact of enrolment rates on expenditure on educational institutions as a percentage of GDP (1999)

A. Estimated increase/decrease in expenditure on educational institutions as a percentage of GDP if enrolment patterns in each country (all levels of education combined) were at the country mean

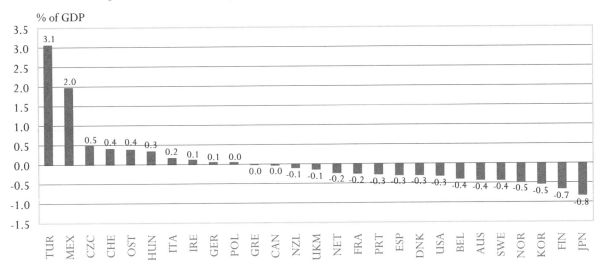

B. Estimated increase/decrease in expenditure on educational institutions as a percentage of GDP if enrolment patterns at the primary and secondary levels in each country were at the country mean

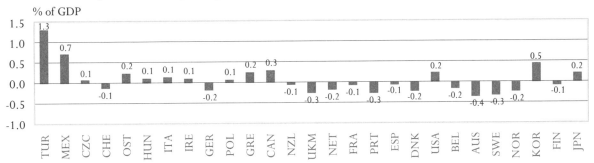

C. Estimated increase/decrease in expenditure on educational institutions as a percentage of GDP if enrolment patterns at the tertiary level in each country were at the country mean

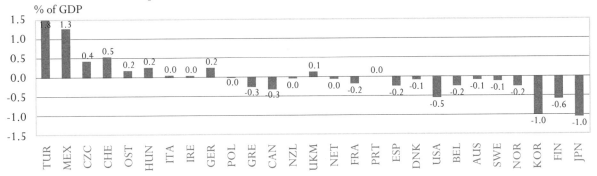

Note: Please refer to the Reader's Guide for list of country codes and country names used in this chart.
Countries are ranked in descending order of the estimated increase/decrease in expenditure as a percentage of GDP if enrolment patterns in each country (all levels of education combined) were at the country mean.
Source: OECD. See Annex 3 for notes *(www.oecd.org/els/education/eag2002).*

B₂

If enrolment patterns were equal in all OECD countries, expenditure as a percentage of GDP would be expected to be more than 1.8 per cent of GDP higher in Mexico and Turkey, and 0.5 per cent or more lower in Finland, Japan, Korea and Norway, assuming constant expenditure on education per student in each of these countries (Chart B2.3).

In some OECD countries, demographic effects on educational spending are outweighed by the effects of enrolment patterns.

B₂

The impact of enrolment rates on educational spending is most clearly visible in tertiary education, where both enrolment rates (see Indicator C1) and expenditure on education per student (Indicator B1) differ widely between OECD countries. If tertiary enrolment patterns in Japan and Korea were at the level of the OECD average, expenditure on tertiary institutions as a percentage of GDP would be expected to be 1.0 percentage points lower, while in Finland and the United States this difference would be 0.6 and 0.5 percentage points, respectively (Chart B2.3). At the other end of the scale are Mexico and Turkey, where expenditure on tertiary institutions as a percentage of GDP would be expected to be 1.3 and 1.8 percentage points higher, respectively, if enrolment patterns were at the OECD average.

Definitions and methodologies

Data refer to the financial year 1999 and are based on the UOE data collection on educational statistics administered by the OECD in 2001 (for details see Annex 3).

Expenditure on educational institutions, as covered by this indicator, includes expenditure on instructional educational institutions as well as expenditure on non-instructional educational institutions. Instructional educational institutions are educational institutions which directly provide instructional programmes (*i.e.*, teaching) to individuals in an organised group setting or through distance education. Business enterprises or other institutions providing short-term courses of training or instruction to individuals on a "one-to-one" basis are not included. Non-instructional educational institutions provide administrative, advisory or professional services to other educational institutions, although they do not enrol students themselves. Examples include national, state, and provincial ministries or departments of education; other bodies that administer education at various levels of government or analogous bodies in the private sector; and organisations that provide such education-related services as vocational or psychological counselling, placement, testing, financial aid to students, curriculum development, educational research, building operations and maintenance services, transportation of students, and student meals and housing.

This broad definition of institutions ensures that expenditure on services, which are provided in some OECD countries by schools and universities and in others by agencies other than schools, are covered on a comparable basis.

The distinction by source of funds is based on the initial source of funds and does not reflect subsequent public-to-private or private-to-public transfers. For this reason, subsidies to households and other entities, such as subsidies for tuition fees and other payments to educational institutions, are included in public expenditure in this indicator. Payments from households and other private entities to educational institutions include tuition and other fees, net of offsetting public subsidies. A detailed discussion of public subsidies can be found in Indicator B5.

Tables B2.1a, B2.1b and B2.2 show expenditure on educational institutions for the financial year 1995. The data on expenditure for 1995 were obtained by a special survey in 2000 in which expenditure for 1995 was adjusted to methods and definitions used in the 1999 UOE data collection.

Data for the financial year 1995 are based on a special survey carried out among OECD countries in 2000.

Chart B2.2 and Table B2.2 present an index of change in expenditure on institutions and GDP between 1995 and 1999. All expenditure, as well as 1995 GDP, is adjusted to 1999 prices using the GDP deflator.

Data for 1995 are expressed in 1999 price levels.

B2

For comparisons over time, the country mean accounts only for those OECD countries for which data are available for all reported reference years.

Note that data appearing in earlier editions of this publication may not always be comparable to data shown in the 2002 edition due to changes in definitions and coverage that were made as a result of the OECD expenditure comparability study (see Annex 3 at *www.oecd.org/els/education/eag2002* for details on changes).

Table B2.1a.
Expenditure on educational institutions as a percentage of GDP (1995, 1999)
Expenditure on educational institutions from public and private sources for all levels of education, by source of fund and year

		1999			1995		
		Public [1]	Private [2]	Total	Public [1]	Private [2]	Total
OECD COUNTRIES	Australia*	4.5	1.4	5.8	4.5	1.0	5.5
	Austria[1]*	6.0	0.3	6.3	6.3	0.3	6.6
	Belgium*	5.3	0.3	5.5	m	m	m
	Canada*	5.3	1.3	6.6	6.2	0.7	6.9
	Czech Republic*	4.2	0.6	4.7	4.9	0.5	5.4
	Denmark[1]*	6.4	0.3	6.7	6.4	0.3	6.7
	Finland*	5.7	0.1	5.8	6.3	x	6.3
	France*	5.8	0.4	6.2	5.9	0.4	6.3
	Germany*	4.3	1.2	5.6	4.5	1.3	5.8
	Greece[1]*	3.6	0.3	3.9	2.9	m	m
	Hungary	4.5	0.6	5.2	4.9	0.6	5.5
	Iceland	m	m	m	m	m	m
	Ireland	4.1	0.4	4.6	4.7	0.5	5.3
	Italy	4.4	0.4	4.8	4.5	m	m
	Japan*	3.5	1.1	4.7	3.6	1.2	4.8
	Korea*	4.1	2.7	6.8	m	m	m
	Luxembourg	m	m	m	m	m	m
	Mexico	4.4	0.8	5.2	4.6	1.0	5.6
	Netherlands*	4.3	0.4	4.7	4.6	0.1	4.7
	New Zealand	5.9	m	m	4.9	m	m
	Norway	6.5	0.1	6.6	7.0	0.2	7.2
	Poland	5.1	m	5.3	5.5	m	m
	Portugal[1]*	5.6	0.1	5.7	5.3	0.0	5.3
	Slovak Republic[1]	4.3	0.1	4.4	m	m	m
	Spain	4.4	0.9	5.3	4.6	1.0	5.5
	Sweden	6.5	0.2	6.7	6.3	0.1	6.4
	Switzerland	5.4	0.5	5.9	m	m	m
	Turkey[1]*	3.9	0.0	3.9	2.4	0.1	2.5
	United Kingdom*	4.4	0.7	5.2	4.8	m	m
	United States*	4.9	1.6	6.5	5.0	1.7	6.4
	Country mean	*4.9*	*0.6*	*5.5*	*~*	*~*	*~*
	OECD total	*4.6*	*1.1*	*5.8*	*~*	*~*	*~*
	Country mean for countries with 1995 and 1999 data (19 countries)	***5.1***	***0.5***	***5.6***	***5.2***	***0.5***	***5.7***
NON-OECD COUNTRIES	Argentina[3]	4.5	1.3	5.8	m	m	m
	Brazil[3, 4]	5.1	m	m	m	m	m
	Chile	4.1	3.1	7.2	m	m	m
	China	2.0	1.6	3.7	m	m	m
	India[4]	3.2	0.1	3.3	m	m	m
	Indonesia[3, 5, 6]	0.8	0.4	1.2	m	m	m
	Israel	7.0	1.4	8.4	7.0	1.5	8.5
	Jamaica	6.3	3.6	9.9	m	m	m
	Jordan[5]	5.0	1.0	6.0	m	m	m
	Malaysia[3]	5.0	m	m	m	m	m
	Paraguay	4.8	3.7	8.5	m	m	m
	Peru[3, 7]	3.3	1.3	4.6	m	m	m
	Philippines[4]	4.2	1.7	5.9	m	m	m
	Russian Federation[3, 6]	3.0	m	m	m	m	m
	Thailand[3]	4.5	0.3	4.7	m	m	m
	Tunisia[3, 6]	6.8	m	m	m	m	m
	Uruguay[3, 5]	2.9	m	m	m	m	m
	Zimbabwe[3]	6.9	m	m	m	m	m

1. Including public subsidies to households attributable for educational institutions. Including direct expenditure on educational institutions from international sources.
2. Net of public subsidies attributable for educational institutions.
3. Public subsidies to households not included in public expenditure, but in private expenditure.
4. Year of reference 1998.
5. Direct expenditure on educational institutions from international sources exceeds 1.5 per cent of all public expenditure.
6. Year of reference 2000.
7. Excluding post-secondary non-tertiary education.
* See Annex 3 for notes (*www.oecd.org/els/education/eag2002*).
Source: OECD.

Table B2.1b.
Expenditure on educational institutions as a percentage of GDP (1995, 1999)
Expenditure on educational institutions from public and private sources, by level of education, source of fund and year

		Primary, secondary and post-secondary non-tertiary education				Tertiary education			
		1999			1995	1999			1995
		Public [1]	Private [2]	Total	Total	Public [1]	Private [2]	Total	Total
OECD COUNTRIES	Australia*	3.6	0.6	4.2	3.7	0.8	0.7	1.5	1.7
	Austria[1]*	4.0	0.2	4.2	4.2	1.4	n	1.5	1.5
	Belgium*	3.5	m	m	m	1.3	m	m	m
	Canada[4]*	3.5	0.3	3.8	4.3	1.6	1.0	2.5	2.2
	Czech Republic*	2.8	0.4	3.2	3.7	0.8	0.1	0.9	1.0
	Denmark[3]*	4.1	0.1	4.2	4.1	1.5	n	1.6	1.6
	Finland*	3.6	n	3.6	4.0	1.8	n	1.8	1.9
	France*	4.1	0.2	4.4	4.4	1.0	0.1	1.1	1.1
	Germany*	2.8	0.9	3.7	3.5	1.0	0.1	1.1	1.1
	Greece[3]*	2.4	0.3	2.6	2.3	1.0	n	1.0	0.7
	Hungary	2.9	0.2	3.1	3.6	0.8	0.2	1.1	1.0
	Iceland	m	m	m	m	m	m	m	m
	Ireland[5]	3.0	0.1	3.1	3.7	1.1	0.3	1.4	1.3
	Italy	3.2	0.1	3.2	m	0.7	0.1	0.8	0.8
	Japan[6]*	2.7	0.2	3.0	3.1	0.5	0.6	1.0	1.0
	Korea*	3.2	0.8	4.0	m	0.5	1.9	2.4	m
	Luxembourg	m	m	m	m	m	m	m	m
	Mexico	3.1	0.5	3.6	4.0	0.8	0.3	1.1	1.1
	Netherlands*	2.9	0.2	3.1	3.1	1.0	0.3	1.3	1.2
	New Zealand	4.6	m	m	3.7	0.9	m	m	1.1
	Norway	4.0	n	4.0	4.2	1.4	0.1	1.5	1.7
	Poland	3.6	m	m	m	0.8	0.2	1.0	m
	Portugal[3]*	4.2	n	4.2	3.8	1.0	0.1	1.1	0.9
	Slovak Republic[3,5]	3.0	n	3.0	m	0.8	0.1	0.8	m
	Spain	3.2	0.4	3.7	3.9	0.9	0.3	1.1	1.0
	Sweden[5]	4.4	n	4.4	4.3	1.5	0.2	1.7	1.6
	Switzerland	3.9	0.5	4.4	m	1.2	n	1.2	m
	Turkey[3]*	2.9	m	2.9	1.8	1.0	n	1.0	0.7
	United Kingdom*	3.3	0.4	3.7	m	0.8	0.3	1.1	1.2
	United States[4]*	3.5	0.4	3.8	m	1.1	1.2	2.3	m
	Country mean	3.4	0.3	3.6	~	1.0	0.3	1.3	~
	OECD total	3.3	0.4	3.7	~	0.9	0.7	1.6	~
	Country mean for countries with 1995 data only	~	~	3.6	3.7	~	~	1.3	1.2
NON-OECD COUNTRIES	Argentina[3]	3.3	0.4	3.7	m	0.8	0.4	1.1	m
	Brazil[3,7]	3.7	m	m	m	1.1	m	m	m
	Chile	3.1	1.4	4.5	m	0.6	1.6	2.2	m
	China	1.4	1.1	2.6	m	0.5	0.4	0.8	m
	India[6,7]	2.5	0.1	2.6	m	0.6	n	0.6	m
	Indonesia[3,5,8]	0.6	0.2	0.8	m	0.2	0.2	0.4	m
	Israel	4.6	0.2	4.8	5.0	1.3	0.7	2.0	1.8
	Jamaica	4.7	2.4	7.2	m	1.2	0.5	1.7	m
	Jordan[5]	4.1	0.1	4.1	m	1.0	0.9	1.9	m
	Malaysia[3]	3.7	m	m	m	1.2	0.1	1.3	m
	Paraguay	4.0	2.7	6.8	m	0.8	0.7	1.5	m
	Peru[3,9]	2.3	0.7	2.9	m	0.7	0.6	1.2	m
	Philippines[7]	3.4	1.7	5.1	m	0.7	m	m	m
	Thailand[3]	2.8	0.1	2.9	m	0.9	0.2	1.1	m
	Tunisia[3,8]	5.4	m	m	m	1.5	m	m	m
	Uruguay[3,5]	2.0	0.1	2.1	m	0.6	m	m	m
	Zimbabwe[6]	5.9	m	m	m	1.0	m	m	m

1. Including public subsidies to households attributable for educational institutions. Including direct expenditure on educational institutions from international sources.
2. Net of public subsidies attributable for educational institutions.
3. Public subsidies to households not included in public expenditure, but in private expenditure.
4. Post-secondary non-tertiary included in tertiary education.
5. Direct expenditure on tertiary-level educational institutions from international sources exceeds 1.5 per cent of all public expenditure. International sources at primary and secondary level exeed 1.5 per cent in Uruguay.
6. Post-secondary non-tertiary included in both upper secondary and tertiary education.
7. Year of reference 1998.
8. Year of reference 2000.
9. Excluding post-secondary non-tertiary education.
* See Annex 3 for notes (*www.oecd.org/els/education/eag2002*).
Source: OECD.

B2

Table B2.1c.
Expenditure on educational institutions as a percentage of GDP (1999)
Expenditure on educational institutions from public and private sources[1], by level of education

	Pre-primary education (for children 3 years and older)	Primary, secondary and post-secondary non-tertiary education				Tertiary education			All levels of education combined (including undistributed and advanced research programmes)
		All primary, secondary and post-secondary non-tertiary education	Primary and lower secondary education	Upper secondary education	Post-secondary non-tertiary education	All tertiary education	Tertiary-type B education	Tertiary-type A education	
	(1)	(2)	(3)	(4)	(5)	(6)	(7)	(8)	(9)
Australia*	0.1	4.2	3.2	0.9	0.1	1.5	0.2	1.3	5.8
Austria	0.5	4.2	2.8	1.3	n	1.5	0.3	1.2	6.3
Belgium*	0.5	3.5	1.2	2.3	x(4)	1.3	x(6)	x(6)	5.3
Canada*	0.2	3.8	x(2)	x(2)	x(7)	2.5	1.1	1.4	6.6
Czech Republic*	0.5	3.2	2.0	1.2	n	0.9	0.1	0.9	4.7
Denmark*	0.8	4.2	2.7	1.4	m	1.6	x(6)	x(6)	6.7
Finland*	0.4	3.6	2.4	1.3	x(4)	1.8	0.1	1.7	5.8
France*	0.7	4.4	2.8	1.5	n	1.1	0.3	0.9	6.2
Germany*	0.6	3.7	2.1	1.3	0.3	1.1	0.1	1.0	5.6
Greece*	x(2)	2.6	1.1	1.4	0.2	1.0	0.2	0.8	3.9
Hungary	0.8	3.1	1.8	1.1	0.2	1.1	n	1.1	5.2
Iceland	m	m	m	m	m	m	m	m	m
Ireland	n	3.1	2.3	0.7	0.1	1.4	x(6)	x(6)	4.6
Italy	0.4	3.2	1.8	1.3	0.1	0.8	n	0.8	4.8
Japan*	0.2	3.0	2.0	0.9	x(4,6)	1.0	0.1	0.9	4.7
Korea*	0.1	4.0	2.7	1.3	a	2.4	0.6	1.8	6.8
Luxembourg	m	m	m	m	m	m	m	m	m
Mexico	0.5	3.6	2.8	0.8	a	1.1	x(6)	x(6)	5.2
Netherlands*	0.4	3.1	2.3	0.8	n	1.3	n	1.3	4.7
New Zealand[1]	0.2	4.6	3.3	1.2	0.1	0.9	0.1	0.8	5.9
Norway	0.8	4.0	2.8	1.3	x(4)	1.5	n	1.5	6.6
Poland	0.5	3.7	2.5	1.2	m	1.0	n	1.0	5.3
Portugal*	0.3	4.2	2.8	1.2	a	1.1	x(6)	x(6)	5.7
Slovak Republic	0.5	3.0	1.8	1.2	x(4)	0.8	x(8)	0.8	4.4
Spain	0.4	3.7	3.7	x(3)	x(3)	1.1	0.1	1.0	5.3
Sweden	0.6	4.4	3.0	1.4	n	1.7	x(6)	x(6)	6.7
Switzerland	0.2	4.4	2.8	1.6	0.1	1.2	0.1	1.1	5.9
Turkey*	m	2.9	2.1	0.8	a	1.0	x(8)	1.0	3.9
United Kingdom*	0.4	3.7	1.2	2.4	x(4)	1.1	x(6)	x(6)	5.2
United States*	0.4	3.8	x(2)	x(2)	x(6)	2.3	x(6)	x(6)	6.5
Country mean	*0.4*	*3.6*	*2.3*	*1.3*	*0.1*	*1.3*	*0.2*	*1.1*	*5.5*
OECD total	*0.4*	*3.7*	*2.3*	*1.3*	*0.1*	*1.6*	*x*	*x*	*5.8*
Argentina	0.3	3.7	2.9	0.8	a	1.1	0.5	0.7	5.8
Brazil[3,4]	0.4	3.7	3.0	0.6	m	1.1	m	1.1	5.1
Chile	0.5	4.5	3.1	1.4	a	2.2	0.2	2.0	7.2
China	0.1	2.6	1.7	0.9	a	0.8	x(6)	x(6)	3.7
India[4]	n	2.6	2.4	0.2	x(4,6)	0.6	0.1	0.5	3.3
Indonesia[5]	n	0.8	0.6	0.2	a	0.4	x(6)	x(6)	1.2
Israel	0.8	4.8	2.5	2.3	n.	2.0	x(6)	x(6)	8.4
Jamaica	1.1	7.2	5.7	1.4	0.1	1.7	0.4	1.2	9.9
Jordan	n	4.1	3.5	0.6	a	1.9	x(6)	x(6)	6.0
Malaysia[2]	0.1	3.7	1.6	2.0	0.2	1.3	0.2	1.1	5.1
Paraguay[2]	x(2)	6.8	4.0	2.8	a	1.5	0.3	1.3	8.5
Peru	0.4	2.9	2.6	0.4	m	1.2	0.3	1.0	4.6
Philippines[4]	n	5.0	4.1	0.3	n	m	a	m	m
Russian Federation[5]	x(9)	x(9)	x(9)	x(9)	x(9)	x(9)	x(9)	x(9)	3.0
Thailand	0.2	2.9	2.4	0.5	m	1.1	0.2	0.9	4.7
Tunisia[3,5]	m	5.4	x(2)	x(2)	a	1.5	x(6)	x(6)	6.8
Uruguay	0.3	2.1	1.6	0.5	a	0.6	m	0.6	3.0
Zimbabwe	n	5.9	3.9	2.0	x(4,6)	1.0	0.4	0.6	6.9

Note: x indicates that data are included in another column. The column reference is shown in brackets after "x". *e.g.*, x(2) means that data are included in column 2.

1. Including international sources.

2. Column 3 only refers to primary education and column 4 refers to all secondary education.

3. Including only direct public expenditure on educational institutions.

4. Year of reference 1998.

5. Year of reference 2000.

* See Annex 3 for notes *(www.oecd.org/els/education/eag2002)*.

Source: OECD.

Table B2.2.
Change of expenditure on educational institutions (1995, 1999)
Index of change between 1995 and 1999 in public and private expenditure on educational institutions, by level of education (1995=100)

	All levels of education			Primary, secondary and post-secondary non-tertiary education			Tertiary education		
	Direct public expenditure for educational institutions	Direct private expenditure for educational institutions	Total direct expenditure from both public and private sources for educational institutions	Direct public expenditure for educational institutions	Direct private expenditure for educational institutions	Total direct expenditure from both public and private sources for educational institutions	Direct public expenditure for educational institutions	Direct private expenditure for educational institutions	Total direct expenditure from both public and private sources for educational institutions
	(1)	(2)	(3)	(4)	(5)	(6)	(7)	(8)	(9)
Australia	123	140	126	136	137	136	88	143	107
Austria	107	80	105	108	101	108	107	54	106
Canada[1]	106	116	108	101	124	103	117	113	116
Czech Republic	92	75	90	85	78	89	116	51	98
Denmark[2]	110	103	109	110	114	110	102	406	104
Finland	109	x(1)	111	109	x(4)	109	108	x(7)	111
France	109	102	108	109	104	108	110	99	108
Germany	102	102	102	103	103	104	102	119	104
Greece	143	x(1)	149	121	x(4)	123	182	x(7)	173
Hungary	107	120	109	101	95	98	117	145	123
Ireland	124	128	124	115	110	115	160	134	151
Italy	103	m	m	96	m	m	112	133	116
Japan[1]	106	106	106	104	103	104	116	108	111
Mexico	114	114	114	111	100	109	119	159	128
Netherlands	113	163	116	116	116	116	105	229	119
New Zealand	134	m	m	142	m	m	96	m	m
Norway	104	88	104	109	88	109	102	88	101
Poland	116	m	m	127	m	m	113	m	m
Portugal	124	262	125	128	187	128	127	265	132
Spain	112	110	111	111	99	110	123	125	124
Sweden	114	201	116	115	119	115	108	206	116
Switzerland	m	m	m	m	m	m	m	m	m
Turkey	186	m	m	194	m	m	167	231	169
United Kingdom	106	m	m	107	m	m	100	103	101

Note: x indicates that data are included in another column. The column reference is shown in brackets after "x". *e.g.*, x(2) means that data are included in column 2.
1. Post-secondary non-tertiary included in tertiary education.
2. Post-secondary non-tertiary data are missing.
3. Post-secondary non-tertiary included in both upper secondary and tertiary education.
Source: OECD.

TOTAL PUBLIC EXPENDITURE ON EDUCATION

- On average, OECD countries devote 12.7 per cent of total public expenditure to educational institutions.

- Public funding of education is a social priority, even in OECD countries with little public involvement in other areas.

- In real terms, public expenditure on education increased by more than 5 per cent in four out of five OECD countries between 1995 and 1999.

- Public expenditure on education tended to grow faster than total public spending, but not as fast as GDP. In Italy, the Netherlands, Sweden and the United Kingdom, public expenditure on education increased between 1995 and 1999 despite public budgets falling in real terms.

B3

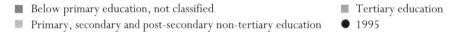

Chart B3.1.

Public expenditure on education as a percentage of total public expenditure (1999)

Direct public expenditure on educational institutions plus public subsidies to households (including subsidies for living costs, and public subsidies for other private entities) as a percentage of total public expenditure, by level of education and year

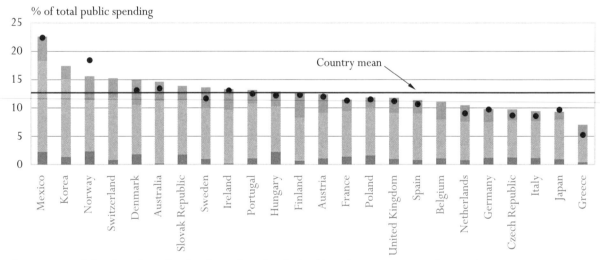

Countries are ranked in descending order of total expenditure from both public and private sources on educational institutions.
Source: OECD. Table B3.1. See Annex 3 for notes *(www.oecd.org/els/education/eag2002).*

Policy context

Governments become involved in providing services to the public for different reasons. If the public benefit from a particular service is greater than the private benefit, then markets alone may fail to provide these services adequately. Education is one area where all governments intervene to fund or direct the provision of services. As there is no guarantee that markets will provide equal access to educational opportunities, government funding of educational services ensures that education is not beyond the reach of some members of society. Public expenditure on education as a percentage of total public expenditure indicates the value of education relative to that of other public investments such as health care, social security, defence and security.

This indicator focuses on public expenditure on education.

B3

Since the second half of the 1990s, most OECD countries made serious efforts to consolidate public budgets. Education had to compete for public financial support against a wide range of other areas covered in government budgets. To portray this, this indicator also evaluates the change in educational expenditure in absolute terms and relative to changes in the size of public budgets.

It also evaluates how public expenditure has changed over time in absolute terms and relative to total governmental spending.

Evidence and explanations

What this indicator covers and what it does not cover

This indicator shows total public expenditure on education. This expenditure includes direct public expenditure on educational institutions as well as public subsidies to households (*e.g.*, scholarships and loans to students for tuition fees and student living costs) and to other private entities for education (*e.g.*, subsidies to companies or labour organisations that operate apprenticeship programmes). Unlike the preceding indicators, this indicator also includes public subsidies that are not attributable to household payments for educational institutions, such as subsidies for student living costs.

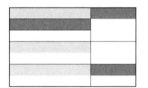

Coverage diagram (see page 144 for explanations)

OECD countries differ in the ways in which they use public money for education. Public funds may flow directly to schools or be channelled to institutions via households; they may also be restricted to the purchase of educational services or be used to support student living costs.

It is important to examine public investment in education in conjunction with private investment, as shown in Indicator B4.

Overall level of public resources invested in education

On average, OECD countries devote 12.7 per cent of total public expenditure to education. However, the values for individual countries range between 7 and 23 per cent. Korea and Mexico allocate 17 and 23 per cent, respectively, of total public spending to education (Chart B3.1). By contrast, in the Czech Republic, Germany, Greece, Italy and Japan, the proportion of public expenditure on education is less than 10 per cent. As in the case of spending on education in

On average, OECD countries devote 12.7 per cent of total public expenditure to education.

relation to GDP per capita, these values need to be interpreted in the light of student demography and enrolment rates.

Between 4.5 and 16.0 per cent of total public expenditure in OECD countries is allocated to primary, secondary and post-secondary non-tertiary education.

The public-sector proportion of the funding of the different levels of education varies widely between OECD countries. In 1999, OECD countries spent between 4.5 and 16.0 per cent of total public expenditure on primary, secondary and post-secondary non-tertiary education, and between 1.2 and 4.3 per cent on tertiary education. Australia, Korea, Portugal and Switzerland spend between about 10 and 15 per cent or more of total public expenditure on primary, secondary, and post-secondary non-tertiary education, and Mexico over 15 per cent. By contrast, Belgium, the Czech Republic, Germany, Greece, Italy, Japan and the Netherlands spend about 7 per cent or less on education below the tertiary level (Table B3.1).

Public funding of education is a social priority, even in OECD countries with little public involvement in other areas.

When public expenditure on education is examined as a proportion of total public spending, the relative sizes of public budgets (as measured by public spending in relation to GDP) need to be taken into account.

In OECD countries where public spending is low relative to overall GDP, such as Australia, Ireland, Korea, Mexico and the Slovak Republic, the proportion of public expenditure devoted to education is relatively high. However, in the remaining OECD countries, where public spending accounts for over 35 per cent of GDP, there seems to be no relation between the size of the public budget and how much of it is spent on education (Charts B3.1 and B3.2).

Chart B3.2.

Total public expenditure as a percentage of GDP (1995, 1999)

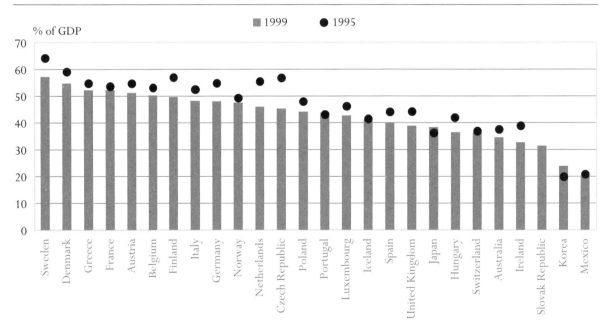

Countries are ranked in descending order of total public expenditure as a percentage of GDP in 1999.
Source: OECD. Annex 2.

Sweden, the OECD country with the highest proportion of GDP spent by government, spends the same high proportion of public budgets on education, as does Portugal, an OECD country with a relatively small public sector. Norway spends the third highest proportion of public budgets of all OECD countries on education, and Italy the third lowest, but in these two OECD countries, public spending accounts for 47 and 48 per cent, respectively, of GDP (Chart B3.2).

The process of budget consolidation puts pressure on education as on every other service. Nevertheless, with the exception of Japan and Norway, spending on education grew faster than spending in other public areas; the proportion of public budgets spent on education growing, on average, from 12.0 per cent in 1995 to 12.7 per cent in 1999. Public spending in Greece increased by nearly one-third, from 5.2 per cent to 7.0 per cent. In Denmark, the education share of public spending increased from 13.1 per cent in 1995 to 14.9 per cent in 1999, in Sweden from 11.6 to 13.6 per cent and in the Netherlands, from 9.1 to 10.4 per cent.

Typically, public expenditure on education grew faster than total public spending, but not as fast as national income.

B3

Definitions and methodologies

Educational expenditure is expressed as a percentage of a country's total public sector expenditure and as a percentage of GDP. Public educational expenditure includes expenditure on educational institutions and subsidies for students' living costs and for other private expenditure outside institutions. Public expenditure on education includes expenditure by all public entities, including ministries other than the ministry of education, local and regional governments and other public agencies.

Data refer to the financial year 1999 and are based on the UOE data collection on educational statistics administered by the OECD in 2001 (for details see Annex 3).

Total public expenditure, also referred to as total government spending, corresponds to the non-repayable current and capital expenditure of all levels of government: central, regional and local. Current expenditure includes final consumption expenditure, property income paid, subsidies and other current transfers (*e.g.*, social security, social assistance, pensions and other welfare benefits). Figures for total public expenditure have been taken from the OECD National Accounts Database (see Annex 2) and use the System of National Accounts 1993. In previous editions of *Education at a Glance*, total public expenditure was based on the System of National Accounts 1968. The change in the system of national accounts may explain differences in this indicator in comparison with previous editions of this publication.

Note that data appearing in earlier editions of this publication may not always be comparable to data shown in the 2002 edition due to changes in definitions and coverage that were made as a result of the OECD expenditure comparability study (see Annex 3 at *www.oecd.org/els/education/eag2002* for details on changes).

B3

Table B3.1.
Total public expenditure on education (1995, 1999)
Public expenditure on educational institutions plus public subsidies to households (which include subsidies for living costs, and other private entities) as a percentage of GDP and as a percentage of total public expenditure, by level of education and year

	Public expenditure on education as a percentage of total public expenditure				Public expenditure[1] on education as a percentage of GDP			
	1999			1995	1999			1995
	Primary, secondary and post-secondary non-tertiary education	Tertiary education	All levels of education combined	All levels of education combined	Primary, secondary and post-secondary non-tertiary education	Tertiary education	All levels of education combined	All levels of education combined
OECD COUNTRIES								
Australia*	11.0	3.4	14.6	13.4	3.8	1.2	5.0	5.0
Austria*	8.0	3.2	12.4	12.0	4.1	1.7	6.3	6.5
Belgium*	6.9	3.0	11.0	m	3.5	1.5	5.5	m
Canada[3]*	m	m	m	12.9	3.5	1.9	5.7	6.5
Czech Republic*	6.6	1.9	9.7	8.7	3.0	0.8	4.4	4.9
Denmark*	8.7	4.3	14.9	13.1	4.8	2.4	8.1	7.7
Finland*	7.6	4.2	12.5	12.3	3.8	2.1	6.2	7.0
France*	8.0	2.0	11.5	11.3	4.2	1.1	6.0	6.0
Germany*	6.2	2.3	9.7	9.7	3.0	1.1	4.7	4.7
Greece*	4.5	2.0	7.0	5.2	2.4	1.1	3.6	2.9
Hungary	8.0	2.6	12.8	12.2	2.9	0.9	4.7	5.0
Iceland	m	m	m	m	m	m	m	m
Ireland	9.4	3.6	13.2	13.0	3.1	1.2	4.3	5.1
Italy	6.6	1.7	9.4	8.6	3.2	0.8	4.5	4.6
Japan[1]*	7.1	1.2	9.3	9.7	2.7	0.5	3.5	3.6
Korea*	13.7	2.4	17.4	m	3.2	0.6	4.1	m
Luxembourg	m	m	m	m	m	m	m	m
Mexico	16.0	4.3	22.6	22.4	3.1	0.8	4.4	4.6
Netherlands*	6.8	2.9	10.4	9.1	3.1	1.3	4.8	5.0
New Zealand	m	m	m	14.4	4.8	1.2	6.3	5.7
Norway	9.0	4.2	15.6	18.4	4.3	2.0	7.4	9.1
Poland	8.3	1.9	11.8	11.5	3.6	0.8	5.2	5.5
Portugal*	9.7	2.4	13.1	12.5	4.2	1.0	5.7	5.4
Slovak Republic	9.6	2.5	13.8	m	3.0	0.8	4.3	m
Spain	8.2	2.3	11.3	10.6	3.3	0.9	4.5	4.7
Sweden	8.9	3.7	13.6	11.6	5.1	2.1	7.7	7.5
Switzerland	11.0	3.4	15.2	m	4.0	1.2	5.5	m
Turkey*	m	m	m	m	2.9	1.1	4.0	2.4
United Kingdom*	8.1	2.6	11.8	11.2	3.3	1.1	4.7	5.2
United States[3]*	m	m	m	m	3.5	1.4	5.2	m
Country mean	*8.7*	*2.8*	*12.7*	*12.0*	*3.5*	*1.2*	*5.2*	*5.4*
NON-OECD COUNTRIES								
Argentina	9.7	2.3	13.3	m	3.3	0.8	4.5	m
Brazil[4]	8.6	2.6	12.3	m	3.7	1.1	5.2	m
Chile	12.8	2.7	17.0	m	3.1	0.7	4.2	m
China	9.1	3.1	13.0	m	1.5	0.5	2.1	m
India[2,4]	9.8	2.4	12.6	m	2.5	0.6	3.2	m
Indonesia[5]	4.0	1.2	5.2	m	0.6	0.2	0.8	m
Israel	9.1	2.5	13.8	13.3	4.6	1.3	7.0	7.0
Jamaica	8.1	2.0	10.8	m	4.7	1.2	6.3	m
Jordan	16.7	3.8	20.6	m	4.1	0.9	5.0	m
Malaysia	16.5	8.3	25.2	m	3.7	1.9	5.7	m
Paraguay	7.3	1.5	8.8	m	4.0	0.8	4.8	m
Peru[6]	14.3	4.3	21.1	m	2.3	0.7	3.3	m
Philippines[4]	16.8	3.4	20.6	m	3.4	0.7	4.2	m
Russian Federation[5]	x	x	10.4	m	x	x	3.0	m
Thailand	16.9	6.7	28.0	m	3.0	1.2	4.9	m
Tunisia[5]	13.6	3.8	17.4	m	5.4	1.5	6.8	m
Uruguay	9.1	2.7	13.0	m	1.9	0.6	2.8	m
Zimbabwe[2]	m	m	m	m	5.8	1.2	7.0	m

1. Public expenditure presented in this table include public subsidies to households for living costs, which are not spent on educational institutions. Thus the figures presented here exceed those on public spending on institutions found in Table B2.1b.
2. Post-secondary non-tertiary is included in tertiary education and excluded from primary, secondary and post-secondary non-tertiary education.
3. Excluding public subsidies to the private sector. Post-secondary non-tertiary included in both upper secondary and tertiary education.
4. Year of reference 1998.
5. Year of reference 2000.
6. Excluding post-secondary non-tertiary education.
* See Annex 3 for notes (*www.oecd.org/els/education/eag2002*).
Source: OECD.

RELATIVE PROPORTIONS OF PUBLIC AND PRIVATE INVESTMENT IN EDUCATIONAL INSTITUTIONS

- The private share of total payments to educational institutions ranges from about 3 per cent or less in Finland, Norway, Portugal, the Slovak Republic, Sweden and Turkey to as much as 40 per cent in Korea.

- In a number of OECD countries, governments pay most of the costs of primary, secondary and post-secondary non-tertiary education but leave the management of educational institutions to the private sector, to provide a wider range of learning opportunities without creating barriers to the participation of students from low-income families.

- Private institutions that are predominantly financed by households are far less common at the primary, secondary and post-secondary non-tertiary levels than government-funded institutions.

B4

- Tertiary institutions tend to mobilise a much higher proportion of their funds from private sources than primary, secondary and post-secondary non-tertiary institutions. The private share includes private payments that are subsidies ranging from about 3 per cent or less in Austria, the Flemish Community of Belgium, Denmark, Finland, Greece and Switzerland to 78 per cent in Korea.

- In ten out of 19 OECD countries, private expenditure on tertiary education grew by more than 30 per cent between 1995 and 1999, but in most countries this did not lead to a decrease in public-sector spending on tertiary education.

Distribution of public and private expenditure on educational institutions, by level of education (1999)

■ Private payments to educational institutions excluding public subsidies to households and other private entities
□ Total public subsidies to households and other private entities excluding public subsidies for student living costs
■ Direct public expenditure on educational institutions

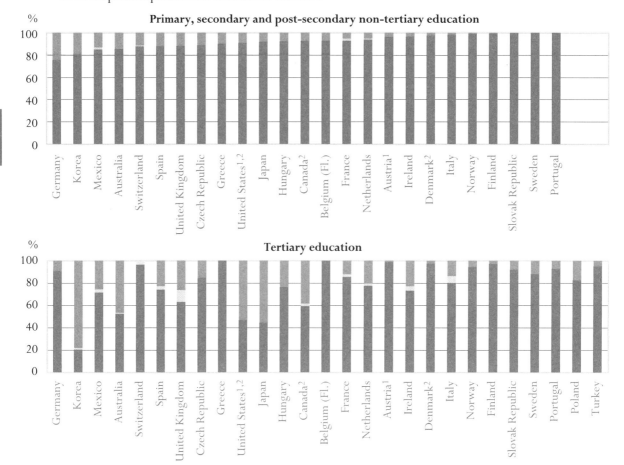

1. Total public subsidies to households partially included in private payments.
2. Post-secondary non-tertiary data are included in tertiary education or are missing.
Countries are ranked in ascending order of the proportion of direct public expenditure in primary, secondary and post-secondary non-tertiary education.
Source: OECD. Table B4.2. See Annex 3 for notes *(www.oecd.org/els/education/eag2002).*

Policy context

Cost-sharing between participants in the education system and society as a whole is an issue that is under discussion in many OECD countries. This question is especially relevant at the beginning and ending stages of initial education – pre-primary and tertiary education – where full or nearly full public funding is less common.

As new client groups participate increasingly in a wide range of educational programmes and have more opportunities made available by increasing numbers of providers, governments are forging new partnerships to mobilise the necessary resources to pay for education. New policies are designed to allow the different actors and stakeholders to participate more fully and to share costs and benefits more equitably.

As a result, public funding is now seen increasingly as providing only a part, although a very important part, of investment in education. The role of private sources is becoming more and more important in the funding of education. Some stakeholders are concerned that this balance should not become so tilted as to lead potential learners away from learning, instead of towards it.

This indicator shows the relative proportions of public and private spending on educational institutions...

...and how these proportions have changed since 1995.

B4

Evidence and explanations

What this indicator covers and what it does not cover

Governments can spend public funds directly on educational institutions or use them to provide subsidies to private entities for the purpose of education. When reporting on the public and private proportions of educational expenditure, it is therefore important to distinguish between the initial sources of funds and the final direct purchasers of educational goods and services.

Initial public spending includes both direct public expenditure on educational institutions and transfers to the private sector. To gauge the level of public expenditure, the components showing direct public expenditure on educational institutions and public subsidies for education therefore need to be added together. Initial private spending includes tuition fees and other student or household payments to educational institutions, less the portion of such payments offset by public subsidies.

The final public and private proportions are the percentages of educational funds spent directly by public and private purchasers of educational services. Final public spending includes direct public purchases of educational resources and payments to educational institutions and other private entities. Final private spending includes tuition fees and other private payments to educational institutions (whether offset or not by public subsidies).

Not all spending on instructional goods and services occurs within educational institutions. For example, families may purchase textbooks and materials commercially or seek private tutoring for their children outside educational institutions. At the tertiary level, student living costs and forgone earnings

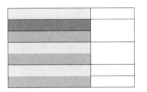

Coverage diagram (see page 144 for explanations)

can also account for a significant proportion of the costs of education. All such expenditure outside educational institutions, even if it is publicly subsidised, is excluded from this indicator. Public subsidies for educational expenditure outside institutions are discussed in Indicators B3 and B5.

Public and private proportions of expenditure on educational institutions

Educational institutions are still mainly funded by public sources…

Schools, universities and other educational institutions are still mainly publicly funded, although there is a substantial and growing degree of private funding. On average across OECD countries, 88 per cent of all funds for educational institutions come directly from public sources. In addition, 0.7 per cent are channelled to institutions via public subsidies to households (Table B4.1).

…but OECD countries vary significantly in the extent to which they draw on private funds.

Among the OECD countries reporting data, the proportion of private payments to educational institutions, including private payments that are subsidies, ranges from about 3 per cent or less in Finland, Norway, Portugal, the Slovak Republic, Sweden and Turkey to between 22 and 40 per cent in Australia, Germany, Japan, Korea and the United States (Table B4.1).

In pre-primary education, the private share of total payments to educational institutions represents on average 18 per cent and exceeds 50 per cent in Ireland, Japan and Korea.

Investment in early childhood education is of key importance in order to build a strong foundation for lifelong learning and to ensure equitable access to learning opportunities later in school. In pre-primary education, the private share of total payments to educational institutions ranges from 5 per cent or less in the Flemish Community of Belgium, France, Italy, the Netherlands, the Slovak Republic, Switzerland and the United Kingdom, to more than 37 per cent in Australia and Germany and more than 50 per cent in Ireland, Japan and Korea (Table B4.2).

The way in which education is financed differs between the primary/secondary and tertiary levels.

At the primary, secondary and post-secondary non-tertiary levels of education, between 10 and 18 per cent of funding comes from private sources in Australia, the Czech Republic, Mexico, Spain, Switzerland and the United Kingdom, and more than 18 per cent in Germany and Korea (Chart B4.1).

In most OECD countries, private expenditure is comprised mainly of household expenditure on tuition and other fees at tertiary institutions, while in Germany and Switzerland nearly all private expenditure is accounted for by contributions from the business sector to the dual system of apprenticeship at the upper secondary and post-secondary non-tertiary levels.

In some OECD countries, governments pay most of the costs of primary, secondary and post-secondary non-tertiary education but leave the management of educational institutions to the private sector…

New funding strategies aim not only at mobilising the required resources from a wider range of public and private sources, but also at providing a broader range of learning opportunities and improving the efficiency of schooling. In the majority of OECD countries, publicly funded primary, secondary and post-secondary non-tertiary education is also organised and delivered by public institutions, but in a fair number of OECD countries the public funds are finally transferred to private institutions or given directly to households to spend in the institution of their choice. In the former case, the final spending and delivery of education can be regarded as subcontracted by governments to non-governmental institutions, whereas in the latter instance, students and their families are left to decide which type of institution best meets their requirements.

On average across OECD countries, more than 10 per cent of primary, secondary and post-secondary non-tertiary students combined are enrolled in privately managed educational institutions that are predominantly publicly funded. In Belgium and the Netherlands, the majority of primary, secondary and post-secondary non-tertiary students are in fact enrolled in government-dependent private institutions, and in Australia, France, Korea, Spain and the United Kingdom the proportion is still more than 20 per cent (Chart B4.2). Although these institutions are privately managed, the financial support from governments can have attendant conditions. For example, teachers may be required to meet some minimum level of qualification, and students may be required to pass a government-regulated examination in order to graduate.

…thus seeking to provide a wider range of learning opportunities without creating barriers to the participation of students from low-income families.

B4

On average across OECD countries, 10 per cent of the public funds designated for educational institutions are spent in institutions that are privately managed (Table B4.3). In the Netherlands, where the central government is the major final source of funds, 71 per cent of public money for primary, secondary and post-secondary non-tertiary educational institutions and 36 per cent of public money for tertiary institutions are transferred from the government to private institutions. In Belgium, 55 per cent of the funds for educational institutions are transferred to private institutions at the primary, secondary and post-secondary non-tertiary levels (Chart B4.2).

An alternative form of final spending is the transfer of public money to private institutions.

In Australia, France, Korea, Spain and the United Kingdom, the share of public funds transferred to private institutions ranges at the primary/secondary and post-secondary level of education from 10 to 21 per cent.

At the primary, secondary and post-secondary non-tertiary levels of education, private educational institutions that are financed mainly by household payments are far less common and sometimes seen as thwarting the participation of students from low-income families. Only in Mexico and the United States are around 10 per cent of students enrolled in private institutions that are predominantly financed through unsubsidised household payments (Chart B4.2).

Private institutions that are predominantly financed by households are far less common at the primary, secondary and post-secondary non-tertiary levels.

Thus, at the primary, secondary and post-secondary non-tertiary levels of education, government funding transferred to the private sector (see Table B4.3 and Indicator B5) represents, on average, 3.5 per cent in OECD countries and exceeds 10 per cent only in Denmark and Sweden. It is more usual for households/students to receive some public funding at the tertiary level. Twenty per cent or more of public funds designated for tertiary educational institutions are transferred to the private sector in Australia, Canada, Denmark, the Netherlands, New Zealand, Norway, Sweden and the United Kingdom.

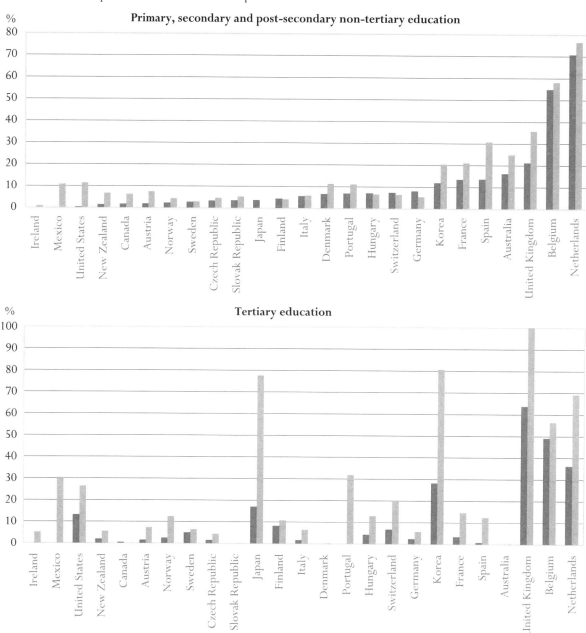

Chart B4.2.

Public support to private educational institutions (1999)

■ Proportion of public expenditure on educational institutions transferred to private institutions
▨ Proportion of students enrolled in private institutions

B4

Primary, secondary and post-secondary non-tertiary education

Tertiary education

Countries are ranked in ascending order of the proportion of direct public expenditure transferred to private institutions in primary, secondary and post-secondary non-tertiary education.
Source: OECD. Tables B4.3, C2.3 and C2.4. See Annex 3 for notes *(www.oecd.org/els/education/eag2002).*

With four countries constituting exceptions, the private proportion of educational expenditure is far higher at the tertiary level than at the primary, secondary and post-secondary non-tertiary levels. While primary, secondary and post-secondary non-tertiary education are usually perceived as a public good with mainly public returns, at the tertiary level the high private returns in the form of better employment and income opportunities (see Indicators A3 and A13) suggest that a greater contribution by individuals to the costs of tertiary education may be justified, provided of course, that governments can ensure that funding is accessible to students irrespective of their economic background (see also Indicator B5).

Tertiary institutions tend to mobilise a much higher proportion of their funds from private sources…

The proportion of expenditure on tertiary institutions covered by individuals, businesses and other private sources including private payments that are subsidies, ranges from about 3 per cent or less in Austria, the Flemish Community of Belgium, Denmark, Finland, Greece and Switzerland, to over one-third in Australia, Canada, Japan, Korea, the United Kingdom and the United States. In Japan and the United States, more than half of all final funds originate from private sources, and in Korea the figure exceeds 78 per cent (Chart B4.1). In Korea, over 80 per cent of students are enrolled in private universities, where more than 95 per cent of budgets are derived from tuition fees.

…but the private share, including private payments that are subsidies, ranges from about 3 per cent or less in Austria, the Flemish Community of Belgium, Denmark, Finland, Greece and Switzerland, to 78 per cent in Korea.

B4

The amounts paid by students and their families to cover tuition fees and other education-related expenditure differ between OECD countries according to taxation and spending policies, and the willingness of governments to support students. This willingness, in turn, is influenced by students' enrolment status (full-time or part-time), age and residency (whether they are living at home). To some extent, however, the guidelines used in establishing eligibility for these subsidies are breaking down. Mature students, whose numbers are increasing, are more likely to have established their own households and to prefer part-time or distance learning to full-time, on-campus study.

Changes in public and private investment in education

Direct private expenditure on educational institutions increased by over 10 per cent in absolute terms between 1995 and 1999 in nine out of 16 OECD countries with comparable data. Increases range from about 2 per cent in France and Germany to 100 per cent or more in Portugal and Sweden. Only three OECD countries – Austria, the Czech Republic and Norway – saw a decline in the private proportion of more than 5 per cent (Chart B4.3).

The scale of private-sector funding of education has increased.

Four OECD countries – Australia, Denmark, Canada and the Netherlands – saw a significant growth in private spending in primary, secondary and post-secondary non-tertiary education between 1995 and 1999. In Australia, Canada and the Netherlands, private funds grew by between 16 and 37 per cent, with private funds now representing more than 5 per cent of total spending on educational institutions in these three countries (Chart B4.3 and Table B4.2).

In Australia, Canada and Denmark, private spending on primary, secondary and post-secondary non-tertiary education increased faster than public spending…

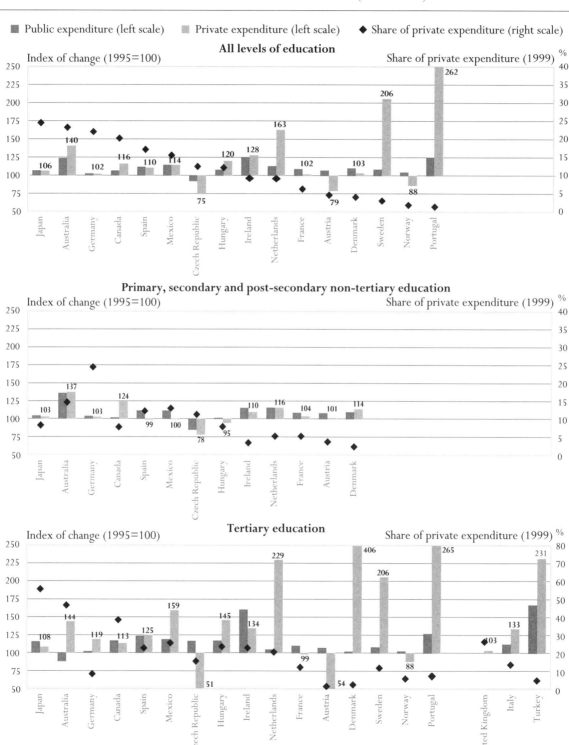

Chart B4.3.

Index of change in public and private expenditure on educational
institutions between 1995 and 1999 (1995=100)

■ Public expenditure (left scale)   ■ Private expenditure (left scale)   ◆ Share of private expenditure (right scale)

All levels of education

Primary, secondary and post-secondary non-tertiary education

Tertiary education

B4

Note: Countries with a share of total funding from private sources of 1 per cent or less are not represented in the chart.
Countries are ranked in descending order of the share of private expenditure in 1999 for all levels of education.
Source: OECD. Tables B2.2, B4.1 and B4.2. See Annex 3 for notes *(www.oecd.org/els/education/eag2002).*

In many OECD countries, the growth in tertiary participation (Indicator C2) represents a response to heavy demand, both individual and social. But, just as many tertiary structures and programmes were designed for a different era, so too were its funding mechanisms. As demand for tertiary education has increased in many OECD countries, so has the share of the financial burden borne by families. With the exception of Canada and France, in every OECD country with available data, the change in private expenditure on educational institutions is much greater with respect to tertiary institutions than with respect to primary, secondary and post-secondary non-tertiary institutions.

…but changes are most striking in tertiary education, where a dramatic growth in participation is accompanied by a growing share of private expenditure…

The increase in private household spending at the tertiary level is explained by one or more of four factors: *i*) an increase in enrolments, *ii*) increased or newly imposed fees, charges or contributions, *iii*) a rise in the costs of education-related goods and services other than institutions, and *iv*) growth in enrolment in private institutions with higher fees.

…which is explained by four main factors.

B4

Ten out of 19 OECD countries reported an increase in private spending on tertiary educational institutions of more than 30 per cent between 1995 and 1999. Some OECD countries, most notably Australia, Hungary, Mexico and the Netherlands, saw a clear shift in the relative proportions of public and private investment in tertiary education institutions between 1995 and 1999. In Australia, the private-sector proportion increased from 36 to 48 per cent, in Hungary from 20 to 23 per cent, in Mexico from 23 to 28 per cent and in the Netherlands, from 12 per cent in 1995 to 22 per cent in 1999. However, there are exceptions to this pattern: in Ireland, an increase of 34 per cent in private-sector funding of tertiary institutions between 1995 and 1999 was outpaced by an increase in public funds of 60 per cent. In Austria and the Czech Republic, private funding of tertiary education decreased by around half between 1995 and 1999. As a consequence, the proportion of private funding of educational institutions relative to total spending on education decreased from almost 29 per cent in 1995 to less than 15 per cent in the Czech Republic, and from 2.4 to 1.3 per cent in Austria (Chart B4.3 and Table B4.2).

In 10 out of 19 OECD countries, the private proportion of tertiary education funding grew by more than 30 per cent between 1995 and 1999…

It is important to note that rises in private educational expenditure have not generally been accompanied by falls in public expenditure on education, either in primary, secondary and post-secondary non-tertiary education or at the tertiary level. On the contrary, Chart B4.3 shows that public investment in education has increased in most of the OECD countries for which 1995 to 1999 data are available, regardless of changes in private spending. In fact, some of the OECD countries with the highest growth in private spending have also shown the highest increase in public funding of education. This indicates that increasing private spending on tertiary education tends to complement, rather than replace, public investment.

…but in most OECD countries, this did not lead to a decrease in public-sector spending on tertiary education.

New funding strategies aim not only at mobilising the required resources from a wider range of public and private sources, but also at influencing

Many OECD countries in which students or their

families contribute to the funding of tertiary education show some of the highest participation rates...

B4

...while several OECD countries with predominantly public funding show only low levels of participation.

Data refer to the financial year 1999 and are based on the UOE data collection on educational statistics administered by the OECD in 2001 (for details see Annex 3).

Data for the financial year 1995 are based on a special survey carried out among OECD countries in 2000.

student behaviour in ways that make education more cost-effective. It is hard to determine the precise impact of tuition fees on learners' behaviour, partly because fees cannot be seen in isolation from grants, taxation and implicit subsidies through loans. But many OECD countries in which students and their families spend more on tertiary education show some of the highest tertiary participation and completion rates (Indicators A2 and C2).

Conversely, in the six OECD countries with the lowest entry rates to tertiary-type A education – the Czech Republic, Denmark, Germany, Mexico, Switzerland and Turkey – private sources of funds account for between 2 and 28 per cent of total educational spending on tertiary institutions (Tables B4.2 and C2.1). It is therefore not obvious that the participation of the beneficiaries of tertiary studies in the financing of their education creates economic barriers – provided, of course, that governments develop appropriate strategies to make funding accessible to students from all income groups.

Definitions and methodologies

The public and private proportions of expenditure on educational institutions are the percentages of total spending originating in, or generated by, the public and private sectors. Private spending includes all direct expenditure on educational institutions, whether partially covered by public subsidies or not. Public subsidies attributable to households, included in private spending, are shown separately.

Parts of the budgets of educational institutions are related to ancillary services offered to students, which are usually student welfare services, such as student meals, housing and transportation. Some of the costs for these services are covered by fees collected from students, which are included.

The change in private and public spending on educational institutions is shown as an index and compares the proportion of private spending in 1995 with that in 1999. The data on expenditure for 1995 were obtained by a special survey in 2000 in which expenditure for 1995 was adjusted to methods and definitions used in the 1999 UOE data collection.

Note that a large increase or decrease in private spending (Chart B4.3) in OECD countries where private spending is small in relation to total spending may only represent a small additional burden on households, while a comparatively small change in spending applied to a high level of private funding can translate into substantial additional funds for educational institutions.

The glossary at the end of this volume gives a definition of public, government-dependent private and independent private institutions.

Note that data appearing in earlier editions of this publication may not always be comparable to data shown in the 2002 edition due to changes in definitions and coverage that were made as a result of the OECD expenditure comparability study (see Annex 3 at *www.oecd.org/els/education/eag2002* for details on changes).

Table B4.1.
Relative proportions of public and private expenditure on educational institutions for all levels of education (1995, 1999)
Distribution of public and private sources of funds for educational institutions after transfers from public sources, by year

	1999			1995		
	Public sources	Private sources[1]	Private: of which subsidised	Public sources	Private sources[1]	Private: of which subsidised
Australia*	76.5	23.5	0.3	78.7	21.3	3.0
Austria*	95.4	4.6	x	93.9	6.1	1.4
Belgium*	95.0	5.0	m	m	m	m
Canada[2]*	79.8	20.2	m	82.3	17.7	a
Czech Republic*	87.6	12.4	n	85.0	15.0	6.2
Denmark[2]*	96.0	4.0	m	95.7	4.3	n
Finland*	97.8	2.2	n	m	m	m
France*	91.9	8.1	1.8	91.4	8.6	2.6
Germany*	77.9	22.1	0.1	77.8	22.2	0.1
Greece*	93.4	6.6	m	m	m	n
Hungary	87.9	12.1	n	89.0	11.0	n
Iceland	m	m	m	m	m	m
Ireland	89.6	10.4	1.2	89.8	10.2	m
Italy	90.3	9.7	1.1	m	m	m
Japan[3]*	75.6	24.4	a	75.5	24.5	a
Korea*	58.7	41.3	1.1	m	m	m
Luxembourg	m	m	m	m	m	m
Mexico	82.6	17.4	1.9	82.6	17.4	m
Netherlands*	89.7	10.3	1.2	92.6	7.4	4.8
New Zealand	m	m	a	m	m	m
Norway	98.2	1.8	n	97.9	2.1	m
Poland	m	m	m	m	m	m
Portugal*	98.7	1.3	m	99.4	0.6	m
Slovak Republic	97.8	2.2	m	m	m	m
Spain	82.3	17.7	0.7	82.1	17.9	0.4
Sweden	97.0	3.0	a	98.3	1.7	m
Switzerland	90.0	10.0	1.7	m	m	m
Turkey*	98.8	1.2	m	94.7	5.3	1.2
United Kingdom*	83.7	16.3	2.2	m	m	m
United States[2]*	75.0	25.0	x	m	m	m
Country mean	*88.0*	*12.0*	*0.7*	~	~	~
Argentina	77.2	22.8	0.1	m	m	m
Chile	55.1	44.9	1.9	m	m	m
China	55.8	44.2	n	m	m	m
India[2,4]	96.2	3.8	x	m	m	m
Indonesia[5]	64.5	35.5	m	m	m	m
Israel	80.9	19.1	2.0	80.5	19.5	1.4
Jamaica	62.3	37.7	1.0	m	m	m
Jordan	83.7	16.3	x	m	m	m
Paraguay	56.4	43.6	x	m	m	m
Peru[2]	71.6	28.4	m	m	m	m
Thailand	94.6	5.4	m	m	m	m

OECD COUNTRIES / NON-OECD COUNTRIES

1. Including subsidies attributable to payments to educational institutions received from public sources.
2. Post-secondary non-tertiary included in tertiary education or missing.
3. Post-secondary non-tertiary included in both upper secondary and tertiary education.
4. Year of reference 1998.
5. Year of reference 2000.
* See Annex 3 for notes (*www.oecd.org/els/education/eag2002*).
Source: OECD.

Table B4.2.
Relative proportions of public and private expenditure on educational institutions (1995, 1999)
Distribution of public and private sources of funds for educational institutions after transfers from public sources, by level of education and year

| | Pre-primary education (for children 3 years and older) | | | Primary, secondary and post-secondary non-tertiary education | | | | | | Tertiary education | | | | | |
| | 1999 | | | 1999 | | | 1995 | | | 1999 | | | 1995 | | |
	Public sources	Private sources[1]	Private: of which subsidised	Public sources	Private sources[1]	Private: of which subsidised	Public sources	Private sources[1]	Private: of which subsidised	Public sources	Private sources[1]	Private: of which subsidised	Public sources	Private sources[1]	Private: of which subsidised
Australia[*]	62.9	37.1	n	85.4	14.6	n	85.6	14.4	0.7	52.4	47.6	1.1	64.2	35.8	8.1
Austria[*]	86.5	13.5	0.2	96.4	3.6	x	96.1	3.9	x	98.7	1.3	x	97.6	2.4	x
Belgium	m	m	m	m	m	m	m	m	m	m	m	m	m	m	m
Belgium (Fl.)[*]	95.2	4.8	m	92.7	7.3	m	m	m	m	100.0	n	m	m	m	m
Canada[2*]	92.3	7.7	x	92.3	7.7	m	93.7	6.3	a	59.3	40.7	2.4	59.1	40.9	a
Czech Republic[*]	89.3	10.7	n	88.8	11.2	n	88.6	11.4	6.8	84.7	15.3	n	71.0	29.0	8.6
Denmark[2*]	81.9	18.1	m	97.8	2.2	m	97.8	2.2	n	97.7	2.3	m	m	m	n
Finland[*]	84.8	15.2	n	99.4	0.6	n	m	m	m	97.4	2.6	n	m	m	m
France[*]	95.8	4.2	n	92.8	7.2	2.0	92.5	7.5	2.4	85.7	14.3	2.3	84.3	15.7	5.0
Germany[*]	62.2	37.8	n	75.6	24.4	n	75.5	24.5	n	91.5	8.5	0.3	92.7	7.3	0.7
Greece[*]	x	x	m	90.2	9.8	m	m	m	n	99.9	0.1	m	m	m	n
Hungary	89.1	10.9	n	92.2	7.8	n	91.7	8.3	n	76.6	23.4	n	80.3	19.7	n
Iceland	m	m	m	m	m	m	m	m	m	m	m	m	m	m	m
Ireland	32.3	67.7	m	96.7	3.3	m	96.5	3.5	m	73.4	26.6	4.0	69.7	30.3	x
Italy	98.7	1.3	n	98.3	1.7	n	m	m	m	80.3	19.7	6.2	82.8	17.2	0.1
Japan[1*]	48.6	51.4	a	91.8	8.2	a	91.7	8.3	a	44.5	55.5	a	42.8	57.2	a
Korea[*]	23.2	76.8	0.5	80.2	19.8	1.0	m	m	m	20.7	79.3	1.3	m	m	m
Luxembourg	m	m	m	m	m	m	m	m	m	m	m	m	m	m	m
Mexico	87.5	12.5	0.2	85.2	14.8	1.9	83.8	16.2	m	71.8	28.2	2.7	77.4	22.6	m
Netherlands[*]	96.9	3.1	a	93.9	6.1	1.0	93.9	6.1	3.0	77.6	22.4	2.1	88.3	11.7	10.2
New Zealand	m	m	m	m	m	a	m	m	m	m	m	a	m	m	m
Norway	100.0	n	n	99.1	0.9	x	98.9	1.1	m	94.4	5.6	n	93.6	6.4	m
Poland[4]	m	m	m	m	m	m	m	m	m	82.8	17.2	m	m	m	m
Portugal[*]	m	m	m	99.9	0.1	m	100.0	0.0	m	92.9	7.1	m	96.5	3.5	m
Slovak Republic	98.6	1.4	m	99.6	0.4	m	m	m	m	91.9	8.1	m	m	m	m
Spain	77.9	22.1	n	87.9	12.1	n	86.6	13.4	n	74.2	25.8	3.2	74.4	25.6	2.0
Sweden	100.0	a	m	99.8	0.2	m	99.8	0.2	m	88.4	11.6	a	93.6	6.4	m
Switzerland	99.9	0.1	0.1	87.7	12.3	1.2	m	m	m	96.7	3.3	3.3	m	m	m
Turkey[*]	m	m	m	m	m	m	94.0	6.0	n	95.3	4.7	m	96.6	3.4	4.2
United Kingdom[*]	95.6	4.4	a	88.2	11.8	0.0	m	m	m	63.2	36.8	10.7	63.9	36.1	16.0
United States[3*]	90.3	9.7	m	90.7	9.3	x	m	m	m	46.9	53.1	x	m	m	m
Country mean	*82.2*	*17.8*	*0.1*	*92.1*	*7.9*	*0.5*	~	~		*79.2*	*20.8*	*2.1*	~	~	
Argentina	m	m	m	88.6	11.4	m	m	m	m	67.4	32.6	0.6	m	m	m
Chile	70.2	29.8	n	69.2	30.8	a	m	m	m	22.8	77.2	6.3	m	m	m
China	54.6	45.4	n	55.8	44.2	a	m	m	m	56.8	43.2	n	m	m	m
India[2,5]	95.3	4.7	m	95.3	4.7	x	m	m	m	99.7	0.3	x	m	m	m
Indonesia[6]	5.3	94.7	m	76.6	23.4	m	m	m	m	43.8	56.2	m	m	m	m
Israel	75.5	24.5	n	94.9	5.1	1.0	m	m	m	58.1	41.9	5.2	m	m	m
Jamaica	33.9	66.1	n	64.7	35.3	1.2	m	m	m	70.4	29.6	1.0	m	m	m
Jordan	m	m	m	98.4	1.6	a	m	m	m	48.1	51.9	x	m	m	m
Malaysia	m	m	m	m	m	m	m	m	m	92.7	7.3	m	m	m	m
Paraguay	m	m	m	59.5	40.5	x	m	m	m	51.2	48.8	x	m	m	m
Peru[2]	80.3	19.7	a	76.8	23.2	a	m	m	m	54.5	45.5	m	m	m	m
Philippines[5]	m	m	m	66.8	33.2	x	m	m	m	m	m	m	m	m	m
Thailand	92.6	7.4	m	97.8	2.2	m	m	m	m	83.3	16.7	m	m	m	m
Uruguay	87.4	12.6	m	93.6	6.4	m	m	m	m	m	m	m	m	m	m

1. Including subsidies attributable to payments to educational institutions received from public sources.
 To calculate private funds net of subsidies, subtract public subsidies (columns 3,6,9) from private funds (columns 2,5,8).
 To calculate total public funds, including public subsidies, add public subsidies (columns 3,6,9) to direct public funds (columns 1,4,7).
2. Post-secondary non-tertiary included in tertiary education or missing.
3. Post-secondary non-tertiary included in both upper secondary and tertiary education.
4. Public institutions only.
5. Year of reference 1998.
6. Year of reference 2000.
* See Annex 3 for notes (*www.oecd.org/els/education/eag2002*).
Source: OECD.

EDUCATION AT A GLANCE © OECD 2002

Table B4.3.
Distribution of total public expenditure on education (1999)
Public expenditure on education transferred to educational institutions and public transfers to the private sector as a percentage of
total public expenditure on education, by level of education

B4

	Primary, secondary and post-secondary non-tertiary education			Tertiary education			All level of education combined		
	Direct public expenditure on public institutions	Direct public expenditure on private institutions	Indirect public transfers and payments to the private sector	Direct public expenditure on public institutions	Direct public expenditure on private institutions	Indirect public transfers and payments to the private sector	Direct public expenditure on public institutions	Direct public expenditure on private institutions	Indirect public transfers and payments to the private sector
Australia[*]	79.6	16.1	4.3	67.7	n	32.3	75.9	12.1	10.8
Austria[*]	96.7	1.8	1.5	85.5	1.5	13.1	92.5	2.7	4.7
Belgium[*]	44.9	54.7	0.4	35.0	49.0	15.9	43.3	52.1	4.6
Canada[1*]	98.3	1.7	x	77.7	0.4	21.8	91.5	1.2	7.3
Czech Republic[*]	91.5	3.2	5.3	91.1	1.4	7.6	92.3	2.6	5.1
Denmark[1*]	78.9	6.5	14.6	64.8	n	35.2	75.3	4.1	20.6
Finland[*]	91.8	4.2	3.9	74.9	8.1	17.1	86.1	5.8	8.2
France[*]	83.0	13.3	3.7	88.7	3.3	8.0	85.2	10.9	4.0
Germany[*]	85.4	7.9	6.7	85.4	2.4	12.3	82.1	10.7	7.2
Greece[*]	99.9	a	0.1	96.6	a	3.4	98.9	a	1.1
Hungary	92.5	6.9	0.6	83.2	4.3	12.6	91.3	5.7	2.9
Iceland	m	m	m	m	m	m	m	m	m
Ireland	96.9	n	3.1	85.2	n	14.8	93.7	n	6.3
Italy	93.7	5.4	0.9	81.3	1.6	17.1	91.6	4.4	4.0
Japan[2*]	96.5	3.5	m	83.0	17.0	m	93.6	6.4	m
Korea[*]	86.6	11.7	1.7	59.8	28.1	12.1	83.7	13.0	3.2
Luxembourg	m	m	m	m	m	m	m	m	m
Mexico	97.2	0.1	2.7	94.3	m	5.7	96.9	0.1	3.1
Netherlands[*]	21.9	70.7	7.4	39.3	36.1	24.6	27.4	61.0	11.6
New Zealand	95.5	1.4	3.2	75.9	1.9	22.2	90.9	2.1	7.0
Norway	91.9	2.2	5.9	69.0	2.4	28.6	83.3	4.6	12.2
Poland	m	m	m	m	m	m	m	m	m
Portugal[*]	92.0	6.7	1.3	94.0	n	6.0	91.8	6.2	2.1
Slovak Republic	96.6	3.4	0.0	95.6	m	4.4	96.7	2.5	0.9
Spain	85.5	13.5	1.0	89.9	0.7	9.3	86.9	10.4	2.7
Sweden	83.7	2.7	13.6	64.7	4.9	30.4	78.9	3.9	17.1
Switzerland	90.0	7.1	2.8	89.3	6.6	4.1	89.6	6.8	3.6
Turkey[*]	99.8	a	0.2	87.8	0.4	11.8	96.5	0.1	3.4
United Kingdom[*]	78.7	21.1	0.2	a	73.3	26.7	64.7	29.8	5.5
United States[1*]	99.7	0.3	x	67.6	13.2	19.2	90.5	4.5	5.0
Country mean	87.0	9.9	3.5	75.1	9.9	16.4	84.0	9.7	6.4
Argentina	85.7	12.5	1.8	96.2	2.5	1.3	88.1	10.4	1.6
Brazil[3]	98.2	1.8	n	93.1	0.8	6.1	97.2	1.5	1.3
Chile	67.8	31.8	0.4	42.2	33.9	23.9	63.8	32.0	4.1
China	99.2	a	0.8	93.7	a	6.3	97.9	a	2.1
India[1, 3]	70.7	29.1	0.2	78.2	21.5	0.3	72.2	27.6	0.2
Indonesia[4]	90.0	6.6	3.5	m	m	m	m	m	m
Israel	75.0	24.0	1.1	6.9	83.4	9.6	64.1	33.1	2.7
Jamaica	98.2	n	1.8	98.3	n	1.7	95.6	2.7	1.7
Jordan	100.0	a	a	88.1	a	11.9	97.8	a	2.2
Malaysia	98.9	0.6	0.5	66.1	n	33.9	88.2	0.4	11.5
Paraguay	92.5	7.4	0.1	m	m	m	m	m	m
Philippines[3]	98.7	a	1.3	97.5	a	2.5	98.5	a	1.5
Thailand	93.3	2.2	4.5	74.9	n	25.1	88.9	2.0	9.1
Uruguay	99.9	a	0.1	100.0	a	n	100.0	a	n

OECD COUNTRIES

NON-OECD COUNTRIES

1. Post-secondary non-tertiary included in tertiary education or missing.
2. Post-secondary non-tertiary included in both upper secondary and tertiary education.
3. Year of reference 1998.
4. Year of reference 2000.
* See Annex 3 for notes (*www.oecd.org/els/education/eag2002*).
Source: OECD.

SUPPORT FOR STUDENTS AND HOUSEHOLDS THROUGH PUBLIC SUBSIDIES

- An average of 16 per cent of public spending on tertiary education is devoted to supporting students, households and other private entities. In Australia, Denmark and the United Kingdom, public subsidies account for about one-third or more of public tertiary education budgets.

- Subsidies are particularly important in systems where students are expected to pay for at least part of the cost of their education.

- In most OECD countries, the beneficiaries of public subsidies have considerable discretion regarding the spending of subsidies. In all reporting OECD countries, subsidies are spent mainly outside educational institutions, and in one out of three countries exclusively outside.

B5

Chart B5.1.

Public subsidies for education at the tertiary level (1999)

Public subsidies for education to the private sector as a percentage of total government expenditure on education, by type of subsidy

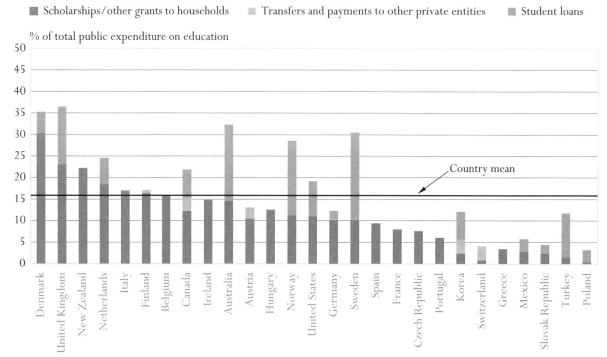

Countries are ranked in descending order of scholarships/other grants to households and transfers and payments to other private entities in tertiary education.
Source: OECD. Table B5.2. See Annex 3 for notes (www.oecd.org/els/education/eag2002).

Policy context

Through subsidies to students and their families, governments can encourage participation in education, particularly among students from low-income families, by covering part of the cost of education and related expenses. Furthermore, public subsidies play an important role in indirectly financing educational institutions.

Channelling funding for institutions through students may also help to increase competition between institutions and result in greater efficiency in the financing of education. Since aid for student living costs can serve as a substitute for work as a financial resource, public subsidies may enhance educational attainment by enabling students to study full-time and to work fewer hours or not at all.

Public subsidies come in many forms: as means-based subsidies, as family allowances for all students, as tax allowances for students or their parents, or as other household transfers. Unconditional subsidies such as tax reductions or family allowances may provide less of an incentive for low-income students to participate in education than means-tested subsidies. However, they may still help to reduce disparities between households with and without children in education.

A key question is whether financial subsidies for households should be provided in the form of grants or loans. Are loans an effective means to help increase the efficiency of financial resources invested in education and shift some of the cost of education to the beneficiaries of educational investment? Or are student loans less appropriate than grants in encouraging low-income students to pursue their education? This indicator cannot answer this question but portray the policies for subsidies that the different OECD countries pursue.

Evidence and explanations

What this indicator covers and what it does not cover

This indicator shows the proportion of public spending on education that is transferred to students, families and other private entities. Some of these funds are spent indirectly on educational institutions, for example, when subsidies are used to cover tuition fees. Other subsidies for education do not relate to educational institutions, such as subsidies for student living costs.

The indicator distinguishes between scholarships and grants, which are non-repayable subsidies, on the one hand, and loans on the other. The indicator does not, however, distinguish between different types of grants or loans, such as scholarships versus family allowances and subsidies in kind.

Governments can also support students and their families by providing tax reductions and tax credits. These types of subsidy are not covered by this indicator.

This indicator examines direct and indirect public spending on educational institutions as well as public subsidies to households for student living costs.

B5

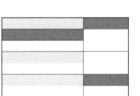

Coverage diagram (see page 144 for explanations)

It is also common for governments to guarantee the repayment of loans to students made by private lenders. In some OECD countries, this indirect form of subsidy is as significant as, or more significant than, direct financial aid to students. However, for reasons of comparability, the indicator only takes into account public transfers to private entities relating to private loans, not the total value of loans generated.

In the case of student loans, the indicator reports the full volume of loans in order to provide information on the level of support which current students receive. The indicator does not take repayments into account, even though these can reduce the real costs of loans substantially. Some OECD countries also have difficulties quantifying the amount of loans attributable to students. Therefore data on student loans should be treated with some caution.

Public subsidies to households and other private entities

OECD countries spend an average of 0.4 per cent of their GDP on public subsidies to households and other private entities.

OECD countries spend an average of 0.4 per cent of their GDP on public subsidies to households and other private entities. In Denmark and Sweden, this figure is more than 1 per cent of GDP. Furthermore, on average across OECD countries, 7.0 per cent of public budgets for education is spent on transfers to the private sector (Tables B3.1, B5.1 and B5.2). Most of these amounts are devoted to the tertiary level of education, except in the Czech Republic, France, Germany, Mexico, Sweden and Switzerland, where more than 50 per cent of transfers to the private sector are devoted to primary, secondary and post-secondary non-tertiary education.

At the primary, secondary and post-secondary non-tertiary levels, public subsidies account for a comparatively small proportion of public spending on education.

Most OECD countries offer public subsidies to households from upper secondary education onwards. There are usually few subsidies available before the upper secondary level, since in most OECD countries education up to that level is compulsory, free of charge, predominantly provided by the public sector and largely provided at the point of residence of students and their families. In 10 out of 26 OECD countries, subsidies to households and private entities therefore account for 1 per cent or less of total public spending on primary, secondary and post-secondary non-tertiary education. However, in Australia, the Czech Republic, Germany, the Netherlands and Norway, public subsidies account for between 4 and 8 per cent of public expenditure on primary, secondary and post-secondary non-tertiary education; and in Denmark and Sweden for 15 and 14 per cent respectively (Chart B5.2). In most of the OECD countries with high proportions of subsidies at the primary, secondary and post-secondary non-tertiary levels of education, these subsidies are directed at adults re-entering secondary education.

Australia, Denmark and the United Kingdom spend about one-third or more of their public education budget at the

The proportion of educational budgets spent on subsidies to households and private entities is much higher at the tertiary level. OECD countries spend, on average, 16 per cent of their public budgets for tertiary education on subsidies to households and other private entities (Chart B5.1). In Australia, Denmark and the United Kingdom, public subsidies account for about one-third or

Public subsidies for education in primary, secondary and post-secondary non-tertiary education (1999)

Public subsidies for education to the private sector as a percentage of total government expenditure on education, by type of subsidy

■ Scholarships/other grants to households ■ Transfers and payments to other private entities ■ Student loans

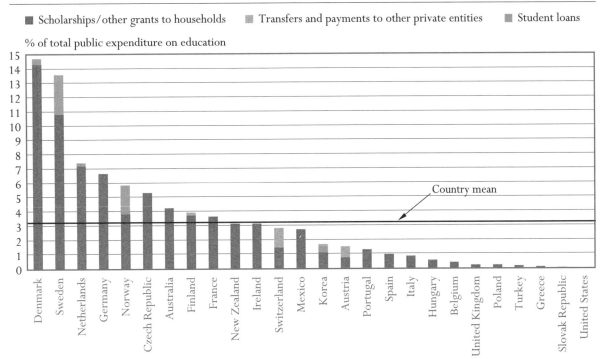

Countries are ranked in descending order of total public subsidies for primary, secondary and post-secondary non-tertiary education.
Source: OECD. Table B5.1. See Annex 3 for notes *(www.oecd.org/els/education/eag2002)*.

B5

more of public spending on tertiary education. Only Greece, Poland, the Slovak Republic and Switzerland spend less than 5 per cent of their total public spending on tertiary education on subsidies (Table B5.1).

tertiary level on subsidies to the private sector.

A key question in many OECD countries is whether financial subsidies for households should primarily be provided in the form of grants or loans. Governments choose to subsidise students' living costs or educational costs through different mixtures of grants and loans. Advocates of student loans argue that money spent on loans goes further, that is, if the amount spent on grants were used to guarantee or subsidise loans instead, more aid would be available to students in total, and overall access would be increased. Loans also shift some of the cost of education to those who benefit most from educational investment. Opponents of loans argue that student loans will be less effective than grants in encouraging low-income students to pursue their education. They also argue that loans may be less efficient than anticipated because of the various subsidies provided to borrowers or lenders, and of the costs of administration and servicing.

OECD countries use different mixtures of grants and loans to subsidise students' educational costs.

Chart B5.1 presents the proportion of public educational expenditure spent on loans, grants and scholarships and other subsidies to households. Grants and scholarships include family allowances and other specific subsidies, but exclude tax reductions. Thirteen out of 27 reporting OECD countries rely exclusively on grants or scholarships and transfers and payments to other private entities. The remaining OECD countries provide both grants or scholarships and loans to students. With two exceptions, the highest subsidies to students are provided by those OECD countries which also offer student loans. Most of them spend an above-average proportion of their budgets on grants and scholarships (Chart B5.1 and Table B5.2).

Repayments of loans reduce the real cost of loan programmes to the public budget; at the same time they increase the burden on households for education.

B5

Repayments of public loans can be a substantial source of income for governments and can decrease the costs of loan programmes significantly. The current reporting of household expenditure on education (Indicator B4) does not take into account the repayment by previous recipients of public loans. These repayments can be a substantial burden to individuals and have an impact on the decision to participate in tertiary education. However, many OECD countries make the repayment of loans dependent on the later level of income of graduates.

Given that repayments to loan programmes are made by former students who took out loans several years previously, it is difficult to estimate the real costs of loan programmes; net of repayments and loans are therefore reported on a gross basis only. International comparisons of total repayments in the same reference period cannot be made, since they are heavily influenced by changes in schemes for the distribution of loans and by changes in the numbers of students receiving loans.

How subsidies are used: student living costs and tuition fees

In most OECD countries, the beneficiaries of subsidies have considerable discretion about how they spend public subsidies.

In most OECD countries, the bulk of public payments to households for education are not earmarked, that is, their use is determined by the beneficiaries, namely the students and their families. In a few OECD countries, however, public subsidies are earmarked for payments to educational institutions. Australia, New Zealand and the United Kingdom, for example, earmark public subsidies for tuition fees. In Australia, loans and tuition fees are closely related through the Higher Education Contribution Scheme (HECS). Under HECS, students can elect to pay their contributions for their university education in advance, semester by semester, and receive a 25 per cent discount, or, they can repay their accumulated contribution through the tax system when their annual income exceeds a minimum threshold. For the purpose of the OECD education indicators, HECS is counted as a loan scheme, although students may not see the delayed payments as a loan. In OECD countries where tuition fees are substantial, a proportion of the public subsidy to households is effectively earmarked for payments to educational institutions, even without an official policy.

Scholarships and other grants attributable to students are largely spent outside educational institutions. They support educational expenses other than tuition fees. In Finland and the Netherlands, scholarships and other grants not attributable for tuition fees to educational institutions account for more than 15 per cent of the total public spending on tertiary education. Korea, Poland and Switzerland are the only OECD countries where scholarships and other grants attributable for expenditure outside institutions amount to less than 1 per cent of total public spending on education (Table B5.2).

In all reporting OECD countries subsidies are spent mainly outside educational institutions, and in one out of three OECD countries exclusively outside.

In OECD countries where students are required to pay tuition fees, access to public subsidies is of particular importance in order to provide students with access to educational opportunities, regardless of their financial situation. Indicator B4 shows what proportion of funding of educational institutions originates from private sources.

Subsidies are particularly important in systems where students are expected to pay at least part of the cost of their education.

B5

In OECD countries with low levels of private involvement in the funding of educational institutions, the level of public subsidies tends to be lower also (Tables B5.2 and B4.2). On the other hand, in the United Kingdom, more than 10 per cent of public expenditure on subsidies at tertiary level is designated to help students and households to pay for tuition fees. An exception is Korea, where despite the fact that more than 80 per cent of all expenditure on tertiary institutions originates from private sources, the level of subsidies to support tuition payments to institutions is, at 2 per cent, comparatively low (Tables B5.2 and B4.2).

Definitions and methodologies

Public subsidies to households include the following categories: *i*) grants/scholarships; *ii*) public student loans; *iii*) family or child allowances contingent on student status; *iv*) public subsidies in cash or kind specifically for housing, transportation, medical expenses, books and supplies, social, recreational and other purposes; *v*) interest-related subsidies for private loans.

Data refer to the financial year 1999 and are based on the UOE data collection on educational statistics administered by the OECD in 2001 (for details see Annex 3).

Expenditure on student loans is reported on a gross basis, that is, without subtracting or netting out repayments or interest payments from the borrowers (students or households). This is because the gross amount of loans including scholarships and grants is the relevant variable for measuring financial aid to current participants in education.

Public costs related to private loans guaranteed by governments are included as subsidies to other private entities. Unlike public loans, only the net cost of these loans is included.

The value of tax reductions or credits to households and students is not included.

Note that data appearing in earlier editions of this publication may not always be comparable to data shown in the 2002 edition due to changes in definitions and coverage that were made as a result of the OECD expenditure comparability study (see Annex 3 at *www.oecd.org/els/education/eag2002* for details on changes).

Table B5.1.

Public subsidies to the private sector as a percentage of total public expenditure on education and GDP for primary, secondary and post-secondary non-tertiary education (1999)

Direct public expenditure on educational institutions and subsides for households and other private entities as a percentage of total public expenditure on education and GDP

		Subsidies for education to private entities					Transfers for education to private entities as percentage of GDP
	Direct expenditure for institutions	Financial aid to students			Transfers and payments to other private entities	Total	
		Scholarships/ other grants to households	Student loans	Total			
OECD COUNTRIES Australia	95.7	4.3	n	4.3	n	4.3	0.16
Austria	98.5	0.7	a	0.7	0.8	1.5	0.06
Belgium	99.6	0.4	n	0.4	n	0.4	0.01
Canada[1*]	m	m	m	m	m	m	m
Czech Republic*	94.7	5.3	a	5.3	n	5.3	0.16
Denmark[1*]	85.3	14.3	0.4	14.7	n	14.7	0.70
Finland	96.1	3.7	n	3.7	0.2	3.9	0.15
France	96.3	3.7	a	3.7	a	3.7	0.15
Germany*	93.3	6.7	n	6.7	n	6.7	0.20
Greece	99.9	0.1	m	0.1	a	0.1	0.00
Hungary	99.4	0.6	a	0.6	n	0.6	0.02
Iceland	m	m	m	m	m	m	m
Ireland*	96.9	3.1	n	3.1	n	3.1	0.10
Italy	99.1	0.9	a	0.9	n	0.9	0.03
Japan	m	a	m	m	n	m	m
Korea	98.3	1.1	0.5	1.6	0.1	1.7	0.06
Luxembourg	m	m	m	m	m	m	m
Mexico	97.3	2.7	a	2.7	n	2.7	0.09
Netherlands	92.6	7.2	0.2	7.4	n	7.4	0.23
New Zealand	96.8	3.2	a	3.2	n	3.2	0.15
Norway	94.1	3.8	2.0	5.9	n	5.9	0.25
Poland	99.8	0.2	x	0.2	m	0.2	0.01
Portugal	98.7	1.3	m	1.3	m	1.3	0.06
Slovak Republic	100.0	n	a	n	a	n	n
Spain	99.0	1.0	n	1.0	n	1.0	0.03
Sweden	86.4	10.8	2.8	13.6	a	13.6	0.69
Switzerland*	97.2	1.5	n	1.5	1.3	2.8	0.11
Turkey	99.8	0.2	a	0.2	a	0.2	0.00
United Kingdom	99.8	0.2	n	0.2	n	0.2	0.01
United States[1]	100.0	n	a	n	n	n	x
Country mean	*96.7*	*3.0*	*0.3*	*3.2*	*0.1*	*3.3*	*0.14*
NON-OECD COUNTRIES Argentina	98.2	1.8	n	1.8	n	1.8	0.06
Brazil[2]	100.0	n	n	n	n	n	n
Chile	99.6	n	a	n	a	n	n
China	99.2	0.8	x	0.8	a	0.8	n
India[1,2]	99.8	0.2	n	0.2	x	0.2	n
Indonesia[3]	96.5	3.5	m	3.5	x	3.5	n
Israel	98.9	1.1	n	1.1	n	1.1	n
Jamaica	98.2	1.8	n	1.8	n	1.8	0.08
Jordan	100.0	a	a	a	a	a	a
Malaysia	99.5	0.5	a	0.5	a	0.5	n
Paraguay	99.9	n	a	n	a	n	n
Peru[1]	99.9	0.1	n	0.1	n	0.1	n
Philippines[2]	98.7	1.3	a	1.3	a	1.3	n
Thailand	95.5	n	4.4	4.5	m	4.5	0.13
Uruguay	99.9	n	a	n	a	n	n

1. Excluding post-secondary non-tertiary education or missing.
2. Year of reference 1998.
3. Year of reference 2000.
* See Annex 3 for notes (*www.oecd.org/els/education/eag2002*).
Source: OECD.

B5

Table B5.2.
Public subsidies to the private sector as a percentage of total public expenditure on education and GDP for tertiary education (1999)

Direct public expenditure on educational institutions and subsidies for households and other private entities as a percentage of total public expenditure on education and GDP

B5

		Subsidies for education to private entities						
		Financial aid to students			Scholarships/ other grants to households attributable to educational institutions	Transfers and payments to other private entities	Total	Transfers for education to private entities as percentage of GDP
	Direct expenditure for institutions	Scholarships/ other grants to households	Student loans	Total				
OECD COUNTRIES Australia	67.7	14.6	17.7	32.3	1.4	n	32.3	0.38
Austria	86.9	10.4	a	10.4	x	2.6	13.1	0.22
Belgium	84.1	15.9	n	15.9	m	n	15.9	0.24
Canada[1]*	78.2	12.2	6.4	18.6	m	3.2	21.8	0.41
Czech Republic*	92.4	7.6	a	7.6	n	n	7.6	0.06
Denmark*	64.8	30.3	4.9	35.2	m	n	35.2	0.83
Finland	82.9	16.4	n	16.4	n	0.7	17.1	0.36
France	92.0	8.0	a	8.0	2.4	a	8.0	0.08
Germany*	87.7	10.1	1.9	12.0	n	0.3	12.3	0.13
Greece	96.6	3.4	m	3.4	m	a	3.4	0.04
Hungary	87.4	12.6	a	12.6	n	n	12.6	0.12
Iceland	m	m	m	m	m	m	m	m
Ireland*	85.2	14.8	n	14.8	4.7	n	14.8	0.17
Italy	82.9	16.9	n	16.9	6.3	0.1	17.1	0.14
Japan	m	m	m	m	m	n	m	m
Korea	87.9	2.4	6.4	8.8	2.4	3.3	12.1	0.07
Luxembourg	m	m	m	m	m	m	m	m
Mexico	94.3	2.8	2.9	5.7	m	n	5.7	0.05
Netherlands	75.4	18.4	6.2	24.6	2.0	n	24.6	0.32
New Zealand	77.8	22.2	a	22.2	x	n	22.2	0.27
Norway	71.4	11.3	17.3	28.6	n	n	28.6	0.57
Poland	96.8	0.4	2.7	3.2	n	m	3.2	0.03
Portugal	94.0	6.0	m	6.0	m	m	6.0	0.06
Slovak Republic	95.6	2.5	1.9	4.4	m	a	4.4	0.03
Spain	90.7	9.3	n	9.3	3.9	n	9.3	0.08
Sweden	69.6	10.1	20.3	30.4	x	a	30.4	0.63
Switzerland*	95.9	0.8	n	0.8	n	3.3	4.1	0.05
Turkey	88.2	1.5	10.2	11.8	m	n	11.8	0.14
United Kingdom	63.6	23.1	13.3	36.4	10.7	n	36.4	0.39
United States[1]	80.8	11.1	8.1	19.2	x	m	19.2	0.26
Country mean	*84.1*	*10.9*	*4.7*	*15.4*	*2.0*	*0.6*	*15.9*	*0.23*
NON-OECD COUNTRIES Argentina	98.7	n	n	n	x	0.9	1.3	n
Brazil[2]	93.9	4.3	1.8	6.1	x	n	6.1	0.07
Chile	76.1	10.8	13.1	23.9	21.0	a	23.9	0.16
China	93.7	6.3	x	6.3	n	a	6.3	n
India[2]	99.7	0.3	x	0.3	x	x	0.3	n
Israel	90.4	8.1	1.6	9.6	8.1	n	9.6	0.12
Jamaica	98.3	1.7	m	1.7	1.3	n	1.7	n
Jordan	88.1	11.9	a	11.9	x	a	11.9	0.11
Malaysia	66.1	13.2	20.7	33.9	x	a	33.9	0.63
Paraguay	98.0	2.0	m	2.0	x	a	2.0	n
Peru	98.9	n	0.9	1.1	x	n	1.1	n
Philippines[2]	97.5	1.0	1.6	2.5	x	a	2.5	n
Thailand	74.9	m	25.1	25.1	m	m	25.1	0.29
Uruguay	100.0	n	a	n	x	a	n	n
Zimbabwe[1]	87.3	4.0	8.7	12.7	x	a	12.7	0.15

1. Including post-secondary non-tertiary education.
2. Year of reference 1998.
* See Annex 3 for notes (*www.oecd.org/els/education/eag2002*).
Source: OECD.

EXPENDITURE ON INSTITUTIONS
BY SERVICE CATEGORY AND BY RESOURCE CATEGORY

B6

- On average, one quarter of expenditure on tertiary education is attributable to R&D at tertiary educational institutions. Significant differences between OECD countries in the emphasis on R&D in tertiary institutions explain part of the large differences in expenditure per tertiary student.

- In primary, secondary, and post-secondary non-tertiary education combined, current expenditure accounts, on average across all OECD countries, for 92 per cent of total spending. In all but four OECD countries, 70 per cent or more of primary, secondary and post-secondary non-tertiary current expenditure is spent on staff salaries.

Chart B6.1.

Expenditure on instruction, research and development (R&D) and ancillary services
in tertiary educational institutions as a percentage of GDP (1999)

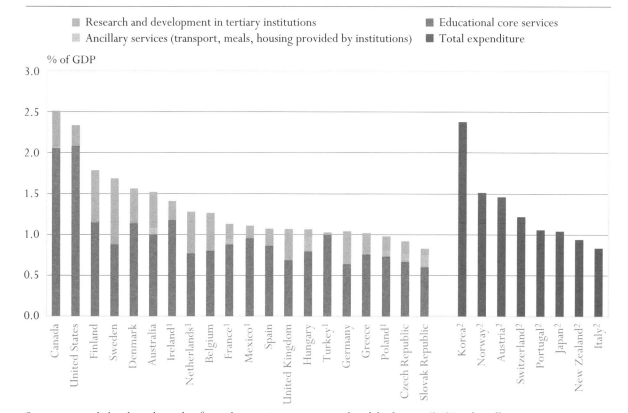

Countries are ranked in descending order of expenditure on instruction, research and development (R&D) and ancillary services in tertiary educational institutions.
1. Research and development expenditure at tertiary level and thus total expenditure are underestimated.
2. The bar represents total expenditure at tertiary level and includes research and development expenditure.
Source: OECD. Table B6.1. See Annex 3 for notes *(www.oecd.org/els/education/eag2002).*

Policy context

How spending is apportioned between different categories of expenditure can affect the quality of services (*e.g.*, through teachers' salaries), the condition of educational facilities (*e.g.*, school maintenance) and the ability of the education system to adjust to changing demographic and enrolment trends (as in the construction of new schools).

Comparisons of how different OECD countries apportion educational expenditure between the various resource categories can provide some insight into variation in the organisation and operation of educational institutions. Decisions on the allocation of resources made at the system level, both budgetary and structural, eventually feed through to the classroom and affect the nature of instruction and the conditions under which it is provided.

Educational institutions offer a range of educational services besides instruction. At the primary, secondary and post-secondary non-tertiary levels of education, institutions may offer meals, free transport to and from school or boarding facilities. At the tertiary level, institutions may offer housing and often perform a wide range of research activities as an integral part of tertiary education.

This indicator compares OECD countries with respect to the division of spending between current and capital expenditure and the distribution of current expenditure by resource category.

B6

It also compares how OECD countries' spending is distributed by different functions of educational institutions.

Evidence and explanations

What this indicator covers and what it does not cover

This indicator breaks down educational expenditure by current and capital expenditure and the three main functions which educational institutions typically fulfil. This includes, first, costs directly attributable to instruction, such as teachers' salaries or school materials, and costs indirectly related to the provision of instruction, such as expenditure on administration, instructional support services, development of teacher, student counselling, or on the construction and/or provision of school facilities. Second, it includes spending on ancillary services, such as student welfare services provided by educational institutions. Third, it includes spending attributable to research and development (R&D) performed at tertiary educational institutions, either in the form of separately funded R&D activities or in the form of those proportions of salaries and current expenditure in general education budgets that are attributable to the research activities of staff.

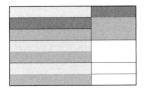

Coverage diagram (see page 144 for explanations)

The indicator does not include public and private R&D spending outside educational institutions, such as R&D spending in industry. A comparative review of R&D spending in sectors other than education is provided in the OECD Science and Technology Indicators. Expenditure on student welfare services at educational institutions only includes public subsidies for those services. Expenditure by students and their families on services that are provided by institutions on a self-funding basis are not included.

B6

Significant differences among OECD countries in the emphasis on R&D in tertiary institutions explain part of the large variation in expenditure per tertiary student.

Student welfare services are integral functions of schools and universities.

Expenditure on ancillary services at primary, secondary, and post-secondary non-tertiary levels represents 5 per cent of total spending on educational institutions.

Expenditure on instruction, R&D and ancillary services

Below the tertiary level, educational expenditure is dominated by spending on educational core services. At the tertiary level other services, particularly those related to R&D activities, can account for a significant proportion of educational spending. Differences between OECD countries in expenditure on R&D activities can therefore explain a significant part of the differences between OECD countries in overall educational expenditure per tertiary student (Chart B6.1). High levels of R&D spending in tertiary educational institutions in Australia, Belgium, Canada, Denmark, Finland, Germany, the Netherlands and Sweden (between 0.40 and 0.80 of GDP), for example, imply that spending on education per student in these OECD countries would be considerably lower if the R&D component were excluded (Table B6.1).

Student welfare services and, sometimes, services for the general public, are integral functions of schools and universities in many OECD countries. Countries finance these ancillary services with different combinations of public expenditure, public subsidies and fees paid by students and their families.

On average, OECD countries spend 0.2 per cent of their GDP on subsidies for ancillary services provided by primary, secondary and post-secondary non-tertiary institutions. This represents 5 per cent of total spending on these institutions. At the high end, the Czech Republic, Finland, France, Hungary and the Slovak Republic spend about 10 per cent or more of total spending on educational institutions on ancillary services, which translates into more than US$ 500 (PPP) per student in Finland and France and more than US$ 250 (PPP) per student in Canada, the Czech Republic, Hungary, Sweden and the United States (Tables B6.1 and B6.2).

In more than two-thirds of OECD countries, the amount spent on ancillary services is higher than the amount spent on subsidies to households at the primary, secondary and post-secondary non-tertiary levels. Exceptions to this pattern are Australia, Ireland, the Netherlands and Sweden, where expenditure on subsidies to households is higher (Tables B5.1 and B6.1).

On average, expenditure on subsidies for ancillary services at the tertiary level amounts to just 0.04 per cent of GDP. Nevertheless, on a per student basis this can translate into significant amounts, as in Australia, the Czech Republic, France, Hungary and the Slovak Republic, where subsidies for ancillary services amount to over US$ 450 (PPP). At the tertiary level, ancillary services are more often provided on a self-financed basis (Tables B6.1 and B6.2).

Current and capital expenditure, and the distribution of current expenditure by resource category

Educational expenditure can first be divided into current and capital expenditure. Capital expenditure comprises spending on assets that last longer than one year and includes spending on the construction, renovation and major repair of buildings. Current expenditure comprises spending on school resources used each year for the operation of schools.

Current expenditure can be further sub-divided into three broad functional categories: compensation of teachers, compensation of other staff, and other current expenditure (on, for example, teaching materials and supplies, maintenance of school buildings, preparation of student meals and renting of school facilities). The amount allocated to each of these functional categories will depend in part on current and projected changes in enrolment, on the salaries of educational personnel and on costs of maintenance and construction of educational facilities.

B6

Education takes place mostly in school and university settings. The labour-intensive technology of education explains the large proportion of current spending within total educational expenditure. In primary, secondary, and post-secondary non-tertiary education combined, current expenditure accounts, on average across all OECD countries, for 92 per cent of total spending.

There is some noticeable variation between OECD countries with respect to the relative proportions of current and capital expenditure: at the primary, secondary and post-secondary non-tertiary levels combined, the proportion of current expenditure ranges from less than 86 per cent in Greece, Korea and Turkey, to 96 per cent or more in Canada, the Flemish Community of Belgium, Mexico and the Slovak Republic (Chart B6.2).

The salaries of teachers and other staff employed in education account for the largest proportion of current expenditure in OECD countries. On average across OECD countries, expenditure on the compensation of educational personnel accounts for 80 per cent of current expenditure at the primary, secondary and post-secondary non-tertiary levels of education combined. Although 70 per cent or less of expenditure in the Czech Republic, Finland, Sweden and the United Kingdom is devoted to the compensation of educational personnel, the proportion is 90 per cent or more in Greece, Mexico, Portugal and Turkey (Chart B6.2).

In all except four OECD countries, 70 per cent or more of current expenditure at the primary, secondary and post-secondary non-tertiary levels is spent on staff salaries.

OECD countries with relatively small education budgets (Mexico, Portugal and Turkey, for example) tend to devote a larger proportion of current educational expenditure to the compensation of personnel and a smaller proportion to services which are sub-contracted or bought in, such as support services (*e.g.*, maintenance of school buildings), ancillary services (*e.g.*, preparation of meals for students) and renting of school buildings and other facilities.

OECD countries with smaller education budgets invest relatively more in personnel and less in other services.

In Denmark and the United States, around one quarter of staff expenditure in primary, secondary and post-secondary non-tertiary education combined goes towards compensation of non-teaching staff, while in Austria, Ireland, Korea and Spain this figure is 10 per cent or less. These differences are likely to reflect the degree to which educational personnel specialise in non-teaching activities

OECD countries vary in the proportions of current expenditure which they allocate to the compensation of teachers and other staff.

Distribution of total and current expenditure on educational institutions, by resource category and level of education (1999)

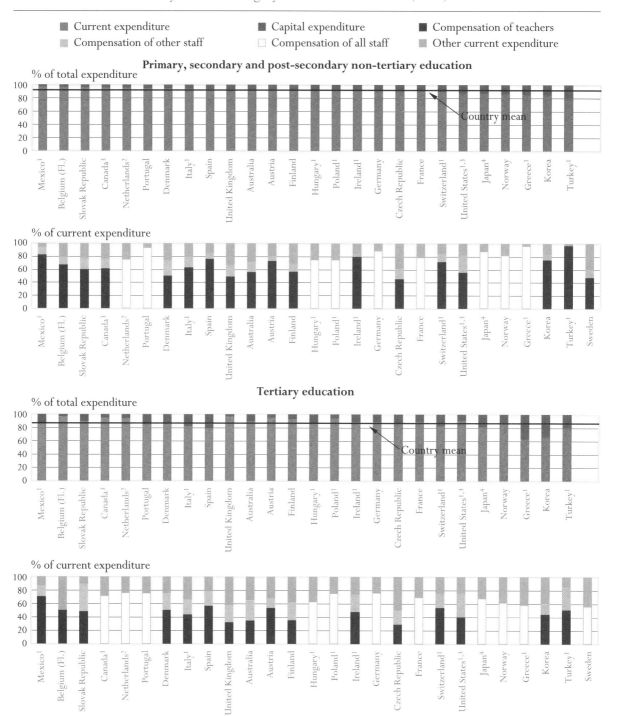

B6

1. Public institutions only.
2. Public and government-dependent private institutions only.
3. Excluding post-secondary non-tertiary education.
4. Post-secondary non-tertiary included in both upper secondary and tertiary education.
Countries are ranked in ascending order of current expenditure on primary, secondary and post-secondary non-tertiary education.
Source: OECD. Table B6.3. See Annex 3 for notes *(www.oecd.org/els/education/eag2002).*

in a particular country (for example, principals who do not teach, guidance counsellors, bus drivers, school nurses, janitors and maintenance workers) (Table B6.3).

At the tertiary level, the proportion of total expenditure spent on capital outlays is larger than at the primary, secondary and post-secondary non-tertiary levels, generally because of more differentiated and advanced teaching facilities. In 18 out of 26 OECD countries, the proportion spent on capital expenditure at the tertiary level is 10 per cent or more, and in Greece, Korea, Spain and Turkey it is above 20 per cent (Chart B6.2).

Differences are likely to reflect how tertiary education is organised in each OECD country, as well as the degree to which expansion in enrolments requires the construction of new buildings.

OECD countries, on average, spend 31 per cent of current expenditure at the tertiary level on purposes other than the compensation of educational personnel. This is explained by the higher cost of facilities and equipment in higher education (Chart B6.2).

Definitions and methodologies

The distinction between current and capital expenditure is the standard one used in national income accounting. Current expenditure refers to goods and services consumed within the current year, and must be made recurrently in order to sustain the production of educational services. Capital expenditure refers to assets which last longer than one year, including spending on construction, renovation or major repair of buildings and on new or replacement equipment. The capital expenditure reported here represents the value of educational capital acquired or created during the year in question – that is, the amount of capital formation – regardless of whether the capital expenditure was financed from current revenue or by borrowing. Neither current nor capital expenditure includes debt servicing.

Calculations cover expenditure by public institutions or, where available, that of public and private institutions combined.

Current expenditure other than on the compensation of personnel includes expenditure on services which are sub-contracted or bought in, such as support services (*e.g.*, maintenance of school buildings), ancillary services (*e.g.*, preparation of meals for students) and renting of school buildings and other facilities. These services are obtained from outside providers (unlike the services provided by the education authorities or educational institutions themselves using their own personnel).

Expenditure on R&D includes all expenditure on research performed at universities and other tertiary education institutions, regardless of whether the research is financed from general institutional funds or through separate grants

At the tertiary level, the proportion of capital expenditure is generally larger because of differentiated and advanced teaching facilities.

B6

Data refer to the financial year 1999 and are based on the UOE data collection on educational statistics administered by the OECD in 2001 (for details see Annex 3).

B6

or contracts from public or private sponsors. The classification of expenditure is based on data collected from the institutions carrying out R&D rather than on the sources of funds.

"Ancillary services" are services provided by educational institutions that are peripheral to the main educational mission. The two main components of ancillary services are student welfare services and services for the general public. At primary, secondary, and post-secondary non-tertiary levels, student welfare services include meals, school health services, and transportation to and from school. At the tertiary level, it includes halls of residence (dormitories), dining halls and health care. Services for the general public include museums, radio and television broadcasting, sports, and recreational and cultural programmes. Expenditure on ancillary services including fees from students or households are excluded.

Educational core services are estimated as the residual of all expenditure, *i.e.* total expenditure on educational institutions net of expenditure on R&D and ancillary services.

Note that data appearing in earlier editions of this publication may not always be comparable to data shown in the 2002 edition due to changes in definitions and coverage that were made as a result of the OECD expenditure comparability study (see Annex 3 at *www.oecd.org/els/education/eag2002* for details on changes).

Table B6.1.
Expenditure on instruction, research and development (R&D) and ancillary services in educational institutions as a percentage of GDP and private expenditure on educational goods purchased outside educational institutions as a percentage of GDP (1999)

	Primary, secondary and post-secondary non-tertiary education				Tertiary education				
	Expenditure on educational institutions			Private payments on instructional services/ goods outside educational institutions	Expenditure on educational institutions				Private payments on instructional services/ goods outside educational institutions
	Educational core services	Ancillary services (transport, meals, housing provided by institutions)	Total		Educational core services	Ancillary services (transport, meals, housing provided by institutions)	Research and development at tertiary institutions	Total	
	(1)	(2)	(3)	(4)	(5)	(6)	(7)	(8)	(9)
Australia	4.07	0.16	4.23	0.16	1.00	0.09	0.43	1.52	0.16
Austria	x(3)	x(3)	4.18	m	x(8)	x(8)	x(8)	1.45	m
Belgium	x(3)	x(3)	3.45	m	x(8)	x(8)	0.46	1.26	m
Canada[1*]	3.66	0.19	3.84	m	2.05	0.02	0.43	2.51	0.40
Czech Republic	2.68	0.48	3.17	m	0.67	0.10	0.15	0.92	m
Denmark	x(3)	x(3)	4.17	0.07	1.14	x(5)	0.43	1.56	0.83
Finland	3.25	0.38	3.63	m	1.14	0.01	0.63	1.78	m
France[2*]	3.76	0.60	4.35	0.14	0.88	0.07	0.18	1.13	0.08
Germany	3.68	n	3.68	0.20	0.65	n	0.40	1.06	0.13
Greece[1]	2.41	0.04	2.45	0.00	0.77	0.02	0.23	1.02	n
Hungary[1]	2.61	0.37	2.97	m	0.80	0.13	0.13	1.07	m
Iceland	m	m	m	m	m	m	m	m	m
Ireland[2*]	3.02	0.07	3.08	m	1.17	n	0.23	1.40	m
Italy	3.08	0.09	3.17	0.07	0.80	0.03	x(6)	0.83	0.40
Japan[4]	x(3)	x(3)	2.95	0.80	x(8)	x(8)	x(8)	1.04	m
Korea	x(3)	x(3)	3.98	m	x(8)	x(8)	x(8)	2.38	m
Luxembourg	m	m	m	m	m	m	m	m	m
Mexico[2*]	x(3)	x(3)	3.59	0.22	0.93	m	0.18	1.11	0.07
Netherlands[1*]	3.05	0.03	3.08	0.18	0.77	0.01	0.50	1.28	0.06
New Zealand	x(3)	x(3)	4.63	m	x(8)	x(8)	x(8)	0.94	m
Norway	x(3)	x(3)	4.04	m	x(8)	x(8)	x(8)	1.51	n
Poland[2, 3]	3.45	0.19	3.63	m	0.74	0.07	0.15	0.97	m
Portugal	x(3)	x(3)	4.17	0.06	x(8)	x(8)	x(8)	1.05	0.06
Slovak Republic	2.68	0.35	3.03	m	0.60	0.16	0.07	0.83	m
Spain	3.60	0.08	3.68	m	0.84	x(5)	0.27	1.10	m
Sweden	4.18	0.21	4.39	0.69	0.88	a	0.81	1.69	0.63
Switzerland	x(3)	x(3)	4.39	m	x(8)	x(8)	x(8)	1.21	m
Turkey[2, 3]	2.82	0.06	2.88	m	1.00	0.01	0.02	1.03	m
United Kingdom	3.55	0.14	3.68	m	0.68	n	0.38	1.07	0.09
United States[1]	3.67	0.14	3.81	0.02	2.08	n	0.26	2.33	0.10
Country mean	*3.29*	*0.20*	*3.65*	*0.22*	*0.97*	*0.04*	*0.32*	*1.32*	*0.22*

Note: x indicates that data are included in another column. The column reference is shown in brackets after "x". *e.g.*, x(2) means that data are included in column 2.

1. Post-secondary non-tertiary included in both upper secondary and tertiary education.

2. Ancillary services in public institutions only. Other ancillary services included in instructional services.

3. Research and development expenditure and thus total expenditure are underestimated.

4. Post-secondary non-tertiary is included in tertiary education and excluded from primary, secondary and post-secondary non-tertiary education.

* See Annex 3 for notes *(www.oecd.org/els/education/eag2002)*.

Source: OECD.

Table B6.2.
Expenditure per student on instruction, ancillary services and research and development (R&D) (1999)
Expenditure per student on educational institutions in US dollars converted using PPPs from public and private sources, by type of service and level of education

| | Primary, secondary and post-secondary non-tertiary education | | | Tertiary education | | | |
| | Expenditure on educational institutions | | | Expenditure on educational institutions | | | |
	Educational core services	Ancillary services (transport, meals, housing provided by institutions)	Total	Educational core services	Ancillary services (transport, meals, housing provided by institutions)	Research and development	Total
	(1)	(2)	(3)	(4)	(5)	(6)	(7)
Australia	5 592	217	5 809	7 714	674	3 338	11 725
Austria	x(3)	x(3)	7 818	x(7)	x(7)	x(7)	12 070
Belgium	x(3)	x(3)	5 329	x(7)	x(7)	3 565	9 724
Canada[1*]	5 691	289	5 981	12 443	146	2 622	15 211
Czech Republic	2 286	413	2 699	4 124	606	958	5 688
Denmark	x(3)	x(3)	7 226	7 753	x(4)	2 904	10 657
Finland	4 559	535	5 093	5 196	30	2 888	8 114
France[*]	5 129	815	5 944	6 123	514	1 231	7 867
Germany	5 955	n	5 955	6 438	n	3 955	10 393
Greece[1]	2 837	49	2 886	3 199	93	968	4 260
Hungary[2]	2 046	288	2 334	4 398	726	736	5 861
Iceland	m	m	m	m	m	m	m
Ireland[*]	3 550	76	3 626	8 089	n	1 585	9 673
Italy[1]	5 905	173	6 078	7 292	260	x(4)	7 552
Japan[1]	x(3)	x(3)	5 668	x(7)	x(7)	x(7)	10 278
Korea	x(3)	x(3)	3 137	x(7)	x(7)	x(7)	5 356
Luxembourg	m	m	m	m	m	m	m
Mexico[*]	x(3)	x(3)	1 240	4 018	n	771	4 789
Netherlands[4*]	4 890	45	4 934	7 383	77	4 825	12 285
New Zealand	x(3)	x(3)	m	x(7)	x(7)	x(7)	m
Norway[2]	x(3)	x(3)	6 665	x(7)	x(7)	x(7)	12 096
Poland[2,3]	1 685	92	1 778	2 993	301	618	3 912
Portugal	x(3)	x(3)	4 483	x(7)	x(7)	x(7)	4 802
Slovak Republic	1 639	212	1 852	3 854	1003	468	5 325
Spain	4 241	90	4 331	4 331	x(4)	1 376	5 707
Sweden	553	278	5 832	7 395	a	6 828	14 222
Switzerland[1]	x(3)	x(3)	8 192	x(7)	x(7)	x(7)	17 997
Turkey[1]	m	m	m	4 206	21	100	4 328
United Kingdom	4 354	208	4 563	6 120	n	3 434	9 554
United States[1,6]	7 131	266	7 397	17 115	n	2 105	19 220
Country mean	*4 297*	*238*	*4 879*	*6 493*	*247*	*2 264*	*9 210*

Note: x indicates that data are included in another column. The column reference is shown in brackets after "x". *e.g.,* x(2) means that data are included in column 2.
1. Public and government-dependent private institutions only.
2. Post-secondary non-tertiary included in tertiary education.
3. Primary, secondary and post-secondary education includes tertiary-type B education.
4. Public institutions only.
5. Public and independent private institutions only.
6. Post-secondary non-tertiary included in both upper secondary and tertiary education.
* See Annex 3 for notes *(www.oecd.org/els/education/eag2002).*
Source: OECD.

B6

Table B6.3.
Expenditure on educational institutions by resource category (1999)
Distribution of total and current expenditure on educational institutions from public and private sources, by resource category and level of education

		Primary, secondary and post-secondary non-tertiary education						Tertiary education					
		Percentage of total expenditure		Percentage of current expenditure				Percentage of total expenditure		Percentage of current expenditure			
		Current	Capital	Compensation of teachers	Compensation of other staff	Compensation of all staff	Other current	Current	Capital	Compensation of teachers	Compensation of other staff	Compensation of all staff	Other current
		(1)	(2)	(3)	(4)	(5)	(6)	(7)	(8)	(9)	(10)	(11)	(12)
OECD COUNTRIES	Australia	93.7	6.3	56.3	15.6	71.9	28.1	89.9	10.1	35.1	30.2	65.3	34.7
	Austria	93.5	6.5	73.3	7.9	81.2	18.8	95.4	4.6	53.6	14.2	67.8	32.2
	Belgium	m	m	m	m	m	m	m	m	m	m	m	m
	Belgium (Fl.)	97.2	2.8	67.4	11.7	79.1	20.9	97.3	2.7	50.6	0.7	51.4	48.6
	Canada[1*]	96.4	3.6	61.7	15.1	76.8	23.2	95.4	4.6	x(11)	x(11)	71.7	28.3
	Czech Republic	91.9	8.1	45.5	16.5	62.1	37.9	87.6	12.4	29.2	21.1	50.3	49.7
	Denmark	95.1	4.9	50.3	25.0	75.3	24.7	87.3	12.7	50.8	24.8	75.6	24.4
	Finland	92.9	7.1	56.8	12.1	68.9	31.1	93.2	6.8	35.4	26.4	61.8	38.2
	France	91.4	8.6	x(5)	x(5)	78.6	21.4	89.2	10.8	x(11)	x(11)	70.0	30.0
	Germany	92.3	7.7	x(5)	x(5)	88.8	11.2	88.9	11.1	x(11)	x(11)	76.2	23.8
	Greece[2]	85.8	14.2	x(5)	x(5)	96.4	3.6	62.9	37.1	x(11)	x(11)	58.4	41.6
	Hungary[2*]	92.6	7.4	x(5)	x(5)	75.2	24.8	86.9	13.1	x(11)	x(11)	63.2	36.8
	Iceland	m	m	m	m	m	m	m	m	m	m	m	m
	Ireland[2]	92.2	7.8	80.0	4.8	84.9	15.1	88.9	11.1	48.1	24.6	72.7	27.3
	Italy[2*]	94.8	5.2	63.6	16.6	80.2	19.8	82.7	17.3	43.8	22.5	66.3	33.7
	Japan[1*]	87.6	12.4	x(5)	x(5)	88.1	11.9	81.5	18.5	x(11)	x(11)	68.4	31.6
	Korea	85.6	14.4	75.3	8.5	83.8	16.2	66.9	33.1	44.8	15.0	59.8	40.2
	Luxembourg	m	m	m	m	m	m	m	m	m	m	m	m
	Mexico[2]	97.6	2.4	82.9	12.0	94.9	5.1	86.7	13.3	71.0	15.3	86.3	13.7
	Netherlands[4]	95.7	4.3	x(5)	x(5)	75.9	24.1	94.0	6.0	m	m	76.2	23.8
	New Zealand	m	m	m	m	m	m	m	m	m	m	m	m
	Norway	86.3	13.7	x(5)	x(5)	82.3	17.7	88.7	11.3	x(11)	x(11)	62.1	37.9
	Poland[2]	92.7	7.3	x(5)	x(5)	74.9	25.1	94.4	5.6	x(11)	x(11)	75.2	24.8
	Portugal	95.4	4.6	x(5)	x(5)	93.7	6.3	85.1	14.9	x(11)	x(11)	75.9	24.1
	Slovak Republic	96.8	3.2	60.6	16.8	77.4	22.6	89.9	10.1	48.8	40.4	89.3	10.8
	Spain	93.9	6.1	76.1	9.5	85.6	14.4	79.1	20.9	57.1	21.1	78.2	21.8
	Sweden[*]	m	m	47.8	13.7	61.8	38.2	m	m	x(11)	x(11)	56.6	43.4
	Switzerland[2]	90.4	9.6	72.4	12.9	85.3	14.7	83.2	16.8	54.4	21.5	75.8	24.2
	Turkey[2]	80.6	19.4	96.8	m	96.8	3.2	79.7	20.3	51.1	34.1	85.2	14.8
	United Kingdom	93.9	6.1	49.0	18.1	67.2	32.8	97.2	2.8	32.5	25.0	57.6	42.4
	United States[1,3]	88.1	11.9	55.9	26.4	82.3	17.7	90.7	9.3	40.4	35.5	75.9	24.1
	Country mean	*92.1*	*7.9*	*65.1*	*14.3*	*80.3*	*19.7*	*87.0*	*13.0*	*46.7*	*23.3*	*69.4*	*30.6*
NON-OECD COUNTRIES	Argentina[2]	93.4	6.6	67.1	24.9	92.0	8.0	97.9	2.1	56.2	34.9	91.1	8.9
	Brazil[2,5]	94.8	5.2	x(5)	x(5)	81.9	18.1	97.6	2.4	x(11)	x(11)	86.3	13.7
	Chile[2]	91.2	8.8	x(5)	x(5)	57.9	42.1	91.8	8.2	x(11)	x(11)	69.4	30.6
	China	91.2	8.8	x(5)	x(5)	64.3	35.7	77.6	22.4	x(11)	x(11)	46.0	54.0
	India[1,2,5]	97.2	2.8	79.5	8.4	87.8	12.2	96.9	3.1	x(11)	x(11)	99.6	0.4
	Indonesia[2,6]	93.9	6.1	78.0	7.6	85.6	14.4	82.0	18.0	87.2	11.8	99.0	1.0
	Israel	91.0	9.0	x(5)	x(5)	76.9	23.1	89.7	10.3	x(11)	x(11)	76.5	23.5
	Jamaica[2]	90.9	9.1	57.4	10.0	67.3	32.7	92.3	7.7	53.6	29.2	82.7	17.3
	Jordan[2]	89.0	11.0	77.8	14.7	92.5	7.5	76.5	23.5	x(11)	x(11)	67.6	32.4
	Malaysia[2]	77.3	22.7	65.8	14.8	80.6	19.4	61.7	38.3	42.1	9.2	51.4	48.6
	Paraguay[2]	90.7	9.3	59.6	11.3	70.9	29.1	87.0	13.0	m	m	m	m
	Peru[2,7]	89.2	10.9	89.3	2.0	91.3	8.7	88.8	11.2	46.0	9.0	55.0	45.0
	Tunisia[2,6]	88.7	11.3	x(5)	x(5)	95.1	4.9	74.1	25.9	x(11)	x(11)	70.0	30.0
	Uruguay[2]	92.7	7.3	72.9	12.3	85.2	14.8	94.2	5.8	64.0	21.6	85.6	14.4

Note: x indicates that data are included in another column. The column reference is shown in brackets after "x". *e.g.,* x(2) means that data are included in column 2.
1. Post-secondary non-tertiary education included in tertiary education.
2. Public institutions only.
3. Post-secondary non-tertiary included in both upper secondary and tertiary education.
4. Public and government-dependent private institutions only.
5. Year of reference 1998.
6. Year of reference 2000.
7. Excluding post-secondary non tertiary education.
* See Annex 3 for notes (*www.oecd.org/els/education/eag2002*).
Source: OECD.

ACCESS TO EDUCATION, PARTICIPATION AND PROGRESSION

OVERVIEW

Indicator C1: School expectancy and enrolment rates

Table C1.1. School expectancy (2000)

Table C1.2. Enrolment rates (2000)

Indicator C2: Entry to and expected years in tertiary education and participation in secondary education

Table C2.1. Entry rates to tertiary education and age distribution of new entrants (2000)

Table C2.2. Expected years in tertiary education and changes in total tertiary enrolment (2000)

Table C2.3. Students enrolled in public and private institutions and full-time and part-time programmes in tertiary education (2000)

Table C2.4. Students in public and private institutions and full-time and part-time programmes in primary and secondary education (2000)

Table C2.5. Upper secondary enrolment patterns (2000)

Indicator C3 Foreign students in tertiary education

Table C3.1. Exchange of students in tertiary education (2000)

Table C3.2. Proportion of foreign students in tertiary education in the country of study (2000)

Table C3.3. Proportion of citizens in tertiary education studying abroad (2000)

Indicator C4: Participation in continuing education and training in the adult population

Table C4.1. Participation rate in continuing education and training during one year for 25 to 64-year-olds, by level of education, type of training and gender

Indicator C5: Education and work of the youth population

Table C5.1. Percentage of the youth population in education and not in education, by age group and work status (2001)

Table C5.1a. Percentage of young men in education and not in education, by age group and work status (2001)

Table C5.1b. Percentage of young women in education and not in education, by age group and work status (2001)

Table C5.2.Percentage of unemployed non-students in the total population, by level of educational attainment, age group and gender (2001)

Indicator C6: The situation of the youth population with low levels of education

Table C6.1. Percentage of 20 to 24-year-olds not in education, by level of educational attainment, gender and work status (2001)

Chapter C looks at access to education, participation and progression, in terms of the expected duration of schooling, overall and at different levels of education as well as entry to and participation in different types of educational programmes and institutions,…

…cross-border movements of students…

C

…and learning beyond initial education.

SCHOOL EXPECTANCY AND ENROLMENT RATES

- In 25 out of 27 OECD countries, individuals participate in formal education for between 15 and 20 years, on average. Most of the variation between countries derives from differences in enrolments in upper secondary education.

- School expectancy increased between 1995 and 2000 in 18 out of 20 OECD countries.

- The majority of primary and secondary students are enrolled in public institutions. However, privately managed schools now enrol, on average, 11 per cent of primary students, 14 per cent of lower secondary students and 19 per cent of upper secondary students.

- In two-fifths of OECD countries, more than 70 per cent of three to four-year-olds are enrolled in either pre-primary or primary programmes. At the other end of the spectrum, a 17-year-old can expect to spend an average of 2.5 years in tertiary education.

- In the majority of OECD countries, women can expect to receive 0.5 more years, on average, of education than men.

Chart C1.1.

School expectancy (2000)

*Expected years of schooling under current conditions, excluding education
for children under five years of age, by level of education*

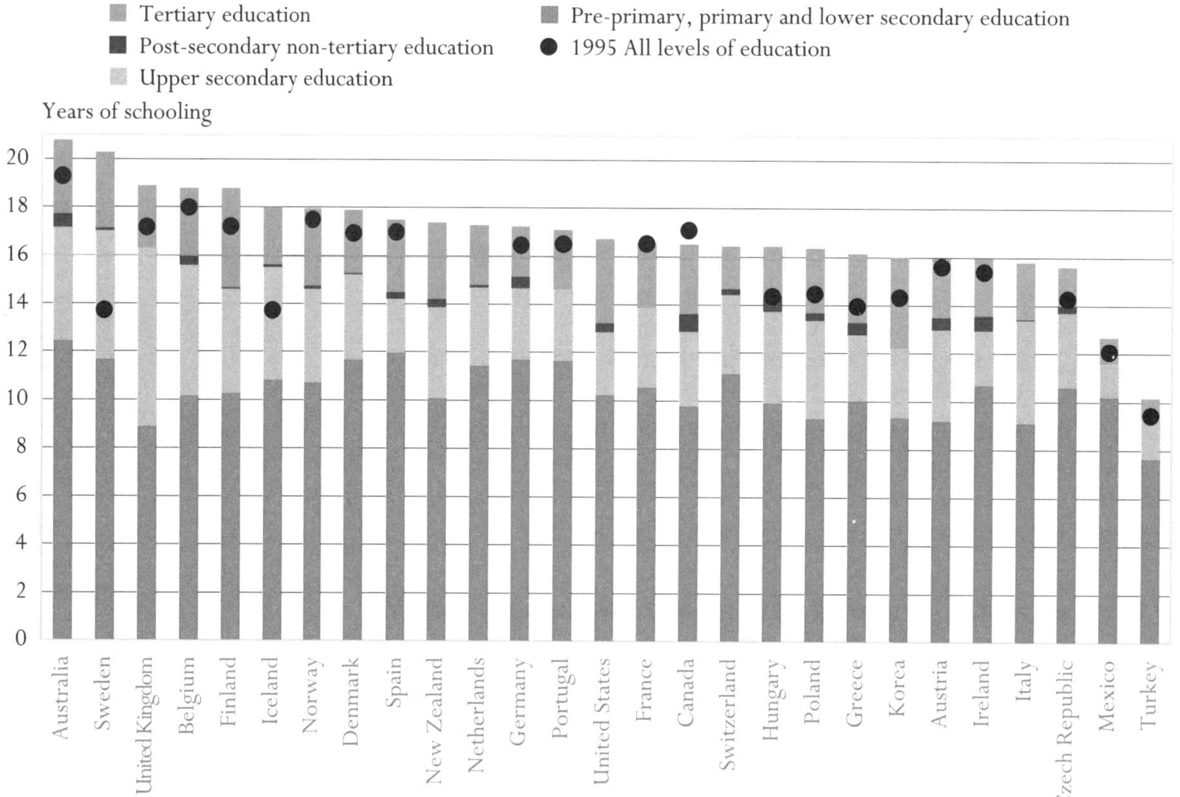

C1

Legend:
- Tertiary education
- Post-secondary non-tertiary education
- Upper secondary education
- Pre-primary, primary and lower secondary education
- 1995 All levels of education

Years of schooling

Countries are ranked in descending order of the total school expectancy for all levels of education in 2000.
Source: OECD. Table C1.1. See Annex 3 for notes (www.oecd.org/els/education/eag2002).

Policy context

A well-educated population is critical for a country's economic and social development, present and future. Societies, therefore, have an intrinsic interest in ensuring broad access to a wide variety of educational opportunities for children and adults. Early childhood programmes prepare children for primary education. They can provide help to combat linguistic and social disadvantages and provide opportunities to enhance and complement home educational experiences. Primary and secondary education lay the foundations for a wide range of competencies and prepare young people to become lifelong learners and productive members of society. Tertiary education provides a range of options for acquiring advanced knowledge and skills, either immediately after school or later.

This indicator examines enrolments at all levels of education.

This indicator presents several measures of participation in education to elucidate levels of access to education in different OECD countries. Enrolment trends at different levels of education are also presented as an indicator of the evolution of access to education.

Evidence and explanations

Overall participation in education

One way of looking at participation in education is to estimate the number of years during which a five-year-old child can expect to be in either full or part-time education during his/her lifetime, given current enrolment rates. *School expectancy* is estimated therefore by taking the sum of enrolment rates for each single year of age, starting at age five (Chart C1.1). In OECD countries, a child in Mexico and Turkey can expect to be in education for 12 years or less compared to more than 18 years in Australia, Belgium, Finland, Sweden and the United Kingdom.

In 25 out of 27 OECD countries, individuals participate in formal education for between 15 and 20 years, on average.

C₁

Most of the variation in school expectancy among OECD countries comes from differences in enrolment rates in upper secondary education. Relative differences in participation are large at the tertiary level, but apply to a smaller proportion of the cohort and therefore have less of an effect on school expectancy.

Most of the variation comes from differences in enrolment rates in upper secondary education.

Measures of the average length of schooling like *school expectancy* are affected by participation rates over the life cycle and therefore underestimate the actual number of years of schooling in systems where access to education is expanding. Nor does this measure distinguish between full-time and part-time participation. OECD countries with relatively large proportions of part-time enrolments will therefore tend to have relatively high values. In Australia, Belgium, New Zealand, Portugal, Sweden and the United Kingdom, part-time education accounts for two or more years of school expectancy (Table C1.1).

In OECD countries where school expectancy at a given level of education exceeds the number of grades at that level, repeating a level (or, in the case of Australia, the number of adults enrolling in those programmes) has a greater impact on school expectancy than the proportion of students leaving school before completing that level of education.

Enrolment rates are influenced by entry rates to a particular level of education and by the typical duration of studies. A high number of expected years in education, therefore, does not necessarily imply that all young people will participate in education for a long time. Belgium and Sweden, where five-year-olds can expect to be in school for more than 18 years, have nearly full enrolment (rates over 90 per cent) for 15 and 13 years of education, respectively. Conversely, Australia and Finland, which have equally high school expectancy, have nearly full enrolment (rates over 90 per cent) for only 12 and 11 years of education, respectively (Table C1.2).

In most OECD countries, virtually all young people have access to 11 years of formal education. At least 90 per cent of students are enrolled in an age band spanning 14 or more years in Belgium, France, Japan and the Netherlands. Mexico and Turkey, by contrast, have enrolment rates exceeding 90 per cent for a period of seven years or less (Table C1.2).

C₁

In the majority of OECD countries, women can expect to receive 0.5 more years, on average, of education than men. The variation in school expectancy is generally greater for women than for men. Some OECD countries show sizeable gender differences. In Korea, Switzerland and Turkey, men can expect to receive between 0.7 and 2.8 years more education than women. The opposite is true in Finland, Iceland, New Zealand, Norway, Sweden and the United Kingdom, where the expected duration of enrolment for women exceeds that of men by more than one year (Table C1.1).

Trends in participation in education

School expectancy increased between 1995 and 2000 in 18 out of the 20 OECD countries for which comparable trend data are available. In Greece, Hungary, Korea, Poland and the United Kingdom, the increase was 10 per cent or more over this relatively short period.

Participation in early childhood education

In the majority of OECD countries, universal enrolment, which is defined here as enrolment rates exceeding 90 per cent, starts between the ages of five and six years. However, in Belgium, the Czech Republic, Denmark, France, Hungary, Iceland, Italy, Japan, New Zealand, Norway, Spain, Sweden and the United Kingdom, over 70 per cent of three to four-year-olds are already enrolled in either pre-primary or primary programmes (Table C1.2). Their enrolment rates range from under 21 per cent in Canada, Korea, Switzerland and Turkey, to over 90 per cent in Belgium, France, Iceland, Italy and Spain.

Given the impact of early childhood education and care for building a strong foundation for lifelong learning and for ensuring equitable access to learning opportunities later, pre-primary education is very important. However, institutionally based pre-primary programmes covered by this indicator are not the only form of quality early childhood education and care. Inferences about access to and quality of pre-primary education and care should therefore be made very carefully.

Participation towards the end of compulsory education and beyond

Several factors, including a higher risk of unemployment and other forms of exclusion for young people with insufficient education, influence the decision to stay enrolled beyond the end of compulsory education. In many OECD countries, the transition from education to employment has become a longer and more complex process which provides the opportunity or the obligation for students to combine learning and work to develop marketable skills (see Indicator C5).

Compulsory education in OECD countries ends between the ages of 14 (Korea, Portugal and Turkey) and 18 (Belgium, Germany and the Netherlands), and in most countries at age 15 or 16 (Table C1.2). However, the statutory age at which compulsory education ends does not always correspond to the age at which enrolment is universal.

Compulsory education ends between the ages of 14 and 18 in OECD countries, and in most countries at age 15 or 16.

While participation rates in most OECD countries are high until the end of compulsory education, they drop below 90 per cent before the age at which students are no longer legally required to be enrolled in school in Mexico, Turkey and the United States. In the United States, this may be due in part to the fact that compulsory education ends at age 17, which is comparatively high. By contrast, in 22 OECD countries, virtually all children remain in school beyond the age at which compulsory education ends (Table C1.2).

Participation in education tends to be high until the end of compulsory education, but in three OECD countries, more than 10 per cent of students never finish compulsory education.

In most OECD countries, enrolment rates gradually decline starting in the last years of upper secondary education. There are several noteworthy exceptions, however where enrolment rates remain relatively high until the age of 20 to 29. In Australia and the Nordic countries, for example, enrolment rates for 20 to 29-year-olds still exceed 25 per cent (Table C1.2)

In Australia and the Nordic countries, one out of four 20 to 29-year-olds participates in education.

The transition to post-secondary education

Graduates of upper secondary programmes who decide not to enter the labour market upon graduation and people who are already working and want to upgrade their skills can choose from a wide range of post-secondary programmes. In OECD countries, tertiary programmes vary in the extent to which they are theoretically based and designed to prepare students for advanced research programmes or professions with high skill requirements (tertiary-type A), or focus on occupationally specific skills so that students can directly enter the labour market (tertiary-type B). The institutional location of

C1

programmes used to give a relatively clear idea of their nature (*e.g.*, university versus non-university institutions of higher education), but these distinctions have become blurred and are therefore not applied in the OECD indicators.

Post-secondary non-tertiary programmes are offered in 26 out of 30 OECD countries.

Upper secondary graduates in many systems can also enrol in relatively short programmes (less than two years) to prepare for trades or specific vocational fields. These programmes are offered as advanced or second cycle upper secondary programmes in some OECD countries (*e.g.,* Austria, Germany, Hungary and Spain); in others they are offered in post-secondary education (*e.g.*, Canada and the United States). From an internationally comparative point of view, these programmes straddle upper secondary and tertiary education and are therefore classified as a different level of education (post-secondary non-tertiary education). In 26 out of 30 OECD countries, these kinds of programmes are offered to upper secondary graduates (see Table C1.1).

Participation in tertiary education

On average in OECD countries, a 17-year-old can expect to receive 2.5 years of tertiary education.

On average in OECD countries, a 17-year-old can expect to receive 2.5 years of tertiary education. Both tertiary entry rates and the typical duration of study affect the expectancy of tertiary education. In Australia, Finland, Korea, New Zealand, Norway, Spain, Sweden and the United States, the figure is three years or more. In the Czech Republic, Mexico, the Slovak Republic and Turkey, by contrast, the expectancy of tertiary education is 1.5 years or less (see Table C1.1 and Indicator C2).

C1

Policies to expand education have, in many OECD countries, increased pressure for greater access to tertiary education.

Policies to expand education have increased pressure for greater access to tertiary education in many OECD countries. Thus far, this pressure has more than compensated for declines in cohort sizes which had led, until recently, to predictions of stable or declining demand from school leavers in several OECD countries. Whereas some OECD countries are now showing signs of a levelling demand for tertiary education, the overall trend remains upward.

Definitions and methodologies

Data refer to 1999-2000 and are based on the UOE data collection on education statistics, which is administered annually by the OECD, and the 2001 World Education Indicators Programme.

Except where otherwise noted, figures are based on head counts, that is, they do not distinguish between full-time and part-time study. A standardised distinction between full-time and part-time participants is very difficult because in several OECD countries, the concept of part-time study is not recognised, although in practice, at least some students would be classified as part-time by other countries. For some OECD countries, part-time education is not completely covered by the reported data.

The average length of time a five-year-old can expect to be formally enrolled in school during his/her lifetime, or *school expectancy*, is calculated by adding the net enrolment percentages for each single year of age from five onwards. The average duration of schooling for the cohort will reflect any tendency to lengthen (or shorten) studies in subsequent years. When comparing data on school expectancy, however, it must be borne in mind that neither the length of the school year nor the quality of education is necessarily the same in each country.

Net enrolment rates expressed as percentages in Table C1.2 are calculated by dividing the number of students of a particular age group enrolled in all levels of education by the size of the population of that age group. Table C1.1 shows the index of change in school expectancy between 1995 and 2000. Enrolment data for 1994-1995 were obtained through a special survey in 2000 and follow the ISCED-97 classification.

C₁

Table C1.1.
School expectancy (2000)
Expected years of schooling under current conditions, excluding education for children under the age of five

	2000							Full-time	Part-time	Index of change in school expectancy for all levels of education combined (1995 = 100)
	Full-time and part-time							All levels of education combined	All levels of education combined	
	All levels of education combined			Primary and lower secondary education	Upper secondary education	Post-secondary non-tertiary education	Tertiary education			
	M+F	Males	Females	M+F				M+F		M+F
	(1)	(2)	(3)	(4)	(5)	(6)	(7)	(8)	(9)	(10)
OECD COUNTRIES										
Australia*	20.7	20.1	20.1	11.8	4.7	0.6	3.0	14.6	6.2	108
Austria*	15.9	15.9	15.9	8.2	3.8	0.5	2.4	15.7	0.2	102
Belgium*	18.7	18.3	19.2	9.1	5.4	0.4	2.7	16.2	2.6	104
Canada	16.5	16.2	16.8	8.8	3.1	0.8	2.8	15.5	0.9	96
Czech Republic	15.6	15.5	15.6	9.1	3.1	0.3	1.5	15.4	0.2	109
Denmark	17.8	17.4	18.3	9.7	3.5	n	2.6	17.8	n	105
Finland*	18.7	18.1	19.2	9.1	4.4	0.1	4.1	18.7	n	109
France	16.5	16.3	16.7	9.4	3.3	n	2.6	16.5	n	100
Germany*	17.2	17.3	17.0	10.1	3.0	0.5	2.0	17.1	0.1	105
Greece	16.1	15.9	16.3	9.2	2.8	0.5	2.8	15.9	0.2	116
Hungary*	16.4	16.2	16.6	8.2	3.8	0.6	2.0	14.9	1.5	114
Iceland	18.0	17.3	18.6	9.9	4.7	0.1	2.3	16.0	1.9	m
Ireland*	15.9	15.5	16.4	10.8	2.3	0.6	2.3	15.3	0.6	103
Italy*	15.8	15.6	15.9	8.2	4.3	0.1	2.3	15.8	n	m
Japan	m	m	m	9.2	3.0	m	m	m	m	m
Korea	16.0	16.9	15.5	8.9	2.9	a	3.7	16.0	n	111
Luxembourg	m	m	m	9.2	3.6	0.1	m	m	m	m
Mexico	12.6	12.7	12.6	9.4	1.4	a	1.0	12.6	n	105
Netherlands	17.2	17.4	17.0	10.5	3.3	0.1	2.4	16.5	0.7	m
New Zealand	17.3	16.6	18.1	10.1	3.8	0.3	3.1	15.4	2.0	m
Norway	17.9	17.3	18.6	9.9	3.9	0.1	3.2	16.6	1.3	102
Poland	16.3	15.9	16.8	8.0	4.1	0.3	2.6	14.4	1.9	113
Portugal	17.0	16.7	17.4	10.8	3.0	n	2.4	13.9	3.1	103
Slovak Republic	m	m	m	m	m	0.1	1.5	m	m	m
Spain*	17.5	17.1	17.9	11.0	2.2	0.3	3.0	16.8	0.6	103
Sweden	20.2	18.6	22.0	9.8	5.4	0.1	3.1	16.1	4.1	m
Switzerland	16.4	16.7	16.0	9.6	3.3	0.2	1.7	16.0	0.4	m
Turkey*	10.1	11.6	8.8	7.5	1.7	a	0.8	10.1	n	107
United Kingdom	18.9	17.9	19.8	8.9	7.4	x(5)	2.5	14.6	4.3	110
United States	16.7	16.2	17.1	9.4	2.6	0.4	3.4	15.0	1.7	m
Country mean	*16.8*	*16.6*	*17.1*	*9.4*	*3.6*	*0.2*	*2.5*	*15.5*	*1.2*	*106*
NON-OECD COUNTRIES										
Argentina[1]	16.4	m	m	10.6	2.1	a	2.7	10.6	5.8	m
Brazil[1]	15.7	m	m	10.9	2.6	a	0.9	10.9	4.8	m
Chile[1]	14.5	m	m	8.4	3.5	a	1.7	14.5	n	m
China	10.1	m	m	8.5	1.2	0.1	0.4	10.8	n	m
Egypt	10.0	10.3	9.8	7.8	1.9	n	0.2	9.8	n	m
Indonesia[2]	9.9	m	m	7.8	1.1	a	0.6	7.8	2.1	m
Israel	15.5	m	m	8.6	3.1	0.1	2.6	8.6	6.9	m
Jamaica	14.4	m	m	9.3	1.6	0.1	0.7	9.3	5.2	m
Jordan	11.9	11.7	12.0	8.8	1.4	a	1.3	8.8	a	m
Malaysia[1]	12.8	m	m	8.8	1.8	0.2	1.1	8.8	4.0	m
Paraguay[1]	11.8	11.8	11.9	9.2	1.4	a	0.6	11.8	n	m
Peru[1]	13.3	13.4	13.2	10.2	1.4	m	0.9	13.2	n	m
Philippines[1]	12.0	m	m	9.6	0.7	0.2	1.4	12.0	n	m
Russian Federation[2]	14.5	14.5	15.2	x(1)	x(1)	0.7	3.1	14.5	n	m
Thailand[3]	13.1	13.0	13.1	9.5	2.2	n	1.8	9.5	5.0	m
Tunisia	13.2	m	m	10.0	2.1	n	0.9	13.2	n	m
Uruguay[1]	15.4	m	m	9.9	2.4	a	1.8	9.9	5.5	m
Zimbabwe	12.0	12.4	11.6	9.2	1.3	n	0.1	11.9	n	m

Note: x indicates that data are included in another column. The column reference is shown in brackets after "x". *e.g.*, x(2) means that data are included in column 2.
1. Year of reference 1999.
2. Year of reference 2001.
3. Full-time participation only. Participation by adults in part-time education accounts for approximately 5 per cent.
* See Annex 3 for notes (*www.oecd.org/els/education/eag2002*).
Source: OECD.

Table C1.2.
Enrolment rates (2000)
Full-time and part-time students in public and private institutions, by age

	Ending age of compulsory education	Number of years at which over 90% of the population are enrolled	Age range at which over 90% of the population are enrolled	Students aged:					
				4 and under as a percentage of the population of 3 to 4-year-olds	5-14 as a percentage of the population of 5 to 14-year-olds	15-19 as a percentage of the population of 15 to 19-year-olds	20-29 as a percentage of the population of 20 to 29-year-olds	30-39 as a percentage of the population of 30 to 39-year-olds	40 and over as a percentage of the population of over 40-year-olds
	(1)	(2)	(3)	(4)	(5)	(6)	(7)	(8)	(9)
Australia	15	12	5 - 16	34.2	100.0	81.8	28.2	14.9	7.1
Austria	15	11	6 - 16	60.6	98.2	76.4	17.9	3.1	x(8)
Belgium*	18	15	3 - 17	118.7	99.1	90.5	25.2	8.4	1.4
Canada	16	12	6 - 17	20.1	97.1	74.2	21.7	4.6	1.2
Czech Republic	15	12	5 - 16	70.6	99.8	80.8	14.2	1.1	n
Denmark	16	13	4 - 16	81.4	99.2	80.4	29.9	5.6	0.9
Finland	16	11	7 - 17	38.0	91.6	84.8	37.9	9.7	1.8
France*	16	15	3 - 17	117.7	99.8	86.4	19.1	1.7	x(8)
Germany	18	12	6 - 17	67.9	99.4	88.3	23.6	2.8	0.2
Greece	14.5	12	6 - 19	28.9	99.8	87.4	16.9	0.1	n
Hungary	16	12	5 - 16	79.2	99.9	81.1	18.7	4.2	0.1
Iceland*	16	13	4 - 16	123.9	98.5	78.9	30.5	6.5	1.8
Ireland	15	12	5 - 16	26.9	100.5	79.8	15.6	3.4	x(8)
Italy*	14	12	3 - 14	97.5	99.7	65.5	18.7	2.3	0.1
Japan	15	14	4 - 17	77.4	101.2	m	m	m	m
Korea	14	12	6 - 17	17.5	92.3	78.6	23.9	1.4	0.3
Luxembourg	15	12	4 - 15	65.8	95.3	73.7	4.6	0.4	n
Mexico	15	7	6 - 12	35.5	94.8	41.0	9.1	2.8	0.7
Netherlands	18	14	4 - 17	49.9	99.4	86.6	22.9	3.0	0.6
New Zealand	16	13	4 - 16	86.8	99.0	72.4	21.4	9.0	3.1
Norway	16	12	6 - 17	74.5	97.4	85.5	27.5	6.1	1.3
Poland	15	11	6 - 16	29.2	93.6	84.2	24.4	3.0	m
Portugal	14	10	6 - 15	63.9	105.2	80.3	19.9	3.0	0.5
Slovak Republic	15	m	m	m	m	m	m	m	m
Spain*	16	13	4 - 16	98.1	104.4	79.5	24.3	2.7	0.4
Sweden*	16	13	6 - 18	70.5	97.8	86.4	33.4	15.0	3.4
Switzerland	15	11	6 - 16	20.8	98.8	83.5	18.9	3.3	0.1
Turkey*	14	5	7 - 11	n	80.2	28.4	5.2	0.2	n
United Kingdom*	16	12	4 - 15	81.1	98.9	73.3	23.8	13.2	5.4
United States	17	10	6 - 15	49.9	99.3	73.9	21.2	5.4	1.5
Country mean	*16*	*12*		*63.8*	*97.9*	*77.3*	*21.4*	*4.9*	*1.3*
Argentina[1]	14	10	5 - 14	37.4	103.8	62.5	20.8	4.8	1.2
Brazil[1]	14	8	7 - 14	24.6	90.1	78.0	20.7	5.9	1.5
Chile[1]	14	9	6 - 14	23.6	92.7	66.7	m	m	m
China	14	5	7 - 11	m	79.6	m	m	n	n
Egypt	13	6	6 - 11	6.4	83.5	31.4	m	n	n
Indonesia[2]	15	4	8 - 11	n	76.5	38.5	3.0	n	n
Israel	16	11	6 - 16	99.6	96.6	63.6	20.1	4.3	0.9
Jamaica	12	9	6 - 14	n	88.6	39.6	a	a	a
Jordan	15	m	m	13.7	83.6	45.0	m	m	m
Malaysia[1]	16	7	6 - 12	8.1	97.3	46.5	6.0	0.5	0.1
Paraguay[1]	14	5	7 - 11	6.3	86.6	46.6	m	m	m
Peru[1]	16	9	6 - 14	48.4	98.0	57.3	15.9	2.3	0.4
Philippines[1]	12	8	m	16.0	84.3	m	m	n	n
Russian Federation[2]	15	8	8 - 15	m	82.5	70.8	15.4	m	m
Thailand	14	9	4 - 13	61.5	97.4	60.2	m	m	m
Tunisia	16	6	6 - 11	19.1	87.4	52.5	4.6	n	n
Uruguay[1]	15	9	6 - 14	23.5	97.8	60.7	18.7	3.6	0.4
Zimbabwe	12	7	7 - 13	m	82.2	45.3	m	m	m

OECD COUNTRIES / NON-OECD COUNTRIES

C₁

Note: Ending age of compulsory education is the age at which compulsory schooling ends. For example, an ending age of 18 indicates that all students under 18 are legally obliged to participate in education.

Note: x indicates that data are included in another column. The column reference is shown in brackets after "x". *e.g.,* x(2) means that data are included in column 2.

1. Year of reference 1999.
2. Year of reference 2001.
* See Annex 3 for notes (*www.oecd.org/els/education/eag2002*).

Source: OECD.

ENTRY TO AND EXPECTED YEARS IN TERTIARY EDUCATION AND PARTICIPATION IN SECONDARY EDUCATION

- Today, four out of ten school leavers are likely to attend tertiary programmes leading to the equivalent of a bachelors' or higher tertiary-type A degree. In some OECD countries, every second school leaver is likely to attend such a programme.

- On average in OECD countries, a 17-year-old can now expect to receive 2.5 years of tertiary-type A education, of which 2 years will be full-time.

- With the exception of France, Germany and Turkey, participation in tertiary education grew in all OECD countries between 1995 and 2000.

- The majority of tertiary students are enrolled in public institutions, but in Belgium, Japan, Korea, the Netherlands and the United Kingdom, most students are enrolled in privately managed institutions.

- In three out of four OECD countries, the majority of upper secondary students are enrolled in programmes that are primarily designed to prepare them for a wide range of tertiary education.

C2

Chart C2.1.

Entry rates to tertiary education (2000)

Sum of net entry rates over single years of age in tertiary-type A and tertiary-type B education

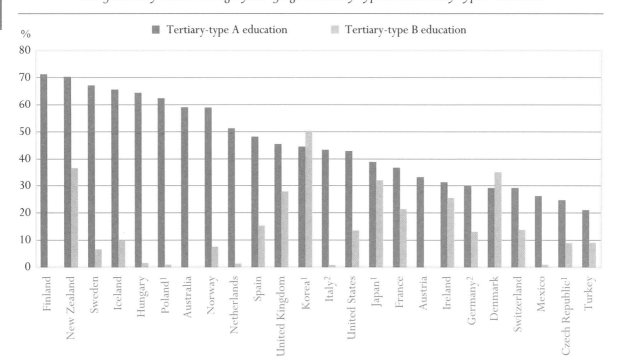

Note: Net entry rates for tertiary-type A and B programmes cannot be added due to double counting.
1. Entry rate for type A and B programmes calculated as gross entry rate.
2. Entry rate for type B programmes calculated as gross entry rate.
Countries are ranked in descending order of the total entry rates for tertiary-type A education.
Source: OECD. Table C2.1. See Annex 3 for notes *(www.oecd.org/els/education/eag2002).*

Policy context

High tertiary entry and participation rates help to ensure the development and maintenance of a highly educated population and labour force. Tertiary education is associated with better access to employment and higher earnings (see Indicator A13). Rates of entry to tertiary education are a partial indication of the degree to which a population is acquiring high-level skills and knowledge that the labour market in knowledge societies values.

This indicator shows the percentage of youth that will enter different types of tertiary education during their lives.

As students have become more aware of the economic and social benefits of tertiary education, entry rates into tertiary type A and tertiary-type B education have risen. Continued growth in participation, and a widening diversity of backgrounds and interests of the people aspiring to tertiary studies, will require a new kind of provision. Tertiary institutions will need to meet growing demand by expanding the number of places that they offer and by adapting their programmes, teaching and learning to the diverse needs of new generations of students.

Entry and participation rates reflect both the accessibility of tertiary education and the perceived value of attending tertiary programmes.

Graduation from upper secondary education is becoming the norm in most OECD countries, but the curricular content in upper secondary programmes can vary, depending on the type of education or occupation for which the programmes are designed. Most upper secondary programmes in OECD countries are designed primarily to prepare students for tertiary studies, and their orientation can be general, pre-vocational or vocational. In addition to preparing students for further education, most OECD countries also have upper secondary programmes which prepare students to enter the labour market directly. Some OECD countries, however, delay vocational training until after graduation from upper secondary education, although these post-secondary programmes often resemble upper secondary level programmes.

The indicator also shows patterns of participation at the secondary level of education.

C_2

Evidence and explanations

Overall access to tertiary education

Today, almost every second young person in the OECD area will enter tertiary-type A education during his/her lifetime, assuming that current entry rates continue. In fact, in Finland, Hungary, Iceland, New Zealand, Poland and Sweden, over 60 per cent of young people enter tertiary-type A education (Table C2.1).

45 per cent of today's young people in OECD countries will enter tertiary-type A programmes.

In other OECD countries, the rates of first-time entry to tertiary-type A education are considerably lower: the estimated first-time entry rates for the Czech Republic, Denmark, Germany, Mexico, Switzerland and Turkey are 30 per cent or below.

The proportion of people who enter tertiary-type B education is generally smaller than the proportion entering tertiary-type A programmes. In 23 OECD countries with available data, 15 per cent of young people, on average, will enter tertiary-type B education. The figures range from 1 per cent in

Fifteen per cent of today's young people will enter tertiary-type B programmes.

Italy, Mexico, the Netherlands and Poland to over 30 per cent in the Flemish Community of Belgium, Denmark, Japan and New Zealand, and 50 per cent in Korea (Table C2.1 and Chart C2.1).

In the Flemish Community of Belgium and Denmark, wide access to tertiary-type B education counterbalances comparatively low rates of entry to tertiary-type A education. Other OECD countries, most notably Korea and the United Kingdom, have entry rates around the OECD average for tertiary-type A education, and comparatively high rates of entry to tertiary-type B education. New Zealand stands out as a country with entry rates at both levels that are the highest among OECD countries.

Net rates of entry to tertiary education should be seen in the light of participation in post-secondary non-tertiary programmes, which are an important alternative to tertiary education in some OECD countries (Indicator C1).

People entering tertiary-type B programmes may also enter tertiary-type A programmes later in their lives. Tertiary-type A and B entry rates cannot be added together to obtain overall tertiary-level entry rates because entrants might be double counted.

Participation in tertiary education

Enrolment rates provide another perspective on participation in tertiary education. They reflect both the total number of individuals entering tertiary education and the duration of their studies. The sum of net enrolment rates for each single year of age, referred to as the *expectancy of tertiary education*, gives an overall measure of the amount of tertiary education undertaken by an age cohort rather than by individual participants. In contrast to entry rates, expectancy of tertiary education, which is based on enrolments in tertiary-type A and tertiary-type B education, can be summed.

In Australia, Finland, Korea, New Zealand, Norway, Sweden and the United States, young people can expect to receive at least three years of tertiary education during their lifetime.

On average in OECD countries, a 17-year-old can expect to receive 2.5 years of tertiary education, of which two years will probably be full-time. In Australia, Finland, Korea, New Zealand, Norway, Sweden and the United States, 17-year-olds can expect to receive at least three years of full or part-time tertiary education during their lifetimes. In Finland and Korea, students can expect to receive about four years of full-time studies. By contrast, the expectancy of tertiary education is less than two years in the Czech Republic, Mexico, the Slovak Republic, Switzerland and Turkey (Table C2.2).

The longer duration tertiary–type A programmes tends to increase the stock of enrolments, and therefore the volume of resources required.

On average in OECD countries, expectancy of tertiary-type A education (2 years) is far higher than that of tertiary-type B education (0.4 years). Because tertiary-type A programmes tend to be longer, they increase the stock of enrolments and therefore the volume of resources required, all other things being equal (see Indicator B1, Table B1.3). However, the majority of tertiary graduates in Denmark are enrolled in tertiary-type B programmes (see Indicator A2). Higher rates of participation in tertiary-type A programmes relative to tertiary-type B in Denmark (Table C2.2) result from longer programmes, and not higher entry rates.

In the majority of OECD countries, public institutions provide and manage tertiary-type A programmes. However, in Belgium, the Netherlands and the United Kingdom, the majority of students are enrolled in privately managed institutions that draw predominantly on public funds. In Japan and Korea, over 70 per cent of students are enrolled in institutions that are privately managed and financed predominantly from private sources. In Mexico, Poland and the United States (Table C2.3), over 30 per cent of students are enrolled in such institutions.

The majority of tertiary students are enrolled in public institutions, but in some OECD countries the majority are in privately managed institutions.

Trends in participation

With the exception of France, Germany and Turkey, participation in tertiary education grew in all OECD countries between 1995 and 2000. In half of the OECD countries with available data, the number of students enrolled in tertiary education increased by over 15 per cent, and in the Czech Republic, Hungary, Korea and Poland, it grew by 50, 80, 48 and 108 per cent, respectively.

Participation in tertiary education grew in most OECD countries between 1995 and 2000.

At the tertiary level, changes in enrolment rates are less closely tied to changes in the size of the relevant age cohort than is true for primary and secondary education. Chart C2.2 breaks down the change in the number of students enrolled into two components: changes in cohort sizes and changes in enrolment rates. Growing demand, reflected in higher enrolment rates, is the main factor driving expansion in tertiary enrolments. Hungary, Ireland and Poland are the only OECD countries where population increases significantly contributed to higher tertiary enrolments, but in all cases, higher enrolment rates were even more significant. Conversely, the actual increase in tertiary students would have been significantly higher in many OECD countries (in particular Austria, Korea and Spain) had the population not decreased. In France and Germany, these decreases were actually more significant than increases in enrolment rates, meaning that overall, there was a slight drop in tertiary enrolment, despite a 7 per cent increase in enrolment rates.

Growing demand, reflected in higher participation rates, is the main factor driving expansion in tertiary enrolments.

C_2

Age of entrants

Traditionally, students typically enter tertiary-type A education immediately after having completed upper secondary education, and this remains true in many OECD countries. In the Czech Republic, France, Ireland and the Slovak Republic, for example, more than 80 per cent of all first-time entrants are under 22 years of age (Table C2.1).

In other OECD countries, the transition to the tertiary level is often delayed, in some cases by some time spent in the labour force. In these countries, first-time entrants to tertiary-type A programmes are typically older and show a much wider range of entry ages. In Denmark, Iceland, New Zealand and Sweden, for example, more than half the students enter this level for the first time after the age of 22 (Table C2.1). The proportion of older first-time entrants to tertiary-

In the Czech Republic, France, Ireland and the Slovak Republic, more than 80 per cent of all entrants to tertiary-type A programmes are under 22 years of age whereas in Denmark, Iceland, New Zealand and Sweden, more than half the students enter this level for the first time after the age of 22.

type A programmes may, among other factors, reflect the flexibility of these programmes and their suitability to students outside the typical or modal age cohort. It may also reflect a specific view of the value of work experience for higher education studies, which is characteristic of the Nordic countries and common in Australia and New Zealand where a sizeable proportion of new entrants is much older than the typical age of entry. In Australia, Denmark, Iceland, New Zealand, Norway and Sweden, more than 20 per cent of first-time entrants are 27 years of age or older.

Chart C2.2.

Change in the number of tertiary students in relation to changing enrolment rates and demography (2000)

Index of change in the number of students at the tertiary level between 1995 and 2000, and the relative contribution of demographic changes and changing enrolment rates (1995=100)

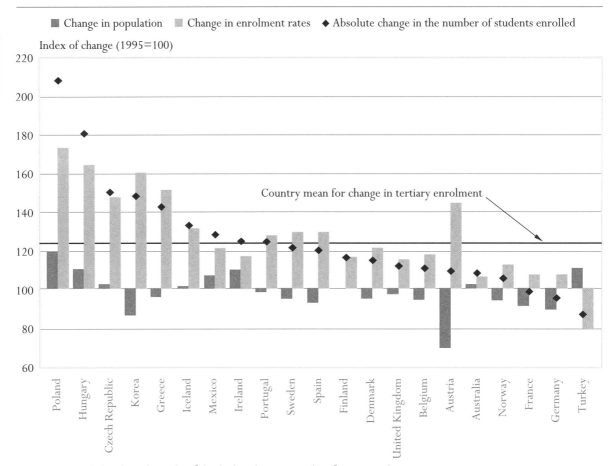

Countries are ranked in descending order of the absolute change in number of tertiary students.
Source: OECD. Table C2.2. See Annex 3 for notes *(www.oecd.org/els/education/eag2002)*.

Participation in upper secondary programmes by programme destination

In most OECD countries, students do not follow a uniform curriculum at the upper secondary level. Different types of curriculum can be distinguished by the type of educational or labour market "career" for which the programme has been designed. The International Standard Classification of Education (ISCED) distinguishes three types of upper secondary programmes by programme *destination*:

ISCED 3A programmes are designed to allow students direct access to tertiary programmes, thus providing students with sufficient qualifications to enter highly-skilled professions or advanced research programmes (tertiary-type A);

ISCED 3B programmes are designed to provide students with direct access to tertiary programmes focused on occupationally specific skills (tertiary-type B);

ISCED 3C programmes are not designed to lead directly to tertiary-type A or B programmes but to prepare students directly for the labour market, post-secondary non-tertiary programmes (ISCED 4) or other upper secondary programmes.

Direct access refers neither to a strict legal interpretation of programme destination nor to the actual destinations of students (which can be strongly influenced by the current labour market situation). Programmes are designated A, B, or C according to the orientation of the *design* of the curriculum, that is, by the type of tertiary programme for which the curriculum of the upper secondary programme is intended to prepare students.

In almost all OECD countries, more than half of the students leave formal education at the end of upper secondary education and enter the labour market. For the remaining students, upper secondary education is mainly preparation for further study at the tertiary level.

In 22 out of 29 OECD countries, the majority of students are enrolled in programmes designed to prepare them for further education at the tertiary-type A level (Table C2.5). In most OECD countries, entry rates to tertiary-type A education are significantly lower than the graduation rates from upper secondary programmes designed to prepare students for entry to tertiary-type A programmes. This implies an underlying need for these programmes to prepare students for the transition to other forms of further education as well as for direct entry into the world of work.

In Germany and Switzerland, around 60 per cent of all students (48 per cent in Austria) are enrolled in programmes that provide access to further education at the tertiary-type B level. These are primarily dual-system apprenticeship programmes. After graduating from these programmes, most students enter

Upper secondary programmes are classified according to the destination for which they have been designed to prepare students.

C₂

In 22 out of 29 countries, the majority of students are enrolled in programmes preparing for entry to tertiary-type A programmes...

...but in some countries, tertiary-type B is the most common destination.

the labour market since many of these programmes require work experience before entry.

Participation in and graduation from upper secondary vocational education

Programmes can also be classsified based on whether they are...

Programmes at the upper secondary level, regardless of their destination, can also be subdivided into three categories based on the degree to which they are oriented towards a specific class of occupations or trades and lead to a labour-market relevant qualification:

...general,...

Type 1 (general) education programmes are not designed explicitly to prepare participants for specific occupations or trades, or for entry into further vocational or technical education programmes;

...pre-vocational...

Type 2 (pre-vocational or pre-technical) education programmes are mainly designed to introduce participants to the world of work and to prepare them for entry into further vocational or technical education programmes. Successful completion of such programmes does not lead to a labour-market relevant vocational or technical qualification. At least 25 per cent of the programme content should be vocational or technical; and

...or vocational.

Type 3 (vocational) education programmes prepare participants for direct entry into specific occupations without further training. Successful completion of such programmes leads to a labour-market relevant vocational qualification.

The degree to which a programme has a vocational or general orientation does not necessarily determine whether participants have access to tertiary education. In several OECD countries, vocationally oriented programmes are designed to prepare for further studies at the tertiary level, while in other countries, many general programmes do not provide direct access to further education.

In more than half of the OECD countries, the majority of upper secondary students attend vocational or apprenticeship programmes.

In all OECD countries, students can choose between vocational, pre-vocational and general programmes. In more than half of the OECD countries, the majority of upper secondary students attend vocational or apprenticeship programmes. In OECD countries with dual-system apprenticeship programmes (Austria, Germany, Luxembourg, the Netherlands and Switzerland), and in Australia, Belgium, the Czech Republic, Poland, the Slovak Republic and the United Kingdom, 60 per cent or more of upper secondary students are enrolled in vocational programmes. The exception is Iceland, where the majority of students are enrolled in general programmes even though dual-system apprenticeship programmes are offered (Table C2.5).

In most OECD countries, vocational education is school-based. In Austria, the Czech Republic, Iceland and the Slovak Republic, however, about half of the vocational programmes have combined school-based and work-based elements. In Denmark, Germany, Hungary and Switzerland, the majority of vocational programmes have both school-based and work-based elements.

C₂

Percentage of primary and secondary students enrolled in private institutions (2000)

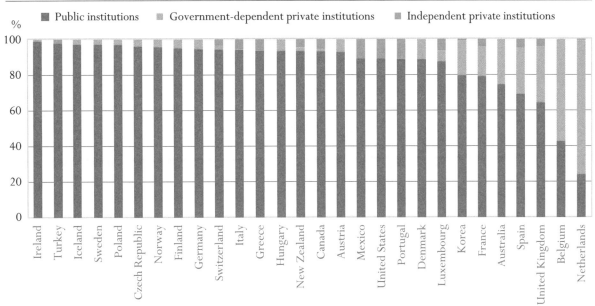

Countries are ranked in descending order of percentage of students enrolled in public institutions
Source: OECD. Table C2.4. See Annex 3 for notes *(www.oecd.org/els/education/eag2002).*

Upper secondary enrolment by type of institution

Although the majority of primary and secondary students are enrolled in publicly managed and financed schools, in OECD countries, 20 per cent of upper secondary students on average are now enrolled in privately managed schools (Table C2.4 and Chart C2.3).

The majority of upper secondary students in Belgium, Korea, the Netherlands and the United Kingdom are enrolled in government-dependent private institutions (60, 55, 90 and 67 per cent respectively). Private educational institutions that are financed mainly by household payments are far less common at the upper secondary level and below, and are occasionally perceived as imposing barriers to the participation of students from low income families. However, in France, Mexico, Portugal and Spain, between 10 and 20 per cent of upper secondary students are enrolled in private institutions that are financed predominantly by unsubsidised household payments (Table C2.4).

The majority of upper secondary students are enrolled in public institutions…

…but enrolments in privately managed primary and secondary institutions account for the majority of students in Belgium, Korea, the Netherlands and the United Kingdom.

Definitions and methodologies

Pre-vocational and vocational programmes include both school-based programmes and combined school and work-based programmes that are recognised as part of the education system. Entirely work-based education and training that is not overseen by a formal education authority is not taken into account.

Data refer to the school year 1999-2000 and are based on the UOE data collection on

C₂

*education statistics,
which is administered
annually by the OECD
(for details, see Annex 3).*

Table C2.1 shows, for all ages, the sum of net entry rates. The net entry rate of a specific age is obtained by dividing the number of first-time entrants to each type of tertiary education of that age by the total population in the corresponding age group (multiplied by 100). The sum of net entry rates is calculated by adding the rates for each single year of age. The result represents the proportion of people in a synthetic age-cohort who enter tertiary education, irrespective of changes in population sizes and of differences between OECD countries in the typical entry age. Table C2.1 shows also the 20th, 50th and 80th percentiles of the age distribution of first-time entrants, *i.e.*, the age below which 20 per cent, 50 per cent and 80 per cent of first-time entrants are to be found.

New (first-time) entrants are students who are enrolling at the relevant level of education for the first time. Foreign students enrolling for the first time in a post-graduate programme are considered first-time entrants.

Not all OECD countries can distinguish between students entering a tertiary programme for the first time and those transferring between different levels of tertiary education or repeating or re-entering a level after an absence. Thus, first-time entry rates for each level of tertiary education cannot be added up to total tertiary-level entrance rate because it would result in double-counting entrants.

Table C2.2 shows the expected number of years for which 17-year-olds will be enrolled in tertiary education, or the sum of net enrolment rates for people aged 17 and over (divided by 100). This measure is a function of the number of participants in tertiary education and the duration of tertiary studies. Since the denominator also includes those who have never participated in tertiary education, the indicator cannot be interpreted as the average number of years an individual student requires to complete tertiary education.

*Data for 1994–1995 are
based on a special survey
carried out in OECD
member countries in 2000.*

Data on tertiary enrolment in 1994-1995 were obtained from a special survey carried out in 2000. OECD countries were asked to report according to the ISCED-97 classification.

Table C2.1.
Entry rates to tertiary education and age distribution of new entrants (2000)
Sum of net entry rates for each year of age, by gender and programme destination

		Tertiary-type B			Tertiary-type A					
		Net entry rates			Net entry rates			Age at:		
		M+F	Males	Females	M+F	Males	Females	20th percentile[1]	50th percentile[1]	80th percentile[1]
		(1)	(2)	(3)	(4)	(5)	(6)	(7)	(8)	(9)
OECD COUNTRIES	Australia	m	m	m	59	52	66	18.4	19.9	27.4
	Austria	m	m	m	33	30	37	19.1	20.5	23.6
	Belgium (Fl.)	34	28	39	36	36	36	18.3	18.9	22.7
	Canada	m	m	m	m	m	m	m	m	m
	Czech Republic*	9	6	12	25	26	24	18.7	19.7	21.8
	Denmark	35	26	45	29	27	32	20.8	22.4	27.9
	Finland	a	a	a	71	62	81	19.9	21.6	26.9
	France	21	22	21	37	30	44	18.3	18.9	20.2
	Germany[2]	13	9	18	30	30	30	20.1	21.4	24.3
	Greece	m	m	m	m	m	m	m	m	m
	Hungary*	2	1	2	65	60	70	19.2	21.0	26.5
	Iceland	10	11	9	66	48	84	20.9	22.7	28.5
	Ireland	26	23	28	31	29	34	18.3	19.0	19.9
	Italy[1]	1	1	1	43	38	49	m	m	m
	Japan[1]	32	22	43	39	47	30	m	m	m
	Korea[1]	50	51	49	45	48	41	m	m	m
	Luxembourg	m	m	m	m	m	m	m	m	m
	Mexico	1	1	1	26	27	26	18.3	19.5	25.7
	Netherlands	1	1	2	51	48	54	18.5	19.8	22.8
	New Zealand	37	31	42	70	57	84	18.9	22.7	<40
	Norway	7	9	6	59	45	74	20.1	21.6	29.6
	Poland[1]	1	n	2	62	x(4)	x(4)	m	m	m
	Portugal	m	m	m	m	m	m	m	m	m
	Slovak Republic[2]	3	1	5	37	38	36	18.6	19.5	21.3
	Spain	15	15	16	48	42	54	18.4	19.2	22.1
	Sweden	7	7	6	67	54	81	20.2	22.7	32.1
	Switzerland	14	15	13	29	32	26	20.3	21.8	26.3
	Turkey*	9	11	8	21	26	17	18.3	19.6	23.2
	United Kingdom	28	24	32	46	42	49	18.4	19.4	25.4
	United States	14	12	15	43	37	49	18.4	19.4	26.8
	Country mean	*15*	*14*	*17*	*45*	*40*	*48*			
NON-OECD COUNTRIES	Argentina[4]	30	18	41	50	31	70	m	m	m
	Chile[3,4]	14	14	14	38	40	35	m	m	m
	China[3,4]	6	x(1)	x(1)	8	x(4)	x(4)	m	m	m
	Indonesia[5]	8	7	9	14	16	11	m	m	m
	Israel	31	26	36	49	44	54	m	m	m
	Jamaica	16	10	22	9	6	13	m	m	m
	Jordan[3]	14	9	20	30	29	30	m	m	m
	Malaysia[4]	24	24	25	22	19	25	m	m	m
	Paraguay[3,4]	8	5	12	m	m	m	m	m	m
	Philippines[4]	a	a	a	41	36	45	m	m	m
	Thailand[3]	23	25	21	40	36	44	m	m	m
	Tunisia[3]	x(4)	x(5)	x(6)	27	27	27	m	m	m
	Uruguay[3,4]	17	8	26	26	21	31	m	m	m
	Zimbabwe[3,5]	4	5	3	1	2	1	m	m	m

Note: x indicates that data are included in another column. The column reference is shown in brackets after "x". *e.g.*, x(2) means that data are included in column 2.
1. 20/50/80 per cent of new entrants are below this age.
2. Entry rate for type B programmes calculated as gross entry rate.
3. Entry rate for type A and B programmes calculated as gross entry rate.
4. Year of reference 1999.
5. Year of reference 2001.
* See Annex 3 for notes (*www.oecd.org/els/education/eag2002*).
Source: OECD.

C₂

Table C2.2.
Expected years in tertiary education and changes in total tertiary enrolment (2000)
Expected years of tertiary education under current conditions, by gender and mode of study, and index of change in total enrolment in tertiary education (1995=100)

		Tertiary-type B education			Tertiary-type A education			Total tertiary education (type A, B and advanced research programmes)			Change in enrolment (1995 = 100)		
		Full-time and part-time		Full-time	Full-time and part-time		Full-time	Full-time and part-time		Full-time		Attributable to:	
		M + F	Females	M + F	M + F	Females	M + F	M + F	Females	M + F	Total tertiary education	Change in population	Change in enrolment rates
		(1)	(2)	(3)	(4)	(5)	(6)	(7)	(8)	(9)	(10)	(11)	(12)
OECD COUNTRIES	Australia	0.7	0.7	0.2	2.2	2.5	1.4	3.0	3.3	1.7	108	102	106
	Austria	0.2	0.3	0.1	2.0	2.0	2.0	2.3	2.4	2.3	109	69	144
	Belgium	1.4	1.6	1.1	1.3	1.3	1.3	2.7	2.9	2.3	111	94	117
	Canada	0.7	0.8	0.6	2.0	2.4	1.4	2.8	3.2	2.1	101	m	m
	Czech Republic	0.2	0.3	0.2	1.2	1.2	1.1	1.5	1.6	1.4	150	102	147
	Denmark	1.1	1.5	1.1	1.4	1.4	1.4	2.6	3.0	2.6	115	95	121
	Finland	0.2	0.3	0.2	3.6	3.9	3.6	4.1	4.4	4.1	116	100	116
	France	0.6	0.7	0.6	1.8	2.0	1.8	2.6	2.8	2.6	98	91	107
	Germany*	0.3	0.4	0.3	1.7	1.6	1.7	2.0	2.0	2.0	95	89	107
	Greece	0.9	0.9	0.9	1.9	2.0	1.9	2.8	2.9	2.8	143	96	151
	Hungary*	n	n	n	1.9	2.1	1.1	2.0	2.2	1.1	180	110	164
	Iceland	0.2	0.2	0.1	2.1	2.7	1.7	2.3	2.9	1.9	133	101	131
	Ireland	x(7)	x(8)	x(9)	x(7)	x(8)	x(9)	2.3	2.4	1.8	125	109	116
	Italy	n	n	n	2.2	2.4	2.2	2.2	2.5	2.2	103	m	m
	Japan	m	m	m	m	m	m	m	m	m	m	m	m
	Korea	1.5	1.1	1.5	2.2	1.6	2.2	3.7	2.7	3.7	148	87	161
	Luxembourg	m	m	m	m	m	m	m	m	m	m	m	m
	Mexico	n	n	n	1.0	1.0	1.0	1.0	1.0	1.0	128	106	121
	Netherlands	n	n	n	2.4	2.4	2.0	2.4	2.5	2.1	m	m	m
	New Zealand	0.8	0.9	0.4	2.3	2.7	1.6	3.1	3.6	2.0	m	m	m
	Norway	0.3	0.2	0.2	2.9	3.5	2.1	3.2	3.7	2.4	105	94	112
	Poland[1]	n	n	n	2.6	3.0	1.3	2.6	3.1	1.4	208	119	173
	Portugal	0.6	0.6	0.6	1.7	2.0	1.7	2.4	2.7	2.4	124	98	127
	Slovak Republic	0.1	0.1	n	1.3	1.4	1.0	1.5	1.5	1.0	m	m	m
	Spain	0.3	0.3	0.3	2.6	2.8	2.4	2.9	3.2	2.7	120	93	129
	Sweden	0.1	0.1	0.1	2.8	3.4	1.6	3.1	3.6	1.7	122	95	129
	Switzerland	0.4	0.3	0.1	1.2	1.1	1.2	1.7	1.5	1.4	m	m	m
	Turkey	0.2	0.1	0.2	0.6	0.5	0.6	0.8	0.6	0.8	86	110	79
	United Kingdom	0.7	0.8	0.2	1.7	1.9	1.4	2.5	2.8	1.7	112	97	115
	United States	0.7	0.8	0.3	2.6	3.0	1.7	3.4	3.8	2.1	m	m	m
	Country mean	*0.4*	*0.5*	*0.3*	*2.0*	*2.1*	*1.6*	*2.5*	*2.7*	*2.0*	*124*	*98*	*127*
NON-OECD COUNTRIES	Argentina[2]	0.7	1.0	m	2.0	2.4	m	2.7	3.4	m	m	m	m
	Brazil[2]	x(4)	x(5)	x(6)	0.8	0.9	0.8	0.9	0.9	0.9	m	m	m
	Indonesia[1]	0.1	0.1	0.1	0.4	0.4	0.4	0.6	0.5	0.6	m	m	m
	Israel	0.5	0.6	0.5	2.1	2.4	1.6	2.6	3.0	2.2	m	m	m
	Malaysia[2]	0.5	0.5	0.5	0.6	0.6	0.5	1.1	1.2	1.0	m	m	m
	Paraguay[2]	0.2	0.3	0.2	m	m	m	m	m	m	m	m	m
	Peru[2]	1.0	1.1	1.0	m	m	m	m	m	m	m	m	m
	Philippines[2]	a	a	a	1.4	1.6	1.4	1.4	1.6	1.4	m	m	m
	Russian Federation[1,3]	1.0	1.1	3.3	2.1	2.4	5.4	3.2	3.6	7.7	m	m	m
	Uruguay[1,2]	0.5	0.7	0.5	1.3	1.6	1.3	1.8	2.2	1.8	m	m	m

Note: x indicates that data are included in another column. The column reference is shown in brackets after "x". *e.g.*, x(2) means that data are included in column 2.
1. Excludes advanced research programmes.
2. Year of reference 1999.
3. Year of reference 2001.
* See Annex 3 for notes (*www.oecd.org/els/education/eag2002*).
Source: OECD.

C₂

Table C2.3.
Students enrolled in public and private institutions and full-time and part-time programmes in tertiary education (2000)
Distribution of students, by mode of study, type of institution and programme destination

	Type of institution						Mode of study			
	Tertiary-type B education			Tertiary-type A and advanced research programmes			Tertiary-type B education		Tertiary-type A and advanced research programmes	
	Public	Government-dependent private	Independent private	Public	Government-dependent private	Independent private	Full-time	Part-time	Full-time	Part-time
	(1)	(2)	(3)	(4)	(5)	(6)	(7)	(8)	(9)	(10)
Australia	98.9	1.1	a	100.0	a	a	32.3	67.7	62.1	37.9
Austria	64.4	35.6	n	95.8	4.2	n	66.1	33.9	100.0	a
Belgium	48.7	51.3	n	38.7	61.3	n	74.4	25.6	94.9	5.1
Canada	100.0	n	n	100.0	n	n	85.2	14.8	68.2	31.8
Czech Republic	66.3	33.7	a	100.0	a	a	100.0	n	92.4	7.6
Denmark	99.6	0.4	a	100.0	a	a	100.0	a	100.0	a
Finland	81.3	18.7	a	89.7	10.3	a	100.0	a	100.0	a
France	73.2	9.1	17.7	89.4	0.8	9.8	100.0	a	100.0	a
Germany	63.2	36.8	x(2)	100.0	a	a	84.9	15.1	100.0	a
Greece	100.0	a	a	100.0	a	a	100.0	a	100.0	a
Hungary	100.0	n	a	87.0	13.0	a	87.7	12.3	58.0	42.0
Iceland	43.8	56.2	n	95.4	4.6	n	71.2	28.8	80.9	19.1
Ireland	94.2	n	5.8	95.3	n	4.7	60.7	39.3	86.8	13.2
Italy	85.3	a	14.7	93.8	a	6.2	100.0	a	100.0	a
Japan	9.4	a	90.6	27.3	a	72.7	96.7	3.3	90.6	9.4
Korea	14.0	a	86.0	23.2	a	76.8	100.0	a	100.0	a
Luxembourg	100.0	a	a	100.0	a	a	99.3	0.7	100.0	a
Mexico	100.0	a	a	69.0	a	31.0	100.0	a	100.0	a
Netherlands	8.9	91.1	m	31.3	68.7	m	69.3	30.7	82.6	17.4
New Zealand	81.3	18.2	0.5	99.0	1.0	n	45.0	55.0	69.7	30.3
Norway	74.9	25.1	x(2)	88.6	11.4	x(5)	87.2	12.8	72.8	27.2
Poland	89.0	10.2	0.7	72.2	a	27.8	78.0	22.0	53.9	46.1
Portugal	80.0	a	20.0	64.3	a	35.7	m	m	m	m
Slovak Republic	94.9	5.1	n	100.0	n	n	64.8	35.2	71.9	28.1
Spain	77.3	16.3	6.3	88.7	n	11.3	99.6	0.4	91.5	8.5
Sweden	71.4	1.6	27.0	94.6	5.4	a	93.0	7.0	54.0	46.0
Switzerland	37.7	39.2	23.1	92.4	6.1	1.5	32.9	67.1	94.5	5.5
Turkey*	97.6	a	2.4	95.7	a	4.3	100.0	a	100.0	a
United Kingdom	a	100.0	n	a	100.0	n	30.5	69.5	76.0	24.0
United States	92.5	a	7.5	68.7	a	31.3	44.2	55.8	64.7	35.3
Country mean	*71.6*	*18.3*	*10.1*	*80.0*	*9.6*	*10.4*	*79.4*	*20.6*	*85.0*	*15.0*
Argentina[1]	m	m	m	85.2	a	14.8	m	m	m	m
Brazil[1]	m	a	m	36.9	a	63.1	m	m	100.0	a
Chile[1]	7.2	6.8	86.0	33.0	23.3	43.7	100.0	n	100.0	n
China	m	m	m	m	m	m	59.4	40.6	89.4	10.6
Egypt	31.1	m	68.9	m	m	m	68.9	31.1	m	m
Indonesia[2]	37.1	a	62.9	31.4	a	68.6	100.0	a	100.0	a
Israel	22.0	78.0	x(2)	12.8	79.6	7.9	100.0	a	83.6	19.1
Jamaica	97.7	a	2.3	81.4	a	18.6	71.6	28.4	m	m
Jordan	44.7	a	55.3	69.2	a	30.8	100.0	a	100.0	a
Malaysia[1]	56.4	a	43.6	77.0	a	23.0	89.8	10.2	85.5	14.5
Paraguay[1]	51.7	1.7	46.5	m	a	m	100.0	a	m	m
Peru[1]	56.2	m	43.8	62.3	a	37.7	100.0	a	m	m
Philippines[1]	a	a	a	26.9	a	73.1	a	a	100.0	a
Russian Federation[2]	97.8	a	2.2	90.3	a	9.7	m	m	m	m
Thailand	56.7	a	43.3	88.3	a	11.7	100.0	a	m	m
Tunisia	100.0	a	a	100.0	a	a	100.0	a	100.0	a
Uruguay[1]	91.0	a	9.0	88.4	a	11.6	100.0	a	100.0	a
Zimbabwe[2]	91.0	9.0	a	76.0	24.0	a	m	m	m	m

OECD COUNTRIES / NON-OECD COUNTRIES

C2

Note: x indicates that data are included in another column. The column reference is shown in brackets after "x". *e.g.*, x(2) means that data are included in column 2.
1. Year of reference 1999.
2. Year of reference 2001.
* See Annex 3 for notes (*www.oecd.org/els/education/eag2002*).
Source: OECD.

Table C2.4.
Students enrolled in public and private institutions and full-time and part-time programmes in primary and secondary education (2000)
Distribution of students, by mode of study and type of institution

	Type of institution									Mode of study	
	Primary education			Lower secondary education			Upper secondary education			Primary and secondary education	
	Public	Govern-ment-dependent private	Inde-pendent private	Public	Govern-ment-dependent private	Inde-pendent private	Public	Govern-ment-dependent private	Inde-pendent private	Full-time	Part-time
	(1)	(2)	(3)	(4)	(5)	(6)	(7)	(8)	(9)	(10)	(11)
Australia	72.8	27.2	a	69.1	30.9	a	82.9	17.1	a	74.0	26.0
Austria	95.8	4.2	x(2)	92.6	7.4	x(5)	90.6	9.4	x(9)	99.4	0.6
Belgium	45.6	54.4	n	41.9	58.1	n	39.9	60.1	n	84.1	15.9
Canada	93.5	1.4	5.1	92.1	1.1	6.7	94.4	0.7	4.9	99.2	0.8
Czech Republic	99.1	0.9	a	98.3	1.7	a	89.5	10.5	a	99.7	0.3
Denmark	89.2	10.8	a	78.4	21.6	a	98.0	2.0	a	100.0	a
Finland	98.9	1.1	a	96.0	4.0	a	89.8	10.2	a	100.0	a
France	85.4	14.3	0.2	79.2	19.8	1.0	69.7	16.6	13.7	100.0	a
Germany	97.8	2.2	x(2)	93.3	6.7	x(5)	93.2	6.8	x(9)	99.8	0.2
Greece	93.0	a	7.0	95.0	a	5.0	93.9	a	6.1	98.3	1.7
Hungary	94.9	5.1	a	95.0	5.0	a	90.6	9.4	a	97.0	3.0
Iceland	98.6	1.4	n	99.0	1.0	n	94.2	5.8	n	92.9	7.1
Ireland	98.8	n	1.2	100.0	n	n	98.8	n	1.2	99.9	0.1
Italy	93.4	a	6.6	96.5	a	3.5	93.7	0.9	5.4	100.0	a
Japan	99.1	a	0.9	94.4	a	5.6	69.4	a	30.6	99.0	1.0
Korea	98.5	a	1.5	77.6	22.4	a	45.0	55.0	a	100.0	a
Luxembourg	93.2	1.0	5.8	79.0	14.0	7.0	85.0	7.7	7.4	100.0	n
Mexico	92.6	a	7.4	86.6	a	13.4	78.6	a	21.4	100.0	a
Netherlands	31.4	68.6	a	24.6	75.3	0.2	7.8	90.0	2.2	97.6	2.4
New Zealand	98.0	a	2.0	95.9	a	4.1	83.0	7.9	9.1	95.2	4.8
Norway	98.5	1.5	x(2)	98.1	1.9	x(5)	89.1	10.9	x(9)	98.6	1.4
Poland	99.2	0.8	a	99.0	1.0	a	93.9	6.1	0.1	95.5	4.5
Portugal	90.4	a	9.6	90.1	a	9.9	85.0	a	15.0	93.5	6.5
Slovak Republic	96.1	3.9	n	95.2	4.8	n	93.3	6.7	n	98.8	1.2
Spain	66.6	30.2	3.2	67.1	29.8	3.2	78.9	10.0	11.1	96.2	3.8
Sweden	96.6	3.4	a	97.3	2.7	a	98.0	2.0	a	84.8	15.2
Switzerland	96.7	1.2	2.2	93.2	2.5	4.3	91.4	3.6	5.0	99.7	0.3
Turkey	98.2	a	1.8	a	a	a	97.5	a	2.5	100.0	a
United Kingdom	95.3	a	4.7	93.6	0.3	6.1	29.6	67.4	3.0	77.0	23.0
United States	88.4	a	11.6	90.1	a	9.9	90.6	a	9.4	100.0	n
Country mean	*89.9*	*7.8*	*2.7*	*83.6*	*10.4*	*3.1*	*81.2*	*13.9*	*5.7*	*96.0*	*4.0*
Argentina[1]	80.5	19.5	x(2)	77.5	22.5	x(5)	72.2	27.8	x(8)	100.0	a
Brazil[1]	91.9	a	8.1	89.9	a	10.1	83.2	a	16.8	100.0	a
Chile[1]	56.8	35.7	7.5	57.8	34.1	8.1	51.4	32.4	16.1	100.0	a
China	m	m	m	m	m	m	m	m	m	96.7	3.3
Egypt	92.4	1.1	7.6	95.8	1.2	4.2	93.8	0.2	6.2	100.0	a
India[1]	75.6	9.9	8.0	57.0	30.4	10.8	42.5	44.5	8.7	95.3	4.7
Indonesia[2]	92.7	a	7.3	72.1	a	27.9	47.2	a	52.8	100.0	a
Israel	100.0	n	n	100.0	n	n	100.0	n	n	98.9	1.1
Jamaica	96.0	a	4.0	97.0	a	3.0	97.0	a	3.0	a	a
Jordan	70.0	a	30.0	80.5	a	19.5	91.3	a	8.7	100.0	a
Malaysia[1]	94.3	a	5.7	92.6	a	7.4	92.1	a	7.9	100.0	a
Paraguay[1]	85.0	9.3	5.7	72.5	10.9	16.7	67.4	7.4	25.2	100.0	a
Peru[1]	87.4	3.2	9.4	84.9	4.7	10.4	82.2	5.1	12.7	100.0	a
Philippines[1]	92.5	a	7.5	74.8	a	25.2	69.5	a	30.5	100.0	a
Russian Federation[2]	99.6	a	0.4	99.7	a	0.3	99.6	a	0.4	m	m
Thailand	86.9	13.1	n	93.6	6.4	n	87.7	3.0	9.3	m	m
Tunisia	99.3	a	0.7	94.5	a	5.5	88.8	a	11.2	100.0	a
Uruguay[1]	85.8	a	14.2	86.1	a	13.9	88.3	a	11.7	100.0	a
Zimbabwe	12.0	88.0	a	27.6	72.4	a	42.6	57.4	a	100.0	a

OECD COUNTRIES

NON-OECD COUNTRIES

Note: x indicates that data are included in another column. The column reference is shown in brackets after "x". *e.g.*, x(2) means that data are included in column 2.
1. Year of reference 1999.
2. Year of reference 2001.

Source: OECD. See Annex 3 for notes on methodology (*www.oecd.org/els/education/eag2002*).

C2

Table C2.5.
Upper secondary enrolment patterns (2000)
Enrolment in public and private upper secondary institutions by programme destination and type of programme

	Distribution of enrolment by programme destination			Distribution of enrolment by type of programme			
	ISCED 3A	ISCED 3B	ISCED 3C	General	Pre-vocational	Vocational	of which: combined school and work-based
	(1)	(2)	(3)	(4)	(5)	(6)	(7)
OECD COUNTRIES							
Australia	34.3	a	65.7	34.3	a	65.7	x(6)
Austria	43.5	48.1	8.5	21.7	7.2	71.1	36.4
Belgium	53.7	a	46.3	33.2	a	66.8	2.8
Canada	90.9	a	9.1	90.9	9.1	a	a
Czech Republic	63.5	0.5	36.0	18.6	1.1	80.2	40.5
Denmark	45.3	a	54.7	45.1	0.2	54.7	54.1
Finland	100.0	a	a	44.7	a	55.3	10.7
France	67.0	a	33.0	42.6	a	57.4	11.7
Germany	36.8	63.2	a	36.8	a	63.2	48.7
Greece	67.9	a	32.1	67.9	a	32.1	a
Hungary	74.6	1.7	23.6	36.0	53.7	10.3	10.3
Iceland	66.8	0.5	32.7	66.6	1.1	32.3	14.4
Ireland	78.1	a	21.9	76.6	23.4	a	a
Italy	80.8	1.3	17.9	35.7	39.8	24.6	m
Japan	73.9	0.8	25.3	73.9	0.8	25.3	a
Korea	63.9	a	36.1	63.9	a	36.1	a
Luxembourg	61.2	14.4	24.3	36.5	a	63.5	13.7
Mexico	87.0	a	13.0	87.0	a	13.0	a
Netherlands	64.8	a	35.2	31.7	a	68.3	20.4
New Zealand	65.0	17.4	17.6	m	m	m	m
Norway	42.7	a	57.3	42.7	a	57.3	m
Poland	78.0	a	22.0	35.7	a	64.3	a
Portugal	75.9	17.0	7.0	72.2	a	27.8	m
Slovak Republic	78.1	a	21.9	21.4	a	78.6	39.7
Spain	66.5	n	33.5	66.5	n	33.5	5.8
Sweden*	49.0	a	0.4	51.2	a	48.8	m
Switzerland	30.0	60.0	10.0	34.3	a	65.7	57.9
Turkey	90.1	a	9.9	51.0	a	49.0	9.9
United Kingdom	24.3	a	75.7	32.7	x(6)	67.3	x(6)
United States	m	m	m	m	m	m	m
Country mean	*63.9*	*7.8*	*26.6*	*48.3*	*5.1*	*46.9*	*17.1*
NON-OECD COUNTRIES							
Argentina[1]	100.0	a	a	41.6	a	58.4	x(6)
Brazil[1]	m	m	a	82.3	a	17.7	m
Chile[1]	58.2	41.8	a	58.2	a	41.8	a
China	47.0	a	53.0	47.0	x(6)	53.0	m
Egypt	35.2	64.8	a	35.2	a	64.8	a
India[1]	m	a	m	95.8	a	4.2	m
Indonesia[2]	60.3	39.7	a	m	a	m	m
Israel	95.8	x(1)	4.2	67.1	a	32.9	m
Jamaica	99.1	0.9	a	99.1	a	0.9	a
Jordan	93.9	a	6.1	74.9	a	25.1	n
Malaysia[1]	14.9	a	85.1	84.9	a	15.1	x(6)
Paraguay[1]	m	a	m	81.5	a	18.5	a
Peru[1]	m	m	a	75.1	a	24.9	a
Philippines[1]	100.0	a	a	100.0	a	a	a
Thailand	70.0	30.0	a	70.0	a	30.0	x(6)
Tunisia	94.1	3.7	2.2	94.1	3.7	2.2	a
Uruguay[1]	90.3	a	9.7	81.3	a	18.7	a
Zimbabwe[2]	54.9	45.1	x(2)	m	m	m	m

Note: x indicates that data are included in another column. The column reference is shown in brackets after "x". *e.g.*, x(2) means that data are included in column 2.
1. Year of reference 1999.
2. Year of reference 2001.
* See Annex 3 for notes (*www.oecd.org/els/education/eag2002*).
Source: OECD.

FOREIGN STUDENTS IN TERTIARY EDUCATION

- Five countries (Australia, France, Germany, the United Kingdom and the United States) receive 70 per cent of all foreign students studying in the OECD area.

- In absolute numbers, students from Greece, Japan and Korea represent the largest sources of intakes from OECD countries. Students from China and Southeast Asia comprise the largest numbers of foreign students from non-OECD countries.

- In relative terms, the percentage of foreign students enrolled in OECD countries ranges from below 1 to almost 17 per cent. Proportional to their size, Australia, Austria, Belgium, Switzerland and the United Kingdom take in the most foreign students, when measured as a percentage of their tertiary enrolments.

Chart C3.1.

Percentage of tertiary students enrolled who are not citizens of the country of study (2000)

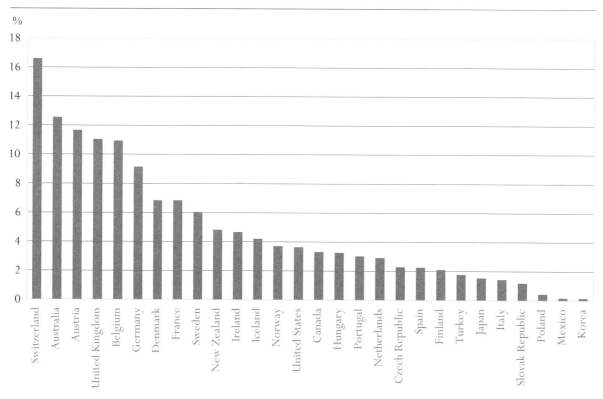

Countries are ranked in descending order of the percentage of students enrolled who are not citizens of the country of study.
Source: OECD. Table C3.1. See Annex 3 for notes *(www.oecd.org/els/education/eag2002).*

Policy context

The international dimension of higher education is receiving increasing attention. The general trend towards freely circulating capital, goods and people coupled with changes in the openness of labour markets have increased the demand for new kinds of skills and knowledge in OECD countries. Governments are looking increasingly to higher education to play a role in broadening the horizons of students and allowing them to develop a deeper understanding of the multiplicity of languages, cultures and business methods in the world.

This indicator shows the mobility of students between countries.

One way for students to expand their knowledge of other cultures and societies is to study in tertiary education institutions in countries other than their own. International student mobility involves costs and benefits to students and institutions in sending and host countries alike. While the direct short-term monetary costs and benefits of this mobility are relatively easy to measure, the long-term social and economic benefits to students, institutions and countries are more difficult to quantify. The number of students studying in other countries, however, provides some idea at least of the extent of student mobility.

It is worth noting that in addition to student flows across borders, cross-border electronic delivery of highly flexible educational programmes is also relevant for capturing the internationalisation of higher education. Today, we see cross-border mobility among participants in and providers of education. In the future, it will be important to develop ways to quantify and measure these components of the internationalisation of education.

C₃

Evidence and explanations

Proportion of foreign students studying abroad, by host countries

A relatively small number of countries enrols the vast majority of foreign students studying in the OECD area and in other non-OECD countries reporting such data. The United States receives the most foreign students (in absolute terms) with 28 per cent of the total, followed by the United Kingdom and Germany (14 and 12 per cent respectively), France and Australia (8 and 7 per cent, respectively) (Chart C3.2). These five host countries account for about 70 per cent of all foreign students studying abroad.

Five OECD countries attract seven out of ten foreign students.

This indicator defines a foreign student as someone who is not a citizen of the country of study. In most countries, it has not been possible to distinguish between foreign students who are residents in the country but who have immigrated (or whose parents have immigrated), and students who came to the country expressly to pursue their education. This leads to a potential overestimation of the foreign student body in countries with comparatively stringent naturalisation policies.

Not all non-national students came to the host country to study.

For example, Germany is a high-ranking destination for foreign students but the actual number of non-resident students registered in German tertiary education

Chart C3.2.

Distribution of students who are not citizens of the country of study, by host country (2000)

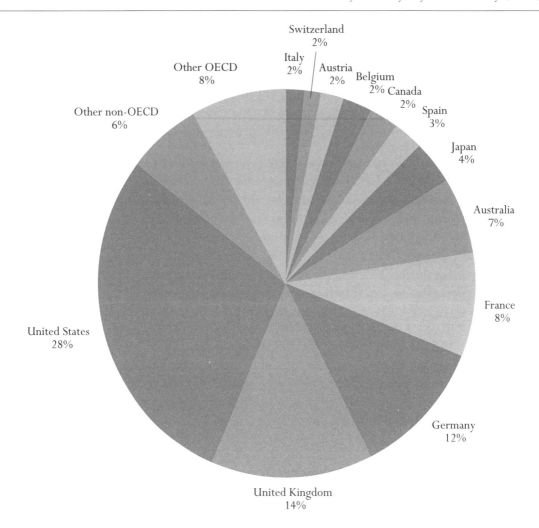

Source: OECD.

C3

institutions accounts for only two-thirds of all foreign students. This is because a significant number of "domestic foreigners", that is mainly children of migrant workers, are considered foreign for the purposes of this indicator, despite having grown up in Germany.

Language of instruction is a critical factor in selecting a country in which to study.

The language of instruction is critical for selecting a foreign country in which to study. Countries whose language of instruction is widely spoken and read (English, French, German) dominate in hosting foreign students in absolute and relative terms. The dominance of English-speaking countries such as Australia, the United Kingdom and the United States may be largely attributable to the fact that students intending to study abroad are most likely to have learned English in their home country. An increasing number of institutions in non-English-speaking countries now offer courses in English to attract overseas students.

Proportion of foreign students studying in OECD countries by sending countries

In 2000, 1.62 million foreign students were enrolled outside their country of origin, of which 1.52 million (or 94 per cent) studied in the OECD area. This represented a 14 per cent increase in student mobility towards the OECD compared to 1998. This increase was balanced between students coming from OECD and non-OECD countries, that is the geographic composition of the intake remained stable: 44 per cent of the foreign students originate from the OECD area and 56 per cent come from non-OECD countries.

Asian students represent the largest group of foreign students studying in OECD countries, with 41 per cent of the total, followed by Europeans (33 per cent).

The predominance of students from Asia and Europe among foreign intakes is also observed when focusing on OECD countries. Students from Japan and Korea comprise the largest groups, at 4.6 and 3.9 per cent respectively, of all foreign students, followed by students from Greece (3.6 per cent), Germany (3.5 per cent), France (3.4 per cent) and Italy (2.7 per cent). Together, these countries account for nearly 20 per cent of all foreign students in OECD countries.

With respect to non-OECD countries with students studying abroad, students from China represent 7.1 per cent of all foreign students studying in OECD countries, followed by students from India (3.4 per cent), Morocco (2.7 per cent) and Malaysia (2.4 per cent). 4.2 per cent of all foreign students originate from Southeast Asia – Indonesia, Singapore and Thailand.

International trade, finance and economic issues are likely to be important factors underlying student mobility. For example, the promotion of regional economic integration by organisations and treaties such as the EU, NAFTA, ASEAN and APEC may provide incentives for students to develop their understanding of partner countries' cultures and languages, and to build bilateral or multilateral networks. Some national governments have made international student mobility an explicit part of their socio-economic development strategies. For example, several governments in the Asia-Pacific region, such as Australia, Japan and New Zealand, have initiated policies to attract foreign students to study in their higher education institutions, often on a revenue-generating or at least self-financing basis.

Foreign student intakes as a proportion of total enrolments

The foregoing analysis is focused on the distribution of absolute numbers of foreign students by countries of destination and origin. This leads to larger countries receiving the most importance, *ceteris paribus*. One way to take this into account is to examine the intake of tertiary students in a particular country with the number of students studying abroad, relative to its tertiary enrolments.

In 2000, 1.62 million foreign students were enrolled outside their country of origin, of which 1.52 million (or 94 per cent) studied in the OECD area.

Students from Greece, Japan and Korea represent the largest intakes from other OECD countries...

C₃

...while students from China and Southeast Asia make up the largest proportion of foreign students from non-OECD countries.

The percentage of foreign students enrolled in OECD countries ranges from below 1 to almost 17 per cent.

Australia, Austria and Switzerland receive the largest proportion of foreign students relative to total tertiary enrolment (between 12 and 17 per cent), followed by Belgium, Germany and the United Kingdom (see Chart C3.1). By contrast, in Italy, Japan, Korea, Mexico, Poland, the Slovak Republic and Turkey, the proportion of foreign students remains below 2 per cent in tertiary enrolment (see Chart C3.1).

In comparison with OECD countries, non-OECD countries participating in the World Education Indicators project receive marginal numbers of foreign students relative to their size, with the exception of Jordan (9 per cent), which reflects the presence of a large Palestinian refugee community, and to a lesser extent Jamaica (2 per cent), due to the presence of one of the three campuses of the regional University of West Indies.

C3

Students studying abroad relative to total enrolments

It is also possible to estimate the extent to which students leave their country and study abroad by comparing the proportion of students studying abroad to national tertiary enrolments. The measure used here only covers students leaving their country to study in OECD and non-OECD countries that report data; it does not cover students who study abroad in countries other than those reporting their intakes in Table C3.1. The indicator is thus likely to underestimate the proportion of students studying abroad. Another potential source of underestimation may be that the indicator is calculated on a full-year basis whereas many students study abroad for less than a full academic year. For example, more than half of the students from the United States who study abroad leave for half a year or less, and only 14 per cent stay in the host country for a full academic year.

Greece, Iceland, Ireland and Luxembourg send a large proportion of their students abroad, while Australia, Mexico and the United States send relatively few.

The ratio of students studying abroad to total enrolment in the country of origin varies widely, from below 1 per cent in Australia (0.6 per cent), Mexico (0.7 per cent) and the United States (0.3 per cent), to as much as 25 per cent in Iceland and 226 per cent in Luxembourg. The latter case is specific, however, because Luxembourg only offers post-secondary non-university programmes or the first year of university at the tertiary level. Since students in Luxembourg must continue their studies abroad, a large number of students are enrolled outside the country.

Net balance of international student exchange

Proportional to their size, Australia, Switzerland and the United Kingdom show the largest net intake of foreign students.

Although the United States receives over 441 000 students more than the total number of American students going abroad for study, other countries have much larger net intakes of students in proportion to their size. In Australia, Switzerland and the United Kingdom, the net intake is between 4.6 and 6.5 per cent of their tertiary enrolment (see Table C3.1, column 4). Conversely, Iceland, Ireland, Norway and Turkey show the highest relative net outflow of students, at 22, 7, 5 and 4 per cent of total tertiary enrolments, respectively. The balances of student flows take only students to and from reporting OECD and non-OECD countries into account. The absolute balance of countries that accept a significant number of students from non-reporting countries or that send students to non-reporting countries may differ from these figures.

For non-OECD countries, the balance of incoming and outgoing students is negative in all cases except the Russian Federation (2 per cent), Tunisia (3 per cent) and Uruguay (1 per cent).

Given the numerous benefits that foreign students may bring to their host countries, it is important to identify the factors likely to enhance student mobility.

Student mobility patterns can be attributed to a variety of push-pull factors, such as language barriers, the academic reputation of particular institutions or programmes, the flexibility of programmes with respect to counting time spent abroad toward degree requirements, the limitations of higher education provision in the home country, restrictive university admission policies at home, financial incentives and tuition costs.

Various push–pull factors help to explain student mobility patterns

These patterns also reflect geographical and historical links between countries, future job opportunities, cultural aspirations, and government policies to facilitate credit transfer between home and host institutions. The transparency and flexibility of courses and degree requirements also count.

Trade effects and economic benefits of the internationalisation of higher education

A first direct benefit of the intake of foreign students is the tuition fee revenue that is generated and the related domestic consumption by foreign students, which appear in the balance of current accounts as exports of educational services. The magnitude of this gain is further increased when host countries adopt a full-fee tuition policy for overseas students. Exports of educational services were estimated at US$ 30 billion in 1998, or 3 per cent of total OECD trade in services. In a top receiving country such as Australia, exports of education services were the third largest service sector export earner in 2000-2001, representing nearly 12 per cent of total service exports.

The net intake of foreign students indicates the magnitude of the benefits countries can potentially reap from the international exchange of tertiary students.

In addition to the direct benefits of internationalised higher education, a higher client-base of tertiary education may result in indirect gains, whereby net receiving countries generate economies of scale in tertiary education, and can therefore diversify their range of programmes or reduce their unit costs. This can be particularly important for host countries with a relatively small population.

The presence of a foreign student client-base also compels higher education institutions to offer quality programmes that stand out among competitors, which contributes to the development of a highly reactive, client-driven higher education.

Finally, the intake of foreign students can to some extent involve technology transfers (especially in advanced research programmes), foster intercultural contacts and help to build social networks for the future.

Definitions and methodologies

Data refer to the academic year 1999-2000 and are based on the UOE data collection on education statistics, which is administered annually by the OECD.

Students are classified as foreign students if they are not citizens of the country in which the data are collected. While pragmatic and operational, this classification may create inconsistencies resulting from national policies regarding naturalisation of immigrants and the inability of several countries to report separately foreign students net of permanent resident students. Countries that naturalise immigrants stringently and which cannot identify non-resident foreign students therefore over-estimate the size of their foreign student body, compared to more lenient countries. Bilateral comparisons of the data on foreign students should therefore be made with caution, since some countries differ in the definition and coverage of their foreign students (see Annex 3 at *www.oecd.org/els/education/eag2002*).

Foreign student data are collected by host countries and therefore relate to students that are coming in rather than to students going from that country to study abroad. Host countries covered by this indicator are OECD countries, with the exception of Luxembourg and the Slovak Republic, and the following non-OECD countries: Argentina, Chile, India, Indonesia, Jamaica, Jordan, Malaysia, the Philippines, the Russian Federation, Tunisia and Uruguay. This indicator does not include students studying in OECD countries which did not report to the OECD, or non-OECD countries other than those mentioned above. All statements on students studying abroad therefore underestimate the real number of students abroad.

The method of obtaining data on the number of foreign students is the same as that used for collecting data on total enrolments, that is to say, records of regularly enrolled students in an educational programme were used. Domestic and foreign students are usually counted on a specific day or period of the year. This procedure measures the proportion of foreign enrolments in an education system, but the actual number of individuals involved in foreign exchange may be much higher, since many students study abroad for less than a full academic year, or participate in exchange programmes that do not require enrolment (*e.g.,* inter-university exchange or advanced research short-term mobility).

Tables C3.1, C3.2 and C3.3 show foreign enrolment as a proportion of the total enrolment in the host country or country of origin (the sending country). Total enrolment, used as a denominator, includes all foreign students in the country and excludes all students from that country studying abroad. The proportions of students abroad given in Table C3.2 do not include the proportion of all students of a certain nationality studying abroad, but expresses the numbers of students of a given nationality as a proportion of the total domestic and foreign enrolment at the tertiary level, excluding students who are nationals of that country who are not studying in their home country.

Table C3.1.
Exchange of students in tertiary education (2000)
Foreign students enrolled as a percentage of all students (foreign plus domestic), and exchange of students as a percentage of total tertiary enrolment

Reading the first column: 2.2 per cent of all students in tertiary education in the Czech Republic are foreign students (from OECD and non-OECD countries).
Reading the second column: Foreign tertiary students from other countries, which report foreign students, represent 1.0 per cent of all tertiary students in the Czech Republic.
Reading the third column: 1.2 per cent of all tertiary students in the Czech Republic study in other countries, which report foreign students.
Column 4 represents the difference between column 2 and column 3.

	Foreign students as a percentage of all students (foreign and domestic students)	Exchange of students[1]			Foreign enrolment by gender	
		Students from other countries relative to total tertiary enrolment	Students studying abroad relative to total tertiary enrolment	Net intake of foreign students relative to total tertiary enrolment	% males	% females
OECD COUNTRIES						
Australia	12.5	6.1[2]	0.6[2]	5.5[2]	52.9	47.1
Austria	11.6	7.6[2]	4.4[2]	3.2[2]	49.9	50.1
Belgium	10.9	5.8	2.8	3.1	52.4	47.6
Canada	3.3	1.5[2]	2.4[2]	-0.9[2]	55.8	44.2
Czech Republic	2.2	1.0	1.2	-0.2	58.8	41.2
Denmark	6.8	2.6	3.5	-0.9	44.5	55.5
Finland	2.1	0.7	3.6	-2.9	57.5	42.5
France	6.8	1.9	2.6	-0.6	m	m
Germany	9.1	4.5	2.6	1.9	53.1	46.9
Greece	m	m	13.1	m	m	m
Hungary	3.2	m	2.2	m	46.7	53.3
Iceland	4.2	3.5	25.4	-21.9	35.5	64.5
Ireland	4.6	3.9	11.0	-7.2	47.8	52.2
Italy	1.4	0.2	2.3	-2.1	48.8	51.2
Japan	1.5	0.6	1.5	-0.9	55.6	44.4
Korea	0.1	n	2.3	-2.3	57.6	42.4
Luxembourg	m	m	225.6	m	m	m
Mexico	0.1	m	0.7	m	m	m
Netherlands	2.9	1.7	2.6	-0.8	52.9	47.1
New Zealand	4.8	2.4	3.5	-1.0	49.3	50.7
Norway	3.7	2.2	7.0	-4.8	44.7	55.3
Poland	0.4	0.1	1.1	-1.0	47.2	51.2
Portugal	3.0	0.8	2.8	-2.0	49.7	50.3
Slovak Republic	1.2	0.3	2.9	-2.6	62.8	37.2
Spain	2.2	1.4	1.5	-0.1	49.3	50.7
Sweden	6.0	4.3	4.4	-0.1	44.1	55.9
Switzerland	16.6	11.8	5.3	6.5	56.0	44.0
Turkey	1.7	0.1	4.3	-4.3	73.7	26.3
United Kingdom	11.0	6.0	1.4	4.6	52.8	47.2
United States	3.6	1.8	0.3	1.5	58.1	41.9
Country mean[3]	*4.9*	*2.9*	*4.1*	*-1.2*	*52.2*	*47.7*
NON-OECD COUNTRIES						
Argentina[4]	0.2	n	0.4	-0.4	m	m
Brazil	m	m	0.6	m	m	m
Chile[4]	0.4	0.1	1.1	-1.0	m	m
China	m	m	1.5	m	m	m
Egypt	m	m	2.2	m	m	m
Indonesia[5]	n	n	1.1	-1.0	m	m
Jamaica	2.2	6.3	12.0	-5.7	m	m
Jordan	8.5	1.1	3.6	-2.5	m	m
Malaysia[4]	0.7	0.3	8.0	-7.7	m	m
Paraguay	m	m	0.8	m	m	m
Peru	m	m	0.6	m	m	m
Philippines[4]	0.2	0.1	0.2	-0.1	m	m
Russian Federation[5]	0.9	2.4	0.3	2.1	m	m
Thailand	m	m	0.9	m	m	m
Tunisia	1.5	4.4	1.5	2.8	m	m
Uruguay[4]	0.9	2.8	1.5	1.4	m	m
Zimbabwe	m	m	7.0	m	m	m

1. Only those OECD and non-OECD countries which report the inflow into their system are included in the sum.
2. Tertiary-type A and advanced research programmes only.
3. Country mean excludes Luxembourg.
4. Year of reference 1999.
5. Year of reference 2001.
Source: OECD. See Annex 3 for notes (*www.oecd.org/els/education/eag2002*).

C3

Table C3.2.
Proportion of foreign students in tertiary education in the country of study (2000)
Number of foreign students enrolled in tertiary education as a percentage of students in the country of destination, based on head counts

The table shows the share of students in each country that have citizenship of another country.

Example: Reading the second column: 0.03 per cent of Austrian tertiary students are Belgian citizens, 0.02 per cent of Austrian students are Canadian citizens, etc.

Reading the first row: 0.03 per cent of Canadian tertiary students are Australian citizens, 0.04 per cent of Irish tertiary students are Australian citizens, etc.

Countries of destination

Countries of origin	Australia	Austria	Belgium	Canada	Czech Republic	Denmark	Finland	France	Germany	Iceland	Ireland	Italy	Japan	Korea	Netherlands	New Zealand	Norway	Poland	Portugal	Slovak Republic	Spain	Sweden	Switzerland	Turkey	United Kingdom	United States
OECD COUNTRIES																										
Australia	a	0.01	n	0.03	n	0.02	0.01	0.01	0.01	0.01	0.01	0.01	n	0.01	n	0.01	n	0.01	n	0.01	n	0.05	0.03	n	0.06	0.02
Austria	0.01	a	0.01	0.01	n	0.02	0.01	0.02	0.32	0.05	0.03	n	n	n	0.02	n	0.02	n	n	n	0.03	0.10	0.46	n	0.06	0.01
Belgium	0.01	0.03	a	0.01	n	0.01	0.01	0.10	0.05	0.01	0.04	0.01	n	n	0.28	n	0.01	n	0.02	n	0.07	0.05	0.17	n	0.12	0.01
Canada	0.13	0.02	0.02	a	0.01	0.02	0.03	0.05	0.02	0.08	0.08	n	n	n	0.01	0.04	0.02	0.01	0.07	n	0.08	0.11	n	0.15	0.16
Czech Republic	0.01	0.13	0.01	n	a	n	0.01	0.02	0.07	0.05	n	n	n	n	0.01	n	0.01	0.02	n	0.21	0.01	0.03	0.08	n	0.01	0.01
Denmark	0.02	0.03	0.01	0.01	n	a	0.02	0.01	0.03	0.44	0.01	n	n	n	0.01	0.02	0.40	n	n	n	0.02	0.25	0.06	n	0.09	0.01
Finland	0.01	0.07	0.02	0.01	n	0.06	a	0.02	0.03	0.05	0.36	0.05	n	n	0.01	n	0.11	n	n	n	0.02	0.97	0.05	n	0.13	0.01
France	0.03	0.19	2.77	0.37	n	0.06	0.03	a	0.31	0.17	0.35	0.02	n	n	0.06	0.03	0.06	n	0.26	n	0.25	0.27	1.80	n	0.62	0.05
Germany	0.13	2.25	0.15	0.06	0.01	0.29	0.08	0.27	a	0.42	0.30	0.04	0.01	n	0.47	0.14	0.21	0.01	0.10	0.01	0.21	0.54	3.51	0.01	0.67	0.07
Greece	0.02	0.12	0.20	0.01	0.21	0.01	0.01	0.13	0.40	n	0.02	0.46	n	n	0.02	n	0.01	n	n	0.18	0.02	0.07	0.17	0.13	1.45	0.02
Hungary	0.01	0.42	0.03	n	n	0.01	0.03	0.02	0.13	n	n	n	n	n	0.01	n	n	n	0.02	n	0.01	0.06	0.10	n	0.02	0.01
Iceland	n	0.01	n	n	n	0.37	0.01	n	0.03	a	n	n	n	n	0.13	n	n	n	n	n	0.10	0.01	n	0.01	0.01	n
Ireland	0.04	0.02	0.01	0.01	n	0.02	0.01	0.03	0.03	n	a	n	n	n	0.01	n	n	n	n	n	0.02	0.03	0.03	n	0.71	0.01
Italy	0.02	2.70	0.92	0.02	n	0.04	0.03	0.20	0.36	0.21	0.08	a	n	n	0.07	n	0.03	n	0.03	n	0.25	0.16	2.56	n	0.30	0.02
Japan	0.26	0.12	0.05	0.12	n	0.02	0.03	0.07	0.10	0.05	0.02	n	a	0.02	0.01	0.40	0.02	n	n	n	0.01	0.04	0.10	n	0.30	0.33
Korea	0.28	0.12	0.01	0.09	0.01	n	0.01	0.08	0.24	n	n	n	0.46	a	0.26	n	n	n	n	n	0.01	0.02	0.04	n	0.11	0.29
Luxembourg	n	0.12	0.41	n	n	n	n	0.06	0.07	n	0.01	n	n	n	0.01	n	n	n	0.01	n	n	n	0.12	n	0.03	n
Mexico	0.01	0.02	0.02	0.06	n	0.01	n	0.02	0.02	n	n	n	n	n	0.01	n	n	n	0.00	0.08	0.01	0.05	n	0.06	0.07
Netherlands	0.04	0.04	0.76	0.01	n	0.05	0.02	0.03	0.10	0.05	0.04	n	n	n	a	0.01	0.06	n	0.01	n	0.05	0.16	0.17	n	0.13	0.01
New Zealand	0.51	n	n	0.01	n	0.01	n	n	n	0.01	n	n	n	n	n	a	n	n	n	n	0.01	0.01	n	0.02	0.01
Norway	0.20	0.03	0.01	0.01	0.02	0.68	0.02	0.02	0.05	0.29	0.07	n	n	n	0.02	0.06	a	0.02	n	n	0.02	0.35	0.08	n	0.20	0.02
Poland	0.01	0.31	0.07	0.01	0.05	0.11	0.02	0.09	0.43	0.09	0.01	0.02	n	n	0.03	n	0.05	a	0.01	0.03	0.02	0.19	0.20	n	0.03	0.02
Portugal	0.01	0.02	0.17	0.01	n	0.01	n	0.15	0.08	0.02	0.01	n	n	n	0.01	n	n	n	a	n	0.05	0.03	0.27	n	0.11	0.01
Slovak Republic	n	0.34	0.01	n	0.70	n	n	0.01	0.00	n	n	n	n	n	0.01	n	n	n	n	a	0.01	0.06	n	0.01	n	n
Spain	0.01	0.15	0.40	0.01	n	0.04	0.02	0.19	0.27	0.16	0.14	0.01	n	n	0.10	n	0.03	n	0.10	n	a	0.18	0.96	n	0.37	0.03
Sweden	0.11	0.10	0.02	0.02	0.02	0.31	0.20	0.05	0.04	0.39	0.04	n	n	n	0.02	0.07	0.47	0.01	n	n	0.02	a	0.14	n	0.20	0.03
Switzerland	0.02	0.10	0.03	0.02	n	0.02	0.01	0.05	0.10	0.02	0.01	0.04	n	n	0.01	0.01	0.02	n	0.01	n	0.01	0.05	a	n	0.07	0.01
Turkey	0.02	0.45	0.14	0.01	n	0.10	0.01	0.11	1.29	0.01	n	n	n	n	0.24	n	0.02	n	n	n	0.04	0.33	a	0.09	0.07	
United Kingdom	0.52	0.08	0.06	0.10	0.09	0.20	0.05	0.16	0.13	0.18	1.13	0.01	0.01	n	0.14	0.07	0.20	n	0.03	n	0.15	0.24	0.19	0.01	a	0.06
United States	0.38	0.14	0.05	0.36	0.02	0.11	0.06	0.12	0.18	0.34	0.98	0.01	0.03	0.01	0.05	0.27	0.15	0.02	0.08	n	0.04	0.26	0.22	n	0.55	a
NON-OECD COUNTRIES																										
Argentina	0.01	0.01	0.01	0.01	n	n	n	0.02	0.02	0.01	n	0.01	n	n	n	0.01	n	n	n	n	0.08	0.01	0.05	n	0.02	0.02
Brazil	0.02	0.03	0.04	0.03	n	0.02	0.01	0.07	0.07	n	n	0.01	0.01	n	0.01	0.02	0.01	n	0.36	n	0.06	0.02	0.11	n	0.05	0.06
Chile	0.02	0.01	0.03	0.01	n	0.01	0.01	0.02	0.02	0.01	n	n	n	n	0.01	0.01	0.04	n	n	n	0.04	0.06	0.04	n	0.01	0.01
China	0.59	0.16	0.18	0.32	n	0.07	0.30	0.10	0.32	0.09	0.03	n	0.71	0.04	0.04	0.66	0.08	n	0.01	n	0.01	0.18	0.27	0.01	0.30	0.38
Egypt	0.01	0.08	0.01	0.01	n	n	n	0.03	0.05	n	0.01	n	n	n	0.01	n	0.01	n	0.02	n	n	0.03	0.01	n	0.05	0.01
India	0.54	0.04	0.03	0.07	0.01	0.01	0.02	0.01	0.06	0.01	0.01	n	n	n	0.01	0.12	0.05	n	0.01	n	n	0.02	0.06	n	0.20	0.30
Indonesia	1.18	0.02	0.01	0.03	n	n	0.01	0.01	0.10	n	n	n	0.03	n	0.08	0.21	0.01	n	n	n	n	0.02	0.05	n	0.05	0.08
Jamaica	n	n	n	0.02	n	n	n	n	n	n	n	n	n	n	n	n	n	n	n	n	n	n	n	n	0.03	0.03
Jordan	0.01	0.03	n	0.01	0.01	n	n	0.01	0.05	0.01	0.01	0.01	n	n	n	n	n	n	0.02	n	0.01	0.01	0.03	0.04	0.01	
Malaysia	1.52	n	n	0.06	n	n	n	n	0.01	n	0.39	n	0.05	n	n	0.69	n	n	n	n	n	0.01	0.01	n	0.51	0.06
Paraguay	n	n	n	n	n	n	n	n	n	n	n	n	n	n	n	n	n	n	n	n	n	n	n	n	n	n
Peru	0.01	0.03	0.02	n	n	0.01	0.01	0.02	0.04	n	n	0.01	n	n	n	n	0.01	n	n	n	0.06	0.02	0.10	n	0.01	0.02
Philippines	0.08	n	0.02	0.01	n	n	0.01	0.01	0.01	n	0.01	n	n	n	0.03	0.01	n	n	n	n	n	0.01	0.01	n	0.01	0.02
Russian Federation	0.02	0.11	0.04	0.02	0.04	0.06	0.24	0.07	0.32	0.10	0.02	0.01	0.01	n	0.01	0.01	0.18	0.02	n	0.01	0.13	0.21	0.10	0.05	0.05	
Thailand	0.32	0.01	0.01	0.02	n	0.01	n	0.01	0.02	0.01	n	n	0.03	n	n	0.19	n	n	n	n	0.02	0.01	0.03	n	0.13	n
Tunisia	n	0.02	0.08	0.05	n	0.01	n	n	0.05	n	n	n	n	n	n	n	n	n	n	n	n	n	0.01	n	0.01	n
Uruguay	n	n	n	n	n	n	n	n	n	n	n	n	n	n	n	n	n	n	n	n	0.01	n	0.01	n	n	n
Zimbabwe	0.03	n	n	0.01	n	n	n	n	n	n	n	n	n	n	n	0.01	0.01	n	n	n	n	n	n	n	0.09	0.01
TOTAL: OECD AND NON-OECD COUNTRIES																										
Africa	0.37	0.38	3.32	0.48	0.08	0.17	0.24	3.36	0.89	0.02	0.19	0.10	0.02	n	0.49	0.07	0.33	0.02	1.63	0.12	0.26	0.20	1.06	0.04	0.82	0.21
Asia	8.03	1.44	0.71	1.18	0.27	0.52	0.52	0.87	3.12	0.30	0.79	0.12	1.37	0.09	0.60	3.24	0.53	0.07	0.04	0.23	0.07	0.67	1.26	1.18	3.49	2.21
Europe	1.32	9.41	6.33	0.78	1.29	2.86	1.14	2.04	4.53	3.22	2.41	0.91	0.05	0.01	1.49	0.44	2.51	0.26	0.62	0.79	1.29	4.50	12.55	0.51	5.54	0.54
North America	0.52	0.21	0.13	0.56	0.03	0.14	0.10	0.27	0.26	0.46	1.09	0.02	0.04	0.01	0.06	0.33	0.20	0.02	0.16	0.01	0.20	0.38	0.44	n	0.89	0.38
Oceania	0.72	0.01	n	0.04	n	0.02	0.01	0.01	0.01	0.02	0.02	0.04	n	0.01	n	0.01	0.01	n	m	n	0.05	0.03	0.09	n	0.03	0.03
South America	0.10	0.12	0.18	0.11	0.03	0.06	0.02	0.20	0.20	0.04	0.01	0.04	0.02	n	0.21	0.05	0.04	n	0.49	0.01	0.40	0.15	0.51	n	0.14	0.22
Not specified	1.46	0.06	0.23	0.13	0.46	3.01	0.03	0.05	0.09	0.01	0.09	0.21	n	n	0.01	a	0.90	0.01	0.04	a	a	1.41	0.72	n	0.04	n
All countries	12.51	11.63	10.91	3.28	2.25	6.80	2.06	6.80	9.10	4.17	4.62	1.41	1.50	0.11	2.87	4.77	3.66	0.39	2.99	1.16	2.22	6.00	16.58	1.74	11.01	3.60

Source: OECD. See Annex 3 for notes *(www.oecd.org/els/education/eag2002).*

Table C3.3.
Proportion of citizens in tertiary education studying abroad (2000)
Number of students enrolled in tertiary education in other countries as a percentage of students enrolled in the country of origin, based on head counts

The table shows the share of students from each country that are studying in other countries.
Example: Reading the first column: 0.06 per cent of Japanese tertiary students study in Australia, 0.08 per cent of Korean students study in Australia, etc.
Reading the first row: 0.05 per cent of Australian students study in Canada, 0.03 per cent of Australian students study in Germany, etc.

Countries of destination

Countries of origin	Australia	Austria	Belgium	Canada	Czech Republic	Denmark	Finland	France	Germany	Iceland	Ireland	Italy	Japan	Korea	Netherlands	New Zealand	Norway	Poland	Portugal	Slovak Republic	Spain	Sweden	Switzerland	Turkey	United Kingdom	United States	Total
Australia	a	n	n	0.05	n	n	n	0.02	0.03	n	0.01	n	0.04	n	n	n	n	n	n	n	0.01	0.02	n	n	0.15	0.29	**0.63**
Austria	0.04	a	0.02	0.03	n	0.01	0.01	0.17	2.52	n	0.02	0.02	0.01	n	0.04	n	0.01	n	n	n	0.24	0.13	0.28	0.01	0.47	0.37	**4.41**
Belgium	0.02	0.02	a	0.04	n	0.01	n	0.54	0.28	n	0.02	0.03	0.01	n	0.39	n	0.01	n	0.02	n	0.35	0.05	0.07	n	0.67	0.23	**2.77**
Canada	0.09	n	0.01	a	n	n	0.01	0.08	0.03	n	0.01	n	0.01	n	n	n	0.01	n	0.01	0.02	n	0.02	0.01	n	0.26	1.78	**2.38**
Czech Republic	0.02	0.13	0.02	0.02	a	n	0.01	0.13	0.0	n	n	0.03	0.01	n	0.01	n	0.01	0.10	n	0.11	0.18	0.45	0.05	n	0.11	0.34	**3.47**
Denmark	0.08	0.04	0.03	0.08	n	a	0.02	0.15	0.33	0.02	0.01	0.01	0.01	n	0.03	0.02	0.08	n	0.01	n	0.14	1.25	0.03	n	1.01	0.52	**3.61**
Finland	0.03	0.07	0.02	0.05	n	0.04	a	0.12	0.41	0.01	0.03	0.02	0.01	n	0.03	n	0.08	n	n	n	0.14	1.25	0.03	n	0.95	0.31	**3.61**
France	0.01	0.02	0.49	0.22	n	0.01	n	a	0.32	n	0.03	0.02	0.01	n	0.01	n	0.01	n	0.05	n	0.23	0.05	0.14	n	0.62	0.32	**2.55**
Germany	0.05	0.29	0.03	0.04	n	0.03	0.01	0.26	a	n	0.02	0.03	0.01	n	0.11	0.01	0.02	0.01	0.02	n	0.19	0.09	0.27	n	0.66	0.44	**2.60**
Greece	0.03	0.08	0.17	0.03	0.13	0.01	0.01	0.60	1.95	n	0.01	1.92	n	n	0.03	n	n	0.01	n	0.06	0.08	0.06	0.06	0.31	6.94	0.61	**13.09**
Hungary	0.01	0.36	0.04	0.01	n	0.01	0.02	0.15	0.86	n	n	0.03	0.02	n	0.02	n	0.01	0.02	n	0.01	0.04	0.06	0.05	n	0.13	0.35	**2.21**
Iceland	0.05	0.16	0.10	0.40	0.03	7.17	0.34	0.61	2.14	a	0.04	0.09	0.06	n	0.16	n	2.47	0.01	0.01	n	0.37	3.62	0.10	n	2.30	5.14	**25.38**
Ireland	0.20	0.03	0.03	0.05	0.01	0.02	0.02	0.37	0.37	n	a	0.01	0.01	n	0.02	n	0.01	n	0.01	n	0.19	0.06	0.03	n	8.93	0.67	**11.04**
Italy	0.01	0.40	0.19	0.01	n	n	n	0.22	0.41	n	0.01	a	n	n	0.02	n	n	n	0.01	n	0.26	0.03	0.23	n	0.34	0.17	**2.33**
Japan	0.06	0.01	n	0.04	n	n	n	0.04	0.05	n	n	0.02	a	0.02	n	n	n	n	n	n	n	n	n	n	0.15	1.09	**1.48**
Korea	0.08	0.01	n	0.04	n	n	n	0.05	0.17	n	n	n	0.61	a	n	0.01	n	n	n	n	n	n	n	n	0.07	1.27	**2.32**
Luxembourg	0.21	12.47	60.24	0.86	n	0.04	n	51.29	61.30	n	0.70	0.86	0.16	n	0.70	n	0.04	n	0.90	n	0.57	0.12	7.71	n	24.66	2.61	**225.47**
Mexico	n	n	n	0.04	n	n	n	0.02	n	n	n	n	0.01	n	n	n	n	n	n	n	0.07	n	n	n	0.06	0.50	**0.72**
Netherlands	0.08	0.02	0.55	0.03	n	0.02	0.01	0.12	0.43	n	0.01	0.01	0.01	n	a	n	0.02	n	0.01	n	0.19	0.12	0.05	n	0.52	0.33	**2.55**
New Zealand	2.48	n	n	0.06	n	0.01	n	0.02	0.03	n	n	n	0.05	n	0.01	a	n	n	n	n	n	0.01	0.01	n	0.27	0.51	**3.49**
Norway	0.88	0.04	0.01	0.08	0.02	0.68	0.03	0.18	0.50	0.01	0.06	0.02	0.01	n	0.05	0.05	a	0.16	n	n	0.19	0.64	0.06	n	2.13	1.13	**6.94**
Poland	0.01	0.05	0.02	0.01	0.01	0.01	n	0.12	0.56	n	n	0.02	0.01	n	n	n	0.01	a	n	n	0.02	0.04	0.02	n	0.04	0.13	**1.08**
Portugal	0.02	0.01	0.17	0.02	n	n	0.01	0.81	0.46	n	0.01	0.01	0.01	n	0.03	n	0.01	n	a	n	0.24	0.03	0.11	n	0.60	0.23	**2.77**
Slovak Republic	0.02	0.66	0.03	0.01	1.30	n	n	0.15	0.00	n	0.05	0.01	n	n	0.01	n	0.01	n	n	a	0.03	0.06	n	n	0.41	0.22	**2.86**
Spain	n	0.02	0.08	0.01	n	n	n	0.21	0.31	n	0.01	0.01	n	n	0.03	n	n	n	0.02	n	a	0.03	0.08	n	0.41	0.22	**1.46**
Sweden	0.26	0.08	0.02	0.08	0.01	0.17	0.16	0.27	0.26	0.01	0.02	0.02	0.02	n	0.03	0.03	0.26	0.02	n	n	0.12	a	0.07	n	1.16	1.33	**4.40**
Switzerland	0.11	0.17	0.06	0.16	n	0.03	0.02	0.62	1.25	n	0.01	0.47	0.02	n	0.05	0.01	0.03	0.01	0.02	n	0.12	0.12	a	n	0.91	1.11	**5.32**
Turkey	0.02	0.12	0.05	0.02	n	0.02	n	0.21	2.62	n	n	0.01	0.01	n	0.11	n	n	n	n	n	n	0.01	0.05	a	0.17	0.92	**4.34**
United Kingdom	0.22	0.01	0.01	0.06	0.01	0.02	0.01	0.16	0.13	n	0.09	n	0.02	n	0.03	0.01	0.02	n	n	n	0.13	0.04	0.01	0.01	a	0.36	**1.35**
United States	0.02	n	n	0.03	n	n	n	0.02	0.03	n	0.01	n	0.01	n	n	n	n	n	n	n	0.01	0.01	n	n	0.08	a	**0.25**
Argentina	0.01	n	n	0.01	n	n	n	0.03	0.02	n	n	0.01	0.01	n	n	n	n	n	n	n	0.10	n	0.01	n	0.03	0.17	**0.39**
Brazil	0.01	n	0.01	0.02	n	n	n	0.06	0.06	n		0.02		n		0.05			0.04		n	0.01		n	0.04	0.32	**0.65**
Chile	0.05	n	0.03	0.02	n	0.01	n	0.08	0.11	n		0.01	0.01		0.01		0.02				0.18	0.05	0.01		0.06	0.31	**0.98**
China	0.07	0.01	0.01	0.05		n	0.01	0.03	0.09	n			0.38	0.02	0.02						0.01	0.01			0.08	0.68	**1.47**
Egypt	0.02	0.09	0.02	0.06	n		n	0.23	0.46	n		0.07		0.02			n		0.01		0.03	0.01	0.02	0.02	0.39	0.74	**2.21**
Indonesia	0.38	n	n	0.02	n		n	0.01	0.08	n		0.04		0.02	0.01						n			n	0.04	0.40	**1.01**
Jamaica	0.01	0.01	0.01	0.58	n	0.01	n	0.04	0.02	n	n	0.01	n	n	0.01	0.01	n				0.01				1.65	9.65	**12.01**
Jordan	0.04	0.05	0.01	0.13	0.02	n	0.01	0.13	0.79		0.01	0.10	0.01					0.04		0.02		0.01	0.01	0.19	0.57	1.35	**3.49**
Malaysia	2.72	n		0.15		n		0.02	0.03	n	0.13		0.41	0.01		0.25									2.19	1.77	**7.69**
Paraguay	n	n	0.01	0.02	0.01	n	n	0.04	0.05		n	0.01	0.05	0.04	0.01	n					0.08		n		0.03	0.43	**0.79**
Peru	n	0.01	0.01	0.01	n	n	n	0.03	0.07	n	n	0.02									0.11	0.01	0.02	n	0.01	0.25	**0.56**
Philippines	0.03	n	n	n	n		n		0.01		n	0.02		n							0.01				0.01	0.13	**0.22**
Russian Federation	n	n	n	n		n	0.01	0.02	0.09		n		n								0.01		0.01	0.01	0.01	0.09	**0.28**
Thailand	0.14	n		0.01		n		0.01	0.02		n		0.05		0.02					n		0.02			0.13	0.53	**0.94**
Tunisia	n	0.03	0.15	0.35	n	0.01	n	0.03	0.62	n	0.05	0.02	n	0.01	n						0.02	0.01	0.01	0.01	0.02	0.18	**1.52**
Uruguay	0.02	0.01	0.01	0.02	0.01	n	n	0.05	0.04	n	0.01	0.01	n	n	0.01						0.24	0.02	0.02	n	0.04	0.40	**0.92**
Zimbabwe	0.47	0.01	0.01	0.13	0.01	n	n	0.02	0.14		n	0.01		n	0.02	0.04	0.02	0.03		0.01	0.02	0.01			3.78	2.24	**7.01**

*(Row labels at left margin: **OECD COUNTRIES** for Australia through United States; **NON-OECD COUNTRIES** for Argentina through Zimbabwe.)*

C3

Source: OECD. See Annex 3 for notes *(www.oecd.org/els/education/eag2002)*.

PARTICIPATION IN CONTINUING EDUCATION AND TRAINING IN THE ADULT POPULATION

- For half of the reporting OECD countries, more than 40 per cent of the adult population participated in some form of continuing education and training within a 12-month period.

- The incidence and intensity of continuing education and training varies greatly between OECD countries. Participation rates range from 18 per cent or below in Hungary, Poland and Portugal, to more than 50 per cent in Denmark, Finland, Sweden and the United States.

- In 11 out of 19 OECD countries, adults with tertiary qualifications are between two and three times more likely to participate in job-related training than adults who have not completed upper secondary education. Education is thus one of several influences making adult training least common among those who need it most.

Chart C4.1.

Participation rate in continuing education and training during one year for 25 to 64-year-olds, by gender and type of training

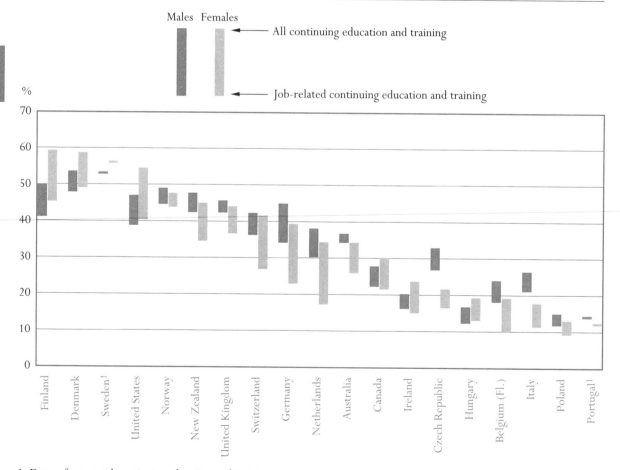

1. Data refer to total continuing education and training.
Countries are ranked in descending order of the participation of women in all continuing education and training.
Source: OECD. Table C4.1. See Annex 3 for notes *(www.oecd.org/els/education/eag2002).*

Policy context

A skilled labour force is a prerequisite for success in today's economy. The education and training of current workers is likely to be the most effective means of maintaining and upgrading the skills of the current labour force. Given swiftly changing technologies, work methodologies and markets, policy-makers in many OECD countries are encouraging enterprises to invest more in training, and to promote more general work-related training of adults.

This indicator brings together evidence on adult education and training.

While much is known about what governments and individuals expend to promote learning within formal education institutions, far less is known about the extent of learning at the workplace or in other settings outside formal education and after the completion of initial education.

Evidence and explanations

Previous editions of *Education at a Glance* have revealed consistent patterns of adult participation in continuing education and training among OECD countries. For example, younger workers spend, on average, more hours in training than older workers; employees in the service sector receive, on average, more training than employees in the manufacturing sector; and employees in large firms or in the public sector receive, on average, more training hours than employees in small firms.

What this indicator covers…

This indicator seeks to expand this picture by relating data on the incidence of adult participation in continuing education and training, both job-related and otherwise, with the participants' educational experiences during initial education.

C_4

Continuing education and training activities covered by this indicator include courses, private lessons, correspondence courses, workshops, on-the-job training, apprenticeship training, arts, crafts, recreation courses and any other organised and sustained education.

This indicator does not include informal learning activities, such as informal, "on the job" or other self-organised learning.

…and what it does not cover.

Participation in job-related training activities among all training activities

Participation rates in job-related training activities are, on average, 8 percentage points lower than participation rates in all continuing education and training activities combined. The difference is higher for women (by 10 percentage points), whose labour force participation rates are generally lower than those of men. The proportion of job-related training among all training activities is particularly high in Denmark, Norway and the United Kingdom.

Participation rates in job–related training activities are, on average, 8 percentage points lower than participation rates in all continuing education and training activities combined.

Women appear to participate in continuing education and training activities at levels not very different from those of men. Women's participation is even higher, in the four OECD countries with the highest total participation rate. However, in the Czech Republic, Germany, Italy, the Netherlands and Switzerland, the gap is significant, even for job-related education and training. (Chart C4.1).

For half of the reporting OECD countries, more than 40 per cent of the adult population participated in some form of continuing education and training within a 12-month period.

For half of the reporting OECD countries, more than 40 per cent of the adult population participated in some form of continuing education and training within a 12-month period. However the incidence and intensity of continuing education and training vary greatly between OECD countries. International comparisons are difficult to make but there is evidence that participation in formal continuing education and training is much higher in the Nordic countries compared with Southern or Eastern European countries. Adult participation rates in continuing education and training range from 18 per cent or below in Hungary, Poland and Portugal, to more than 50 per cent in Denmark, Finland, Sweden and the United States.

Participation rates by level of educational attainment

In 11 out of 19 OECD countries, adults with tertiary qualifications are between two and three times more likely to participate in job-related training than adults who have not completed upper secondary education...

Training tends to reinforce skill differences resulting from unequal participation in initial education. Participation rates in both job-related continuing education and training and in all continuing education and training (Table C4.1) rise with levels of educational attainment. In 11 of the 19 OECD countries with available data, adults with tertiary qualifications are between two and three times more likely to participate in job-related training than adults who have not completed upper secondary education. This relative advantage tends to be between four and eight times larger in the OECD countries where the incidence of training is particularly low. In other words, the OECD countries where there is broad continuing education and training were more successful in securing the participation of individuals with different educational qualifications (Chart C4.2).

...thus education is one of several factors making adult training least common among those who need it most.

The positive association between initial education and participation in continuing education and training remains strong even after controlling for other characteristics affecting participation in training. Workers tend to receive more training in OECD countries with higher overall average levels of educational attainment, as well as in OECD countries which devote a larger share of GDP to research and development or which achieve a strong trade performance in high tech industries. These patterns suggest that initial education and continuing education and training are mutually reinforcing, and that education combines with other factors to make adult training least common among those who need it most.

Women with lower levels of educational attainment tend to receive less job-related continuing education and training...

On average, only 12 per cent of women with less than an upper secondary qualification compared with 17 per cent of men have participated in some job-related continuing and training over the course of a year.

Chart C4.2.

Participation rate in continuing education and training and ratio of participation based on educational attainment for 25 to 64-year-olds (2001)

■ Total participation in continuing education and training

◆ Ratio of participation in continuing education and training for individuals with tertiary education relative to individuals who have not completed lower secondary education

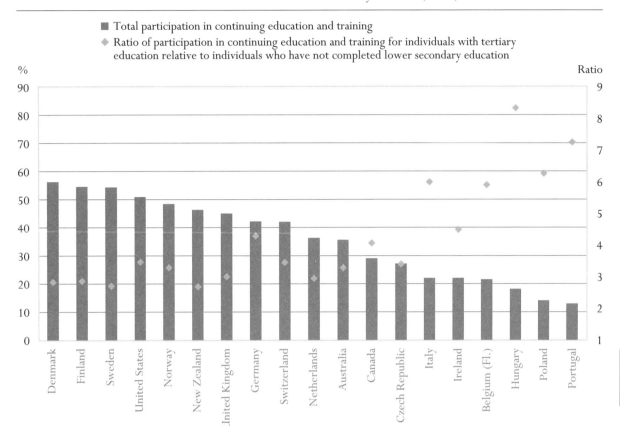

Countries are ranked in descending order of total participation in all continuing education and training.
Source: OECD. Table C4.1. See Annex 3 for notes *(www.oecd.org/els/education/eag2002).*

By contrast, gender differences in participation rates for individuals with tertiary qualifications are less pronounced. For example, for 25 to 64-year-olds with upper secondary education, the participation rate of women in job-related continuing education and training is, on average, 28 per cent compared to 31 per cent for men. At the tertiary level, the average participation rate of women is 45 per cent, while that of men is 46 per cent (Table C4.1).

…but the pattern becomes less pronounced for individuals with upper secondary and tertiary qualifications.

Definitions and methodologies

For this indicator, comparable data on continuing education and training were compiled from national surveys in seven OECD countries that all have the same *reference period of 12 months.* The *sample sizes* in these surveys ranged from 5 000 to 40 000 respondents. *Data collection* was based on face-to-face interviews or telephone interviews. The coverage of *job-related continuing education and training* in these surveys extended to "all measures which the interviewed persons identify as job or career-related". For this indicator, *informal types* of training have not been included. (See Annex 3 at *www.oecd.org/els/education/*

Data are based on national surveys on continuing education and training of the adult population…

eag2002 for a list of sources on national household surveys on adult education and training.)

...as well as the International Adult Literacy Survey (IALS), carried out by the OECD and Statistics Canada between 1994 and 1998, were substituted.

Where comparable data could not be obtained from recent national surveys, data from the International Adult Literacy Survey (IALS), which was carried out by the OECD and Statistics Canada between 1994 and 1998, were substituted. The background questionnaire of the International Adult Literacy Survey records participation in education or training during the 12 months preceding the survey. The survey asks: "During the past 12 months, did you receive any training or education including courses, private lessons, correspondence courses, workshops, on-the-job training, apprenticeship training, arts, crafts, recreation courses or any other training or education?" This very broad definition of education and training covers a wide category of training types. A further question distinguishes between education or training taken for "career or job-related purposes" (shown in this indicator as "job-related training"); education or training undertaken for "personal interest"; and education and training undertaken for "other" reasons.

C4

Table C4.1.
Participation rate in continuing education and training during one year for 25 to 64–year-olds, by level of education, type of training and gender

		Job-related continuing education and training				All continuing education and training			
		Lower secondary education	Upper secondary and post-second-ary non-tertiary education	Tertiary education	All levels of education	Lower secondary education	Upper secondary and post-second-ary non-tertiary education	Tertiary education	All levels of education
Australia	M+F	19	33	55	30	23	39	60	36
IALS 95/96	Males	23	35	57	34	25	38	41	37
	Females	16	30	52	26	22	41	61	34
Belgium (Fl.)	M+F	4	19	33	14	9	28	47	22
IALS 95/96	Males	6	24	36	18	9	30	26	24
	Females	2	15	28	10	8	26	44	19
Canada	M+F	8	19	33	22	12	25	43	29
1997	Males	10	20	33	22	13	25	40	28
	Females	6	18	34	22	12	26	45	30
Czech Republic	M+F	15	29	38	22	18	36	49	27
IALS 98/99	Males	22	29	44	27	27	37	35	33
	Females	7	29	30	17	9	35	44	22
Denmark	M+F	29	51	70	49	36	59	75	56
IALS 98/99	Males	33	48	66	48	38	55	64	54
	Females	25	53	76	49	35	64	81	59
Finland	M+F	24	41	65	43	36	52	76	55
2000	Males	24	39	64	41	32	46	76	50
	Females	24	43	65	45	41	58	76	59
Germany	M+F	9	26	43	29	16	39	60	42
2000	Males	15	30	46	34	20	40	60	45
	Females	6	22	38	23	14	39	58	39
Hungary	M+F	5	11	35	13	6	17	49	18
IALS 98/99	Males	5	11	32	12	7	16	18	17
	Females	5	11	37	13	5	18	56	19
Ireland	M+F	9	21	41	16	13	30	50	22
IALS 95/96	Males	11	21	39	16	12	28	32	20
	Females	6	21	43	15	13	32	55	24
Italy	M+F	6	27	46	16	9	37	52	22
IALS 98/99	Males	10	32	46	21	13	41	33	26
	Females	3	21	45	11	7	33	53	18
Netherlands	M+F	14	27	40	24	24	42	52	36
IALS 94/95	Males	18	35	44	30	24	44	39	38
	Females	10	19	34	17	24	39	52	34
New Zealand	M+F	29	45	62	38	36	55	69	46
IALS 95/96	Males	32	49	67	43	38	54	55	48
	Females	26	42	58	35	35	55	67	45
Norway	M+F	22	44	62	44	26	47	67	48
IALS 98/99	Males	25	44	59	45	30	48	46	49
	Females	17	43	65	44	21	46	70	48
Poland	M+F	5	18	27	11	6	23	37	14
IALS 94/95	Males	7	20	26	12	8	25	22	15
	Females	2	16	27	9	4	22	39	13
Portugal*	M+F	m	m	m	m	8	39	55	13
IALS 98/99	Males	m	m	m	m	10	41	37	14
	Females	m	m	m	m	6	37	61	12
Sweden*	M+F	m	m	m	m	36	58	70	54
IALS 94/95	Males	m	m	m	m	39	56	61	53
	Females	m	m	m	m	34	61	74	56
Switzerland	M+F	11	32	48	32	20	44	55	42
1998/99	Males	12	35	49	36	16	41	55	42
	Females	11	30	44	27	22	47	55	42
United Kingdom	M+F	28	52	70	40	33	58	75	45
IALS 95/96	Males	30	51	68	43	33	54	64	46
	Females	27	54	72	37	33	64	80	44
United States	M+F	14	35	58	40	24	46	69	51
2001	Males	13	34	57	39	23	41	65	47
	Females	15	35	59	41	25	51	73	55

C₄

* See Annex 3 for notes *(www.oecd.org/els/education/eag2002)*.

Source: International Adult Literacy Survey 1994-1998 and national household surveys on adult education and training (see Annex 3 for details).

EDUCATION AND WORK STATUS OF THE YOUTH POPULATION

- The percentage of 20 to 24-year-olds not in education ranges, in most OECD countries, between 50 and 70 per cent.

- In some countries, education and work largely occur consecutively, while in other countries they are concurrent. Work-study programmes, relatively common in European countries, offer coherent vocational education routes to recognised occupational qualifications.

- In some countries, many young people also combine paid work out of school hours with education. In other countries, initial education and work are rarely associated.

Chart C5.1.

Percentage of 20 to 24-year-olds in education and not in education, by work status (2001)

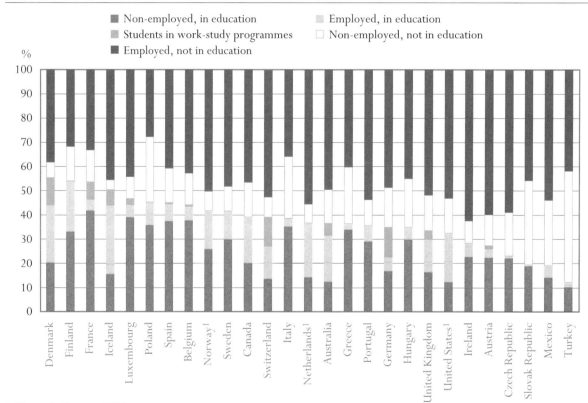

1. Year of reference 2000.
Countries are ranked in descending order of the percentage of 20 to 24-year-olds in education.
Source: OECD. Table C5.1. See Annex 3 for notes *(www.oecd.org/els/education/eag2002).*

Policy context

All OECD countries are experiencing rapid social and economic changes that are making the transition to working life more uncertain. In some OECD countries, education and work largely occur consecutively, while in other OECD countries they may be concurrent. The ways in which education and work are combined can significantly affect the transition process. Of particular interest, for example, is the extent to which working while studying may facilitate the eventual definitive entry into the labour force. On the other hand, many hours of work while studying may result in dropping out rather than successful transition.

This indicator examines the education and employment status of young men and women.

Evidence and explanations

Combining work and education

Table C5.1 reveals the education and work status of young people in the age groups 15 to 19, 20 to 24 and 25 to 29, and the overall situation for all young people aged 15 to 29. Working while studying can occur as part of work-study programmes or in the form of part-time jobs out of school hours. Work-study programmes are relatively common in European countries such as Austria, the Czech Republic, Denmark, Germany and Switzerland, and offer coherent vocational education routes to recognised occupational qualifications. Many young people also combine paid work out of school hours with education. This form of initial contact with the labour market is a major feature of the transition from education to work in Australia, Canada, Denmark, the Netherlands, the United States and, to a lesser extent, Finland, Sweden and Switzerland. Finally, in Belgium, France, Mediterranean and Eastern European countries, initial education and work are rarely associated.

Work-study programmes and other ways of combining work and education are common in some OECD countries, but rare in others.

C5

The employment status of men and women is broadly similar during the years spent in education, with the exception of Austria and Germany, where men participate more in work-study programmes. In Australia, Canada, Denmark, Finland, Iceland and Sweden, more women than men in the 15 to 29-year-old age group combine work outside school hours with education (Tables C5.1a and C5.1b).

During the years spent in education, the employment status of men and women is broadly similar in most OECD countries.

Entry into the labour market after initial education

As they grow older, young people participate decreasingly in education and increasingly in the labour force. The percentage of young people not in education in most OECD countries is between 10 and 35 per cent for 15 to 19-year-olds, rises to between 50 and 70 per cent for 20 to 24-year-olds and reaches 80 to 95 per cent for 25 to 29-year-olds (Chart C5.2). However, in many OECD countries young people begin their transition to work later, and in some cases over a longer period. This trend reflects not only the demand for education, but also the general state of the labour market, the length and orientation of educational programmes in relation to the labour market and the prevalence of part-time education.

The transition from education to work occurs at different points of time in different OECD countries, depending on various educational and labour market factors.

Chart C5.2.

Percentage of the youth population in education and not in education,
by age group and work status (2001)

■ Non-employed, in education   ▪ Employed, in education   ▪ Students in work-study programmes
□ Non-employed, not in education   ■ Employed, not in education

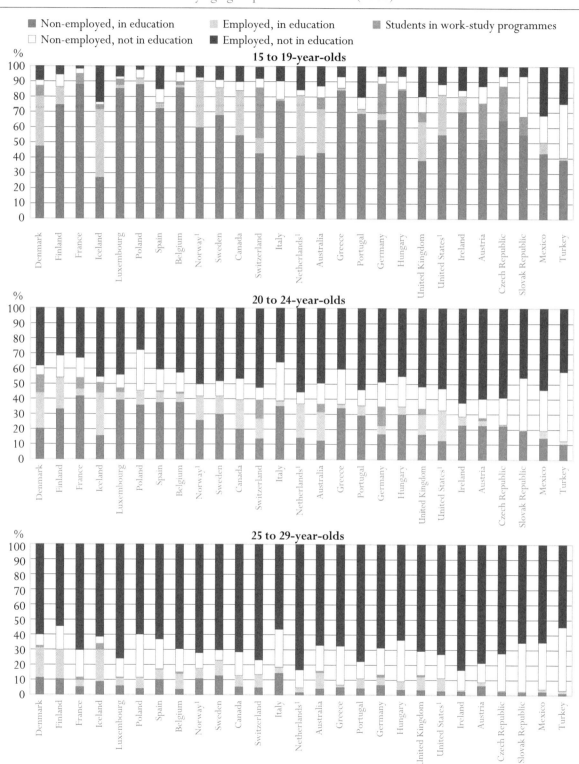

1. Year of reference 2000.
Countries are ranked in descending order of the percentage of 20 to 24-year-olds in education.
Source: OECD. Table C5.1. See Annex 3 for notes *(www.oecd.org/els/education/eaa2002).*

The age at which people enter the labour market after completing initial education has consequences for employment. Overall, older non-students are more likely to be employed than non-students in the age group 15 to 19 years, while a higher percentage of male than female non-students are working. In relative terms, more women than men are out of the labour force, particularly during the years associated with child-bearing and child-rearing, captured by the age group 25 to 29 years in this indicator (Tables C5.1a and C5.1b).

Employment-to-population ratios among young adults who are not in education provide information on the effectiveness of transition frameworks and thus help policy-makers to evaluate transition policies. In two-thirds of OECD countries, fewer than 65 (and in some even fewer than 50) per cent of 15 to 19-year-olds not in education are working, which may suggest that because these young people have left school early, they are not viewed by employers as having the skills necessary for productive employment. Employment-to-population ratios for 20 to 24-year-olds generally exceed 70 per cent, but ratios in some OECD countries such as Greece, Italy, Poland and Turkey are still around or below 65 per cent. For the 25 to 29 age group, most OECD countries have ratios of between 70 and 80 per cent, with the exception of Italy, Mexico, Poland, the Slovak Republic and Turkey. Employment-to-population ratios for men tend to be higher than for women after completion of initial education, probably because of family-related reasons and because the social acceptability of being unemployed is still higher for women than for men in many OECD countries (Table C5.1a and C5.1b).

C5

Unemployment rate and ratio of unemployed non-students to the total youth population

Young people represent the principal source of new skills in OECD countries. In most OECD countries, education policy seeks to encourage young people to complete at least upper secondary education. Since jobs on offer in the labour market require ever higher general skill levels and more flexible learning skills, persons with low attainment are often severely penalised. Differences in the ratio of unemployed non-students to the total youth population, by level of educational attainment, are an indicator of the degree to which further education improves the economic opportunities of any young man or woman.

The youth unemployment rate by age group is the most common measure available for describing the labour market status of young people. However, unemployment rates do not take educational circumstances into account. Consequently, an unemployed young person counted in the numerator may, in some OECD countries, be enrolled in education. The denominator may include young people in vocational training, provided they are apprenticed, but not those in school-based vocational courses. Hence, if almost all the young people in a particular age group are still in education, the employment rate will reflect only the few in the labour market and therefore appear very high,

Traditional unemployment measures overestimate unemployment in the transition period and are insensitive to different systems of combining education and work in the transition period

particularly among the youngest cohort who have usually left the education system with very low qualifications.

The ratio of unemployed non-students to the total age cohort is therefore a more appropriate way to reflect the likelihood of youth unemployment. This is because young people who are looking for a job while still in education are usually seeking part-time or temporary work while studying, unlike those entering the labour market after leaving school.

The ratio of unemployed people with no upper secondary education to the total youth population is 1.5 times higher on average than for upper secondary graduates.

On average, completing upper secondary education reduces the unemployment-to-population ratio (*e.g.,* unemployment among non-students as a percentage of the entire age cohort) of 20 to 24-year-olds by about 6 percentage points, and that of 25 to 29-year-olds by about 4 percentage points (Table C5.2). In 20 out of 27 OECD countries, the unemployment-to-population ratio among 20 to 24-year-olds not in education is less than 8 per cent if they have completed upper secondary or post-secondary non-tertiary education. This proportion remains below 8 per cent for people who have not attained upper secondary

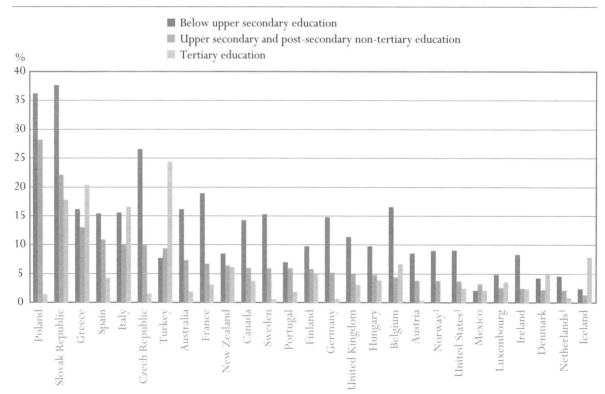

Chart C5.3.

Ratio of unemployed non-students to the population of 20 to 24-year-olds, by level of educational attainment (2001)

■ Below upper secondary education
■ Upper secondary and post-secondary non-tertiary education
▨ Tertiary education

1. Year of reference 2000.
Countries are ranked in descending order of the ratio of unemployed non-students to the population of 20 to 24-year-olds having attained upper secondary and post-secondary non-tertiary education.
Source: OECD. Table C5.2. See Annex 3 for notes *(www.oecd.org/els/education/eag2002).*

education in only six OECD countries. Since it has become the norm in most OECD countries to complete upper secondary education, many young persons who do not are much more likely to have employment problems during their working lives.

Nevertheless, in a number of OECD countries, for upper secondary graduates aged 20 to 24, the ratio of unemployed non-students to the total youth population is above 7 per cent (Chart C5.3). In a few OECD countries, even young people who have completed tertiary-level education, probably a first degree given the age band involved, are subject to considerable unemployment when they enter the labour market. The ratio of unemployed non-students to the total youth population among this age group is up to 16 per cent or more in Greece, Italy, the Slovak Republic and Turkey, and higher than 13 per cent for 25 to 29-year-olds in Greece and Italy (Table C5.2).

Upper secondary education, and even tertiary-level education, does not guarantee a job.

Definitions and methodologies

Data for this indicator were obtained from a special OECD data collection usually implemented during the first quarter or the average of the first three months of the calendar year, and therefore exclude summer employment. The labour force status categories shown in this section are defined according to ILO guidelines, with one exception. For the purposes of these indicators, persons in work-study programmes (see below) have been classified separately as *in education* and *employed*, without reference to their ILO labour force status during the survey reference week, since they may not necessarily be in the work component of their programmes during the reference week, and may therefore not be employed then.

Data for this indicator were obtained from a special OECD data collection in the first quarter of the year.

C5

Work-study programmes combine work and education as parts of an integrated, formal education or training activity, such as the dual system in Germany; *apprentissage* or *formation en alternance* in France and Belgium; internship or co-operative education in Canada; apprenticeship in Ireland; and youth training in the United Kingdom. Vocational education and training take place in school settings and working environments. Students or trainees can be paid or not, usually depending on the type of job and the course or training.

The enrolment rates shown in Table C5.1 are estimated on the basis of self-reports collected during labour force surveys that often correspond only imprecisely with enrolment counts obtained from administrative sources shown elsewhere in this publication, for several reasons. First, age may not be measured in the same way. For example, in administrative data, both enrolment and age are measured on January 1st in OECD countries in the northern hemisphere, whereas in some labour force surveys, enrolment is measured in the reference week, while the age recorded is the age that will be attained at the end of the calendar year, even if the survey is conducted in the early part of the year. This means that recorded enrolment rates may occasionally reflect a population that is almost one year younger than the specified age range. At ages when movements out of education may be significant, this affects enrolment rates. Second, young people may be enrolled in several programmes and can sometimes be counted twice in administrative statistics but only once in a labour force survey. Moreover, not all enrolments may be captured in administrative statistics, particularly in profit-making institutions. Third, the programme classification used in the self-reports in labour force surveys do not always correspond to the qualification standards used for administrative data collections.

C₅

Table C5.1.
Percentage of the *youth population* in education and not in education, by age group and work status (2001)

	Age group	In education					Not in education				Total in education and not in education
		Students in work-study programmes[1]	Other employed	Unemployed	Not in the labour force	Sub-total	Employed	Unemployed	Not in the labour force	Sub-total	
Australia	15-19	7.3	29.0	6.4	36.7	79.5	13.0	4.3	3.3	20.5	100
	20-24	5.1	18.8	2.3	10.2	36.5	49.6	6.9	7.0	63.5	100
	25-29	0.8	10.6	0.9	3.6	15.8	67.0	4.5	12.7	84.2	100
Austria	15-19	22.7	0.6	0.4	52.2	75.8	12.9	2.2	9.1	24.2	100
	20-24	1.6	3.3	0.4	22.1	27.4	59.8	3.4	9.4	72.6	100
	25-29	0.1	2.1	0.2	6.4	8.7	78.5	3.0	9.8	91.3	100
Belgium	15-19	2.0	1.7	0.3	85.7	89.7	4.1	1.8	4.5	10.3	100
	20-24	0.9	5.4	0.9	36.9	44.2	42.8	6.9	6.1	55.8	100
	25-29	0.9	10.2	0.4	3.5	15.0	69.5	7.3	8.1	85.0	100
Canada	15-19	a	29.1	5.2	49.5	83.9	10.2	2.6	3.3	16.1	100
	20-24	a	19.0	1.5	18.7	39.1	46.6	6.3	8.0	60.9	100
	25-29	a	7.2	0.2	5.4	12.8	71.4	6.1	9.7	87.2	100
Czech Republic	15-19	21.9	0.2	n	64.8	87.0	6.2	4.1	2.8	13.0	100
	20-24	0.1	0.6	0.2	22.2	23.1	58.9	9.3	8.7	76.9	100
	25-29	n	0.3	n	2.6	3.0	72.1	7.2	17.7	97.0	100
Denmark	15-19	6.6	32.9	3.4	44.0	86.8	9.4	1.2	2.5	13.2	100
	20-24	11.4	23.6	3.5	16.8	55.3	38.1	2.9	3.6	44.7	100
	25-29	1.0	19.8	1.0	10.5	32.4	60.0	1.9	5.7	67.6	100
Finland	15-19	a	11.6	5.9	68.7	86.3	5.7	2.1	5.9	13.7	100
	20-24	a	20.6	4.4	28.9	53.9	31.7	6.1	8.3	46.1	100
	25-29	a	19.0	1.8	8.9	29.8	54.5	6.3	9.4	70.2	100
France	15-19	6.2	0.4	n	88.2	94.9	1.7	1.8	1.6	5.1	100
	20-24	7.3	4.4	0.6	41.3	53.6	33.1	8.5	4.9	46.4	100
	25-29	1.6	4.4	0.4	5.0	11.4	70.3	9.1	9.2	88.6	100
Germany	15-19	19.4	4.0	0.6	64.5	88.5	6.4	1.4	3.7	11.5	100
	20-24	12.6	5.5	0.3	16.7	35.0	48.7	5.6	10.8	65.0	100
	25-29	1.4	5.0	0.2	6.8	13.5	68.5	5.8	12.2	86.5	100
Greece	15-19	0.2	1.1	0.6	83.8	85.7	6.8	3.9	3.6	14.3	100
	20-24	0.1	2.4	1.3	32.8	36.5	40.2	14.0	9.3	63.5	100
	25-29	0.1	1.2	0.5	5.0	6.7	67.4	12.7	13.2	93.3	100
Hungary	15-19	a	0.6	0.2	84.3	85.1	6.5	2.1	6.3	14.9	100
	20-24	a	4.8	0.5	29.5	34.8	45.0	5.5	14.7	65.2	100
	25-29	a	5.3	0.2	3.7	9.1	63.4	5.3	22.1	90.9	100
Iceland	15-19	2.8	44.6	3.7	23.4	74.4	23.7	1.6	0.3	25.6	100
	20-24	6.5	28.3	1.0	14.6	50.3	45.6	2.0	2.1	49.7	100
	25-29	3.9	21.0	n	8.9	33.8	61.5	1.4	3.4	66.2	100
Ireland	15-19	a	9.9	0.5	69.8	80.3	15.5	1.9	2.2	19.7	100
	20-24	a	5.5	0.4	22.4	28.3	62.4	3.3	6.0	71.7	100
	25-29	a	0.5	n	2.7	3.3	83.1	2.8	10.7	96.7	100
Italy	15-19	n	0.6	0.8	76.8	78.2	9.6	4.9	7.3	21.8	100
	20-24	0.1	3.1	1.8	33.6	38.6	35.8	11.8	13.8	61.4	100
	25-29	0.1	3.6	1.2	13.5	18.4	56.4	9.9	15.3	81.6	100
Luxembourg	15-19	3.6	2.3	0.2	85.2	91.2	7.0	0.6	1.2	8.8	100
	20-24	2.6	4.9	0.3	38.9	46.7	44.2	3.5	5.5	53.3	100
	25-29	0.4	5.0	0.2	5.9	11.6	75.9	1.8	10.7	88.4	100
Mexico	15-19	a	7.1	0.3	42.8	50.2	32.0	1.6	16.3	49.8	100
	20-24	a	4.7	0.2	14.1	19.1	53.8	2.0	25.1	80.9	100
	25-29	a	1.6	n	2.5	4.1	64.8	1.6	29.4	95.9	100
Netherlands[2]	15-19	m	39.3	4.7	36.4	80.4	15.8	1.2	2.6	19.6	100
	20-24	m	22.3	1.4	12.9	36.6	55.2	2.1	6.0	63.4	100
	25-29	m	3.3	0.3	1.9	5.5	82.6	2.5	9.4	94.5	100
Norway[2]	15-19	a	30.4	6.9	53.0	90.3	7.5	1.1	1.1	9.7	100
	20-24	a	15.8	2.6	23.4	41.7	50.3	3.3	4.7	58.3	100
	25-29	a	6.6	1.3	9.7	17.5	72.1	3.2	7.2	82.5	100
Poland	15-19	a	3.9	1.2	86.7	91.8	2.4	3.4	2.4	8.2	100
	20-24	a	9.4	6.7	29.2	45.2	27.7	18.9	8.2	54.8	100
	25-29	a	7.1	1.5	2.9	11.4	59.9	15.7	13.0	88.6	100
Portugal	15-19	a	2.9	0.4	68.7	72.0	20.3	2.8	4.9	28.0	100
	20-24	a	6.5	0.6	28.5	35.6	53.7	5.1	5.6	64.4	100
	25-29	a	6.3	0.4	4.4	11.0	77.6	3.6	7.8	89.0	100
Slovak Republic	15-19	11.4	0.1	n	55.7	67.3	6.3	11.0	15.5	32.7	100
	20-24	a	0.4	0.6	18.5	19.4	45.7	22.8	12.1	80.6	100
	25-29	a	0.1	n	2.2	2.3	65.0	16.9	15.7	97.7	100
Spain	15-19	0.5	3.0	1.6	70.7	75.8	15.1	5.4	3.6	24.2	100
	20-24	0.7	6.8	2.6	34.9	45.0	40.7	8.7	5.6	55.0	100
	25-29	0.2	6.4	2.2	8.2	17.0	63.1	8.6	11.2	83.0	100
Sweden	15-19	a	17.9	4.4	63.4	85.8	9.1	1.9	3.3	14.2	100
	20-24	a	11.6	2.0	28.0	41.6	48.2	5.1	5.1	58.4	100
	25-29	a	9.9	1.2	11.8	22.9	70.2	3.2	3.8	77.1	100
Switzerland	15-19	32.5	10.3	3.9	38.9	85.7	7.5	m	6.2	14.3	100
	20-24	12.1	13.2	m	13.7	39.3	52.3	2.8	5.6	60.7	100
	25-29	m	8.3	m	5.1	13.5	76.8	m	9.7	86.5	100
Turkey	15-19	a	1.4	38.5	0.3	40.3	24.3	5.8	29.7	59.7	100
	20-24	a	1.9	9.5	0.9	12.2	41.9	9.2	36.7	87.8	100
	25-29	a	1.6	1.2	0.3	3.0	54.7	7.3	35.0	97.0	100
United Kingdom	15-19	6.1	25.6	2.8	35.5	70.0	19.7	5.6	4.7	30.0	100
	20-24	3.8	13.2	1.2	15.3	33.5	51.7	5.0	9.7	66.5	100
	25-29	1.0	8.7	0.4	3.2	13.3	70.6	3.6	12.5	86.7	100
United States[2]	15-19	a	25.9	3.3	52.1	81.3	11.7	2.4	4.6	18.7	100
	20-24	a	20.0	1.0	11.5	32.5	53.1	4.0	10.4	67.5	100
	25-29	a	8.4	n	2.9	11.4	72.8	3.0	12.8	88.6	100
Country mean	*15-19*	*5.3*	*12.5*	*3.6*	*58.6*	*79.9*	*11.5*	*2.9*	*5.6*	*20.1*	*100*
	20-24	*2.4*	*10.2*	*1.8*	*22.8*	*37.2*	*46.5*	*6.9*	*9.4*	*62.8*	*100*
	25-29	*0.4*	*6.8*	*0.6*	*5.5*	*13.3*	*68.5*	*5.7*	*12.5*	*86.7*	*100*

1. Students in work-study programmes are considered to be both in education and employed, irrespective of their labour market status according to the ILO definition.
2. Year of reference 2000.
Source: OECD. See Annex 3 for national data sources (*www.oecd.org/els/education/eag2002*).

OECD COUNTRIES

C5

Table C5.1a.
Percentage of *young men* in education and not in education, by age group and work status (2001)

	Age group	In education					Not in education				Total in education and not in education
		Students in work-study programmes[1]	Other employed	Unemployed	Not in the labour force	Sub-total	Employed	Unemployed	Not in the labour force	Sub-total	
Australia	15-19	10.8	25.2	5.8	37.6	79.4	12.8	5.2	2.7	20.6	100
	20-24	7.9	16.5	2.5	11.1	38.1	50.5	7.8	3.6	61.9	100
	25-29	1.1	10.3	1.0	3.5	15.8	74.7	5.3	4.1	84.2	100
Austria	15-19	28.2	0.3	0.4	46.3	75.2	11.8	2.2	10.9	24.8	100
	20-24	2.2	2.9	0.2	19.0	24.3	61.2	4.3	10.2	75.7	100
	25-29	0.1	2.6	n	7.6	10.4	81.6	3.4	4.7	89.6	100
Belgium	15-19	3.1	1.3	0.3	83.5	88.2	5.7	2.2	3.8	11.8	100
	20-24	1.6	6.2	1.1	34.3	43.3	45.8	7.4	3.5	56.7	100
	25-29	1.0	12.6	0.6	3.0	17.2	73.4	6.3	3.1	82.8	100
Canada	15-19	a	27.0	5.3	49.3	81.6	11.7	3.5	3.2	18.4	100
	20-24	a	16.6	1.7	18.3	36.6	49.0	8.6	5.8	63.4	100
	25-29	a	6.2	n	5.0	11.3	76.4	7.2	5.1	88.7	100
Czech Republic	15-19	27.6	0.2	n	58.5	86.3	7.3	4.1	2.3	13.7	100
	20-24	0.2	0.6	n	20.7	21.6	65.8	10.5	2.2	78.4	100
	25-29	a	0.2	n	3.0	3.3	88.5	6.2	2.0	96.7	100
Denmark	15-19	9.6	30.7	2.3	44.8	87.4	7.9	2.0	2.7	12.6	100
	20-24	12.6	21.2	3.2	13.5	50.5	45.7	2.6	1.2	49.5	100
	25-29	0.6	22.8	1.1	8.4	32.8	62.8	1.5	2.8	67.2	100
Finland	15-19	a	9.2	4.8	68.8	82.7	5.3	2.5	9.5	17.3	100
	20-24	a	17.7	4.3	26.5	48.5	35.6	7.3	8.7	51.5	100
	25-29	a	19.6	1.6	8.1	29.3	61.6	4.8	4.3	70.7	100
France	15-19	8.6	0.2	n	85.6	94.5	2.1	1.9	1.5	5.5	100
	20-24	8.0	3.1	0.5	38.9	50.5	38.5	8.2	2.7	49.5	100
	25-29	1.5	3.8	0.5	4.7	10.5	78.4	8.3	2.8	89.5	100
Germany	15-19	21.6	3.7	0.7	61.6	87.6	7.5	1.6	3.3	12.4	100
	20-24	12.0	5.0	0.3	15.6	32.9	52.8	7.0	7.3	67.1	100
	25-29	1.7	5.9	0.3	8.1	16.1	72.3	6.7	4.9	83.9	100
Greece	15-19	0.4	1.4	0.6	83.4	85.8	8.6	3.2	2.4	14.2	100
	20-24	n	2.2	0.6	31.3	34.2	48.2	11.8	5.9	65.8	100
	25-29	n	1.3	0.3	5.6	7.2	79.4	10.5	2.8	92.8	100
Hungary	15-19	a	0.9	n	83.4	84.3	6.9	2.6	6.2	15.7	100
	20-24	a	4.6	0.6	27.5	32.7	51.7	7.3	8.3	67.3	100
	25-29	a	5.3	0.2	2.6	8.1	76.0	7.0	8.9	91.9	100
Iceland	15-19	3.8	36.7	4.2	24.5	69.2	28.4	2.0	0.5	30.8	100
	20-24	7.4	26.0	0.9	13.9	48.3	48.3	2.4	0.9	51.7	100
	25-29	3.7	18.8	n	5.7	28.2	70.3	1.0	0.5	71.8	100
Ireland	15-19	a	9.2	0.6	65.6	75.4	20.3	2.4	1.9	24.6	100
	20-24	a	4.9	0.4	19.5	24.8	68.5	3.7	3.0	75.2	100
	25-29	a	0.4	n	2.7	3.2	89.0	3.3	4.5	96.8	100
Italy	15-19	n	0.6	0.5	75.6	76.7	11.5	5.0	6.8	23.3	100
	20-24	n	2.9	1.4	30.6	34.9	41.1	11.7	12.2	65.1	100
	25-29	0.2	3.5	0.9	13.3	17.9	65.7	9.5	6.9	82.1	100
Luxembourg	15-19	4.3	3.1	0.3	83.7	91.3	7.1	0.8	0.8	8.7	100
	20-24	3.4	5.0	0.3	37.5	46.1	46.7	4.4	2.8	53.9	100
	25-29	0.6	6.3	0.5	6.8	14.1	80.5	2.1	3.3	85.9	100
Mexico	15-19	a	9.4	0.3	40.5	50.1	42.7	1.8	5.4	49.9	100
	20-24	a	5.9	0.2	14.7	20.8	73.6	2.6	3.0	79.2	100
	25-29	a	2.0	n	2.8	4.8	90.5	2.1	2.6	95.2	100
Netherlands	15-19	m	38.4	3.6	36.2	78.2	17.7	1.1	3.0	21.8	100
	20-24	m	22.6	1.5	13.7	37.8	57.1	1.9	3.2	62.2	100
	25-29	m	4.1	0.4	2.0	6.4	87.8	2.0	3.8	93.6	100
Norway	15-19	a	26.1	6.6	55.3	88.0	9.1	1.7	1.2	12.0	100
	20-24	a	11.9	2.5	18.3	32.7	60.2	4.3	2.8	67.3	100
	25-29	a	6.5	1.4	8.5	16.4	75.3	3.8	4.4	83.6	100
Poland	15-19	a	4.5	1.1	85.2	90.9	2.9	3.9	2.4	9.1	100
	20-24	a	9.3	6.7	27.0	43.0	31.4	20.6	5.0	57.0	100
	25-29	a	7.1	1.3	2.6	11.0	69.9	15.0	4.1	89.0	100
Portugal	15-19	a	2.7	0.3	66.4	69.5	25.0	1.5	4.0	30.5	100
	20-24	a	6.8	0.4	23.1	30.2	61.5	4.2	4.1	69.8	100
	25-29	a	6.5	0.3	4.7	11.5	82.1	2.3	4.0	88.5	100
Slovak Republic	15-19	15.3	0.1	n	52.6	68.0	4.1	10.6	17.3	32.0	100
	20-24	a	0.2	0.5	15.8	16.5	47.6	28.4	7.5	83.5	100
	25-29	a	0.1	n	2.3	2.4	72.7	20.0	4.9	97.6	100
Spain	15-19	0.7	3.3	1.3	64.8	70.2	21.2	5.4	3.2	29.8	100
	20-24	0.7	6.5	2.1	31.7	40.9	48.3	7.4	3.3	59.1	100
	25-29	n	6.0	1.8	7.9	15.8	72.1	7.3	4.8	84.2	100
Sweden	15-19	a	15.3	3.7	66.4	85.4	8.1	1.8	4.6	14.6	100
	20-24	a	10.4	1.9	24.9	37.2	52.6	5.8	4.4	62.8	100
	25-29	a	9.0	1.2	10.6	20.8	74.1	3.6	1.5	79.2	100
Switzerland	15-19	34.7	9.0	m	38.8	86.8	6.8	m	5.7	13.2	100
	20-24	15.3	14.6	m	11.8	42.2	48.5	m	6.9	57.8	100
	25-29	m	10.1	m	5.0	16.4	79.2	m	m	83.6	100
Turkey	15-19	a	2.0	43.2	0.3	45.5	31.4	7.8	15.3	54.5	100
	20-24	a	2.3	11.7	1.2	15.2	57.9	12.6	14.3	84.8	100
	25-29	a	2.1	1.2	0.3	3.6	78.4	10.5	7.6	96.4	100
United Kingdom	15-19	8.8	21.8	2.9	35.0	68.6	21.0	7.1	3.4	31.4	100
	20-24	4.6	11.4	1.6	15.6	33.1	56.4	6.1	4.4	66.9	100
	25-29	0.6	7.5	0.3	2.5	10.9	79.6	4.2	5.3	89.1	100
United States[2]	15-19	a	24.8	3.2	52.2	80.2	13.0	2.5	4.3	19.8	100
	20-24	a	18.2	1.1	11.5	30.8	58.6	4.7	5.8	69.2	100
	25-29	a	7.7	n	2.2	10.0	81.0	3.1	5.8	90.0	100
Country mean	*15-19*	*6.6*	*11.4*	*3.4*	*57.3*	*78.8*	*13.3*	*3.2*	*4.8*	*21.2*	*100*
	20-24	*2.8*	*9.5*	*1.8*	*21.0*	*35.1*	*52.0*	*7.5*	*5.3*	*64.9*	*100*
	25-29	*0.4*	*7.0*	*0.5*	*5.2*	*13.2*	*76.8*	*5.8*	*4.1*	*86.8*	*100*

1. Students in work-study programmes are considered to be both in education and employed, irrespective of their labour market status according to the ILO definition.
2. Year of reference 2000.
Source: OECD. See Annex 3 for national data sources (*www.oecd.org/els/education/eag2002*).

C5

Table C5.1b.
Percentage of *young women* in education and not in education, by age group and work status (2001)

	Age group	In education					Not in education				Total in education and not in education
		Students in work-study programmes[1]	Other employed	Unemployed	Not in the labour force	Sub-total	Employed	Unemployed	Not in the labour force	Sub-total	
Australia	15-19	3.7	33.0	7.1	35.8	79.7	13.2	3.3	3.9	20.3	100
	20-24	2.3	21.2	2.2	9.2	34.9	48.6	6.0	10.5	65.1	100
	25-29	0.4	10.9	0.8	3.7	15.7	59.3	3.7	21.2	84.3	100
Austria	15-19	16.9	0.9	0.3	58.3	76.5	14.1	2.2	7.2	23.5	100
	20-24	1.0	3.6	0.6	25.3	30.5	58.4	2.6	8.5	69.5	100
	25-29	0.0	1.7	0.3	5.1	7.1	75.5	2.7	14.7	92.9	100
Belgium	15-19	0.9	2.1	0.2	88.0	91.1	2.4	1.3	5.2	8.9	100
	20-24	0.2	4.6	0.8	39.6	45.1	39.7	6.4	8.8	54.9	100
	25-29	0.8	7.8	0.3	4.0	12.9	65.5	8.4	13.3	87.1	100
Canada	15-19	a	31.4	5.1	49.7	86.2	8.7	1.7	3.3	13.8	100
	20-24	a	21.4	1.3	19.0	41.8	44.1	4.0	10.2	58.2	100
	25-29	a	8.2	0.2	5.9	14.3	66.4	4.9	14.3	85.7	100
Czech Republic	15-19	15.9	0.2	0.2	71.3	87.7	5.0	4.1	3.2	12.3	100
	20-24	a	0.7	0.3	23.7	24.6	51.7	8.1	15.6	75.4	100
	25-29	a	0.3	n	2.3	2.6	55.1	8.3	34.1	97.4	100
Denmark	15-19	3.4	35.2	4.5	43.2	86.3	11.0	0.4	2.3	13.7	100
	20-24	10.1	26.0	3.7	20.1	59.9	30.8	3.3	6.0	40.1	100
	25-29	1.6	16.7	1.0	12.8	32.0	57.0	2.3	8.7	68.0	100
Finland	15-19	a	14.3	7.2	68.7	90.2	6.0	1.6	2.1	9.8	100
	20-24	a	23.5	4.5	31.2	59.2	27.9	5.0	7.9	40.8	100
	25-29	a	18.4	2.1	9.8	30.3	46.6	8.1	15.1	69.7	100
France	15-19	3.7	0.5	n	90.9	95.3	1.2	1.8	1.7	4.7	100
	20-24	6.5	5.8	0.7	43.6	56.6	27.6	8.7	7.1	43.4	100
	25-29	1.7	4.9	0.4	5.3	12.3	62.3	9.9	15.5	87.7	100
Germany	15-19	17.0	4.3	0.6	67.5	89.3	5.3	1.3	4.0	10.7	100
	20-24	13.2	6.0	0.3	17.7	37.2	44.1	4.1	14.6	62.8	100
	25-29	1.1	4.1	0.2	5.3	10.7	64.6	4.7	20.0	89.3	100
Greece	15-19	n	0.7	0.6	84.2	85.6	4.8	4.7	4.9	14.4	100
	20-24	n	2.5	1.9	34.1	38.5	33.1	16.0	12.4	61.5	100
	25-29	n	1.0	0.7	4.5	6.3	55.0	14.9	23.9	93.7	100
Hungary	15-19	a	0.4	0.3	85.2	85.9	6.1	1.6	6.3	14.1	100
	20-24	a	5.1	0.3	31.5	37.0	38.5	3.7	20.8	63.0	100
	25-29	a	5.2	0.2	4.8	10.2	51.3	3.7	34.8	89.8	100
Iceland	15-19	1.8	52.7	3.2	22.2	79.9	18.8	1.3	0.0	20.1	100
	20-24	5.5	30.6	1.1	15.3	52.4	42.6	1.6	3.3	47.6	100
	25-29	4.1	23.4	n	12.3	39.8	52.0	1.8	6.4	60.2	100
Ireland	15-19	a	10.7	0.5	74.3	85.6	10.5	1.4	2.6	14.4	100
	20-24	a	6.1	0.3	25.4	31.8	56.2	3.0	9.0	68.2	100
	25-29	a	0.5	n	2.8	3.4	77.1	2.4	17.1	96.6	100
Italy	15-19	n	0.7	1.0	78.1	79.8	7.7	4.7	7.8	20.2	100
	20-24	n	3.3	2.1	36.7	42.3	30.4	11.9	15.4	57.7	100
	25-29	n	3.8	1.4	13.8	19.0	47.0	10.2	23.8	81.0	100
Luxembourg	15-19	2.9	1.4	n	86.7	91.1	6.8	0.4	1.6	8.9	100
	20-24	1.9	4.8	0.2	40.3	47.3	41.8	2.7	8.1	52.7	100
	25-29	n	3.7	n	5.1	9.2	71.3	1.5	18.0	90.8	100
Mexico	15-19	a	4.8	0.3	45.2	50.3	21.4	1.3	27.0	49.7	100
	20-24	a	3.7	0.2	13.6	17.5	36.4	1.6	44.5	82.5	100
	25-29	a	1.2	n	2.2	3.5	42.3	1.2	53.0	96.5	100
Netherlands[3]	15-19	m	40.2	5.9	36.6	82.7	13.8	1.2	2.2	17.3	100
	20-24	m	22.0	1.3	12.1	35.4	53.4	2.3	8.9	64.6	100
	25-29	m	2.5	0.1	1.9	4.5	77.3	3.1	15.2	95.5	100
Norway[2]	15-19	a	26.1	6.6	55.3	88.0	9.1	1.7	1.2	12.0	100
	20-24	a	11.9	2.5	18.3	32.7	60.2	4.3	2.8	67.3	100
	25-29	a	6.5	1.4	8.5	16.4	75.3	3.8	4.4	83.6	100
Poland	15-19	a	3.3	1.3	88.2	92.8	1.8	2.8	2.5	7.2	100
	20-24	a	9.4	6.6	31.4	47.4	24.1	17.3	11.2	52.6	100
	25-29	a	7.0	1.6	3.2	11.9	49.6	16.5	22.0	88.1	100
Portugal	15-19	a	3.0	0.5	71.0	74.5	15.5	4.1	5.9	25.5	100
	20-24	a	6.2	0.8	34.0	41.0	46.0	5.9	7.1	59.0	100
	25-29	a	6.1	0.5	4.0	10.6	73.0	4.8	11.5	89.4	100
Slovak Republic	15-19	7.4	0.1	n	58.9	66.5	8.6	11.3	13.6	33.5	100
	20-24	a	0.5	0.6	21.2	22.4	43.8	16.9	16.9	77.6	100
	25-29	a	0.2	n	2.0	2.2	57.2	13.8	26.9	97.8	100
Spain	15-19	0.3	2.7	1.9	76.9	81.8	8.7	5.5	4.0	18.2	100
	20-24	0.7	7.2	3.2	38.2	49.3	32.8	10.0	7.9	50.7	100
	25-29	0.4	6.9	2.7	8.5	18.4	53.8	10.0	17.9	81.6	100
Sweden	15-19	a	20.7	5.2	60.3	86.1	10.1	1.9	1.8	13.9	100
	20-24	a	12.8	2.1	31.4	46.3	43.6	4.3	5.8	53.7	100
	25-29	a	10.8	1.1	13.1	25.0	66.1	2.8	6.1	75.0	100
Switzerland	15-19	30.4	11.5	m	39.0	84.5	8.3	m	6.7	15.5	100
	20-24	8.6	11.8	m	15.7	36.2	56.3	m	m	63.8	100
	25-29	m	5.3	m	m	10.5	71.0	m	16.1	89.5	100
Turkey	15-19	a	0.8	33.2	0.2	34.2	16.1	3.5	46.2	65.8	100
	20-24	a	1.4	7.4	0.6	9.4	25.9	5.8	59.0	90.6	100
	25-29	a	1.0	1.1	0.2	2.3	26.7	3.5	67.5	97.7	100
United Kingdom	15-19	3.2	29.6	2.7	36.1	71.5	18.5	3.9	6.1	28.5	100
	20-24	2.9	15.1	0.8	15.1	33.9	46.9	3.9	15.2	66.1	100
	25-29	1.3	9.9	0.5	4.0	15.8	61.4	2.9	19.9	84.2	100
United States[2]	15-19	a	10.4	4.1	63.8	78.3	12.8	2.8	6.1	21.7	100
	20-24	a	18.9	0.9	11.9	31.7	49.3	3.5	15.5	68.3	100
	25-29	a	7.3	n	3.7	11.1	66.3	3.0	19.6	88.9	100
Country mean	*15-19*	*4.0*	*12.7*	*3.4*	*60.6*	*80.8*	*9.9*	*2.7*	*6.6*	*19.2*	*100*
	20-24	*2.0*	*10.6*	*1.7*	*24.3*	*38.6*	*42.0*	*6.0*	*13.1*	*61.4*	*100*
	25-29	*0.4*	*6.5*	*0.6*	*5.5*	*13.3*	*60.2*	*5.7*	*20.8*	*86.7*	*100*

1. Students in work-study programmes are considered to be both in education and employed, irrespective of their labour market status according to the ILO definition.
2. Year of reference 2000.
Source: OECD. See Annex 3 for national data sources (*www.oecd.org/els/education/eag2002*).

Table C5.2.
Percentage of unemployed non-students in the total population, by level of educational attainment, age group and gender (2001)

		Below upper secondary education			Upper secondary and post-secondary non-tertiary education			Tertiary education		All levels of education			
		15-19	20-24	25-29	15-19	20-24	25-29	20-24	25-29	15-19	20-24	25-29	15-29
Australia	Males	7.6	17.5	11.0	3.3	8.1	4.1	1.8	2.9	5.8	7.8	5.3	6.3
	Females	3.9	14.7	6.6	4.2	6.3	4.5	1.7	1.5	4.0	6.0	3.7	4.6
	M+F	5.8	16.1	8.7	3.7	7.3	4.3	1.7	2.1	5.0	6.9	4.5	5.5
Austria	Males	9.1	11.8	5.4	0.6	4.2	3.4	0.2	1.9	2.3	4.3	3.4	3.3
	Females	11.3	5.2	4.0	0.6	3.3	2.9	0.3	0.8	2.4	2.6	2.7	2.6
	M+F	10.1	8.4	4.6	0.6	3.8	3.2	0.2	1.4	2.4	3.4	3.0	3.0
Belgium	Males	2.3	17.9	10.9	1.9	3.7	5.3	8.4	4.9	2.2	7.4	6.3	5.4
	Females	1.2	14.2	13.0	1.7	5.0	10.2	5.6	4.4	1.3	6.4	8.4	5.5
	M+F	1.8	16.5	11.9	1.8	4.3	7.6	6.6	4.6	1.8	6.9	7.4	5.4
Canada	Males	2.7	17.1	15.5	6.1	7.7	7.5	5.1	4.7	3.5	8.6	7.2	6.5
	Females	1.4	9.3	6.0	2.6	4.0	6.5	2.6	3.7	1.7	4.0	4.9	3.6
	M+F	2.1	14.2	11.4	4.3	6.0	7.1	3.6	4.1	2.7	6.3	6.1	5.1
Czech Republic	Males	9.1	33.0	19.7	2.9	10.5	5.7	1.5	1.9	4.2	10.5	6.2	7.2
	Females	7.6	18.7	18.7	3.5	9.2	8.1	1.4	1.7	4.2	8.1	8.3	7.1
	M+F	8.5	26.5	19.2	3.2	9.9	6.9	1.4	1.8	4.2	9.3	7.2	7.1
Denmark	Males	0.4	4.6	5.7	m	2.6	1.8	1.8	1.6	0.4	3.3	2.3	2.1
	Females	1.9	3.6	1.8	m	1.7	0.6	7.9	3.9	2.0	2.6	1.5	2.0
	M+F	1.2	4.1	3.7	6.7	2.2	1.1	5.0	2.6	1.2	2.9	1.9	2.0
Finland	Males	2.0	11.8	10.6	5.8	6.4	4.5	7.6	2.0	2.5	7.3	4.8	4.8
	Females	0.7	5.8	15.4	7.7	5.1	8.5	4.1	6.0	1.6	5.0	8.1	4.8
	M+F	1.4	9.7	12.3	6.7	5.7	6.2	4.9	4.3	2.1	6.1	6.3	4.8
France	Males	1.8	20.0	15.3	3.0	5.5	7.3	2.3	5.6	1.9	8.2	8.3	6.1
	Females	1.5	17.4	16.4	4.1	8.0	10.7	3.6	6.1	1.8	8.7	9.9	6.8
	M+F	1.6	18.9	15.9	3.6	6.7	8.9	3.1	5.9	1.9	8.4	9.1	6.5
Germany	Males	2.5	18.6	17.1	0.5	6.4	6.7	0.4	1.5	1.5	7.1	6.7	5.1
	Females	2.0	10.9	7.4	0.6	3.6	5.0	0.7	2.4	1.3	4.1	4.7	3.4
	M+F	2.3	14.7	12.0	0.5	5.2	5.8	0.5	1.9	1.4	5.7	5.7	4.3
Greece	Males	2.5	14.3	9.0	5.4	11.2	10.6	9.2	12.8	3.2	11.8	10.5	8.5
	Females	2.9	18.7	13.9	9.3	14.4	14.4	27.3	16.8	4.7	16.0	14.9	12.2
	M+F	2.7	16.1	10.9	7.5	13.0	12.5	20.3	15.2	3.9	14.0	12.7	10.4
Hungary	Males	1.7	14.4	15.2	6.4	6.0	6.0	6.0	0.3	2.6	7.3	7.0	5.8
	Females	0.8	5.1	5.7	4.4	3.6	4.0	2.3	0.5	1.6	3.7	3.7	3.1
	M+F	1.3	9.7	10.3	5.3	4.8	5.0	3.8	0.4	2.1	5.5	5.3	4.5
Iceland	Males	1.3	1.2	3.6	a	2.2	a	a	2.2	1.3	1.6	1.8	1.6
	Females	2.0	3.2	1.4	a	a	a	20.0	2.6	2.0	2.4	1.0	1.8
	M+F	1.7	2.3	2.4	a	1.2	a	7.8	2.3	1.6	2.0	1.4	1.7
Ireland	Males	2.3	10.0	7.3	2.3	2.0	2.8	2.1	1.4	2.3	3.7	3.3	3.1
	Females	1.2	5.6	4.6	1.7	2.8	2.5	2.3	1.4	1.3	3.0	2.4	2.2
	M+F	1.8	8.3	6.1	1.9	2.4	2.7	2.3	1.4	1.8	3.3	2.8	2.7
Italy	Males	4.7	15.5	11.0	8.0	9.6	8.2	13.9	10.9	5.0	11.7	9.5	9.0
	Females	4.0	15.5	10.2	9.5	10.5	9.2	17.9	14.2	4.7	11.9	10.2	9.3
	M+F	4.3	15.5	10.6	8.8	10.1	8.7	16.5	12.9	4.9	11.8	9.9	9.1
Luxembourg	Males	0.6	2.3	2.1	a	3.2	0.0	3.1	2.4	0.5	2.8	1.4	1.6
	Females	0.9	7.2	3.5	a	1.7	0.5	4.1	2.2	0.8	4.3	2.1	2.4
	M+F	0.8	4.8	2.8	a	2.5	0.3	3.5	2.3	0.7	3.5	1.8	2.0
Mexico	Males	1.9	2.6	1.8	0.9	5.9	4.2	2.0	2.8	1.9	2.5	2.1	2.1
	Females	1.2	1.4	1.0	4.2	2.1	1.2	2.1	2.3	1.3	1.6	1.2	1.4
	M+F	1.5	2.0	1.4	3.1	3.1	1.8	2.0	2.5	1.6	2.0	1.6	1.7
Netherlands[1]	Males	1.8	4.0	3.4	0.6	1.9	1.1	0.4	2.1	1.1	1.9	2.0	1.7
	Females	2.5	5.1	5.2	0.7	2.0	2.5	1.2	2.3	1.2	2.3	3.1	2.3
	M+F	2.1	4.5	4.2	0.7	2.0	1.8	0.8	2.2	1.2	2.1	2.5	2.0
Norway[1]	Males	3.1	9.0	6.7	1.1	4.7	4.1	n	2.7	1.7	4.3	3.8	3.4
	Females	1.3	8.9	7.1	n	2.5	3.1	n	1.2	0.5	2.2	2.5	1.9
	M+F	2.2	8.9	6.9	0.6	3.7	3.7	n	1.8	1.1	3.3	3.2	2.7
Poland	Males	7.3	39.1	25.9	3.2	27.9	16.1	1.0	6.1	4.0	20.6	15.0	13.3
	Females	4.7	31.6	27.5	2.7	28.5	18.8	1.5	7.8	3.0	17.3	16.5	12.6
	M+F	6.1	36.1	26.6	2.9	28.2	17.4	1.3	7.1	3.5	18.9	15.7	12.9
Portugal	Males	2.7	6.0	2.9	0.3	4.2	1.2	0.4	2.2	1.7	4.3	2.5	2.9
	Females	8.1	8.3	5.6	1.2	7.4	4.3	2.6	3.7	4.5	5.9	4.9	5.2
	M+F	5.1	6.9	4.2	0.8	5.9	2.7	1.8	3.0	3.0	5.1	3.7	4.0
Slovak Republic	Males	3.7	50.7	43.8	32.2	27.3	19.5	17.5	12.4	10.6	28.4	20.0	19.9
	Females	1.5	19.8	19.3	37.1	16.7	15.0	17.9	4.8	11.3	16.9	13.8	14.1
	M+F	2.6	37.5	30.0	34.8	22.1	17.4	17.7	8.2	11.0	22.8	16.9	17.0
Spain	Males	10.7	13.1	9.1	1.5	8.2	8.5	2.8	5.4	6.2	7.6	7.6	7.3
	Females	14.8	18.7	13.9	2.0	13.7	10.7	5.5	8.0	7.1	10.5	10.6	9.8
	M+F	12.3	15.3	11.1	1.7	10.8	9.6	4.2	6.8	6.6	9.0	9.0	8.5
Sweden	Males	18.6	17.5	9.8	1.0	6.4	4.1	0.1	0.5	1.9	5.9	3.7	3.9
	Females	21.2	12.2	9.0	1.1	5.4	3.3	0.8	0.8	2.0	4.4	2.9	3.1
	M+F	19.8	15.2	9.5	1.0	5.9	3.7	0.5	0.7	1.9	5.2	3.3	3.5
Switzerland	Males	m	m	m	m	m	m	m	m	m	m	m	m
	Females	m	m	m	m	m	m	m	m	m	m	m	m
	M+F	m	m	m	m	m	m	m	m	m	m	m	1.7
Turkey	Males	6.7	13.6	10.8	11.4	10.0	11.4	23.3	7.6	7.8	12.6	10.5	10.1
	Females	2.4	2.7	2.1	8.5	8.5	6.4	25.1	8.4	3.5	5.8	3.5	4.3
	M+F	4.6	7.6	6.3	10.2	9.4	9.6	24.3	7.9	5.8	9.2	7.3	7.4
United Kingdom	Males	10.4	15.2	13.9	5.9	5.8	4.1	3.2	2.0	7.0	6.1	4.3	5.7
	Females	4.3	7.2	6.3	3.8	3.9	3.0	2.7	1.4	3.9	3.9	2.8	3.5
	M+F	7.6	11.3	10.1	4.9	4.9	3.5	3.0	1.7	5.5	5.0	3.5	4.6
United States[1]	Males	8.5	10.7	5.3	1.4	4.0	3.3	3.3	2.0	2.6	4.7	3.1	3.5
	Females	9.3	6.9	8.7	1.4	3.3	3.1	1.7	1.0	2.5	3.4	3.0	2.9
	M+F	8.9	9.0	7.0	1.4	3.6	3.2	2.4	1.4	2.5	4.0	3.0	3.2
Country mean	*Males*	4.7	14.5	10.8	3.9	7.2	5.6	4.3	3.7	3.2	7.5	5.9	5.6
	Females	4.2	10.3	8.7	4.2	6.4	5.9	6.0	4.0	2.9	6.0	5.6	4.9
	M+F	4.4	12.6	9.6	4.3	6.8	5.7	5.2	3.9	3.0	6.7	5.7	5.3

1. Year of reference 2000.

Source: OECD. See Annex 3 for national data sources (*www.oecd.org/els/education/eag2002*).

C5

THE SITUATION OF THE YOUTH POPULATION WITH LOW LEVELS OF EDUCATION

- Most persons aged 15 to 19 are still in school. In many OECD countries, a high percentage of those who are not are either unemployed or not in the labour force.

- In Austria, Italy, Mexico, the Slovak Republic, Turkey and the United Kingdom, over 10 per cent of persons aged 15 to 19 are neither at school nor in the workforce.

- This situation is true mainly for young men in Austria, Denmark, Finland, the Slovak Republic and Sweden, and young women in Greece, Mexico, Portugal and Turkey.

Chart C6.1.

Percentage of 15 to 19-year-olds not in education or work, by gender (2001)

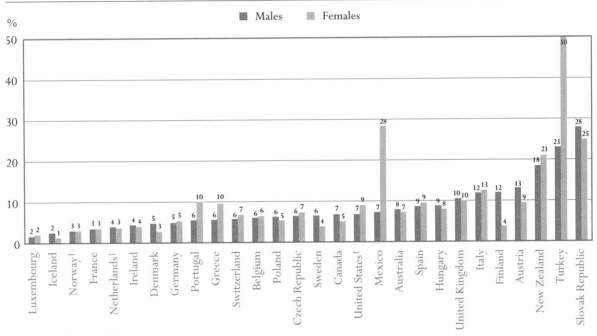

C6

1. Year of reference 2000.
Countries are ranked in ascending order of 15 to 19-year-old males not in education or work.
Source: OECD. Tables C5.1a and C5.1b. See Annex 3 for notes *(www.oecd.org/els/education/eag2002).*

Policy context

This indicator reflects on the situation of young people who are no longer in education but who are not yet in employment.

Entering the labour market is often a difficult period of transition. While the length of time spent in education has increased, a significant proportion of young people still remain marginal if they are neither in education or working, *i.e.*, they are either unemployed or in non-employment. This situation gives particular cause for concern for younger age groups, many of whom have no unemployment status or welfare cover (see *A Caring World*, OECD, 1999).

As the interrelationships between education, the economy and the well-being of nations become ever closer, providing for effective educational careers of young people and for successful transitions from initial education to working life become major policy concerns. Rising skill demands in OECD countries have made upper secondary diplomas a minimum for successfully entering the labour market and a basis for further participation in lifelong learning. Young people with lower qualifications run a higher risk of long-term unemployment or unstable or unfulfilling employment, which can have additional consequences such as social exclusion.

Evidence and explanations

Young people not in education or work

Most 15 to 19-year-olds are still at school. In many OECD countries, a high percentage of those who are not, are either unemployed or not in the labour force.

Over 80 per cent of persons between the ages of 15 and 19 are in education in most OECD countries. A small proportion of this age group is employed after having left school, although this figure is as high as 10 or 20 per cent in some OECD countries (Table C5.1).

There is, however, a group of young people who are no longer in education but not yet at work. Some are officially unemployed if they are actively seeking work, while those who are not doing so for some reason are considered to be in non-employment. Their reasons may be many and varied, such as discouragement because of the difficulty of finding work or voluntary withdrawal because of family circumstances. In 18 out of 27 OECD countries, the proportion of these young people is higher than the proportion of those with unemployment status.

To be out of education or out of employment is very uncommon in Denmark, France, Iceland, Luxembourg, the Netherlands and Norway yet common in Austria, Italy, Mexico, the Slovak Republic, Turkey and the United Kingdom. In these OECD countries, over 10 per cent of young people aged 15 to 19 are neither at school nor in work (Table C5.1). In other OECD countries, the proportion is lower but not insignificant, ranging from 4 to 10 per cent. The problem mainly affects young men in Austria, Denmark, Finland, the Slovak Republic and Sweden, and young women in Greece, Mexico, Portugal and Turkey (Chart C6.1).

Between the ages of 20 and 24, the scale

Young people with low qualifications may run an increased risk of long-term unemployment or of unstable, unfulfilling employment, which can have other negative consequences such as social exclusion. Early drop-out has become one of the most important educational policy problems. For students between 20 and 24 years, the scale of the problem grows and changes since most young people are entering the labour market at that age. Most have just completed initial education. There is often a period of unemployment before finding a job (Chart C6.2).

of the problem grows and changes since most young people enter the labour market at that age.

Chart C6.2.

Percentage of 20 to 24-year-olds who are not in education and who have not attained upper secondary education, by gender (2001)

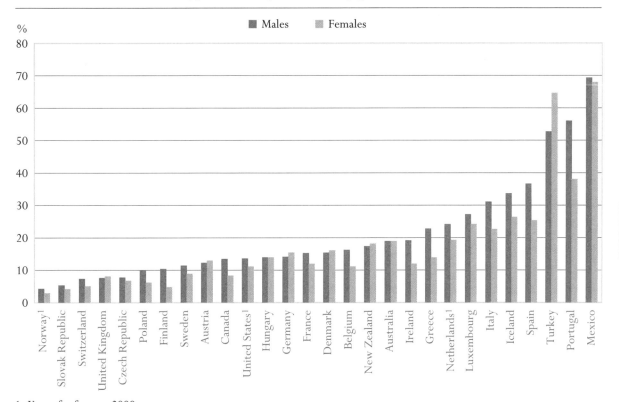

■ Males   ■ Females

C6

1. Year of reference 2000.
Countries are ranked in ascending order of the percentage of 20 to 24-year-old males who are not in education and who have not completed upper secondary education.
Source: OECD. Table C6.1. See Annex 3 for notes *(www.oecd.org/els/education/eag2002).*

Three different patterns exist. In a first group of eight OECD countries including Nordic and Eastern European countries as well as Switzerland and the United Kingdom, the proportion of young people without upper secondary education in the age group remains under 10 per cent. This particular group is certainly in a difficult position, but its extent is limited. For a second group of 12 out of 27 OECD countries, this potentially "at risk" group represents between 10 and 20 per cent of the age group. The challenge in terms of increasing upper secondary graduation rates is significant here. For the third group of eight OECD countries, more than 20 per cent of the age group falls under this category.

The consequences of having left school without an upper secondary qualification can be observed by comparing the work status of those with and those without an upper secondary qualification. In all OECD countries except one, higher educational attainment is associated with an average increase in the employment rate of 19 percentage points. The comparison also reveals some patterns related to the specific organisation of the labour market. The gap between those who have attained upper secondary education and those who have not is remarkably small in all Mediterranean countries, which suggests a good match between qualifications - even if these are low - and employment. The United Kingdom is an interesting case in that the prevalence of low qualifications is among the lowest among OECD countries, but the unemployment differentials are particularly high, suggesting that the few persons who have not obtained an upper secondary qualification are particularly disadvantaged.

C6

Chart C6.3.

Employment rates for 20 to 24-year-olds who are not in education,
by level of educational attainment (2001)

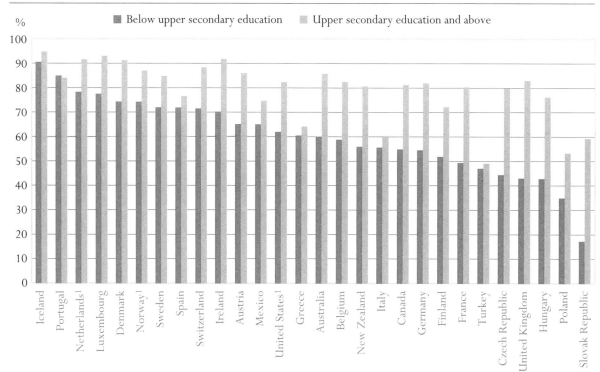

1. Year of reference 2000.
Countries are ranked in descending order of the employment rate of 20 to 24-year-olds who are not in education and who have not completed upper secondary education.
Source: OECD. Table C6.1. See Annex 3 for notes *(www.oecd.org/els/education/eag2002).*

Definitions and methodologies

The indicator is based on labour force survey data on age-specific proportions of young people in each of the specified categories. The definitions of the labour force statuses of those not in education (and not enrolled in work-study programmes) are based on ILO guidelines. Data for this indicator were calculated from the special OECD data collection on transition from education to work (see Indicator A12).

An "early school leaver" could broadly be defined as "a young person who has not attained upper secondary education and is not in education, or in a work-study programme leading to an upper secondary qualification or higher". However, such a definition needs to include the specification of an age group within which very few people can still be attending school at the primary or secondary level. Young people aged 18 and 19, in a significant number of OECD countries, are still enrolled in upper secondary education. Very early leavers may eventually return to school. Moreover, labour market outcomes at early ages may not be representative of outcomes at later ages. The OECD therefore defines a young adult with low level of education as "a person aged 20-24 years who has not attained upper secondary education and who is not enrolled in education nor in a work-study programme".

C6

Table C6.1.
Percentage of 20 to 24-year-olds not in education, by level of educational attainment, gender and work status (2001)

		Below upper secondary education				Upper secondary education and above				In education	Total 20 to 24-year-olds
		Employed	Unemployed	Not in the labour force	Sub-total	Employed	Unemployed	Not in the labour force	Sub-total		
Australia	Males	13.4	4.0	1.6	18.9	37.1	3.9	2.0	43.0	38.1	100
	Females	9.2	3.2	6.4	18.9	39.4	2.8	4.1	46.2	34.9	100
	M+F	11.3	3.6	4.0	18.9	38.2	3.3	3.0	44.6	36.5	100
Austria	Males	8.6	1.4	2.2	12.2	52.6	2.8	8.0	63.5	24.3	100
	Females	7.8	0.7	4.5	12.9	50.6	1.9	4.1	56.6	30.5	100
	M+F	8.2	1.1	3.3	12.6	51.6	2.4	6.0	60.0	27.4	100
Belgium	Males	10.9	3.9	1.5	16.2	35.0	3.5	2.0	40.5	43.3	100
	Females	5.2	2.0	4.0	11.1	34.5	4.4	4.8	43.8	45.1	100
	M+F	8.0	2.9	2.7	13.7	34.8	4.0	3.4	42.1	44.2	100
Canada	Males	8.4	2.7	2.4	13.5	40.6	5.9	3.4	49.9	36.6	100
	Females	3.5	0.9	3.9	8.3	40.6	3.1	6.3	49.9	41.8	100
	M+F	6.0	1.8	3.1	10.9	40.6	4.5	4.8	49.9	39.1	100
Czech Republic	Males	4.2	2.5	1.0	7.7	61.6	7.9	1.2	70.7	21.6	100
	Females	2.2	1.3	3.3	6.7	49.5	6.9	12.3	68.6	24.6	100
	M+F	3.2	1.9	2.1	7.2	55.7	7.4	6.6	69.7	23.1	100
Denmark	Males	13.6	1.2	0.5	15.4	32.1	1.4	0.7	34.2	50.4	100
	Females	9.8	1.6	4.7	16.1	20.9	1.7	1.4	23.9	60.0	100
	M+F	11.7	1.4	2.6	15.7	26.4	1.5	1.0	29.0	55.3	100
Finland	Males	5.8	1.8	2.7	10.4	29.8	5.4	5.9	41.1	48.5	100
	Females	2.1	0.5	2.2	4.8	25.8	4.5	5.6	36.0	59.2	100
	M+F	3.9	1.2	2.5	7.6	27.8	5.0	5.8	38.6	53.9	100
France	Males	8.9	4.5	1.9	15.2	29.6	3.7	0.8	34.2	50.6	100
	Females	4.5	3.3	4.2	12.0	23.0	5.4	2.9	31.4	56.7	100
	M+F	6.7	3.9	3.0	13.6	26.3	4.6	1.9	32.8	53.6	100
Germany	Males	9.1	2.8	2.2	14.1	44.0	4.4	4.4	52.8	33.1	100
	Females	6.8	1.8	6.9	15.4	37.9	2.4	7.0	47.2	37.4	100
	M+F	8.0	2.3	4.4	14.7	41.1	3.4	5.6	50.1	35.2	100
Greece	Males	17.4	3.4	1.9	22.8	30.7	8.4	3.9	43.0	34.2	100
	Females	5.1	2.8	6.0	13.9	27.5	13.2	6.5	47.2	38.9	100
	M+F	10.9	3.1	4.0	18.1	29.0	10.9	5.3	45.2	36.7	100
Hungary	Males	7.8	2.2	3.9	13.9	43.9	5.1	4.5	53.4	32.7	100
	Females	4.1	0.8	9.0	14.0	34.3	2.9	11.8	49.1	37.0	100
	M+F	6.0	1.5	6.5	14.0	39.0	4.0	8.2	51.2	34.8	100
Iceland	Males	31.8	1.9	0.0	33.7	16.8	0.5	0.5	17.7	48.6	100
	Females	22.5	0.5	3.3	26.4	19.8	1.1	0.0	20.9	52.7	100
	M+F	27.3	1.3	1.6	30.1	18.3	0.8	0.2	19.3	50.6	100
Ireland	Males	15.3	2.0	1.8	19.1	53.2	1.6	1.2	56.1	24.8	100
	Females	6.5	0.8	4.8	12.0	49.7	2.2	4.2	56.1	31.8	100
	M+F	10.9	1.4	3.3	15.6	51.5	1.9	2.7	56.1	28.3	100
Italy	Males	20.3	5.6	5.2	31.1	20.8	6.2	7.0	34.0	34.9	100
	Females	9.5	4.1	9.1	22.6	20.9	7.8	6.4	35.1	42.3	100
	M+F	14.9	4.8	7.1	26.9	20.8	7.0	6.7	34.6	38.6	100
Luxembourg	Males	22.4	3.1	1.6	27.1	26.1	1.2	1.3	28.6	44.3	100
	Females	17.4	0.5	6.2	24.2	25.1	2.3	2.0	29.3	46.5	100
	M+F	19.9	1.8	4.0	25.6	25.6	1.8	1.6	29.0	45.4	100
Mexico	Males	64.7	1.9	2.7	69.3	8.9	0.6	0.3	9.9	20.8	100
	Females	26.9	1.0	40.0	68.0	9.5	0.6	4.5	14.5	17.5	100
	M+F	44.6	1.5	22.5	68.6	9.2	0.6	2.5	12.4	19.1	100
Netherlands[1]	Males	21.1	1.0	1.9	24.0	36.0	0.9	1.3	38.2	37.8	100
	Females	12.7	1.0	5.6	19.3	40.6	1.3	3.3	45.3	35.4	100
	M+F	17.0	1.0	3.7	21.7	38.3	1.1	2.3	41.7	36.6	100
Norway[1]	Males	3.6	0.4	0.2	4.3	56.6	3.9	2.5	63.0	32.7	100
	Females	1.7	0.3	0.9	2.9	38.2	1.9	5.9	46.0	51.1	100
	M+F	2.7	0.4	0.6	3.6	47.6	2.9	4.2	54.7	41.7	100
Poland	Males	4.0	3.8	2.0	9.8	27.4	16.7	3.0	47.2	43.0	100
	Females	1.6	2.0	2.6	6.2	22.5	15.3	8.6	46.4	47.4	100
	M+F	2.8	2.9	2.3	8.0	24.9	16.0	5.9	46.8	45.2	100
Portugal	Males	49.6	3.4	3.0	56.0	12.9	0.9	0.4	14.2	29.8	100
	Females	30.3	3.2	4.6	38.0	16.9	2.8	1.6	21.2	40.7	100
	M+F	39.9	3.3	3.8	47.0	14.9	1.8	1.0	17.7	35.3	100
Slovak Republic	Males	0.8	3.1	1.4	5.3	46.7	25.3	6.1	78.2	16.5	100
	Females	0.8	0.9	2.4	4.2	43.0	16.0	14.4	73.4	22.4	100
	M+F	0.8	2.1	1.9	4.8	44.9	20.7	10.2	75.8	19.4	100
Spain	Males	29.5	4.9	2.3	36.7	20.3	2.7	1.2	24.3	39.1	100
	Females	14.9	4.9	5.5	25.3	19.6	5.6	2.8	28.0	46.7	100
	M+F	22.4	4.9	3.8	31.2	20.0	4.1	2.0	26.1	42.8	100
Sweden	Males	8.4	2.0	1.0	11.4	45.1	3.9	3.5	52.5	36.1	100
	Females	6.1	1.1	1.6	8.8	38.3	3.3	4.3	45.9	45.3	100
	M+F	7.3	1.6	1.3	10.2	41.8	3.6	3.9	49.3	40.6	100
Switzerland	Males	4.7	m	m	7.3	43.9	m	m	50.1	42.6	100
	Females	m	m	m	m	51.9	m	m	58.3	36.7	100
	M+F	4.4	m	m	6.2	47.8	m	4.1	54.1	39.8	100
Turkey	Males	38.5	7.3	7.0	52.8	19.5	5.3	7.3	32.1	15.2	100
	Females	16.8	1.8	46.0	64.6	9.1	4.0	13.0	26.0	9.4	100
	M+F	27.6	4.5	26.6	58.7	14.3	4.7	10.1	29.1	12.2	100
United Kingdom	Males	4.5	1.3	1.7	7.6	52.4	4.8	2.5	59.7	32.8	100
	Females	2.1	0.6	5.3	8.1	45.3	3.3	9.5	58.1	33.8	100
	M+F	3.4	1.0	3.5	7.8	48.9	4.0	6.0	58.9	33.3	100
United States[1]	Males	10.3	1.5	1.8	13.6	48.3	3.3	4.0	55.6	30.8	100
	Females	5.0	0.8	5.4	11.1	42.5	2.6	9.6	54.7	34.1	100
	M+F	7.7	1.1	3.6	12.4	45.4	2.9	6.8	55.1	32.5	100
Country mean	*Males*	*16.2*	*2.7*	*2.0*	*21.1*	*36.0*	*4.8*	*2.9*	*44.0*	*34.9*	*100*
	Females	*8.7*	*1.6*	*7.3*	*17.6*	*32.5*	*4.4*	*5.8*	*42.9*	*39.3*	*100*
	M+F	*12.5*	*2.2*	*4.7*	*19.5*	*34.2*	*4.6*	*4.5*	*43.5*	*37.1*	*100*

Note: Students in work-study programmes are considered to be both in education and employed, irrespective of their labour market status according to the ILO definition.

1. Year of reference 2000.

Source: OECD. See Annex 3 for national data sources (*www.oecd.org/els/education/eag2002*).

C6

Chapter

THE LEARNING ENVIRONMENT AND ORGANISATION OF SCHOOLS

OVERVIEW

Indicator D1: Total intended instruction time for students 9 to 14 years of age

Table D1.1. Intended instruction time in public institutions (2000)
Table D1.2a. Intended instruction time for 9 to 11-year-olds in public institutions, by subject (2000)
Table D1.2b. Intended instruction time for 12 to 14-year-olds in public institutions, by subject (2000)
Table D1.3. Additional instruction time and learning time of 15-year-olds (2000)

Chapter D examines the learning environment and organisation of schools, in terms of…

Indicator D2: Class size and ratio of students to teaching staff

Table D2.1. Average class size, by type of institution and level of education (2000)
Table D2.2. Ratio of students to teaching staff in public and private institutions by level of education, calculations based on full-time equivalents (2000)

…student learning conditions,…

Indicator D3: Use and availability of computers at school and in the home

Table D3.1. Ratio of students to computers (2000)
Table D3.2. Availability of computers and computer networks in schools in which 15-year-olds are enrolled (2000)
Table D3.3. The extent to which learning is hindered by a lack of computers for instruction or lack of multi-media resources for instruction in schools in which 15-year-olds are enrolled (2000)
Table D3.4. Availability of computers to use at home and at school for 15-year-olds (2000)
Table D3.5. Frequency of use of computers at home and at school by 15-year-olds (2000)
Table D3.6. 15-year-olds who use computers to help them learn school material (2000)

…the availability and use of information technology at school and at home,…

Indicator D4: Attitudes and experiences of males and females using information technology (2000)

Table D4.1. Perceived comfort with and ability to use computers of 15year-olds, by gender (2000)
Table D4.2. 15-year-old students' interest in using computers, by gender (2000)

Indicator D5: Classroom and school climate

Table D5.1. Classroom climate for 15year-olds (2000)
Table D5.2. Homework policy and pressure on 15-year-olds to achieve (2000)
Table D5.3. Quality and use of school resources for 15-year-olds (2000)
Table D5.4. Broader engagement of 15-year-olds with school (2000)

…the classroom and school climate …

...and teacher working conditions.

Indicator D6: Salaries of teachers in public primary and secondary schools

Table D6.1. Teachers' salaries (2000)
Table D6.2. Adjustments to base salary for teachers in public schools (2000)

Indicator D7: Teaching time and teachers' working time

Table D7.1. The organisation of teachers' working time (2000)
Table D7.2. Number of teaching hours per year (1996, 2000)

Indicators D1 on instruction time, D6 on teachers' salaries and bonus systems, and D7 on teacher working time draw on system-level information on teachers and the curriculum collected annually. Annex 3 (see *www.oecd.org/els/education/eag2002)* adds to this a rich source of qualitative information on differences and similarities between countries in instruction time, teachers' pay scales and bonus systems, and definitions of teaching and working time. It also helps readers to interpret comparisons and data on individual countries.

Indicators D3 to D5 and part of indicator D1 draw on data from the Programme of International Student Assessment (PISA). For detailed information on PISA, see *www.pisa.oecd.org*.

TOTAL INTENDED INSTRUCTION TIME
FOR STUDENTS 9 TO 14 YEARS OF AGE

- Students between the ages of 9 and 11 spend, on average, 841 hours per year in the classroom, while students between the ages of 12 and 14 spend nearly 100 hours more per year. However, the figure varies significantly across countries.

- On average across countries, reading and writing in the language of instruction, mathematics and science comprise about half of the compulsory curriculum for 9 to 11-year-olds and 40 per cent for 12 to 14-year-olds.

- 15-year-old students spend an average of 4.6 hours per week on homework and learning in the language of instruction, mathematics and science in addition to the instruction time spent in the classroom.

- On average, one in three 15-year-olds receive private instruction outside school at least occasionally.

- The degree to which schools and local and regional authorities can specify curricular content and timetables varies widely from country to country.

Intended instruction time in public institutions, by school subject (2000)

Percentage of total intended instruction time allocated for the compulsory core curriculum, by subject, compulsory flexible curriculum and non-compulsory curriculum, for 9 to 11-year-olds and 12 to 14-year-olds

Intended instruction time for 9 to 11-year-olds (Average total intended instruction time 841 hours)

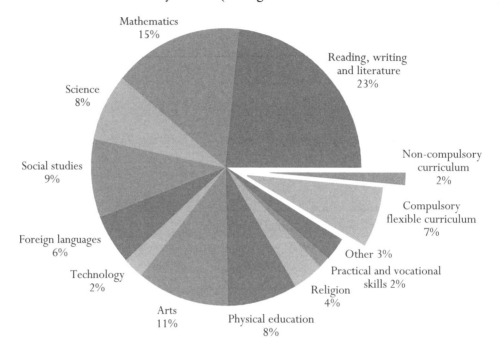

Intended instruction time for 12 to 14-year-olds (Average total intended instruction time 936 hours)

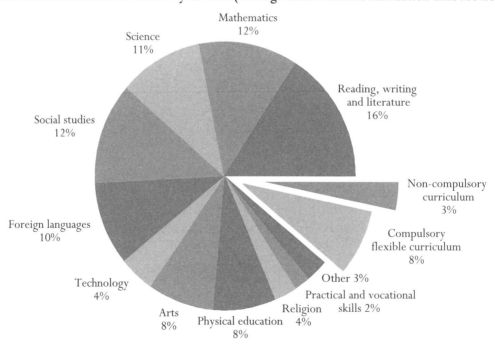

Source: OECD. Tables D1.2a and D1.2b. See Annex 3 for notes (*www.oecd.org/els/education/eag2002*).

Policy context

The amount and quality of the time that people spend learning between early childhood and the start of their working lives are decisive for shaping their lives, socially and economically. Instruction time in formal classroom settings comprises a large part of the public investment in student learning. Matching resources with students' needs and using time in an optimal manner, from the perspective of the learner and of public investment, are major challenges for education policy. The costs of resources depend primarily on the costs of teacher labour, of institutional maintenance, and of other educational resources. The length of time during which resources are made available to students, as shown in this indicator on instruction time in classroom settings in the formal education system, are therefore important.

This indicator shows intended instruction time in classroom settings in the formal education system…

Student learning time includes hours spent in the formal classroom setting as well as time spent on homework and in other learning activities organised by the school such as remedial tutoring, enrichment classes and interest clubs. It often also includes private lessons, tutoring and other forms of out-of-school learning that are much more difficult to quantify. The indicator does report on two important aspects of extra-curricular learning, namely the incidence of organised instruction in addition to the formal curriculum both inside and outside school, and the time that 15-year-olds report spending on homework.

…and sheds some light on the incidence of learning outside school.

Evidence and explanations

What this indicator shows

This indicator captures intended instruction time as a measure of exposure to learning in formal classroom settings as per public regulations. It also shows how instruction time is allocated to different curricular areas. The indicator is calculated as the intended net hours of instruction for the grades in which the majority of students are 9 to 14 years of age. Although such data are difficult to compare across countries because of different curriculum policies, they nevertheless provide an indication of how much contact time countries consider students need in order to achieve the educational goals that have been set for them.

Intended instruction time is an important indicator of the public resources invested in education…

D1

In some countries, intended instruction time varies considerably between regions or different types of school. In many countries, local education authorities or schools can determine the number and allocation of hours. Additional teacher time is often planned for individual remedial teaching or enhancement of the curriculum. On the other hand, time may be lost because too few qualified substitutes exist to replace absent teachers or because students are absent.

…but needs to be interpreted in the context of often considerable variation between regions and schools…

Annual instruction time should also be seen together with the length of compulsory education, which measures the time during which young people receive full-time educational support from public resources, or during which more than 90 per cent of the population participates in education (see Indicator

…and in the context of other measures of learning time and of the quality of teaching that

are not captured by this indicator. C1). Intended instruction time also does not capture the quality of learning opportunities that are being provided or the level or quality of human and material resources involved. Other indicators in this section tackle the problem of the availability of educational resources (Indicators D3 and D5) and of teachers relative to the student population (Indicator D2), and the quality of the learning climate in schools and classrooms (Indicator D5).

Curriculum policies

Responsibilities for curriculum provision are distributed in different ways. Decision-making responsibilities for planning students' programmes of learning vary greatly from country to country. Two basic models exist in OECD countries, with several variants.

In some OECD countries, subjects and content are defined, and time is allocated at a national (or sub-national) level... In one model of curriculum regulation, national or regional authorities specify subject areas, the time allocated to them and the content, and schools must respect with a greater or lesser degree of flexibility these national or sub-national curricular specifications. In Austria, England, France, Germany, Greece and Spain, the national authorities (German *Länder*, Spanish Autonomous Communities) establish curricula for all types of schools, grades and subjects. Typically, the documents define subjects, the time allocated to them and content in more or less detail by grade level and type of programme, while the school is responsible for managing and delivering the curriculum.

Curriculum regulation in Spain

In Spain, the governments of Autonomous Communities state the curriculum for their community by specifying the subjects and number of hours per school year to be devoted to each subject. The governments must necessarily include the compulsory curriculum prescribed by the central government (65 per cent of the total compulsory curriculum, or 55 per cent if the community has its own language).

...while in others, local school authorities, or the schools themselves, are primarily responsible for providing the curricula, with attainment targets set at the national level... In the second model of curriculum regulation, national authorities establish attainment targets or standards, while local authorities or schools are responsible for planning and implementing curricula. For example, in Belgium (Flemish Community), the Czech Republic, New Zealand and Portugal (primary level), national policy documents describe the targets, and local authorities or schools specify the subjects, content and time allocated to them.

Curriculum guidance in New Zealand

In New Zealand, the national curriculum is specified by seven learning area statements for mathematics, science, English, technology, social studies, health and physical education and the arts. State and state-integrated schools are required to provide programmes of learning based on the statements for all students in grades 1 to 10. However, how schools do this is not prescribed either in terms of time allocations or programme/timetable arrangements. Modern foreign languages are not compulsory at any level, and in New Zealand, community languages and international languages are considered foreign languages.

Primary education curricula in Portugal

In Portugal, the primary education curriculum does not specify the amount of hours per week allocated to each subject area; it only indicates the total amount of hours per week. Study areas include physical education, music, drama and plastic education; environmental studies; Portuguese language; mathematics and religion or personal and social development. Teachers may allocate the time for each subject area up to a total amount of 25 hours per week.

Finland, Hungary, Ireland and Sweden combine these two models. Local authorities and schools are required to develop the programme of learning, but they are guided by national curriculum documents on subject and content, which provide broad directions concerning time allocations to study areas at the national level. Schools in these countries enjoy a fair degree of flexibility in offering additional instruction and even individual tutoring for students.

…and yet in others, combinations of the two models exist.

D1

Primary education curriculum in Ireland

In Ireland, the primary school curriculum is integrated and envisages an integrated learning experience for children. Learning experiences are organised to foster cross-curricular activity. Schools are required to develop their own curricula, but are assisted in planning and implementing them by a framework allocating minimal times to each of the main study areas.

Curriculum regulations in Sweden

In Sweden, the curriculum prescribed by legislation states the total number of hours per subject or group of subjects for the nine years of compulsory education. Municipalities and schools decide in which year a given subject should be introduced and how many hours are needed for each subject in any academic year.

Compulsory intended instruction time in classroom settings in the formal education system

On average, 8 per cent of compulsory instruction time belongs to the flexible part of the curriculum in the grades where most students are 9 to 14 years of age.

In most OECD countries, the number of hours of compulsory instruction is defined. Within the compulsory part of the curriculum, students have varying degrees of freedom to choose the subjects they want to learn. On average, the flexible part of the curriculum comprises 7 per cent of compulsory instruction time in the grades where most students are 9 to 11 years old, and 9 per cent for students 12 to 14 years of age. However, in Australia, the flexible part of the curriculum is 60 and 28 per cent in the two age groups respectively, whereas it is zero in one-third of OECD countries. For 12 to 14-year-old students in Belgium, the Czech Republic, Finland, Iceland, the Netherlands, Portugal, Scotland and Spain, at least 10 per cent of the compulsory curriculum is flexible (Tables D1.2a and D1.2b).

Chart D1.2.

Average number of hours per year devoted to foreign language instruction in public institutions for 9 to 14-year-olds (2000)

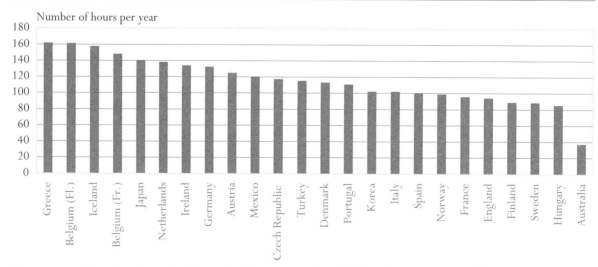

Countries are ranked in descending order of the number of hours per year devoted to foreign language instruction for 9 to 14-year-olds.
Source: OECD. Tables D1.2a and D1.2b. See Annex 3 for notes *(www.oecd.org/els/education/eag2002)*.

For students 9 to 11 years of age, 48 per cent of the compulsory curriculum on average is devoted to the three basic subject areas: reading and writing (23 per cent), mathematics (15 per cent) and science (8 per cent). On average, 9 per cent of the compulsory curriculum is devoted to social studies and 6 per cent to modern foreign languages (Chart D1.2). Arts account for 11 per cent and physical education accounts for 8 per cent of the total compulsory curriculum time. These seven study areas form part of the curriculum in all OECD countries for these age cohorts. Religion or moral education is included in the curriculum in about half of the countries. At this level, classroom activities in the study areas are not necessarily organised as separate subject classes (Tables D1.2a and D1.2b).

About half of compulsory instruction time tends to be devoted to reading and writing, mathematics and science for all students 9 to 11 years of age...

For 12 to 14-year-old students in OECD countries, 40 per cent of the compulsory curriculum, on average, is devoted to three basic subject areas: reading and writing (16 per cent), mathematics (12 per cent) and science (11 per cent). In these age cohorts, a relatively larger part of the curriculum is devoted to social studies (12 per cent) and modern foreign languages (10 per cent) (Chart D1.2), whereas somewhat less time is devoted to arts (8 per cent). Physical education accounts for 8 per cent. These seven study areas form part of the curriculum in all OECD countries for lower secondary students. Technology is included in about two-thirds of the countries, and religion is included in about half of the OECD countries as part of the compulsory curriculum (Tables D1.2a and D1.2b).

...and 40 per cent for students 12 to 14 years of age.

Total intended instruction time in classroom settings in the formal education system

Intended instruction time is an estimate of the number of hours during which students are taught both the compulsory and non-compulsory parts of the curriculum. Total intended instruction time in classroom settings in the formal education system for 9 to 11-year-old students ranges from a yearly average of less than 700 hours in Finland and Iceland to 1 000 hours or more in Italy, the Netherlands and Scotland. These figures do not include individualised instruction outside classroom settings, which is considerable in many countries, including Finland and Iceland (Table D1.1).

Total intended instruction time for 9 to 11-year-olds averages to 841 hours...

For 12 to 14-year-old students, the average intended instruction time per year ranges from less than 800 hours in Sweden and Turkey to more than 1 100 hours in Austria and Mexico. The OECD average for the 12 to 14 age cohorts is 936 hours per year (Table D1.1).

...and to 936 hours for 12 to 14-year-olds.

On average, the non-compulsory part of the curriculum comprises 2 per cent of the total instruction time for 9 to 11-year-old students and 4 per cent for 12 to 14-year-old students. However, a considerable amount of additional non-compulsory instruction time can sometimes be provided. In primary schools, all intended instruction time is compulsory for students in most OECD countries, but the additional non-compulsory part is as high as 20 per cent in Hungary and around 10 per cent in New Zealand and Turkey. At the lower secondary level,

On average, the non-compulsory part of the curriculum accounts for 3 per cent of total intended instruction time, but this varies greatly across countries.

a sizeable non-compulsory fraction of instruction time is provided in Australia, Belgium Denmark, England, France, Hungary, Ireland, New Zealand and Turkey, which ranges from 5 per cent in Australia and New Zealand to 28 per cent in Hungary (Tables D1.2a and D1.2b and Chart D1.1).

In most OECD countries, total intended instruction time for 12 to 14-year-old students remained unchanged between 1996 and 2000.

In most OECD countries, total intended instruction time for students aged 12 to 14 did not change between 1996 and 2000. However, it increased by 11 per cent in the Czech Republic and New Zealand (see Annex 3 at *www.oecd.org/els/education/eag2002*).

Homework

Homework and other out-of-school learning play an important part for 15-year-olds…

Practices and policies concerning homework are other elements in this equation that can substantially influence how much time students spend learning. In many countries, homework constitutes a major part of students' learning time. In PISA 2000, 15-year-olds were asked to specify how much time they spend each week on homework in the language of assessment, mathematics and science.

…with close to the equivalent of one-third of instruction time in the language of instruction, mathematics and science devoted to homework.

In PISA, 15-year-olds reported spending an average of 4.6 hours on homework and learning in the language of instruction, mathematics and science. Students in Greece, however, reported spending about 7 hours per week. Students in Australia, Canada, Denmark, France, Hungary, Iceland, Ireland, Italy, Mexico, New Zealand, Poland, Portugal, Spain and the United Kingdom reported spending more time on homework in the core subjects than the OECD average. Students in Austria, the Czech Republic, Finland, Japan, Korea, Luxembourg, Sweden and Switzerland, by contrast, reported spending less than the OECD average time on homework (Table D1.3).

Additional instruction time

School principals and students in PISA were asked about the additional instruction offered by the school for 15-year-old students.

A policy on a flexible curriculum is often used to respond to students' specific interests or to their need for remedial instruction in OECD countries. In addition, parents often seek tutoring and instruction for their children beyond what the school can offer. In PISA, school principals in secondary schools were asked whether their school offers *i)* extra courses on academic subjects for gifted students, *ii)* special training in the test language for low achievers, *iii)* special courses in study skills for low achievers, *iv)* special tutoring by staff members and *v)* room(s) where students can do their homework with staff help. 15-year-old students in the same schools were asked whether they had attended additional extension or enrichment courses or remedial courses in the test language and in other subjects or training to improve their study skills, and whether they received additional instruction outside of the school. The responses to these questions give some hints of further learning opportunities beyond formal classroom instruction. Although the age cohort responding to the questions in the PISA student questionnaire is somewhat older than that referred to in the first part of this indicator, the characteristic differences between countries may suggest policy issues that warrant attention (Table D1.3).

On average across OECD countries, the schools of about half of the 15-year-olds offer additional instruction, and about two-thirds of schools offer individual tutoring for students. Schools in Australia, Canada, Finland, Iceland, Italy, Luxembourg, New Zealand, Portugal, Sweden and the United Kingdom offer additional instruction for interested students and remedial teaching for students in need relatively more frequently. For example, over 90 per cent of 15-year-olds attend schools where remedial courses for low achievers are offered in the language of instruction in Iceland, Italy, New Zealand, Norway, Portugal and Sweden (Table D1.3).

By contrast, only half of 15-year-olds go to such schools in Belgium, Germany, Korea, Mexico and Poland. Where more than 90 per cent of students receive individual tutoring from staff members in Denmark, Finland, Japan, New Zealand and the United Kingdom, less than 40 per cent are offered such help in Austria, Germany and France (Table D1.3).

Comparing these findings with the intended instruction time reported on the system level, one finds that a relatively low amount of intended instruction time does not necessarily equate with an insufficient amount of instruction. For example, Austria, France, Greece and Mexico are among the countries with the highest amount of intended instruction time, yet fewer schools reported offering additional instruction time. By contrast, Finland, Iceland, Norway, Sweden and Portugal appear to have the fewest classroom instruction hours among the OECD countries, yet belong to the group of countries where most schools reported offering additional courses to meet special needs of students (Tables D1.1 and D1.3).

Students seek not only additional courses in schools, but also additional instruction outside school. In Japan, 30 and 55 per cent of 15-year-olds, respectively, reported regularly receiving out-of-school instruction in the language of instruction and other subjects during the last three years. These percentages are also high in Korea (27 and 34 per cent respectively). Somewhat fewer students in Hungary and Poland – 25 and 10 per cent – reported regularly attending extension or additional courses outside school during the last three years (for data see *www.pisa.oecd.org*). Finally, 11 per cent or more of 15-year-olds receive private tutoring in Hungary, Japan, Korea, New Zealand, Ireland, Poland, Portugal and Spain.

Including the students who only occasionally seek instruction outside of the school, fewer than 10 per cent of 15-year-old students in Finland, Italy, Norway, Switzerland and Sweden attended courses in the test language or in other subjects, or additional extension courses outside of the school during the last three years. By contrast, in Mexico, Poland, Korea and Japan, more than half of the students received private instruction in addition to instruction in the school. Furthermore, while less than 10 per cent received remedial (private) instruction in Finland and Sweden, in Hungary, Ireland, Italy, Mexico, New

Most schools in Australia, Canada, Finland, Iceland, Italy, Luxembourg, New Zealand, Portugal, Sweden and the United Kingdom offer additional courses for interested students or students needing remedial help while only about half of the schools or fewer in Belgium, Germany, Korea, Mexico and Poland do so.

In some cases, additional courses in schools compensate for below-average intended instruction time.

One-third of 15-year-olds in Korea and more than half the 15-year-olds in Japan reported receiving private instruction outside school in subjects other than those in the language of instruction during the last three years.

D1

Zealand, Poland, Portugal and Spain 40 per cent of 15-year-olds or more receive some during the last three years (Table D1.3).

Definitions and methodologies

Data on instruction time are from the 2001 OECD-INES survey on Teachers and the Curriculum and refer to the school year 1999-2000.

Instruction time for 9 to 14-year-olds refers to the formal number of class 60 minute-hours per school year organised by the school for instructional activities for students in the reference school year 1999-2000. For countries that have no formal policy on instruction time, the number of hours was estimated from survey data. Hours lost when schools are closed for festivities and celebrations, such as national holidays, are excluded. Intended instruction time does not include non-compulsory time outside the school day, homework, individual tutoring, or private study done before or after school.

Compulsory curriculum refers to the amount and allocation of instruction time that every school must provide and all students must attend.

Compulsory flexible curriculum refers to the part of the compulsory curriculum where schools or students have some flexibility or choice. For example, a school may choose to offer more than the minimum number of science classes and only minimum required number of art classes within the compulsory time frame.

The *non-compulsory part of the curriculum* is that which is defined entirely at the school level or eventually at the programme level if various programme types exist. Students are usually not required to attend the non-compulsory part of the curriculum.

Intended instruction time refers to the number of hours per year during which students receive instruction in the compulsory and non-compulsory parts of the curriculum.

The amount of time spent on homework by 15-year-olds in the language of assessment, mathematics and science was estimated based on self-reports administered as part of PISA 2000. In PISA, students rated the amount on a four-point scale for each subject area with response categories 'no time', 'less than 1 hour per week', 'between 1 and 3 hours per week' and '3 hours or more per week'. Student responses were then added across subject areas with 'no time' recoded as 0, 'less than 1 hour per week' recoded as 0.5, 'between 1 and 3 hours per week' recoded as 2 and '3 hours or more per week' recoded to 4 hours.

For the classification of subject areas and specific notes on countries, see *www.oecd.org/els/education/eag2002*.

Table D1.1.
Intended instruction time in public institutions (2000)
Total intended instruction time in hours per year for 9 to 14-year-olds

		Ages			Average (Ages 9-11)	Ages			Average (Ages 12-14)
		9	10	11		12	13	14	
OECD COUNTRIES	Australia*	986	987	987	987	1 014	1 020	1 023	1 019
	Austria	m	m	m	m	1 013	1 169	1 262	1 148
	Belgium (Fl.)*	831	831	831	831	955	955	a	955
	Belgium (Fr.)	m	m	m	m	1 044	1 106	a	1 075
	Czech Republic*	716	738	803	752	828	886	886	867
	Denmark	750	810	810	790	840	900	930	890
	England	890	890	890	890	940	940	940	940
	Finland*	684	684	713	694	713	855	855	808
	France	802	802	837	814	960	1 100	1 066	1 042
	Germany	752	774	862	796	874	915	918	903
	Greece*	928	928	928	928	1 064	1 064	1 064	1 064
	Hungary*	733	867	902	834	971	902	902	925
	Iceland	630	700	747	692	793	817	817	809
	Ireland*	941	941	941	941	891	891	891	891
	Italy	1 020	1 020	1 020	1 020	1 020	1 020	m	1 020
	Japan	761	761	761	761	875	875	875	875
	Korea	706	752	752	737	867	867	867	867
	Mexico	800	800	800	800	1 167	1 167	1 167	1 167
	Netherlands*	1 000	m	1 000	1 000	1 067	1 067	1 067	1 067
	New Zealand	985	985	985	985	985	930	930	948
	Norway	m	770	770	770	770	855	855	827
	Portugal	815	842	842	833	842	842	842	842
	Scotland*	1 000	1 000	1 000	1 000	1 000	1 000	1 000	1 000
	Spain*	795	795	795	795	795	870	870	845
	Sweden*	741	741	741	741	741	741	741	741
	Turkey	796	796	796	796	796	796	m	796
	United States	m	m	m	m	m	m	m	m
	Country mean	*829*	*835*	*855*	*841*	*916*	*944*	*944*	*936*
NON-OECD COUNTRIES	Argentina	729	729	729	729	912	936	936	928
	Brazil	800	800	800	800	800	800	800	800
	Chile	1 140	1 140	900	1 060	990	990	1 260	1 080
	China	771	771	771	771	893	893	1 020	935
	Egypt	1 026	1 053	1 026	1 035	1 026	999	a	1 013
	India	1 051	1 051	1 051	1 051	1 176	1 176	1 176	1 176
	Indonesia	1 064	1 120	1 176	1 120	1 176	1 323	1 323	1 274
	Jamaica	950	808	808	855	798	798	798	798
	Jordan	802	945	974	907	974	945	974	965
	Malaysia	964	964	964	964	1 230	1 230	1 230	1 230
	Paraguay	753	753	753	753	1 011	1 011	1 011	1 011
	Peru[1]	783	783	783	783	914	914	914	914
	Philippines	1 067	1 067	1 067	1 067	1 467	1 467	1 467	1 467
	Russian Federation	630	893	919	814	971	998	998	989
	Thailand	1 080	1 200	1 200	1 160	1 167	1 167	1 167	1 167
	Tunisia	960	960	960	960	900	900	900	900
	Uruguay	455	455	455	455	863	863	1011	913
	Zimbabwe	753	753	753	753	753	1 375	1375	1167

1. Year of reference 1999.
* See Annex 3 for notes (*www.oecd.org/els/education/eag2002*).
Source: OECD.

D1

Table D1.2a.
Intended instruction time for 9 to 11-year-olds in public institutions, by subject (2000)

Intended instruction time as a percentage of total compulsory instruction time, by subject, and division of instruction time into compulsory and non-compulsory parts of the curriculum, for 9 to 11-year-olds

| | Compulsory core curriculum | | | | | | | | | | | Com-pulsory flexible curricu-lum | TOTAL compul-sory cur-riculum | Non-com-pulsory curricu-lum |
| | Reading, writing and lit-erature | Math-ematics | Science | Social studies | Modern foreign lan-guages | Tech-nology | Arts | Physical educa-tion | Reli-gion | Practi-cal and vocational skills | Other | TOTAL compulsory core cur-riculum | | | |
	(1)	(2)	(3)	(4)	(5)	(6)	(7)	(8)	(9)	(10)	(11)	(12)	(13)	(14)	(15)
Australia*	12	8	2	3	2	2	4	4	1	n	n	40	60	100	n
Austria	m	m	m	m	m	m	m	m	m	m	m	m	m	m	m
Belgium (Fl.)*	m	m	m	m	m	m	m	m	m	m	m	m	m	m	m
Belgium (Fr.)	m	m	m	m	m	m	m	m	m	m	m	m	m	m	m
Czech Republic[1]*	23	18	15	5	12	n	14	9	n	2	n	98	2	100	m
Denmark*	24	15	8	4	10	n	22	10	4	n	4	100	n	100	n
England	27	22	11	10	n	9	10	7	5	n	n	100	n	100	n
Finland*	23	16	11	2	6	n	9	9	6	6	n	86	14	100	4
France	29	21	5	8	9	4	9	16	n	n	n	100	n	100	n
Germany	20	17	7	8	7	n	16	11	7	n	2	96	4	100	n
Greece*	29	14	11	11	10	n	8	7	7	n	2	100	n	100	n
Hungary*	28	17	n	9	7	n	16	12	n	7	4	100	n	100	20
Iceland	20	13	4	7	2	n	17	10	7	3	n	84	16	100	n
Ireland*	29	12	x(4)	12	n	n	12	4	10	n	14	92	8	100	n
Italy	17	10	8	11	10	3	13	7	6	n	n	84	16	100	n
Japan*	23	17	10	10	n	5	14	10	n	n	10	100	n	100	n
Korea	19	14	12	11	6	n	12	9	n	3	3	91	9	100	n
Mexico	30	25	15	20	n	n	5	5	n	n	n	100	n	100	n
Netherlands[2,3]	30	19	x(4)	15	2	2	10	7	4	n	12	100	n	100	n
New Zealand*	42	19	7	8	x(1)	7	9	9	m	n	m	100	n	100	10
Norway[1]*	19	14	8	8	7	n	17	7	9	n	9	100	n	100	n
Portugal[1]*	16	13	10	10	13	16	10	10	3	n	n	100	n	100	n
Scotland*	20	15	5	5	x(1)	5	10	5	15	x(13)	n	80	20	100	n
Spain*	24	17	9	9	13	n	11	11	x(13)	n	n	93	7	100	n
Sweden*	22	14	12	13	12	x[1]	7	8	x[4]	7	n	94	6	100	n
Turkey	19	13	10	10	9	n	7	6	7	10	1	91	9	100	10
United States	m	m	m	m	m	m	m	m	m	m	m	m	m	m	m
Country mean	*24*	*16*	*8*	*9*	*6*	*2*	*11*	*8*	*4*	*2*	*3*	*93*	*7*		*2*
Argentina	19	19	15	15	7	4	7	7	a	a	n	93	7	100	m
Chile	x(12)	x(12)	x(12)	x(12)	x(12)	x(12)	x(12)	x(12)	x(12)	x(12)	x(12)	81	19	100	m
China	26	18	6	9	n	n	12	9	n	3	12	94	6	100	m
Egypt	30	15	9	6	9	2	5	7	7	5	5	100	a	100	m
India	19	17	12	12	19	a	4	6	a	a	6	96	4	100	m
Indonesia	22	22	13	11	a	a	5	5	5	13	5	100	a	100	m
Jamaica	25	23	9	9	a	a	6	6	6	a	16	100	n	100	m
Jordan	24	16	13	8	12	a	3	6	9	5	3	100	a	100	m
Malaysia	21	15	11	9	15	n	4	4	13	4	4	100	a	100	m
Paraguay	26	13	8	10	x(13)	7	10	7	3	x(7)	10	93	7	100	m
Peru[5]	x(12)	x(12)	x(12)	x(12)	x(12)	x(12)	x(12)	x(12)	x(12)	x(12)	a	70	30	100	m
Philippines	13	13	13	13	13	a	8	4	a	13	13	100	a	100	m
Russian Federation	31	15	4	9	6	6	6	6	a	m	m	85	15	100	m
Thailand	14	10	x(11)	x(11)	x(15)	x(15)	x(11)	x(11)	x(11)	23	39	86	14	100	m
Tunisia	62	13	5	7	n	2	3	3	4	n	n	100	a	100	m
Uruguay	28	29	13	19	a	a	9	3	a	a	a	100	a	100	m
Zimbabwe	17	17	14	11	17	n	5	5	8	3	3	100	n	100	m

Note: x indicates that data are included in another column. The column reference is shown in brackets after "x". *e.g.*, x(2) means that data are included in column 2.

1. For 9 to 10-year-olds, social studies is included in science.
2. Includes 9 to 11-year-olds only.
3. Includes 10 to 11-year-olds only.
4. Included in various subjects.
5. Year of reference 1999.
* See Annex 3 for notes (*www.oecd.org/els/education/eag2002*).
Source: OECD.

Table D1.2b.

Intended instruction time for 12 to 14-year-olds in public institutions, by subject (2000)

Intended instruction time as a percentage of total compulsory instruction time, by subject, and division of instruction time into compulsory and non-compulsory parts of the curriculum, for 12 to 14-year-olds

	Compulsory core curriculum														
	Reading, writing and literature	Mathematics	Science	Social studies	Modern foreign languages	Technology	Arts	Physical education	Religion	Practical and vocational skills	Other	TOTAL compulsory core curriculum	Compulsory flexible curriculum	TOTAL compulsory curriculum	Non-compulsory curriculum
	(1)	(2)	(3)	(4)	(5)	(6)	(7)	(8)	(9)	(10)	(11)	(12)	(13)	(14)	(15)
OECD COUNTRIES															
Australia*	11	11	9	8	5	7	7	8	1	n	3	72	28	100	5
Austria	11	14	13	11	9	5	11	10	5	2	9	100	n	100	n
Belgium (Fl.)*[1]	14	13	5	9	14	6	6	6	6	n	n	80	20	100	n
Belgium (Fr.)[1]	15	14	6	12	12	3	3	9	6	n	5	85	15	100	6
Czech Republic*	13	14	16	13	10	n	8	7	n	6	n	87	13	100	n
Denmark*	23	15	14	13	11	n	10	8	4	n	4	100	n	100	11
England	14	14	13	13	11	13	9	9	4	n	n	100	n	100	10
Finland*	13	12	13	5	13	n	5	7	4	6	2	79	21	100	1
France	17	15	12	13	12	6	7	11	n	n	n	93	7	100	10
Germany	14	13	11	12	16	3	10	10	5	1	3	98	2	100	n
Greece*	12	11	10	10	15	5	6	8	6	1	16	100	n	100	n
Hungary*	13	13	12	16	9	4	12	9	n	8	5	100	n	100	28
Iceland	15	12	8	7	15	n	14	9	3	6	n	88	12	100	n
Ireland*	28	14	11	22	11	x(13,15)	x(13,15)	6	8	x(13,15)	n	100	n	100	11
Italy[1]	22	10	10	15	10	10	13	7	3	n	n	100	n	100	n
Japan*	14	12	11	12	13	7	11	10	n	n	7	98	2	100	n
Korea	14	12	12	11	12	5	8	9	n	4	6	91	9	100	n
Mexico	14	14	19	21	9	9	6	6	n	n	n	97	3	100	n
Netherlands	10	10	8	11	14	5	7	9	n	3	n	78	22	100	n
New Zealand*	24	17	12	12	x(1)	12	11	11	n	n	n	100	n	100	5
Norway*	16	13	9	11	10	n	8	10	7	n	10	94	6	100	n
Portugal*	13	13	15	17	10	n	10	10	3	n	n	90	10	100	n
Scotland*	19	10	9	9	x(1)	8	8	5	5	x(13)	n	73	27	100	n
Spain*	18	13	10	10	11	5	12	8	x(13)	x(13)	x(13)	88	12	100	n
Sweden*	22	14	12	13	12	x[2]	7	8	x[2]	7	n	94	6	100	n
Turkey[1]	17	13	10	12	13	n	7	3	7	10	2	93	7	100	10
United States	m	m	m	m	m	m	m	m	m	m	m	m	m	m	m
Country mean	*16*	*13*	*11*	*12*	*11*	*4*	*8*	*8*	*3*	*2*	*3*	*91*	*9*		*4*
NON-OECD COUNTRIES															
Argentina	13	13	13	15	8	8	8	8	a	a	5	90	10	100	m
Chile	x(12)	x(12)	x(12)	x(12)	x(12)	x(12)	x(12)	x(12)	x(12)	x(12)	x(12)	92	8	100	m
China	14	12	9	17	11	n	5	7	n	5	11	92	8	100	m
Egypt	24	13	11	8	13	5	5	5	5	5	4	100	a	100	m
India	11	13	15	13	13	a	4	6	a	a	9	83	17	100	m
Indonesia	16	16	14	13	6	a	5	5	5	15	5	100	a	100	m
Jamaica	17	14	14	14	6	17	6	6	6	3	n	100	n	100	m
Jordan	21	13	15	9	16	2	3	4	9	6	3	100	a	100	m
Malaysia	13	11	11	13	11	n	4	4	9	9	13	100	a	100	m
Paraguay	20	12	14	13	x(13)	12	10	5	2	x(7)	7	95	5	100	m
Peru[3]	14	14	12	23	6	a	6	6	6	7	a	93	7	100	m
Philippines	9	9	9	9	9	18	6	3	a	a	9	82	18	100	m
Russian Federation	23	13	14	13	8	6	4	5	a	a	m	87	13	100	m
Thailand	11	6	9	11	x(13)	x(13)	3	9	x(11)	6	14	69	31	100	m
Tunisia	33	13	5	15	7	5	7	10	5	n	n	100	a	100	m
Uruguay	13	13	19	18	8	a	5	5	a	a	a	81	19	100	m
Zimbabwe	14	14	11	9	14	9	7	4	7	10	2	100	n	100	m

Note: x indicates that data are included in another column. The column reference is shown in brackets after "x". *e.g.*, x(7) means that data are included in column 7.

1. Includes 12 to 13-year-olds only.
2. Included in various subjects.
3. Year of reference 1999.

* See Annex 3 for notes (*www.oecd.org/els/education/eag2002*).

Source: OECD.

D1

Table D1.3.
Additional instruction time and learning time of 15-year-olds (2000)
Percentage of students attending schools where additional courses are offered and percentage of students attending additional courses at and outside school, estimated average amount of hours spent on homework

	Percentage of students attending schools which offer...					Percentage of students reporting *regular* participation in extra-curricular courses *at school*				Percentage of students reporting *regular* attendance of courses *outside school*							Percentage of students who have *sometimes or regularly* attended courses *outside of school* in the language of assessment, courses in other subjects, or extension or additional courses in the last three years	Percentage of students who have *sometimes or regularly* attended remedial courses *outside of school* in the language of assessment, in other subjects, received training to improve study skills or private tutoring in the last three years	Estimated mean number of hours spent on homework in the language of assessment, mathematics and science courses
	extra courses on academic subjects for gifted students	special training in test language for low achievers	special courses in study skills for low achievers	special tutoring by staff members	room(s) where students can do their homework with staff help	Extension or additional courses	Remedial courses in test language	Remedial courses in other subjects	Training to improve study skills	Courses in test language	Courses in other subjects	Extension or additional courses	Remedial courses in test language	Remedial courses in other subjects	Training to improve study skills	Private tutoring			
OECD COUNTRIES																			
Australia	61	86	71	76	46	2	2	2	2	2	5	2	1	2	2	9	23	32	4.7
Austria	42	68	32	32	26	1	2	4	1	n	n	2	1	7	1	n	11	35	3.5
Belgium	12	51	63	67	43	2	2	4	2	1	4	n	n	1	1	3	22	17	4.3
Canada	50	77	68	79	61	3	1	2	3	n	n	3	1	1	2	6	14	32	5.0
Czech Republic	31	60	16	83	22	1	9	8	1	2	6	n	n	n	n	7	19	20	3.6
Denmark	9	78	19	96	32	n	4	3	n	1	2	1	2	2	n	1	15	14	4.7
Finland	78	80	14	93	35	1	n	3	1	n	n	1	n	1	n	1	5	9	3.5
France	4	70	59	39	41	2	5	8	2	3	7	2	2	4	1	7	m	m	4.9
Germany	45	46	15	14	25	2	2	5	2	n	n	3	1	5	1	9	10	36	4.5
Greece	4	76	n	70	17	n	13	12	n	n	n	n	n	10	n	n	m	25	7.0
Hungary	76	71	43	60	31	3	6	13	3	n	n	25	3	9	2	12	47	47	5.8
Iceland	27	93	45	82	57	3	8	11	3	1	3	1	2	4	1	6	18	27	4.7
Ireland	7	89	45	54	33	4	2	3	4	1	5	6	1	2	2	14	31	41	5.4
Italy	49	91	93	77	31	3	3	8	3	n	1	1	1	5	2	8	6	48	5.2
Japan	37	59	53	94	38	2	3	6	2	30	55	n	n	n	n	11	71	17	2.9
Korea	10	29	46	56	29	1	3	8	1	27	34	9	5	14	3	11	64	58	4.4
Luxembourg	18	89	54	83	61	2	4	7	2	3	4	1	2	4	6	2	22	37	4.0
Mexico	22	51	48	62	43	5	2	5	5	1	3	8	1	3	2	4	51	47	5.2
New Zealand	59	94	78	93	55	5	2	3	5	n	n	3	3	4	4	12	18	40	4.7
Norway	9	93	24	72	29	1	3	5	1	n	n	1	1	2	1	n	6	11	4.3
Poland	55	24	24	70	28	3	5	4	3	7	8	10	3	3	3	15	51	53	5.3
Portugal	1	99	42	87	75	2	6	7	2	2	5	1	n	4	1	14	21	45	5.0
Spain	8	54	52	79	28	2	2	7	2	3	12	n	3	11	1	22	31	54	5.4
Sweden	19	97	39	86	61	n	3	5	n	n	1	n	n	1	n	1	8	8	3.3
Switzerland	47	73	35	46	32	2	5	9	2	n	n	2	2	6	1	6	7	30	3.9
United Kingdom	52	83	65	91	79	7	2	6	7	2	5	n	n	n	3	8	20	24	5.4
United States	62	53	49	69	46	5	6	6	5	3	3	2	1	n	2	3	25	29	4.6
OECD total	*41*	*58*	*49*	*68*	*41*	*4*	*4*	*6*	*4*	*8*	*13*	*4*	*2*	*4*	*2*	*8*	*34*	*34*	*4.6*
Country average	*35*	*71*	*46*	*72*	*41*	*3*	*4*	*6*	*3*	*5*	*9*	*4*	*2*	*4*	*2*	*8*	*25*	*32*	*4.6*
NON-OECD COUNTRIES																			
Brazil	14	58	28	62	20	10	3	6	10	n	n	4	2	5	6	5	14	51	4.4
Latvia	76	48	48	94	48	3	6	10	3	3	9	9	2	4	2	11	55	56	m
Liechtenstein	71	63	16	57	31	2	6	6	2	4	n	4	2	3	1	5	10	29	m
Russian Federation	62	62	45	94	39	5	10	15	5	6	12	n	n	n	n	8	45	21	m
Netherlands[1]	15	55	60	60	54	m	2	4	2	m	m	m	m	m	m	5	m	18	4.1

1. Response rate is too low to ensure comparability (see Annex 3 at *www.oecd.org/els/education/eag2002*).

Source: OECD PISA database, 2001. See Annex 3 for notes on methodology (*www.oecd.org/els/education/eag2002*) and *www.pisa.oecd.org*.

D1

CLASS SIZE AND RATIO OF STUDENTS TO TEACHING STAFF

- The average class size in primary education is 22, but varies between countries from 36 students in Korea per class to less than half of that number in Greece, Iceland and Luxembourg.

- The number of students per class increases by an average of two students between primary and lower secondary education but ratios of students to teaching staff tend to decrease with increasing levels of education due to more annual instruction time.

Chart D2.1.

Average class size in public and private institutions, by level of education (2000)

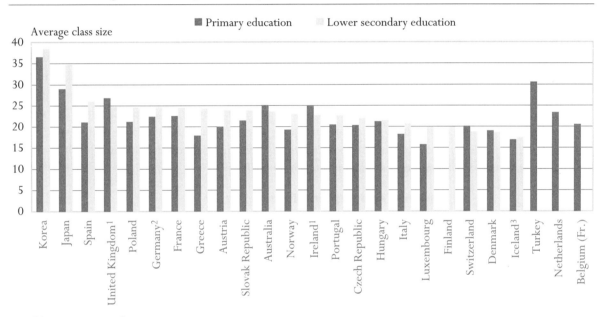

1. Public institutions only.
2. Year of reference 2001.
3. Including multi-grade classes.
Countries are ranked in descending order of average class size in lower secondary education.
Source: OECD. Table D2.1. See Annex 3 for notes *(www.oecd.org / els / education / eag2002).*

D2

Policy context

This indicator shows class sizes and ratios of students to teaching staff.

Class sizes are widely debated in many OECD countries. Smaller classes are valued because they may allow students to receive more individual attention from their teachers and reduce the disadvantage of managing large numbers of students and their work. Smaller class sizes may also influence parents when they choose schools for their children. However, the predominance of teacher costs in educational expenditure means that reducing class sizes leads to sharp increases in the costs of education.

Another important indicator of the resources devoted to education is the ratio of students to teaching staff. Because of the difficulty of constructing direct measures of educational quality, especially at higher levels of education, this indicator is often used as a proxy for quality, on the assumption that a smaller ratio of students to teaching staff means better student access to teaching resources. However, a smaller ratio of students to teaching staff may have to be weighed against higher salaries for teachers, greater investment in teaching technology, or more widespread use of assistant teachers and other paraprofessionals whose salaries are often considerably lower than those of qualified teachers. Moreover, as larger numbers of children with special educational needs are integrated into normal classes, more use of specialised personnel and support services may limit the resources available for reducing the ratio of students to teaching staff.

Evidence and explanations

Average class size in primary and lower secondary education

The average class size in primary education is 22, but varies between countries from 36 students per class to less than half of that.

The average class size in primary education varies widely between OECD countries. It ranges from 36 students per primary class in Korea to fewer than 20 in Denmark, Greece, Iceland, Italy, Luxembourg and Norway. At the lower secondary level, the average class size varies from 38 students per class in Korea to fewer than 20 in Denmark, Finland, Iceland, Luxembourg and Switzerland (Table D2.1).

The number of students per class increases by an average of two between primary and lower secondary education.

The number of students per class tends to increase, on average, by two students between primary and lower secondary education. In Greece, Japan, Luxembourg and Spain, the increase in average class size exceeds four students, while Australia, Denmark, Ireland, Switzerland and United Kingdom show a drop in the number of students per class between these two levels (Chart D2.1). The indicator on class size is limited to primary and lower secondary education because class sizes are difficult to define and compare at higher levels of education, where students often attend several different classes, depending on the subject area.

Public institutions have three students or more per class than private institutions in the Czech Republic, Greece, Norway, Poland, Switzerland and Turkey.

In nine out of the 20 countries with comparable data, the difference in class sizes between public and private institutions exceeds three students at the primary level. Differences tend to be smaller at the lower secondary level but the average class size in private lower secondary schools is still lower than in public schools in eight out of the 18 countries (Table D2.1).

Ratio of students to teaching staff

The indicator also provides the ratio of students to teaching staff, which is obtained by dividing the number of full-time equivalent students at a given level of education by the number of full-time equivalent "teachers" at that level and in similar types of institutions. The relationship between the ratio of students to teaching staff and average class size is influenced by many factors, including the number of hours during which a student attends class each day, the length of a teacher's working day, the number of classes or students for which a teacher is responsible, the subject taught, the division of the teacher's time between teaching and other duties, the grouping of students within classes and the practice of team-teaching.

Many factors contribute to differences in the ratio of students to teaching staff.

In primary education, the ratio of students to teaching staff, expressed in full-time equivalents, ranges from 32 students per teacher in Korea to 10 in Denmark. The country mean in primary education is 18 students per teacher. There is slightly more variation between countries in the ratio of students to teaching staff at the secondary level, ranging from more than 21 students per full-time equivalent teacher in Korea and Mexico to below 11 in Belgium, Greece, Italy, Luxembourg and Portugal. On average across countries, the ratio of students to teaching staff at the secondary level of education is 14, which is close to the ratios in Finland (14), Germany (15), Japan (15), Poland (15), Sweden (14), Turkey (14), the United Kingdom (15) and the United States (15) (Table D2.2).

In Korea and Turkey, the ratio of students to teaching staff in primary education is approximately three times as high as in Denmark and Hungary.

As the difference in the mean ratio of students to teaching staff between primary and secondary education indicates, there are fewer students per teacher as the level of education rises. With the exception of Canada, Denmark, Hungary, Mexico, the Netherlands, Poland and Sweden, the ratio of students to teaching staff in every OECD country decreases between primary and secondary levels of education, despite a tendency for class sizes to increase. This is mostly because instruction time tends to increase with the level of education.

There are fewer students per teacher as the level of education rises.

In France, Korea and Turkey, the decrease in the ratio of students to teaching staff from the primary to the secondary levels is between seven and 16 students per full-time equivalent teacher, which is more marked compared to other countries. In France and Korea, this mainly reflects differences in the annual instruction time, but it may also result from delays in matching the teaching force to demographic changes, or from differences in teaching hours for teachers at different levels of education. The general trend is consistent across countries, but it is not obvious from an educational perspective why a smaller ratio of students to teaching staff should be more desirable at higher levels of education (Table D2.2).

Chart D2.2.

Ratio of students to teaching staff in public and private institutions, by level of education (2000)

Primary education
Number of students per teacher in full-time equivalents

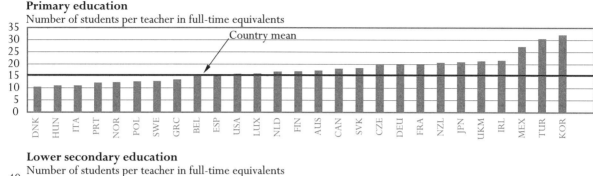

Lower secondary education
Number of students per teacher in full-time equivalents

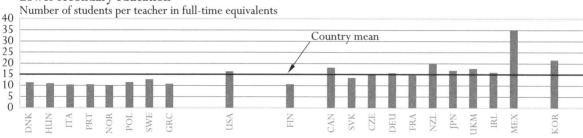

Upper secondary education
Number of students per teacher in full-time equivalents

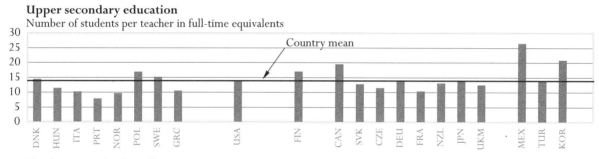

Tertiary-type B education
Number of students per teacher in full-time equivalents

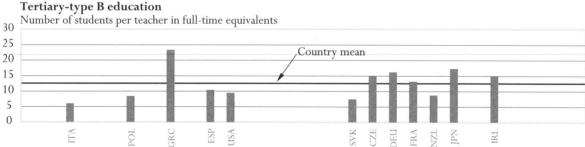

Tertiary-type A and advanced research programmes
Number of students per teacher in full-time equivalents

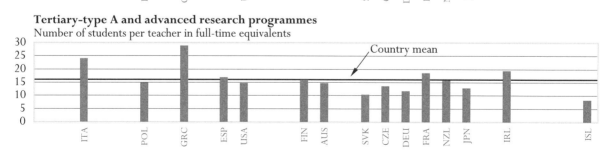

Note: Please refer to the Reader's Guide for list of country codes and country names used in this chart.
Countries are ranked in ascending order of number of students per teacher in primary education.
Source: OECD. Table D2.2. See Annex 3 for notes *(www.oecd.org/els/education/eag2002).*

The ratio of students to teaching staff in public and private tertiary institutions ranges from 27 students per teacher in Greece to 12 or below in Canada, Germany, Iceland, Japan, the Slovak Republic and Sweden (Table D2.2). Such comparisons in tertiary education, however, should be made with caution since it is still difficult to calculate full-time equivalent students and teachers on a comparable basis at this level.

In 11 out of the 12 countries for which data are available for both tertiary-type A and advanced research programmes and tertiary-type B education, the ratio of students to teaching staff is lower, at 12, in the generally more occupationally specific tertiary-type B programmes than in tertiary-type A and advanced research programmes, which have an average ratio of 16 (Chart D2.2). Germany is the only country with a higher ratio in tertiary-type B programmes.

The ratio of students to teaching staff in pre-primary education tends to be lower than in primary education, but slightly higher than in secondary education. In pre-primary education, the ratio ranges from fewer than seven students per teacher in Denmark and Iceland to over 22 students per teacher in Germany, Korea and Mexico. There is little apparent relationship between the ratio of students to teaching staff in pre-primary and primary education, suggesting that the staffing requirements or emphases at these levels differ within countries (Table D2.2).

Definitions and methodologies

Class sizes have been calculated by dividing the number of students enrolled by the number of classes. In order to ensure comparability between countries, special needs programmes have been excluded. Data include only regular programmes at primary and lower secondary levels of education and exclude teaching in sub-groups outside the regular classroom setting.

"Teaching staff" refers to professional personnel directly involved in teaching students. The classification includes classroom teachers; special education teachers; and other teachers who work with a whole class of students in a classroom, in small groups in a resource room, or in one-to-one teaching situations inside or outside a regular classroom. Teaching staff also includes department chairpersons whose duties include some teaching, but excludes non-professional personnel who support teachers in providing instruction to students, such as teachers' aides and other paraprofessional personnel.

In general, the ratio of students to teaching staff at the tertiary level tends to be similar to that in secondary education.

The ratio of students to teaching staff in pre-primary education tends to be between that in primary and secondary education.

Data refer to the school year 1999-2000, and are based on the UOE data collection on education statistics that is administered annually by the OECD.

D2

Table D2.1.
Average class size, by type of institution and level of education (2000)

	Primary education				Lower secondary education			
	Public institutions	Government-dependent private institutions	Independent private institutions	Total: Public and private institutions	Public institutions	Government-dependent private institutions	Independent private institutions	Total: Public and private institutions
	(1)	(2)	(3)	(4)	(5)	(6)	(7)	(8)
Australia	24.9	25.9	a	25.0	23.6	22.2	a	23.5
Austria	19.9	22.7	x(2)	20.0	23.8	25.3	x(6)	23.9
Belgium (Fl.)	m	m	m	m	m	m	m	m
Belgium (Fr.)	20.2	21.0	m	20.5	21.1	m	m	m
Canada	m	m	m	m	m	m	m	m
Czech Republic	20.4	12.7	a	20.3	22.0	18.7	a	21.9
Denmark	19.0	m	m	19.0	18.6	m	m	18.6
Finland	m	m	a	m	m	m	a	19.9
France	22.3	23.9	n	22.6	24.4	24.8	x(6)	24.5
Germany[1]	22.4	24.0	x(2)	22.4	24.5	26.0	x(6)	24.6
Greece	17.7	a	21.3	17.9	24.1	a	27.4	24.2
Hungary	21.3	19.9	a	21.2	21.5	22.2	a	21.5
Iceland*[1]	16.9	18.9	n	16.9	17.4	14.3	n	17.4
Ireland	24.8	m	m	m	22.7	m	m	m
Italy	18.1	a	20.7	18.2	20.7	a	20.8	20.7
Japan	28.9	a	34.8	29.0	34.5	a	37.9	34.7
Korea	36.5	a	36.4	36.5	38.7	37.9	a	38.5
Luxembourg	15.5	21.0	19.6	15.7	19.9	20.8	19.1	19.9
Mexico	m	m	m	m	m	m	m	m
Netherlands	m	m	m	23.9	m	m	m	m
New Zealand	m	m	m	m	m	m	m	m
Norway	19.3	16.1	x(2)	19.3	22.9	19.1	x(6)	22.8
Poland	21.3	12.7	a	21.2	24.8	13.0	a	24.6
Portugal	20.2	23.6	x(2)	20.5	22.7	22.0	x(6)	22.6
Slovak Republic	21.4	21.5	n	21.4	23.8	24.5	n	23.8
Spain	19.7	25.0	21.6	21.1	25.0	29.0	22.6	26.0
Sweden	m	m	m	m	m	m	m	m
Switzerland	20.2	12.5	15.8	20.1	18.9	18.0	16.4	18.8
Turkey	30.9	a	21.1	30.6	a	a	a	a
United Kingdom	26.8	m	m	m	24.7	a	m	m
United States	m	m	m	m	m	m	m	m
Country mean	*22.1*	*20.1*	*23.9*	*21.9*	*23.6*	*22.5*	*24.0*	*23.6*
Israel	m	m	m	26.7	m	m	m	31.6

OECD COUNTRIES / *NON-OECD COUNTRY*

*See Annex 3 for notes (*www.oecd.org/els/education/eag2002*).

Note: x indicates that data are included in another column. The column reference is shown in brackets after "x". *e.g.*, x(2) means that data are included in column 2.
1. Year of reference 2001.
2. Including multi-grade classes.
Source: OECD.

Table D2.2.
Ratio of students to teaching staff in public and private institutions by level of education, calculations based on full-time equivalents (2000)

	Pre-primary education	Primary education	Lower secondary education	Upper secondary education	All secondary education	Post secondary non-tertiary education	Tertiary-type B education	Tertiary-type A and advanced research programmes	All tertiary education
	(1)	(2)	(3)	(4)	(5)	(6)	(7)	(8)	(9)
OECD COUNTRIES									
Australia[1]	m	17.3	m	m	12.6	m	m	14.8	m
Austria	m	m	m	m	m	m	m	m	m
Belgium*	x(2)	15.0	x(5)	x(5)	9.7	x(5)	x(9)	x(9)	19.9
Canada	18.1	18.1	18.1	19.5	18.8	x(9)	x(9)	x(9)	9.8
Czech Republic	13.1	19.7	14.7	11.5	13.1	11.0	12.1	13.7	13.5
Denmark	6.6	10.4	11.4	14.4	12.8	m	m	m	m
Finland*	12.2	16.9	10.7	17.0	13.8	x(4)	x(4)	16.1	m
France	19.1	19.8	14.7	10.4	12.5	11.4	16.2	18.6	18.3
Germany*	23.6	19.8	15.7	13.9	15.2	14.3	14.9	11.7	12.1
Greece	15.8	13.4	10.8	10.5	10.7	m	23.3	28.9	26.8
Hungary	11.6	10.9	10.9	11.4	11.2	x(4)	x(9)	x(9)	13.1
Iceland	5.4	x(3)	12.7	9.7	m	m	m	8.3	7.9
Ireland*	15.1	21.5	15.9	x(3)	x(3)	x(3)	14.8	19.4	17.4
Italy*	13.0	11.0	10.4	10.2	10.3	m	6.0	24.1	22.8
Japan	18.8	20.9	16.8	14.0	15.2	m	8.8	12.9	11.4
Korea	23.1	32.1	21.5	20.9	21.2	a	m	m	m
Luxembourg[2]	20.2	15.9	x(5)	x(5)	9.2	m	m	m	m
Mexico	22.4	27.2	34.8	26.5	31.7	m	x(9)	x(9)	15.1
Netherlands	x(2)	16.8	x(5)	x(5)	17.1	x(5)	m	m	12.6
New Zealand	7.5	20.6	19.9	13.1	16.3	12.6	13.2	15.8	15.2
Norway	m	12.4	9.9	9.7	m	x(4)	x(9)	x(9)	12.7
Poland	13.1	12.7	11.5	16.9	15.5	17.1	8.4	14.9	14.7
Portugal	16.4	12.1	10.4	7.9	9.0	m	x(9)	x(9)	m
Slovak Republic	10.1	18.3	13.5	12.8	13.2	9.0	7.4	10.3	10.2
Spain	16.1	14.9	x(5)	x(5)	11.9	x(5)	10.5	16.9	15.9
Sweden	m	12.8	12.8	15.2	14.1	m	x(9)	x(9)	9.3
Switzerland[2]	m	m	m	m	m	m	m	m	m
Turkey	16.0	30.5	m	14.0	14.0	m	m	m	m
United Kingdom*[1]	21.0	21.2	17.6	12.5	14.8	m	x(9)	x(9)	17.6
United States	18.7	15.8	16.3	14.1	15.2	10.1	9.5	14.8	13.5
Country mean	*15.5*	*17.7*	*15.0*	*13.9*	*14.3*	*12.2*	*12.1*	*16.1*	*14.7*
NON-OECD COUNTRIES									
Argentina[2,3]	19.9	22.7	13.2	9.0	11.2	a	12.1	8.0	9.3
Brazil[3]	18.5	26.6	34.2	38.7	35.6	m	x(9)	x(9)	14.1
Chile[3]	39.3	34.0	33.4	28.5	30.2	a	m	m	m
China[3]	26.7	20.2	17.6	13.8	16.4	10.1	31.0	8.5	12.3
Egypt	a	23.0	22.0	12.8	17.1	m	m	m	m
India[2,3]	m	43.0	22.0	9.2	16.1	20.8	m	m	m
Indonesia[4]	33.0	27.1	19.6	17.8	18.9	a	x(9)	x(9)	15.0
Jamaica	22.1	30.4	x(5)	x(5)	18.5	x(7)	19.4	13.4	16.5
Jordan[2]	19.4	x(3)	21.2	16.9	20.6	a	15.6	34.9	29.5
Malaysia[3]	26.9	21.3	17.7	18.3	17.9	24.7	17.3	20.2	19.1
Paraguay[3]	x(2)	18.0	x(5)	x(5)	30.6	a	17.2	m	m
Peru[3]	25.9	26.8	x(5)	x(5)	18.5	m	m	m	m
Philippines[3]	32.9	34.7	40.5	21.2	34.1	m	a	23.6	23.6
Russian Federation[4]	7.0	17.3	m	m	m	10.2	15.1	15.3	15.2
Tunisia[2]	19.8	23.3	24.9	17.4	21.5	a	x(9)	x(9)	19.2
Uruguay[3]	31.3	20.4	11.9	22.6	14.9	a	x(9)	x(9)	8.1
Zimbabwe[4]	m	37.0	x(5)	x(5)	24.7	m	m	m	m

*See Annex 3 for notes (*www.oecd.org/els/education/eag2002*).

Note: x indicates that data are included in another column. The column reference is shown in brackets after "x". *e.g.*, x(2) means that data are included in column 2.

1. Includes only general programmes in lower and upper secondary education.
2. Public institutions only.
3. Year of reference 1999.
4. Year of reference 2001.

Source: OECD.

D₂

USE AND AVAILABILITY OF COMPUTERS AT SCHOOL AND IN THE HOME

- On average in OECD countries, the typical 15-year-old attends a school where there are 13 students for every computer. However, the figure varies widely across countries and in some countries it varies between regions and schools.

- On average across countries, about one-third of 15-year-olds reported using a computer at school every day or at least a few times per week, but the frequency of computer use at home is almost twice that proportion. However, the percentage of 15-year-olds who say that they never have a computer available to use is 10 points higher in the home than at school, suggesting that schools may play an important role in bridging the educational gap between the "information-haves and have-nots".

Chart D3.1.

Ratio of students to computers (2000)

Total number of students enrolled in the school divided by the total number of computers for the school in which 15-year-olds are enrolled, weighted by student enrolment, by quartile

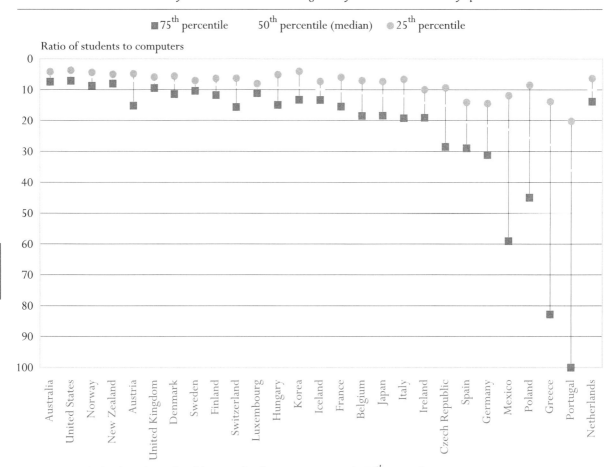

Countries are ranked in descending order of the ratio of students to computers at the 50th percentile.
Source: OECD PISA database, 2001. Table D3.1. See Annex 3 for notes on methodology *(www.oecd.org/els/education/eag2002)* and *www.pisa.oecd.org.*

Policy context

OECD economies depend increasingly on technological knowledge and skills in the labour force. Students with little or no exposure to computers and information technology may face difficulties in making a smooth transition to the modern labour market. The integration of computers into the learning environment at school has important implications in the classroom, but the increasing availability of affordable home computers, software, and access to the Internet and e-mail means that students are often more likely to come into frequent contact with computers at home than at school. The way in which students use computers in the home is also taking on a greater educational role, increasingly incorporating non game-playing activities such as word-processing, databases, spreadsheets, programming, the Internet and Web design. Nevertheless, schools have an important role to play, especially in bridging the gap between the "information-haves and have-nots".

PISA 2000 explored three aspects of computer familiarity among 15-year-olds both at school and at home: interest in computers, self-assessment of attitudes and ability to work with computers, and use of and experience with computers. This indicator explores several of these aspects.

This indicator shows the use and availability of information technology to 15-year-olds.

Evidence and explanations

Ratio of students to computers at school

The average number of students per computer is often used as a proxy for the extent to which technology is accessible to students. In PISA, principals of the schools in which 15-year-olds were enrolled were asked the total number of computers available in the school. A ratio of students to computers was then calculated by dividing the total number of computers by the total number of students enrolled in each school. To better explain how computer availability may vary between schools within each country, the 25th, 50th and 75th percentiles of the ratio are also presented. A ratio of students to computers of 20 at the 25th percentile, for example, means that 25 per cent of 15-year-olds attend a school where there are 20 students or less per computer. Similarly, a ratio of 30 students per computer at the 50th percentile means that, among 15-year-olds, 50 per cent of students attend a school where there are 30 students or less per computer. Ratios of students to computers were also calculated separately for public, private government-independent and private government-dependent institutions, and for schools in villages, towns and cities.

The average number of students per computer is a proxy for the extent to which information technologies are accessible to students...

The availability of hardware does not guarantee its effective use by students and teachers, nor does it indicate how easily the technology can be accessed when needed in the classroom, laboratories, school libraries or other locations. Nor does the ratio guarantee the quality of hardware (*e.g.*, compatibility, memory, speed, age of the machine, attached peripheral devices and software) that is appropriate for classroom use. Finally, average ratios may hide variation between schools according to such factors as the geographical or socio-economic location of the school and the type of educational institution.

...although accessibility does not guarantee the effective use of computers.

D3

Across OECD countries, the typical 15–year–old attends a school where 13 students share one computer, but the ratio varies widely.

On average in OECD countries, a typical 15-year-old attends schools where there is one computer for every 13 students, but the ratio varies widely. In Australia and the United States, the ratio is five students per computer and it is six in New Zealand and Norway. On the other hand, in Germany, Greece, Mexico, Poland, Portugal and Spain, 15-year-olds attend schools where, on average, more than 20 students share one computer. In some of these countries, most notably Greece, Mexico, Poland and Portugal, access to computers varies widely across schools, as indicated by large differences between the 25th and 75th percentiles in the ratio of students to computers (Chart D3.1 and Table D3.1).

Access to computers can also be influenced by the extent to which local and regional governments and private stakeholders invest in these new technologies.

Access to computers can also be influenced by the extent to which local, regional and national governments and private decision-making bodies are prepared to finance the purchase of hardware in schools. Related policies and decisions may also target schools in remote geographical areas or in low socio-economic inner-city areas. Further information provided by school principals participating in PISA made it possible to calculate the ratio of students per computer by school location and by type of educational institution.

In some countries, access to computers is markedly better in private schools…

In some countries, 15-year-olds will have better access to computers in private schools. The contrast with public schools is marked in Greece and Mexico, where there are fewer than 10 students per computer in private schools, compared to up to 32 students per computer in public schools. In other countries, access to computers does not vary between types of institutions (Table D3.1).

…and sometimes access differs considerably depending on the school location.

In Australia, Finland, New Zealand, the United Kingdom and the United States, the ratios of students to computers do not differ greatly between geographical locations. Ratios vary between five and six students per computer in Australia and the United States, irrespective of whether the school is located in a village of fewer than 3 000 people, a small town of 15 000 to 100 000 people, close to the centre of a city of over one million people or elsewhere in a city of over one million people. This is not the case in the Czech Republic, Hungary and Ireland, where a student attending a school located in an urban area has greater access to computers than a student attending a school in a rural area. In Ireland, for example, the ratio of students per computer in a school located in a village is 14 (in which 28 per cent of the student population goes to school), but in schools located close to cities of over one million people, there are nine students for every computer in the school. The reverse is true of students studying in schools in rural areas in Korea, Mexico, Poland and Spain, who have far greater access to computers than students who are studying in schools in urban areas (Table D3.1).

Availability and use of computers at school

On average across countries, about one-third of 15-year-olds

Between 45 and 65 per cent of 15-year-olds reported using a computer at school almost every day or a few times each week in Australia, Denmark, Finland, Hungary, Scotland and Sweden. By contrast, in Germany and Switzerland,

D3

this percentage is only 18 and 22 per cent respectively, and in Mexico half of 15-year-olds reported never using a computer at school (Table D3.5).

In most countries, 15-year-olds reported using computers at home far more frequently than at school. On average across countries, 60 per cent of 15-year-olds reported using a computer at home almost every day or a few times each week, and in Australia, Canada, Denmark, Finland, Norway, Sweden and the United States, this is between 66 and 82 per cent. Even in Germany and Switzerland, where computer use at school is comparatively low, almost two-thirds of 15-year-olds reported using a computer at home almost every day or a few times each week. The only exceptions to this pattern are Hungary and Mexico, where 15-year-olds reported using computers more frequently at school than at home (Table D3.5).

reported using a computer at school almost every day or a few times each week, but this varies widely.

Students and teachers are using the Internet and local area networks more widely both as a communication and as a research tool. While a slow, costly connection to the Internet at a school with an insufficiently flexible curriculum may result in little educational value, Internet and computer networks that are effectively used in the classroom can add a new dimension to learning and teaching methodologies. In PISA, school principals were asked how many computers in the school were connected to the Internet and to a local area network. On average, approximately half of all computers in schools in OECD countries are connected to the Internet or a local area network. In Australia and Luxembourg, this proportion is more than 75 per cent, while less than one-quarter of computers in schools in Italy and Mexico are connected to the Internet or a local area network (Table D3.2). In Australia, Austria, Denmark, Finland, Iceland and Sweden, more than 50 per cent of 15-year-olds reported using the Internet at school several times a month or several times a week. For data see *www.oecd.org/els/education/eag2002*.

Around one-third of students use the Internet at school several times per week or at least several times per month.

While measures of availability of computers in schools such as those described in this indicator may provide some indication of the success of national policies for resourcing computers in education, availability alone does not guarantee quality or effective use of computers for learning. To extend the picture, school principals in PISA were asked to what extent they perceived that the lack of computers and multi-media resources for instruction hindered the learning of 15-year-olds. School principals were also asked about the quality of other educational resources, such as instructional material, instruction materials in the library, science laboratory equipment and facilities for the fine arts. On average, more than any other type of instructional material, lack of computers and multi-media resources was perceived by school principals as being the greatest hindrance to learning (Table D5.3). In OECD countries, more than 37 per cent of 15-year-olds were enrolled in schools where principals reported that learning was hindered to some extent or a lot by the lack of computers for instruction. However, while school principals in Greece and Mexico expressed the most concern about the lack of computers and multi-media resources

School principals consider a lack of computers and multi-media resources to be more of an obstacle to learning than a lack of any other type of instructional material.

D3

impeding the learning process, school principals in Australia, Belgium, Hungary, Switzerland and the United States, where levels of computer availability are markedly higher, reported that learning was not hindered at all by a lack of computers and multi-media resources for instruction (Table D3.3).

On average across countries, 15 per cent of computers in schools are exclusively for use by teachers and 12 per cent are exclusively reserved for use by administrative staff.

Computers are also a vital tool for teachers and school administrators, who use computers to complete every day tasks such as updating student records, writing letters to parents and committees, completing electronic student assessments, preparing lessons and updating school and class web sites. In the PISA school questionnaire, school principals were asked how many computers in the school were available for 15-year-old students, for teachers only, and for administrative staff only. Fifteen per cent of computers in schools are for use by teachers only and a further 12 per cent by administrative staff only. In Greece, Korea, Portugal and the United States, more than one-fifth of the total number of computers available in the school are used exclusively by teachers. In Belgium, Greece, Mexico and Portugal, more than 15 per cent of computers in the school are available only to administrative staff (Table D3.2).

Availability and use of computers at home

Access to computers and educational software at home has grown rapidly in many countries with an average of about three quarters of 15-year-olds now reporting having at least one computer at home…

Students' use of computers at home has the potential to complement the learning process at school and improve attitudes towards learning, thus bridging formal classroom learning and informal learning that occurs at home.

Over the last five to 10 years, the home personal computer market has risen dramatically. The marketing of home computers increasingly targets family and educational use rather than games, reflecting the increasing availability of affordable hardware and software, and parents growing awareness of the role that computers can play in their child's education. More recently, inexpensive home Internet connections have become more common. In 2000, an average of 73 per cent of 15-year-old students in OECD countries reported having at least one computer in the home. More than 40 per cent of 15-year-olds in Denmark, Iceland, Norway, Sweden and the United Kingdom reported having two or more computers in the home. Over 55 per cent of 15-year-olds in OECD countries, on average, reported having educational software at home; in Australia, Canada, Iceland, New Zealand, Sweden, United Kingdom and the United States the figure was 75 per cent or more. Forty-five per cent of 15-year-olds in OECD countries reported being connected to the Internet at home. In Iceland and Sweden, more than three-quarters of 15-year-olds have Internet access at home. (For data see *www.oecd.org/els/education/eag2002.*)

D3

…and daily contact with computers much more likely to occur in the home than at school …

This indicator also shows that for many 15-year-olds, daily contact with computers is much more likely to occur in the home than at school. An average of 64 per cent of 15-year-olds in OECD countries reported having home computers available for use every day, but only 27 per cent had this facility at school (Chart D3.2 and Table D3.4).

Chart D3.2.

Availability and frequency of the use of computers for 15-year-olds at home and at school (2000)

Distribution of mean percentages of 15-year-olds who reported having a computer available to use and those who reported using computers at home and at school

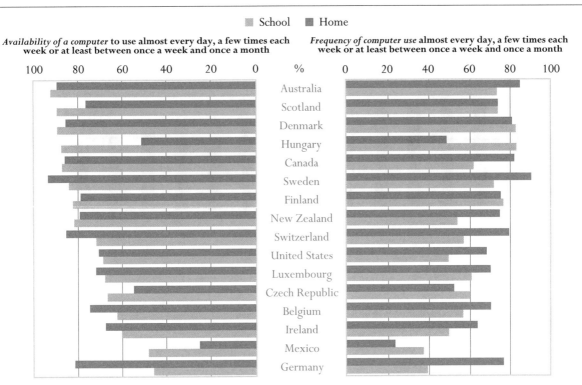

■ School   ■ Home

Countries are ranked in ascending order of the availability of a computer to use almost every day, a few times each week or between once a week and once a month at school.

Source: OECD PISA database, 2001. Tables D3.4 and D3.5. See Annex 3 for notes on methodology *(www.oecd.org/els/education/eag2002)* and *www.pisa.oecd.org.*

Interestingly, the percentage of 15-year-olds who say that they never have a computer available to use is 10 percentage points higher in the home than at school, suggesting that schools may be helping to bridge the educational gap between the "information-haves and have-nots".

In PISA, 15-year-olds were asked how often they used computers to help them learn school material. An average of 11 per cent reported that they used computers almost every day to help them learn school material; 24 per cent use computers a few times each week; and 26 per cent use them between once a week and once a month. However, more than 25 per cent of 15-year-olds in Belgium, the Czech Republic, Hungary, Ireland and Switzerland reported that they never use computers to help them with schoolwork (Chart D3.3 and Table D3.6).

…but in other countries, a large gap remains between the "information haves and have-nots".

Not all computer use at home is related to school-learning.

D3

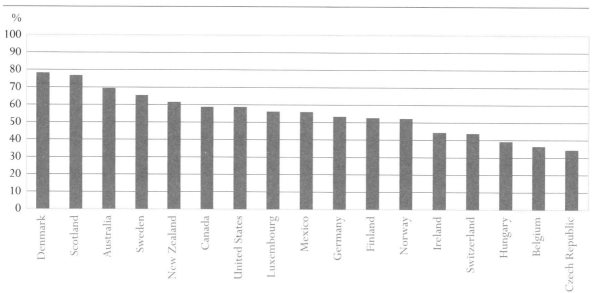

15-year-olds' use of computers to help them learn school material (2000)

Distribution of mean percentages of 15-year-olds who reported using computers to help them learn school material almost every day, a few times each week or at least between once a week and once a month

Countries are ranked in descending order of the percentage of 15-year-olds who reported using computers to help them learn school material almost every day, a few times each week or at least between once a week and once a month.
Source: OECD PISA database, 2001. Table D3.6. See Annex 3 for notes on methodology *(www.oecd.org/els/education/eag2002)* and *www.pisa.oecd.org.*

Definitions and methodologies

Results from this indicator derive from background questionnaires completed by 15-year-old students and their principals as part of the Programme for International Student Assessment (PISA) under-taken by the OECD in 2000.

D3

Data used in this indicator derive from responses of 15-year-old students and school principals to questions related to computer use and availability of computers at home and at school in three background questionnaires used in the 2000 cycle of the OECD Programme for International Student Assessment (PISA).

In addition to a written test, 15-year-olds participating in PISA completed a student questionnaire that was designed to collect information about the student's family, home environment, reading habits, school and everyday activities. Students' responses to questions on the frequency of use of computers and the Internet at school (Table D3.2) derive from this questionnaire. A second background questionnaire on computer familiarity was completed by students in 20 countries as part of an international option exploring students' interest in computers, self-assessment of their attitudes and ability to work with computers, and use of and experience with computers. Data used in this indicator on the availability and use of computers at home and at school (Chart D3.2, Table D3.4 and Table D3.5), and the extent to which students use computers to help them learn school material (Chart D3.3 and Table D3.6) are taken from this questionnaire. Students' responses were weighted to be proportional to the number of 15-year-olds in each school.

The principals of the schools in which students were assessed also completed a questionnaire on the characteristics of their school. Data presented here relating to the availability of computers, including the number of students per computer (Chart D3.1, Table D3.1 and Table D3.2) and principals' perception of quality of educational resources (Table D3.3), derive from principals' responses to this questionnaire. These were weighted to be proportional to the number of 15-year-olds in each school.

D3

Table D3.1.
Ratio of students to computers (2000)
Total number of students enrolled in the school divided by the total number of computers for the school in which 15-year-olds are enrolled, by quartile, type of institution and location of school, weighted by student enrolment

| | | Ratio of students to computers | | Ratio of students to computers, by type of institution | | | | | |
| | | | | Government-independent private schools | | Government-dependent private schools | | Public schools | |
	25th percentile	50th percentile (median)	75th percentile	50th percentile (median)	% students represented in the sample	50th percentile (median)	% students represented in the sample	50th percentile (median)	% students represented in the sample
OECD COUNTRIES									
Australia	4	5	7	m	m	m	m	m	m
Austria	5	7	15	11	7	9	6	7	87
Belgium	7	11	18	10	1	12	75	9	75
Czech Republic	9	15	28	9	n	10	6	17	94
Denmark	6	8	11	a	a	7	24	8	76
Finland	6	8	12	a	a	20	3	8	97
France	6	11	15	11	8	8	13	11	79
Germany	14	22	31	a	a	19	3	22	97
Greece	14	28	83	10	3	a	a	32	97
Hungary	5	9	15	8	1	11	4	9	95
Iceland	7	10	13	10	1	a	a	10	99
Ireland	10	14	19	9	3	15	60	13	37
Italy	7	12	19	8	4	a	a	13	96
Japan	7	12	18	12	29	15	1	11	70
Korea	4	9	13	10	33	7	16	9	51
Luxembourg	8	9	11	a	a	7	11	10	89
Mexico	12	23	59	9	16	a	a	26	84
New Zealand	5	6	8	2	4	4	n	6	96
Norway	4	6	9	a	a	1	1	6	99
Poland	8	26	45	10	3	a	a	27	97
Portugal	20	36	100	32	2	124	5	36	93
Spain	14	21	29	21	9	25	31	18	60
Sweden	7	8	10	a	a	9	3	8	97
Switzerland	6	9	16	16	4	7	2	9	94
United Kingdom	6	8	9	6	5	a	a	8	95
United States	4	5	7	6	4	4	1	5	95
Country mean	*8*	*13*	*24*	*11*	*8*	*17*	*15*	*14*	*84*
NON-OECD COUNTRIES									
Brazil	15	26	39	a	a	15	1	27	99
Latvia	4	5	12	3	4	a	a	6	96
Liechtenstein	31	57	88	a	a	a	a	57	100
Russian Federation	6	10	14	a	a	10	76	8	24
Netherlands[1]	6	10	14	2	4	4	n	6	96

| | Ratio of students to computers, by school location | | | | | | | |
| | Fewer than 3 000 people [village] | | From 15 000 to 100 000 people [town] | | Over 1 000 000 people [close to the centre of a city] | | Over 1 000 000 people [elsewhere in a city] | |
	50th percentile (median)	% students represented in the sample	50th percentile (median)	% students represented in the sample	50th percentile (median)	% students represented in the sample	50th percentile (median)	% students represented in the sample
OECD COUNTRIES								
Australia	6	5	6	23	5	15	5	20
Austria	10	6	6	28	4	5	15	11
Belgium	20	4	10	51	8	1	a	a
Czech Republic	19	6	15	40	13	2	16	10
Denmark	6	29	9	25	9	8	11	3
Finland	7	17	9	34	10	15	8	6
France	9	7	9	52	57	1	8	3
Germany	18	6	23	43	15	2	22	4
Greece	18	8	32	38	33	9	17	6
Hungary	12	1	8	39	10	10	7	9
Iceland	m	m	m	m	m	m	m	m
Ireland	14	28	16	13	12	12	9	8
Italy	9	2	13	54	a	a	12	12
Japan	a	a	13	28	18	9	15	4
Korea	7	3	5	10	11	15	11	29
Luxembourg	a	a	8	19	a	a	a	a
Mexico	11	7	23	26	33	6	22	9
New Zealand	6	14	6	33	7	12	6	13
Norway	5	38	8	20	a	a	a	a
Poland	7	3	27	41	39	7	4	2
Portugal	20	4	27	39	101	7	26	1
Spain	12	2	21	32	22	4	29	5
Sweden	8	23	8	34	10	4	4	1
Switzerland	9	12	9	25	a	a	a	a
United Kingdom	8	10	7	35	8	4	8	4
United States	4	6	6	33	6	5	6	7
Country mean	*11*	*10*	*13*	*33*	*20*	*7*	*12*	*8*
NON-OECD COUNTRIES								
Brazil	91	4	140	26	108	15	223	9
Latvia	19	18	29	27	23	6	a	a
Liechtenstein	4	21	a	a	a	a	a	a
Russian Federation	50	26	54	22	57	9	62	6
Netherlands[1]	a	a	10	63	a	a	a	a

1. Response rate is too low to ensure comparability (see Annex 3 at *www.oecd.org/els/education/eag2002*).
Source: OECD PISA database, 2001. See Annex 3 for notes on methodology (*www.oecd.org/els/education/eag2002*) and *www.pisa.oecd.org*.

D3

Table D3.2.
Availability of computers and computer networks in schools in which 15-year-olds are enrolled (2000)
Percentage of computers available to students, teachers and administrative staff and computers connected to the Internet / WWW and local area networks,
as reported by school principals, weighted by student enrolment

	Percentage of computers available to 15-year-olds	Percentage of computers available only to teachers	Percentage of computers available only to administrative staff	Percentage of computers connected to the Internet/ World Wide Web	Percentage of computers connected to a local area network (LAN)
	%	%	%	%	%
Australia	70	16	8	80	75
Austria	75	9	7	69	56
Belgium	62	9	16	45	33
Czech Republic	63	20	15	40	46
Denmark	63	8	10	65	50
Finland	77	11	8	84	57
France	59	9	13	26	19
Germany	68	10	13	37	25
Greece	51	24	33	26	23
Hungary	72	11	10	58	65
Iceland	51	15	8	83	62
Ireland	69	10	8	47	28
Italy	61	10	13	24	21
Japan	66	20	4	35	40
Korea	56	34	5	61	70
Luxembourg	70	9	7	88	86
Mexico	62	16	17	14	17
New Zealand	72	14	8	62	65
Norway	51	18	14	50	30
Poland	67	14	13	35	25
Portugal	61	28	34	35	31
Spain	58	18	9	41	37
Sweden	55	14	10	74	62
Switzerland	70	14	9	47	37
United Kingdom	78	10	7	51	53
United States	73	22	6	39	61
Country mean	*65*	*15*	*12*	*51*	*46*
Brazil	53	19	34	27	27
Latvia	78	24	19	42	57
Liechtenstein	77	19	8	79	67
Russian Federation	74	10	13	6	18
Netherlands[1]	62	12	10	45	55

OECD COUNTRIES

NON-OECD COUNTRIES

1. Response rate is too low to ensure comparability (see Annex 3 at *www.oecd.org / els / education / eag2002*).

Source: OECD PISA database, 2001. See Annex 3 for notes on methodology (*www.oecd.org / els / education / eag2002*) and *www.pisa.oecd.org.*

D3

Table D3.3.

The extent to which learning is hindered by a lack of computers for instruction or lack of multi-media resources for instruction in schools in which 15-year-olds are enrolled (2000)

Mean percentage of 15-year-olds enrolled in schools where principals reported that learning is hindered a lot, to some extent, very little or not at all by insufficient numbers of computers for instruction and multi-media resources for instruction

		Learning is hindered by a lack of computers for instruction			Learning is hindered by a lack of multi-media resources for instruction			
		Not at all	Very little	To some extent	A lot	Not at all	Very little	To some extent	A lot
		%	%	%	%	%	%	%	%
OECD COUNTRIES	Australia	32	38	27	3	29	39	31	1
	Austria	30	32	23	15	22	35	32	11
	Belgium	49	32	15	3	42	34	17	7
	Canada	33	36	26	4	30	46	22	3
	Czech Republic	37	25	28	10	34	27	31	9
	Denmark	32	40	21	6	48	39	10	3
	Finland	16	41	35	7	15	40	37	9
	France	39	33	23	5	40	26	29	5
	Germany	20	30	35	15	15	33	33	20
	Greece	15	17	40	28	11	21	45	24
	Hungary	69	18	9	4	41	34	23	2
	Iceland	26	29	41	4	16	36	42	5
	Ireland	34	24	30	12	21	26	41	13
	Italy	42	26	26	6	29	25	34	12
	Japan	32	37	26	5	20	38	33	9
	Korea	30	46	18	6	21	39	32	8
	Luxembourg	24	53	23	n	19	58	23	n
	Mexico	16	16	27	42	17	18	23	42
	New Zealand	25	35	35	5	25	44	29	2
	Norway	12	28	52	9	9	29	51	10
	Poland	33	29	27	12	38	32	24	6
	Portugal	27	35	31	8	25	41	27	7
	Spain	43	27	23	7	29	28	32	11
	Sweden	21	29	40	11	18	28	46	8
	Switzerland	40	37	19	4	37	38	19	6
	United Kingdom	18	26	37	19	13	30	42	16
	United States	35	33	24	7	33	39	22	6
	Country mean	*31*	*31*	*26*	*11*	*26*	*34*	*28*	*12*
NON-OECD COUNTRIES	Brazil	20	17	27	36	53	22	13	12
	Latvia	25	35	24	16	13	30	34	22
	Liechtenstein	26	33	41	n	59	20	20	n
	Russian Federation	11	3	31	55	18	11	36	35
	Netherlands[1]	27	34	25	14	26	37	26	11

1. Response rate is too low to ensure comparability (see Annex 3 at *www.oecd.org/els/education/eag2002*).

Source: OECD PISA database, 2001. See Annex 3 for notes on methodology (*www.oecd.org/els/education/eag2002*) and *www.pisa.oecd.org.*

Table D3.4.
Availability of computers to use at home and at school for 15-year-olds (2000)
Mean percentage of 15-year-olds who reported that computers are available to use at home and at school almost every day, a few times each week, between once a week and once a month, less than once a month and never

	Availability of computers to use at *home*					Availability of computers to use at *school*				
	Almost every day	A few times each week	Between once a week and once a month	Less than once a month	Never	Almost every day	A few times each week	Between once a week and once a month	Less than once a month	Never
	%	%	%	%	%	%	%	%	%	%
Australia	85	4	1	1	9	52	30	10	5	2
Belgium	65	11	5	4	16	13	29	26	12	20
Canada	81	4	2	1	12	52	24	12	7	5
Czech Republic	48	6	3	2	41	10	29	30	10	21
Denmark	77	7	4	3	9	49	29	15	6	2
Finland	73	5	3	2	18	19	40	24	12	4
Germany	72	8	4	3	13	6	16	27	21	30
Hungary	41	8	3	3	44	13	58	17	4	7
Ireland	62	4	2	2	29	16	25	20	13	25
Luxembourg	63	11	6	5	14	16	29	32	10	13
Mexico	23	5	3	3	66	22	25	8	9	37
New Zealand	74	4	2	2	18	48	22	13	11	5
Scotland	72	3	2	2	21	43	36	11	5	5
Sweden	90	3	1	1	6	37	31	17	10	5
Switzerland	76	8	3	3	10	22	23	28	14	12
United States	68	7	5	4	15	46	21	12	11	10
Country mean	*64*	*6*	*3*	*3*	*24*	*27*	*29*	*20*	*10*	*14*
Brazil	24	5	4	4	64	8	13	10	13	55
Latvia	23	6	4	4	64	14	35	22	11	18
Liechtenstein	75	8	3	2	12	20	29	41	5	5
Russian Federation	15	5	4	4	73	5	24	24	10	38

OECD COUNTRIES / NON-OECD COUNTRIES

Source: OECD PISA database, 2001. See Annex 3 for notes on methodology (*www.oecd.org/els/education/eag2002*) and *www.pisa.oecd.org*.

D3

Table D3.5.
Frequency of use of computers at home and at school by 15-year-olds (2000)
Mean percentage of 15-year-olds who reported using computers at home and at school almost every day, a few times each week,
between once a week and once a month, less than once a month and never

	Use of computers at *home*					Use of computers at *school*				
	Almost every day	A few times each week	Between once a week and once a month	Less than once a month	Never	Almost every day	A few times each week	Between once a week and once a month	Less than once a month	Never
	%	%	%	%	%	%	%	%	%	%
Australia	44	30	12	5	10	15	35	24	17	8
Belgium	38	26	13	7	17	5	26	32	12	25
Canada	51	21	10	4	13	18	21	23	22	16
Czech Republic	31	15	8	4	41	4	24	34	11	26
Denmark	44	25	14	7	9	23	36	26	11	4
Finland	45	22	10	5	18	6	41	30	16	7
Germany	43	23	14	7	14	4	14	25	20	37
Hungary	29	14	7	4	46	7	58	19	5	10
Ireland	32	23	10	5	30	4	22	25	14	35
Luxembourg	44	22	14	7	13	10	26	34	12	17
Mexico	14	10	4	4	68	8	26	8	8	50
New Zealand	36	27	13	6	18	18	16	21	27	17
Norway	53	22	11	6	9	6	22	33	28	11
Scotland	38	26	10	4	21	18	39	18	14	12
Sweden	60	21	9	3	6	16	29	27	17	11
Switzerland	39	25	17	7	12	5	17	37	20	21
United States	49	18	12	6	15	18	19	23	23	17
Country mean	*39*	*21*	*11*	*5*	*24*	*10*	*28*	*26*	*16*	*19*
Brazil	18	7	7	5	64	5	7	14	15	59
Latvia	16	9	5	4	65	6	35	26	12	21
Liechtenstein	39	24	17	5	14	5	24	50	11	10
Russian Federation	12	6	4	4	74	4	22	24	11	39

Source: OECD PISA database, 2001. See Annex 3 for notes on methodology (*www.oecd.org/els/education/eag2002*) and *www.pisa.oecd.org.*

Table D3.6.
15-year-olds who use computers to help them learn school material (2000)
Mean percentage of 15-year-olds who reported using computers to help them learn school material almost every day, a few times each week,
between once a week and once a month, less than once a month and never

	Almost every day	A few times each week	Between once a week and once a month	Less than once a month	Never
	%	%	%	%	%
Australia	12	30	29	17	12
Belgium	8	16	21	21	35
Canada	10	21	28	21	20
Czech Republic	6	14	21	21	37
Denmark	15	38	28	12	7
Finland	6	18	32	27	17
Germany	11	23	28	21	18
Hungary	9	19	23	20	28
Ireland	7	20	25	22	26
Luxembourg	14	23	25	17	20
Mexico	17	34	17	14	18
New Zealand	13	25	28	21	13
Norway	8	21	28	25	19
Scotland	17	39	25	11	8
Sweden	13	26	29	19	12
Switzerland	6	17	27	24	26
United States	19	26	25	17	12
Country mean	*11*	*24*	*26*	*19*	*19*
Brazil	14	25	21	20	20
Latvia	11	23	22	19	25
Liechtenstein	6	16	33	24	21
Russian Federation	12	27	25	17	18

Source: OECD PISA database, 2001. See Annex 3 for notes on methodology (*www.oecd.org/els/education/eag2002*) and *www.pisa.oecd.org.*

ATTITUDES AND EXPERIENCES OF MALES AND FEMALES USING INFORMATION TECHNOLOGY

- While schools may be helping to bridge inequities in access to computers by males and females at home, 15-year-old males in many countries actually use computers and the Internet more often at school than do females.

- On average in OECD countries, 15-year-old males reported a significantly greater confidence and perceived ability to use computers than females. Gender differences are greatest in Denmark, Finland and Sweden, and smallest in Australia, New Zealand, Scotland and the United States.

Chart D4.1.

Gender differences of comfort with and perceived ability to use computers among 15-year-olds (2000)

PISA index of comfort with and perceived ability to use computers for 15-year-old males and females, based on self-reports of students

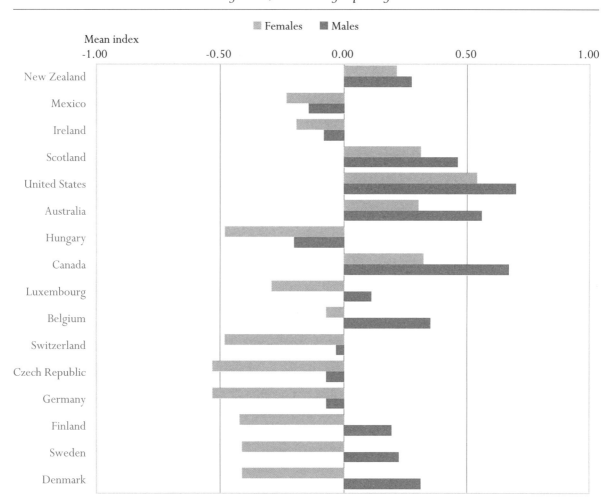

Countries are ranked in ascending order of the difference between males and females on the PISA index of comfort with and perceived ability to use computers.
Source: OECD PISA database, 2001. Table D4.1. See Annex 3 for notes on methodology *(www.oecd.org / els / education / eag2002)* and *www.pisa.oecd.org*.

Policy context

This indicator examines the attitudes towards as well as perceived comfort with and ability to use computers of 15-year-old males and females.

Bridging the "gender gap" in education has received considerable attention over the last decades as policy-makers and education practitioners work together to ensure equitable access to educational opportunities. The widespread introduction of computers into schools raised concerns about whether this new technology would act to moderate or reinforce inequities between males and females in an area that is traditionally perceived as male-dominated.

The relationship between attitudes towards and experiences with computers and gender is not straightforward. Many factors in and beyond a student's classroom experience may influence the differences in knowledge and attitudes towards computers, including gender stereotypes, general patterns of socialisation between males and females, and parents' and teachers' attitudes.

To shed light on these issues, this indicator examines the attitudes and perceived comfort with and ability to use computers of 15-year-old males and females.

Evidence and explanations

The largest gender gaps for 15-year-olds occur in access to computers in the home.

15-year-olds in PISA were asked how often computers were available to use at home, at school, in the library and "at another place". In all countries, more males than females reported that they have a computer available to use at home almost every day, a few times each week or between once a week and once a month. Similarly, in all OECD countries, more males reported having a link to the Internet in the home compared to females – in 23 out of 32 countries this difference was statistically significant. (For data see *www.oecd.org/els/education/eag2002*.)

Gender differences in computer availability at school tend not to be significant...

In most countries, gender differences in computer availability at school are not statistically significant (for data see *www.oecd.org/els/education/eag2002*). While ensuring the provision of equal access to computers is an important policy consideration, the existence of such technologies does not guarantee their equitable use. Ensuring that males and females receive equitable opportunities to use computers at school depends on many factors, including teacher and student attitudes and practices, the structure of educational activities, peer-group pressure, students' familiarity with computers and gender stereotyping.

...but, in most countries, significantly more males than females actually use computers and the Internet at school,...

In PISA, 15-year-old males and females were asked how often they used computers and the Internet at school. On average across OECD countries, 59 per cent of females reported that they use computers several times a month or several times a week or about once a month, compared to 64 per cent of males. In Austria, Ireland, Japan, Korea, Mexico and New Zealand, more females than males reported that they use computers with this frequency, although this gender difference was statistically significant in favour of females only in Korea and New Zealand. Gender differences were most marked in Finland, France, Germany, Greece, Norway, Sweden and Switzerland, where the number of males reporting that they used computers several times a month, several times a week or about once a month exceeded that of females by more than 10 percentage points. Males also dominate the use of the Internet at school in all countries except Austria, Korea, Mexico and New Zealand. Males in Canada, Finland, France, Greece, Hungary, Norway, Poland, Portugal, Sweden, Switzerland and the United Kingdom exceed females in frequency of Internet use by more than 10 percentage points. (For data *see www.oecd.org/els/ education/eag2002.*)

Several factors can influence a student's interest, confidence and perceived ability to use computers, including attitudes and comfort and familiarity with computers. PISA explored aspects related to the self-assessment of 15-year-old students' attitudes and familiarity with computers (Table D4.1 and Chart D4.1). On average in OECD countries, males reported being significantly more confident and having a higher perceived ability to use computers than females. The gender differences on the PISA index of comfort with and perceived ability to use computers are strong in countries such as Denmark, Finland and Sweden, where the comfort with and perceived ability to use computers of males exceeds that of females by more than 0.6 index points (*i.e.*, more than half a standard deviation). In Australia, New Zealand, Scotland and the United States, the differences between genders are smallest, and the indices for males and females are highest (Chart D4.1 and Table D4.1).

…which may have less to do with access to technology than with attitudes and familiarity with computers…

The individual variables that comprise this index reveal that males reported being significantly more comfortable than females at taking a test using a computer in all countries. In Denmark, Finland and Sweden, the difference between males and females who reported being comfortable at taking a test using a computer is more than 24 percentage points.

Similarly, in all countries, more males reported being very comfortable or comfortable using a computer. However, these gender differences were not statistically significant in Mexico, New Zealand, Scotland or the United States. By contrast, gender differences in comfort with using a computer to write a paper were small, and females had a slight advantage (Table D4.1).

PISA also investigated students' interest in computers (Table D4.2 and Chart D4.2). With the exception of Mexico and the United States, males reported consistently higher on the PISA index of interest in computers than females. The difference is statistically significant favouring males in all of these countries, except Ireland. The United States is the only country where more females reported that it is important to work with a computer (89 per cent of females versus 84 per cent of males) and that playing or working with a computer is really fun (94 per cent of females versus 89 per cent of males). On average across countries, 84 per cent of females and 92 per cent of males still believe that playing or working on the computer is fun. Similarly, more males than females reported using a computer because it interests them. Although this difference is small and not statistically significant in Ireland and Mexico, gender

…as well as with differences in interest in computers.

D4

Chart D4.2.

Gender differences in interest of 15-year-olds in computers (2000)

Distribution of mean percentages of 15-year-old males and females who reported that:

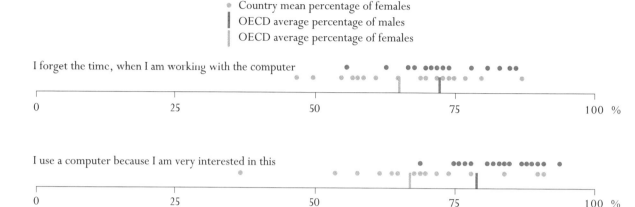

I forget the time, when I am working with the computer

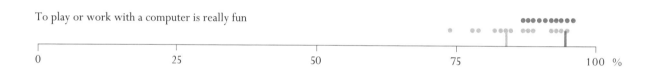

I use a computer because I am very interested in this

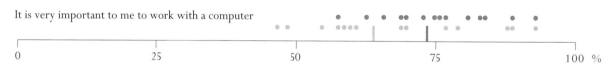

To play or work with a computer is really fun

It is very important to me to work with a computer

Note: Countries are represented by dots.
Source: OECD PISA database, 2001. Table D4.2. See Annex 3 for notes on methodology *(www.oecd.org/els/education/eag2002)* and *www.pisa.oecd.org.*

differences are greatest for this question: on average 66 per cent of females and 80 per cent of males in OECD countries report using the computer because it interests them. Less than 55 per cent of female 15-year-olds in Australia, Denmark and New Zealand reported using a computer because it interests them (Table D4.2 and Chart D4.2).

Males tend to use computers more frequently to access the Internet, for electronic communication and for programming...

15-year-olds in PISA were asked how often they use computers to access the Internet, for electronic communication (*i.e.,* e-mails), to help them learn school material or for programming. In all countries, more males than females reported using the Internet almost every day, a few times each week or between once a week and once a month. Mexico and the United States are the only countries where this difference favouring males is not statistically significant. By contrast, in Germany and Scotland, this difference is more than 14 percentage points. Similarly, in all but two countries, males use programming more frequently than females.

In many countries, however, females are more likely to use computers to help them learn school material. (For data see *www.oecd.org/els/education/eag2002.*)

Students also reported how often they used computer software such as games, word processing, spreadsheets, drawing and painting or graphics or educational software. On average across OECD countries, males use these types of software more frequently than females. Gender differences in frequency of use are particularly marked for computer games, where the frequency of use is significantly higher for males in all countries. In Australia, Denmark, Finland, Sweden and Switzerland, the difference between males and females is over 33 percentage points. Although students use spreadsheet and drawing, painting or graphics software much more infrequently than games and word processing, this is predominantly a male past-time, although gender differences in favour of males for using spreadsheets and graphics software are small and not statistically significant in Ireland, Mexico and New Zealand. (For data see *www.oecd.org/els/education/eag2002.*)

...and the same is true for the use of different types of software, such as games, word processing, spreadsheets, drawing, painting or educational software...

With the exception of Mexico and Scotland, males score significantly higher on the PISA index of computer usage and experience than females. However in Belgium, the Czech Republic, Mexico and Switzerland, negative indices for both males and females indicate that all 15-year-olds reported less frequent use of and experience with computers compared to students in other countries. In Mexico, however, the index for females was higher. Male and female 15-year-olds in Australia, New Zealand, Scotland and the United States rated the highest on the PISA index of computer usage and experience, although the index was still higher for males in these countries. (For data see *www.oecd.org/els/education/eag2002.*)

...as well as for computer use and experience.

Definitions and methodologies

Data used in this indicator derive from responses of 15-year-old students and school principals to questions concerning the use and availability of computers at home and at school in three background questionnaires used in the 2000 cycle of the OECD Programme for International Student Assessment (PISA).

In addition to a written test, 15-year-olds in PISA completed a student questionnaire designed to collect information about the their family, home environment, reading habits, school and everyday activities. Responses to questions on the frequency of use of computers and the Internet at school and the availability of computers in the home (for data see *www.oecd.org/els/education/eag2002*) derive from this student background questionnaire. A second background questionnaire on computer familiarity was completed by students in 20 countries as part of an international option. It explored students' interest in computers, the self-assessment of their attitudes and ability to work with computers, and use and experience with computers. This indicator uses data from this questionnaire on the availability and use of computers at home and at school (for data see *www.oecd.org/els/education/eag2002*), students'

Results from this indicator derive from background questionnaires completed by 15-year-old male and female students as part of the Programme for International Student Assessment (PISA) undertaken by the OECD during 2000.

comfort with and perceived ability to use computers (Chart D4.1 and Table D4.1), their interest in computers (Chart D4.2 and Table D4.2) and use of computers and computer software (for data see *www.oecd.org/els/education/ eag2002*). The responses were weighted to make them proportional to the number of 15-year-olds in each school.

Index of comfort with and perceived ability to use computers

The PISA index of comfort with and perceived ability to use computers is constructed with the average score across countries set at 0 and the standard deviation set at 1. A positive value indicates that students reported more frequently than on average in OECD countries that it is very important to them to work with a computer, that they are comfortable using a computer, that they are comfortable using a computer to write a paper or to take a test, and that they rate their ability to use a computer as higher than that of other 15-year-olds.

Index of interest in computers

The PISA index of interest in computers is constructed with the average score across countries set at 0 and the standard deviation set at 1. A positive value indicates that students reported more frequently than on average in OECD countries that it is very important to them to work with a computer, that playing or working with a computer is fun, that they use a computer because they are very interested, and that they forget the time when they are working with a computer.

Index of computer usage and experience

The PISA index of computer usage and experience is constructed with the average score across countries set at 0 and the standard deviation set at 1. A positive value on the index indicates that students reported more frequently than on average in OECD countries that they use the computer to help them learn school material, for programming, for word processing, spreadsheets, drawing, painting or graphics and educational software.

In the tables and charts used in this indicator, differences between the means of males and females are identified as statistically significant at a confidence level of 95 per cent. This means that a difference of this size or larger would be observed less than 5 per cent of the time if there were really no difference in corresponding population values.

Table D4.1.
Perceived comfort with and ability to use computers of 15-year-olds, by gender (2000)
PISA index of comfort with and perceived ability to use computers, by gender, and mean percentage of 15-year-old males and females who reported that they were very comfortable or comfortable; and somewhat comfortable or not at all comfortable with using a computer, using a computer to write a paper, or taking a test on a computer

		PISA index of comfort with and perceived ability to use computers[1]		Using a computer				Using a computer to write a paper				Taking a test using a computer			
				Very comfortable or comfortable		Somewhat comfortable or not at all comfortable		Very comfortable or comfortable		Somewhat comfortable or not at all comfortable		Very comfortable or comfortable		Somewhat comfortable or not at all comfortable	
		Females	Males	Females	Males	Females	Males	Females	Males	Females	Males	Females	Males	Females	Males
				%	%	%	%	%	%	%	%	%	%	%	%
OECD COUNTRIES	Australia	0.30	0.56	86	91	14	9	90	88	10	12	64	75	36	25
	Belgium	-0.07	0.35	72	86	28	14	76	80	24	20	57	73	43	27
	Canada	0.32	0.67	85	92	15	8	89	88	11	12	67	77	33	23
	Czech Republic	-0.53	-0.07	47	72	53	28	63	65	37	35	57	71	43	29
	Denmark	-0.41	0.31	57	80	43	20	74	84	26	16	34	66	66	35
	Finland	-0.42	0.19	64	84	36	16	69	74	31	26	31	60	69	40
	Germany	-0.53	-0.07	49	73	51	27	56	63	44	37	48	65	52	35
	Hungary	-0.48	-0.20	80	89	20	11	40	45	60	55	57	63	43	37
	Ireland	-0.19	-0.08	73	77	27	23	64	58	36	42	44	51	56	49
	Luxembourg	-0.29	0.11	58	77	42	23	62	67	38	33	52	68	48	32
	Mexico	-0.23	-0.14	70	72	30	28	73	69	27	31	54	61	46	39
	New Zealand	0.21	0.27	85	87	15	13	83	78	17	22	63	67	37	33
	Scotland	0.31	0.46	83	87	17	13	83	82	17	18	65	70	35	30
	Sweden	-0.41	0.22	67	88	33	12	76	86	24	14	19	43	81	57
	Switzerland	-0.48	-0.03	47	73	53	27	61	65	39	35	52	66	48	34
	United States	0.54	0.70	88	91	12	9	93	89	7	11	74	79	26	21
	Country mean	*-0.17*	*0.21*	*70*	*82*	*30*	*18*	*72*	*74*	*28*	*26*	*52*	*66*	*48*	*34*
NON-OECD COUNTRIES	Brazil	-0.62	-0.35	57	68	43	32	51	58	49	42	38	49	62	51
	Latvia	-0.35	-0.07	59	74	41	26	63	66	37	34	52	65	48	35
	Liechtenstein	-0.52	-0.02	43	77	57	23	61	63	39	37	61	68	39	32
	Russian Federation	-0.39	-0.24	53	62	47	38	62	64	38	36	53	59	47	41

Note: Values marked in bold indicate that the difference between the means of males and females is statistically significant.
1. For the definitions of the indices see the Definitions and Methodologies section of this indicator.
Source: OECD PISA database, 2001. See Annex 3 for notes on methodology (*www.oecd.org/els/education/eag2002*) and *www.pisa.oecd.org.*

Table D4.2.
15-year-old students' interest in using computers, by gender (2000)
PISA index of interest in computers, by gender, and mean percentage of 15-year-old males and females who agree that working with computers is important to them, playing or working with computers is really fun, they use computers because they are interested in this, and they forget the time when working on computers

		PISA index of interest in computers[1]		It is important to work with a computer		Playing or working with a computer is really fun		Student uses computer because it interests them		Student forgets the time when working with a computer	
		Females	Males	Females	Males	Females	Males	Females	Males	Females	Males
				%	%	%	%	%	%	%	%
OECD COUNTRIES	Australia	−0.41	−0.04	64	72	74	87	52	71	52	58
	Belgium	−0.22	0.18	60	73	87	94	62	78	58	72
	Canada	−0.24	0.07	58	70	82	90	58	76	65	68
	Czech Republic	−0.21	0.14	61	69	85	93	68	81	57	70
	Denmark	−0.66	0.18	49	75	74	94	37	77	47	70
	Finland	−0.39	0.10	47	66	78	92	68	85	50	63
	Germany	0.04	0.43	69	84	89	96	70	87	73	83
	Hungary	−0.21	0.14	58	69	84	90	64	81	61	71
	Ireland	−0.02	0.02	55	58	92	94	72	75	75	74
	Luxembourg	0.12	0.45	70	83	88	93	74	88	77	86
	Mexico	0.29	0.27	88	89	87	88	84	84	87	85
	New Zealand	−0.41	−0.15	55	63	78	87	54	69	55	56
	Scotland	0.03	0.26	69	76	87	95	69	83	72	73
	Sweden	−0.18	0.29	59	81	79	95	74	88	59	67
	Switzerland	−0.12	0.24	60	76	83	91	65	82	70	78
	United States	0.33	0.29	89	84	94	89	78	83	73	73
	Country mean	*−0.14*	*0.18*	*63*	*74*	*84*	*92*	*66*	*80*	*64*	*72*
NON-OECD COUNTRIES	Brazil	0.34	0.39	93	93	95	95	**91**	**94**	69	70
	Latvia	0.28	0.34	79	77	93	92	90	91	**74**	**81**
	Liechtenstein	**−0.02**	**0.35**	**69**	**81**	**84**	**92**	68	89	69	78
	Russian Federation	0.18	0.18	77	75	92	92	90	90	**80**	**85**

Note: Values marked in bold indicate that the difference between the means of males and females is statistically significant.

1. For the definitions of the indices see the Definitions and Methodologies section of this indicator.

Source: OECD PISA database, 2001. See Annex 3 for notes on methodology (*www.oecd.org/els/education/eag2002*) and *www.pisa.oecd.org*.

SCHOOL AND CLASSROOM CLIMATE

- Compared to the OECD mean, 15-year-olds reported receiving more support from their teachers in Australia, Canada, New Zealand, Portugal, Sweden, the United Kingdom and the United States and less in Austria, Belgium, the Czech Republic, Germany, Italy, Korea, Luxembourg and Poland.

- On average, one 15-year-old in three reported that more than five minutes are spent at the start of the class doing nothing, and more than one in four complained that there is noise and disorder.

- More than half of the 15-year-olds in Australia, Denmark, Ireland, New Zealand, Norway, Sweden and the United Kingdom reported that they regularly use the science laboratory compared to less than 10 per cent in Finland and Hungary.

- School resources tend to be used more frequently, schools tend to be more autonomous, teachers' morale and commitment tend to be higher, and teacher-student relations tend to be relatively better in high performing countries. In countries with relatively low performance, negative school climate indices tend to cluster, and the indices on the use of school resources, teachers' morale and commitment, school autonomy and teacher-student relations tend to fall below the OECD average.

Chart D5.1.

Broader engagement of 15-year-olds with school (2000)

Distribution of mean percentages of 15-year-olds who agreed or strongly agreed that "School is a place where...

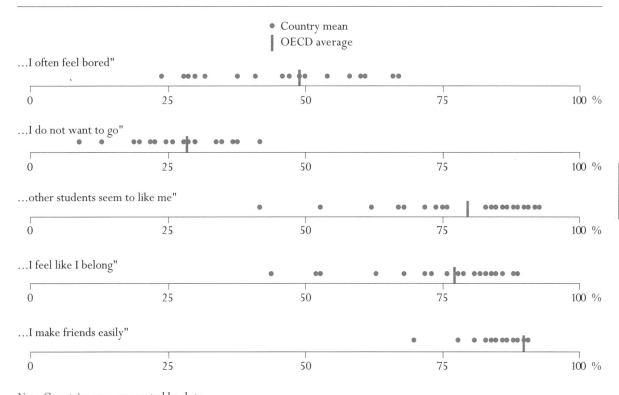

D5

Note: Countries are represented by dots.
Source: OECD PISA database, 2001. Table D5.4. See Annex 3 for notes on methodology *(www.oecd.org/els/education/eag2002)* and *www.pisa.oecd.org.*

Policy context

This indicator shows various aspects of the classroom and learning climate as well as student engagement with school.

Students between the ages of six and 15 spend on average about 900 hours a year in the classroom, where they co-operate with teachers and with each other (see Indicator D1). The quality of these interactions and the use that is made of classroom time determine to a large extent how much students can profit from schooling.

Classroom experiences affect the substance and the mode of learning, and can influence students' motivation and learning styles. PISA provides evidence that both teacher and student-related factors of classroom climate and practice closely relate to students' individual performance.

In addition, students' attitudes towards and involvement with school are important aspects of the learning climate. Research shows that negative attitudes may lead to poor attendance and disruptive behaviour and, conversely, that if students become involved in their school curricula or extra-curricular activities and develop strong ties with other students and teachers, they are more likely to do well in their studies.

This indicator shows various aspects of the classroom and learning climate and reports on student attitudes towards school.

Evidence and explanations

Learning climate in the classroom

In PISA, 15-year-olds were asked about several aspects of their classroom experiences in their language classes: their teacher's supportiveness, the disciplinary climate, the use of school resources, and homework policies in the school. Based on their responses a *teacher support index*, a *disciplinary climate index*, an *achievement press index*, and a *use of school resources index* were developed (Chart D5.2).

PISA indices of classroom learning climate

The PISA indices on the learning climate of the classroom summarise responses from 15-year-olds to a series of related questions and are standardised so that the OECD mean is 0 and the standard deviation is 1. A negative value for a country on an index does not necessarily imply that 15-year-olds in a country responded negatively to the underlying questions but merely indicates that they responded less positively than all 15-year-olds across OECD countries. For the content of the indices and for more technical explanation, see the Definitions and methodologies section of this indicator.

Indices of classroom climate for 15-year-olds (2000)

PISA indices of teacher support, disciplinary climate, achievement press and use of school resources, based on self-reports of students

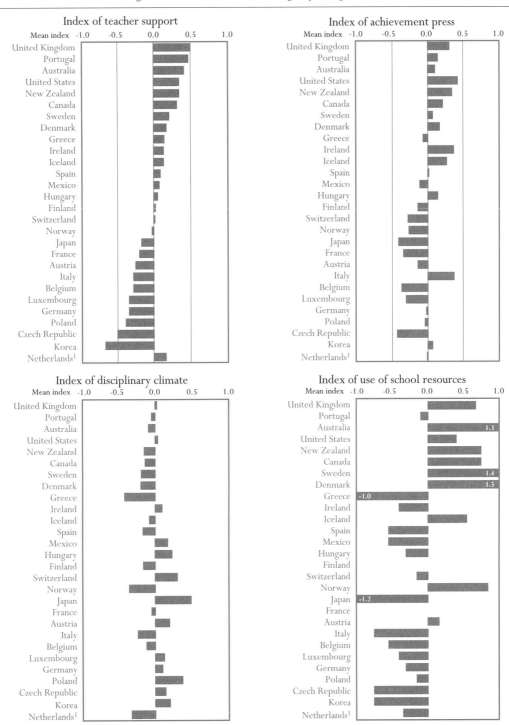

D5

1. Response rate is too low to ensure comparability (see Annex 3 at *www.oecd.org/els/education/eag2002*).
Data are ranked in descending order of the value on the PISA index of teacher support.
Source: OECD PISA database, 2001. Tables D5.1, D5.2 and D5.3. See Annex 3 for notes on methodology
(www.oecd.org/els/education/eag2002) and *www.pisa.oecd.org*.

Teacher support

On average, six 15-year-olds in ten reported that their teacher shows an interest in all students' learning most of the time, whereas one in ten says this never happens, but the perceived level of teacher support varies widely between countries.

On average across OECD countries, about six 15-year-olds in ten reported that their teacher of language of instruction classes shows an interest in every student's learning in most or all lessons, gives students an opportunity to express themselves, helps them with their work, continues teaching until all students understand, helps with learning and checks homework (Table D5.1).

The average level of perceived teacher support varies between countries. For example, more than three 15-year-olds in four in Australia, Portugal and the United Kingdom reported that their teachers are interested in every student's progress always or at least most of the time and only 5 per cent or less say that this never happens. By contrast, in Italy, Korea and Poland, only one 15-year-old in three reported that the teacher shows an interest in all students' learning, and nearly as many think that this never happens. Similarly, in Australia, Iceland, New Zealand and the United Kingdom, four 15-year-olds in five or more reported that their language teacher helps them with their work most of the time or always, but only about one in three say so in the Czech Republic, Korea or Mexico. Between two-thirds and three-quarters of the 15-year-olds in Australia, Canada, Denmark, Iceland, New Zealand, Portugal, Sweden and the United Kingdom reported that their language teacher teaches them until all students understand, compared to less than half of the 15-year-olds in the Czech Republic, Japan, Korea and Poland (Table D5.1)

Fifteen-year-olds in the Czech Republic, Germany, Korea, Luxembourg and Poland reported the least support from their teachers, whereas 15-year-olds in Australia, Canada, New Zealand, Portugal, the United Kingdom and the United States report high levels of teacher support. There is more than a standard deviation difference between the country mean PISA teacher support index in the United Kingdom (0.50) and Korea (-0.67). On average, therefore, 15-year-olds in the United Kingdom reported that they perceive receiving at least as much or more support from their teachers as the top third of all 15-year-olds in OECD countries. By contrast, 15-year-olds in Korea reported that they receive as much or less support from their language teachers than the bottom third of all 15-year-olds in the OECD (Table D5.1).

Disciplinary climate

On average in OECD countries, one 15-year-old in three reported that more than five minutes are spent at the start of the class doing nothing, and 28 per cent complained that there is noise and disorder.

In all countries, there is a positive link between the disciplinary climate in the language (of instruction) classes and student performance. The relationship is strong in Australia, Japan, Hungary, Poland and the United Kingdom, and weaker in Belgium, France, Luxembourg and Mexico. Even after accounting for other factors (including home background), disciplinary climate seems to be one of the factors that relate to learning outcomes. When students themselves say they cannot work very well in class, or that students do not listen to the teacher, whatever the cause, work is hindered. PISA suggests that discipline problems disturb students' learning quite frequently. For example, 28 per cent of all 15-year-olds in OECD countries reported noise and disorder in most or every language (of instruction) class and a particularly large proportion of 15-year-olds – 40 per cent or more – reported this in Finland, France, Greece and Italy. According to students' reports, time wasted at the beginning of lessons is the most frequent disciplinary problem. Of all students in OECD countries, over one-third reported that most or all language (of instruction) classes start by spending more than five minutes doing nothing. However, while more than half of 15-year-olds in Belgium, Denmark, Greece, Iceland and Norway reported frequent loss of time at the beginning of lessons, fewer than one in four 15-year-olds reported the same in Hungary, Japan and Mexico (Table D5.1).

Pressure to achieve

Schools offer a variety of subjects and no student is equally interested in all of them. Students optimise their learning efforts according to their personal interests and goals, the demands of their parents, and the requirements of their teachers. Setting desirable and attainable goals and encouraging students to reach them are major challenges of the teaching profession. In PISA, 15-year-olds were asked how frequently their teacher in the language of instruction wants them to work hard and do their work with care, encourages them to do better, and makes them learn a lot. From students' responses a 'pressure to achieve' index was created. Compared to the OECD average, 15-year-olds in Australia, Canada, Finland, Hungary, Iceland, Ireland, Italy, New Zealand, the United Kingdom and the United States reported higher pressure to achieve from the teacher (Table D5.2).

15-year-olds in Australia, Canada, New Zealand, the United Kingdom and the United States feel more pressure to achieve…

Interestingly, 15-year-olds in Australia, Canada, New Zealand, the United Kingdom and the United States seem to experience a lot of pressure to achieve while enjoying a relatively high level of teacher support, suggesting that teacher supportiveness and achievement pressure do not necessarily work against each other.

…and, at the same time, enjoy a high level of teacher support.

By contrast, in Austria, Belgium, the Czech Republic, Japan, Korea and Luxembourg, teacher support and pressure to achieve are below the OECD average. In a third group of countries including France, Italy and Poland, higher than average pressure to achieve is coupled with lower than average support from teachers. In Denmark, Finland, Norway and Sweden, the mean pressure to achieve and the mean teacher support index both appear to be near the OECD average (Tables D5.1 and D5.2).

The pattern is different in other countries.

D5

Use of educational resources

In PISA, school principals were asked the extent to which learning is hindered by lack of textbooks, computers, instruction materials in the library, multi-media equipment, science laboratories, and facilities for art activities. Furthermore, 15-year-olds were asked how frequently they use these resources. Educational resources can enhance learning opportunities in schools and their availability is a pre-requisite to effective teaching, but the integration of educational resources into classroom work and school learning mainly depends on teachers. Access

One 15-year-old in three reported using the school library regularly in Australia, Denmark, Mexico, New Zealand, Portugal and Sweden…

...while less than one in ten in Austria, Belgium, the Czech Republic, Finland, Greece, Ireland and Italy do so.

to books and other media in school and encouragement to use them is a major issue. In addition to the adults in the home, teachers are in a unique position to develop students' reading and information use habits. The library, which is becoming a multimedia centre increasingly in OECD countries, can be an important tool for this. Over one-third of 15-year-olds in Australia, Denmark, Mexico, New Zealand, Portugal and Sweden reported in PISA that they use the school library regularly (at least several times a month).

By contrast, less than one 15-year-old in ten reported using the school library regularly in Austria, Belgium, the Czech Republic, Finland, Greece, Ireland and Italy (Table D5.3).

Shortage of educational material in the school library may also hinder the use of the library.

It is difficult to discern the extent to which curriculum and textbook policy are linked to habits of library use in a country. For example, in Austria, 15-year-olds are given a large set of textbooks and other instructional material, while students in Hungary must buy their own textbooks. In other countries, like Sweden for example, students typically are loaned textbooks from the school library.

While owning many books may be one reason not to use the school library, insufficient resources may be another. In Finland, Greece, Ireland, Mexico and Norway, more than 40 per cent of 15-year-olds go to schools where principals report that the shortage of instructional material in the library hinders learning to some extent or a lot. By contrast, in Australia, Denmark, France, Hungary, Luxembourg, New Zealand, Portugal and Switzerland, less than 20 per cent of 15-year-olds go to schools where, according to principals, the shortage of educational material hinders learning (Table D5.3).

More than half of 15-year-olds in Australia, Denmark, Ireland, New Zealand, Norway, Sweden and the United Kingdom reported using the science laboratory regularly, compared to less than 10 per cent in Finland and Hungary.

Differences between countries in the reported use of science laboratories are even more marked than those for using school libraries. On average across OECD countries, one 15-year-old in three reported using the science laboratory regularly. In Australia, Denmark, Ireland, New Zealand, Norway, Sweden and the United Kingdom, six to eight 15-year-olds in ten reported using the science laboratory at least several times a month, compared to less than two 15-year-olds in ten in the Czech Republic, Greece and Japan, and less than 1 in Finland and Hungary (Table D5.3).

To become efficient users of school resources, students need the encouragement and support of teachers. PISA suggests that in countries where teacher support is above the OECD average, the mean index on the use of school resources also tends to be above the OECD average. Conversely, in countries with a relatively low teacher support index, the use of school resources also tends to be low. Further research and analysis is needed to explore whether and to what extent professional development and the specification of teachers' working time influence teachers' efforts to use school resources effectively.

Homework policy

In PISA, 15-year-olds were asked about their school's homework policy. Two-thirds or more of 15-year-olds in Austria, Canada, Iceland, Korea, Mexico, Portugal and the United States reported that homework always or at least most of the time counts towards their school marks. By contrast, homework is less likely to be used in the formal evaluation of students in the Czech Republic, France, Germany, Hungary, Ireland, Italy, Luxembourg, New Zealand, Switzerland and the United Kingdom (Table D5.2).

In Belgium, Ireland, Korea, Mexico, New Zealand, the United Kingdom and the United States, more than half of the 15-year-olds reported that teachers grade their homework regularly. By contrast, in Germany and Switzerland only about 10 per cent and in Hungary only 4 per cent of the 15-year-olds reported that their homework is graded regularly. In Germany, Greece, Switzerland and the United Kingdom, more than 36 per cent of 15-year-olds reported that their teachers make useful comments on their homework most of the time. By contrast, only 15 per cent of 15-year-olds in the Czech Republic, Finland, Hungary, Iceland or Japan reported that they receive useful comments on their homework from teachers (Table D5.2).

In about half of OECD countries, 90 per cent or more of 15-year-olds reported that homework counts in students' marks at least sometimes.

In some countries, teachers grade homework regularly while in others, they rarely do so.

School climate

Learning conditions affect students' progress directly and are part of the wider school context in which teachers and students interpret assignments and evaluate teaching-learning situations. In PISA, over and above the relationships between individual student performance and school climate, the extent to which school climate factors are related to performance differences among schools was explored. Seven indices of school climate and practice were found to have a statistically significant association with school-level performance in the three subject domains assessed in PISA. Three of these (the indices on teacher related factors affecting of school climate, the school principal's perception of teachers' morale and commitment, and the school's autonomy) represent the school principal's view of the learning climate of the school. Three other indices (students' perception of teacher-student relations, disciplinary climate of the classroom and students' perception of pressure to achieve) represent students' views of the classroom and of the learning climate in the school. The seventh indicator refers to the frequency of the use of school resources.

D5

Overall, the set of seven school climate indices explains around 30 per cent of the variation in reading literacy performance among schools and around 20 per cent of the variation among countries. The joint effect of the factors underlying these indices and the average economic social and cultural status of the student populations explain around 70 per cent of the variation between schools and around 40 per cent of the variation between countries.

The PISA indices on school climate

The PISA indices on school climate summarise responses from students and school principals to a series of related questions (See the Definitions and methodologies section of this indicator for a description of the indices.)

The PISA index on **teacher-related factors affecting school climate** was derived from principals' responses to questions about the hindrances to learning in the school.

The index on **teachers' morale and commitment** is based on principals' agreement with statements like 'the morale of teachers in this school is high'; 'teachers work with enthusiasm', 'teachers take pride in this school' and 'teachers value academic achievement'.

The PISA index on **school autonomy** is based on principals' information on the areas in which the school (principal) has no responsibility.

The PISA index on **teacher-student relations** is based on 15-year-olds' agreement with statements like 'students get along well with most teachers', 'most teachers are interested in students' well-being', 'most teachers listen to what students have to say', 'if students need extra help, they get it from their teachers' and 'most teachers treat students fairly'.

The PISA index on the classroom's **disciplinary climate** is based on 15-year-olds responses to questions about the frequency of noise and disorder, wasting classroom time doing nothing, students not listening to teachers.

The PISA index on **pressure to achieve** is based on 15-year-olds' responses to questions on how often their teacher wants them to work hard, tells students that they can do better, makes them learn a lot and disapproves of careless work.

The PISA index on the **use of school resources** is also based on 15-year-olds' responses concerning the frequency with which they use the library, computers, the science laboratory and other educational resources.

D5

In most high performing countries, 15-year-olds tend to use school resources more frequently, schools tend to have a higher level of autonomy, teachers' morale and commitment tend to be higher, and teacher-student relations tend to be better.

The majority of countries performing above the OECD average on the PISA scales have high or average values on five of the seven school climate indices: the school-level mean indices of *the use of educational resources*, *school autonomy*, *teachers' morale and commitment*, *pressure to achieve* and *teacher-student relations*.

In Australia, Canada, Denmark, Finland, Iceland, New Zealand, Sweden, the United Kingdom and the United States, all five of these school climate indices have values above or around the OECD mean. The coincidence of these five factors are related to a regulation type that can be characterised by substantial school autonomy and an orientation to outcomes rather than control over school inputs and content. (For data see *www.oecd.org/els/education/eag2002*.)

In countries where the average performance of 15-year-olds is below the OECD average, more than half of the school climate indices also tend to have values below the OECD average. In Germany and Greece, for example, all but one of the seven indices are negative. Five indices in Italy, Luxembourg, Portugal and Spain, and four of the seven indices in the Czech Republic, Japan and Mexico are below the OECD mean. The two exceptions are Hungary and Poland, where six and four respectively of the school climate indices have values above the OECD mean. (For data see *www.oecd.org/els/education/eag2002.*)

In countries with below-average performance, negative school climate indices tend to cluster...

In this latter group of countries, with the exception of Portugal, the use of school resources index is significantly lower than the OECD average. The school autonomy index is negative in seven of these countries (except the Czech Republic, Hungary and Poland). In Germany, Greece, Portugal and Mexico, principals perceive teacher-related problems as hindering learning (although the same problems are also reported in some of the high performing countries, including Australia, Canada, Finland, Ireland and New Zealand). Teacher-student relations are less favourable than the OECD mean in the Czech Republic, Germany, Greece, Italy, Luxembourg and Poland. In five of these countries (the Czech Republic, Italy, Spain, Poland and Portugal), principals perceive low teacher morale and commitment. Similar problems also exist in Belgium, Korea and the United States although the performance level in these countries is around or above the OECD average. (For data see *www.oecd.org/els/education/eag2002.*)

...and the indices on the use of school resources, teachers' morale and commitment, school autonomy and teacher-student relations tend to fall below the OECD average.

PISA provides evidence that school climate indices in most countries are associated with the socio-economic composition of the student population (for data see *www.oecd.org/els/education/eag2002),* which can be critical in countries with relatively large overall differences in student performance and where a substantial part of these differences is attributable to differences between schools. For example, in Germany, the variation in performance between schools is well above the OECD average. The significant positive correlations between the mean socio-economic status of schools and teacher-related factors affecting school climate, teacher-student relations, school autonomy, and disciplinary climate indicate that schools with a more affluent student intake tend to have fewer problems with teacher and student discipline, better teacher-student relations and more autonomy. This also means that students with a lower socio-economic status are less likely to be enrolled in schools where the learning climate is more favourable.

School climate factors are often associated with the social, economic and cultural status of the school's intake.

Broader engagement with school

School and school-related work constitutes a large proportion of a 15-year-old's time. Can schools focus young students' attention amidst competing stimuli? Evidence from PISA suggests that, on average, 48 per cent of 15-year-olds often feel bored at school and 29 per cent say school is a place where they do not want to go (Chart D5.1 and Table D5.4).

Half of the 15-year-olds in PISA report that they often feel bored at school...

...yet for most 15-year-olds school is an important social sphere where they make connections with peers.

At the same time, PISA suggests that schools play an important role in the social life of 15-year-olds, and schools remain an important place for teenagers to meet. PISA asked 15-year-olds to what extent they feel they belong in school. Table D5.4 summarises their responses and suggests that for the majority of 15-year-olds, school is a place where they make friends easily (82 per cent), where they feel they belong (75 per cent), and where other 15-year-olds seem to like them (77 per cent). However, on average in OECD countries, 9 per cent feel like an outsider or feel left out of things, 14 per cent feel awkward and out of place, and 10 per cent feel lonely (Chart D5.1 and Table D5.4).

Definitions and methodologies

Results from this indicator derive from background questionnaires completed by 15-year-olds and their school principals as part of the Programme for International Student Assessment (PISA) undertaken by the OECD during 2000.

The PISA indices reported in this section summarise responses from students and school principals to a series of related questions. Responses were weighted to represent the school's population of 15-year-olds. The questions were selected from larger constructs on the basis of theoretical considerations and previous research. Structural equation modelling was used to confirm the theoretically expected attributes of the indices and to validate their comparability across countries. A separate model was estimated for each country and, collectively, for all OECD countries.

Negative values on an index do not necessarily imply that students and school principals responded negatively to the underlying questions. Rather they indicate that a group of students (or all students collectively in one country) or principals responded less positively than did students or principals on average across OECD countries. A positive value on an index indicates that a group of students or principals responded more favourably, or more positively, than all students or principals, on average, in OECD countries.

Indices based on students' responses

Index of teacher support

The PISA index of *teacher support* was derived from students' reports on the frequency with which the teacher: shows an interest in every student's learning; gives students an opportunity to express opinions; helps students with their work; continues teaching until students understand; does a lot to help students; and helps students with their learning. A four-point scale with response categories 'never', 'some lessons', 'most lessons' and 'every lesson' was used.

Index of disciplinary climate

The PISA index of *disciplinary climate* summarises students' reports on the frequency with which in their <language class>: the teacher has to wait a long time for students to <quieten down>; students cannot work well; students don't listen to what the teacher says; students don't start working for a long time after the lesson begins; there is noise and disorder; and at the start of class, more than five minutes are spent doing nothing. A four-point scale with response categories 'never', 'some lessons', 'most lessons' and 'every lesson' was used. This index was inverted so that low values indicate a poor disciplinary climate.

D5

The PISA index of pressure to achieve was derived from students' reports on the frequency with which the teacher in their <language class> wants students to work hard, tells students that they can do better, does not like it when students deliver <careless> work; and students have to learn a lot. A four-point scale with response categories 'never', 'some lessons', 'most lessons' and 'every lesson' was used.

Index of pressure to achieve

The PISA index on the *use of school resources* was derived from the frequency with which students reported using the following resources in their school: the school library, calculators, the Internet and <science> laboratories. Students responded on a five-point scale with the following categories: 'never or hardly ever', 'a few times a year', 'about once a month', 'several times a month', and 'several times a week'. The indices were derived using the WARM method.

Index of the use of school resources

The PISA index of *time spent on homework* is derived from students' reports on the frequency with which homework is completed: never, sometimes, most of the time, or always; and the amount of time spent per week doing homework for <test language>, mathematics and science classes using a four-point scale with categories: 'never', 'less than 1 hour a week', 'between 1 and 3 hours a week' and '3 hours or more a week.' High values mean that the student reported investing a large amount of time in homework and completes it on time.

Index of the time spent on homework

The PISA index of *teacher-student relations* was derived from students' reports on their agreement with the following statements using a four-point scale with response categories 'strongly disagree', 'disagree', 'agree' and 'strongly agree': students get along well with most teachers; most teachers are interested in students' well being; most of my teachers really listen to what I have to say; if I need extra help, I will receive it from my teachers; and most of my teachers treat me fairly.

Index of teacher-student relations

To capture wider aspects of a student's family and home background, the PISA index of economic, social and cultural status was created on the basis of the following variables: the International Socio-Economic Index of Occupational Status; parents' highest level of education converted into years of schooling; the PISA index of family wealth; the PISA index of home educational resources; and the PISA index of possessions related to "classical" culture in the family home. For a detailed description of these variables see the *PISA Technical Report* on *www.pisa.oecd.org*.

Index of economic, social and cultural status (ESCS)

D5

PISA indices based on principals' responses

The PISA index of *principals' perceptions of teacher-related factors affecting school climate* was based on principals' reports on the extent to which the learning of 15-year-olds is hindered by: low expectations of teachers; poor student-teacher relations; teachers not meeting individual students' needs; teacher absenteeism; staff resisting change; teachers being too strict with students; and students not being encouraged to achieve their full potential. A four-point scale

Index of school principals' perceptions of teacher-related factors affecting school climate

with categories 'not at all', 'very little', 'to some extent' and 'a lot' was used. This index was inverted so that low values indicate a poor disciplinary climate.

Index of school principals' perception of teachers' morale and commitment

The PISA index of *principals' perception of teachers' morale and commitment was* based on the extent to which school principals agreed with the following statements: the morale of the teachers in this school is high; teachers work with enthusiasm; teachers take pride in this school; and teachers value academic achievement. A four-point scale with response categories 'strongly disagree', 'disagree', 'agree' and 'strongly agree' was used.

Index of school autonomy

School principals were asked to report whether teachers, department heads, the school principal, an appointed or elected board, or education authorities at higher levels have the main responsibility for: hiring and firing teachers; establishing starting salaries; determining salary increases; formulating school budgets; allocating budgets within the school; establishing student disciplinary policies; establishing student assessment policies; approving student admissions; choosing textbooks; determining course content; and deciding which courses are offered. The PISA index of *school autonomy* was based on the categories which principals classified as not being a school responsibility.

D5

Table D5.1.
Classroom climate for 15-year-olds (2000)
PISA indices of teacher support and disciplinary climate and change in the PISA reading literacy score

		Teacher support							PISA index of teacher support[1]	Change in the PISA reading literacy score per unit of the PISA index of teacher support[2]
		Percentage of students who report that in most or every test language lesson, the teacher …								
		shows an interest in every student's learning	gives students an opportunity to express opinions	helps students with their work	continues teaching until the students understand	does a lot to help students	helps students with their learning	checks students' homework	Mean index	
OECD COUNTRIES	Australia	72	77	80	72	70	77	49	0.41	**7.37**
	Austria	48	67	54	56	52	32	64	-0.25	-0.62
	Belgium	42	56	44	58	54	60	60	-0.28	**-4.83**
	Canada	69	73	76	68	67	75	49	0.31	**4.42**
	Czech Republic	47	57	32	41	51	24	47	-0.50	0.77
	Denmark	62	76	74	67	66	67	49	0.17	**11.65**
	Finland	52	72	72	59	57	66	42	0.02	**5.48**
	France	55	61	50	57	48	42	44	-0.20	-2.53
	Germany	41	62	52	53	51	34	61	-0.34	**-12.55**
	Greece	69	77	41	62	65	69	53	0.14	2.20
	Hungary	58	71	73	58	67	51	52	0.05	-2.43
	Iceland	53	51	79	72	69	75	61	0.13	**8.87**
	Ireland	70	66	62	64	64	61	63	0.13	-0.13
	Italy	22	72	50	63	61	41	50	-0.28	**-11.46**
	Japan	48	58	61	48	48	51	35	-0.17	**6.23**
	Korea	31	43	17	41	49	41	54	-0.67	**5.56**
	Luxembourg	45	57	46	56	49	32	51	-0.34	**-5.13**
	Mexico	70	76	36	62	53	61	76	0.07	-2.60
	New Zealand	69	73	79	67	69	76	56	0.34	**5.26**
	Norway	48	62	69	59	60	70	41	-0.03	**14.95**
	Poland	38	60	41	43	44	35	46	-0.39	**9.20**
	Portugal	83	77	71	68	70	79	51	0.47	-1.33
	Spain	62	63	59	66	57	63	68	0.09	2.53
	Sweden	64	71	74	69	70	76	51	0.21	**6.20**
	Switzerland	56	68	66	66	63	47	56	0.01	**-13.40**
	United Kingdom	75	76	80	75	75	79	69	0.50	**6.66**
	United States	66	66	70	63	63	69	65	0.34	**6.87**
	OECD total	*56*	*65*	*58*	*59*	*58*	*57*	*57*	*0.00*	*2.82*
	Country mean	*56*	*66*	*59*	*60*	*60*	*56*	*54*	*0.02*	*2.96*
NON-OECD COUNTRIES	Brazil	73	70	62	69	74	75	49	0.38	**4.60**
	Latvia	40	60	56	54	53	53	59	-0.20	**15.56**
	Liechtenstein	51	69	72	70	65	42	65	0.09	**-14.19**
	Russian Federation	55	69	65	61	65	70	64	0.16	**6.40**
	Netherlands[3]	38	57	67	65	57	39	30	-0.21	-5.54

		Disciplinary climate						PISA index of disciplinary climate[1]	Change in the PISA reading literacy score per unit of the PISA index of disciplinary climate[2]
		Percentage of students who report that in most or every test language lesson …							
		the teacher has to wait a long time for students to quieten down	students cannot work well	students don't listen to what the teacher says	students don't start working for a long time after the lesson begins	there is noise and disorder	at the start of class, more than five minutes are spent doing nothing	Mean index	
OECD COUNTRIES	Australia	31	18	21	26	32	42	-0.09	**16.69**
	Austria	32	20	21	29	19	38	0.19	**4.98**
	Belgium	35	14	23	30	36	51	-0.12	3.15
	Canada	35	16	23	29	33	46	-0.14	**13.28**
	Czech Republic	32	17	26	21	26	27	0.14	**12.37**
	Denmark	27	17	19	22	33	55	-0.20	**9.71**
	Finland	39	15	29	21	42	44	-0.16	**9.56**
	France	35	15	27	36	42	38	-0.05	1.53
	Germany	36	23	24	27	22	34	0.10	**10.13**
	Greece	43	39	29	34	46	58	-0.42	2.96
	Hungary	34	25	22	16	23	16	0.23	**16.05**
	Iceland	34	16	20	20	28	50	-0.08	**8.90**
	Ireland	29	16	25	25	26	41	0.09	**15.41**
	Italy	48	22	35	29	46	49	-0.24	**14.11**
	Japan	9	20	16	17	17	25	0.49	**17.15**
	Korea	17	21	32	23	29	32	0.20	**6.88**
	Luxembourg	31	21	24	26	27	36	0.12	2.41
	Mexico	28	17	19	19	24	23	0.17	2.03
	New Zealand	33	22	23	26	32	46	-0.15	**12.47**
	Norway	42	23	27	33	39	56	-0.36	**7.79**
	Poland	26	13	19	19	18	27	0.37	**20.88**
	Portugal	25	19	20	24	24	42	-0.05	**10.57**
	Spain	41	18	24	35	34	48	-0.17	**12.18**
	Sweden	43	23	29	31	38	30	-0.19	**12.44**
	Switzerland	27	18	18	23	18	27	0.30	**9.81**
	United Kingdom	31	17	20	23	27	41	0.02	**20.10**
	United States	26	17	24	23	28	37	0.03	**13.17**
	OECD total	*28*	*18*	*23*	*24*	*28*	*35*	*0.09*	*11.99*
	Country mean	*32*	*19*	*24*	*25*	*30*	*39*	*0.00*	*9.45*
NON-OECD COUNTRIES	Brazil	36	24	28	38	40	50	-0.34	**-5.95**
	Latvia	19	17	19	16	17	21	0.38	**9.04**
	Liechtenstein	25	21	15	15	10	21	0.35	-2.59
	Russian Federation	19	16	16	13	12	27	0.45	**10.06**
	Netherlands[3]	39	16	21	37	39	69	-0.33	2.63

1. For the definitions of the indices see the Definitions and Methodologies section of this indicator.

2. Unit changes marked in bold are statistically significant.

3. Response rate is too low to ensure comparability (see Annex 3 at *www.oecd.org/els/education/eag2002*).

Source: OECD PISA database, 2001. See Annex 3 for notes on methodology (*www.oecd.org/els/education/eag2002*) and *www.pisa.oecd.org*.

Table D5.2.
Homework policy and pressure on 15-year-olds to achieve (2000)

| | Homework policy | | | | Achievement press | | | | PISA index of achievement press[1] | | | Change in the PISA reading literacy score per unit of the PISA index of achievement press[2] | Correlation of the PISA school's mean achievement press index with the school index of economic, social and cultural status (ESCS)[2] |
| | Percentage of students who report that most of the time or always... | | | | Percentage of students who report that in most or all test language lessons... | | | | Mean index | | | | |
	My teachers grade my homework	My teachers make useful comments on my homework	I am given interesting homework	My homework is counted as part of my marks	The teacher wants students to work hard	The teacher tells students that they can do better	The teacher does not like it when students deliver careless work	Students have to learn a lot	All students	Bottom quarter	Top quarter		
Australia	43	24	11	53	85	41	57	54	0.09	-0.22	0.40	**-10.06**	0.14
Austria	47	19	15	77	64	42	49	57	-0.14	-0.62	0.39	**-6.39**	0.04
Belgium	63	23	16	57	52	32	47	40	-0.36	-0.79	0.04	1.95	**0.52**
Canada	41	22	10	66	84	41	62	59	0.20	-0.19	0.56	**-9.71**	0.07
Czech Republic	19	13	10	27	28	51	35	52	-0.43	-0.94	0.11	-3.41	-0.10
Denmark	38	29	8	54	83	21	66	74	0.16	-0.13	0.45	2.97	-0.04
Finland	15	12	8	51	72	36	47	56	-0.14	-0.47	0.21	**-14.69**	-0.24
France	32	24	19	43	45	49	40	43	-0.34	-0.68	0.02	-5.84	m
Germany	12	42	8	43	71	50	48	57	-0.02	-0.43	0.38	**-11.07**	-0.12
Greece	43	39	35	58	61	70	42	41	-0.07	-0.48	0.34	**11.73**	0.19
Hungary	4	11	16	16	64	61	61	57	0.13	-0.22	0.47	-2.31	-0.04
Iceland	46	15	8	74	80	51	65	64	0.26	-0.14	0.68	**-13.21**	-0.01
Ireland	53	27	11	12	85	54	65	59	0.36	0.09	0.62	**-7.32**	-0.03
Italy	22	30	23	34	84	83	50	60	0.37	0.06	0.68	**-6.31**	0.04
Japan	35	10	3	64	74	29	16	66	-0.41	-0.91	0.15	4.36	0.04
Korea	63	17	4	72	72	47	53	58	0.06	-0.34	0.41	**13.27**	**0.76**
Luxembourg	15	21	9	24	57	42	41	46	-0.30	-0.49	-0.09	1.48	-0.20
Mexico	71	23	28	81	50	63	40	49	-0.11	-0.54	0.26	-0.37	**0.27**
New Zealand	53	31	15	33	89	52	63	61	0.34	0.05	0.66	**-18.04**	**0.51**
Norway	30	16	8	56	67	36	35	53	-0.26	-0.59	0.05	**-11.93**	0.06
Poland	21	18	17	48	59	47	49	58	-0.04	-0.43	0.38	3.37	**0.51**
Portugal	45	20	18	75	59	65	48	63	0.13	-0.15	0.41	-5.10	-0.05
Spain	48	26	17	55	48	56	53	66	0.01	-0.41	0.48	2.04	0.14
Sweden	30	28	9	62	84	39	47	67	0.06	-0.22	0.33	**-16.33**	0.15
Switzerland	10	36	14	25	62	35	41	50	-0.27	-0.67	0.13	**-9.58**	-0.33
United Kingdom	76	50	14	22	91	49	55	63	0.30	0.04	0.58	**-12.88**	0.07
United States	61	24	13	79	83	50	58	59	0.42	0.09	0.78	-1.51	0.20
OECD total	*47*	*24*	*14*	*61*	*71*	*49*	*47*	*58*	*0.06*	*-0.31*	*0.45*	*-0.95*	
Country mean	*39*	*24*	*14*	*50*	*68*	*48*	*49*	*57*	*0.00*	*-0.36*	*0.37*	*-2.34*	*0.18*
Brazil	50	30	40	51	68	77	57	79	0.61	0.15	1.06	**8.02**	**0.23**
Latvia	57	17	12	50	46	53	49	59	-0.10	-0.54	0.38	1.55	m
Liechtenstein	8	44	9	22	65	33	34	56	-0.27	-0.57	0.32	-12.31	-0.30
Russian Federation	39	22	21	42	59	60	61	82	0.47	0.11	0.81	**-4.99**	-0.01
Netherlands[3]	7	15	8	18	70	29	49	44	-0.26	-0.55	-0.26	-10.38	-0.17

1. For the definition of the index see the Definitions and Methodologies section of this indicator.

2. Unit changes and correlations marked in bold are statistically significant.

3. Response rate is too low to ensure comparability (see Annex 3 at *www.oecd.org/els/education/eag2002*).

Source: OECD PISA database, 2001. See Annex 3 for notes on methodology (*www.oecd.org/els/education/eag2002*) and *www.pisa.oecd.org*.

Table D5.3.
Quality and use of school resources for 15-year-olds (2000)

	Quality and use of the school library			Availability and use of computers			Quality and use of science laboratory equipment			PISA index of use of school resources[2]	
	Percentage of students enrolled in schools where principals report that learning is hindered to some extent or a lot by lack of instructional material in the library[1]	Percentage of students who report that they[2]...		Percentage of students enrolled in schools where principals report that learning is hindered to some extent or a lot by lack of computers[1]	Percentage of students who report that they[2]...		Percentage of students enrolled in schools where school principals report that learning is hindered to some extent or a lot by inadequate science laboratory equipment[1]	Percentage of students who report that they[2]...			Change in the PISA reading literacy score per unit of the PISA index of use of school resources[3]
		never use the school library	use the school library at least several times a month		never use computers in the school	use computers in the school at least several times a month		never use the science laboratory	use the science laboratory at least several times a month	Mean index[2]	
OECD COUNTRIES											
Australia	17	11	35	30	8	60	16	16	61	1.27	11.98
Austria	22	67	4	38	15	68	34	57	25	0.16	28.06
Belgium	24	69	4	19	27	48	19	43	27	-0.57	49.50
Canada	20	19	22	31	14	50	19	20	44	0.73	8.44
Czech Republic	25	74	4	31	33	47	22	62	17	-0.76	34.30
Denmark	14	14	43	28	2	79	21	11	77	1.47	10.35
Finland	43	53	6	43	6	64	43	67	9	0.02	3.75
France	15	31	20	28	35	22	13	43	33	m	m
Germany	35	73	10	50	38	32	32	41	37	-0.29	-0.94
Greece	50	60	6	68	31	37	64	50	14	-1.00	-14.67
Hungary	12	42	11	13	15	72	27	70	8	-0.30	31.51
Iceland	37	29	21	45	10	66	53	47	23	0.54	2.95
Ireland	48	69	7	41	35	42	42	22	59	-0.38	16.24
Italy	34	71	3	32	26	53	37	51	21	-0.78	7.48
Japan	24	50	16	31	60	22	34	50	19	-1.17	12.43
Korea	35	65	13	24	30	57	28	25	40	-0.76	-2.80
Luxembourg	16	51	11	23	22	49	14	55	24	-0.40	**-65.96**
Mexico	60	16	33	68	49	30	66	33	35	-0.55	33.89
New Zealand	11	10	32	40	16	41	19	15	65	0.75	14.53
Norway	59	20	22	61	11	44	49	10	62	0.86	5.52
Poland	32	19	21	39	27	55	43	37	33	-0.18	53.20
Portugal	17	16	38	39	30	33	23	47	33	-0.09	-3.57
Spain	27	44	14	30	40	37	32	37	29	-0.53	9.46
Sweden	27	15	36	51	10	60	16	6	83	1.38	3.60
Switzerland	15	46	12	23	23	43	16	44	29	-0.13	22.42
United Kingdom	38	31	18	56	9	63	42	7	67	0.70	14.04
United States	21	21	20	31	12	44	23	23	34	0.38	39.74
OECD total	*29*	*36*	*18*	*38*	*29*	*41*	*32*	*33*	*34*		
Country mean	*30*	*39*	*18*	*38*	*24*	*49*	*32*	*37*	*37*	*0.00*	*16.18*
NON-OECD COUNTRIES											
Brazil	36	21	28	63	61	14	55	57	11	-1.25	**20.00**
Latvia	47	14	28	40	30	45	60	50	18	m	m
Liechtenstein	21	43	9	41	12	57	58	33	41	0.40	m
Russian Federation	78	12	42	86	52	32	79	17	50	-0.18	34.20
Netherlands[4]	*31*	48	18	*39*	28	44	*20*	65	11	-0.34	52.39

1. Based on school principals' responses.
2. Based on students' responses. For the description of the index of the use of school resources see the section on Definitions and Methodologies of this indicator.
3. Unit changes marked in bold are statistically significant.
4. Response rate is too low to ensure comparability (see Annex 3 at *www.oecd.org/els/education/eag2002*).
Source: OECD PISA database, 2001. See Annex 3 for notes on methodology (*www.oecd.org/els/education/eag2002*) and *www.pisa.oecd.org.*

D5

Table D5.4.

Broader engagement of 15-year-olds with school (2000)

Percentage of 15-year-olds who agree or strongly agree with the following statements relating to their broader engagement with school

		Percentage of students who agree or strongly agree with the statement that "My school is a place where...							
		I feel like an outsider (or left out of things)"	I make friends easily"	I feel like I belong"	I feel awk-ward and out of place"	other students seem to like me"	I feel lonely"	I do not want to go"	I often feel bored"
OECD COUNTRIES	Australia	9	89	85	11	92	8	34	60
	Austria	7	86	85	18	72	10	29	49
	Belgium	10	86	53	19	87	7	42	46
	Canada	9	89	81	12	93	9	37	58
	Czech Republic	11	86	73	9	84	9	29	47
	Denmark	6	85	84	10	75	10	19	41
	Finland	6	84	86	11	84	8	26	60
	France	8	87	44	16	86	7	37	32
	Germany	6	81	82	15	67	8	25	49
	Greece	10	88	83	13	85	10	22	66
	Hungary	10	87	89	9	85	9	38	29
	Iceland	10	81	85	11	86	10	23	30
	Ireland	7	89	83	9	93	8	34	67
	Italy	7	90	73	9	88	16	38	54
	Japan	6	70	76	22	62	9	25	32
	Korea	15	83	68	15	42	10	30	46
	Luxembourg	9	84	72	19	68	11	30	50
	Mexico	10	84	88	11	76	12	9	28
	New Zealand	9	90	83	12	91	9	34	60
	Norway	6	85	79	10	86	8	23	58
	Poland	10	78	63	14	53	12	28	38
	Portugal	8	91	83	19	90	8	13	24
	Spain	5	90	52	12	89	7	30	66
	Sweden	6	87	78	7	88	9	20	58
	Switzerland	7	85	76	14	74	8	28	38
	United Kingdom	7	91	83	9	93	6	28	54
	United States	11	81	78	14	83	12	35	61
	OECD total	*9*	*82*	*75*	*14*	*77*	*10*	*29*	*48*
	Country mean	*8*	*85*	*77*	*13*	*80*	*9*	*28*	*48*
NON-OECD COUNTRIES	Brazil	5	89	86	10	88	8	20	30
	Latvia	9	79	86	15	63	14	18	31
	Liechtenstein	9	83	83	17	69	9	31	47
	Russian Federation	6	82	86	13	50	10	17	27
	Netherlands[1]	5	89	76	10	91	4	100	38

1. Response rate is too low to ensure comparability (see Annex 3 at *www.oecd.org/els/education/eag2002).*

Source: OECD PISA database, 2001. See Annex 3 for notes on methodology (*www.oecd.org/els/education/eag2002*) and *www.pisa.oecd.org.*

D5

SALARIES OF TEACHERS IN
PUBLIC PRIMARY AND SECONDARY SCHOOLS

- The mid-career salaries of lower secondary teachers range from less than US$ 10 000 in the Czech Republic and Hungary to US$ 40 000 and more in Germany, Japan, Korea, Switzerland and the United States. Some countries make a major investment in human resources despite lower levels of national income.

- An upper secondary teacher's salary per teaching hour is, on average, 42 per cent higher than that of a primary teacher, but the difference between these two levels of education is 10 per cent or less in Australia, New Zealand, Scotland and the United States, and more than 80 per cent in Spain and Switzerland.

- Teachers in Australia, Denmark, England, New Zealand and Scotland reach the highest step on the salary scale in 11 years or less, while a teacher in Austria, the Czech Republic, France, Greece, Hungary, Italy, Japan, Korea and Spain must teach for more than 30 years before reaching the maximum.

- Schools have at least some responsibility in deciding on the levels and extent of compensation for additional responsibilities and overtime in about half of the OECD countries.

Chart D6.1.

Teachers' salaries in lower secondary education (2000)

Annual statutory teachers' salaries in public institutions in lower secondary education, in equivalent US dollars converted using PPPs, and the ratio of salary after 15 years of experience to GDP per capita

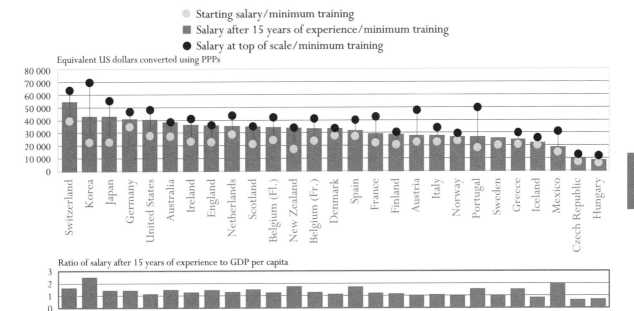

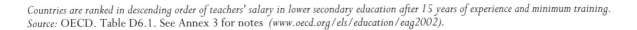

Countries are ranked in descending order of teachers' salary in lower secondary education after 15 years of experience and minimum training.
Source: OECD. Table D6.1. See Annex 3 for notes *(www.oecd.org/els/education/eag2002).*

Policy context

This indicator shows the starting, mid-career and maximum statutory salaries of teachers in public primary and secondary education, as well as various incentive schemes used in teacher rewards systems.

Education systems employ a large number of professionals in an increasingly competitive market. Ensuring that there is a sufficient number of skilled teachers is a key concern in all OECD countries. Salaries and working conditions of teachers, including starting salaries and pay scales, and the costs incurred by individuals in becoming teachers, compared to salaries and costs in other high-skill occupations are key factors in determining the supply of qualified teachers. Both affect the career decisions of potential teachers and the types of people who are attracted to the teaching profession.

Teachers' salaries are the largest single cost in providing education, making this compensation a critical consideration for policy-makers seeking to maintain the quality of teaching and a balanced education budget. The size of education budgets naturally reflects trade-offs between many interrelated factors, including teachers' salaries, the ratio of students to teaching staff, the instruction time planned for students, and the designated number of teaching hours.

Evidence and explanations

Comparing teachers' salaries

The first part of this indicator compares the starting, mid-career and maximum statutory salaries of teachers with the minimum level of qualifications required for certification in public primary and secondary education. First, teachers' salaries are examined in absolute terms at starting, mid-career and top-of-the-scale salary points, expressed in equivalent US dollars converted using purchasing power parities. This provides information on the influence of teaching experience on national salary scales, and on the cost of teaching time in different countries. Second, teachers' salaries are compared to GDP per capita to assess the value of teachers' salaries in terms of affordability for countries. Third, bonus schemes are examined.

The annual statutory salaries of lower secondary teachers with 15 years of experience range from below US$ 10 000 in the Czech Republic and Hungary, to over US$ 50 000 in Switzerland. This difference, which appears even after an adjustment for purchasing power parities has been made, can be explained to some extent by differences in GDP per capita between OECD countries, but it has a large impact on the variation in education costs per student (Table D6.1).

Statutory salaries, as reported in this indicator, refer to scheduled salaries according to official pay scales. These must be distinguished from the actual wage bills incurred by governments and teachers' average salaries, which are also influenced by other factors such as the age structure of the teaching force or the prevalence of part-time work. Furthermore, since teaching time and teachers' workload can vary considerably between countries, these factors

D6

should be considered when comparing statutory salaries for teachers in countries.

An alternative measure of salaries and the cost of teaching time is the statutory salary for a full-time classroom teacher relative to the number of hours per year which that teacher is required to spend teaching students (see Indicator D7). Although this measure does not adjust salaries for the amount of time that teachers spend in various teaching-related activities, it can nonetheless provide a rough estimate of the cost of the actual time teachers spend in the classroom. The average statutory salary per teaching hour after 15 years of experience is US$ 36 in primary, US$ 44 in lower secondary, and US$ 53 in upper secondary general education. In primary education, the Czech Republic, Hungary, Mexico and Turkey have relatively low salary costs per teaching hour (US$ 22 or less). By contrast, costs are relatively high (more than US$ 50 in Japan, Korea and Switzerland). There is even more variation in salary cost per teaching hour in general upper secondary schools, ranging from US$ 20 or less in the Czech Republic and Hungary to US$ 80 or more in Japan, Korea and Switzerland (Table D6.1).

The average statutory salary per teaching hour after 15 years of experience is US$ 36 in primary, US$ 44 in lower secondary, and US$ 53 in upper secondary general education.

Among other considerations, countries invest in teaching resources relative to their ability to fund educational expenditure. Comparing statutory salaries to GDP per capita is, therefore, another way of assessing the relative value of teachers' salaries across countries.

Comparing statutory salaries relative to GDP per capita adds a further perspective on teachers' salaries across countries. Mid-career salaries for primary teachers relative to GDP per capita are comparatively low in the Czech Republic, Hungary and Iceland, and relatively high in Korea, New Zealand and Turkey.

Mid-career salaries for primary teachers relative to GDP per capita are lowest in the Czech Republic (0.65), Hungary (0.71) and Iceland (0.80) and highest in Korea (2.49), New Zealand (1.70) and Turkey (2.06). The mid-career salary of a primary teacher in Spain is around the OECD average but its ratio to GDP per capita is relatively high compared with other OECD countries. In lower secondary education, mid-career salaries relative to GDP are highest in Korea (2.48) and Mexico (2.05). In upper secondary general education, the lowest ratios are found in the Czech Republic (0.80), Hungary (0.89) and Norway (0.92), and mid-career salaries relative to the GDP are highest in Korea (2.48), Mexico (2.18) and Turkey (1.91) (Table D6.1).

D6

There is a significant association between teachers' salaries and GDP per capita (the correlation is approximately 0.60), although the relationship is not straightforward. Some countries, such as the Czech Republic and Hungary, have both relatively low GDP per capita and low teachers' salaries. Others there have a relatively low GDP per capita and teachers' salaries that are comparable to those in countries with much higher GDP (*e.g.,* Greece, Korea, Mexico, Portugal and Turkey). Yet other countries with relatively high GDP per capita have lower than OECD average teachers' salaries (Iceland and Norway), whereas others have a high GDP per capita and high teachers' salaries (Switzerland and the United States) (Chart D6.1).

Some countries make a major investment in human resources despite lower levels of national income.

Teachers' salary scales and enhancements

In most countries, salaries increase with the level of education.

In Australia, England, Greece, Ireland, Japan, Korea, New Zealand, Norway, Portugal, Scotland and the United States, upper secondary and primary teachers' salaries are comparable, while in the remaining OECD countries, teachers' salaries increase with the level of education in absolute terms. For example, in Belgium, Hungary, the Netherlands and Switzerland, the mid-career salary of an upper secondary teacher is at least 25 per cent higher than that of a primary school teacher (Table D6.1).

An upper secondary teacher's salary per contact hour is, on average, 42 per cent higher than that of a primary teacher.

Even in countries where statutory salaries are the same in primary and secondary education, salaries per teaching hour are usually higher in upper secondary education than in primary education, since in most countries, secondary teachers are required to teach fewer hours than primary teachers. On average across countries, upper secondary teachers' salary per hour exceeds that of primary teachers by 42 per cent. However, in Australia, New Zealand, Scotland and the United States, this difference is only 10 per cent or less, whereas it is between 50 to 87 per cent in Belgium, France, Hungary, Iceland, Korea, the Netherlands, Portugal, Spain and Switzerland (Table D6.1).

Teaching experience and qualifications influence teachers' salary scales in many OECD countries.

Comparing gross teachers' salaries between countries at the point of entry into the teaching profession, after 15 years of experience, and at the top of the salary scale, provides information on the extent to which teaching experience influences salary scales within countries. The difference between statutory starting salaries and subsequent increases is an indication of the financial return to experience. On average, across OECD countries, statutory salaries for primary and lower secondary teachers with 15 years of experience are 37 to 39 per cent higher than starting salaries.

Teachers in Australia, Denmark, England, New Zealand and Scotland reach the highest step on the salary scale within 8 to 11 years. In Belgium, Finland, Germany, Ireland, the Netherlands, Norway and Portugal, the curve flattens after 20 to 28 years. In Austria, the Czech Republic, France, Greece, Hungary, Italy, Japan, Korea and Spain, teachers reach the top of the salary scale after more than 30 years of service (Table D6.1).

D6

Teachers in Austria, Japan, Korea, Mexico or Portugal start with a relatively low salary level, but the ratio of the top to the starting salary is 2:1 or more. By contrast, top salaries of teachers in Denmark, Norway and Iceland are less than 30 per cent higher than starting salaries. In Iceland, long service is rewarded by a reduction in the number of statutory teaching hours rather than by higher salaries. In Greece, salary increments and reduced teaching time are both used to reward long service (Table D6.1).

In addition, bonus schemes can compensate for permanent or

In addition to basic pay scales, many school systems have developed incentive schemes for teachers, which may take the form of financial remuneration and/or a reduction in the number of teaching hours. Together with the starting salary, such incentive schemes affect a person's decision to enter the teaching profession. Initial incentives for graduate teachers may include family allowances and bonuses for working in certain locations, higher initial salaries for higher than minimum teaching certification or qualifications, and additional compensation for those holding educational qualifications in multiple subjects or with certification to teach students with special educational needs.

temporary special duties and responsibilities that teachers take on …

In most countries, allowances are paid to all or most teachers for taking on management responsibilities; teaching more classes or hours than are required under a full-time contract (*e.g.*, acting duties); and involvement in special tasks such as guidance counselling or training student teachers. Although in many countries, there are country level regulations for payment of allowances for overtime work, management responsibilities, and special tasks and activities, in about half of the OECD countries with comparable data (Australia, the Czech Republic, Denmark, England, France, Greece, Hungary, Iceland, Ireland, Italy, Mexico, New Zealand, Portugal and Sweden), schools have at least some responsibility in deciding on the levels and extent of compensation for such activities (Table D6.2).

Once in the teaching profession, teaching personnel must be recognised and rewarded for good teaching. Schools can provide incentives by awarding additional remuneration for completing professional development activities, for involvement in special activities, for taking on extra management responsibilities or for outstanding performance in teaching (Table D6.2).

…as well as for educational qualifications or outstanding performance.

In Sweden, teachers' salaries are based upon collective agreements. Educational qualifications, development activities and outstanding performance in teaching are criteria for raising salaries above base levels. In New Zealand, school principals dispose of a number of salary units in addition to the annual entitlement for teaching positions, which they can use to recruit, retain or reward teachers (Table D6.2 and Annex 3 at *www.oecd.org/els/education/eag2002*).

In Spain, in addition to the triennial salary supplement constituting the steps of the salary ladder, teachers may earn salary supplements by participating in professional development and earn an in-service qualification, which also increases their salary further (Table D6.2 and Annex 3 at *www.oecd.org/els/education/eag2002*).

D6

Salary supplements in Spain

All teachers in public and private institutions receive a small salary supplement (*trienios*) every three years. In pre-primary and primary education, teachers begin their careers at 22 years of age and can teach for a maximum of 43 years (*i.e.*, 14 *trienios*). In uppersecondary education, longer initial training requirements mean that teachers start their careers two years later and can obtain a maximum experience of 41 years (*i.e.*, 13 *trienios*). Teachers in public education can receive a salary supplement every six years (*sexenio*), which is related to in-service training. Teachers must complete 100 hours of recognised in-service training courses during that time period to receive this supplement. Teachers in public education can receive a maximum of 5 *sexenios*. Since 1990, teachers in general secondary education can receive *catedrático condition*, which is a salary supplement for a specific in-service attained qualification. *Catedráticos* formerly referred to a distinct teacher with the same qualifications but higher entry requirements. In upper secondary general education, only teachers of non-technical subjects can receive this supplement, which refers to only 15 per cent of teachers.

Operation of salary units in
New Zealand State and Integrated Schools

In 1996, salary units were introduced in the Secondary Teacher Collective Employment Contract and translated to the primary school sector in subsequent negotiations.

In addition to an annual entitlement to a specific number of teaching positions calculated according to national staffing regulations, schools receive entitlement to a number of salary units to be allocated to teaching staff. The value of each salary unit is set in the negotiation of the national collective employment contracts/collective agreements, and was $2 750 per annum from 19 April 2000.

Each school determines the basis for allocating units, which are typically assigned on the basis of responsibilities (largely managerial; *i.e.*, Deputy Principal, Heads of Department, Deans), however they can also be used to recruit, retain or reward individual teachers.

Units may be allocated on a permanent or a fixed-term basis subject to the limitations prescribed in the relevant collective employment contract/collective agreement.

In addition to the effect on the immediate salary, teachers who are allocated one or more units permanently are entitled to progress beyond their maximum qualification salary step to the top step of the base scale.

In practice, approximately half of the entitlement units in primary schools were given as a single unit to teachers. In secondary schools, 56 per cent of units were allocated in one or two unit bundles to teachers. Due in part to the larger number of units able to be allocated in secondary schools, over half of all secondary teachers receive one or more units.

Pay scales are based on the simple principles of qualification levels and years of service but in reality, the structure of the teacher compensation system is far more complex. Many countries include regional allowances for teaching in remote regions, or a family allowance as part of the annual gross salary. Entitlements may include reduced rates on public transportation, tax allowances on purchasing cultural goods, and other quasi-pecuniary entitlements that contribute to teacher's basic income. There are large differences between the taxing and social benefit systems in OECD countries. This makes it important to compare teachers' salaries with caution.

Differences in tax wedges, social benefit systems, allowances and entitlements may enhance basic salaries of all teachers differently in OECD countries.

Definitions and methodologies

Data on statutory teachers' salaries and bonuses (Table D6.1) derives from the 2001 OECD-INES Survey on Teachers and the Curriculum and refer to the school year 1999-2000, and are reported in accordance with formal policies for public institutions.

Data are from the 2001 OECD-INES survey on Teachers and the Curriculum and refer to the school year 1999-2000.

Statutory salaries (Table D6.1) refer to scheduled salaries according to official pay scales. The salaries reported are gross (total sum of money paid by the employer) less the employer's contribution to social security and pension (according to existing salary scales). Salaries are "before tax", *i.e.*, before deductions for income taxes.

Gross teachers' salaries were converted using GDP and Purchasing Power Parities (PPPs) exchange rate data from the OECD National Accounts database. The reference date for GDP per capita is the calendar year 2000, while the period of reference for teachers' salaries is 30 June 1999 to 30 June 2000. The reference date for PPPs is 1999-2000. Data are adjusted for inflation with reference to January 2000 for countries with different financial years (*i.e.*, Australia and New Zealand) and for countries with slightly different salary periods (*e.g.*, Hungary, Iceland, Norway and Spain) only if this results in an adjustment of over 1 per cent. Small adjustments have been discounted because even for salaries referring to 1999-2000, the exact period for which they apply will only be slightly different. Reference statistics and reference years for teachers' salaries are provided in Annex 2.

Starting salaries refer to the average scheduled gross salary per year for a full-time teacher with the minimum training necessary to be fully qualified at the beginning of the teaching career.

Salaries after 15 years of experience refer to the scheduled annual salary of a full-time classroom teacher with the minimum training necessary to be fully qualified and have 15 years of experience. The maximum salaries reported refer to the scheduled maximum annual salary (top of the salary scale) of a full-time classroom teacher with the minimum training to be fully qualified for the job.

An adjustment to base salary is defined as any difference in salary between what a particular teacher actually receives for work performed at a school and the amount that he or she would be expected to receive on the basis of level of experience (*i.e.*, number of years in the teaching profession). Adjustments may be temporary or permanent, and they can effectively move a teacher "off-scale", on to a different salary, or to a higher step on the same salary scale.

D6

Table D6.1.
Teachers' salaries (2000)
Annual statutory teachers' salaries in public institutions at starting salary, after 15 years of experience and at the top of the salary scale, by level of education, in equivalent US dollars converted using PPPs

	Primary education				Lower secondary education				Upper secondary education, general programmes			
	Starting salary/ minimum training	Salary after 15 years of experience/ minimum training	Salary at top of scale/ minimum training	Ratio of salary after 15 years of experience to GDP per capita	Starting salary/ minimum training	Salary after 15 years of experience/ minimum training	Salary at top of scale/ minimum training	Ratio of salary after 15 years of experience to GDP per capita	Starting salary/ minimum training	Salary after 15 years of experience/ minimum training	Salary at top of scale/ minimum training	Ratio of salary after 15 years of experience to GDP per capita
OECD COUNTRIES												
Australia	26 887	38 297	38 300	1.43	26 946	38 312	38 314	1.43	26 946	38 312	38 314	1.43
Austria	21 953	26 570	44 461	1.03	22 574	27 691	47 055	1.07	24 192	30 584	53 808	1.19
Belgium (Fl.)	24 122	32 318	38 328	1.22	24 336	34 079	41 547	1.28	30 194	43 580	52 383	1.64
Belgium (Fr.)	22 983	31 282	37 459	1.18	23 466	33 173	40 666	1.25	29 275	42 707	51 540	1.61
Czech Republic	7 043	9 339	12 524	0.65	7 043	9 339	12 524	0.65	8 570	11 381	15 221	0.80
Denmark	29 116	32 883	32 883	1.16	29 116	32 883	32 883	1.16	28 825	38 279	40 931	1.35
England	22 428	35 487	35 487	1.48	22 428	35 487	35 487	1.48	22 428	35 487	35 487	1.48
Finland	18 489	25 183	26 140	1.03	20 720	28 690	30 124	1.18	21 517	30 124	31 878	1.23
France	20 199	27 172	40 091	1.17	22 358	29 331	42 357	1.26	22 358	29 331	42 357	1.26
Germany	31 213	37 905	41 021	1.52	3 4891	40 561	46 180	1.63	37 394	43 881	52 004	1.76
Greece	20 065	24 336	29 358	1.50	2 0387	24 658	29 680	1.52	20 387	24 658	29 680	1.52
Hungary	6 086	8 659	11 805	0.71	6 086	8 659	11 805	0.71	7 375	10 896	14 562	0.89
Iceland	20 222	22 202	25 738	0.80	20 222	22 202	25 738	0.80	21 071	26 162	31 394	0.95
Ireland	22 063	35 760	40 365	1.24	23 163	36 145	40 750	1.25	23 163	36 145	40 750	1.25
Italy	20 927	25 115	30 306	1.03	22 657	27 507	33 510	1.13	22 657	28 329	35 138	1.16
Japan	22 670	42 820	54 663	1.62	22 670	42 820	54 663	1.62	22 670	42 845	56 307	1.62
Korea	26 300	43 952	69 818	2.49	26 148	43 800	69 666	2.48	26 148	43 800	69 666	2.48
Mexico	11 235	14 824	24 536	1.62	14 383	18 760	30 859	2.05	m	m	m	m
Netherlands	27 411	32 686	39 563	1.18	28 443	34 985	43 466	1.26	28 713	48 840	57 907	1.77
New Zealand	17 354	33 653	33 653	1.70	17 354	33 653	33 653	1.70	17 354	33 653	33 653	1.70
Norway	23 752	26 831	29 051	0.92	23 752	26 831	29 051	0.92	23 752	26 831	29 051	0.92
Portugal	17 914	26 607	49 492	1.52	17 914	26 607	49 492	1.52	17 914	26 607	49 492	1.52
Scotland	20 931	34 798	34 798	1.45	20 931	34 798	34 798	1.45	20 931	34 798	34 798	1.45
Spain	25 029	29 261	37 238	1.52	27 046	31 616	39 804	1.65	29 081	33 985	42 521	1.77
Sweden	19 893	25 553	m	1.05	19 893	25 553	m	1.05	21 663	27 241	m	1.12
Switzerland	34 808	45 728	54 308	1.53	41 048	54 763	63 534	1.83	49 123	65 041	73 946	2.18
Turkey	12 410	14 094	15 760	2.06	a	a	a	a	11 354	13 038	14 704	1.91
United States	27 631	40 072	48 782	1.12	27 643	40 072	47 908	1.12	27 751	40 181	48 037	1.12
Country mean	*21 469*	*29 407*	*36 145*	*1.32*	*22 727*	*31 221*	*38 674*	*1.35*	*23 808*	*33 582*	*41 366*	*1.45*
NON-OECD COUNTRIES												
Argentina	9 027	12 545	14 897	1.00	14 623	21 188	25 742	1.69	14 623	21 188	25 742	1.69
Brazil	7 420	10 176	11 309	1.48	14 820	16 240	18 723	2.36	15 500	16 121	19 776	2.35
Chile	10 716	12 038	16 122	1.39	10 716	12 038	16 122	1.39	10 716	12 582	16 883	1.45
China	2 835	2 952	3 595	0.88	2 835	2 952	3 595	0.88	2 835	2 952	3 595	0.88
Egypt	2 269	5 065	m	1.58	2 269	5 065	m	1.58	2 269	5 065	m	1.58
India[1]	10 678	15 236	16 375	7.22	12 992	19 373	21 074	9.18	15 798	23 205	24 914	11.00
Indonesia	1 357	2 148	4 093	0.77	1 357	2 148	4 093	0.77	1 412	2 586	4 093	0.93
Jamaica	8 332	9 927	9 927	2.82	8 332	9 927	9 927	2.82	8 332	9 927	9 927	2.82
Jordan	7 838	10 200	26 475	2.66	7 838	10 200	26 475	2.66	7 838	10 200	26 475	2.66
Malaysia	6 158	10 225	14 623	1.33	11 784	18 632	25 775	2.43	11 784	18 632	25 775	2.43
Paraguay	8 874	8 874	8 874	2.00	13 911	13 911	13 911	3.13	13 911	13 911	13 911	3.13
Peru[2]	5 523	5 523	5 523	1.19	5 462	5 462	5 462	1.18	5 462	5 462	5 462	1.18
Philippines	10 409	11 491	12 374	3.10	10 409	11 491	12 374	3.10	10 409	11 491	12 374	3.10
Russian Federation	3 735	3 735	3 735	0.54	3 735	3 735	3 735	0.54	3 735	3 735	3 735	0.54
Thailand	5 756	14 145	26 977	2.42	5 756	14 145	26 977	2.42	5 756	14 145	26 977	2.42
Tunisia[3]	13 186	14 505	15 149	2.60	16 965	18 549	19 340	3.30	20 540	22 270	23 177	4.00
Uruguay[4]	5 749	6 891	8 317	0.76	5 749	6 891	8 317	0.76	6 257	7 398	8 824	0.82
Zimbabwe	35 725	50 011	50 011	17.42	35 725	50 011	50 011	17.42	35 725	50 011	50 011	17.42

1. Salaries in National Capital Territory of Delhi. Teachers' salaries vary from state to state.
2. Year of reference 1999.
3. Including additional bonuses.
4. Salaries for a position of 20 hours per week. Most teachers hold two positions.
Source: OECD. See Annex 3 for sources and methodologies (*www.oecd.org/els/education/eag2002*).

D6

Table D6.1. (*continued*)
Teachers' salaries (2000)
Annual statutory teachers' salaries in public institutions at starting salary, after 15 years of experience and at the top of the salary scale, by level of education, in equivalent US dollars converted using PPPs

	Ratio of salary after 15 years of experience to starting salary			Years from starting to top salary (lower secondary education)	Salary per hour of net contact (teaching) time after 15 years of experience			Ratio of salary per teaching hour of upper secondary and primary teachers (after 15 years of experience)
	Primary education	Lower secondary education	Upper secondary education, general programmes		Primary education	Lower secondary education	Upper secondary education, general programmes	
OECD COUNTRIES								
Australia	1.42	1.42	1.42	8	43	47	48	1.10
Austria	1.21	1.23	1.26	34	39	42	49	1.27
Belgium (Fl.)	1.34	1.40	1.44	27	39	48	65	1.67
Belgium (Fr.)	1.36	1.41	1.46	27	39	46	64	1.64
Czech Republic	1.33	1.33	1.33	32	14	14	18	1.28
Denmark	1.13	1.13	1.33	8	51	51	68	1.33
England	1.58	1.58	1.58	8	m	m	m	m
Finland	1.36	1.38	1.40	20	38	50	57	1.49
France	1.35	1.31	1.31	34	30	46	48	1.60
Germany	1.21	1.16	1.17	28	48	55	64	1.31
Greece	1.21	1.21	1.21	33	31	39	39	1.26
Hungary	1.42	1.42	1.48	40	11	16	20	1.76
Iceland	1.10	1.10	1.24	18	35	35	56	1.60
Ireland	1.62	1.56	1.56	22	39	49	49	1.26
Italy	1.20	1.21	1.25	35	34	45	46	1.38
Japan	1.89	1.89	1.89	31	67	77	90	1.33
Korea	1.67	1.68	1.68	37	53	77	80	1.52
Mexico	1.32	1.30	m	14	19	16	m	m
Netherlands	1.19	1.23	1.70	22	35	40	56	1.60
New Zealand	1.94	1.94	1.94	10	34	35	35	1.04
Norway	1.13	1.13	1.13	28	38	42	53	1.41
Portugal	1.49	1.49	1.49	26	33	45	52	1.58
Scotland	1.66	1.66	1.66	11	37	39	39	1.06
Spain	1.17	1.17	1.17	42	33	56	62	1.87
Sweden	1.28	1.28	1.26	a	a	a	a	a
Switzerland	1.31	1.33	1.32	23	52	64	96	1.87
Turkey	1.14	a	1.15	a	22	a	26	1.17
United States	1.45	1.45	1.45	m	35	36	36	1.02
Country mean	*1.37*	*1.39*	*1.42*	*25*	*37*	*44*	*53*	*1.42*
NON-OECD COUNTRIES								
Argentina	1.35	1.41	1.41	21-24	2	2	3	1.71
Brazil	1.37	1.10	1.04	25	m	m	m	m
Chile	1.09	1.09	1.12	30	14	14	15	1.04
China	1.04	1.04	1.04	m	m	m	m	m
Egypt	2.11	2.11	2.11	m	8	8	8	1.00
India[1]	1.42	1.48	1.46	20	16	19	22	1.37
Indonesia	1.81	1.81	2.09	32	2	4	4	2.20
Jamaica	2.53	2.53	2.53	12	10	14	15	1.47
Jordan	1.30	1.30	1.30	43	13	13	15	1.17
Malaysia	1.67	1.59	1.59	22	13	24	24	1.79
Paraguay	1.15	1.15	1.15	a	12	17	15	1.25
Peru[2]	1.00	1.00	1.00	at least 20	8	10	10	1.19
Philippines	1.09	1.09	1.09	22	10	10	12	1.20
Russian Federation	1.00	1.00	1.00	m	m	m	m	m
Thailand	2.46	2.46	2.46	37	19	22	22	1.17
Tunisia[3]	1.10	1.09	1.08	30	25	40	48	1.92
Uruguay[4]	1.19	1.19	1.21	24	9	14	15	1.61
Zimbabwe	1.40	1.40	1.40	21	51	53	53	1.04

1. Salaries in National Capital Territory of Delhi. Teachers' salaries vary from state to state.
2. Year of reference 1999.
3. Including additional bonuses.
4. Salaries for a position of 20 hours per week. Most teachers hold two positions.
Source: OECD. See Annex 3 for sources and methodologies (*www.oecd.org/els/education/eag2002*).

D6

Table D6.2.
Adjustments to base salary for teachers in public schools (2000)
Types of adjustments to base salary awarded to teachers in public schools, by authority responsible for making the decision regarding the adjustment

▲ Decision for additional bonus made by the head teacher/school principal ■ Decision for additional bonus made by the local or regional authority ● Decision for additional bonus made by the national authority

	Holding an initial educational qualification higher than the minimum qualification required to enter the teaching profession	Reaching high scores in the qualification examination	Holding an educational qualification in multiple subjects (e.g., history and mathematics)	Successful completion of professional development activities	Management responsibilities in addition to teaching duties (e.g., serving as a head of department or co-ordinator of teachers in a particular class/grade)	Holding a higher than minimum level of teacher certification or training obtained during professional life (e.g., master teacher; holding an advanced certificate rather than an ordinary certificate)	Outstanding performance in teaching (e.g., based on higher student achievement, independent assessment of teaching skills, etc.)	Teaching courses in a particular field (e.g., mathematics or science)
Australia*	■				▲ ■	■		
Austria								
Belgium (Fl.)*								
Belgium (Fr.)*								
Czech Republic*					▲ ●		▲	
Denmark*	▲ ■ ●		▲ ■ ●	▲	▲	▲	▲	
England*	●				▲	●	▲	▲
Finland	■		■		■	■	■	■
France*						●		
Germany*								
Greece*	●							
Hungary*	▲		▲	▲	▲	▲	▲	▲
Iceland*					▲			▲
Ireland*	●				▲	●	●	
Italy				▲	▲			
Japan*					■	●		
Korea								●
Mexico*	▲ ■		●		▲ ■	■	●	
Netherlands*	●							
New Zealand*	●		●		▲	●	▲	●
Norway*	●					●		
Portugal*				●	▲	●	▲ ●	
Scotland*	■				■			
Spain				■	■		■	
Sweden*					▲ ■			
Switzerland						●		
Turkey*	●					●	■	
United States*	■			■	■	■	■	■

	Teaching students with special educational needs (in regular schools)	Teaching more classes or hours than required by full-time contract (e.g., overtime compensation)	Special activities (e.g., sports and drama clubs, homework clubs, Summer school etc.)	Special tasks (e.g., training student teachers, guidance counselling)	Teaching in a disadvantaged, remote or high cost area (location allowance)	Family status (e.g., married, number of children)	Age (independent of years of teaching experience)	Other
Australia*				▲ ■	■ ●		▲	
Austria							●	●
Belgium (Fl.)*								●
Belgium (Fr.)*								●
Czech Republic*	▲	●		●	▲	●	▲	
Denmark*		▲	▲					
England*	▲	▲	▲		▲	●		
Finland	■		■	■	■			
France*		●	▲		●	●		
Germany*		■				● ●	●	
Greece*		▲						
Hungary*	▲	▲	▲	▲	▲		▲	▲
Iceland*	▲	▲	▲	▲	■		■	
Ireland*								●
Italy			▲	▲				
Japan*		■	■			●		■
Korea		●	●		●	●		
Mexico*					●			▲ ■
Netherlands*		●						
New Zealand*		●		▲	▲			●
Norway*			●		●		●	
Portugal*		●	▲		●			
Scotland*					■			
Spain					■		■	
Sweden*		▲ ■		▲ ■				
Switzerland	■		■	■	●	●		■
Turkey*		●		●	●			
United States*	■		■		■			

* See Annex 3 for notes (*www.oecd.org/els/education/eag2002*).

Source: OECD.

TEACHING TIME AND TEACHERS' WORKING TIME

- The number of teaching hours per year in public primary schools averages 792 hours but ranges from 583 to 1 139 hours.

- The average number of teaching hours in the lower secondary education is 720 hours but ranges from 555 to 1 182 hours.

- Regulations of teachers' working time vary across countries. In most countries, teachers are formally required to work a specific number of hours; in others teaching time in lessons per week is specified. In some countries, time is set aside for non-teaching activities at school, while in others, teachers are required to be at school for a certain number of hours.

Chart D7.1.

Number of teaching hours per year (2000)

Net contact time in hours per year in public institutions, by level of education

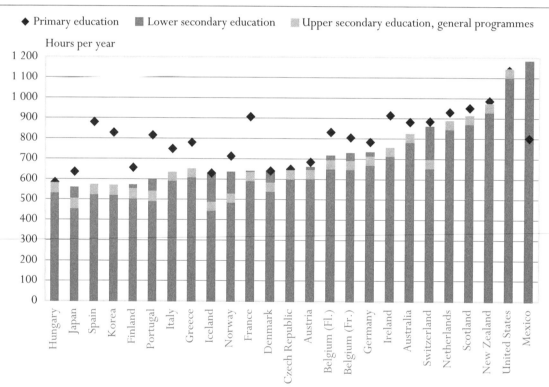

Countries are ranked in ascending order of the number of teaching hours in lower secondary education.
Source: OECD. Table D7.1. See Annex 3 for notes *(www.oecd.org/els/education/eag2002).*

D7

Policy context

In addition to class size and ratio of students to teaching staff (Indicator D2), students' hours of instruction (Indicator D1) and teachers' salaries (Indicator D6), the amount of time teachers spend teaching influences the financial resources which countries need to invest in education. Teaching hours and the extent of non-teaching duties are also important elements of teachers' working conditions and are related to the attractiveness of the teaching profession.

This indicator shows the number of hours per year that a full-time teacher is required to spend teaching according to formal policy in his/her country.

Evidence and explanations

Teaching time

A primary school teacher teaches an average of 792 hours per year but this varies from 650 hours or less in the Czech Republic, Denmark, Hungary, Iceland, Japan and Turkey to 950 hours or more in New Zealand, Scotland and the United States (Table D7.2).

At the lower secondary level of education, a teacher teaches on average 720 hours per year. The teaching load here ranges from around 555 hours in Finland, Hungary, Japan, Spain and Korea to over 900 hours in Mexico, New Zealand and the United States (Table D7.2).

A public primary school teacher teaches an average of 792 hours per year, but the figure ranges from 583 hours to 1 139 hours. A lower secondary teacher teaches an average of 720 hours per year, but this figure ranges from 555 hours to 1 182 hours

An upper secondary teaching load is equal to or less than that in lower secondary education. A teacher of general subjects has an average statutory load of 648 hours per year across OECD countries. Teaching loads range from less than 500 hours in Iceland and Japan to over 900 hours in New Zealand and the United States (Table D7.2).

In France, Korea, Portugal and Spain, a primary teacher is required to teach almost more than 300 hours more than an upper secondary teacher (general programmes). By contrast, in Austria, Australia, the Czech Republic, Denmark, Finland, Germany, the Netherlands, New Zealand, Scotland and the United States the difference is less than 100 hours (Chart D7.1).

In most countries, a primary school teacher teaches for more hours than a lower and upper secondary teacher, but the differentials vary widely between countries

D7

In interpreting the differences in teaching hours between countries, it needs to be taken into account that net contact time, as used for the purpose of this indicator, does not correspond to the number of lessons a teacher has during the week. Whereas contact time in itself is a substantial component of workload, the preparation for classes and necessary follow-up (including correcting students' work) relates more closely to the number of lessons per week. Other elements of teaching load (like the number of subjects taught, the number of students taught, and the number of years a teacher teaches the same students should also be taken account when establishing the average teaching load of teachers within a country. These factors, however, can often only be assessed at school level.

With the exception of the Czech Republic, Hungary, Portugal and Spain (upper secondary education), teaching time in most OECD countries was about the

With the exception of the Czech Republic,

Hungary, Portugal and Spain, teaching time did not change substantially between 1996 and 2000.

same in 1996 and 2000. It increased by about 6 per cent in primary education, and 17 per cent in lower and upper secondary education in Hungary. In the Czech Republic, teachers in secondary education were required to teach 7 per cent more in 2000 than in 1996. By contrast, in Portugal net contact time dropped by 8 and 10 per cent in lower and upper secondary education, respectively. In Spain, teaching time in upper secondary education also decreased by 13 per cent (Table D7.2).

Teachers' working time

Regulations of teachers' working time vary widely across countries.

The regulations of teachers' working time vary widely across countries. While some countries formally regulate contact time only, others establish working hours as well. In some countries, time is allocated for teaching and non-teaching activities within the formally established working time. Within the framework of statutory working time and teaching time, teachers' actual workload may vary widely.

In most countries, teachers are formally required to work a specified number of hours…

In most countries, teachers are formally required to work a specified number of hours per week to earn their full-time salary including teaching and non-teaching time. Within this framework, however, countries vary regarding what they specify in terms of allocating time to teaching and non-teaching activities. Typically, the number of hours for teaching is specified, but some countries also regulate at national level the time that a teacher has to be present in the school.

…in some countries, teachers' working time is specified only in the general regulations on civil servants' working time…

In Japan and Korea, teachers are required to work the same number of hours as civil servants. No further regulations are provided at the national level concerning teaching or non-teaching hours. However, in Korea, teachers are required to work during the school vacation on their own schedule on professional development (Table D7.1).

…in some, teaching time in lessons per week is also specified…

As part of the mandatory working time, teaching time in lessons per week is specified in Austria, Belgium, the Czech Republic, Denmark, France, Greece, Hungary, Iceland, Italy, Korea, Mexico, the Netherlands, Norway, Portugal, Scotland, Spain, Switzerland and Turkey (Table D7.1).

D7

Austria

The Education Act governing teachers stipulates only teaching hours (20 to 24 periods of 50 minutes per week). Provisions concerning teaching time are based on the assumption that a teacher's duties (including preparing lessons, test marking, correcting papers and examinations and administrative tasks) amount to a total of 40 hours a week.

In Belgium, the Czech Republic, Finland, France, Ireland, New Zealand, Portugal and Turkey, teachers are required to be at school only for scheduled teaching hours. However, teaching assignments and school related non-teaching activities may be specified at the school level.

…in some, time is set aside at the national level for non-teaching activities at school…

Hungary

The mandatory 40 hours working hours conforms to the work week of public employees and is a formal requirement for teachers. Most preparation takes place outside school. School-related activities (*e.g.*, staff meetings, meetings with parents, preparation for school festivities, etc.) are specified at the school level. Pre-primary teachers are required to teach 32 lessons per week (of 60 minutes each), primary teachers teach 21 lessons (of 45 minutes each), and secondary teachers teach 20 lessons (45 minutes each) to earn a full-time salary. Overtime is paid and is often required.

In Scotland and Spain, in addition to teaching hours, time is stipulated for specific non-teaching activities at school.

Teaching and non-teaching time in Spain

Primary teachers are required to work for 37.5 hours per week, including 22.5 hours of net contact time and 7.5 additional hours for school activities (breaks, meetings and pedagogical activities). The remaining 7.5 hours may be spent out of school to prepare classes, for professional development, etc. Secondary teachers are required to teach 16.5 hours per week, and are expected to be available at school for 30 hours per week.

D7

Regulation of teachers' working time in Scotland

The working hours of teachers come under the overall direction of the Head teacher, and include 27.5 hours per week in school, of which the maximum class contact time is 25 hours in primary education, 23.5 hours in lower secondary education, and 22.5 hours in special schools. Except for teachers in special schools and units, the balance between the specified class contact time and the 27.5 hours are available to teachers for work relevant to individual teaching duties. The Head teacher can use this time for other purposes only under exceptional circumstances. The hours of

---

part-time teachers include class contact time, and a *pro-rata* element for non-class contact time. A teacher's working hours also include an additional maximum of up to 30 hours during the school year for parent meetings, stipulated as the total including preparatory work and provision of travelling time up to a maximum of six meetings within the school year.

…and in some countries, formal agreements regulate teaching and non-teaching duties.

In some countries, including Denmark and Iceland, detailed formal agreements between teachers' unions and public authorities regulate the methods that schools are supposed to use in calculating hours for teaching and non-teaching duties.

Allocation of working time in Denmark

The formal demands of 37 working hours per week in primary and lower secondary education include, for every hour of teaching, one hour of preparation time and an average of 30 minutes of non-teaching time in the reference year. In upper secondary education (general programmes), a collective agreement between the county authorities and the teachers' union defines lesson preparation time as 75 per cent of the number of lessons * 1.33 hours, and the hours to be used for examinations as an average of 110 hours per annum. Remaining duties are defined at the local level. In upper secondary education (vocational programmes), the management of the school and the teachers' representative must agree on the principles for allocating working hours for preparation, etc. in accordance with the collective agreement between the teachers' union and the Ministry of Finance. Preparation time is limited to between 13 and 126 minutes per 60 minutes of teaching. Norms for correcting written work, examination work, etc., are regulated by the collective agreement or by local agreement within the school. As a minimum, each teacher is allowed 50 hours per year for pedagogical, theoretical and skills development.

Calculating the teaching workload in Iceland

A teacher's workload in primary and lower secondary education is divided into teaching (K), preparing lessons (U), and other work (Ö). If other work is increased for a particular teacher, s/he can either choose to teach less or to receive overtime pay; a part-time teacher is entitled to a higher percentage of a full-time job. In upper secondary education, the teacher's workload is divided into five categories: work at school under the supervision of the head teacher (130 hours), teaching and teaching-related work (1 177 hours), work during the six examination weeks (258 hours), preparation and follow-up at the beginning and end of the school year (32 hours), and professional development. In some countries, teachers' working time – including teaching time – is regulated at regional, local or school levels.

In Australia, England, Finland, Germany, New Zealand, Sweden and the United States, teachers' working time – including the allocation of teaching time – is defined at sub-national levels. In Sweden, for example, within the general framework of 40 hours per week required of public employees, schools negotiate with teachers on an individual basis regarding teaching and non-teaching duties. However, a formal agreement between the Swedish Association of Local Authorities and teachers' unions limits the number of working hours during the school year. Within these limits, teaching time is not regulated so as to allow for teaching non-compulsory subjects.

Working time regulations in Sweden

Working time is regulated in formal agreements between the Swedish Association of Local Authorities and teachers' unions. According to the Teacher Agreement 2000, working time is regulated at 1 360 hours per school year. Teachers themselves are responsible for how they spend the remaining working time. Teaching time in hours is not regulated so as to allow for teaching non-compulsory subjects.

Definitions and methodologies

Teaching time

The number of teaching hours is defined as net contact hours calculated on the basis of the annual number of weeks of instruction multiplied by the minimum/maximum number of periods that a teacher is supposed to spend teaching a class or a group, multiplied by the length of a period in minutes and divided by 60. This excludes break periods between lessons and days when schools are closed for public holidays and festivities. In primary education, however, short breaks that teachers spend with the class are typically included.

Data are from the 2001 OECD-INES Survey on Teachers and the Curriculum and refer to the school year 1999–2000.

Working time

Working time refers to the normal working hours of a full-time teacher. According to the formal policy in a given country, working time can refer:

- only to the time directly associated with teaching (and other curricular activities for students such as assignments and tests, but excluding annual examinations);

- or to time directly associated with teaching and to hours devoted to other activities related to teaching, such as lesson preparation, counselling students, correcting assignments and tests, professional development, meetings with parents, staff meetings and general school tasks.

Working time does not include paid overtime.

Working time in school

Working time in school refers to the working time teachers are supposed to be at school, including teaching time and non-teaching time.

Number of teaching weeks and days

The number of teaching weeks refers to the number of weeks of instruction excluding holiday weeks, and is calculated as the number of teaching weeks less the days that the school is closed for festivities.

D7

Table D7.1.
The organisation of teachers' working time (2000)
Number of teaching weeks, teaching days, net teaching hours, and teacher working time over the school year

		Number of weeks of instruction		Number of days of instruction		Net teaching time in hours			Working time required at school in hours			Total statutory working time in hours		
		Primary education	Secondary education	Primary education	Secondary education	Primary education	Lower secondary education	Upper secondary education, general programmes	Primary education	Lower secondary education	Upper secondary education	Primary education	Lower secondary education	Upper secondary education
OECD COUNTRIES	Australia	40	40	196	196	882	811	803	a	a	a	1 310[2]	1 310[2]	1 310[2]
	Austria	38	38	187	187	684	658	623	m	m	m	a	a	a
	Belgium (Fl.)	37	37	178	179	831	716	671	m[3]	m[3]	m[3]	a	a	a
	Belgium (Fr.)	38	38	182	182	804	728	673	871[3]	734[3]	673[3]	a	a	a
	Czech Republic	40	40	197	197	650	650	621	650[3]	650[3]	621[3]	1 700	1 700	1 700
	Denmark	42	42	200	200	640	640	560	a	a	a	1 680[1]	1 680[1]	1 680[1]
	England	38	38	190	190	a	a	a	a	a	a	1 265[2]	1 265[2]	1 265[2]
	Finland	38	38	190	190	656	485 - 656	428 - 627	964[3]	905[3]	901[3]	a	a	a
	France	35	35	m	m	907	639	611	907[3]	639[3]	611[3]	a	a	a
	Germany	39	39	188	188	783	732	690	a	a	a	1702 - 1760[1]	1702 - 1760[1]	1702 - 1760[1]
	Greece	40	38	195	185	780	629	629	1 000[3]	798[3]	798[3]	1 500[1]	1 425[1]	1 425[1]
	Hungary	37	37	185	185	777	555	555	a	a	a	1 664[1]	1 664[1]	1 664[1]
	Iceland	38	38	170	170	629	629	464	a	a	a	1 800[1]	1 800[1]	1 800[1]
	Ireland	37	33	183	167	915	735	735	a	735[3]	735[3]	1 036[2]	a	a
	Italy	34	34	m	m	748	612	612	m[3]	m[3]	m3	a	a	a
	Japan	35	35	193	193	635	557	478	a	a	a	1 940[5]	1 940[5]	1 940[5]
	Korea	37	37	220	220	829	565	545	a	a	a	1 613[5]	1 613[5]	1 613[5]
	Mexico	42	42	200	200	800	1 182	m	a	a	m	900[2]	1 680[1]	m
	Netherlands	40	40	195	195	930	867	867	a	a	a	1 659[1]	1 659[1]	1 659[1]
	New Zealand	39	39	197	192	985	968	950	985[3]	968[3]	950[3]	a	a	a
	Norway	38	38	190	190	713	633	589	a	a	a	1 718[1]	1 718[1]	1 718[1]
	Portugal	34	34	163	163	815	595	515	815[3]	595[3]	515[3]	1 596[1]	1 596[1]	1 596[1]
	Scotland	38	38	190	190	950	893	893	1 075[2]	1 075[2]	1 075[2]	1 153[1]	1 153[1]	1 153[1]
	Spain	37	36	176	171	880	564	548	1 110	1 080	1 050	1 418[2]	1 418[2]	1 418[2]
	Sweden	a	a	a	a	a	a	a	1 360[2]	1 360[2]	1 360[2]	1 767[1]	1 767[1]	1 767[1]
	Switzerland	38	38	m	m	884	859	674	884[3]	859[3]	674[3]	m	m	m
	Turkey	38	a	180	180	639	639	504	639[3]	6 39[3]	504[3]	a	a	a
	United States[6]	36	36	180	180	1 139	1 127	1 121	1 353[4]	1 371[4]	1371[4]	1 353[4]	1 371[4]	1 371[4]
NON-OECD COUNTRIES	**Argentina**	38	38	m	m	765	850	755	m	m	m	m	m	m
	Brazil	40	40	m	m	800	800	800	m	m	m	m	m	m
	Chile	40	40	m	m	860	860	860	m	m	m	m	m	m
	Egypt	36	36	m	m	748	748	748	m	m	m	m	m	m
	India	42	42	m	m	743	825	825	m	m	m	m	m	m
	Indonesia	44	44	m	m	1 260	738	738	m	m	m	m	m	m
	Jamaica	38	38	m	m	950	703	646	m	m	m	m	m	m
	Jordan	44	44	m	m	774	774	659	m	m	m	m	m	m
	Malaysia	41	41	m	m	758	774	774	m	m	m	m	m	m
	Paraguay	35	37	m	m	720	801	900	m	m	m	m	m	m
	Peru[7]	36	36	m	m	783	626	626	m	m	m	m	m	m
	Philippines	40	40	m	m	1 176	1 176	980	m	m	m	m	m	m
	Russian Federation	45	45	m	m	860	774	774	m	m	m	m	m	m
	Thailand	40	40	m	m	760	652	652	m	m	m	m	m	m
	Tunisia	33	31	m	m	730	544	544	m	m	m	m	m	m
	Uruguay[8]	38	38	m	m	732	489	489	m	m	m	m	m	m
	Zimbabwe	39	39	m	m	975	936	936	m	m	m	m	m	m

1. Full-time teachers work a specified number of hours per week to earn their full-time salary and working time is allocated for both teaching and non-teaching activities (such as lesson preparation, examinations, meetings and general school tasks) completed at school or outside school.
2. Full-time teachers are required to be at school for specified number of hours per week to earn their full-time salary, and working time is allocated for both teaching and non-teaching activities (such as lesson preparation, examinations, meetings and general school tasks), of which a specified amount of hours has to be spent at school.
3. Full-time teachers are only required to be at school for a specified number of hours. (*i.e.*, the teaching hours plus breaks between teaching hours). There is no requirement for how much time must be spent on non-teaching activities.
4. Teacher working time is set at the individual, local or school level. It includes teaching and non-teaching activities.
5. Statutory working time for public employees. In Korea, working time is calculated only for the school-year period.
6. The number of teaching weeks is estimated on the basis of the PISA average. Teachers' working time required in school is estimated from teachers' reports of the number of hours they are required to be at school.
7. Year of reference 1999.
8. Teaching time for a position of 20 hours per week. Most teachers hold two positions.

Source: OECD. See Annex 3 for notes, sources and methodologies (*www.oecd.org/els/education/eag2002*).

D7

Table D7.2.
Number of teaching hours per year (1996, 2000)
Net contact time in hours per year in public institutions, by level of education, and index of change from 1996 to 2000

	Primary education			Lower secondary education			Upper secondary education, general programmes		
	2000	1996	Index of change 1996-2000	2000	1996	Index of change 1996-2000	2000	1996	Index of change 1996-2000
Australia	882	m	m	811	m	m	803	m	m
Austria	684	684	n	658	658	n	623	623	n
Belgium (Fl.)	831	841	-1%	716	724	-1%	671	679	-1%
Belgium (Fr.)	804	858	-6%	728	734	-1%	668	677	-1%
Czech Republic	650	635	2%	650	607	7%	621	580	7%
Denmark	640	640	n	640	640	n	560	560	n
Finland	656	m	m	570	m	m	527	m	m
France	907	900	1%	639	647	-1%	611	m	m
Germany	783	772	1%	732	715	2%	690	671	3%
Greece	780	780	n	629	629	n	629	629	n
Hungary	583	551	6%	555	473	17%	555	473	17%
Iceland	629	m	m	629	m	m	464	m	m
Ireland	915	915	n	735	735	n	735	735	n
Italy	748	748	n	612	612	n	612	612	n
Japan	635	m	m	557	m	m	478	m	m
Korea	829	m	m	565	m	m	545	m	m
Mexico	800	800	n	1 182	1 182	n	m	m	m
Netherlands	930	930	n	867	867	n	867	867	n
New Zealand	985	985	n	968	968	n	950	950	n
Norway	713	713	n	633	611	4%	505	505	n
Portugal	815	783	4%	595	644	-8%	515	574	-10%
Scotland	950	975	-3%	893	m	m	893	917	-3%
Spain	880	900	-2%	564	m	m	548	630	-13%
Sweden	a	624	m	a	576	m	a	528	m
Switzerland	884	871	1%	859	850	1%	674	669	1%
Turkey	639	m	m	a	a	m	504	m	m
United States	1 139	958	19%	1 127	964	17%	1 121	942	19%
Country mean	*792*	*802*	*n*	*720*	*728*	*n*	*648*	*674*	*n*

OECD COUNTRIES

Source: OECD. See Annex 3 for notes, sources and methodologies (*www.oecd.org/els/education/eag2002*).

Annex

TYPICAL GRADUATION AGES

The typical graduation age is the age at the end of the last school/academic year of the corresponding level and programme when the degree is obtained. The typical age is based on the assumption of full-time attendance in the regular education system without grade repetition. (Note that at some levels of education the term "graduation age" may not translate literally and is used here purely as a convention.)

Table X1.1a
Typical graduation ages in upper secondary education

	Programme orientation		Educational/labour market destination			
	General programmes	Pre-vocational or vocational programmes	ISCED 3A programmes	ISCED 3B programmes	ISCED 3C short programmes[1]	ISCED 3C long programmes[1]
OECD COUNTRIES						
Australia	m	m	17	m	m	m
Belgium	18	18	18	a	18	18
Czech Republic	18	18	18	18	a	17
Denmark	19-20	19-20	19-20	a	a	19-20
Finland	19	19	19	a	a	a
France	18-19	17-20	18-19	19-20	17-20	18-21
Germany	19	19	19	19	a	a
Greece	18	17-18	18	a	a	17-18
Hungary	18-20	16-17	18-20	20-22	16-17	18
Iceland	19	19	19	18	17	19
Ireland	18	18	18	a	a	18
Italy	19	19	19	19	17	a
Japan	18	16-18	18	18	16	16
Korea	17-18	17-18	17-18	a	a	17-18
Luxembourg	19	17-19	17-19	19	n	17-19
Mexico	18	19	18	a	19	19
Netherlands	17-18	18-20	17-18	a	a	18-20
New Zealand	m	m	18	17	17	17
Norway	18-19	18-19	18-19	a	18-19	16-18
Poland	19	20	19-20	a	18	a
Slovak Republic	18	16-18	18	a	17	16
Spain	17	15-17	17	a	15-17	17
Sweden	19	19	19	a	a	19
Switzerland	m	m	18-20	18-20	17-19	17-19
Turkey	16	16	16	a	a	m
United States	18	a	18	a	a	a
NON-OECD COUNTRIES						
Argentina	17	17	17	a	a	a
Brazil	17	17	17	17	a	17
Chile	18	18	18	18	a	a
China	18	18	18	a	17-18	18
Egypt[2]	17	17	17	17	a	17
India	18	18	18	a	m	m
Indonesia	18	18-19	18	18	a	a
Israel	18	18	18	18	18	18
Jamaica	17	17	17	17	a	a
Jordan[2]	18	18	18	a	18	18
Malaysia[1]	17-19	17	19	a	a	17
Paraguay[2]	17	17	17	a	a	17
Peru	17	17	17	17	a	a
Philippines[2]	16	a	16	a	a	a
Russian Federation[2]	17	17-18	17	a	m	m
Thailand	17	17	17	17	a	a
Tunisia[2]	19	19	19	19	a	19
Uruguay[2]	17	18	18	18	a	a
Zimbabwe[2]	19	17	19	a	a	17

1. Duration categories for ISCED 3C - Short: at least one year shorter than ISCED 3A/3B programmes; Long: of similar duration to ISCED 3A or 3B programmes.
2. OECD estimate.
3. OECD estimate for general and pre-vocational/vocational programmes.
Source: OECD.

Table X1.1b
Typical graduation ages in post-secondary non-tertiary education

		Educational/labour market destination	
	ISCED 4A programmes	ISCED 4B programmes	ISCED 4C programmes
OECD COUNTRIES			
Belgium	19	a	19-21
Canada	a	a	20
Czech Republic	20	a	20
Denmark	21-22	a	21-22
Finland	a	a	25-29
France	18-21	a	19-21
Germany	22	22	a
Greece	a	a	19-20
Hungary	20-22	a	19-22
Iceland	a	a	21
Ireland	a	a	19
Italy	a	a	20
Korea	a	a	a
Luxembourg	a	a	20-25
Mexico	a	a	a
Netherlands	a	a	18-20
New Zealand	18	18	18
Norway	20-25	a	20-25
Poland	a	21	a
Slovak Republic	20-21	a	a
Spain	18	18	a
Sweden	m	m	19-20
Switzerland	19-21	21-23	a
Turkey	a	a	a
United States	a	a	20
NON-OECD COUNTRIES			
Argentina	a	a	a
Brazil	a	a	a
China	a	20	20
Indonesia	a	a	a
Jordan[1]	a	a	a
Malaysia[1]	20	18	19
Paraguay	a	a	a
Peru	a	a	m
Philippines[1]	19	19	17
Russian Federation	a	a	18
Thailand[1]	a	a	19
Tunisia	a	21	a

1. OECD estimate.
Source: OECD.

Table X1.1c
Typical graduation ages in tertiary education

	Tertiary-type B (ISCED 5B)	Tertiary-type A (ISCED 5A)			Advanced research programmes (ISCED 6)
		3 to less than 5 years	5 years	6 years or more	
Australia	m	20	22-23	a	25-29
Austria	m	22	23	a	25
Belgium	m	m	m	m	25-29
Canada	m	22	26	26	29
Czech Republic	22	22	24	a	27
Denmark	21-25	22-24	25-26	27	30
Finland	21-22	25-29	25-29	30-34	29
France	20-21	21-22	23-24	25	25-26
Germany	21	25	26	a	28
Hungary	m	m	m	m	30
Iceland	22-24	23	25	27	29
Ireland	20	22	23	24	27
Italy	22-23	22	23-25	25-27	27-29
Japan	20	22	22	23	27
Korea	m	m	m	m	26
Netherlands	m	m	m	m	25
New Zealand	m	m	m	m	28
Norway	m	m	m	m	29
Poland	m	24	25	26	m
Portugal	m	m	m	m	27-29
Slovak Republic	20-21	m	m	m	27
Spain	19	m	m	m	25-27
Sweden	22-23	23-25	25-26	a	27-29
Switzerland	m	23-26	23-26	28	29
Turkey	m	m	m	m	28-29
United Kingdom	m	21	23	24	24
United States	20	21	23	25	28

OECD COUNTRIES

Source: OECD.

Table X1.2a
School years and financial years as used for the calculation of the indicators

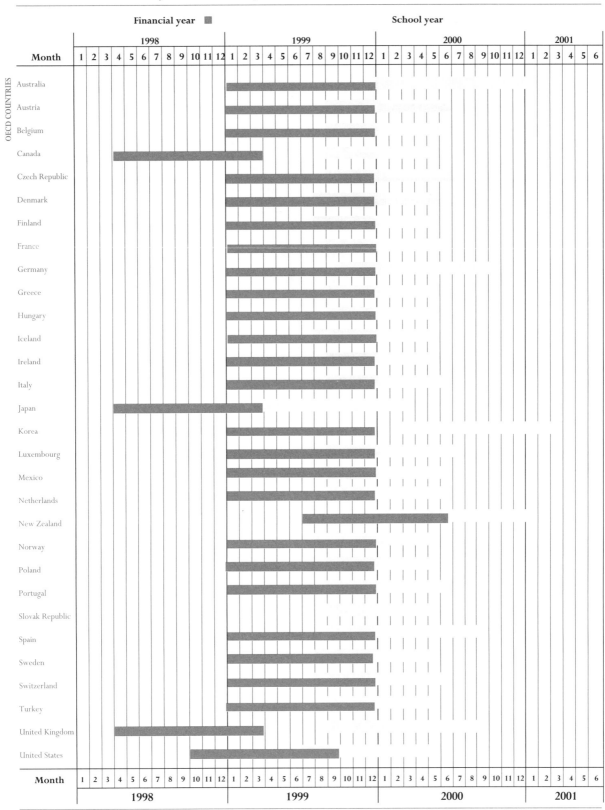

Source : OECD.

Table X1.2b
School years and financial years as used for the calculation of the indicators

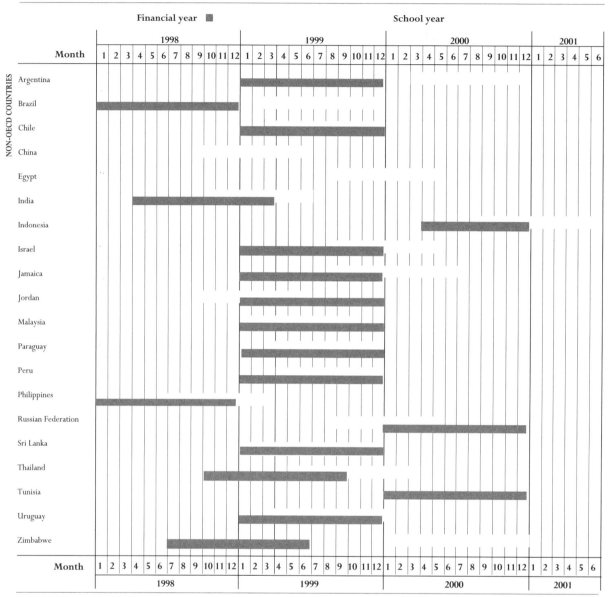

Source : OECD.

BASIC REFERENCE STATISTICS

Table X2.1.
Overview of the economic context using basic variables (reference period: calendar year 1999, 1999 current prices)

	Total public expenditure as a percentage of GDP	GDP per capita (in equivalent US dollars converted using PPPs)	GDP deflator (1995 =100)	Labour force participation rate[1]	Unemployment rate[1]
Australia	34.4	25 559	105.28	73.9	7.0
Austria	51.1	25 704	103.50	72.2	4.7
Belgium	50.1	24 669	105.45	65.0	8.6
Canada	m	26 462	103.68	76.9	7.6
Czech Republic	45.2	13 553	134.16	73.1	8.7
Denmark	54.6	27 679	108.60	81.1	5.1
Finland	49.5	23 429	104.72	74.0	10.2
France[2]	52.2	23 155	104.00	68.1	11.8
Germany	47.8	24 627	103.30	71.8	8.7
Greece	52.1	15 799	124.29	64.1	10.8
Hungary	36.3	11 505	175.32	60.2	7.0
Iceland	40.9	27 695	114.74	89.8	2.0
Ireland	32.6	26 006	117.51	67.6	5.8
Italy	48.0	23 952	112.59	60.6	11.3
Japan	38.2	24 933	98.06	78.1	4.7
Korea	23.8	13 647	110.29	66.9	6.3
Luxembourg	42.6	43 069	110.18	63.3	2.4
Mexico	19.6	8 357	203.94	65.3	2.0
Netherlands	45.8	26 440	106.78	74.1	3.6
New Zealand	m	19 423	103.56	76.4	6.8
Norway	47.4	29 013	113.41	82.0	3.2
Poland	44.0	8 991	161.57	67.6	12.5
Portugal	43.7	17 063	114.81	74.4	4.4
Slovak Republic	31.3	11 152	124.80	m	m
Spain	39.7	19 044	111.57	64.4	15.8
Sweden	57.1	23 476	104.76	79.5	7.1
Switzerland	36.1	28 778	100.75	84.9	3.1
Turkey	m	5 966	882.32	59.2	7.3
United Kingdom	38.8	23 303	112.24	77.6	6.0
United States	m	33 725	106.73	79.5	4.2

OECD COUNTRIES

1. Austria, Greece and the Netherlands: Reference period calendar year 1998.
2. Excluding Over Sea Departments (DOM).

Table X2.2.
Basic reference statistics (reference period: calendar year 1999, 1999 current prices)

	Gross Domestic Product reported for the calendar year (in millions of local currency)[1]	Gross Domestic Product (adjusted to the national financial year)[2]	Total public expenditure (in millions of local currency)	Total population in thousands (mid-year estimates)	Purchasing Power Parity (PPP)
Australia[1]	629 212	629 212	216 602	18 937	1.30
Austria	2 706 068	2 706 068	1 381 502	8 092	13.01
Belgium	9 501 583	9 501 583	4 761 994	10 222	37.68
Canada	960 206	915 981	m	30 493	1.19
Czech Republic	1 887 325	1 887 325	852 242	10 285	13.54
Denmark	1 213 595	1 213 595	663 051	5 321	8.24
Finland	716 370	716 370	354 936	5 165	5.92
France[1]	8 730 475	8 730 475	4 554 093	59 099	6.38
Germany	3 861 200	3 861 200	1 847 510	82 087	1.91
Greece	38 389 050	38 389 050	20 011 550	10 534	230.68
Hungary	11 393 499	11 393 499	4 140 835	10 067	98.37
Iceland	623 419	623 419	255 283	277	81.21
Ireland	70 116	70 116	22 832	3 745	0.72
Italy	2 146 350 000	2 146 350 000	1 031 140 000	57 646	1 554.48
Japan	511 837 100	514 835 375	195 575 600	126 686	162.04
Korea	482 744 175	482 744 175	114 685 126	46 858	754.89
Luxembourg	744 232	744 232	316 780	436	39.66
Mexico	4 583 762	4 583 762	898 886	97 428	5.63
Netherlands	823 446	823 446	377 144	15 809	1.97
New Zealand[1]	105 852	105 852	m	3 811	1.43
Norway	1 197 457	1 197 457	567 018	4 462	9.25
Poland	615 115	615 115	270 619	38 654	1.77
Portugal	21 694 862	21 694 862	9 475 440	9 990	127.27
Slovak Republic	815 330	815 330	255 396	5 396	13.55
Spain	94 088 400	94 088 400	37 335 000	39 626	124.68
Sweden	2 004 651	2 004 651	1 144 257	8 858	9.64
Switzerland	388 569	388 569	140 395	7 144	1.89
Turkey	77 415 272 000	77 415 272 000	m	65 819	197 156.62
United Kingdom	901 269	870 171	349 235	59 501	0.65
United States	9 206 900	9 085 225	m	272 996	1.00

1. Australia and New Zealand: GDP calculated for the financial year.
2. For countries where GDP is not reported for the same reference period as data on educational finance, GDP is estimated as: (wt-1)* (GDPt - 1) + (wt)* (GDPt), where wt and wt-1 are the weights for the respective portions of the two reference periods for GDP which fall within the educational financial year. Adjustments were made in Chapter B for Canada, Japan, the United Kingdom and the United States.
3. Excluding Over Sea Departments (DOM).

Table X2.3.
Basic reference statistics (reference period: calendar year 1995, 1995 current prices)

	Gross Domestic Product reported for the calendar year (in millions of local currency)[1]	Gross Domestic Product (adjusted to the national financial year)[2]	Gross Domestic Product (1999 constant prices, base year=1995)[1]	Total public expenditure (in millions of local currency)	Total population in thousand (mid-year estimates)	Purchasing Power Parity (PPP)
Australia[1]	502 828	502 828	597 681	188 394	18 072	1.29
Austria	2 370 726	2 370 726	2 614 606	1 294 685	8 047	13.73
Belgium	8 161 733	8 161 733	9 010 388	4 330 957	10 137	36.74
Canada	800 334	755 180	926 160	386 082	29 354	1.18
Czech Republic	1 381 049	1 381 049	1 406 725	783 678	10 327	10.81
Denmark	1 009 756	1 009 756	1 117 464	596 033	5 222	8.42
Finland	564 566	564 566	684 100	321 141	5 108	5.86
France[1]	7 662 391	7 662 391	8 401 029	4 104 369	58 020	6.46
Germany	3 523 000	3 523 000	3 737 800	1 928 460	81 661	2.02
Greece	27 235 205	27 235 205	30 885 829	14 895 505	10 454	203.08
Hungary	5 614 042	5 614 042	6 498 680	2 327 299	10 229	60.55
Iceland	451 372	451 372	543 328	186 846	267	75.87
Ireland	41 502	41 502	59 670	16 111	3 601	0.63
Italy	1 787 278 000	1 787 278 000	1 906 388 000	936 613 000	57 301	1 550.31
Japan	497 739 400	483 738 700	521 986 724	180 014 200	125 570	169.94
Korea	377 349 800	377 349 800	437 709 420	74 550 100	45 093	730.50
Luxembourg	533 300	533 300	675 464	245 719	413	38.87
Mexico	1 837 019	1 837 019	2 247 589	380 924	90 903	2.96
Netherlands	666 035	666 035	771 195	368 872	15 460	2.03
New Zealand[1]	92 679	92 679	102 215	36 441	3 656	1.47
Norway	928 745	928 745	1 055 851	457 033	4 358	9.14
Poland	308 104	308 104	380 701	147 561	38 588	1.14
Portugal	16 201 007	16 201 007	18 896 766	6 970 107	9 917	119.07
Slovak Republic	546 032	546 032	653 309	m	5 364	11.90
Spain	72 841 700	72 841 700	84 332 000	32 046 100	39 223	122.08
Sweden	1 713 316	1 713 316	1 913 547	1 098 782	8 827	9.73
Switzerland	363 329	363 329	385 666	133 827	7 041	2.01
Turkey	7 762 456 000	7 762 456 000	8 774 067 634	m	61 646	22 334.21
United Kingdom	719 176	678 972	803 019	317 104	58 612	0.65
United States	7 338 400	7 166 250	8 626 700	m	263 073	1.00

1. Australia and New Zealand: GDP calculated for the financial year.
2. For countries where GDP is not reported for the same reference period as data on educational finance, GDP is estimated as: (wt-1)*(GDPt - 1) +(wt)* (GDPt), where wt and wt-1 are the weights for the respective portions of the two reference periods for GDP which fall within the educational financial year. Adjustments were made in Chapter B for Canada, Japan, the United Kingdom and the United States.
3. Excluding Over Sea Departments (DOM).

Table X2.4.
Reference statistics used in the calculation of teachers' salaries

	Purchasing Power Parity (PPP) (1999/2000)[1]	Purchasing Power Parity (PPP) (2000)[2]	Gross Domestic Product (in millions of local currency, calendar year 2000)	Total population in thousands (calendar year 2000)	GDP per capita (in equivalent US dollars converted using PPPs, calendar year 2000)	Reference year for salary data	Adjustments for inflation
Australia	1.30	1.31	672 796	19 157	26 800	2000	0.978
Austria	13.53	13.48	2 818 695	8 110	25 788	1998/1999	1.012
Belgium (Fl.)	36.92	36.77	10 017 934	10 254	26 570	1999/2000	1.000
Belgium (Fr.)	36.92	36.77	10 017 934	10 254	26 570	1999/2000	1.000
Czech Republic	13.44	13.38	1 959 479	10 272	14 262	1999/2000	1.000
Denmark	8.60	8.66	1 315 526	5 338	28 448	April 1 2000	0.991
England	0.65	0.65	934 924	59 766	23 966		1.000
Finland	6.17	6.20	782 876	5 176	24 414	2000	0.984
France	6.59	6.55	9 214 720	60 431	23 276	1999/2000	1.000
Germany	1.96	1.93	3 961 600	82 168	24 931	1999/2000	1.000
Greece	240.21	241.44	41 406 732	10 558	16 244	1999	1.017
Hungary	103.61	106.48	13 075 210	10 024	12 251	1999/2000	1.000
Iceland	86.09	86.74	673 660	281	27 608	1999	1.015
Ireland	0.73	0.74	81 489	3 787	28 895	1999/2000	1.000
Italy	1 601.18	1 602.74	2 257 066 000	57 728	24 395	1999/2000	1.000
Japan[3]	155.19	152.27	511 835 900	126 919	26 484	1999	1.000
Korea[3]	631.57	620.22	517 096 590	47 275	17 636	2000	1.000
Mexico	5.85	6.09	5 426 786	97 221	9 164		1.000
Netherlands	2.00	2.01	883 884	15 920	27 662	1999/2000	1.000
New Zealand	1.47	1.47	111 776	3 831	19 808	1999/2000	1.000
Norway	10.16	10.82	1 423 864	4 491	29 311	1999	1.078
Portugal	129.45	130.15	22 860 162	10 005	17 556	1999/2000	1.000
Scotland	0.65	0.65	934 924	59 766	23 966	1999/2000	1.000
Spain	131.27	132.17	101 293 600	39 927	19 194	1999	1.017
Sweden	9.72	9.66	2 082 748	8 871	24 308	1999/2000	1.000
Switzerland	1.89	1.88	404 392	7 185	29 892	1998/1999	1.011
Turkey	229 780.57	273 987.20	124 982 454 000	66 835	6 825	1999	1.227
United States	1.00	1.00	9 839 200	275 423	35 724	1999/2000	1.000

OECD COUNTRIES

1. Used in the calculation of teachers' salaries at starting, mid and top levels.
2. Used in the calculation of teachers' salaries relative to GDP per capita.
3. No adjustment for inflation.

Annex 2

General notes

Definitions

Gross Domestic Product (GDP) refers to the producers' value of the gross outputs of resident producers, including distributive trades and transport, less the value of purchasers' intermediate consumption plus import duties. GDP is expressed in local money (in millions). For countries which provide this information for a reference year that is different from the calendar year (such as Australia and New Zealand), adjustments are made by linearly weighting their GDP between two adjacent national reference years to match the calendar year.

The GDP deflator is obtained by dividing the GDP expressed at current prices by the GDP expressed at constant prices. This provides an indication of the relative price level in a country. Data are based on the year 1995.

GDP per capita is the Gross Domestic Product (in equivalent US dollars converted using PPPs) divided by the population.

Purchasing Power Parity exchange rates (PPP) are the currency exchange rates that equalise the purchasing power of different currencies. This means that a given sum of money when converted into different currencies at the PPP rates will buy the same basket of goods and services in all countries. In other words, PPPs are the rates of currency conversion which eliminate the differences in price levels among countries. Thus, when expenditure on GDP for different countries is converted into a common currency by means of PPPs, it is, in effect, expressed at the same set of international prices so that comparisons between countries reflect only differences in the volume of goods and services purchased.

Total public expenditure as used for the calculation of the education indicators, corresponds to the non-repayable current and capital expenditure of all levels of government. Current expenditure includes final consumption expenditure (*e.g.*, compensation of employees, consumption intermediate goods and services, consumption of fixed capital, and military expenditure), property income paid, subsidies, and other current transfers paid (*e.g.*, social security, social assistance, pensions and other welfare benefits). Capital expenditure is spending to acquire and/or improve fixed capital assets, land, intangible assets, government stocks, and non-military, non-financial assets, and spending to finance net capital transfers.

The unemployment rate is calculated as the percentage of unemployed people in the labour force, where unemployment is defined according to the guidelines of the International Labour Office (ILO). The labour force participation rate for a particular age group relates to the percentage of individuals in the population of that age group who are either employed or unemployed, where these terms are defined according to the ILO guidelines. Rates for age groups are defined correspondingly.

Sources

The 2002 edition of the National Accounts of OECD countries: Main Aggregates, Volume I

The theoretical framework underpinning national accounts has been provided for many years by the United Nations' publication A System of National Accounts, which was released in 1968. An updated version was released in 1993 (commonly referred to as SNA93).

OECD Analytical Data Base, January 2002

Annex

SOURCES, METHODS
AND TECHNICAL NOTES

Annex 3 on sources and methods is available in electronic form only. It can be found at *www.oecd.org / els / education / eag 2002*.

GLOSSARY

Additional bonuses to base salary: Additional bonuses to base salary refer to additional payments that teachers may acquire in addition to the amount received on the basis of educational qualification and experience (salary scale). These bonuses may be awarded for teaching in remote areas, for participating in school improvement projects or special activities or for excellence in teaching performance. See also *Teacher's salaries*.

Advanced Research Qualifications (ISCED 6): Advanced Research Qualifications refer to tertiary programmes that lead directly to the award of an advanced research qualification, *e.g.*, Ph.D. The theoretical duration of these programmes is three years full-time in most countries (for a cumulative total of at least seven years full-time at the tertiary level), although the actual enrolment time is typically longer. The programmes are devoted to advanced study and original research. See also *International Standard Classification of Education (ISCED)*.

Age: See *Theoretical age*, *Typical age*, *Typical ending age*, *Typical graduation age* and *Typical starting age*.

Ancillary services: See *Expenditure on ancillary services*.

Capital expenditure: Capital expenditure represents the value of educational capital acquired or created during the year in question - that is, the amount of capital formation - regardless of whether the capital outlay was financed from current revenue or by borrowing. Capital expenditure includes outlays on construction, renovation, and major repair of buildings and expenditure for new or replacement equipment. Although capital investment requires a large initial expenditure, the plant and facilities have a lifetime that extends over many years.

Class size: Class size is the average number of students per class, which is calculated by dividing the number of students enrolled by the number of classes. In order to ensure comparability between countries, special needs programmes have been excluded. Data include only regular programmes at these two levels of education and also exclude teaching in sub-groups outside the regular classroom setting. See also *Class*.

Combined school and work-based programmes: In combined school and work-based programmes, instruction is shared between school and the workplace, although instruction may take place primarily in the workplace. Programmes are classified as combined school and work-based if less than 75 per cent of the curriculum is presented in the school environment or through distance education. Programmes that are more than 90 per cent work-based are excluded. See also *General programmes, Programme orientation*, *School-based programmes* and *Vocational education*.

Comprehensive private internal rate of return: See *Private internal rate of return*.

Compulsory core curriculum: Compulsory core curriculum is the minimum required time devoted to core subjects and study areas within the compulsory curriculum. See also *Compulsory curriculum*, *Compulsory flexible curriculum*, *Intended instruction time* and *Non-compulsory curriculum*.

Compulsory curriculum: Compulsory curriculum refers to the amount and allocation of instruction time that has to be provided in every school and must be attended by all students. See also *Compulsory core curriculum*, *Compulsory flexible curriculum*, *Intended instruction time* and *Non-compulsory curriculum*.

Compulsory education: The legal age from which children are no longer compelled to attend school (*e.g.*, 15th birthday). The ending age of compulsory schooling is thus different from the ending age of an educational programme.

Compulsory flexible curriculum: Compulsory flexible curriculum refers to the part of the compulsory curriculum in which there is flexibility or choice for schools or students. For example, a school may choose to offer more classes than the minimum in science and only the minimum required number of classes in art within the compulsory time frame. See also *Compulsory core curriculum*, *Compulsory curriculum*, *Intended instruction time* and *Non-compulsory curriculum*.

Continuing education and training: For the purpose of these indicators, continuing education and training for adults is defined as all kinds of general and job-related education and training that is organised, financed or sponsored by authorities, provided by employers or self-financed.

Core services: See *Expenditure on educational core services*.

Country of birth: See *Native students*, *First-generation students* and *Non-native students*.

Current expenditure: Current expenditure is expenditure on goods and services consumed within the current year, which needs to be made recurrently to sustain the production of educational services. Minor expenditure on items of equipment, below a certain cost threshold, is also reported as current spending. Current expenditure includes final consumption expenditure, property income paid, subsidies and other current transfers (*e.g.*, social security, social assistance, pensions and other welfare benefits). See also *Final consumption expenditure*, *Property income paid*, and *Other current transfers*.

Direct expenditure on educational institutions: Direct expenditure on educational institutions are purchases by a government agency of educational resources to be used by educational institutions (*e.g.*, direct payments of teachers' salaries by a central or regional education ministry, direct payments by a municipality to building contractors for the construction of school buildings, and procurement of textbooks by a central or regional authority for subsequent distribution to local authorities or schools) and payments by a government agency to educational institutions that have the responsibility for purchasing educational resources themselves (*e.g.*, a government appropriation or block grant to a university, which the university then uses to pay staff salaries and to buy other resources; government allocations of funds to fiscally autonomous public schools; government subsidies to private schools; and government payments under contract to private companies conducting educational research). Direct expenditure by a government agency does not include tuition payments received from students (or their families) enrolled in public schools under that agency's jurisdiction, even if the tuition payments flow, in the first instance, to the government agency rather than to the institution in question. See also *Instructional educational institutions* and *Non-instructional educational institutions*.

Dropouts: Dropouts are defined as those students who leave the specified level in the educational system without obtaining a first qualification. See also *Survival rates*.

Duration of programme: Programme duration refers to the standard number of years in which a student can complete the education programme.

Earnings: Earnings are annual money earnings as direct payment for labour services provided, before taxes. Income from other sources, such as government social transfers, investment income, net increase in the value of an owner operated business and any other income not directly related to work are not to be included. See also *Relative earnings*.

Educational attainment: Educational attainment is expressed by the highest completed level of education, defined according to the International Standard Classification of Education (ISCED).

Educational institution: An educational institution is an entity that provides instructional services to individuals or education-related services to individuals and other educational institutions. See *Private institution* and *Public institution*.

Educational personnel: The classification is based on function and organises staff into four main functional categories. The classification is: *i*) Instructional personnel; *ii*) Professional support for students; *iii*) Management/Quality control/ Administration; and *iv*) Maintenance and operations personnel. Teaching staff (teachers) and teachers' aides make up the category instructional personnel. For the purposes of Indicator D2, only teaching staff is taken into account. See also *Full-time teacher*, *Full-time equivalent teacher*, *Instructional personnel*, *Maintenance* and *operations personnel*, *Management/Quality control/ Administration*, *Part-time teacher*, *Professional support for students*, *Ratio of students to teaching staff*, *Teaching staff* and *Teaching time*.

Employed: The employed, which is defined according to the guidelines of the International Labour Office (ILO), are those who during the survey reference week: work for pay (employees) or profit (self-employed and unpaid family workers) for at least one hour or; have a job but are temporarily not at work (through injury, illness, holiday or vacation, strike or lock-out, educational or training leave, maternity or parental leave, etc.) and have a formal attachment to their job. See also *Labour force*, *Participation rate*, *Unemployed*, *Unemployment rate* and *Work status*.

Enrolment rate: Enrolment rates are expressed as net enrolment rates, which are calculated by dividing the number of students of a particular age group enrolled in all levels of education by the number of people in the population in that age group.

Entry rates: Entry rates are expressed as net entry rates, which represent the proportion of people of a synthetic age-cohort who enter the tertiary level of education, irrespective of changes in the population sizes and of differences between OECD countries in the typical entry age. The net entry rate of a specific age is obtained by dividing the number of first-time entrants to each type of tertiary education of that age by the total population in the corresponding age group (multiplied by 100). The sum of net entry rates is calculated by adding the net entry rates for each single year of age. See also *New entrants*.

Expected years of schooling: See *School expectancy*.

Expenditure on Research and Development (R&D): Expenditure on Research and Development (R&D) refers to all expenditure on research performed at universities and at other institutions of tertiary education, regardless of whether the research is funded from general institutional funds or through separate grants or contracts from public or private sponsors. This includes all research institutes and experimental stations operating under the direct control of, or administered by, or associated with, higher education institutions. See also *Expenditure on ancillary services* and *Expenditure on educational core services*.

Expenditure on ancillary services: Ancillary services are services provided by educational institutions that are peripheral to the main educational mission. The two main components of ancillary services are student welfare services and services for the general public. At ISCED levels 0-3, student welfare services include such things as meals, school health services, and transportation to and from school. At the tertiary level, they include halls of residence (dormitories), dining halls, and health care. Services for the general public include such things as museums, radio and television broadcasting, sports, and recreational or cultural programmes. Day or evening childcare provided by pre-primary and primary institutions is not included as an ancillary service. Entities providing ancillary services cover separate organisations that provide such education-related services as vocational and psychological counselling, placement, transportation of students, and student meals and housing. See also *Expenditure on educational core services* and *Expenditure on Research and Development (R&D)*.

Expenditure on educational core services: Expenditure on educational core services includes all expenditure that is directly related to instruction and education. This should cover all expenditure on teachers, school buildings, teaching materials, books, tuition outside schools, and administration of schools. See also *Expenditure on ancillary services* and *Expenditure on Research and Development (R&D)*.

Expenditure on educational institutions: Expenditure on educational institutions includes expenditure on instructional educational institutions as well as expenditure on non-instructional educational institutions. See also *Direct expenditure on educational institutions*, *Instructional educational institutions* and *Non-instructional educational institutions*.

Expenditure on non-instruction: Expenditure on non-instruction is all expenditure broadly related to student living costs.

Expenditure outside educational institutions: Expenditure outside educational institutions is expenditure on educational services purchased outside institutions, *e.g.*, books, computers, external tuition, etc. It also deals with student living costs and costs of student transport not provided by institutions.

Expenditure over the average duration of tertiary studies: Expected expenditure over the average duration of tertiary studies is calculated by multiplying current annual expenditure by the typical duration of tertiary studies.

Field of study: Field of study is defined in International Standard Classification of Education (ISCED) as the subject matter taught in an education programme. For details and implementation, see the *Fields of Education and Training - Manual* (EUROSTAT, 1999).

Final consumption expenditure: Final consumption expenditure of government services is the value of goods and services produced for their own use on current account, *i.e.*, the value of their gross output less the value of their commodity and non-commodity sales and the value of their own-account capital formation which is not segregated as an industry. The value of their gross output is equal to the sum of the value of their intermediate consumption of goods and services (including indirect taxes paid), compensation of employees, and consumption of fixed capital (*i.e.*, its depreciation due to normal wear and tear and to foreseen obsolescence). See also *Current expenditure*, *Property income paid* and *Other current transfers*.

Financial aid to students: Financial aid to students comprises: *i*) Government scholarships and other government grants to students or households. These include, in addition to scholarships and similar grants (fellowships, awards, bursaries, etc.), the following items: the value of special subsidies provided to students, either in cash or in kind, such as free or reduced-price travel on public transport systems; and family allowances or child allowances that are contingent on student status. Any benefits provided to students or households in the form of tax reductions, tax subsidies, or other special tax provisions are not included; *ii*) Student loans, which are reported on a gross basis, that is, without subtracting or netting out repayments or interest payments from the borrowers (students or households).

First-generation students: "First-generation" are those students who reported in PISA that they were born in the country of assessment but whose parents were born in another country. See *Native students* and *Non-native students*.

Foreign students: Foreign students are students who do not hold the citizenship of the country for which the data are collected. While pragmatic and operational, this classification may give rise to inconsistencies resulting from national policies regarding naturalisation of immigrants, combined with the inability of several countries to report separately foreign students net of those holding permanent residence permits. As a result, countries where naturalisation of immigrants is stringent and identification of non-resident foreign students impossible over-estimate the size of the foreign student body, compared to countries granting citizenship to their immigrants more easily.

Full-time equivalent student: A full-time equivalent (FTE) measure attempts to standardise a student's actual course load against the normal course load. Calculating the full-time/part-time status requires information on the time periods for actual and normal course loads. For the reduction of head-count data to FTEs, where data and norms on individual participation are available, course load is measured as the product of the fraction of the normal course load for a full-time student and the fraction of the school/academic year. [FTE = (actual course load/normal course load) * (actual duration of study during reference period/normal duration of study during reference period).] When actual course load information is not available, a full-time student is considered equal to one FTE. See also *Full-time student*, *Mode of study*, *Part-time student*, *Student* and *Study load*.

Full-time equivalent teacher: A full-time equivalent (FTE) attempts to standardise a full-time teacher's teaching load against that of a part-time teacher. The basis for the calculation are the "statutory working hours" and not the "total or actual working hours" or "total or actual teaching hours". The full-time equivalence of part-time educational personnel is then determined by calculating the ratio of hours worked by part-time personnel over the statutory hours worked by a full-time employee during the school year. See also *Educational personnel*, *Full-time teacher*, *Instructional personnel*, *Part-time teacher*, *Ratio of students to teaching staff*, *Teaching staff*, *Working time* and *Teaching time*.

Full-time student: Students enrolled in primary and secondary level educational programmes are considered to participate full-time if they attend school for at least 75 per cent of the school day or week (as locally defined) and would normally be expected to be in the programme for the entire academic year. This includes the work-based component in combined school and work-based programmes. At the tertiary level, an individual is considered full-time if he or she is taking a course load or educational programme considered requiring at least 75 per cent of a full-time commitment of time and resources. Additionally, it is expected that the student will remain in the programme for the entire year. See also *Full-time equivalent student*, *Mode of study*, *Part-time student*, *Student* and *Study load*.

Full-time teacher: A teacher employed for at least 90 per cent of the normal or statutory number of hours of work for a full-time teacher over a complete school year is classified as a full-time teacher. See also *Educational personnel*, *Full-time equivalent teacher*, *Instructional personnel*, *Part-time teacher*, *Ratio of students to teaching staff* and *Teaching staff* and *Working time*.

General programmes: General programmes are programmes that are not designed explicitly to prepare participants for a specific class of occupations or trades or for entry into further vocational or technical education programmes. Less than 25 per cent of the programme content is classified as vocational or technical. See also *Pre-vocational programmes*, *Programme orientation*, *Upper secondary education (ISCED 3)* and *Vocational programmes*.

Government-dependent private institution: A government-dependent private institution is an institution that receives more than 50 per cent of its core funding from government agencies. The term "government dependent" refers only to the degree of a private institution's dependence on funding from government sources; it does not refer to the degree of government direction or regulation. See also *Educational institution*, *Government-dependent private institution*, *Private institution* and *Public institution*.

Graduates: Graduates are those students who enrolled and successfully completed the final year of a level of education (*e.g.,* upper secondary education) during the reference year, regardless of their age. However, there are exceptions (especially in tertiary education) where graduation can also be recognised by the awarding of a certificate without the requirement that the participants are enrolled. See also *Graduation/Successful completion*, *Gross graduation rates*, *Net graduation rates* and *Unduplicated total count of graduates*.

Graduation/Successful completion: Successful completion is defined by each country. In some countries, completion is defined in terms of passing an examination or a series of examinations. In other countries, completion occurs after a requisite number of course hours have been accumulated (although completion of some or all of the course hours may also involve examinations). See also *Graduates*, *Gross graduation rates*, *Net graduation rates* and *Unduplicated total count of graduates*.

Graduation rate: See *Gross graduation rates* and *Net graduation rates*.

Gross Domestic Product (GDP): Gross Domestic Product (GDP) refers to the producers' value of the gross outputs of resident producers, including distributive trades and transport, less the value of purchasers' intermediate consumption plus import duties. GDP is expressed in local money (in millions). For countries which provide this information for a reference year that is different to the calendar year (*e.g.*, Australia and New Zealand), adjustments are made by linearly weighting GDP between two adjacent national reference years to match the calendar year. Data for GDP are provided in Annex 2.

Gross graduation rates: Gross graduation rates refer to the total number of graduates (the graduates themselves may be of any age) at the specified level of education divided by the population at the typical graduation age from the specified level. In many countries, defining a typical age of graduation is difficult, however, because graduates are dispersed over a wide range of ages. See also *Graduates*, *Graduation/Successful completion*, *Net graduation rates* and *Unduplicated total count of graduates*.

Head count: This refers to the method of data collection: the number of individuals are counted, regardless of the intensity of participation/length of their programme. See also *Full-time student*, *Part-time student*, *Full-time teacher* and *Part-time teacher*.

Human capital: Human capital is productive wealth embodied in labour, skills and knowledge.

IEA Civic Education Study: The International Association for the Evaluation (IEA) Civic Education Study tested 14-year-olds in 28 countries, including 17 OECD countries, on their knowledge of civic-related content, their skills in understanding political communication, their concepts and attitudes towards civics, and their participation or practice in this area. The test was designed to identify and examine the ways in which young people are prepared to undertake their role as citizens in democracies, both inside and outside the school.

Independent private institution: An independent private institution is an institution that receives less than 50 per cent of its core funding from government agencies. The term "independent" refers only to the degree of a private institution's dependence on funding from government sources; it does not refer to the degree of government direction or regulation. See also *Educational institution*, *Government-dependent private institution*, *Private institution* and *Public institution*.

Instruction time: See *Intended instruction time*.

Instructional educational institutions: Instructional educational institutions are educational institutions that directly provide instructional programmes (*i.e.*, teaching) to individuals in an organised group setting or through distance education. Business enterprises or other institutions providing short-term courses of training or instruction to individuals on a "one-to-one" basis are not included. See also *Expenditure on educational institutions* and *Non-instructional educational institutions*.

Instructional personnel: Instructional Personnel comprises two sub-categories: Classroom teachers at ISCED 0-4 and academic staff at ISCED 5-6; and teacher aides at ISCED 0-4 and teaching / research assistants at ISCED 5-6. See also *Educational personnel*, *Maintenance* and *operations personnel*, *Management/Quality control/Administration*, *Professional support for students*, *Ratio of students to teaching staff*, *Teaching staff* and *Teaching time*.

Intended instruction time: Intended instruction time refers to the number of hours per year for which students receive instruction in both the compulsory and non-compulsory parts of the curriculum. For countries that have no formal policy on instruction time, the number of hours was estimated from survey data. Hours lost when schools are closed for festivities and celebrations, such as national holidays, are excluded. Intended instruction time does not include non-compulsory time outside the school day. It does not include homework, individual tutoring or private study taken before or after school. See also *Compulsory core curriculum*, *Compulsory curriculum*, *Compulsory flexible curriculum* and *Non-compulsory curriculum*.

Intergovernmental transfers: Intergovernmental transfers are transfers of funds designated for education from one level of government to another. The restriction to funds earmarked for education is very important in order to avoid ambiguity about funding sources. General-purpose intergovernmental transfers are not included (*e.g.*, revenue sharing grants, general fiscal equalisation grants, or distributions of shared taxes from a national government to provinces, states, or *Länder*), even where such transfers provide the funds that regional or local authorities draw on to finance education.

International Standard Classification of Education (ISCED): The International Standard Classification of Education (ISCED-97) is used to define the levels and fields of education used in this publication. For details on ISCED 1997 and how it is nationally implemented see *Classifying Educational Programmes: Manual For ISCED-97 Implementation in OECD Countries* (Paris, 1999). See also *Pre-primary education (ISCED 0)*, *Primary education (ISCED 1)*, *Lower secondary education (ISCED 2)*, *Upper secondary education (ISCED 3)*, *Post-secondary non-tertiary level of education (ISCED 4)*, *Tertiary-type A education (ISCED 5A)*, *Tertiary-type B education (ISCED 5B)* and *Advanced Research Qualifications (ISCED 6)*.

International Standard Classification of Occupations (ISCO): The International Standard Classification of Occupations (1998) classifies persons according to their actual and potential relation with jobs. Jobs are classified with respect to the type of work performed or to be performed. The basic criteria used to define the system of major, sub-major, minor and unit groups is the "skill" level and "skill specialisation" required to carry out the tasks and duties of the occupations, with separate major groups for "Legislators, senior officials and managers" and for "Armed forces".

Internet: The Internet is an electronic communications network that connects computer networks and organisational computer facilities around the world. See also Local Area Network and World Wide Web.

Job-related continuing education and training: Job-related continuing education and training refers to all organised, systematic education and training activities in which people take part in order to obtain knowledge and/or learn new skills for a current or a future job, to increase earnings, to improve job and/or career opportunities in a current or another field and generally to improve their opportunities for advancement and promotion.

Labour force: The total labour force or currently active population, which is defined according to the guidelines of the International Labour Office (ILO), comprises all persons who fulfil the requirements for inclusion among the employed or the unemployed as defined in OECD Labour Force Statistics. See also *Work status*.

Language spoken at home: In PISA, students were asked if the language spoken at home most of the time is the language of assessment, another official national language, other national dialect or language, or another language. The responses were then grouped into two categories: the language spoken at home most of the time is different from the language of assessment, from other official national languages, and from other national dialects or languages, and; the language spoken at home most of the time is the language of assessment, other official national languages, or other national dialects or languages.

Local area network (LAN): A Local Area Network is a network of personal computers in a small area (as an office) that are linked by cable, can communicate directly with other devices in the network, and can share resources. See also *Internet* and *WorldWideWeb*.

Lower secondary education (ISCED 2): Lower secondary education (ISCED 2) generally continues the basic programmes of the primary level, although teaching is typically more subject-focused, often employing more specialised teachers who conduct classes in their field of specialisation. Lower secondary education may either be "terminal" (*i.e.*, preparing students for entry directly into working life) and/or "preparatory" (*i.e.*, preparing students for upper secondary education). This level usually consists of two to six years of schooling (the mode of OECD countries is three years). See also *International Standard Classification of Education (ISCED)*.

Maintenance and operations personnel: Maintenance and operations personnel refers to personnel who support the maintenance and operation of schools, school security and ancillary services, such as the transportation of students to and from school and food services operations. This category includes the following types of personnel: masons, carpenters, electricians, locksmiths, maintenance repairers, painters and paperhangers, plasterers, plumbers, and vehicle mechanics. It also includes bus drivers and other vehicle operators, construction workers, gardeners and groundskeepers, bus monitors and crossing guards, cooks/food carers, custodians, food servers, dormitory supervisors, and security guards. See also *Educational personnel*, *Instructional personnel*, *Management/Quality control/Administration*, *Professional support for students*, *Ratio of students to teaching staff* and *Teaching staff*.

Management/Quality control/Administration: Management/Quality control/Administration comprises four categories: School Level Management, Higher Level Management, School Level Administrative Personnel and Higher Level Administrative Personnel at all ISCED levels. See also *Educational personnel*, *Instructional personnel*, *Maintenance and operations personnel*, *Professional support for students*, *Ratio of students to teaching staff* and *Teaching staff*.

Mathematical literacy: Mathematical literacy is defined in PISA as the capacity to identify, understand and engage in mathematics, and to make well-founded judgements about the role that mathematics plays in an individual's current and future private life, occupational life, social life with peers and relatives, and life as a constructive, concerned and reflective citizen. See also *Reading literacy* and *Scientific literacy*.

Mode of study: Mode of study refers to the study load of the student, whether full-time or part-time. See also *Full-time student*, *Full-time equivalent student*, *Part-time student*, *Student* and *Study load*.

Native students: "Native" students are those students who reported in PISA that they were born in the country of assessment and who had at least one parent born in that country. See also *First-generation students* and *Non-native students*.

Net capital transfers paid: Net capital transfers paid are capital transfers to the resident private sector and to the rest of the world minus capital transfers received from the resident private sector and the rest of the world.

Net contact hours of teaching: See *Teaching time*.

Net graduation rates: Net graduation rates is the percentage of persons within a virtual age cohort who obtain a tertiary qualification, thus being unaffected by changes in population size or typical graduation age. The net graduation rate is calculated by dividing the number of graduates by the population for each single year of age. See also *Graduates*, *Graduation / Successful completion*, *Net graduation rates* and *Unduplicated total count of graduates*.

New entrants: New entrants to a level of education are students who are entering any programme leading to a recognised qualification at this level of education for the first time, irrespective of whether the students enter the programme at the beginning or at an advanced stage of the programme. See also *Entry rates*.

Non-compulsory curriculum: The non-compulsory curriculum is that which is defined entirely at the school level or eventually at the programme level if various programme types exist. See also *Compulsory core curriculum*, *Compulsory curriculum*, *Compulsory flexible curriculum* and *Intended instruction time*.

Non-instructional educational institutions: Non-instructional educational institutions are educational institutions that provide administrative, advisory or professional services to other educational institutions, although they do not enrol students themselves. Examples include national, state, and provincial ministries or departments of education; other bodies that administer education at various levels of government or analogous bodies in the private sector; and organisations that provide such education-related services as vocational or psychological counselling, placement, testing, financial aid to students, curriculum development, educational research, building operations and maintenance services, transportation of students, and student meals and housing. See also *Expenditure on educational institutions* and *Instructional educational institutions*.

Non-native students: "Non-native" students are those students who reported in PISA that they were born outside the country of assessment and whose parents were also born in another country. See also *Native students* and *First-generation students*.

Non-salary compensation: Non-salary compensation includes expenditure by employers or public authorities on retirement programmes, health care or health insurance, unemployment compensation, disability insurance, other forms of social insurance, non-cash supplements (*e.g.*, free or subsidised housing), maternity benefits, free or subsidised child care, and such other fringe benefits as each country may provide. This expenditure does not include contributions made by the employees themselves, or deducted from their gross salaries. See also *Salaries* and *Staff compensation*.

Other current transfers: Other current transfers paid are net casualty insurance premiums, social security benefits, social assistance grants, unfunded employee pension and welfare benefits (paid directly to former or present employees without having special funds, reserves or insurance for this purpose), current transfers to private non-profit institutions serving households and current transfers to the rest of the world. See also *Current expenditure*, *Final consumption expenditure* and *Property income paid*.

Participation rate: The labour force participation rate, which is defined according to the guidelines of the International Labour Office (ILO), refers to the percentage of individuals in the population of the same age group who are either employed or unemployed. See also *Employed*, *Labour force*, *Unemployed* and *Unemployment rate*.

Part-time student: Students enrolled in primary and secondary-level educational programmes are considered to participate part-time if they attend school for less than 75 per cent of the school day or week (as locally defined) and would normally be expected to be in the programme for the entire academic year. At the tertiary level, an individual is considered part-time if he or she is taking a course load or educational programme that requires less than 75 per cent of a full-time commitment of time and resources. See also *Full-time equivalent student*, *Full-time student*, *Mode of study*, *Student* and *Study load*.

Part-time teacher: A teacher employed for less than 90 per cent of the normal or statutory number of hours of work for a full-time teacher over a complete school year is classified as a part-time teacher. See also *Educational personnel*, *Full-time equivalent teacher*, *Full-time teacher*, *Instructional personnel*, *Ratio of students to teaching staff and Teaching staff*, *Teaching time* and *Working time*.

PISA index of achievement press: The PISA index of achievement press was derived from students' reports on the frequency with which, in their <class of the language of assessment>: the teacher wants students to work hard; the teacher tells students that they can do better; the teacher does not like it when students deliver <careless> work; and, students have to learn a lot. A four-point scale with the response categories 'never', 'some lessons', 'most lessons' and 'every lesson' was used. The index was derived using the WARM estimator described above with 'never' coded as 1 and all other response categories coded as 0.

PISA index of comfort with and perceived ability to use computers: The PISA index of comfort with and perceived ability to use computers was derived from students' responses to the following questions: How comfortable are you with using a computer?; How comfortable are you with using a computer to write a paper?; How comfortable are you with taking a test on a computer?; and, If you compare yourself with other 15-year-olds, how would you rate your ability to use a computer? For the first three questions, a four-point scale was used with the response categories 'very comfortable', 'comfortable', 'somewhat comfortable' and 'not at all comfortable'. For the last questions, a four-point scale was used with the response categories 'excellent', 'good', 'fair' and 'poor'. The index was derived using the WARM estimator described above. For information on the conceptual underpinning of the index see Eignor *et al.* (1998).

PISA index of disciplinary climate: The PISA index of disciplinary climate summarises students' reports on the frequency with which, in their <class of the language of assessment>: the teacher has to wait a long time for students to <quieten down>; students cannot work well; students don't listen to what the teacher says; students don't start working for a long time after the lesson begins; there is noise and disorder; and, at the start of class, more than five minutes are spent doing nothing. A four-point scale with the response categories 'never', 'some lessons', 'most lessons' and 'every lesson' was used. This index was inverted so that low values indicate a poor disciplinary climate.

PISA index of economic, social and cultural status (ESCS): The PISA index of economic, social and cultural status was created on the basis of the following variables: the International Socio-Economic Index of Occupational Status (ISEI); the highest level of education of the student's parents, converted into years of schooling; the PISA index of family wealth; the PISA index of home educational resources; and the PISA index of possessions related to "classical" culture in the family home.

PISA index of interest in computers: The PISA index of interest in computers was derived from the students' responses to the following statements: it is very important to me to work with a computer; to play or work with a computer is really fun; I use a computer because I am very interested in this; and, I forget the time, when I am working with the computer. A two-point scale with the response categories 'yes' and 'no' was used. The index was derived using the WARM estimator described above. For information on the conceptual underpinning of the index see Eignor *et al.* (1998).

PISA index of teacher support: The PISA index of teacher support was derived from students' reports on the frequency with which: the teacher shows an interest in every student's learning; the teacher gives students an opportunity to express opinions; the teacher helps students with their work; the teacher continues teaching until the students understand; the teacher does a lot to help students; and, the teacher helps students with their learning. A four-point scale with the response categories 'never', 'some lessons', 'most lessons' and 'every lesson' was used. The index was derived using the WARM estimator (Warm, 1985) described above.

PISA index of the use of school resources: The PISA index of the use of school resources was derived from the frequency with which students reported using the following resources in their school: the school library; calculators; the Internet; and <science> laboratories. Students responded on a five-point scale with the following categories: 'never or hardly ever', 'a few times a year', 'about once a month', 'several times a month' and 'several times a week'. The index was derived using the WARM estimator described above.

PISA International Socio-Economic Index of Occupational Status (ISEI): The PISA International Socio-Economic Index of Occupational Status (ISEI) was derived from students' responses on parental occupation. The index captures the attributes of occupations that convert parents' education into income. The index was derived by the optimal scaling of occupation groups to maximise the indirect effect of education on income through occupation and to minimise the direct effect of education on income, net of occupation (both effects being net of age). For more information on the methodology, see Ganzeboom *et al.* (1992). The PISA International Socio-Economic Index of Occupational Status is based on either the father or mother's occupations, whichever is the higher.

PISA mean score: To facilitate the interpretation of the scores assigned to students in PISA, the PISA mean score for combined reading, mathematical and scientific literacy performance across OECD countries was set at 500 and the standard deviation at 100, with the data weighted so that each OECD country contributed equally.

PISA population: The PISA population refer to 15-year-old students, or students aged between 15 years and 3 (completed) months and 16 years and 2 (completed) months at the beginning of the testing period, and enrolled in an educational institution, regardless of the grade level or type of institution in which they were enrolled and of whether they participated in school full-time or part-time. See also *Population*.

Population: Population refers to all nationals present in or temporarily absent from the country and aliens permanently settled in the country. For further details, see OECD Labour Force Statistics. See also *PISA population*.

Post-secondary non-tertiary level of education (ISCED 4): Post-secondary non-tertiary education straddles the boundary between upper secondary and post-secondary education from an international point of view, even though it might clearly be considered upper secondary or post-secondary programmes in a national context. Although their content may not be significantly more advanced than upper secondary programmes, they serve to broaden the knowledge of participants who have already gained an upper secondary qualification. The students tend to be older than those enrolled at the upper secondary level. See also *International Standard Classification of Education (ISCED)*.

Pre-primary education (ISCED 0): Pre-primary education (ISCED 0) is defined as the initial stage of organised instruction, designed primarily to introduce very young children to a school-type environment, that is, to provide a bridge between home and a school-based atmosphere. ISCED level 0 programmes should be centre or school-based, be designed to meet the educational and developmental needs of children at least three years of age, and have staff that are adequately trained (*i.e.*, qualified) to provide an educational programme for the children. See also *International Standard Classification of Education (ISCED)*.

Pre-vocational programmes: Pre-vocational education is mainly designed to introduce participants to the world of work and to prepare them for entry into further vocational or technical programmes. Successful completion of such programmes does not lead to a labour-market relevant vocational or technical qualification. See also *General programmes*, *Programme orientation*, *Upper secondary education (ISCED 3)* and *Vocational programmes*.

Primary education (ISCED 1): Primary education (ISCED 1) usually begins at ages five, six or seven and lasts for four to six years (the mode of the OECD countries being six years). Programmes at the primary level generally require no previous formal education, although it is becoming increasingly common for children to have attended a pre-primary programme before entering primary education. The boundary between pre-primary and primary education is typically the beginning of systematic studies characteristic of primary education, *e.g.*, reading, writing and mathematics. It is common, however, for children to begin learning basic literacy and numeracy skills at the pre-primary level. See also *International Standard Classification of Education (ISCED)*.

Private expenditure: Private expenditure refers to expenditure funded by private sources, *i.e.*, households and other private entities. "Households" means students and their families. "Other private entities" include private business firms and non-profit organisations, including religious organisations, charitable organisations, and business and labour associations. Private expenditure comprises school fees; materials such as textbooks and teaching equipment; transport to school (if organised by the school); meals (if provided by the school); boarding fees; and expenditure by employers on initial vocational training. Note that private educational institutions are considered service providers, not funding sources.

Private institution: An institution is classified as private if it is controlled and managed by a non-governmental organisation (*e.g.*, a Church, Trade Union or business enterprise), or if its Governing Board consists mostly of members not selected by a public agency. See also *Educational institution*, *Government-dependent private institution*, *Independent private institution* and *Public institution*.

Private internal rate of return: The private internal rate of return is equal to the discount rate that equalises the real costs of education during the period of study to the real gains from education thereafter. In its most comprehensive form, the costs equal tuition fees, foregone earnings net of taxes adjusted for the probability of being in employment minus the resources made available to students in the form of grants and loans. See also *Social rate of return*.

Professional support for students: Professional support for students comprises pedagogical support at ISCED 0-4 and academic support at ISCED 5-6; and health and social support at ISCED 0-6. See also *Educational personnel*, *Instructional personnel*, *Maintenance and operations personnel*, *Management/Quality control/Administration*, *Ratio of students to teaching staff* and *Teaching staff*.

Programme destination: Programme destination is defined according to International Standard Classification of Education (ISCED) as the destination for which programmes have been designed to prepare students, such as tertiary education, the labour market or other programmes at the same or other levels of education.

- A programmes are designed to prepare students for direct access to the next level of education;
- B programmes are designed to prepare students for access to certain types of but not all programmes at the next level of education; and
- C programmes are designed to prepare students for direct access to the labour market or other programmes at the same level of education.

Programme duration: See *Duration of programme*.

Programme for International Student Assessment (PISA): The Programme for International Student Assessment is an international study conducted by the OECD which measures how well young adults, at age 15 and therefore approaching the end of compulsory schooling, are prepared to meet the challenges of today's knowledge societies.

Programme orientation: Programme orientation is defined according to International Standard Classification of Education (ISCED) as the degree to which a programme is specifically oriented towards a certain class of occupations or trades and leads to a labour-market relevant qualification. See also *General programmes*, *Pre-vocational programmes* and *Vocational programmes*.

Property income paid: Property income paid is defined as interest, net land rent and royalties paid. See also *Current expenditure*, *Final consumption expenditure* and *Other current transfers*.

Public expenditure: Public expenditure refers to spending of public authorities at all levels. Expenditure that is not directly related to education (*e.g.*, culture, sports, youth activities, etc.) is, in principle, not included. Expenditure on education by other ministries or equivalent institutions, for example Health and Agriculture, is included.

Public institution: An institution is classified as public if it is controlled and managed directly by a public education authority or agency or; is controlled and managed either by a government agency directly or by a governing body (Council, Committee etc.), most of whose members are appointed by a public authority or elected by public franchise. See *Educational institution* and *Public institution*.

Purchasing Power Parities (PPP): Purchasing Power Parities (PPP) are the currency exchange rates that equalise the purchasing power of different currencies. This means that a given sum of money, when converted into different currencies at the PPP rates, will buy the same basket of goods and services in all countries. In other words, PPPs are the rates of currency conversion, which eliminate the differences in price levels among countries. Thus, when expenditure on GDP for different countries is converted into a common currency by means of PPPs, it is, in effect, expressed at the same set of international prices so that comparisons between countries reflect only differences in the volume of goods and services purchased. The purchasing power parities used in this publication are given in Annex 2.

Ratio of students to computers: In PISA, the ratio of students per computer was calculated by dividing the total number of computers in each school by the total number of students enrolled in each school.

Ratio of students to teaching staff: The ratio of students to teaching staff is calculated as the total number of full-time equivalent students divided by the total number of full-time equivalent educational personnel. See also *Educational personnel*, *Full-time equivalent student*, *Full-time equivalent teacher*, *Instructional personnel Maintenance and operations personnel*, *Management/ Quality control/Administration*, *Professional support for students*, *Teaching staff* and *Teaching time*.

Reading literacy: Reading literacy is defined in PISA as the ability to understand, use and reflect on written texts in order to achieve one's goals, to develop one's knowledge and potential, and to participate effectively in society. See also *Mathematical literacy* and *Scientific literacy*.

Relative earnings: Relative earnings from work are the mean annual earnings from employment of individuals with a certain level of educational attainment divided by the mean annual earnings from employment of individuals whose highest level of education is the upper secondary level. See also *Earnings*.

Research and development: See *Expenditure on Research and Development (R&D)*.

Retirement expenditure: Retirement expenditure is the cost incurred currently, exclusive of any contribution by employees, in providing future retirement benefits for persons currently employed in education. This cost can be measured by actual or imputed employers (or third party) contributions to retirement systems. The reason for not counting employee's contributions is that they are already counted in the gross salary component of total compensation.

Salaries: Salaries are the gross salaries of educational personnel, before deduction of taxes, contributions for retirement or health care plans, and other contributions or premiums for social insurance or other purposes. See also *Non-salary compensation* and *staff compensation*.

School expectancy: School expectancy is the average duration of formal education in which a five-year-old child can expect to enrol over his or her lifetime. It is calculated by adding the net enrolment percentages for each single year of age from the age of five onwards.

School location: In PISA, school location refers to the community in which the school is located, such as a <village, hamlet or rural area> (fewer than 3 000 people), a <small town> (3 000 to about 15 000 people), a <town> (15 000 to about 100 000 people), a <city> (100 000 to about 1 000 000 people), close to the centre of a <city> with over 1 000 000 people or elsewhere in a <city> with over 1 000 000 people.

School-based programmes: In school-based (vocational and technical) programmes, instruction takes place (either partly or exclusively) in educational institutions. This includes special training centres for vocational education run by public or private authorities or enterprise-based special training centres if these qualify as educational institutions. These programmes can have an on-the-job training component, *i.e.*, a component of some practical experience in the workplace. See also *Combined school and work-based programmes*, *General programmes*, *Programme orientation* and *Vocational programmes*.

Scientific literacy: PISA defines scientific literacy as the capacity to use scientific knowledge, to identify questions, and to draw evidence-based conclusions in order to understand and help make decisions about the natural world and the changes made to it through human activity. See also *Mathematical literacy* and *Reading literacy*.

Secondary education (ISCED 23): See *Lower secondary education* and *Upper secondary education*.

Social internal rate of return: The social internal rate of return refers to the costs and benefits to society of investment in education, which includes the opportunity cost of having people not participating in the production of output and the full cost of the provision of education rather than only the cost borne by the individual. The social benefit includes the increased productivity associated with the investment in education and a host of possible non-economic benefits, such as lower crime, better health, more social cohesion and more informed and effective citizens. See also *Private rate of return*.

Spending on educational services other than instruction: Spending on educational services other than instruction includes public spending on ancillary services such as meals, transport to schools, or housing on the campus; private spending on fees for ancillary services; subsidised private spending on student living costs or reduced prices for transport; and private spending on student living costs or transport. See also *Expenditure on ancillary services*, *Expenditure on educational core services* and *Expenditure on Research and Development (R&D)*.

Staff compensation: Expenditure on staff compensation includes gross salaries plus non-salary compensation (fringe benefits). See also *Non-salary compensation* and *Salaries*.

Standard error: The standard errors used in PISA are expressions of the degree of uncertainty of an estimate, which are estimates of national performance based on samples of students rather than the values that could be calculated if every student in every country had answered every question. Consequently, it is important to know the degree of uncertainty inherent in the estimates.

Statistical significance: Differences are reported as statistically significant when a difference of that size, or larger, would be observed less than 5 per cent of the time, if there was actually no difference in corresponding population values. Similarly, the risk of reporting as significant if there is, in fact, no correlation between to measures is contained at 5 per cent.

Statutory teachers' salaries: See *Teachers' salaries*.

Student: A student is defined as any individual participating in educational services covered by the data collection. The number of students enrolled refers to the number of individuals (head count) who are enrolled within the reference period and not necessarily to the number of registrations. Each student enrolled is counted only once. See also *Full-time student*, *Full-time equivalent student*, *Part-time student* and *Study load*.

Study load: There are two basic measures of study load: time in the classroom and progress towards a qualification. Time in classroom attempts to measure the amount of instruction time that a student receives and can be counted as hours of instruction per day or year, counts of the number of courses taken, or a combination of the two. These measures are based on characteristics of the course or on patterns of attendance, not on the programme in which the student is enrolled. Because of this, such measures of study load will be useful when there is no programme structure or when programme structures are not comparable. The second measure of study load is the unit used to measure progress towards a qualification. Such measures focus less on the amount of instruction and more on the "academic value" of that instruction. It is conceivable, therefore, those courses with the same quantity of instruction may have different academic values and they would only be the same if measures of academic progress were made in amounts of instruction. See also *Full-time equivalent student*, *Full-time student*, *Mode of study* and *Part-time student*.

Support services: Entities providing support services to other educational institutions include institutions that provide educational support and materials as well as operation and maintenance services for buildings. These are commonly part of the general-purpose units of public authorities.

Survival rates: Survival rate at the tertiary level is defined as the proportion of new entrants to the specified level of education who successfully complete a first qualification. It is calculated as the ratio of the number of students who are awarded an initial degree to the number of new entrants to the level *n* years before, *n* being the number of years of full-time study required to complete the degree. See also *Dropout*.

Teachers' salaries: Teachers' salaries are expressed as statutory salaries, which are scheduled salaries according to official pay scales. The salaries reported are defined as gross salaries (total sum of money that is paid by the employer for the labour supplied) minus the employer's contribution to social security and pension (according to existing salary scales).

- Starting salaries refer to the average scheduled gross salary per year for a full-time teacher with the minimum training necessary to be fully qualified at the beginning of his or her teaching career.

- Salaries after 15 years of experience refer to the scheduled annual salary of a full-time classroom teacher with the minimum training necessary to be fully qualified and with 15 years of experience.

- Maximum salaries reported refer to the scheduled maximum annual salary (top of the salary scale) of a full-time classroom teacher with the minimum training to be fully qualified for his or her job.

Salaries are "before tax", *i.e.*, before deductions for income taxes. See also *Additional bonuses to base salary*.

Teaching days: The number of teaching days is the number of teaching weeks minus the days when the school is closed for festivities. See also *Teaching time*, *Teaching weeks*, *Working time* and *Working time in school*.

Teaching staff: Teaching staff refer to professional personnel directly involved in teaching students, including classroom teachers; special education teachers; and other teachers who work with students as a whole class in a classroom, in small groups in a resource room, or in one-to-one teaching inside or outside a regular classroom. Teaching staff also includes chairpersons of departments whose duties include some amount of teaching, but it does not include non-professional personnel who support teachers in providing instruction to students, such as teachers' aides and other paraprofessional personnel. See also *Educational personnel*, *Full-time teacher*, *Full-time equivalent teacher*, *Instructional personnel Maintenance and operations personnel*, *Management/ Quality control/Administration*, *Part-time teacher*, *Professional support for students*, *Ratio of students to teaching staff* and *Teaching time*.

Teaching time: Teaching time is defined as the net contact hours of teaching. It is calculated on the basis of the annual number of weeks of instruction multiplied by the minimum/maximum number of periods, which a teacher is supposed to spend teaching a class or a group, multiplied by the length of a period in minutes and divided by 60. Periods of time formally allowed for breaks between lessons or groups of lessons, and days when schools are closed for public holidays and festivities, are excluded. In primary education, however, short breaks that teachers spend with the class are typically included. See also *Teaching days*, *Teaching weeks*, *Working time* and *Working time in school*.

Teaching weeks: The number of teaching weeks is defined as the number of weeks of instruction not counting holiday weeks. See also *Teaching days*, *Teaching time*, *Working time* and *Working time in school*.

Tertiary education (ISCED 56): See *Tertiary-type A education (ISCED 5A)* and *Tertiary-type B education (ISCED 5B)*.

Tertiary-type A education (ISCED 5A): Tertiary-type A programmes (ISCED 5A) are largely theory-based and are designed to provide sufficient qualifications for entry to advanced research programmes and professions with high skill requirements, such as medicine, dentistry or architecture. Tertiary-type A programmes have a minimum cumulative theoretical duration (at tertiary level) of three years' full-time equivalent, although they typically last four or more years. These programmes are not exclusively offered at universities. Conversely, not all programmes nationally recognised as university programmes fulfil the criteria to be classified as tertiary-type A. Tertiary-type A programmes include second-degree programmes like the American Master. First and second programmes are sub-classified by the cumulative duration of the programmes, *i.e.*, the total study time needed at the tertiary level to complete the degree. See also *International Standard Classification of Education (ISCED)* and *Tertiary-type B education (ISCED 5B)*.

Tertiary-type B education (ISCED 5B): Tertiary-type B programmes (ISCED 5B) are typically shorter than those of tertiary-type A and focus on practical, technical or occupational skills for direct entry into the labour market, although some theoretical foundations may be covered in the respective programmes. They have a minimum duration of two years full-time equivalent at the tertiary level. See also *International Standard Classification of Education (ISCED)* and *Tertiary-type A education (ISCED 5A)*.

Theoretical age: Theoretical ages refer to the ages as established by law and regulation for the entry and ending of a cycle of education. Note that the theoretical ages may differ significantly from the typical ages. See also *Typical age*, *Typical ending age*, *Typical graduation age* and *Typical starting age*.

Third International Mathematics and Science Study (TIMSS): The Third International Mathematics and Science Study, conducted by the IEA, measured the mathematics and science achievement of fourth and eighth-grade students in 1995, 1999 and 2003.

Transfer and payments to other private entities: Transfer and payments to other private entities are government transfers and certain other payments (mainly subsidies) to other private entities (commercial companies and non-profit organisations). These transfers and payments can take diverse forms, *e.g.*, transfers to business or labour associations that provide adult education; subsidies to companies or labour organisations (or associations of such entities) that operate apprenticeship programmes; and interest rate subsidies or defaults guarantee payments to private financial institutions that provide student loans.

Typical age: Typical ages refer to the ages that normally correspond to the age at entry and ending of a cycle of education. These ages relate to the theoretical duration of a cycle assuming full-time attendance and no repetition of a year. The assumption is made that, at least in the ordinary education system, a student can proceed through the educational programme in a standard number of years, which is referred to as the theoretical duration of the programme. See also *Theoretical age*, *Typical ending age*, *Typical graduation age* and *Typical starting age*.

Typical ending age: The typical ending age should be the age at the beginning of the last school/academic year of the corresponding level and programme. See also *Theoretical age*, *Typical age*, *Typical graduation age* and *Typical starting age*.

Typical graduation age: The typical graduation age should be the age at the end of the last school/academic year of the corresponding level and programme when the degree is obtained. Note that at some levels of education the term "graduation age" may not translate literally and would be equivalent to a "completion age"; it is used here purely as a convention. See also *Theoretical age*, *Typical age*, *Typical ending age* and *Typical starting age*.

Typical starting age: The typical starting age should be the age at the beginning of the first school/academic year of the corresponding level and programme. See also *Theoretical age*, *Typical age*, *Typical ending age* and *Typical graduation age*.

Unduplicated total count of graduates: Unduplicated total count of graduates is calculated by netting out those students who graduated from programmes in a previous year and/or who are earning more than one qualification at the specified level during the reference period. It represents therefore a count of individuals graduating and not certificates being awarded. See also *Graduates*, *Graduation/Successful completion*, *Gross graduation rates* and *Net graduation rates*.

Unemployed: The unemployed, which is defined according to the guidelines of the International Labour Office (ILO), refers to individuals who are without work, actively seeking employment and currently available to start work. See also *Employed*, *Labour force*, *Participation rate*, *Unemployment rate* and *Work status*.

Unemployment rate: The unemployment rate (expressed as a percentage), which is defined according to the guidelines of the International Labour Office (ILO), is the number of unemployed persons divided by the number of labour force participants. See also *Employed*, *Labour force*, *Participation rate* and *Unemployed*.

Upper secondary education (ISCED 3): Upper secondary education (ISCED 3) corresponds to the final stage of secondary education in most OECD countries. Instruction is often more organised along subject-matter lines than at ISCED level 2 and teachers typically need to have a higher level, or more subject-specific, qualifications than at ISCED 2. The entrance age to this level is typically 15 or 16 years. There are substantial differences in the typical duration of ISCED 3 programmes both across and between countries, typically ranging from two to five years of schooling. ISCED 3 may either be "terminal" (*i.e.*, preparing the students for entry directly into working life) and/or "preparatory" (*i.e.*, preparing students for tertiary education). Programmes at level 3 can also be subdivided into three categories based on the degree to which the programme is specifically oriented towards a specific class of occupations or trades and leads to a labour-market relevant qualification: General, Pre-vocational or pre-technical, and Vocational or technical programmes. See also *General programmes*, *International Standard Classification of Education (ISCED)*, *Pre-vocational programmes* and *Vocational programmes*.

Vocational programmes: Vocational education prepares participants for direct entry, without further training, into specific occupations. Successful completion of such programmes leads to a labour-market relevant vocational qualification. Some indicators divide vocational programmes into school-based programmes and combined school and work-based programmes on the basis of the amount of training that is provided in school as opposed to training in the workplace. See also *Combined school and work-based programmes*, *General programmes*, *Pre-vocational programmes*, *Programme orientation*, *School-based programmes* and *Upper secondary education (ISCED 3)*.

Work status: Work status, which is defined according to the guidelines of the International Labour Office (ILO), refers to the position of the population within the labour force as defined in OECD Labour Force Statistics. See also *Employed*, *Labour force* and *Unemployed*.

Work study programmes: 'Work-study programmes' are combinations of work and education in which periods of both form part of an integrated, formal education or training activity. Examples of such programmes include the 'dual system' in Germany; 'apprentissage' or 'formation en alternance' in France and Belgium; internship or co-operative education in Canada; apprenticeship in Ireland; and "youth training" in the United Kingdom.

Working time: Teacher's working time refers to the normal working hours of a full-time teacher. According to the formal policy in a given country, working time can refer only to the time directly associated with teaching (and other curricular activities for students such as assignments and tests, but excluding annual examinations); or to time directly associated with teaching and to hours devoted to other activities related to teaching, such as lesson preparation, counselling of students, correction of assignments and tests, professional development, meetings with parents, staff meetings and general school tasks. Working time does not include paid overtime. See also *Educational personnel*, *Full-time equivalent teacher*, *Full-time teacher*, *Instructional personnel*, *Part-time teacher*, *Ratio of students to teaching staff*, *Teaching days*, *Teaching staff*, *Teaching time*, *Teaching weeks* and *Working time in school*.

Working time in school: Working time in school refers to the working time teachers are supposed to be at school including teaching time and non-teaching time. See also *Teaching days*, *Teaching time*, *Teaching weeks* and *Working time*.

World Wide Web (WWW): The World Wide Web is a part of the Internet designed to allow easier navigation of the network through the use of graphical user interfaces and hypertext links between different addresses. See also *Internet* and *Local Area Network*.

CONTRIBUTORS TO THIS PUBLICATION

Many people have contributed to the development of this publication. The following lists the names of the country representatives, researchers and experts who have actively taken part in the preparatory work leading to the publication of this edition of *Education at a Glance - OECD Indicators 2002*. The OECD wishes to thank them all for their valuable efforts.

National Co-ordinators

Mr. Dan ANDERSSON (Sweden)

Ms. Ikuko ARIMATSU (Japan)

Ms. Hatice BAL (Turkey)

M. Dominique BARTHÉLÉMY (Belgium)

Mr. H.H. DALMIJN (Netherlands)

Mr. Antonio Manuel Pinto FAZENDEIRO (Portugal)

Mr. Michael FEDEROWICZ (Poland)

Mr. Guillermo GIL (Spain)

Mr. Heinz GILOMEN (Switzerland)

Ms. Margrét HARÐARDÓTTIR (Iceland)

Mr. G. Douglas HODGKINSON (Canada)

Mr. Gregory KAFETZOPOULOS (Greece)

Ms. Maki KUBO (Japan)

Mr. Matti KYRÖ (Finland)

Mr. Antonio Giunta LA SPADA (Italy)

Ms. Kye Young LEE (Korea)

Mr. Jérôme LEVY (Luxembourg)

Mr. Dittrich MAGERKURTH (Germany)

Mr. Victor MANUEL VELÁZQUEZ CASTAÑEDA (Mexico)

Mr. Lubomir MARTINEC (Czech Republic)

Ms. Elizabetta MIDENA (Italy)

Mr. Gerardo MUÑOZ SANCHEZ-BRUNETE (Spain)

Ms. Marion NORRIS (New Zealand)

Mr. Torlach O CONNOR (Ireland)

Mr. Brendan O'REILLY (Australia)

Mr. Laurence OGLE (United States)

Ms. Hyun-Jeong PARK (Korea)

Mr. Elin PEDERSEN (Norway)

Mr. Friedrich H. PLANK (Austria)

Mr. Vladimir POKOJNY (Slovak Republic)

Mr. Imre RADÁCSI (Hungary)

Ms. Janice ROSS (United Kingdom)

Mr. Ingo RUSS (Germany)

Mr. Claude SAUVAGEOT (France)

Mr. Yasuyuki SIMOTUMA (Japan)

Mr. Ole-Jacob SKODVIN (Norway)

Mr. Ken THOMASSEN (Denmark)

Ms. Ann VAN DRIESSCHE (Belgium)

Ms. Angela VEGLIANTE (European Commission)

Mr. Arturo VILLARUEL (Mexico)

Technical Group on Education Statistics and Indicators

Mr. R.R.G. ABELN (Netherlands)

Mr. Paul AMACHER (Switzerland)

Ms. Birgitta ANDREN (Sweden)

Ms. Karin ARVEMO-NOTSTRAND (Sweden)

Ms. Alina BARAN (Poland)

Ms. Eva BOLIN (Sweden)

Mr. John CANLIN (United Kingdom)

Mr. Fernando CELESTINO REY (Spain)

Mr. Fernando CORDOVA CALDERON (Mexico)

Mr. Eduardo DE LA FUENTE (Spain)

Mr. Douglas LYND (UNESCO)

Mr. Dittrich MAGERKURTH (Germany)

Mr. Robert MAHEU (Canada)

Mr. Joaquim MAIA GOMES (Portugal)

Ms. Giuliana MATTEOCCI (Italy)

Mr. Konstantinos MITROGIANNIS (Greece)

Mr. Yoshiro NAKAYA (Japan)

Mr. Geir NYGARD (Norway)

Mr. Muiris O'CONNOR (Ireland)

Mr. Brendan O'REILLY (Australia)

Ms. Gemma DE SANCTIS (Italy)

Ms. Ritsuko DOKO (Japan)

Ms. Maria DOKOU (Greece)

Mr. J. Douglas DREW (Canada)

Ms. Mary DUNNE (EUROSTAT)

Mr. Michele EGLOFF (Switzerland)

Mr. Timo ERTOLA (Finland)

Mr. Pierre FALLOURD (France)

Mrs. Esin FENERCIOGLU (Turkey)

Mr. Paul GINI (New Zealand)

Mr. Bengt GREF (Sweden)

Ms. Yonca GUNDUZ-OZCERI (Turkey)

Mr. Heikki HAVEN (Finland)

Mr. Walter HOERNER (Germany)

Mr. Jesus IBANEZ MILLA (Spain)

Mr. Klaus Fribert JACOBSEN (Denmark)

Ms. Michèle JACQUOT (France)

Ms. Nathalie JAUNIAUX (Belgium)

Mr. Felix KOSCHIN (Czech Republic)

Mr. Karsten KUHL (Denmark)

Ms. Kye Young LEE (Korea)

Mr. Jérôme LEVY (Luxembourg)

Ms. Judit KOZMA LUKACS (Hungary)

Ms. Michaela KLENHOVÁ (Czech Republic)

Ms. Hyun-Jeong PARK (Korea)

Mr. Wolfgang PAULI (Austria)

Mr. João PEREIRA DE MATOS (Portugal)

Ms. Marianne PERIE (United States)

Mr. Spyridon PILOS (EUROSTAT)

Mr. Jean Paul REEFF (Luxembourg)

Mr. Ron ROSS (New Zealand)

Mr. Jean-Claude ROUCLOUX (Belgium)

Mr. Ingo RUSS (Germany)

Mr. Joel SHERMAN (United States)

Mr. Thomas SNYDER (United States)

Ms. Maria Pia SORVILLO (Italy)

Mr. Konstantinos STOUKAS (Greece)

Mr. Dick TAKKENBERG (Netherlands)

Mr. Ken THOMASSEN (Denmark)

Mr. Mika TUONONEN (Finland)

Mr. Shuichi UEHARA (Japan)

Ms. Ásta URBANCIC (Iceland)

Mr. Matti VAISANEN (Finland)

Ms. Erika VALLE BUTZE (Mexico)

Ms. Ann VAN DRIESSCHE (Belgium)

Mr. Juraj VANTUCH (Slovak Republic)

Ms. Elisabetta VASSENDEN (Norway)

Mr. Erik VERSTRAETE (Belgium)

Network A on Educational Outcomes

Lead Country: United States
Network Leader: Mr. Eugene OWEN

Ms. Lorna BERTRAND (United Kingdom)

Ms. Christiane BLONDIN (Belgium)

Ms. Müfie CALISKAN (Turkey)

Ms. Sunhee CHAE (Korea)

Mr. Fernando CORDOVA CALDERON (Mexico)

Ms. Chiara CROCE (Italy)

Mr. Guillermo GIL (Spain)

Mrs. Jacqueline LEVASSEUR (France)

Mr. Pirjo LINNAKYLA (Finland)

Mr. Jay MOSKOWITZ (United States)

Mr. Jerry MUSSIO (Canada)

Mr. Michael O'GORMAN (Canada)

Mr. Jules PESCHAR (Netherlands)

Mr. Vladislav ROSA (Slovak Republic)

Ms. Eva SCHOEYEN (Norway)

Mr. Jochen SCHWEITZER (Germany)

Mr. Gerry SHIEL (Ireland)

Mr. Joern SKOVSGAARD (Denmark)

Mr. Arnold A. J. SPEE (Netherlands)

Ms. Maria STEPHENS (United States)

Mrs. Jana STRAKOVÁ (Czech Republic)

Mr. P. Benedek TÓTA (Hungary)

Mr. Luc VAN DE POELE (Belgium)

Ms. Evangelia VARNAVA-SKOURA (Greece)

Mr. Ryo WATANABE (Japan)

Ms. Anita WESTER (Sweden)

Mr. Friedrich H. PLANK (Austria)

Ms. Glória RAMALHO (Portugal)

Mr. Erich RAMSEIER (Switzerland)

Mr. Jean-Paul REEFF (Luxembourg)

Ms. Wendy WHITHAM (Australia)

Ms. Lynne WHITNEY (New Zealand)

Ms. Marta ZVALOVA (Slovak Republic)

Network B on Student Destinations

Lead country: Sweden
Network Leader: Mr. Jonas BÖRJESSON

Ms. Yupin BAE (United States)

Ms. Ariane BAYE (Belgium)

Ms. Irja BLOMQVIST (Finland)

Ms. Anna BORKOWSKY (Switzerland)

Mr. Richard BRIDGE (Australia)

Mr. Fernando CELESTINO REY (Spain)

Ms. Jihee CHOI (Korea)

Mr. Erik DAHL (Norway)

Mr. H.H. DALMIJN (Netherlands)

Mr. Patrice DE BROUCKER (Canada)

Ms. Pascaline DESCY (CEDEFOP)

Mr. Kjetil DIGRE (Norway)

Ms. Isabelle ERAUW (Belgium)

Ms. Lisa HUDSON (United States)

Mr. Evangelos INTZIDIS (Greece)

Mr. Olof JOS (Sweden)

Ms. Christiane KRÜGER-HEMMER (Germany)

Mr. Pavel KUCHAR (Czech Republic)

Mr. Karsten KÜHL (EUROSTAT)

Mr. Jérôme LEVY (Luxembourg)

Ms. Anne-France MOSSOUX (CEDEFOP)

Mr. Philip O'CONNELL (Ireland)

Ms. Simona PACE (Italy)

Mr. Ali PANAL (Turkey)

Mr. Kenny PETERSSON (Sweden)

Ms. Cheryl REMINGTON (New Zealand)

Ms. Aila REPO (Finland)

Ms. Véronique SANDOVAL (France)

Ms. Emilia SAO PEDRO (Portugal)

Ms. Astrid SCHORN-BUCHNER (Luxembourg)

Mr. Peter SCRIMGEOUR (United Kingdom)

Mr. Dan SHERMAN (United States)

Ms. Irena SKRZYPCZAK (Poland)

Mr. Ken THOMASSEN (Denmark)

Ms. Mariá THURZOVÁ (Slovak Republic)

Ms. Éva TÓT (Hungary)

Ms. Paola UNGARO (Italy)

Ms. Stina UTTERSTRÖM (Sweden)

Mr. Johan VAN DER VALK (Netherlands)

Mr. Jaco VAN RIJN (Netherlands)

Network C on School Features and Processes

Lead Country: Netherlands
Network Leader: Mr. Jaap SCHEERENS

Ms. Bodhild BAASLAND (Norway)

Ms. Giovanna BARZANO (Italy)

Ms. Kathryn CHANDLER (United States)

Mr. Vassilios CHARISMIADIS (Greece)

Ms. Maria do Carmo CLÍMACO (Portugal)

Mr. H.H. DALMIJN (Netherlands)

Mr. Philippe DELOOZ (Belgium)

Mr. Gunnar ENEQUIST (Sweden)

Mr. Rainer FANKHAUSER (Austria)

Ms. Esin FENERCIOGLU (Turkey)

Ms. Flora GIL TRAVER (Spain)

Mr. Paul GINI (New Zealand)

Mr. Sean GLENNANE (Ireland)

Mrs. Kerry GRUBER (United States)

Ms. Maria HENDRIKS (Netherlands)

Ms. Maria HRABINSKA (Slovak Republic)

Ms. Anna IMRE (Hungary)

Mr. Raynald LORTIE (Canada)

Mr. Heikki LYYTINEN (Finland)

Ms. Nelly MCEWEN (Canada)

Mr. Lubomir MARTINEC (Czech Republic)

Mr. Gerd MÖLLER (Germany)

Mr. Mario OLIVA RUIZ (Mexico)

Ms. Hyun-Jeong PARK (Korea)

Mr. Jørgen Balling RASMUSSEN (Denmark)

Ms. Olga ROMERO HERNANDEZ (Mexico)

Ms. Marie-Claude RONDEAU (France)

Mr. Ingo RUSS (Germany)

Ms. Astrid SCHORN-BUCHNER (Luxembourg)

Mr. Joel SHERMAN (United States)

Ms. Pavlina STASTNOVA (Czech Republic)

Mr. Eugene STOCKER (Switzerland)

Mr. Jason TARSH (United Kingdom)

Ms. Erika VALLE BUTZE (Mexico)

Mr. Peter VAN PETEGEM (Belgium)

World Education Indicators

Mr. Mark AGRANOVITCH (Russian Federation)

Mr. Ramon BACANI (Philippines)

Mr. C. BALAKRISHNAN (India)

Ms. Valerie BEEN (Jamaica)

Mr. Ade CAHYANA (Indonesia)

Mr. Farai CHOGA (Zimbabwe)

Ms. Jehad Jamil Abu EL-SHAAR (Jordan)

Mrs. Maria Helena GUIMARAES DE CASTRO (Brazil)

Ms. Vivian HEYL (Chile)

Mr. Mohsen KTARI (Tunisia)

Ms. Zhi-Hua LIN (China)

Ms. Khalijah MOHAMMAD (Malaysia)

Ms. Irene OIBERMAN (Argentina)

Ms. Mara PEREZ TORRANO (Uruguay)

Mr. Mohammed RAGHEB (Egypt)

Mr. José RODRIGUEZ (Peru)

Mrs. Sirivarn SVASTIWAT (Thailand)

Ms. Dalia Noemi ZARZA PAREDES (Paraguay)

Others contributors to this publication

Ms. Isabel ABELE (OECD)

Mr. Kai v. AHLEFELD (Layout)

Mr. Gilles BURST (Layout)

Ms. Catherine DUCHENE (OECD)

Ms. Deborah GLASSMAN (Editor)

Ms. Katja HETTLER (Layout)

Mr. Michael JUNG (OECD)

Ms. Christine JUNG (OECD)

Ms. Cécile SLAPE (OECD)

RELATED OECD PUBLICATIONS

Classifying Educational Programmes: Manual for ISCED-97 implementation in OECD countries (1999)

    ISBN 92-64-17037-5   41.00   US$ 43.00   £ 26.00   ¥ 5,050.00

From Initial Education to Working Life: Making transitions work (2000)

    ISBN 92-64-17631-4   39.00   US$ 37.00   £ 23.00   ¥ 3,900.00

Literacy in the Information Age: Final report of the International Adult Literacy Survey (OECD and Statistics Canada) (2000)

    ISBN 92-64-17654-3   33.00   US$ 31.00   £ 19.00   ¥ 3,250.00

Measuring Student Knowledge and Skills: The PISA 2000 assessment of reading, mathematical and scientific literacy (2000)

    ISBN 92-64-17646-2   20.00   US$ 20.00   £ 12.00   ¥ 2,100.00

Where are the Resources for Lifelong Learning? (2000)

    ISBN 92-64-17677-2   26.00   US$ 26.00   £ 16.00   ¥ 2,700.00

Education Policy Analysis (2001)

    ISBN 92-64-18636-0   20.00   US$ 18.00   £ 12.00   ¥ 2,000.00

Knowledge and Skills for Life: First Results from PISA 2000 (2001)

    ISBN 92-64-19671-4   21.00   US$ 19.00   £ 13.00   ¥ 2,110.00

Starting Strong: Early Childhood Education and Care (2001)

    ISBN 92-64-18675-1   45.00   US$ 40.00   £ 28.00   ¥ 4,550.00

Teachers for Tomorrow's Schools: Analysis of the 2000 World Education Indicators (2001)

    ISBN 92-64-18699-9   22.00   US$ 20.00   £ 14.00   ¥ 2,200.00

Education Policy Analysis (2002)

    To be published in November 2002

Financing Education: Investments and returns – Analysis of the World Education Indicators (2002)

    To be published in 2002

PISA 2000 Technical Report (2002)

    To be published in 2002

Programme for International Student Assessment (PISA): Manual for the PISA 2000 Database (2002)

    ISBN 92-64-19822-9   20.00   US$ 19.00   £12.00   ¥2,300.00

Sample Tasks from the PISA 2000 Assessment: Reading, Mathematical and Scientific Literacy (2002)

    ISBN 92-64-19765-6   20.00   US$ 19.00   £ 12.00   ¥ 2,300.00

These titles are available at the OECD Online Bookshop: *www.oecd.org/bookshop*

OECD PUBLICATIONS, 2, rue André-Pascal, 75775 PARIS CEDEX 16
PRINTED IN FRANCE
(96 2002 03 1 P) ISBN 92-64-19890-3 – No. 52677 2002